ENGLAND
AND THE CONTINENT
IN THE
EIGHTH CENTURY

THE FORD LECTURES

DELIVERED IN

THE UNIVERSITY OF OXFORD IN THE

HILARY TERM, 1943

BY

WILHELM LEVISON

OXFORD
AT THE CLARENDON PRESS
1946

OXFORD UNIVERSITY PRESS
AMEN HOUSE, E.C. 4
London Edinburgh Glasgow New York
Toronto Melbourne Cape Town Bombay
Calcutta Madras
GEOFFREY CUMBERLEGE
PUBLISHER TO THE UNIVERSITY

111202
283. 032 U
L 579

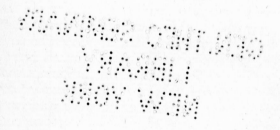

PRINTED IN GREAT BRITAIN

PREFACE

ARLY in February 1942 Professor Powicke to my great surprise informed me that the University of Oxford intended to appoint me Ford's Lecturer in English History during the Academic Year 1942–3. I greatly appreciated the honour conferred on me and accepted the invitation. The lectures were delivered in February and March 1943, when I had the privilege of enjoying the hospitality of Oriel College for three weeks, which gave me an impressive experience of English college life. My sincere thanks are due to Professor Powicke, to W. A. Pantin, M.A., who acted as my special 'guardian', to the other Fellows of Oriel College, and to members of other colleges and halls, who by their kindness and hospitality made those weeks unforgettable to me. I cannot name them all in this preface, but I recall especially the friendliness shown to me by the Provost of Queen's College, Robert H. Hodgkin, and by Dr. Decima Douie of Lady Margaret Hall, formerly of Durham.

My further thanks are due to the staff of the Clarendon Press. The Secretary to the Delegates from the outset encouraged me to adapt these lectures for publication as a book, provided with ample notes and several appendixes on special questions which arose in the preparation of the lectures or which I tried to answer in connexion with them. Mr. Sisam supplied me too with valuable contributions in questions of detail. He also invited Sir Paul Harvey to read the whole manuscript and to give the foreigner's 'English' a more idiomatic flavour. If my book to any extent should prove palatable to English taste, the reader is indebted for this to Sir Paul's kind patience.

Notes and appendixes will show that I had to rely for a large amount of English and Continental literature on assistance from many libraries, public and private. My many requests must have sometimes appeared a burden to the staff of Durham University Library; but their helpfulness never failed. Nor should I forget the aid given, with the permission of the Dean and Chapter, by the Durham Cathedral Library and the assistant librarian, E. H. Knight, and by the valuable library of St. Cuthbert's College at Ushaw, which was made accessible to me through the kindness of the President, the Rt. Rev.

Monsignor C. Corbishley, the librarian, the Rev. B. Payne, and the unceasing aid of my young friend the Rev. Dr. A. Theissen. The libraries of Newcastle-upon-Tyne provided more resources, and many other libraries sent books for me to the Durham University Library. Lecturing and a later stay at Oxford gave me the opportunity to collect further gleanings in the Bodleian. The photographic service of the British Museum furnished me with photostats from several books not available elsewhere. I am indebted for help of various kinds to H. M. Adams, librarian of Trinity College, Cambridge (p. 297); to Dr. H. I. Bell, the then Keeper of the Manuscripts of the British Museum (p. 297), and Dr. S. J. Madge, Honorary Assistant Keeper of the Department of Printed Books; to H. B. Browne, Honorary Secretary of the Whitby Literary and Philosophical Society (p. 17, n. 2); to Dom C. Mohlberg of Rome, once of Maria Laach (p. 303); to the Rev. Dr. W. J. Moore of Cotton College (p. 37, n. 1); to my former colleague of Bonn, Professor Fritz Schulz of Oxford, once of Berlin; to Werner Schwarz of London; to Professor A. Hamilton Thompson of Leeds; and to the Rev. Professor Dr. C. Wampach of Luxemburg, formerly of Bonn (p. 313). His Excellency the Spanish Ambassador, the Duke of Alba, was kind enough (through the mediation of H. W. Acomb, the Durham University Librarian) to lend from his private library the third volume of the late Z. G. Villada's *Historia eclesiástica de España* (1936), few copies of which seem to have reached England in consequence of the civil war in Spain. Dom H. Dumaine, librarian of St. Michael's Abbey, Farnborough, provided me with the edition of the *Sacramentarium Fuldense* (p. 146, n. 3). I have tried to some extent to connect up Continental and English research. May these pages, in their small way, contribute to join again broken links, when the works of peace have resumed their place lost in the turmoil of war.

I use this opportunity to express my gratitude to those also, who, apart from the help of my brother Arthur Levison, have made it possible for me to pursue my studies, when access to every public library was denied me in my native country. It is the University of Durham which gave me this opportunity, since I was able in April 1939 to accept the invitation of the Vice-Chancellor and Warden of the Durham Colleges, J. F.

Duff, to become its Honorary Fellow. My wife and I think with thankfulness of the kindness and humanity of so many, who, in this University and outside it, have striven to persuade us to find a positive answer to the question of Goethe's Iphigenia, whether a foreign country can become to anybody a fatherland ('Kann uns zum Vaterland die Fremde werden?'). The number of these kind helpers has been astonishingly large. I will mention only one of them, Bertram Colgrave, who, since Bodley's Librarian, Dr. Craster, introduced us to each other in the Bodleian in 1929, has been a friend to us and has contributed to this book also in many ways.

I should be untrue to myself if I did not mention my old *alma mater Bonnensis* and the *Monumenta Germaniae historica*. If my present book is of any use at all, it is based on the foundations laid in connexion with the service which I was privileged to perform for these two institutions during many years, and I think with grateful mind of the happy collaboration with old friends, colleagues and pupils, many of whom did not bow the knee to Baal, but remained faithful till the hour of parting could no longer be avoided.

And last not least, there is my wife, who has followed the growth of these pages with understanding and help, as she has done with all my studies now for nearly thirty years. I dedicate this book to her:

UXORI CARISSIMAE
PER LAETA ARDUAQUE COMITI
INDEFESSAE.

W. L.

DURHAM
9 August 1945

CONTENTS

APPENDIX: STUDIES AND SOME TEXTS

ABBREVIATIONS

Abhandl. Berlin = Abhandlungen der (Königl.) Preussischen Akademie der Wissenschaften, Philosophisch-historische Klasse.

Abhandl. Gött. = Abhandlungen der (Königlichen) Gesellschaft der Wissenschaften zu Göttingen, Philologisch-historische Klasse.

Abhandl. München = Abhandlungen der (Königl.) Bayerischen Akademie der Wissenschaften, Philos.–philol. und historische Klasse.

Acta SS. = *Acta Sanctorum* of the Bollandists.

Anal. Boll. = *Analecta Bollandiana.*

Archiv f. Urk. = *Archiv für Urkundenforschung.*

Auct. ant. = *Auctores antiquissimi* of the *MG.*

BECh. = Bibliothèque de l'École des chartes.

Bede Essays = *Bede, his Life, Times, and Writings.* Essays in commemoration of the twelfth centenary of his death edited by A. Hamilton Thompson. Oxford, 1935.

Bede, *H.E.* = *Baedae Historia Ecclesiastica,* ed. C. Plummer.

BHL. = *Bibliotheca hagiographica Latina* of the Bollandists.

Birch = Walter de Gray Birch, *Cartularium Saxonicum.*

CSEL. = *Corpus scriptorum ecclesiasticorum Latinorum,* of Vienna.

Dipl. Karol. = *Diplomata Karolinorum* (*Die Urkunden der Karolinger*) of the *MG.*

Dipl. Merov. = *Diplomatum imperii tomus I* of the *MG.*, ed. K. Pertz.

E.H.R. = *English Historical Review.*

E.P-N.S. = English Place-Name Society.

H. and S. = A. W. Haddan and W. Stubbs, *Councils and Ecclesiastical Documents relating to Great Britain and Ireland.*

H. Br. Soc. = Henry Bradshaw Society.

Holtzmann, *Papsturkunden* = Walther Holtzmann, *Papsturkunden in England,* i, ii (=Abhandl. Gött., Neue Folge xxv, Berlin, 1931; Dritte Folge, No. 14, Berlin, 1935).

Jaffé = Ph. Jaffé, *Regesta pontificum Romanorum,* editio secunda, ed. S. Loewenfeld, F. Kaltenbrunner, P. Ewald.

J.T.S. = *Journal of Theological Studies.*

Kemble = J. M. Kemble, Codex diplomaticus aevi Saxonici.

Kirchenrechtl. Abhandl. = Kirchenrechtliche Abhandlungen, ed. Ulrich Stutz, Stuttgart.

Liebermann, *Gesetze* = *Die Gesetze der Angelsachsen,* ed. Felix Liebermann.

Lowe, *Codices Lat. ant.* = E. A. Lowe, *Codices Latini antiquiores.* Oxford, 1934 ff.

Mabillon, *Acta* = d'Achery and Mabillon, *Acta Sanctorum ordinis S. Benedicti* (first edition).

MG. = *Monumenta Germaniae historica.*

Migne, *P.L.* = Migne, *Patrologiae cursus completus*, Series secunda (Latina).

MIÖG., MÖIG. = *Mitteilungen des Instituts für Österreichische Geschichtsforschung;* later: *Mitteilungen des Österreichischen Instituts für Geschichtsforschung.*

Mon. Angl. = W. Dugdale, *Monasticon Anglicanum*, new edition. London, 1817–30.

Nachrichten Gött. = Nachrichten von der (K.) Gesellschaft der Wissenschaften zu Göttingen, Philologisch-historische Klasse.

Neues Archiv = *Neues Archiv der Gesellschaft für ältere deutsche Geschichtskunde.*

P.B.A. = *Proceedings of the British Academy.*

Poole, *Studies* = Reginald L. Poole, *Studies in Chronology and History.* Oxford, 1934.

Rev. Bén. = *Revue Bénédictine.*

Rev. hist. = *Revue historique.*

Savigny-Zeitschr., Kan. Abt. = Zeitschrift der Savigny-Stiftung für Rechtsgeschichte, Kanonistische Abteilung.

Saxon Chronicle = *Two of the Saxon Chronicles parallel*, ed. C. Plummer on the basis of an edition by J. Earle, 2 vols. Oxford, 1892–9.

SB. Berlin = Sitzungsberichte der (Königl.) Preussischen Akademie der Wissenschaften, Phil.-hist. Klasse.

SB. München = Sitzungsberichte der Bayerischen Akademie der Wissenschaften, Philos.-philol. und hist. Klasse.

SB. Wien = Sitzungsberichte der (Kaiserlichen) Akademie der Wissenschaften in Wien, Philos.-hist. Klasse.

SS. = Scriptores (in folio) of the *MG.*

SS. rer. Germ. = *Scriptores rerum Germanicarum in usum scholarum ex Monumentis Germaniae historicis separatim editi* (in 8vo).

SS. rer. Merov. = *Scriptores rerum Merovingicarum* of the *MG.*

Traube, *Quellen* = *Quellen und Untersuchungen zur lateinischen Philologie des Mittelalters*, herausgegeben (begründet) von Ludwig Traube, 5 vols. Munich, 1906–20.

Traube, *Vorles.* = Ludwig Traube, *Vorlesungen und Abhandlungen*, 3 vols. Munich, 1909–20.

T.R.H.S. = *Transactions of the Royal Historical Society.*

V.C.H. = *Victoria History of the Counties of England.*

Zeitschr. = *Zeitschrift.*

I

INTRODUCTION

TWICE in her history England has exercised a broad, deep, and lasting influence upon continental ways of thought and life. During the last two centuries of modern history, since the days of Montesquieu, her constitution has directly or indirectly served as a standard and given direction to the popular struggle for participation in and control of government, for a constitutional balance of powers, for an adjustment between the efficiency of the State and the liberty of the individual. A millennium earlier English missionaries and scholars, such as Willibrord, Boniface, and Alcuin, left their native country to work in foreign lands and made a large contribution to the spiritual foundations and unity of Western civilization. This first expansion of English activity outside Great Britain, these early medieval relations between England and the European countries overseas, or at least some aspects of them, form the subject of these lectures, a subject which I may briefly describe as 'England and the Continent in the Eighth Century'.

Many have written on this matter. There is no history of early England which has not at least touched on it,[1] no history of Germany and France which has not devoted some space to it: I will mention only the *Ecclesiastical History of Germany* by Albert Hauck[2] and the *History of the Christian Church during the Early Middle Ages* by Hans von Schubert.[3] There are modern biographies of the principal figures, particularly of Boniface and Alcuin. But the essential facts of this chapter of history have been specially and comprehensively surveyed only in a few essays; the lectures delivered by S. J. Crawford in 1931 on *Anglo-Saxon Influence on Western Christendom* and published in 1933[4] after his early death deserve an honourable mention.

[1] I may refer to R. H. Hodgkin, *A History of the Anglo-Saxons*, vols. i and ii, 2nd ed., Oxford, 1939, and to F. M. Stenton, *Anglo-Saxon England*, Oxford, 1943. The latter work was published after my lectures had been delivered.
[2] *Kirchengeschichte Deutschlands*, vols. i and ii, 3rd and 4th eds., Leipzig, 1904–12 (and later reprints).
[3] *Geschichte der christlichen Kirche im Frühmittelalter*, Tübingen, (1917–)1921.
[4] Oxford University Press.

The sources are unequal in quantity and quality as they relate to the principal actors and the different parts of the story; but, on the whole, they are perhaps more plentiful than for any other epoch and subject of English history in the 'dark ages'. One class of these sources is more direct and vivid than most, the collections of letters, a sort of document to which much attention has rightly been paid in recent times. There are two collections, or rather groups of such collections, of the first importance for our subject, inviting and encouraging repeated consideration. One is the correspondence of Boniface and of his successor to the see of Mainz, Lullus, particularly embracing the relations between the former and the Papacy and the connexions of both with their English home country.[1] There are also at the end of our period the letters of Alcuin's last years.[2] Many letters of which we occasionally hear are lost;[3] the 150 pieces of the Boniface and Lullus collections and the 300 Alcuinian letters fall far short of the 850 surviving letters of Pope Gregory the Great, several of which are highly relevant to the beginnings of English Christianity, as was already recognized by the Venerable Bede. But in spite of all losses and deficiencies, the smaller collections under the names of Boniface, Lullus, and Alcuin throw unusual light upon the information from other sources: of these I will call attention only to the series of biographies stretching from Wilfrid of York to Alcuin, different as they are in quality and weight, authority and substance.

The seventh and eighth centuries were decisive epochs in the history of the West. The migration of Germanic peoples, the so-called *Völkerwanderung*, had come to an end, except for the inroads and settlements of the Scandinavians of the Viking age. But the seventh century saw the conquests of Islam; the southern shores of the Mediterranean ceased to be Christian countries. One has only to call to mind names like those of Clement and Origen of Alexandria, of Tertullian and Cyprian of Carthage, and of St. Augustine, to see the part played by these countries in the history of early Christianity and to estimate the significance of their loss; this has been emphasized lately, with some exaggerations, in the suggestive posthumous book of Henri

[1] Cf. Appendix VII, pp. 280 ff.   [2] Cf. Appendix XI, pp. 314 f.
[3] See Tangl's list of 'Acta deperdita' of the Boniface and Lullus correspondence, *Neues Archiv*, xli. 46–71.

Pirenne, *Mahomet et Charlemagne*.[1] But there was some sort of compensation. In 597, a generation before Mohammed roused the fighting forces of his new religion, the missionaries of Pope Gregory I began the conversion of the Anglo-Saxons, thus initiating 'the return of Britain to Europe and to her past'.[2] The conversion was finished after nearly ninety years, when all England had accepted Christianity, at least superficially. These were not years of continual progress; there were moments of reaction, particularly when wars broke out among the Anglo-Saxons, some of whom clung to the gods of their forefathers, and between the Anglo-Saxons and the Britons in the west, who were Christians too but detested the invaders of their native soil. The aim of Gregory seemed to be frustrated for a while not only by these opponents but also by the zeal of the Irish offspring of the old British Church; its monks regained ground lost by the papal emissaries, and won over the larger part of England to the Christian faith and to the peculiarities which the Celtic churches had kept in their separation, and which were opposed by the followers of Rome. But the synod or rather debate of Whitby in 664 gave the victory to the Roman cause; the conversion of Sussex and of the Isle of Wight from heathenism brought Gregory's enterprise after two more decades to a victorious end.

The importance of his mission has recently been contested, its failure asserted;[3] this opinion is tenable only from a narrow point of view, looking at the situation as it was for about thirty years after the death of King Edwin of Northumbria (633). But this and other reverses were overcome at last; Gregory had set the course which not only in the end reached its goal in Britain but also had momentous consequences for the Continent. A new religious superstructure, rudimentary as it was, was built on the foundations of pagan England from materials brought over from the Mediterranean world; a vigorous civilization grew up in a receptive soil, in which the mingling of native and foreign elements yielded a rich harvest. Stone churches and monumental crosses, illuminated manuscripts and the parch-

[1] Paris and Brussels, 1937; English translation, *Mohammed and Charlemagne*, London, 1939.
[2] Chr. Dawson, *The Making of Europe*, London, 1932, p. 209.
[3] Cf., e.g., Johannes Haller, *Das Papsttum: Idee und Wirklichkeit*, i, Stuttgart, 1934, pp. 275, 282, 284, 340 ff., 503.

ments which have handed down the first English literature, Latin as well as vernacular, the names of Aldhelm and Bede, of Cædmon and Beowulf may be mentioned as illustrations of this fresh growth. The first written laws and the introduction of charters as 'a new and a better form of testimony'[1] bear witness to the influence of Roman example. A new chapter was opened in the relations between Great Britain and the lands across the sea. England was, in the main, in the seventh century the recipient of extraneous influences; in the next century the new member of the medieval Western world was herself to become the donor.

Channels of intercourse and trade

Intercourse between Anglo-Saxon Britain and the Continent, even during the periods of invasion and the 'coalescence' of the kingdoms emerging from the chaos, was probably never wholly interrupted; the waters of the Channel were a link as well as a barrier. We must not forget that in late Roman times a *Litus Saxonicum* had to be established against the Teutonic invaders on the Gallic and on the British seaboards; Saxon settlements succeeded not only in Britain but, on a smaller scale, also on the southern coast of the Channel.[2] There were the Saxons of Adovacer in the estuary of the Loire near Angers in the sixties of the fifth century; perhaps it was their descendants who about a century later were won to the Christian faith by Bishop Felix of Nantes.[3] The Saxons of Bayeux in the later Normandy are another example of a Saxon community surviving under Frankish rule. Place-names in use to-day in the proximity of Boulogne-sur-Mer are explained by a settlement from early Saxon Britain,[4] and show that contact across the Straits of Dover existed in this ~~see Stenton on @1765~~

---

[1] H. D. Hazeltine in Dorothy Whitelock, *Anglo-Saxon Wills*, Cambridge, 1930, p. xxvii. On the descent of the Anglo-Saxon charter cf. Appendix I, pp. 226 ff.

[2] H. Prentout, 'Littus Saxonicum, Saxones Bajocassini, Otlinga Saxonia' (*Rev. hist.* cvii, 1911, pp. 285–309); F. Lot, 'Les Migrations saxonnes en Gaule et en Grande-Bretagne' (ib. cxix, 1915, pp. 20 ff.); E. Gamillscheg, *Romania Germanica*, iii, Berlin, 1936, pp. 207 f.; Helmut Ehmer, *Die Sächsischen Siedlungen auf dem Französischen Litus Saxonicum* (Studien zur Englischen Philologie, xcii), Halle, 1937.

[3] Venantius Fortunatus, *Carm.* iii. 9. 103: 'aspera gens, Saxo, vivens quasi more ferino'. The last editor, Fr. Leo (*Auct. ant.* iv. 1, p. 62), printed *saxo*; but W. Meyer has rightly restored the proper name, *Der Gelegenheitsdichter Venantius Fortunatus* (Abhandl. Gött., Neue Folge, iv, no. 5), 1901, p. 82.

[4] Ehmer, loc. cit.

age. Archaeological research has confirmed this inference, particularly as regards Kent, whose geographical position rendered it especially open to continental influences.

The intercourse was no doubt greater than the scanty written sources and archaeological finds suggest; we have to remember that no author before the eighth century, except the writers of a few Lives of saints, belongs to the northern provinces of France. But two facts are relevant. Before Pope Gregory started his missionary effort, he ordered Anglian boys of 17 or 18 years to be bought in Gaul and to be educated in monasteries for the service of God;[1] thus it is certain that slave-trade existed between England and Gaul. And the surest proof of further connexions is the marriage of King Ethelbert of Kent with Bertha, the daughter of a Merovingian king, Charibert I, who had died in 567. The Merovingian kingdom was the greatest power in the West in the sixth century; the marriage of a daughter of its royal house to an English king meant his admission to some equality with the foremost Teutonic rulers. By entering into relations with the political powers of the Continent England was brought into touch with Christianity, the spiritual power that had penetrated the Roman Empire and was its most important heritage. Christianity was spreading more and more to peoples and countries outside the Mediterranean world, and contact with it led to the conversion of the Anglo-Saxons. The intercourse was now increased by the needs and connexions of the Church. The Papacy had secured the position of honorary head of the Western Church and aimed at its authoritative monarchical leadership. In spite of all the disruptive tendencies and antagonisms of the age, its claims were somehow established in theory in the early fifth century; when the Roman Empire disintegrated, the Roman Church inherited a part of its organization and pretensions. The mission of Pope Gregory created links with Britain, now stronger now weaker, which lasted for centuries. Rome became the starting-point or the destination of envoys from both sides. The proximity of Gaul was made conspicuous by her situation as the country of transit to and from Italy. Political and cultural relations increased.

The channels of this intercourse were settled by nature and previous history, as has recently been described by Philip

[1] *Gregorii I Registrum*, vi. 10 (ed. Ewald and Hartmann, *MG. Epist.* i, pp. 388 f.).

Grierson.[1] London, where several Roman roads met for the crossing of the Thames, had regained some importance in the times of Bede, who called the city an emporium of many people coming by land and sea (*H.E.* ii. 3); this 'market for the sale of goods'[2] was one of the shipping-ports for the Continent. St. Boniface embarked there in 716 and 718. The first time his ship crossed the sea he made for the mouths of the Rhine and went up the river to Wijk bij Duurstede near Utrecht; this *Dorstet* was the principal place of sea traffic in Friesland before the age of the Vikings. On the second occasion his ship took Boniface across the Straits of Dover, which naturally carried the larger part of the 'through traffic',[3] the more so because several Roman roads converged in the Boulonnais to this shortest crossing of the sea. Quentavic at the mouth of the Canche, near the modern Étaples, had succeeded Boulogne[4] after Roman times as the main place of embarkation and disembarkation. The crossing by Quentavic was considered in 678 the 'via rectissima' for a man travelling from England to Rome.[5] Forty years later it was the landing-place of Boniface, when he sailed the second time for the Continent, never to return. Farther to the west the estuary of the Seine attracted traffic from the Solent. A kinsman of Boniface, Willibald, the future first bishop of Eichstätt, embarked with his companions in 720 at the 'mercimonium', the market-place, of Hamwih near Southampton, to reach the Continent at another 'mercimonium', Rouen. The names of

---

[1] 'The Relations between England and Flanders before the Norman Conquest' (*T.R.H.S.*, 4th series, xxiii, 1941, pp. 72 ff.).

[2] Willibald, *Vita Bonifatii*, c. 4 (ed. Levison, p. 16).

[3] Grierson, loc. cit., p. 74.

[4] An accidental or rather miraculous crossing from Boulogne to Britain and the 'Saxonica terra' was related about 800 in the *Vitae Audomari, Bertini, Winnoci*, c. 8 (*SS. rer. Merov.* v. 757). The Old English Martyrology of the ninth century does not contain any other extracts from lives of saints of the Merovingian age, but all three parts of this work on the saints of St. Omer are represented there (ib., p. 741, n. 6). An Anglo-Saxon passing through may have taken a copy to England. These three saints are also entered in English calendars as early as Oxford, Digby MS. 63 of the 9th century; see F. Wormald, *English Kalendars before A.D. 1100*, vol. i (H. Br. Soc. lxxii), 1934, pp. 7, 8, 10, 12. The MS. was either written at Winchester or soon taken there; cf. *Palaeographical Society*, Series I, vol. ii, pl. 168 (cf. *Indices*, 1901, p. 2); B. Krusch in *Papsttum und Kaisertum. Forschungen . . . Paul Kehr dargebracht*, München, 1926, pp. 50 ff.

[5] *Vita Wilfridi*, c. 25 (ed. Levison, *SS. rer. Merov.* vi. 219). I refer also to the edition of B. Colgrave, *The Life of Bishop Wilfrid by Eddius Stephanus*, Cambridge, 1927, p. 50.

these places illustrate the main routes of English traffic overseas. We hear also of 'naves Britannicae' which came to the island of Noirmoutier near the mouth of the Loire and to the port of Angoulême;[1] they are rather probably ships of Great Britain than of Brittany, the more so since Irish merchant ships are also found at Nantes and Noirmoutier in the seventh century.[2] But the ships of Britain might have come from the Celtic parts of the island.

There may have been other places in the Merovingian lands where goods were sold and purchased by Englishmen, such as the 'mercimonium' of Rouen. In the eighth century an English merchant settled at Marseilles, one of the most important centres of Mediterranean traffic.[3] We have some documentary evidence in the records of the monastery of Saint-Denis near Paris, whose charters were better preserved than those of any French monastery of this early age. King Dagobert I granted it in 634 the permission to establish an annual fair, to be held after the day of the patron-saint (9 October).[4] 'Saxon' merchants very soon visited this fair; they alone were mentioned by name in the royal charters among the traders of different nations who met there in the seventh century. Frisians, enterprising merchants

[1] *Vita Filiberti*, c. 41 (*SS. rer. Merov.* v. 603) and, of later origin, *Virtutes Eparchii*, c. 10 (ib. iii. 562). In the later 9th century the 'monachus Sangallensis', i. 1, ii. 14 (*MG. SS.* ii. 731, 757) mentions 'mercatores Brittanni'.

[2] Jonas, *Vita Columbani*, i. 23 (ed. Krusch, *SS. rer. Merov.* iv. 97; *Ionae Vitae SS. Columbani, Vedastis, Iohannis*, in the collection *SS. rer. Germ.*, 1905, p. 205); *Vita Filiberti*, c. 42 (p. 603); cf. 'Gallici nautae de Galliarum provinciis adventantes' in Adamnan's *Vita Columbae*, i. 28 (2nd ed. by Fowler, Oxford, 1920, p. 107). I omit the modern literature on this Gallo-Irish traffic.

[3] Addition in the Geneva MS. (from Massay) to the *Annales Petaviani*, 790, *MG. SS.* i. 17, cf. iii. 170; Hieronymus Frank, *Die Klosterbischöfe des Frankenreiches*, Dissertation of Bonn (Beiträge zur Geschichte des alten Mönchtums und des Benediktinerordens, ed. Ildef. Herwegen, xvii), Münster, 1932, p. 57: 'et Audegarius episcopus monasterii sancti Martini (of Tours) obiit XV. Kal. Febr. Fuit autem ex genere Anglorum, sed pater eius Botto nomine negociator fuit in urbe Massiliae. . . .' The commercial activity of the father must be ascribed to the middle of the 8th century rather than to the time of Charles the Great, as was done by F. L. Ganshof, 'Notes sur les ports de Provence du VIIIᵉ au Xᵉ siècle' (*Rev. hist.* clxxxiii, 1938, p. 31). The Anglo-Saxon form of his name was Botta; cf. 'Signum manus Botta' in Kentish charters of 697, Birch, i, nos. 97–8.

[4] *Gesta Dagoberti*, c. 34 (*SS. rer. Merov.* ii. 413), based on a lost charter. The existing charter of King Dagobert I which mentions the ports of Rouen and 'Wicus' (Quentavicus), the merchants 'de ultra mare', and 'Saxones et Wicarii et Rothomenses' (*Dipl. Merov.*, p. 140, no. 23), is a forgery probably of the early 10th century; cf. L. Levillain, 'Études sur l'abbaye de Saint-Denis à l'époque mérovingienne IV' (*BECh.* xci, 1930, pp. 7 ff.).

who also came to England, were added in the charters of the next century.[1] Wine was a special object of commerce at St. Denis,[2] later also honey, which was probably purchased for making mead. We may imagine that at such gatherings the so-called 'Coptic' bronze vessels found in Saxon graves were acquired by English traders, and conjecture a similar source for silver objects such as those discovered in 1939 in the Sutton Hoo ship-burial, and for other pieces of luxury which furnished patterns for imitation in England. English cloaks (*saga*) were sent to the Continent in the eighth century.[3]

There is frequent mention of another kind of traffic, the slave-trade, connected with the internal wars of Great Britain. Bede tells the story of a young Northumbrian warrior who was taken prisoner by the Mercians and sold to a Frisian in London (*H.E.* iv. 22). All know the legend of the English boys whom Pope Gregory the Great found on the slave market at Rome, the sight of whom suggested to him the mission to England (ib. ii. 1);[4] there is an historical foundation for this legend, as

---

[1] Charter of Childebert III of 710 (*Dipl. Merov.*, p. 68, no. 77; Ph. Lauer and Ch. Samaran, *Les Diplômes originaux des Mérovingiens*, Paris, 1908, pl. 31), referring to earlier grants from the reign of Clovis II (639–57) onwards: 'neguciantes aut *Saxonis* vel quascumquelibit nacionis'; *Dipl. Karol.* i, nos. 6, 43, &c. In the time of King Pippin 'quidam Saxo transmarinus ex eis qui Angli dicuntur', being unable to walk, recovered his health at St. Denis; cf. *Miracula S. Dionysii*, ed. A. Luchaire, *Études sur quelques MSS. de Rome et de Paris* (Université de Paris, Bibliothèque de la Faculté des lettres, viii), Paris, 1899, p. 95, and Mabillon, *Acta*, iii. 2, 1672, p. 346 (i. 9).—Of course I do not use 'the Old English charters to St. Denis' (Birch, i, nos. 252, 259, &c.) which W. H. Stevenson has shown to be forgeries of this monastery (*E.H.R.* vi, 1891, pp. 736–42; cf. ib. xxvii, 1912, p. 6, n. 18). But the monks employed a genuine charter of King Offa of Mercia; the list of witnesses in Birch, no. 259 was based on such a document (Stevenson, pp. 741 f.), the charter contains letters of the Anglo-Saxon alphabet (ib., p. 742), and the preamble is also found in an Evesham charter of 706 (Birch, no. 117). To the documents studied by Stevenson a charter of Pope Benedict III has to be added (Jaffé, i. 2666; Migne, *P.L.* cxv. 701); here a genuine charter was also used, but at least retouched; cf. J. Harttung, *Diplomatisch-historische Forschungen*, Gotha, 1879, pp. 110 ff.; A. Hessel, 'Les Plus Anciennes Bulles en faveur de l'abbaye de Saint-Denis' (*Le Moyen Âge*, xiv, 1901, pp. 377, 379, 392 f.). Cf. also H. Bresslau, 'Internationale Beziehungen im Urkundenwesen des Mittelalters' (*Archiv f. Urk.* vi, 1918, p. 47).

[2] Alcuin sent wine (and tin for a bell-tower) as a present to York, cf. his *Epist.* 226 (p. 370).

[3] Letter of Charles the Great to King Offa, ib., *Epist.* no. 100 (p. 145).

[4] In the other version of the story, told by the unknown monk of Whitby who wrote the first Life of Gregory, there is no mention of the English boys in Rome being slaves, ed. Fr. A. Gasquet, *A Life of Pope Gregory the Great*, Westminster, 1904, pp. 13 f. (c. 9); ed. P. Ewald, *Historische Aufsätze dem Andenken an Georg Waitz gewidmet*, Hanover, 1886, p. 48. The two versions do not depend on each other; cf.

already indicated (p. 5), in Gregory's order to purchase pagan
English boys in Gaul. When Archbishop Theodore of Canterbury in his penitential canons laid down rules for husbands and
wives separated by the captivity of one of them, he added that
the same rules should be applied 'de servis transmarinis'.[1] The
redemption of prisoners and slaves was considered a particular
work of Christian charity; therefore several Merovingian saints
are credited with the performance of this 'eleemosyna', and
special mention is sometimes made of slaves brought from overseas, of captives from Great Britain or 'Saxony', as in the Lives
of SS. Richarius, Eligius, Amandus, and Filibertus.[2] Eligius,
the goldsmith and mintmaster and future bishop of Noyon
(641–60), was able to redeem whole shiploads of prisoners, men
and women, up to a hundred: 'praecipue ex genere Saxonorum,
qui abunde eo tempore veluti greges a sedibus propriis evulsi in
diversa distrahebantur.' This relates to the years before Eligius
was made bishop in 641. We must remember the wars of the
Britons, of Wessex, Mercia, and Northumbria, and their vicissitudes in this period; thus the words have been rightly referred
rather to the insular than to the continental Saxons.[3] The most
famous of all these English slaves in France was Balthild.[4] She

H. Moretus, *Anal. Boll.* xxvi, 1907, pp. 66–72; W. Stuhlfath, *Gregor I. der Grosse.
Sein Leben bis zu seiner Wahl zum Papste* (Heidelberger Abhandlungen zur mittleren
und neueren Geschichte, xxxix), Heidelberg, 1913, pp. 63 ff.; C. E. Wright, *The
Cultivation of Saga in Anglo-Saxon England*, Edinburgh, 1939, pp. 43 ff., 85 ff., 255 ff.

[1] H. and S. iii. 201 (c. 24); P. W. Finsterwalder, *Die Canones Theodori Cantuariensis*,
i, Weimar, 1929, pp. 260 (§ 72), 276 (§ 87), 329 (§ 25).

[2] *Vita I. Richarii*, c. 7 (*SS. rer. Merov.* vii. 448) and the derived version of Alcuin,
c. 8 (ib. iv. 393); *Vita Eligii*, i. 10 (ib. iv. 677); *Vita Amandi*, c. 9 (ib. v. 435); *Vita
Filiberti*, c. 23 (ib., p. 596).

[3] Whether Eligius' helper, 'Thille vernaculus eius ex genere Saxonico' (*Vita
Eligii*, i. 10, p. 676), belonged to the insular or to the continental Saxons is uncertain; the *Vita Boniti*, c. 9 (ib. vi. 124) does not mention his origin.

[4] *Vita Balthildis*, ed. Krusch, ib. ii. 475–508 (cf. vii. 798); *Liber historiae Francorum*, cc. 43, 44 (ib. ii. 315 ff.); Jonas, *Vita Iohannis Reomaensis*, pref. (ib. iii. 505;
Ionae Vitae sanctorum Columbani, &c., p. 326); *Vita Eligii*, ii. 32, 37, 38, 41, 48 (*SS. rer.
Merov.* iv. 717 ff.); *Passio I. Leudegarii*, cc. 2, 4, and *Passio II*, c. 3 (ib. v. 284, 286,
326); *Vita Filiberti*, c. 6 (ib., p. 587); *Vita Ansberti*, c. 1 (ib., p. 619); *Vita Bertilae*
(ib. vi. 95–109); *Vita Wilfridi*, c. 6 (ib., p. 199); *Vita Aunemundi* (*Acta SS. Sept.* vii.
744 ff.; cf. A. Coville, *Recherches sur l'histoire de Lyon*, Paris, 1928, pp. 366 ff.); *Dipl.
Merov.*, p. 31, no. 33 (cf. *Vita Frodoberti*, c. 11, *SS. rer. Merov.* v. 77), pp. 35, 37, nos.
38, 40 (L. Levillain, *Examen critique des chartes mérov. et carol. de l'abbaye de Corbie*,
Paris, 1902, pp. 213–20; cf. Krusch, *Neues Archiv*, xxix, 1904, pp. 250 ff., xxxi, 1906,
pp. 338 ff., 367, 372 f.), p. 36, no. 39 (cf. *SS. rer. Merov.* v. 734, n. 11), p. 196, no. 81
(cf. J. Havet, *Œuvres*, i, 1896, p. 271; F. Lot, 'La Nomination du comte à l'époque
mérovingienne', *Nouvelle revue historique du droit français et étranger*, 1924, pp. 272–87).

also came 'ex genere Saxonum' and was sold overseas at a low price into the house of a mayor of the palace; but because of her beauty and charm King Clovis II (639–57) made her his consort. The monasteries of Chelles near Paris and Corbie in Picardy are her foundations; she also practised the redemption of captives, particularly of her own people. When Clovis died, she became regent during the minority of her son Chlothar III, and apparently showed a strong hand in those days of the decline of the Merovingian power and the rise of the Frankish aristocracy. A bishop of Lyons, the patron of Wilfrid (the future bishop of York), was put to death in these struggles; his end, attributed to her command, gave her a bad name in her native country. At last (between 664 and 667) she was forced to surrender the government and to retire to her monastery of Chelles; there, by a life of asceticism and devotion, she gained the reputation of a saint, thus closing (after 677) what was truly an extraordinary career for an English slave sold to the Continent.

The status of slavery could also be imposed as a punishment. According to the laws of King Wihtred of Kent (695) a free man caught in the act of theft could be killed or redeemed for his wergeld or sold over sea by the will of the king. By the laws of King Ine of Wessex (688–726) the selling of countrymen, free and unfree, overseas was forbidden; but the trade, on the whole, persisted for centuries.[1] It became, however, unlawful in Christian England to sell slaves to pagans who might sacrifice them to their gods. Boniface on the Continent likewise opposed this practice.[2]

The continental traffic of England, of which the slave-trade was only one branch, had gained some importance by the end of the eighth century; its interruption meant damage to Anglo-Saxon merchants. When the relations between Charles the Great and King Offa of Mercia became strained, the Frankish king ordered that no Englishman should be admitted into Gaul 'mercimonii causa'; commerce was prohibited by both sides for a while, till normal conditions were restored (below, p. 112).

The growing trade with the Continent in the seventh century

---

[1] Liebermann, *Gesetze*, i. 14, 94; cf. ii. 2, pp. 693, 502. On later times see, e.g., E. I. Bromberg, 'Wales and the Mediaeval Slave Trade' (*Speculum*, xvii, 1942, pp. 263–9).   [2] *Epist.* 28 (ed. Tangl, p. 51).

gave rise to the first English coinage.[1] Late Roman and to a greater extent Merovingian gold coins, *trientes* or *tremisses*, were imported into southern England, as a purse containing forty Frankish coins in the Sutton Hoo finds has recently confirmed;[2] they were imitated by the islanders. Silver coins, also derived from Roman and Merovingian models, followed and replaced them; of these a large variety of types were developed. As Merovingian coins are found in England, so are Anglo-Saxon coins found in the countries of Frankish dominion. For example, a hoard of gold and silver coins was discovered in 1904 at Ilanz on the Vorder-Rhein in remote Grisons, where it had been deposited about 810. Most of the coins were of the last king of the Langobards, Desiderius, and of Charles the Great, his victorious successor in Italy; there were also two dirhems of caliphs of Bagdad, one of them struck at Tunis, and three pennies of the kings Offa of Mercia and Egbert of Kent—the collection thus ranging from England to Moslem countries.[3] One of Offa's gold coins found near Rome is known to be an imitation of a caliph's dinar of 774.

Economic connexions are shown not only by the discovery of Anglo-Saxon money overseas but also by the further history of the English coinage. The silver coins underwent debasement in the eighth century. But Offa, the powerful king of Mercia (757–96), in the later part of his reign introduced a new issue of broader and somewhat heavier silver coins commonly called pennies; they were probably struck at the mint of Canterbury working for the Mercian overlord of Kent. It was most likely from this time that 240 pennies represented a pound. The first Carolingian kings, Pippin, the father of Charles the Great, and Charles himself, had also improved the monetary standard of

---

[1] C. F. Keary, *A Catalogue of English Coins in the British Museum, Anglo-Saxon Series*, i, 1887, Introduction; H. M. Chadwick, *Studies on Anglo-Saxon Institutions*, Cambridge, 1905, pp. 1 ff.; F. Seebohm, *Tribal Custom in Anglo-Saxon Law*, London, 1902, pp. 1 ff.; Liebermann, *Gesetze*, ii. 2, pp. 477 f., 575 f., 591 f., 614, 634, 640 f.; A. Dopsch, *Wirtschaftliche und soziale Grundlagen der europäischen Kulturentwicklung*, ii, 2nd ed., Wien, 1924, pp. 487 ff.; C. Oman, *The Coinage of England*, Oxford, 1931, pp. 1 ff.; George C. Brooke, *English Coins*, London, 1932, pp. 1 ff.

[2] O. G. S. Crawford in *Antiquity*, xiv, 1940, pp. 64 ff.; D. Allen, *The British Museum Quarterly*, xiii, 1938–9, pp. 126 ff.

[3] A. Luschin von Ebengreuth, 'Beiträge zur Münzgeschichte im Frankenreich I' (*Neues Archiv*, xxxiii, 1908, p. 440). On the use of Arab gold coins in the West cf. Marc Bloch, 'Le problème de l'or au moyen âge' (*Annales d'histoire économique et sociale*, v, 1933, pp. 13 f., 19 f.).

the Frankish coinage; the relation of 240 pennies (*denarii*) to the pound is exactly the Frankish system that prevailed under Charles from about 780 at the latest and exerted its influence for centuries. This conformity is a sign of the close connexion of English and Frankish trade in this period.[1] While centesimal systems have been widely introduced under the influence of modern rationalization, conservative England has clung to the old custom. I do not know whether many Englishmen are aware that, when equating 240 pennies to a pound, they are applying a system borrowed from the great Frankish king and emperor of the West.

So far these continental relations of England corresponded with the natural conditions, with the proximity of Gaul, and might have developed on similar lines without Gregory's missionary enterprise. But as a result of this enterprise and its consequences they were expanded and multiplied. We must not forget the difficulties of travelling in this age, particularly across the seas. During the winter the normal traffic ceased; in the Old English poem of the 'Seafarer', those whose 'blissful lot is cast on land' are compared with the man who has to spend the winter 'in paths of exile on the icy sea'. Boniface was in Friesland in 716 during the summer and a part of the autumn, but returned to his English monastery before the winter; he set out again for the Continent in the summer of 718. Similarly two years later Willibald and his companions started from Southampton at the approach of summer. Bede's abbot Ceolfrid left Wearmouth on horseback on the 4th of June in 716. He had to wait for a ship in a monastery near the mouth of the Humber till the 4th of July; it put to shore three times, and Ceolfrid disembarked in Gaul on the 12th of August. Long journeys on land were also often interrupted during the winter; we shall see that this circumstance gave Wilfrid the occasion of his first missionary effort in Frisia during the winter of 678–79. This reduction of winter travel was due to the difficulty of getting fodder for horses. It was for the same reason that the meeting of the Frankish 'campus Martius' was moved in the eighth century from the beginning of March to that of May.

[1] I may also mention the gold coins of Louis the Pious imitated by Archbishop Wigmund of York (837–54). Cf., e.g., Engel and Serrure, *Traité de numismatique du moyen âge*, i, Paris, 1891, pp. 230, 309; Brooke, loc. cit., p. 12 and pl. iii. 1.

Political obstacles sometimes increased the natural difficulties; there were many wars in England, France, and Italy in the seventh and eighth centuries. They hindered an archbishop of Canterbury about 760 from sending a messenger to Lullus of Mainz. An English abbess who wished to go to Rome in the thirties of the same century was warned of the dangers from Arab invaders.[1] Until about 750 everyone passing through Italy on the way to Rome had to cross Byzantine and Lango-bard territory; the malignant ferocity of the Byzantine *milites* is mentioned in this connexion by the biographer of St. Boniface. The travellers were equipped with letters of recommendation addressed to kings and bishops. But the dangers of the road caused Englishmen to wait at the place of disembarkation till a large company had assembled to start together for the journey. About eighty men travelled with Ceolfrid and his company through Gaul in 716, 'diversis collecti de partibus'; two years later 'superveniens collegum multitudo' made the journey with Boniface.

The increasing intercourse occasionally gave rise to political suspicions and created obstacles for travellers. A Byzantine emperor, Constans II, came to the West in 663 to make the last attempt at a reconquest in this age. This successor of Justinian achieved nothing; but the appearance of an emperor in Italy and Sicily during five years, his visits to Naples and Rome, his long stay in Syracuse where he was killed in 668, caused appre-hensions in France. In this same year 668 Archbishop Theodore of Canterbury and Abbot Hadrian were sent by the Pope to England and passed through Gaul. The Byzantines had re-peatedly asked for the help of the Franks against the Langobard invaders of Italy. The suspicion arose that Hadrian, who came from Naples, might have a secret mission from the emperor to the English kings to stir them up against their Frankish neigh-bours, and he was detained for a time by Ebroin, the mighty mayor of the palace. The idea may appear absurd to-day, and was soon dropped by Ebroin.[2] But the incident shows that England by its conversion had been brought into closer con-

[1] Boniface, *Epist.* 27 (p. 48). The Arab invasion of Provence in 737 may be recalled; cf., e.g., *SS. rer. Merov.* v, p. 625, n. 3.

[2] E. Caspar, *Geschichte des Papsttums*, ii, Tübingen, 1933, p. 583, n. 6, has seen the connexion between the Byzantine attempt at a *reconquista* and the detainment of Hadrian.

nexion with the political system of the West. There were some relations with the Langobards, who had been neighbours of the Saxons in their ancient continental homes. A Langobard pretender, Perctarit, was in exile in Gaul, but, fearing for his life, he planned to go overseas to an English king, when the news of the death of the Langobard king, his enemy, induced him to return to Italy, where he himself became king in 672. Wilfrid of York, appealing to the Pope in 679, was received and protected by him. His son and successor Cunincpert (688–700) married an Anglo-Saxon wife; when King Cædwalla of Wessex resigned his throne to go to Rome, he enjoyed Cunincpert's hospitality on his way in 688. Similarly later, Boniface was the guest of King Liutprand.[1]

---

[1] Paulus, *Hist. Langobard.* v. 32, 33, 37, vi. 15 (*MG. SS. rer. Langob.* pp. 155, 157, 169); *Vita Wilfridi*, c. 28 (p. 222); Willibald, *Vita Bonifatii*, cc. 5, 7 (pp. 20, 22, 37).

II

ENGLAND AND THE CHURCH OF ROME

THE occasional contacts with Langobards were of course without consequence. The relations with the Roman Church were quite different. The English Church had been founded and organized by papal emissaries and was conscious of this origin. The connexion with the mother-church was strengthened by the mission of Theodore of Tarsus in Asia Minor, a Greek monk living in Rome; with him came the African Hadrian, who exchanged his monastery near Naples for the Canterbury abbey of SS. Peter and Paul. Theodore was the last continental prelate of England in this age, but not the least. In his twenty-one years as archbishop of Canterbury (669–90), he organized with energy a united English Church which was a 'national' church but did not lose its connexion with Rome. There were limits to papal influence and intervention even in Theodore's time, as appears from the stormy history of Bishop Wilfrid of York and of his Roman appeals. Nevertheless the idea of a universal church under the leadership of the Pope was alive. There were only native bishops and clergy in the England of the eighth century, but the links created in the seventh persisted. In the early ninth century, when the Frankish Church had also come into closer connexion with Rome, the author of a monastic chronicle of northern France could speak of the English people 'qui maxime familia-riores apostolicae sedi semper existunt'.[1]

Papal envoys to England were now the exception. During the dogmatic controversies of the seventh century, before the synod of Constantinople in 680–1 effected the victory of the West over the Monotheletism, Pope Agatho arranged preliminary synods of the occidental countries to strengthen his position with a view to a culminating synod at Rome; the decrees of the Roman synod of 649 were to be confirmed everywhere. Therefore John, the archchanter or precentor of St. Peter's and abbot

---

[1] *Gesta abbatum Fontanellensium*, c. 14, ed. S. Loewenfeld (in *SS. rer. Germ.*), 1886, p. 42; ed. F. Lohier and J. Laporte, *Gesta sanctorum patrum Fontanellensis coenobii*, Rouen–Paris, 1936 (Société de l'histoire de Normandie), p. 75, c. 10. 3.

of St. Martin's, one of the monasteries connected with the Vatican Church,[1] was sent to England with these decrees to bring back a declaration of the orthodox faith of the English Church. The synod of Hatfield, summoned by Archbishop Theodore in September 679, was the result of this mission.[2] Many years passed before we hear again of a papal delegate, when the activity of St. Boniface had initiated reform synods of the Frankish Church and tried to evoke a similar reformative spirit in Britain. Admonitions of Pope Zacharias were read and interpreted at the reform synod of Clovesho in 747; but we do not know the particular circumstances of his intervention nor the text of his letters. Two papal *missi* came to England in 786, accompanied by an abbot of Charles the Great, and caused the two so-called 'Legatine synods' to be convoked in the north and the south for the reform of the Church; the report sent to Pope Hadrian still exists.[3] No other papal delegates are known to have visited England during this century. Pope Leo III sent one in 808 and again in 809 to settle Northumbrian troubles; he had some doubt whether too frequent legations might not have an opposite effect.[4] But a real connexion with the Papacy continued nevertheless: Englishmen went to Rome.

First, there was from the beginning what I may call a routine

---

[1] It is not the church of SS. Silvester and Martin on the Esquiline Hill (S. Martino ai Monti) that is mentioned by the biographer of Ceolfrid, c. 10, and by Bede, *H. E.* iv. 18 and *Hist. abb.* c. 6 (ed. Plummer, pp. 241 f., 369, 391), as W. Bright, *Chapters of Early English Church History*, 3rd ed., 1897, p. 354, n. 5, has suggested, but no doubt the monastery of St. Martin *post S. Petrum* (thus also C. Silva-Tarouca, 'Giovanni "archicantor" di S. Pietro a Roma . . .', *Atti della Pontificia Accademia Romana di archeologia*, Serie III, Memorie I. i, 1923, p. 163). The passages quoted seem to be the earliest evidence for the existence of this monastery; they have to be added to those quoted by P. Kehr, *Italia pontificia*, i. 133, 145, and Chr. Huelsen, *Le chiese di Roma nel medio evo*, Florence, 1927, p. 384.

[2] On the year of the synod (679, not 680) see Poole, *Studies*, p. 44 f., 49; cf. below, pp. 265 f.

[3] The report on the Legatine synods was formerly known from the incomplete text of the Magdeburg Centuries, reprinted by H. and S. iii, pp. 447–62. The MS. was rediscovered at Wolfenbüttel, though a quaternion had been lost in the meantime; see Dümmler's edition, *MG. Epist.* iv. 19–29. Now the year 786 (not 787) is certain, while the identifications with other synods have to be dropped; cf. Helene Tillmann, *Die päpstlichen Legaten in England bis . . . 1218*, Dissertation of Bonn, 1926, pp. 5 ff., 156 ff.; Stenton, *Anglo-Saxon England*, p. 216, n. 5. Cf. also below, pp. 127 ff.

[4] *MG. Epist.* v. 90: 'et ipsi homines dolosi sunt, ut ne, missos super missos suscipientes, in dolositate eveniant'. The papal legate, the deacon Aldulf, was of English origin; see *Annales regni Francorum*, 808 (ed. F. Kurze, *SS. rer. Germ.*, 1895, pp. 126 f.): 'Aldulfus diaconus de ipsa Brittania, natione Saxo.'

intercourse. How far could the laws, rules, and customs of a church that had been established for centuries be applied in the different circumstances of its recent offshoot? Problems and questions arose which the missionaries did not dare answer without instructions from the authority that had sent them forth. The responses given by Gregory I to Augustine are the most famous example of this kind.[1] Such questions, together with reports on the progress and vicissitudes of the mission, had to be taken to Rome by a member of the company or other messenger, who might bring back with the answer other papal letters or the decrees of some Roman synod that had met during the sojourn of the envoy in Rome; there was in fact a correspondence, 'reperta portitoris occasione'.[2] When the new church had struck

[1] The genuineness of the 'responsum Gregorii ad Augustinum' (ed. Hartmann, *MG. Epist.* ii. 331–43; without the introductory part, Bede, *H.E.* i. 27) was contested, after others, by M. Müller, *Theologische Quartalschrift*, cxiii, 1932, pp. 94–118, who sought to show that the document was forged in the last decade before 731. But being quoted in Bede's prose Life of St. Cuthbert, c. 16 (ed. B. Colgrave, p. 208), it must be earlier than 721 (*Bede Essays*, p. 128, n. 2), and being also used by Bede in his Commentary on the Epistle of St. James, c. 1. 15 (Migne, *P.L.* xciii. 14), as Plummer has observed (*Baedae Op. hist.* ii. 54 f.), it must have existed shortly after 709. I do not doubt that it is in fact genuine, as I concede to D. Knowles, *J.T.S.* xxxix, 1938, pp. 127 f. and *The Monastic Order in England*, Cambridge, 1940, p. 619, n. 3. To the MSS. of the complete text (see Hartmann, loc. cit., pp. 331 f.) a volume written in Spanish uncials about 700 has to be added, Copenhagen, Ny Kgl. Saml. 58, 8vo, fols. 86v–117v, according to E. Jørgensen, *Catalogus codicum Latinorum medii aevi Bibliothecae Regiae Hafniensis*, 1926, p. 272; the text seems to be similar to the famous Lucca MS. 490. The MS. also contains among other pieces fols. 1v–35 the Penitential of the Pseudo-Cummeanus (cf. J. T. McNeill and H. M. Gamer, *Medieval Handbooks of Penance*, New York, 1938, p. 63, n. 34; pp. 67, 99, 437, 444) and fols. 52–69v the 'Epitome Hispana' (cf. Fr. Maassen, *Geschichte der Quellen und der Literatur des canonischen Rechts*, i, 1870, pp. 646 ff.), also similar to the Lucensis.

[2] Pope Boniface V to Queen Ethelberg, in Bede, *H.E.* ii. 11 (pp. 106. 12).—I may mention in this connexion the leaden *bulla* found at Whitby and best reproduced, as far as I know, by D. H. Haigh, 'The Monasteries of S. Heiu and S. Hild' (*The Yorkshire Archaeological and Topographical Journal*, iii, London, 1875, p. 371); cf. also Hübner, *Inscriptiones Britanniae Christianae*, p. 81, no. 221; J. Raine, *The Historians of the Church of York*, i. 8, n. 3; Plummer, *Baedae Op. hist.* ii. 321; Colgrave, *The Life of Bishop Wilfrid*, p. 153. The seal, which belongs to the Whitby Museum, is not accessible at present. I am indebted to H. B. Browne, M.A., Hon.
Secretary of the Whitby Literary
and Philosophical Society, for a
photograph taken some years ago
and reproduced here. The inscriptions on the obverse and reverse

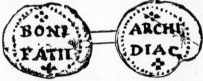

obviously follow the example of the papal bulls of this age, the type of which was constant from Boniface V (619–25) to Leo IV (847–55), and especially of the bulls of

root and lived its own life along the traditional lines, there were
the rights reserved to the head of the Church and no doubt also
other occasions for his intervention. A Northumbrian abbot
Forthreth personally appealed to Pope Paul in 757–8 for the
restoration of three monasteries of which he had been deprived
by the king of Northumbria; we have a letter of the Pope asking
for the restoration of the minsters but do not know the result of
the intervention.[1] When the people of Kent rose in rebellion
against the lordship of the Mercian king in 796 and made a
priest, Eadbert Praen, their ruler, Archbishop Ethelhard of
Canterbury supported the Mercian cause; at his request Pope
Leo anathematized the 'apostate',[2] who soon succumbed to his
enemies. During the quarrels of King Cœnwulf of Mercia
(796–821) with Archbishop Wulfred about two monasteries and
other possessions, the king sent accusations against Wulfred
to the Apostolic See, but also gave out that, if Wulfred would
not comply with his demands, he must go into exile, nor would
letters from the Pope or the Emperor (Louis the Pious) make
any difference. When after some years an (abortive) agreement
was reached, Cœnwulf promised to declare the 'innocence' and
'security' of the Archbishop to the Pope.[3] There may have been
more occasions of papal interference than are mentioned in the
scanty records.

Metropolitans and their Pallia

The division of dioceses and the creation of new bishoprics
was in those days an internal affair which could be managed
without reference to the Pope, if the bishops concerned agreed.
But there was also the higher office of the metropolitan, the

Boniface V himself; cf. C. Serafini, *Le monete e le bolle plumbee pontificie del Medagliere
Vaticano*, i, Milan, 1910, pl. A2. 3. The archdeacon was identified, probably rightly,
with the Roman archdeacon whose friendship Wilfrid gained during his first stay at
Rome about 655 (*Vita Wilfridi*, c. 5, p. 198; cf. c. 53, p. 248), and there has been
some speculation on the document to which this seal may have been attached, and
on the occasion of its coming to England. But it may have protected a mere letter
or a present like that sent 'obsignatum' to St. Boniface by another Roman archdeacon, Theophylactus (Boniface, *Epist.* 84, p. 189). On the use of leaden bulls cf.,
e.g., A. Eitel, *Ueber Blei- und Goldbullen im Mittelalter*, Freiburg i. Br., 1912; Poole,
Studies, pp. 95 ff. They do not mention this seal 'Bonifatii archidiac(oni)'.

[1] Jaffé, i. 2337; H. and S. iii. 394; Birch, i, no. 184.

[2] *MG. Epist.* iv. 188; cf. 189, 192.

[3] H. and S. iii. 586 (n. *a*), 596 ff.; Birch, i, no. 384. Cf. the letter of Pope Leo III
to Charles the Great of 808, *MG. Epist.* v. 90; below, pp. 251 f.

head of an ecclesiastical province, whose function was not only to govern a diocese himself but also to supervise other bishops administering dioceses situated in his province. This system was based on the political organization of the late Roman Empire. The diocese of the bishop corresponded to a *civitas*, a city district, while the ecclesiastical province was analogous to the secular province of the fourth century comprising several *civitates*, with the secular capital of the province, the *metropolis*, as centre. Provinces and *civitates* of the Empire survived in this way and could in general be recognized after the fall of the Empire, for example in Gaul, in the shape of the provinces and dioceses of the Church. Gregory the Great transferred this system to England in his scheme of 601, by which he organized the new Church in two provinces of London (Canterbury took its place) and York. Gregory's plan was premature. When the bishop of York was made metropolitan by the Pope in 634, York was already lost by the fall of King Edwin in the previous year. For a century the English Church formed a single province with the archbishop of Canterbury as its head. No doubt this unity of the Church, particularly from the times of Archbishop Theodore, together with the meetings of the bishops in synods, had a centralizing tendency and prepared the spiritual unity of the English nation, whose political union in these centuries of the so-called Heptarchy was still far off. The position of Canterbury was changed in accordance with Gregory's design in 735, when the province of York and the metropolitan dignity of the bishop were restored. This consummation could not be attained without the participation and consent of the Pope. His intervention was again necessary when the ambition of King Offa of Mercia sought the creation of a third metropolitan see and province, to be vested in the Mercian bishopric of Lichfield at the cost of Canterbury. The Pope complied with this demand in 788.[1] He had to be asked once more for his consent when, Offa having died, the third province was abolished at King Coenwulf's request and the division of the country into two metropolitan sees was restored. This took place in 802, after the archbishop of Canterbury had himself visited Rome.

The part played by the Pope in the provincial organization of the English Church was closely related to the history of the

[1] Cf. Tillmann, loc. cit., pp. 156 ff.

pallium.[1] The pallium is a band of white wool, of a special kind and significance, worn by the Pope; he can confer it on his vicars and on other bishops of merit to be worn in their districts on certain occasions, like a modern decoration. The foundation of the English Church was of particular importance in this connexion, because the theory then emerged that the metropolitan bishop *must* have received the pallium from Rome as a token of his rank to qualify him for the exercise of his functions as the head of the province. In Gregory's scheme of 601 the 'usus pallii' and 'metropolitani honor', the right to institute and consecrate the bishops of the province, were combined in this way for the first time on record. The title of 'archbishop' also was attached to this combination in England. It was given in the Mediterranean countries first to bishops who had a higher position than metropolitans, viz. to those of Rome, Alexandria, Constantinople. Later it was extended to others, such as the bishop of Ravenna. The Popes applied it about 600 to bishops of special importance but on no clear system. The title was quite unusual in the Frankish Church; but in the English Church of the seventh century the metropolitan, the bearer of the pallium, and the archbishop became identical notions, and the terms were used interchangeably by the Popes of the eighth century.[2] The metropolitan or archbishop is attached to the Roman See by the pallium; he is the connecting link between the Pope and the bishops of the province and is called to a share in the papal rights. He does not, of course, enjoy 'plenitudinem potestatis', but he is specially called 'in partem sollicitudinis', to use a famous formula applied in the fifth century to the papal vicars. Before receiving the pallium he is required to send to the Pope a written profession of faith.[3] He convokes and presides over the provincial synods. It is his duty to examine whether the elections of the bishops are in accord with canon law. From the end of the eighth century (796) the bishop elect must make

[1] Cf. Curt-Bogislav Graf von Hacke, *Die Palliumverleihungen bis 1143*, Dissertation of Göttingen, 1898, pp. 102 ff.; E. Lesne, *La hiérarchie épiscopale en Gaule et Germanie 742–882*, Lille and Paris, 1905, pp. 30 ff.; H. Nottarp, *Die Bistumserrichtung in Deutschland im achten Jahrhundert* (Kirchenrechtl. Abhandl. xcvi), Stuttgart, 1920, pp. 176 ff.

[2] Cf., e.g., Lesne, loc. cit., pp. 26 (n. 3), 28 (n. 2), 31 ff.; A. Testi Rasponi, 'Archiepiscopus' (*Bulletin Du Cange*, iii, 1927, pp. 5–11); *Thesaurus linguae Latinae*, ii (1900–6), 461.

[3] Cf. Appendix II, pp. 233 ff., on the profession of Lullus.

a profession of obedience and faith to the archbishop of Canterbury, such as the latter has already been required to make to the Pope.

An archbishop is elected and consecrated in the same way as any other bishop. But the fact that he must have the pallium in order to exercise metropolitan rights obliges a new archbishop (or the king interested and influential in his election) to petition the Pope for the grant of it. A new diocese can be constituted without papal intervention (though the Pope may be asked to confirm the new see), but not an ecclesiastical province, because the metropolitan must receive the pallium from Rome. The restoration of the province of York, for example, was effected by the arrival of the pallium from the Pope in 735 (and, no doubt, of relevant charters, now lost); no bishop of York had received the pallium since the days of Paulinus, a century before. Egbert, the new archbishop, was a relative of the Northumbrian king, and one may suppose, even without Bede's known letter to Egbert, that the king took part in the negotiations which preceded the re-establishment of the Gregorian scheme. Some negotiation, at least the sending of an envoy and of a petition to Rome, necessarily followed the election of every archbishop. There were eight archbishops of Canterbury from the death of Theodore in 690 to the early ninth century, as well as five archbishops of York from Egbert. Thus the question of the pallium must have given rise to negotiations with the Pope thirteen times during this period, apart from those occasioned by the shortlived promotion of the see of Lichfield. We get some inkling of the procedure when we see the election of an archbishop and the receipt of his pallium recorded in annals, and observe a considerable interval between the two events.

There even exists a letter of the bishops and priests of 'all Britain' to a Pope on the subject of the pallium. They object to the requirement that an archbishop should travel in person to Rome to receive the pallium, and hint at the 'Simoniaca haeresis' of payments demanded for the grant; they refer to Bede and to Alcuin to show the different practice of former times. The text is commonly ascribed to the year 805 and referred to Pope Leo III, but wrongly. The archbishops of Canterbury went to Rome to receive the pallium not about 800, but in the tenth century (at least from 927), those of York not till a century later (1026). In my opinion the document belongs to the tenth or more probably to the early eleventh century; it has some significance in the history of the relations between the English Church and the Papacy, but in later times, not in our period.[1]

Monastic Privileges[2]

Application for the pallium is one example of the regular intercourse between England and the Continent, as it resulted from church organization and custom. There was another feature of church life which also called for papal co-operation. This was monasticism, which from the outset had a prominent place in the English Church. Gregory the Great was a patron of the monks; he had himself renounced worldly life to enter one of the monasteries which he had founded. We owe to his 'Dialogues' whatever is known of St. Benedict, legendary as it may be, apart from the *Regula* of the latter, the Rule which was to dominate Western monachism. Augustine and a large number of his companions were monks; Canterbury saw the foundation not only of the cathedral of the Saviour, but also of the monastery of SS. Peter and Paul. The advance of the Roman cause from Kent to the north carried with it the progress of the Rule of St. Benedict; Wilfrid of York was proud of having first introduced it into Northumbria.[3] Monasteries had already been planted there by the Irish missionaries; it is common knowledge that monachism had even greater importance in the Irish than in the Roman Church, and the spiritual influence of Celtic monasticism survived the victory of the Roman party, as the example of St. Cuthbert suggests. Gaul likewise made its contribution to English monastic life: the English double monasteries of nuns and monks ruled by an abbess represented a type

---

[1] See Appendix III, pp. 241 ff.

[2] In general cf. Terence P. McLaughlin, *Le Très Ancien Droit monastique de l'occident* (Archives de la France monastique, xxxviii), Ligugé and Paris, 1935, where earlier literature is indicated.

[3] On the text of the Rule used in early England cf. L. Traube, *Textgeschichte der Regula S. Benedicti*, 2nd ed. (Abhandl. München xxv. 2), 1910, p. 45 and pp. 57 f. on Hatton MS. 48 of the Bodleian Library, the oldest existent copy of the Rule, of about 700. On this manuscript, which comes from Worcester (N. R. Ker, *The Bodleian Library Record*, ii, no. 17, December 1941, pp. 28 f.; Ivor Atkins and N. R. Ker, *Catalogus librorum manuscriptorum bibliothecae Wigorniensis*, Cambridge, 1944, pp. 7 f., 48, 66), cf. also Lowe, *Codices Lat. ant.* ii, no. 240, and his book, *Regula S. Benedicti*, Oxford, 1929.

which was transferred from northern France to England about the middle of the seventh century.[1] They were convents of nuns, but monks helped in building, in organizing, and in celebrating the divine service; the monks lived apart, but were also under the government of the abbess.

The well-devised Rule of St. Benedict had to be interpreted and put into practice; thus the possibility arose of different customs, *consuetudines*, established by the influence of a strong personality or the acknowledged standard of a monastic house. Founders of English monasteries, or monks wishing to join a community based on sound principles and training, sometimes visited the old ascetic centres of the Continent. Benedict Biscop, the founder of Wearmouth and Jarrow, inquired into the *statuta* of ancient monasteries in Gaul and Italy, in the famous insular community of Lérins, and in Rome and its neighbourhood. The Rule of St. Benedict was authoritative in his two houses, but his institutions were based on the experience of seventeen monasteries which he had visited during his travels. When Fulda had been founded by St. Boniface and the Benedictine Rule introduced, Abbot Sturmi and two brethren went to Rome and Monte Cassino to study the customs and traditions of the monasteries in 'Italy' and Tuscany.[2]

The organization of the Western Church in dioceses with fixed frontiers, which generally prevailed, did not exclude the monasteries from the supervision of the bishop, and, as Bede's letter to Egbert of York shows, there were also monks who thought it necessary for the maintenance of the monastic ideal that episcopal interference should be possible. On the other hand, the monasteries had to be protected against arbitrary meddling by the bishop with the monastic life, and against encroachments on their property or on the freedom of the election of the abbot. As early as 672 a canon of the synod of Hertford declared that no bishop was permitted to disturb (*inquietare*) a monastery, or to abstract anything of its property by force. The devotion to and the fear of St. Peter, the door-keeper of Heaven, seemed to give a further guarantee against

---

[1] Cf. Stephanus Hilpisch, *Die Doppelklöster: Entstehung und Organisation*, Dissertation of Bonn (Beiträge zur Geschichte des alten Mönchtums und des Benediktinerordens ed. Ild. Herwegen, xv), Münster, 1928, pp. 44 ff.

[2] Eigil, *Vita Sturmi*, c. 14 (*MG. SS.* ii. 371 f.); *Supplex libellus* of the monks of Fulda of 812, c. 10 (*MG. Epist.* iv. 549); cf. Rudolf's *Vita Leobae*, c. 10 (*MG. SS.* xv. 125).

such encroachments. Therefore the papal authority was invoked to safeguard monastic rights. We have another example of the connexion with Rome in the petitions of monasteries for privileges and in the papal grants of these. Some of the latter, relating to English religious houses, are forged or falsified and must be set on one side; but from the time of Pope Agatho (678–81) we reach safer ground. Benedict Biscop brought back from Rome in 679 a privilege of Agatho for his foundation of Wearmouth; it was confirmed by Pope Sergius (687–701) and was extended to Jarrow (founded in the meantime), perhaps in 700, when Abbot Ceolfrid sent some monks to Rome. These privileges were ratified by the signatures of the king of Northumbria and of certain bishops; it is a way of confirming papal charters, which was also adopted in other cases in this country. The privileges to Wearmouth and Jarrow are lost; but we are reliably informed that they aimed at security against irruption from outside and at liberty for the election of the abbot on his personal merits, and not on the ground of hereditary position.[1] Agatho also granted a privilege to Bishop Wilfrid for his monasteries of Ripon and Hexham, when the latter appealed to the Pope against his deposition and visited Rome in 679 and 680. In this privilege the 'liberty' of the monastery of Ripon was mentioned, which was lost, in Wilfrid's opinion, when it became the see of a bishop; he committed the monasteries with all their properties to St. Peter, and Agatho 'ascribed' both monasteries in one privilege to the Apostolic See. The 'ascription' made the monasteries directly dependent on the Pope, who conferred them on Wilfrid. This privilege also is known only by quotations;[2] it was evidently a privilege not only of protection but also of exemption, substituting the Apostolic See for the regular jurisdiction of the diocesan bishop, in the same way as half a century earlier Bobbio, the Italian foundation of

---

[1] *Vita Ceolfridi*, cc. 16, 20, 25 (ed. Plummer, pp. 393, 395 f.); Bede, *Hist. abb.* cc. 6, 11, 15, 16 (ib., pp. 369, 375, 380 f.) and *H.E.* iv. 18 (p. 241). On the visit of Ceolfrid's monks to Rome about Christmas 700 see Bede, *De temporum ratione*, c. 47 (ed. C. W. Jones, *Bedae Opera de temporibus*, Cambridge, Mass., 1943, p. 267); cf. below, p. 277.

[2] *Vita Wilfridi*, cc. 45, 47, 51 (*SS. rer. Merov.* vi. 239, 242, 245). In the last chapter (ed. Colgrave, p. 106) Wilfrid in his petition presented to Pope John VI mentioned his two monasteries, 'quae a sancto Agathone papa huic apostolicae sedis sub uno privilegio asscripta sunt'. I substitute the dative *sedi* for the reading of the two MSS. *sedis*; the *s* was obviously added under the influence of the following *sub*.

the Irishman St. Columbanus, had been withdrawn from the jurisdiction of the bishop of Tortona.

We have what is probably another early example of such a privilege in England. The charters of SS. Peter and Paul or, as the monastery was afterwards called, St. Augustine's of Canterbury, include evident forgeries; a critical examination of the whole series is a desideratum of English diplomatics. Now there is a privilege granted by the same Pope Agatho to St. Augustine's.[1] Its authenticity has been doubted or denied, and the text, which exists only in later copies, is corrupt in details; there are mistakes in the numerals of the date, and the end of the text is spoilt. But a genuine papal privilege of the early Middle Ages underlies it; for the wording generally corresponds to a formula of the so-called 'Liber Diurnus', the earliest existing formulary of the papal chancery. This collection has sometimes been overrated; it was not *the* formulary of the chancery, but the only one which survived from this age, and it was perhaps not intended for practical use in the chancery but for the instruction of its pupils.[2] The original series was collected from real documents in the seventh century, except that names and dates were omitted to adapt the texts to the purposes of a formulary, and additions were gradually made till the end of the eighth or the beginning of the ninth century. The privilege of Agatho is based on a formula (No. 32) of the earliest part, a text of the seventh century, a privilege by which a monastery was put under the immediate jurisdiction of the Roman Church and the authority of another bishop was entirely excluded; no bishop could even celebrate mass there except on the invitation of the abbot.[3] There is only one addition to the

---

[1] Birch, i, no. 38; cf. Jaffé, ii, p. 741, no. 2105 a. Cf. Appendix I, pp. 187 ff.

[2] Cf. Leo Santifaller, 'Die Verwendung des Liber Diurnus in den Privilegien der Päpste bis zum Ende des 11. Jahrhunderts' (*MÖIG.* xlix, 1935, pp. 225–366). This is not the place to examine the controversies about the origin of the *Liber Diurnus* (cf., e.g., Caspar, loc. cit. ii. 617 ff., 782 ff.). I use the edition by Th. Sickel, Vienna, 1889; but I have also paid attention to the facsimile of the Ambrosianus published by L. Gramatica and G. Galbiati, *Il codice Ambrosiano del Liber diurnus Romanorum pontificum* (Analecta Ambrosiana, vii), Milan, 1921. The missing Codex Claromontanus, which contains the same recension as the Ambrosianus, was recently rediscovered in a monastery in Holland, Egmond-Binnen; see K. Mohlberg, *Theologische Revue,* 1939, nos. 8–9, cols. 297 ff. I have not seen W. M. Peitz, *Das vorephesinische Symbol der Papstkanzlei* (Miscellanea Historiae Pontificiae, i), Rome, 1939.

[3] *Liber Diurnus,* no. 32 (p. 23): 'nisi ab abbate monasterii fuerit invitatus'; so also

formula of Agatho's charter, on the liberty to elect the abbot. It may be a later interpolation designed to safeguard a free election against the interference of the archbishops of Canterbury; a close examination of all the records of St. Augustine's might perhaps give some certainty on this point. But two facts can be adduced in defence of this addition: it corresponds to what we know of the Wearmouth privilege of the same Pope, and there exists a privilege of a Pope Gregory, the second or third of this name (between 715 and 741) rather than the first, for two monasteries near Beneventum, in which the same formula of the *Liber Diurnus* was enlarged by a similar addition on the election of the abbot.[1]

I cannot discuss the few other papal privileges for English monasteries which are ascribed to the later part of the seventh or to the beginning of the eighth century.[2] The charters for Ripon and Hexham and, if it is reliable, that for St. Augustine's, show that at least from about 680 there existed English monastic houses which were put under the direct jurisdiction of the Apostolic See and were exempted from the authority of the diocesan. In the next century St. Boniface strove hard to organize the German Church and to reform the Frankish Church in accordance with the Roman tradition; the establishment or restoration of the diocesan system was one of his objects. There is one fact which might be considered to be in conflict with this aim: in 744 he founded the monastery of Fulda in Hesse which was to be a place of rest to him in old age and death; in 751 Pope Zacharias granted him at his request a privilege, by which

Agatho. Cf. Bede, *Hist. abb.* c. 11 (p. 375): 'Hunc vobis *accito episcopo* rogetis abbatem consueta benedictione firmari'; c. 20 (p. 384): '*advocatur episcopus* Acca et solita illum in abbatis officium benedictione confirmat.' Santifaller, loc. cit., pp. 251, 266, 272 ff., 298, observed the conformity of charter and formula and evidently considered the privilege genuine, while W. Holtzmann, *Papsturkunden*, i, p. 231, called it a forgery. Cf. below, p. 189.

[1] Jaffé, i. 1926; *MG. Epist.* ii. 468 f. Cf. Caspar, loc. cit. ii. 416, n. 4; Santifaller, p. 238, n. 24; McLaughlin, loc. cit., p. 189. In general cf., e.g., K. Brandi, *Ausgewählte Aufsätze*, Oldenburg, 1938, pp. 262 f.

[2] I will only mention the privilege of Pope Constantine for Bermondsey and Woking (Jaffé, i. 2148; Birch, i, no. 133); its authenticity is also accepted by F. M. Stenton, 'Medeshamstede and its colonies' (*Historical Essays in honour of James Tait*, Manchester, 1933, pp. 319 ff.). But the privileges of Agatho for Chertsey and of Constantine for Evesham (Jaffé, i. 2115, 2149; Birch, i, nos. 56, 129) are evident forgeries and cannot be accepted as 'in substance perfectly genuine' (Knowles, *The Monastic Order in England*, p. 576).

the monastery was made subject to the direct jurisdiction of the Roman See and was withdrawn from that of the diocesan bishop.[1] The privilege is based on the same formula of the 'Liber Diurnus' which I have mentioned above; it was interpolated in the early ninth century, but it also exists in its genuine form and is an exact copy of this formula, without any addition. Fulda is the first German example of a monastery thus exempted; Boniface's compatriot and successor at Mainz, Lullus, tried to put an end to this independent position and to subject Fulda to the diocesan authority. How could a man so imbued with a sense of order and regularity as Boniface repudiate this authority where his own foundation was concerned? Psychological explanations suggest themselves; but it may be doubted whether he was aware of any inconsistency at all in his conduct in view of the papal privileges granted to English monasteries at a time when he was himself a member of such communities. Many monasteries were founded in the Frankish countries during the seventh century as a result of the ascetic movement initiated by St. Columbanus and his followers. Here also the tendency towards independence and exemption from the episcopal authority can be observed, and several of these Gallic monasteries did in fact obtain exemption, but usually by a privilege of the diocesan bishop himself, to which a royal privilege was sometimes added; papal privileges of exemption to Gallic monasteries were an exception in this age. They were first granted to Italian houses, next to English, then to German monasteries beginning with Fulda; the further development does not concern us.

We have another kind of papal privileges in connexion with English monasteries. The aristocratic character of the Western Church in the early Middle Ages has been rightly emphasized by Aloys Schulte and his school; England was no exception in this respect, as Heinrich Boehmer has shown.[2] Ceolfrid, when prior of Wearmouth, had difficulties, because monks of noble

[1] Boniface, *Epist.* 89 (ed. Tangl, pp. 203 ff.); Edmund E. Stengel, *Urkundenbuch des Klosters Fulda*, i. 1, Marburg, 1913, pp. 25 ff., nos. 15–16; cf. the articles of both editors quoted there.

[2] Aloys Schulte, *Der Adel und die deutsche Kirche im Mittelalter* (Kirchenrechtl. Abhandl. lxiii–lxiv), Stuttgart, 1910, p. 196, with 'Nachtrag' of the 2nd edition, 1922, pp. 18 f., referring to Heinrich Boehmer, 'Das germanische Christentum' (*Theologische Studien und Kritiken*, lxxxvi, 1913, pp. 193 ff., 278 ff.). Cf. also Plummer, *Baedae Op. hist.* i, p. xxxv, n. 1; Stenton, *Anglo-Saxon England*, p. 162; and, on later times, Knowles, *The Monastic Order in England*, pp. 103, 137, 423 f.

descent resented the practice of discipline according to the monastic Rule. Landowners exerted a predominant influence in this age of prevailing agrarian economy; proprietary churches and monasteries were a result, *Eigenkirchen* and *Eigenklöster*, to use the terms adopted by Ulrich Stutz, whose essay on *Eigenkirchen* has been made more accessible to English readers by the translation of Geoffrey Barraclough.[1] Landowners founded churches and monasteries on their property and thereafter considered them as a part of it in spite of the restrictions set by canon law (c. 24 of the synod of Chalcedon of 451, &c.). The proprietor sometimes claimed his share of the revenue of the church or monastery or to appoint the priest, abbot, or abbess; the modern patronage and advowson are a survival of these proprietary rights and claims. Such tendencies might be a source of danger to the monastic ideals.[2] A number of monasteries and convents were moreover established in England less to realize ascetic conceptions than to settle members of the founder's family, his widow, sons, or daughters, who would enjoy the exemptions from service granted to monastic houses. I may here refer again to Bede's letter to Egbert of York. Even in communities of a high standard the tendency may be observed to 'elect' as successor of an abbot or abbess a member of his or her family, or particularly of the founder's family; it was a natural tendency, and there is no need to attribute it to the influence of Irish monastic practice. There are plenty of examples of this kind of succession in English convents in the seventh and eighth centuries. It may also be no mere chance that in the Lindisfarne Confraternity Book of the ninth century, the *Liber Vitae Dunelmensis*, there are special categories of 'nomina regum vel ducum', 'nomina abbatum', and so on, but the 'nomina reginarum et abbatissarum' are combined: it was evidently a common practice for a queen after the death of her consort to become abbess of a convent of the royal house. One

---

[1] *Mediaeval Germany*, ii (Studies in Mediaeval History, ii), Oxford, 1938, pp. 35–70, translation of U. Stutz, *Die Eigenkirche als Element des mittelalterlich-germanischen Kirchenrechtes*, Berlin, 1895. On further literature cf. Stutz in *Real-Enzyklopädie für protestantische Theologie und Kirche*, ed. Herzog and Hauck, 3rd ed., xxiii, 1913, pp. 364 ff.; McLaughlin, loc. cit., pp. 232 ff.; on England, H. Boehmer, 'Das Eigenkirchentum in England' (*Texte und Forschungen zur Englischen Kulturgeschichte, Festgabe für Felix Liebermann*, Halle, 1921, pp. 301–53). Cf. Stenton, loc. cit., pp. 162 f.
[2] Cf., e.g., the privilege of Wihtred of Kent, Birch, i, no. 91; H. and S. iii, 238.

may also doubt whether Bede and Alcuin, writing on *heredes*, *posteri*, or *successiones legitimas* of monastic founders, were thinking only of spiritual heirs.[1] 'Elections' such as I have indicated were contrary to the spirit of the Rule of St. Benedict, who ordered with regard to the abbot: 'Vitae autem merito et sapientiae doctrina elegatur qui ordinandus est, etiamsi ultimus fuerit in ordine congregationis.' Benedict Biscop warned his monks against electing, 'iuxta successionem generis', even his own brother, and Bede raised his voice against those who founded so-called monasteries, made them hereditary by royal decree, and even obtained the confirmation and signatures of bishops and abbots.[2]

Further than this, even Popes were petitioned to confirm such proprietary rights, which easily conflicted with canon law, though they were established by practice.[3] In the last part of the papal formulary, the *Liber Diurnus*, which was added after 772 in the time of Hadrian I,[4] there is the formula (no. 93) of a 'privilegium' by which a Pope confirmed to somebody,

---

[1] Bede, *H.E.* v. 11 (p. 302. 26); Alcuin, *Vita Willibrordi*, pref. and cc. 1, 21 (*SS. rer. Merov.* vii, pp. 114. 7; 116. 17, 19; 132. 10).

[2] German examples of proprietary monasteries are found in the correspondence of Boniface, nos. 83 and 130 (pp. 186 f., 267 ff.), the latter being partly misinterpreted in the headings of the modern editions (the contents were better represented by H. Hahn, *Bonifaz und Lul*, p. 335). Bishop Megingoz of Würzburg was expecting the death of his sister, an abbess. There were two young daughters of his brother in her convent (*monasteriolum, cellula*); but they were not yet fit for the dignity of abbess which ignorant people might be inclined to confer upon one or the other (obviously in view of family rights). Therefore Megingoz wanted a suitable person quickly made abbess in the interest of the order and stability of the convent, to avoid its dispersal, and asked for Lullus's advice (but not about the 'foundation' of a convent).

[3] As early as A.D. 558–60 Pope Pelagius I acknowledged that 'monachorum electio' and 'possessionis dominus' participated in the appointment of the abbot of an Italian monastery; cf. Jaffé, i. 987.

[4] A fixed point is given by a formula (no. 82) which has been referred by Sickel and others, rightly in my opinion, to the election of Pope Hadrian in 772, as the text is transmitted in the Vatican MS.; it was changed in the recension of the Claromontanus and Ambrosianus (no. 58) on the occasion of the election of Leo III in 795 (but the Ambrosianus agrees with the Vaticanus in *diaconi*, p. 88. 13, and substitutes *presbytero* for *diacono* with the Claromontanus, p. 90. 2 only). H. Steinacker assigned the formula to 795 instead of 772, 'Zum Liber diurnus . . .' (*Miscellanea Francesco Ehrle*, iv=*Studi e Testi*, xl, Rome, 1924, pp. 108 ff.); but the objections of W. Erben, *Historische Zeitschr.* cxlv, 1932, pp. 584 f., are convincing. I refer of course to the date of the recension preserved in the Vatican MS., not to the date of the manuscript itself, which was written in the early 9th century and was therefore omitted by Lowe in the first part of his *Codices Lat. ant.*, the limit of which is A.D. 800.

called 'excellentia vestra', and to his wife and offspring, the possession of monasteries and monastic properties. In such formulas the proper names that occurred in the copied documents were generally omitted; but by chance one name was preserved in transcribing this text, that of the wife of the person addressed: 'Cynedridae regine.'[1] She was the consort of King Offa of Mercia, and is known by his charters and by coins.[2] It follows that the privilege which formed the basis of the formula was granted to Offa by Pope Hadrian, between 772 and 795. We learn from the text that Offa had erected or justly acquired many monasteries and had established and consecrated them all in honour of and in the name of St. Peter. Unfortunately, though naturally, the names of the monasteries and of their possessions were omitted in the *Liber Diurnus*. The formula was later used on several occasions for comprehensive papal confirmations of a similar kind; two may be mentioned. The first, of which the papyrus original exists, is a privilege of Pope Paschalis I granted to the Church of Ravenna in 819; it refers to lost charters of Hadrian I and Leo III.[3] The second is a privilege of the same Pope Paschalis granted to Offa's second successor, King Cœnwulf of Mercia, in 817; it is transcribed in two cartularies of Winchcombe Abbey in Gloucestershire. Evidently only portions of the crumbling papyrus were at the disposal of the copyists; here the list of monasteries and possessions is also missing.[4]

King Offa had manifold connexions with Pope Hadrian. I have mentioned the visit of the papal legates in 786 (p. 16)

---

[1] *Liber Diurnus*, ed. Sickel, p. 122, mentioned by W. H. Stevenson, 'Trinoda Necessitas' (*E.H.R.* xxix, 1914, p. 700, n. 49). The *arenga* or preamble of the formula partly depends on a letter of Gregory I, *Registr.* ix. 216 (*MG. Epist.* ii. 203), or on a similar text. The usual word *ill.* was substituted for the proper name in the second recension of the *Liber Diurnus*, in the Claromontanus and Ambrosianus (no. 73). It is highly improbable that the name of Cynedrida was not transcribed from an underlying charter but is the addition of a copyist, as W. Peitz has assumed, *Liber Diurnus*, i (SB. Wien, clxxxv. 4), 1918, pp. 123 ff.

[2] Cf., e.g., Bruce Dickins, 'Queen Cynethryth of Mercia' (*Proceedings of the Leeds Philosophical and Literary Society, Literary and Historical Section*, iv, 1936–8, p. 54). The identity of the queen mentioned in the formula with King Offa's consort was recognized by Sickel, *Liber Diurnus*, p. xxviii and *Prolegomena zum Liber Diurnus*, ii (SB. Wien, cxvii. 13), 1889, pp. 28 f. Another Cynethryth was the wife of King Wigla of Mercia (827–40); but his reign is too late, not to mention other reasons.

[3] Cf. below, p. 257, n. 2. On charters depending on formula no. 93 cf. Santifaller, loc. cit., p. 269.

[4] See Appendix IV, pp. 255 ff.

and the promotion of Lichfield to a metropolitan see, granted by Hadrian to the king in 788 (p. 19). At the Legatine synod of 786 Offa promised to send the Roman Church a present of 365 mancuses every year;[1] this donation seems to have had a part in the preliminary history of Peter's Pence. Which were the monasteries built or acquired by Offa and all dedicated to St. Peter? Certainly he got by exchange in 781 the monastery of Bath, of which St. Peter was in fact the patron saint.[2] Probably he owned as heir the monastery of Bredon in Worcestershire founded by his grandfather Eanwulf and also dedicated to St. Peter; Offa himself provided it with gifts.[3] He obtained by force the monastery of Cookham in Berkshire.[4] In Winchcombe he is credited with having founded in 787 a convent of nuns, to which King Cœnwulf added a house for monks in 798; here also the original dedication seems to have been to St. Peter, though later St. Mary supplanted him.[5] In any case we have here another type of papal monastic privilege granted to English kings of the late eighth and early ninth centuries. It was of a singular character: the Pope consented that the monasteries and their possessions mentioned in the charter should remain 'sub dicione' of the king, queen, and their descendants ('natorum vestrorum genealogie') 'in perpetuum'. The fragmentary charter of Paschalis was inscribed (if the text is reliable) 'Kenulfo [that is, Cœnwulf] regi suisque heredibus vel ubi largire voluerit'. The Winchcombe cartularies contain also a further privilege which Pope Leo III (795–816) granted to Cœnwulf;[6] it was based on

[1] Letter of Pope Leo III to Cœnwulf of Mercia of 797, *MG. Epist.* iv. 188 f. On the origin of Peter's Pence cf., e.g., Liebermann, *Gesetze*, ii. 2, pp. 608 ff.

[2] Birch, i, no. 241. Cf. W. Hunt, *Two Chartularies of the Priory of St. Peter at Bath*, Somerset Record Society, 1893, p. xxxvii; William of Malmesbury, *Gesta pontificum*, ii. 90 (ed. Hamilton, p. 194). [3] Birch, i, nos. 209–10, 234 (cf. ii, no. 847), 236.

[4] H. and S. iii. 512 f.; Birch, i, no. 291. Cf. F. M. Stenton, *The Early History of the Abbey of Abingdon*, Reading, 1913, pp. 22, 24 f.

[5] See Appendix IV, pp. 257 f. Offa is also said to have restored Westminster (*Mon. Angl.* i. 266), which was likewise dedicated to St. Peter. But there seems to be no early authority in support of this assertion, which may be based on the charter of 785, by which Offa granted or rather sold some land to this church (Birch, i, no. 245). The forged charter of King Edgar of 969 (A. S. Napier and W. H. Stevenson, *The Crawford Collection of Early Charters*, Oxford, 1895, no. 6, p. 13) with its source (cf. ib. p. 90; Birch iii, nos. 1048, 1351) mentions donations ascribed to Offa. Only in the late 11th century Sulcard asserted that Offa (of Essex!) 'opere ampliavit ecclesiam' (*The History of Westminster Abbey by John Flete*, ed. J. A. Robinson, Cambridge, 1909, p. 43; cf. p. 63).

[6] See below, p. 255.

another formula (no. 86) of the latest part of the *Liber Diurnus*.[1]
This formula had been copied from a charter, by which Pope
Hadrian placed the monastery of Piumarola near Monte Cassino
under the authority of the Apostolic See, removed all other
authorities, and confirmed its possessions. A text of this kind was
modified in the privilege which Leo conceded to the Mercian
king; he gave not only protection and immunity to a monastery
destined to be Cœnwulf's burial-place, that is, to Winchcombe,
but he conferred also on him and his 'heredes' the liberty
to dispose of his other monasteries in 'insula Saxonia' at will.

Pope Leo also confirmed in 798 to a son of Cœnwulf, 'King'
Kinelm (that is, Cynehelm), and to his successors the ownership
of the monastery of Glastonbury and of its possessions.[2] William
of Malmesbury found only an English translation of this privilege and retranslated it into Latin, and the wording was of
course changed during this process; but here also a genuine
charter underlies. It was based on the formula no. 93 which
I mentioned previously and which was derived from the privilege granted to Offa by Hadrian. This charter obviously gave
origin to a whole series of papal privileges, by which the proprietary rights of royal lords of monasteries and monastic lands
were recognized, privileges at least spiritually in conflict with
earlier canon law and possibly prejudicial to monastic life. Leo
himself gave Archbishop Ethelhard of Canterbury, who visited
Rome in 801, the mandate that monasteries should not presume
to elect laymen and seculars as lords over God's heredity.[3]
Facts were stronger than theories; the institution of proprietary
churches and monasteries, particularly of royal ownership, had
struck root everywhere in the West, and the Church had to
make the best of it. The chapter of Anglo-Roman diplomatics

[1] Ed. Sickel, pp. 111 ff. A part of the formula depends on no. 32. Cf. Kehr,
Italia pontificia, viii, 1935, p. 195.

[2] Birch, i, no. 284, from William of Malmesbury, *De antiquitate Glastoniensis
ecclesiae*; on the confirmation of this privilege by King Cœnwulf and others (ib.,
no. 285) cf. below, p. 251. Cf. Jaffé, i. 2497 (where Migne, *P.L.* clxxix. 1709 ff.
should be added); Bresslau, *Handbuch der Urkundenlehre*, i², pp. 195 (n. 5), 209 (n. 4),
225 (n. 3); J. A. Robinson, *Somerset Historical Essays*, London, 1921, p. 38, n. 3.

[3] Statute of Archbishop Ethelhard at Clovesho in 803, H. and S. iii. 545; Birch,
i, no. 312. Cf. the decrees of the synod of Chelsea in 816, c. 8 (H. and S., p. 582)
and of Kingston in 838 (ib., p. 617; Birch, i, no. 421), the latter recognizing the
liberty of 'free' monasteries which had elected King Egbert of Wessex and his son
Ethelwulf 'pro suis propriis ac maximis necessitatibus sibi ad protectionem et ad
dominium' and had the bishops as 'spiritual lords'.

which I have touched on is an example of this development. A few years later, in 826, the existence of proprietary churches was practically recognized by a Roman synod.[1]

Relics and Church-dedications

The conferring of the pallium and the granting of monastic privileges by the Popes form part of the 'official' intercourse between England and Rome. There were other links which appealed to the sentiments and interests of all ranks of Christian society. I refer to one of the strongest ingredients in the religious life of this 'magical' age, the cult of saints, particularly as it took practical form in the belief in the miraculous 'virtue' of relics. Relics included parts not only of the body of a holy person but also of his belongings; every object which had been in touch with him or his tomb had the power of transmitting the mysterious strength acquired by a saintly life or death. Dust taken from the tomb of a saint or from the place where he died could afford the same succour as particles of his real body, 'representative relics', as they have been called. The world of Bede was in this respect like that of Gregory of Tours or Gregory the Great, full of evil spirits always bent on doing harm, but also abundant in possibilities of saintly intervention. This belief had an official side, in so far as every church was dedicated to a patron saint, in whose name the principal altar was consecrated, while side-altars might contain relics of other saints. Therefore relics were imported into England from the earliest days of the English Church, and continued to be imported to supply those churches which were still unprovided. Visitors to Rome, like Wilfrid, Benedict Biscop, Willibrord, or Boniface, acquired there not only books and vestments but also relics of apostles and martyrs to be an 'abundant grace to many churches'; in the early eighth century Bishop Acca of Hexham tried to get such relics from 'everywhere' for the altars in the chapels (*porticus*) of his cathedral.

There is a list of English church-dedications by Frances Arnold-Forster[2] and a shorter survey by Francis Bond,[3] besides

---

[1] Roman synod of 826, cc. 21, 24 (*MG. Capitularia*, i. 374 f.; *Concilia*, ii. 576 f.). Cf. U. Stutz, *Geschichte des kirchlichen Benefizialwesens*, i. 1, Berlin, 1895, pp. 259 ff.
[2] *Studies in Church Dedications, or England's Patron Saints*, 3 vols., London, 1899.
[3] *Dedications and Patron Saints of English Churches*, Oxford, 1914.

some papers dealing with particular districts. This matter of *Patrozinienforschung*, a subject that has been much studied recently on the Continent,[1] presents difficulties. The patron saint of many ancient churches is not mentioned until later times and cannot with certainty be regarded as the original patron; in other cases he is not mentioned at all. Therefore a complete survey of church-dedications for any special period of ancient times is impossible. But in spite of all the limits set to our knowledge, if we confine ourselves strictly to such English dedications as can be ascribed to the seventh and eighth centuries with some certainty, one fact emerges clearly: the overwhelmingly Roman character of the dedications, corresponding to the origin of the English Church.[2] The Celtic districts of the west and south-west with their particular problems are here of course left aside.

In England proper the cult of the British martyr St. Alban survived at Verulamium.[3] The early connexion of the British and Gallic churches was based on proximity. A survival of these relations is seen in two churches of St. Martin preserved through the times of Anglo-Saxon heathendom: St. Martin of Canterbury served as the place of worship of Queen Bertha, the Merovingian wife of King Ethelbert of Kent, before her husband's conversion; the north had St. Ninian's church of St. Martin at Whithorn in Galloway.[4] The veneration of the celebrated bishop of Tours, which also spread to Rome, contributed, up to the end of our period, a few chapels in southern England.

But these were exceptions, so far as we can judge from the scanty sources. In the majority of the dedications Roman influence is evident. The first church consecrated at Canterbury by Augustine, Christ Church, was originally called after the Saviour, *Sancti Salvatoris*. This was a fitting name for the earliest cathedral of England; for it was the old name of the papal

---

[1] I may mention the comprehensive studies by Johann Dorn, 'Beiträge zur Patrozinienforschung' (*Archiv für Kulturgeschichte*, xiii, 1917, pp. 9–49, 220–55), by the Bollandist Hippolyte Delehaye, 'Loca Sanctorum' (*Anal. Boll.* xlviii, 1930, pp. 5–64), and by W. Deinhardt, 'Patrozinienkunde' (*Historisches Jahrbuch*, lvi, 1936, pp. 174–207).   [2] See Appendix V, pp. 259 ff.

[3] Cf. my paper 'St. Alban and St. Albans' (*Antiquity*, xv, 1941, pp. 337–59).

[4] Bede, *H.E.* iii. 4 and the *Miracula Nynie episcopi* (ed. K. Strecker, *MG. Poetae*, iv. 2, pp. 943–62). Cf. Strecker, *Neues Archiv*, xliii, 1920–2, pp. 1–26, and my article, *Antiquity*, xiv, 1940, pp. 280–91.

cathedral, San Giovanni in Laterano. The monastic foundation of St. Augustine at Canterbury, later St. Augustine's, had the dedication, not less significant, of SS. Peter and Paul, a double dedication given also to some other English churches. Often St. Peter alone is mentioned where both were patrons; and as regards churches which were dedicated only to him, it may be said that no name was given to so many houses in early England as that of the 'door-keeper of Heaven'. The veneration of St. Peter spread likewise on the Continent in this age.[1] The synod of Whitby in 664 must be recalled, if we are to realize the feelings of anxiety and hope which the idea of the apostle's heavenly office produced on the believers. English kings left their worldly splendour to end their lives abroad near the tomb of the *claviger caeli* (pp. 37 f.). The cathedral of York bears his name. Benedict Biscop dedicated his first monastery, Wearmouth, to St. Peter, his second, Jarrow, to St. Paul. King Naiton of the Picts about 710 asked Ceolfrid, the abbot of these monasteries (which were united under a single government), to send him architects to build a stone church in his country; he promised to give it the name of St. Peter. We learned from a formula in the *Liber Diurnus* (no. 93) that all monasteries founded or acquired by King Offa of Mercia up to the date of the document were consecrated in honour of the same apostle (p. 30).[2]

Other English dedications of these centuries also show the Roman connexion, though they cannot compete with the number of St. Peter's houses. St. Paul became patron of the cathedral of London, of Jarrow monastery, and of a few other churches. St. Andrew was the saint of the Roman monastery founded by

[1] Cf. Theodor Zwölfer, *Sankt Peter Apostelfürst und Himmelspförtner: seine Verehrung bei den Angelsachsen und Franken*, Stuttgart, 1929, pp. 69 ff., 100 ff., and the review by P. W. Finsterwalder, *Savigny-Zeitschr.* l, 1930, *Kan. Abt.* xix. 693 ff. Cf. also Haller, loc. cit. i. 347 ff., 367 f., 379 ff. on the devotion to St. Peter.

[2] The foundation of the monastery of St. Albans, which was referred by tradition to Offa, may have been later than the privilege of Pope Hadrian; the translation of St. Alban is ascribed to the year 793; cf. my paper, loc. cit. (p. 34, n. 3), pp. 350 ff. The record of the dedication of a St. Alban's church on 1 December 805 (rather 804 according to the indiction) in Thorpe's edition of Florence of Worcester (i. 64) is taken from the Chronicle of Marianus Scottus (*MG. SS.* v. 549) written in Mainz (which was the foundation of Florence's work) and refers to the new building of St. Alban's at Mainz, not to the English monastery, as is assumed by W. J. Moore, *The Saxon Pilgrims to Rome and the Schola Saxonum*, Dissertation of Fribourg (Switzerland), 1937, p. 81; cf., e.g., *MG. Poetae*, i. 431 and my edition of the *Vitae S. Bonifatii*, pp. 61, 95 (n. 3).

Gregory the Great *in Clivo Scauri*, that is, the monastery of Augustine and at least several of his companions; Rochester Cathedral, Wilfrid's monasteries of Hexham and Oundle, and some other churches were consecrated to his name. The Roman origin is evident in the dedication of a 'martyrium' at Canterbury to the 'Quattuor Coronati' and of a small number of chapels to St. Lawrence or St. Gregory. Other dedications are less illustrative. But four churches of the Archangel Michael have a Roman counterpart, e.g. in the church of the Castel Sant' Angelo. The widespread veneration of the Virgin is shown by her patronage of many churches (later more numerous than those of St. Peter), a number of them erected in monasteries. It is impossible to trace the origins and wanderings of relics of St. Mary which these dedications suggest; one may imagine for example that Gregory's disciples brought relics from Santa Maria Maggiore. But it is better to abstain from random speculation, and the same applies to relics of St. John the Baptist, whose name was given to Aldhelm's monastery of Frome in Somerset and to a church built by Archbishop Cuthbert at Canterbury about 750. This survey is necessarily incomplete; among the dedications which are known only in later times there may be many that go back to those early days, and others may be entirely forgotten. We may recall the altars of the twelve apostles in an unknown church (perhaps in Malmesbury) which were commemorated in verse by Aldhelm, or his lines on a church of St. Matthias. But the prevailing Roman character of these early dedications is evident. Apart from St. Martin, saints of Gaul were not yet represented, nor were there churches in honour of the first English saints. It was an exception that, at the place near the Roman Wall where King Elfwald of Northumbria was murdered in 788, a church of SS. Cuthbert and Oswald was erected.

Pilgrimages

There were numerous opportunities of acquiring relics. Rome was the destination of many people who set out with the purpose of *peregrinatio*, pilgrimage, which meant originally living abroad (*peregre*). To give up one's native country, to leave one's relatives and friends and all the things one loved, was considered a good means of winning forgiveness for sins and eternal life. Renunciation of the world by entering a monastery or convent was a similar act of piety. But a temporary pilgrimage, with the difficulties, dangers, and hardships of the journey, was also thought to be meritorious when it was made with the object of visiting the tombs and holy shrines of martyrs, there to offer prayers, and presents large or small, and to acquire by personal approach the blessing and help of saints for this and the other world. The miraculous power emanating from their relics was believed to be particularly attached to their last resting-place. Rome had lost its political position of *caput mundi*; but it retained this rank in the sphere of the Church. Containing the tombs of the 'princes of the apostles' and, above all, of St. Peter, besides many other martyrs, it became the destination for innumerable pilgrims even in these centuries of difficult travelling. Englishmen, whose Church originated from Rome, were in the forefront of these pilgrimages. Scanty as our information is, the number of English pilgrims known to have gone to Rome in these centuries is large.[1]

Contemporaries were conscious of this multitude of *Romipetae*, to use a later expression. Bede at the end of his Chronicle of the World of 725 remarked: 'His temporibus multi Anglorum gentis, nobiles et ignobiles, viri et feminae, duces et privati, divini amoris instinctu de Brittania Romam venire consueverant' (cf. *H.E.* v. 7). He then speaks of his own abbot Ceolfrid. In 716, when 74 years old, this nobleman resigned his office as abbot of Wearmouth and Jarrow to end his life near the 'limina apostolorum'. He died during the journey at Langres; companions carried to Rome his gift to St. Peter, the beautiful *Codex Amiatinus* of the Bible. Ceolfrid's anonymous biographer and Bede have left lively descriptions of the departure and travels of the abbot.

Not only did monks like Ceolfrid desire to die near the tombs of the apostles; English kings had the same longing. Oswiu of Northumbria died before he could carry out this intention, in

---

[1] Moore, loc. cit., gives a list of English pilgrims to Rome in the 7th and 8th centuries (I am indebted to the Rev. Dr. Moore, of Cotton College, for kindly sending me a copy of his valuable thesis). See also Æthilwald's poem on the pilgrimage of three men, ed. Ehwald, *Auct. ant.* xv. 528–33. Cf. Zwölfer, loc. cit., pp. 24 ff.; Elisabeth Pfeil, *Die Fränkische und Deutsche Romidee des frühen Mittelalters* (Forschungen zur mittelalterlichen u. neueren Geschichte, iii), München, 1929, pp. 57 ff. See EHD-I-Fn-Quam.

670. The warlike Cædwalla of Wessex, when about 30 years old, left his kingdom in 688 and went to Rome, not only, as his sepulchral inscription states, 'ut Petrum sedemque Petri rex cerneret hospes', but also to be christened there; he died in the next year, a few days after his baptism, falling ill *in albis*, in the baptismal vestments. It was an impressive act, that a prince should relinquish his power to come 'a finibus terrae' to the prince of the apostles; the Pope gave him the distinctive baptismal name of Petrus and a tomb in St. Peter's. In 709 Cœnred of Mercia and Offa of Essex followed the example of Cædwalla; even the official historiographer of the Popes thought this event worthy of record.[1] In 726 King Ine of Wessex resigned after a reign of many years to become a pilgrim (*peregrinari*) near the holy places of Rome and to be received in consequence with readier recognition by the saints in heaven.

Many more went to Rome with the intention of returning to their country. Pilgrimage was not always the real or the only purpose of their journey. Benedict Biscop, the Northumbrian nobleman, who left the 'terrestrial militia' to be a soldier of God, and became the founder and first abbot of Wearmouth and Jarrow, visited Rome six times. In these journeys devotion was combined with other purposes: to learn the ecclesiastical and monastic institutions and customs of Rome and other places; to acquire relics, books, pictures for the ornamentation of his church; to procure a papal privilege for his monastery (p. 24).

The number of English pilgrims to Rome was large, and there was some possibility of abuse. The Carolingian kings Pippin and Charles the Great granted such pilgrims exemption from customs for the necessities of life. But there were merchants who under the pretext of pilgrimage tried to evade the customs, and Charles objected to this kind of fraud in a letter of 796 to King Offa.[2] The care of *peregrini* (that is, originally, aliens) was a biblical precept and a Christian duty. St. Benedict devoted a whole chapter of his Rule to the reception of 'hospites', amongst whom 'peregrini' were prominent; they had their place at the table of the abbot. Pilgrims had to rely largely on hospitality in those times of prevailing agrarian economy. Letters of recommenda-

---

[1] *Liber Pontificalis, Vita Constantini*, c. 9 (ed. Mommsen, p. 225).
[2] *MG. Capitularia*, i. 32 (c. 4), 37 (c. 22); *MG. Epist.* iv. 145. Cf. below, p. 111.

tion therefore served the needs of the pilgrims, while at the same time protecting their hosts against false pilgrims and vagabonds. Nor could the desire for pilgrimage be reconciled with the vow of *stabilitas* of the Benedictine monk except by the permission of the abbot; the worst kind of monks in the eyes of St. Benedict were 'semper vagi et numquam stabiles', the 'gyrovagi'. In spite of precautionary measures there were many stranded English pilgrims, particularly women who went astray. About 720 an English abbess, like so many other women, desired to go to Rome to gain there forgiveness for her sins; but she had numerous critics who found fault with her and emphasized the canonical precept of remaining at the place where the vow had been taken.[1] As for men, the same opinion may perhaps be read between the lines where Bede in 731, speaking of the Roman journey of an English monk in the later part of the seventh century, adds (*H.E.* iv. 23, p. 255): 'quod *eo tempore magnae virtutis aestimabatur*'. Many reached their goal safely; a friend of Boniface, Wiethburg, believed that she had found at Rome spiritual tranquillity, as she had desired.[2] But others failed. Boniface in 747 expressed the opinion that the frequent pilgrimages of English women to Rome should be forbidden, because most of them lapsed from virtue on the journey: 'There are very few cities in Longobardia, in Francia or Gaul, where an English adulteress or prostitute is not to be found. *Quod scandalum est et turpitudo totius ecclesiae vestrae.*'[3]

The dangers of pilgrimage were diminished by a kind of organized hospitality. It could be expected in every monastery, at every bishop's house. Perhaps no description is more impressive than the few words in the Life of St. Willibald on his travels in southern Italy, after he had left Naples:[4] 'And from there he went to the town of Capua, and the archbishop sent him to another town to another bishop. And the bishop sent him to the town of Teano to the bishop. And the bishop sent him to St. Benedict', that is, to the monastery of Monte Cassino. There were *xenodochia*, hostels for poor pilgrims in general, founded in Gaul and Italy on the main roads frequented by

---

[1] Letter of Abbess Eangyth, in Boniface, *Epist.* 14 (ed. Tangl, p. 25).
[2] Ib., no. 27 (p. 48).
[3] Ib., no. 78 (p. 169).
[4] *Vita Willibaldi,* c. 4 (*MG. SS.* xv. 1, p. 102).

them,[1] and special 'hospitalia Scottorum', founded for the Irish predecessors and contemporaries of the Saxon pilgrims,[2] Irishmen, for whom, according to an author of the ninth century,[3] the custom of peregrination had almost turned into a second nature. Near Quentavic, where most Anglo-Saxons landed on the Continent (p. 6), Charles the Great committed to Alcuin the cell of St. Jodocus (Saint-Josse) 'ad elemosinam exhibendam peregrinis'.[4]

In Rome many of them were in need of care. Boniface recommended to a cardinal-deacon in 745 the 'ancillae Dei' who had 'hurried' to Rome.[5] A number of Englishmen settled there,[6] perhaps not only pilgrims but also traders; like other strangers in Rome: Franks, Frisians, and Langobards, they were organized at the end of the eighth century as a military unit, the 'schola Saxonum', who with the other 'scholae peregrinorum' solemnly received Pope Leo III outside Rome when he returned there in 799 after having taken refuge with Charles the Great. They had real military duties when the Saracens invaded in 846. These Anglo-Saxons, like the other foreigners, had a common settlement, as was usual for groups of aliens, in the neighbourhood of St. Peter's near the Tiber: the 'vicus' or 'schola Saxonum', with a hostel and a church of St. Mary, which Pope Leo IV (847–55) erected after a fire had

---

[1] Cf. Walther Schönfeld, 'Die Xenodochien in Italien und Frankreich im frühen Mittelalter' (Savigny-Zeitschr. xliii, 1922, Kan. Abt. xii. 1–54); Siegfried Reicke, Das deutsche Spital und sein Recht im Mittelalter, i (Kirchenrechtl. Abhandl. cxi–cxii), 1932. See e.g. Codex Carolinus 87 (MG. Epist. iii. 623): 'monasterium sancti Ilarii . . . in Calligata [Galeata in the diocese of Forlimpopoli; cf. Kehr, Italia pontificia, v. 138 f.] una cum hospitales qui per calles Alpium [that is, Apennines] siti sunt pro peregrinorum susceptione.' Heiric, Miracula S. Germani, i. 5. 52 (Acta SS. Julii, vii. 266; Duru, Bibliothèque historique de l' Yonne, ii. 139) mentions the monastery of Moutiers-en-Puisaye ('coenobium Meleredense'), dép. Yonne: 'Id coenobium genti Britonum [including Anglo-Saxons?] Romam infatigabiliter expetenti et pervium et familiare est.' Quintilian, the father of the bishop of Auxerre of the same name (about 735), founded it, 'xenodochiumque Brittonum Romam pergentium ibidem esse constituit' (Gesta pontificum Autissiodor. c. 29, MG. SS. xiii. 395).

[2] Cf. Louis Gougaud, Christianity in Celtic Lands, London, 1932, pp. 177 ff.; Reicke, loc. cit. i, p. 9, n. 1.

[3] Walahfrid Strabo, Vita Galli, ii. 46 (SS. rer. Merov. iv. 336).

[4] Alcuin, Epist. 230, 232 (MG. Epist. iv, pp. 375. 19, 376. 29); Lupus of Ferrières, Epist. 11, 53, 55, 71 (ib. vi, pp. 21, 56, 58, 68: 'transmarinorum curam').

[5] Boniface, Epist. 62 (p. 128).

[6] Cf. W. H. Stevenson, Asser's Life of King Alfred, Oxford, 1904, pp. 193 f., 243 ff.; Kehr, Italia pontificia, i. 151, cf. 145; Liebermann, Gesetze, ii. 2, pp. 608 ff.; Chr. Huelsen, Le chiese di Roma, pp. 363 f.; Moore, loc. cit., pp. 90–125.

devastated the Saxon quarter, to-day Santo Spirito in Sassia. The Englishmen called the settlement *burh*; the name has survived to the present day in that of the Borgo. There are other Borghi in Italy: *būrgus* (from the Greek πύργος?) was a military word received into Latin for a small castle, fortress; but there was also the Germanic *bŭrg*,[1] and we are informed that the Anglo-Saxons in Rome called their settlement *burgus* in their own language in the early ninth century.[2] How many Englishmen who pass the Borgo Santo Spirito walking from Ponte Sant' Angelo to St. Peter's, are aware that they are crossing a district which was originally an English 'borough'? It had previously been destroyed by fire in 818; but Pope Paschalis relieved the 'need of the pilgrims' by rich gifts, and 'Angelcynnes scolu'[3] was restored.

On the way to Rome English pilgrims visited other sanctuaries, to obtain the blessings of their saints also. Boniface and his associates in 718, Willibald and his companions in 720, offered their prayers in many churches or oratories of saints, though only in the latter case is San Frediano of Lucca mentioned by name, because Willibald's father was buried there.[4] We may suppose that one of the most famous objects of Anglo-Saxon art was taken to France on such an occasion, the so-called Franks Casket in the British Museum, a box made of the bone of a whale.[5] Its carvings combine runic with Roman letters,

---

[1] Gamillscheg, *Romania Germanica*, i, 1934, p. 35, n. 1; cf. p. 180 and vol. ii, 1935, pp. 65, 108, 138.

[2] *Vita Paschalis I*, c. 7 (*Liber Pontificalis*, ed. Duchesne, ii. 53): '. . . per quorundam gentis Anglorum desidiam ita est omnis illorum habitatio, quae in eorum lingua burgus dicitur, flamma ignis exundante conbusta. . . .'

[3] *Saxon Chronicle*, 816 (ed. Plummer, pp. 60 f.). A letter of a Pope John, referring to 'omnibus Anglorum proceribus, qui tunc ad beatum Petrum degebant apostolum', and containing an order about the vestments of the English clergy, has been ascribed, on the basis of a defective copy from Ripoll used by Baluze, to John VI (701–5) or VII (705–7); cf., e.g., H. and S. iii. 264; Birch, i, no. 119; Moore, loc. cit., p. 106, n. 5. But it belongs to Pope John VIII and to the years 873–5; cf. *MG. Epist.* vii, pp. 293 f., no. 36; on the date, see P. Ewald, *Neues Archiv*, v, 1880, pp. 320 f. Another letter addressed 'Bulgred Fregi Saxonum' and ascribed to John IV, 640–2 (Birch, i, no. 21), also belongs to John VIII (872–4) and refers to King Burgred of Mercia; cf. *MG. Epist.* vii, p. 293, no. 35; Ewald, loc. cit., p. 308.

[4] On the stories referring to Willibald's father, who was provided by legend with the name of Richard, see M. Coens, 'Légende et Miracles du roi S. Richard' (*Anal. Boll.* xlix, 1931, pp. 353–97).

[5] On the Franks Casket cf., e.g., G. Baldwin Brown, *The Arts in Early England*, vi. 1, London, 1930, pp. 18–51. Archbishop Bregwine of Canterbury (761–4) sent Lullus of Mainz as a gift 'capsam unam ad officium quidem sacerdotale ex ossibus fabricatam'; Boniface and Lullus, *Epist.* 117 (p. 253).

biblical and Roman subjects with scenes from Saxon heathen tradition, and may be considered, in virtue of this blend, a true symbol of English civilization about 700. In former days it belonged to the church of St. Julien de Brioude, one of the ancient Christian centres of the Auvergne; Gregory of Tours devoted a whole book to the miracles of the patron saint. An English pilgrim going to Italy may have made a detour to the place and offered his gift at the tomb of the martyr.

The wanderings of pilgrims did not stop at Rome. Christianity and its Bible carried with them some knowledge of the Mediterranean world. This was increased, in England as elsewhere, by other books, such as the histories of Orosius with his introductory geographical survey, the chapter that afterwards induced King Alfred to insert passages on the northern countries into the translation of Orosius. Voyages to and from Rome gave a view of Gaul and Italy and obviously contributed to the interest in geography and connected subjects. Benedict Biscop bought at Rome a volume on cosmography, a 'wonderful work', as Bede calls it; King Aldfrid of Northumbria (685–704), one of the first literate English kings,[1] acquired this manuscript for eight hides of land. About 770 Bishop Lullus of Mainz tried to get from York 'libros cosmografiorum'.[2] Bede also manifested an interest in geographical facts;[3] even during his last illness he translated some extracts from Isidore's 'libri Rotarum',[4] that is, the book De natura rerum, used by Bede also in his earlier text-book of the same title. Biblical geography, as interpreted by the Fathers like Jerome, was naturally of peculiar interest

[1] Cf. V. H. Galbraith, 'The Literacy of the Medieval English Kings' (P.B.A. xxi, 1935, pp. 207 f.). The 'Cosmographiorum codex' (Bede, Hist. abb. c. 15, p. 380) cannot have contained, as has been conjectured, the strange work of the Pseudo-Aethicus, which was composed in the last third of the eighth century; cf. Kurt Hillkowitz, Zur Kosmographie des Aethicus, Dissertation of Bonn, 1934, p. 69.

[2] Boniface, Epist. 124 (p. 261). Lullus was perhaps influenced by Cassiodorus's Institutiones, i. 25 (ed. R. A. B. Mynors, Oxford, 1937, p. 66).

[3] Bede Essays, pp. 141 f. Bede speaks of 'libris cosmographorum authenticis ac nobilissimis' in his book De temporum ratione, c. 35 (ed. Jones, p. 247 ; cf. p. 370).

[4] Not notarum (Plummer, Baedae Op. hist. i, p. clxii, n. 8; cf. p. lxxv, n. 6). E. Van Kirk Dobbie, The MSS. of Caedmon's Hymn and Bede's Death Song (Columbia University Studies in English and Comparative Literature, cxxviii), New York, 1937, p. 123, and N. Ker, Medium Aevum, viii, 1939, p. 42, have restored the right title of Isidore's work in their texts of Cuthbert's letter De obitu Bedae. Cf. M. Manitius, Geschichte der Lateinischen Literatur des Mittelalters, i, München, 1911, pp. 54 f.; Dobbie, pp. 101 f.

to these ecclesiastical scholars. Their knowledge was increased by the personal experience of a Gallic bishop, Arculf, who had visited the Holy Land, Egypt, and Constantinople. On his return he was driven off his course by storms to the west of Great Britain and came to Abbot Adamnan of Iona, who wrote down the report of his guest, tested his veracity by comparison with the Fathers, and thus composed his book on the Holy Places.[1] He gave it to King Aldfrid, and others also read it; Bede from this and a few other sources drew up a shorter survey of the same subject,[2] and even introduced some extracts from it into his *Ecclesiastical History of the English People* in spite of the different theme.

This interest in the geography and topography of Eastern countries soon manifested itself in actual travel. Pilgrimages to the Holy Land had come into fashion in the fourth century. Arculf met there a Burgundian, Peter, who lived in Palestine as a hermit and became his guide. The first Englishman whom we know to have followed his example[3] was Willibald, a Wessex man and relative of Boniface; I have already mentioned (pp. 6, 39, 41) his pilgrimage to Rome in 720. There he conceived the idea of 'a greater peregrination into the unknown country'; after Rome, Jerusalem and the Holy Land became his goal, the scene of the life and sufferings of Christ himself. There is no need to relate here the details of his journey, his dangers, hardships, and adventures in Greek and Moslem countries; he returned to Italy after nearly seven years (723–9) to become a monk in Monte Cassino. When he was bishop of Eichstätt and an old man, an English nun of the monastery of Heidenheim near by, Hugeburc, whose name was discovered only a few years ago, did for him what Adamnan had done for Arculf: she wrote down his recollections and inserted them in his biography. This *Vita Willibaldi* is the earliest extant book of travel written by an English pen.[4] It is mainly concerned, of course, with

---

[1] Best edition by Paul Geyer, 'Itinera Hierosolymitana' (*CSEL*. xxxix), 1898, pp. 219–97.   [2] Ib., pp. 299–324.

[3] He may have had predecessors; cf. *Vita Willibaldi*, c. 4 (*MG. SS*. xv. 1, p. 94): 'Frequenter hic venientes vidi homines de illis terre partibus *istorum contribulos*; non querunt mala, sed legem eorum adimplere cupiunt' (that is, make a pilgrimage). But these words may refer to Occidental Christians in general, not specially to Englishmen.

[4] Best edition of the Lives of Willibald and of his brother Wynnebald by O. Holder-Egger, *MG. SS*. xv. 1, pp. 80–117. On the name of the authoress.

places of devotion, biblical or legendary events, churches and tombs of saints; but occasionally other topics are touched on. I will only mention the volcano of the Lipari Islands, in which Arculf was also interested, the 'infernus Theodrichi', where the Ostrogothic king Theodoric the Great was said by the legend to have been overwhelmed. Willibald tried to reach its summit but had to give up the attempt. He added an impressive description of the eruptions, nor did he forget to mention the pumice thrown up, which the transcribers of manuscripts used for polishing vellum. He went away, 'visionum spectaculis exploratis'; there is something of the curiosity of the explorer in this story from the dawn of medieval geography.

These pilgrims not only manifested religious fervour after the manner of their age, but displayed also qualities of activity and enterprise. It was these which enabled Englishmen of this period to become missionaries, reformers, and teachers on the Continent. Peregrination and pilgrimage were originally the same word. *Peregrinatio* could serve to rescue one's own soul and at the same time to save the souls of others; this is the common foundation of medieval pilgrimage and missionary work. Egbert, one of its originators, left his English native country to live as a pilgrim in Ireland so as to win a home in heaven; but then his purpose developed: 'proposuit animo pluribus prodesse', to preach the Gospel to the heathen of the Continent. If that should prove impossible, he considered going on pilgrimage to Rome:[1] the two purposes were in some sense regarded as equivalents.

discovered by B. Bischoff, see below, p. 294. On the chronology of Willibald's life cf. also Franz Heidingsfelder, *Die Regesten der Bischöfe von Eichstätt*, i, Innsbruck, 1915 ff., pp. 2 f.

[1] Bede, *H.E.* v. 9 (p. 296).

III

THE FRISIAN MISSION

The Situation in the Frankish Kingdom

THE Merovingian kingdom had reached its greatest extent by about the middle of the sixth century; it comprised nearly all Gaul and most of the German countries, but the greater part of the modern Netherlands and north-western Germany, that is, the lands of the Frisians and Saxons, remained outside it.[1] Even these sometimes recognized, in theory, the overlordship of the Frankish kings; the frontier-lines of independent Friesland changed as the strength of her Frankish neighbours waxed or waned. The kingdom of the Merovingians was the largest body politic of the West, too large for the social and economic conditions of this age. Its difficulties were intensified by the lack of strong personalities among the kings after the death of Dagobert I in 639. The pretence of a reign of child kings followed, under the regency of the queen dowagers; the political weight shifted to the local powers of the aristocracy, who combined the lordship over large estates and dependent people with the high offices in state and church. The dukes of the eastern tribes or 'stems' of the Alamanni, Bavarians, and Thuringians became almost independent rulers. The great endeavoured to make of the office of mayor of the palace, the 'maiordomus', an instrument to control the king. But certain strong men, such as Ebroin, went further; they sought so to use this central power as to dominate not only the king but also the other aristocrats. The outcome of these struggles was the ascendancy of an Austrasian, eastern family, the Arnulfings or Carolingians; the victory of Pippin II over the mayor of the palace of the west at Tertry in 687 was the decisive event. It

[1] For literature on continental conditions and events I refer students to the 9th edition of Dahlmann-Waitz, *Quellenkunde der Deutschen Geschichte* (ed. H. Haering), Leipzig, 1931–2, supplemented by the annual *Jahresberichte für Deutsche Geschichte* (ed. A. Brackmann and F. Hartung), ib. 1927 ff.; to the bibliographies in the first volumes of *The Cambridge Medieval History*; and to my survey of the history of the Carolingian age in *Gebhardts Handbuch der Deutschen Geschichte*, 7th ed. (ed. R. Holtzmann), i, Stuttgart, 1930, pp. 131–214. I have largely drawn in this chapter on my lecture on 'St. Willibrord and his Place in History' (*The Durham University Journal*, xxxii, 1940, pp. 23–41).

established the preponderance of Austrasia, the more German east, over the more Romanic parts of the state and initiated its reconstruction. It meant a stronger central power, a reinforcement of the ties that held the different countries together, a renewed control over the loose advanced positions of the tribal dukedoms, which gradually came to an end; the lands of the last independent German tribes, Frisians and Saxons, were incorporated in the kingdom. This work of four generations, begun by Pippin II and finished by Charles the Great, brought to a conclusion what Clovis had originated at the end of the fifth century. The foundations of the Germanic and Romanic medieval world were laid. The continental activity of the Anglo-Saxons is interwoven with this development, whose consequences were immense.

The acceptance of the Catholic form of Christianity was one of the momentous acts of Clovis; in spite of all pagan survivals and paganizing influences Catholicism won a stronghold in his realm, while Arianism in other Germanic kingdoms gradually gave way. The Frankish Church preserved the organization of the Gallic Church. It was divided into provinces and bishoprics corresponding to the secular provinces and cities of the late Roman Empire. But there was one important difference. The influence of the Papacy was very small; the Church became a national or rather a territorial church, with synods composed of the bishops of the kingdom or, in times of divided kingships, of its sections. The king, from the beginning, participated in the selection and institution of the bishops, who were almost all members of the aristocracy, of the Gallo-Roman and before long of the Germanic nobility also. The decay of the royal power intensified the local or territorial influences; episcopacies were in danger of becoming proprietary churches belonging to aristocratic masters. Bishops were involved in the struggles for power, and were instituted and deposed from office for secular considerations—Boniface in his letters deplored the worldliness, immorality, and martial spirit of the Frankish episcopate. The organization of the Church broke down. The monarchic power of the bishop in his diocese declined through the increase of proprietary churches dependent on landlords and by the exemption of monasteries, as a result of Irish influence or otherwise, which sometimes had their own bishops. The

ecclesiastical provinces ceased to exist; the metropolitans lost
their pre-eminence. Concurrently with the disintegration of the
kingdom synods ceased to be held. Boniface in 742 referred to
the opinion of old men that no synod had met for more than
eighty years. This was an exaggeration by almost half. The
signatures of a number of bishops under a monastic privilege
in 696 suggest this as the latest date on which a synod met, and
thereafter we find indeed no trace of any such gathering for
more than forty years.[1] The learning of the clergy declined;
apart from Lives of saints and some rhythmical poems there was
no literature deserving the name. At the time when Anglo-
Latin writing culminated in Aldhelm and Bede, a glance at
the language of original Merovingian charters suffices to show
the different standard of learning that prevailed on the other
side of the Channel.

The conversion of a chieftain or king in these centuries, as
often to-day in primitive tribes, meant the 'conversion' of many
of his followers also, superficial as the simultaneous baptism of
hundreds or thousands must have been; the real religious education remained to be given after the acceptance of the Christian
belief. The great mass of the Franks thus became Christians
in consequence of the conversion of Clovis. Paganism survived
till the early eighth century in the north-east, in parts of Belgium
and the adjoining territory, where the Franks had their ancient
homes. The Irishman Columbanus preached the Gospel about
610 near Lake Constance to Alamanni, whom he found making
offerings to Woden; the town of St. Gall near by has kept alive
the memory of his Irish pupil Gallus. Columbanus's successor
as abbot of Luxeuil, the Frank Eustasius, spread Christianity
among the eastern neighbours of the Alamanni, the Bavarians.
In Franconia, at Würzburg, the name of an Irish martyr,
Kilianus, is connected with the evangelization of the country,
which in the seventh century belonged to the sphere of the
Thuringian dukes. Christianity thus had taken root in the lands
of all German tribes within the Frankish frontiers, though there
remained 'pagan islands', such as in Hesse, amidst Christian
surroundings, and pagan practice was mixed up with Christian

---

[1] Boniface, *Epist.* 50 (ed. Tangl, p. 82). Cf. F. Lot, C. Pfister, F. L. Ganshof,
Histoire du Moyen Age, i (Histoire générale, ed. G. Glotz), Paris, 1928–35, pp. 332
(n. 38), 571 (n. 22).

custom everywhere. And the two tribes who in fact lived outside the Frankish borders, the Frisians and Saxons, clung to the
gods and rituals of their ancestors no less than to political
independence; Frankish domination and the Christian religion
were to them inseparable notions.

The missionary efforts of the Frankish Church were small.
Bishop Eligius of Noyon and Tournai (641–60) worked for the
conversion of Flanders: 'Flandrenses atque Andoverpenses,
Fresiones quoque et Suevi', and barbarians near the coast are
said to have been converted by him. This was the evangelizing
work of a diocesan in the borderland of heathenism. At the
same time St. Amandus devoted a part of his missionary activities
to the Franks near Schelde and Scarpe, where the town of
St. Amand occupies the site of one of his monasteries and of his
tomb (he died about 676). The Italian monk Jonas of Susa,
the biographer of St. Columbanus, was his helper for three
years about 640. Amandus was a real missionary bishop, an
Aquitanian of unusually widely diffused activities; his endeavours, according to his (partly legendary) Life, embraced
the Basques of the Pyrenees in the south and the Slavs near the
Danube in the east. He himself said in his last will that he had
preached the word of God and administered baptism 'longe
lateque per universas provintias seu gentes'. He was peculiarly
devoted to SS. Peter and Paul, in whose honour he consecrated
his churches; a papal letter in 649 shows his close relations
with the Roman See, when he was bishop of Maestricht for a
while. Antwerp was within the range of his activities. He
erected there in the castle a church, which some years after his
death was transferred to Willibrord, the first of the many gifts
to him that we hear of; thus it formed a link connecting the
work of the Anglo-Saxons with that of their Aquitanian predecessor and through him with that of the Irish monks. Antwerp
was in the neighbourhood of the Frisians, though not actually
in their country. The idea of bringing them the Gospel was
alive in the sixth or early seventh century. A church existed
in the castle of Utrecht before 612; King Dagobert I conferred
the castle with the church on the bishop of Cologne on condition
that he preached Christ to the Frisians. But the bishops of
Cologne neglected the task and the pagans destroyed the church;
when the Anglo-Saxons arrived, only its foundations remained.

It was left to their zeal to perform the work that had been imposed upon others.

The Beginnings of the Frisian Mission

The first effort of the Anglo-Saxons originated less in missionary fervour than in the casual opportunity of political circumstances. These arose in connexion with the earliest attempt, doomed to failure, to dethrone the Merovingians of Austrasia. King Sigibert III died in 656 in his youth, like many of the later Merovingians, and left the royal name to a child, Dagobert II. The real ruler was the mayor of the palace, Grimoald, a member of one of the mightiest Austrasian families and, by his sister's marriage, connected with the Carolingian house. He combined secular ambition and the pursuit of power with devotion to the Church; he founded monasteries and was a patron of the Irish monks. After some years he was not satisfied to be lord only in fact, but tried to secure the royal title also, not for himself but for his son. He did not take the life of the young king, but chose the more humane method of deposing him after the fashion of that age. Dagobert was tonsured and sent to Ireland into exile, while it was given out that Grimoald's son had been adopted by the late Sigibert, and he was made king. But the *coup d'état* was premature, the loyalty to the legitimate royal house proved too strong; the attempt ended in disaster and in Grimoald's death, probably in 662. A son of the Anglo-Saxon Balthild (pp. 9 f.) became king of Austrasia. Another son already held the royal title in the rest of the kingdom, where his *maiordomus* Ebroin was the real governor, after Balthild had been obliged to abandon the court and to end her life in the seclusion of her monastery of Chelles.

We need not follow here the vicissitudes of the Frankish kingdoms. The internal troubles reached a climax after 673, when one of these kings died. The succeeding brother was dethroned, the third brother was murdered in 675, and a 'bellum omnium contra omnes' set in, a struggle between several parties of the aristocracy. Now one of the Austrasian factions remembered the royal youth living in Ireland and applied for the help of Bishop Wilfrid of York. We can only guess that personal connexions were at work. The Northumbrian nobleman Wilfrid had been living in Gaul about 660, before and after his Roman pilgrimage, staying with a bishop of Lyons who lost his life in the struggles of the early sixties (p. 10). Wilfrid was spared because he was 'transmarinus de Anglorum gente ex Brittannia'. He returned to his native country to become the champion of the Roman cause and to win in 664 the debate of Whitby.

About 675 he was at the zenith of his life as bishop of York, of a diocese which comprised the whole Northumbrian kingdom stretching then from the Humber to the country of the Picts. He liked to show the splendour of his position; he transferred continental styles of church architecture into the north, where the monasteries of Ripon and Hexham and the restored cathedral of York were the monuments of his aims. Now the Austrasians asked him for his help to bring Dagobert back from Ireland to his home country. He gave it; the young prince was invited to Northumbria and sent overseas by Wilfrid 'magnifice'. In 676 he was made a second time king of Austrasia, only for a few years; some days before the year 679 ended he was killed by the treachery of dukes with the consent of bishops, to use the words of Wilfrid's biographer. It was the end of the Austrasian kingdom, but not of the struggle, till, several years later, Pippin II not only secured the actual rule in the east but was also victor over the *maiordomus* of the west and his king. The recovery of the Frankish state began; the activity of the Anglo-Saxon missionaries had a part in it.

The last years of Dagobert II also marked a crisis in Wilfrid's life. Dagobert returned in 676; two years later Wilfrid was deposed. He had resisted a partition of his large, too large diocese, and opposed the policy of Archbishop Theodore to increase the number of bishops; so he lost everything, and went overseas to appeal to the Pope for the restitution of his bishopric. He could not go the shortest way, the 'via rectissima', by crossing the Straits to Quentavic and passing through France, as did most Englishmen on their way to Rome (p. 6). By helping Dagobert to return from Ireland he had incurred the enmity of the latter's opponents in 'Neustria', particularly of Ebroin, who was fiercely striving for power again. Wilfrid's English adversaries are also said to have asked Ebroin and his king to hinder the journey. So he took a more easterly course, crossed the North Sea, and landed in the delta of the Rhine in the country of the Frisians. We need not follow the progress of his journey nor tell of his stay with Dagobert, who offered him the episcopal see of Strasburg, nor of his longer sojourn at Rome. We need only note that he stayed with the Frisians during the winter 678–9.[1] We do not know the extent of the traffic already existing between England and Friesland, though Anglo-Saxon coins found overseas point to there being trade between the kindred peoples. I have mentioned a Frisian inhabitant of London who about this time bought a Northumbrian prisoner from Mercia as a slave (p. 8). Frisian merchants had some importance in the commerce of the next century and were also found at York.[2] In any case Wilfrid and his companions received hospitality from the Frisian king Aldgisl; he contemptuously declined Ebroin's proposal that he should surrender or kill his guest. With his permission Wilfrid used the opportunity for missionary work; he preached the Gospel to the Frisians, and had some success. According to Wilfrid's biographer most chieftains ('principes') and many thousands of other people were baptized, the more readily since a rich sea and land harvest seemed to confirm the truth of his teaching. He left the Netherlands in the spring to continue his journey to Rome, nor was his work very lasting. But this casual episode in Wilfrid's stormy career was of far-reaching importance. By his missionary zeal he had shown an opening to his fellow countrymen which was not forgotten. In the opinion of the next generation of Northumbrians he laid the foundations on which his pupil Willibrord afterwards built the Frisian Church. When Wilfrid about 703 made his last journey to Rome he stayed some time with Willibrord. This time there was no political need to avoid the shorter route; the route chosen shows Wilfrid's interest in a task which he had himself begun a quarter of a century before.

A new incentive came from another side, from Ireland. It is usual to dwell on the differences and controversies of the Irish and Anglo-Roman clerics, rightly so far as concerns the early times of their contact, when the peculiar customs of the Celtic churches, the paschal reckoning, the different tonsure, and other rites were asserted with zeal by the Irish monks in England as

---

[1] I cannot accept R. L. Poole's date of 677–8. Cf. Appendix VI, pp. 265 ff.

[2] Altfrid, *Vita Liudgeri*, i. 11 (*MG. SS.* ii. 407; ed. W. Diekamp, *Geschichtsquellen des Bisthums Münster*, iv, 1881, p. 17). Cf. also Alcuin, *Carm.* 59 (*MG. Poetae*, i. 273).

on the Continent. But, except for the lack of an organization conforming to the continental ecclesiastical order, these differences disappeared in time; the Irish accepted the Roman usages. Southern Ireland had joined the Roman cause as early as about 630;[1] the debate of Whitby put an end to the struggle in England in 664; only northern Ireland, the island monastery of Iona, and the dependent monasteries continued their opposition till the beginning of the eighth century. The Britons alone went on upholding Celtic church practice together with political independence. But the adherence of southern Ireland about 630 opened the way to Englishmen of the Roman observance to visit Ireland for voluntary exile, a pilgrimage in the original sense, and in order to acquire the monastic custom and learning cultivated in the neighbouring island. So even champions of the Roman cause went there for an austerer life or 'legendarum gratia Scripturarum'. Bede praises the hospitality shown to such Englishmen by the Irish, who supplied them with food, books, and teachers. Relating the invasion of Ireland by King Egfrid of Northumbria in 684, he calls the Irish people 'nationi Anglorum semper amicissimam'. The Irish visionary Furseus founded a monastery first in Ireland, then in East Anglia, lastly in Gaul, where he was buried about 650 at Péronne in Picardy, 'Perrona Scottorum', Péronne of the Irishmen. There exist small fragments of the correspondence of one of the abbots of this monastery, Cellan, with Aldhelm, to which attention was called by the late Ludwig Traube.[2] Irish influences must be borne in mind in connexion with the English continental exploits.

Egbert, a young Englishman of noble birth, was staying in an Irish monastery, when in 664, the year of the Whitby synod, the plague carried off his companions. He made a vow never to return to his native country if God, by sparing his life, gave him time to repent the sins of his earlier years. He kept his promise till the end, for not less than sixty-five years; he died, 90 years old, in 729, a bishop, praised for his humility, kindness, asceticism, and learning. He was a supporter of the Roman

[1] On the probable date cf. D. J. O'Connell, 'Easter Cycles in the Early Irish Church' (*Journal of the Royal Society of Antiquaries of Ireland*, lxvi, 1936, pp. 80 ff.).

[2] 'Perrona Scottorum' (*SB. München*, 1900, pp. 469–538; partly reprinted in Traube's *Vorles.* iii. 95–119). Cf. also my note, 'Zu den Versen des Abtes Cellanus von Péronne' (*Zeitschr. für Celtische Philologie*, xx, 1936, pp. 382–90).

rites, converting to them the monks of Iona and thereby the last reluctant part of the Irish Church. Egbert also had missionary ambitions. But England was closed to him by his vow, and, moreover, ceased to need missionaries; by the conversion of Sussex and the Isle of Wight about 681–6 Wilfrid and his helpers won over the last of Anglo-Saxon lands. So the desire of Egbert to bring salvation to others turned to the kindred tribes beyond the sea, where Angles and Saxons, whose kinship had never been forgotten, had their origin, and where Wilfrid on his journey to Rome had initiated such apostolic work. But Egbert did not go there himself; according to a legendary tradition recorded by Bede, he was prevented by the night visions of one of his monks and by a storm, which seemed to confirm them. He sent Wictbert, another of his companions, to the Frisians. But King Aldgisl had been succeeded by Radbod and heathenism prevailed once more, and Wictbert returned to Ireland after two years without any success. And now Egbert chose the right man to answer his purpose: he sent out Willibrord together with eleven other monks, constituting the number of the apostles, a number favoured by the Irish pilgrims. So the Anglo-Saxon mission set out in 690, a century after Columbanus with twelve companions had begun the continental activity of the Irish, and less than a century after Pope Gregory had initiated the conversion of the Anglo-Saxons.

Willibrord

Our knowledge of Willibrord is dimmer and more limited than our knowledge of Wilfrid or Boniface.[1] We have some valuable but short chapters which Bede devoted to the beginnings of the Anglo-Saxon mission on the Continent in his contemporaneous history of the English Church. We have a

---

[1] The older literature on St. Willibrord is included in the edition of his medieval Lives by the late Bollandist Albert Poncelet, *Acta SS. Novembris*, iii, 1910, pp. 414–500, and in my edition of Alcuin's Prose Life, *SS. rer. Merov.* vii, 1920, pp. 81–141. Cf. Franz Flaskamp, *Die Anfänge friesischen und sächsischen Christentums* (Geschichtliche Darstellungen und Quellen, ed. L. Schmitz-Kallenberg, ix), Hildesheim, 1929; Josef Jung-Diefenbach, *Die Friesenbekehrung bis zum Martertode des hl. Bonifatius* (Missionswissenschaftliche Studien, ed. J. Schmidlin, Neue Reihe, i), Mödling near Vienna, 1931; Gabriel H. Verbist, *Saint Willibrord* (Université de Louvain, Recueil de travaux publiés par les membres des Conférences d'histoire et de philologie, xlix), Louvain, 1939.

calendar of saints which belonged to Willibrord himself,[1] and a few other manuscripts written by some of his companions. There are several charters of his episcopal see of Utrecht and more of his monastery of Echternach.[2] But while a part of the correspondence of Boniface exists, thanks to the care of his pupil Lullus of Mainz, and gives us a lively picture of the man and his work, the correspondence of Willibrord is entirely lost. Nor did he find an early biographer, such as Eddi Stephanus, whose Life of Wilfrid is biased and partial but weighty and full of substantial material, or as Willibald, whose Life of Boniface is incomplete and inadequate but gives parts of a coherent narrative based on contemporary information. In contrast to these Alcuin wrote his Life of Willibrord about half a century after the death of his hero; it is a collection of miracle stories rather than a biography, whereas the miraculous element in the writings of Eddi or Willibald is negligible. Consequently it is almost impossible to give a satisfactory sketch of Willibrord's personality,[3] beyond what can be gathered from his activities, and there remain important gaps which can be seen but not confidently filled, questions which can be raised but answered only with hesitation.

Willibrord continued on the Continent the Northumbrian missionary tradition which Wilfrid had created. He was born in 658, at the time when the expansion of the Northumbrian kingdom was at its greatest, probably in the southern part, in Deira, where his father Wilgils in later years lived as a hermit near the mouth of the Humber in a cell amidst a monastic congregation, over which Alcuin, probably a kinsman, after-

[1] Edited, with a reproduction, by H. A. Wilson, *The Calendar of St. Willibrord* (H. Br. Soc. lv), London, 1918. One page is reproduced in E. A. Lowe, *Codices Lat. ant.* ii, before p. xiii. On impressions made in the MS. (Paris Lat. 10837) by the stylus, which B. Bischoff has discovered, cf. my note, 'A propos du calendrier de S. Willibrord' (*Rev. Bén.* l, 1938, pp. 37–41), and L. Levillain and Ch. Samaran, 'Sur le lieu et la date de la bataille dite de Poitiers de 732' (*BECh.* xcix, 1938, pp. 243–67). 'On the age of the earliest Echternach manuscripts' cf. lastly Carl Nordenfalk, *Acta archaeologica*, iii, Copenhagen, 1932, pp. 57–62.

[2] Edited by Camillus Wampach, *Geschichte der Grundherrschaft Echternach im Frühmittelalter*, i. 2, Luxemburg, 1930; cf. the explanations in vol. i. 1, 1929, and the 'regesta' in Wampach's *Urkunden- und Quellenbuch zur Geschichte der altluxemburgischen Territorien bis zur burgundischen Zeit*, i, Luxemburg, 1935.

[3] Cf. K. Heeringa, 'Willibrord' (*Bijdragen voor Vaderlandsche Geschiedenis en Oudheidkunde*, 8th series, i, Hague, 1940, p. 22): 'Eigenlijk zijn de paus, Pippijn en Radbod duidelijker figuren dan Willibrord', &c.

wards presided.[1] Wilgils offered his son to the monastery of
Ripon, which was also situated in Deira. When he was born,
the struggle between the Celtic and Roman rituals was approaching its end in England; he was six years old when the
debate of Whitby in 664 brought victory to the Roman party.
Being educated at Ripon, Willibrord entered the Roman path
from the outset. The monastery, founded a few years before
for Irish monks, had been made a stronghold of the followers
of Rome and entrusted to Abbot Wilfrid, their champion; the
latter was soon to become bishop of all Northumbria at York,
till his opposition to the division of the vast diocese brought
about his removal and all the troubles of his later life. In the
meantime Willibrord's education at Ripon made him 'filius',
that is, the spiritual son of Wilfrid, as Eddi calls him; he
developed there the attachment to the Roman See which inspired his later achievements, and doubtless also his loyalty to
the monastic life, though we have no explicit statement on the
Rule observed by him.

In the year of Wilfrid's deposition, 678, Willibrord left Ripon,
and one is inclined to presume a connexion between the depar-
tures of bishop and monk. Twelve years followed, spent by
Willibrord in Ireland, a time of preparation like that in Ripon,
devoted to the monastic life in voluntary exile, 'pilgrimage',
and to the monastic learning as communicated by Irish tradition.
Pilgrimage overseas was a prominent ascetic practice of Irish
(and now also of English) monks, who, in the desire for self-
mortification, sought on and across the sea what the desert had
been to the hermits and monks of Egypt (cf. pp. 36 f.). Since
Columbanus went to France about 590, this kind of asceticism
had opened the Continent to Irish monks and had fostered in
France, Germany, and Italy, as in Scotland and northern
England, the missionary and pastoral zeal of these wandering
Irishmen, who worked in this way not only for the salvation of
their own souls but also for the spiritual welfare of others.
Willibrord, in Ireland, was touched by this spirit.

I have already said something of the new master, Egbert,

---

[1] Perhaps we may be justified in identifying Wilgils's monastery with that of
'Cornu Vallis', where Abbot Ceolfrid in 716 waited for a ship to take him down the
estuary of the Humber and overseas to Gaul (*Vita Ceolfridi*, cc. 30, ed. Plummer,
pp. 399 f.; cf. Bede's *Hist. abb.* c. 18, ed. Plummer, p. 383).

whom he found there, and of the latter's missionary efforts, disappointed at first but realized at last when, in 690, he sent Presbyter Willibrord and his companions to Friesland. We have also seen that the country of Willibrord's labours was then in a period of transition, dissolution, and reconstruction; that after many years of internal struggle for influence and power in the Frankish lands the predominance of one family emerged, that of the Carolingians. In 687 Pippin II established his domination by the victory of Tertry in Picardy. After the death of the defeated *maiordomus* of the west he governed in the name of a powerless Merovingian king, in virtue of the same office of mayor of the palace; it was first held by Pippin himself, then by his son Grimoald.[1] The re-establishment of the frontiers, the recovery of contested territories, was the next aim. The first blow was struck at the Frisians and their pagan duke or king Radbod, who, according to a famous legend, had already set one foot in the baptismal font but preferred to join his ancestors in hell, rather than enjoy the bliss of heaven without them.[2] Thus 'citerior Frisia', as Bede calls it, that is, the western part of the Frisian lands, with Utrecht, had returned to Frankish supremacy when Willibrord and his company arrived at the right moment in 690. Knowledge of the changing conditions overseas might have reached Ireland and England very quickly; the battlefield of Tertry was near the main road of English pilgrims to Rome and near the Irish monastery of Péronne previously mentioned.

Willibrord and his companions began their work in the conquered part of Friesland under the protection of Pippin;

[1] Cf. my note, 'Zu den Annales Mettenses' (*Historische Studien*, ed. Ebering ccxxxviii: *Festschrift für Robert Holtzmann*, Berlin, 1933, p. 15, n. 21).

[2] *Vita Vulframni*, c. 9 (*SS. rer. Merov.* v. 668). In spite of all the deficiencies and even impossible statements in this Life, I am inclined to assume that some relation actually existed between the Frisian mission and the monastery of Saint-Wandrille in Normandy, where Bishop Vulframn of Sens died in the last years of the 7th century and where his Life was written about 800, or between the mission and Bishop Vulframn himself (cf. preface and cc. 6, 7, pp. 662, 665 f. on Frisians living in the monastery; c. 8, p. 667 with n. 3, on Frisian paganism; c. 9, p. 668, on Willibrord). A few years later an Anglo-Saxon monk, Baga (the ancient spelling should have been Bacga), lived and died (after 710) in the same monastery (*Gesta abb. Fontanell.* cc. 5, 7, ed. Loewenfeld, pp. 22 f., 25; ed. Lohier and Laporte, pp. 27 f., 35, cc. 3. 3, 3. 6). The conjectures of Gerhard Eis, *Drei deutsche Gedichte des 8. Jahrhunderts aus Legenden erschlossen* (Germanische Studien, clxxxi), Berlin, 1936, pp. 9–26, that the *Vita Vulframni* drew on an Old German poem, are very uncertain.

Frankish dominion and Christian mission assisted each other. But having got the licence to preach and the support of the secular lord, Wilfrid's pupil sought further help: he went to Rome to obtain the sanction, benediction, and advice of Pope Sergius. It was a momentous decision. The Pope as yet was of little importance in the Frankish Church, which was united with the theoretical head of the universal church more in idea than in practice. It has been said, with deliberate exaggeration, that the history of the Frankish Church could be told down to the beginning of the eighth century without any reference to Rome.[1] The English Church was conscious of its Roman origin; now its first continental offspring entered into the same relation at once, an attitude which also became the distinctive mark of Boniface and of the German Church created by him. Willibrord, of course, obtained the permission and the sanction of the Pope, whose name is inscribed in his calendar. He also brought back Roman relics of apostles and martyrs for the churches which were to be erected in their honour.

During his absence the companions elected one of their number, Suidbert, bishop, and sent him to England to be consecrated. Theodore of Canterbury had died in 690, and the metropolitan see was vacant for some time; so Wilfrid, being in exile in Mercia, performed Suidbert's consecration. He who had started the missionary work overseas gave it the first English bishop. But Suidbert soon left Friesland to become the apostle of the Boructvari, the Bructeri of Tacitus and other Roman writers, in southern Westphalia. The expansion of the Saxons, who since the third century had united north-western Germany, had not yet come to a standstill; some time after Suidbert's arrival they conquered the territory of the Boructvari, and the community converted by him dispersed. He left this country. Pippin and his wife Plectrudis gave him a home on the Rhine, later called Kaiserswerth (near the present town of Düsseldorf), the history of which place begins with a monastery founded by Suidbert.[2] He died there in 713; his name also is found in Willibrord's calendar.

---

[1] A. Hauck, loc. cit. i. 419.

[2] On the name mentioned by Bede 'In Litore' (Anglo-Saxon 'on thæm waroðe', for Old German 'up demo waride', that is, 'In Insula') cf. A. Dresen, 'Beda Venerabilis und der älteste Name von Kaiserswerth' (*Düsseldorfer Jahrbuch*, xxviii, 1916, pp. 211–18).

His election as bishop and his going away have raised questions and conjectures. Were there dissensions among the brethren? Did Pippin object to Suidbert's leadership in Frisia? Did his episcopate mean such leadership at all, or did he hold his bishopric subject to Willibrord's guidance in a way not unusual in Irish monasteries, and was it his function only to confer spiritual gifts reserved to a bishop? Was his departure a symptom not of tension but rather of an expansion of the missionary field outside Friesland? The following occurrence supports this last view. Two English priests, both bearing the name of Hewald, who came with Willibrord or followed him from Ireland in the early days of the mission, also tried to find a field of action beyond the Frisian territory in that of the Saxons, but suffered martyrdom there very soon. Their bodies were taken, by order of Pippin, to Cologne, where their relics are still preserved in the church of St. Cunibert on the Rhine;[1] their names also were inscribed in Willibrord's calendar. Suidbert working in the country of the Boructvari, the Hewalds in that of the Saxons—their failure perhaps justifies the conclusion that this enterprise of the English was too daring at the outset and exceeded the limits that could be maintained. A firm footing had first to be secured.

Willibrord after his Roman journey appeared again in the forefront of the Frisian mission. About this time, as previously mentioned (p. 48), a church in the castle of Antwerp erected by St. Amandus was given to him, the first place we hear of assigned as a support and refuge for the missionaries.[2] It was outside Friesland but not far away, and connected their work with that of their Aquitanian forerunner; the name of St. Amandus also is recorded in the calendar.

After a few years of successful achievement Christianity had spread so far that the time had come for organization and establishment. Pippin sent Willibrord to Rome a second time to be consecrated *arch*bishop of the Frisian people. He could have been made bishop by members of the Frankish episcopate, without the participation of the Pope. But there were higher

[1] Cf. *Die Kunstdenkmäler der Rheinprovinz*, ed. Paul Clemen, vi. 4 (Stadt Köln, i. 4), Düsseldorf, 1916, pp. 243, 304.

[2] *MG. SS.* xxiii. 55, 63 f.; Wampach, *Grundherrschaft Echternach*, i. 2, p. 15, no. 1, cf. p. 78, no. 34. Cf. E. de Moreau, *Saint Amand*, Louvain, 1927, pp. 202 f.; Verbist, loc. cit., pp. xxiii f. and 90.

aims. A new province of the Church was to be constituted, comparable to the English Church; the future head of the new church should be able to consecrate other bishops, who were to be subject to his authority. As we have seen, it was necessary that the archbishop should receive the pallium, and this made it imperative to apply for the papal intervention in consequence of the significance of the pallium, a significance which had been developed in connexion with the English Church and was now transferred to the Continent for the first time. There must have been previous negotiations of which we have no record; for Willibrord was sent to Rome, as Bede says, with the favour and consent of all: 'misit Pippin, favente omnium consensu, virum venerabilem Vilbrordum Romam.' A kind of 'witenagemot', a meeting of the great, seems to have given its approval before-hand, and whatever we may conjecturally attribute to Anglo-Saxon suggestions, it was Pippin, not Willibrord, according to Bede, who now took action. It is the first time we hear of the co-operation of a Carolingian and a Pope, a co-operation which was to mark an epoch in the history of the West. The history of St. Boniface will show more signs of this approach, a develop-ment which was promoted from another side by the threat of the Langobards to the papal position in Rome. The establish-ment of the Pontifical State by the Frankish intervention in Italy and the foundation of the Western Empire were culmina-tions of this co-operation; the whole history of Germany and Italy was thereby affected almost up to the present day. These events went far beyond the scope of Willibrord and Pippin; but Willibrord's second journey to Rome at Pippin's behest, the first known occasion of Carolingian and Roman collaboration, was at least a symptom of the new tendency and drift.[1]

Pope Sergius consecrated Willibrord on the 21st day of November 695 in the old church of Santa Cecilia in Trastevere, on the eve of the festival of the patroness of music. He gave Willibrord the name of 'Clemens', because the 23rd was the

---

[1] Pippin also sent presents to Rome (Pope Gregory III to Charles Martel, *Codex Carolinus* 1, MG. *Epist*. iii. 477: 'quae a vestris parentibus vel a vobis offerta sunt') and is mentioned by Pope Paul I together with Charles Martel and Pippin's name-sake, the first Carolingian king, as having been one of the 'fideles Deo et beato Petro' (ib., no. 33, p. 540). Cf. Zwölfer, loc. cit., pp. 85 f. The expression 'fideles' should of course not be stressed.

day of Clement, the Roman saint. In the same way, twenty-four
years later, Wynfrid, when he was given his missionary mandate,
was named 'Bonifatius' after a saint venerated on the Aventine
Hill, whose festival preceded the writing of the papal mandate
by one day.[1] The change of name signified their reception into
the Roman community.

The Frisian Church was now established; the castle of
Traiectum, the modern Utrecht, was given to Willibrord as a
cathedral site and the centre of the ecclesiastical province. He
erected there a cathedral in honour of the Saviour. We may
again note the dedication 'Sancti Salvatoris': it was that of the
cathedrals of the Pope and of Canterbury, to-day San Giovanni
in Laterano and Christ Church (pp. 34 f.); the underlying idea is
obvious. He also found at Utrecht the ruins of a smaller church
which had been destroyed by the heathen (cf. p. 48); he built
a new church on its site in honour of St. Martin—here also a
parallel may be recognized with Canterbury, where a church
of St. Martin of Roman origin existed when the Roman missionaries arrived. At Utrecht monks and other clergy lived side by
side; the monastic ideal of Willibrord and the analogy of
Canterbury explain this dualism.

Willibrord was to England what Columbanus had been to
Ireland. He inaugurated a century of English spiritual influence
on the Continent, which was more than a literary influence
exercised by books; it was made personal by the migration of
English ecclesiastics and monks to the Frankish kingdom. Willibrord's activity was the first step to the more comprehensive

---

[1] Cf. my explanation of both names, Clemens and Bonifatius, *Neues Archiv*, xxxiii,
1908, pp. 525–30. On the date and the scene of Willibrord's consecration cf. *SS. rer.
Merov.* vii. 122, n. 3. The name of Clement may have been considered particularly
appropriate to a pilgrim missionary such as Willibrord; cf. the mass of St. Clement
in the *Sacramentarium Leonianum* (ed. C. L. Feltoe, Cambridge, 1896, p. 152) and in
the so-called *Missale Gothicum*, c. 121 (ed. H. M. Bannister, H. Br. Soc. lii, 1917,
p. 38): 'Vere dignum . . . Sancti Clementis martyris tui natalicia celebrantes, qui
cognationem reliquit et patriam, et post odorem tui nominis terras mariaque
transmittens ("transmeans" Miss. Goth.) abnegansque semet ipsum, crucem pere-
grinationis adsumpsit, ut te per apostolorum tuorum vestigia sequeretur. Cui
tu, Domine, secundum promissionem Filii tui tam in praesenti saeculo quam futuro
centupli ("centuplicata" ib.) muneris praemia repensasti. Nam beatissimi Petri mox
tradito ("traditus" ib.) disciplinis parentes, quos in genitali solo perdiderat, in
externa regione restituis', &c. The legend of the so-called Pseudo-Clementine
Recognitiones underlies this passage; cf., e.g., H. Delehaye, *Étude sur le légendier romain*
(Subsidia hagiographica, xxiii), Brussels, 1936, p. 98.

work and wider scope of Boniface, and to English collaboration in the educational effort of Charles the Great. He formed overseas an English colony which attracted followers in the next generations, and came to an end only in the beginning of the ninth century. His correspondence is lost; so we miss the lively picture of the relations between England and her emigrant sons and daughters which strikes every reader of the letters of Boniface, Lullus, and their correspondents. But a few stories and casual statements show that some personal intercourse and a similar exchange of letters existed between Willibrord and his compatriots in England. When Wilfrid about 703 made his last journey to Rome, he stayed with Willibrord (cf. p. 51). Acca, the future bishop of Hexham, was among his companions and, in later days, liked to recall what Willibrord had told them of relics of St. Oswald and their miraculous power, which he had experienced in Ireland and Friesland (Bede, *H.E.* iii. 13). Oswald is one of the English saints entered in his calendar. About the same time we hear of a member of the 'familia' of Willibrord, one of his monks or clerics, who came across the sea to Northumbria and was hospitably received at Lindisfarne. There he fell ill and regained his health at the tomb of St. Cuthbert,[1] in consequence of which this example of intercourse between the missionaries abroad and their native country came to be recorded. Some words also of Eddi Stephanus and of Bede show the existence of such a connexion and of the warm interest with which the continental achievements of the missionaries and even the sentiments of Willibrord were observed in his homeland,[2] an interest which induced like-minded men to follow the eleven monks whom Willibrord had led across the sea. We know from later tradition the names of a few of his English collaborators, Adalbert (that is, Ethelbert), who became the patron saint of Egmond in north Holland, and Presbyter Werenfrid, whose cult centred at Elst in Gelderland, and we may presume that there are others among Anglo-Saxon names commemorated in his calendar. In Friesland, of course, he began at once to educate a native clergy, ready to take the place

---

[1] *Vita Cuthberti anonyma*, iv. 16 (ed. Colgrave, p. 134); Bede, *Vita Cuthberti* in prose, c. 44 (ib., p. 296).
[2] *Vita Wilfridi*, c. 26 (p. 220); Bede, *Chronica maiora*, c. 566 (*Auct. ant.* xiii. 316) and *H.E.* v. 11 (p. 303).

of the apostles who had come from abroad. The first Frisian priests he ordained were brothers of the grandmother of Liudger, the first bishop of Münster in Westphalia, who carried on Willibrord's tradition in more than one respect.

But Willibrord had been sent to the Pope to be consecrated not bishop but archbishop of a new Frisian Church province and to receive the proper 'palleum dignitatis', as Alcuin calls this symbol and condition of metropolitan rights; it is the first continental precedent for this significance of the pallium as developed in the English Church. We learn from Bede that Willibrord did in fact institute other bishops ('antistites') out of the number of his Anglo-Saxon companions and followers, some of whom had already died when Bede wrote in 731. Not one of them is known. Bede cannot have been thinking of Suidbert or Boniface, who were not made bishops by Willibrord, and there are serious objections to my conjecture that Bishop Theutbert 'de Dorostat', to whom the famous old Vienna MS. of Livy belonged in the eighth century, was one of Willibrord's helpers; others consider him a bishop of Utrecht in the later part of this century.[1] In any case, his bishops had no successors, and a separate Frisian province of the Church did not survive him. But the system and idea lived on. The ancient provincial and metropolitan organization of the Church had struck root in England, while it broke down in the Frankish kingdom. It was transferred to Willibrord's field of work, the first new continental example of a system which was indeed to have a future. A papal mandate to three legates sent to organize the Bavarian Church in 716 was not carried out;[2] but the German archbishopric of another Anglo-Saxon, Boniface, came into

[1] See my note on Theutbert of Wijk bij Duurstede (on the place cf. above, p. 6), *Neues Archiv*, xxxiii, 1908, pp. 517–25; cf. *SS. rer. Merov.* vii. 85 f., 857. Objections are raised and different views held by I. H. Gosses, 'De oude kern van het bisdom Utrecht' (*Historische Avonden*, Derde bundel, Groningen–Den Haag, 1917, pp. 40 ff.), and Paul Lehmann, 'Das älteste Bücherverzeichnis der Niederlande' (*Het Boek*, xii, 1923, pp. 210 f.). Bede's application of the word 'antistes' only to bishops can now be easily examined with the help of P. F. Jones, *A Concordance to the Historia Ecclesiastica of Bede*, Cambridge (Mass.), 1929, pp. 35 f. Cf. also p. 82, n. 2.

[2] *MG. Leges* (in 2°), iii. 451 ff. Cf. Caspar, loc. cit. ii. 692 ff. The date has been restored by B. Krusch, *SS. rer. Merov.* vi. 499, also in *Arbeonis episcopi Frisingensis Vitae sanctorum Haimhrammi et Corbiniani* (in the collection *SS. rer. Germ.*), Hanover, 1920, p. 102 f. Joh. Haller, *Das Papsttum*, i. 505, has erroneously substituted the year of the Pope for that of the Emperor; there were no pontifical years in papal documents before Hadrian I.

being about 732 and swallowed up the very province of Willibrord after his death. This organization then spread to Gaul, where it had disappeared, though the re-establishment of the provinces in Gaul and Germany was not completed before the reign of Charles the Great. Utrecht itself ceased to be a metropolitan see, and after some vicissitudes became an episcopal diocese belonging to the province of Cologne. It was only by the new organization of the Dutch Church in 1559 in the time of Philip II of Spain (with which the Old Catholic Archbishop of Utrecht of modern times is connected), and again by the restoration of the Catholic hierarchy of the Netherlands in 1853, that Utrecht's metropolitan character was revived.

In the missionary field also Willibrord only made a start and set the course. He came to convert the Frisians and succeeded wherever the Frankish supremacy gave him protection. Within these limits the story would have been mostly that of the normal, difficult activities of the head of a missionary church, had not political events interrupted the continuity, as they had done so often in the England of the seventh century. In 714 Pippin died, leaving with his widow Plectrudis a grandson, a child, as heir and even as mayor of the palace, and all the enemies of his house joined to overthrow its power. The Frisians with Duke Radbod took part in the insurrection; their ships went up the Rhine to Cologne. Frankish dominion and Christian Church broke down together; all the work of Willibrord seemed to be undone. But a stronger man emerged from the strife, a son of Pippin by another wife, Charles Martel, the 'hammer', as later times have called the conqueror of the Arabs. Duke Radbod died in 719, and Willibrord was able to resume his work and make good the loss of the years 715–19. A second period of construction followed, ended only by his death in 739, when he had lived on the Continent for forty-nine years and reached the venerable age of 81. But again in his later years Christianity did not spread beyond the borders of Frankish rule; in the east of the Zuider Zee, in the oldest settlements of the Frisians, as far as the lower part of the Weser, the inhabitants clung faithfully to their ancestral traditions. Boniface and his companions suffered martyrdom in this part of Friesland, and these eastern Frisians gave way only when the forced conversion of the Saxons by Charles the Great had removed their last

support. Anglo-Saxons once more took part in their Christianization. Thus Willibrord's Frisian work was no more than a
beginning, though a decisive beginning.

His original aims went far beyond the borderland of Frankish
rule. He tried, though without success, to convert the Danes.
He made a journey to Denmark, bringing back thirty Danish
boys, whom he baptized, no doubt in the hope of establishing
a kind of seminary for future work, thus anticipating the English
missionaries of the next centuries in Scandinavia. It was too
early to make an advance into these strongholds of Germanic
heathenism; not before Charles the Great had pushed forward
the frontiers of his empire to the borders of the Saxons and
Danes, did the time come for such an attempt. There are also
traces of pastoral activity in inner Germany. The last duke of
the Thuringians, Heden, in 704 and 717 conferred on Willibrord
possessions in Thuringia and northern Franconia,[1] on the second
occasion to obtain his advice regarding the erection of a monastery at Hammelburg (south-west of Kissingen). We have no
knowledge beyond that; but the two charters of donation presuppose relations of at least thirteen years, and the question
arises whether Willibrord may not also have been a forerunner
of Boniface in Thuringia. We have no information enabling
us to answer this question.

His success in western Friesland depended greatly on the
protection and favour of the secular arm. The Carolingian
house looked with friendly eye on the new-comers. A few
charters still extant bear witness to this in the case of Utrecht,
and other documents give similar testimony in respect of the
monastery of Echternach in Luxemburg, in the proximity of
Trier. Its territory was given about 700 to Willibrord, partly
by an abbess of Trier, Irmina, partly by Pippin and his consort
Plectrudis. It was to him in his later years what Antwerp perhaps had been in his early continental days, a harbour of rest
and a place of retreat outside his missionary field in times of
danger; in due course it became his last resting-place. Pippin
and his wife, Charles Martel and other members of the ruling
family bestowed many possessions on it, while Willibrord transferred the ownership of the whole monastery to Pippin and

[1] *MG. SS.* xxiii. 55, 60; Wampach, *Grundherrschaft Echternach*, i. 2, pp. 27, 63,
nos. 8, 26.

made it a Carolingian proprietary monastery, 'Eigenkloster'. How much this place became a centre in the life of the archbishop is shown, not only in some stories related by Alcuin but also in Willibrord's calendar which I have repeatedly quoted. This manuscript, written by an English hand in the early eighth century and now in the National Library in Paris, is a calendar of saints, whose choice is clearly connected with the scenes of Willibrord's life, in his native country and during his 'peregrinatio'. There are saints of Northumbria and Kent, of Ireland and Rome, of Gaul and particularly of Trier. The entries point to good neighbourly relations between Echternach and Willibrord on one side and the ancient episcopal city on the other. Three years before Bede in 731 wrote an account of the Frisian mission in his *Ecclesiastical History*, Clemens Willibrordus, as he called himself, made a short entry on the margin of the November page of the calendar, the only lines which to-day can be attributed to his hand. He commemorated there in brief the years of two principal events of his life, his coming overseas 'in Francea' in 690 and his consecration by Pope Sergius in 695, and also the year 728, when this note was written.[1] He was then exactly 70 years old, and that may have been the motive of his writing.

He survived for another eleven years, till 739 (7 November). His province, consisting of a missionary church in the making, was large, and though, according to Bede, he consecrated some bishops, he felt the need of help in his personal work as early as 721, when he tried in vain to induce Boniface, then staying with him, to be consecrated bishop and to assist him in his pastoral duties. There was a difficulty arising out of canon law, at least in theory. The principle from Roman times was that there should be only one bishop in each 'civitas', and that no other bishop should interfere there; a second bishop in the same diocese and the election or designation of a successor during the lifetime of his predecessor were forbidden. But occasionally in the seventh and eighth centuries the illness or old age of a

---

[1] A facsimile of the November page will be found, besides the reproduction of the entire calendar by Wilson (cf. p. 54, n. 1), in Cabrol and Leclercq, *Dictionnaire d'archéologie chrétienne et de liturgie*, iii. 2, after cols. 2603–4, and in Flaskamp, loc. cit. after p. 80. On the entries cf. also W. H. Frere, 'A Relic of St. Willibrord' (*The Church Quarterly Review*, xci, 1921, pp. 356–62); Jung-Diefenbach, loc. cit., pp. 43, 46 f., 54, 90 f.

bishop caused Englishmen to disregard this law and custom.[1]
Boniface desired a similar arrangement for his own succession;
but Pope Zacharias at first insisted on the principle against
him (743), though after some years he gave his permission.[2]
Now Willibrord, having preached till he was aged and infirm,
had, as we learn from Boniface himself,[3] an assistant bishop to
help him, who was known not as bishop, 'episcopus', but as
country bishop, 'chorepiscopus'. Here we see how a man,
though strictly devoted to the canonical rules of Rome, found
an expedient by which to combine the monarchy of the bishop
and the needs of his diocese. In consequence of the tendency
to adapt the ecclesiastical order to the secular organization of
the late Roman Empire, the rule had prevailed that the bishop
must have his see in the πόλις, 'civitas', of his diocese, the
urban centre of the municipal government of Roman times.
Previously, in the East, bishops had also lived in villages, in
the rural districts, the χώρα, and the synodical legislation of
the fourth century strove hard to restrict these rural bishops,
χωρεπίσκοποι, to reduce their rights and functions, and to bring
them into dependence on the bishop of the city, who would
thus govern the whole diocese. The West had seen only a few
exceptional cases of 'chorepiscopi';[4] but name and institution were known from the collections of the eastern synodical
decrees translated into Latin and constituting the first manuals
of canon law. The theoretical justification of Willibrord's
proceeding is to be found here rather than in the model of the
Irish monastic bishops, or in the irregularities of the Frankish
Church of his times. There exists a translation of the Greek

---

[1] Bede, *H.E.* ii. 4, iv. 5, 23, v. 6 (pp. 86 f., 217, 255, 292); Symeon of Durham,
Hist. regum, § 50 (*Opera*, ed. Arnold, ii. 47). Cf. Bede, *Hist. abb.* c. 7 (p. 371).

[2] Boniface, *Epist.* 50, 51, 80 (pp. 83, 89, 180).

[3] Ib., no. 109 (p. 235).

[4] Cf. Theodor Gottlob, *Der abendländische Chorepiskopat* (Kanonistische Studien
und Texte, ed. A. M. Koeniger, i), Bonn, 1928. The author is wrong in referring
the first chorepiscopi of the 8th century to the example of auxiliary bishops residing
at St. Martin's, Canterbury; such bishops are attested there by reliable sources in
the 11th century only. Cf. my review, *Neues Archiv*, xlviii, 1930, pp. 262 f.; W. H.
Frere, *Visitation Articles and Injunctions of the Period of the Reformation*, i (Alcuin Club
Collections, xiv), London, 1910, pp. 35–40; R. A. L. Smith, 'The Place of Gundulf
in the Anglo-Norman Church' (*E.H.R.* lviii, 1943, p. 261). Nor can I connect the
origin of these bishops of St. Martin's with the grant of 867, Birch, ii, no. 516
(H. and S. iii. 656), as have suggested Frere, loc. cit., and M. Deanesly, 'The
Archdeacons of Canterbury under Archbishop Ceolnoth' (*E.H.R.* xlii, 1927, pp. 8 f.).

canons of the fourth century, where the interpreter renders χωρεπίσκοποι by 'vicarii episcoporum, quos Graeci chorepiscopos dicunt'.[1] The chorepiscopi of the East thus found their place in the canon law of the West, the more so because Isidore of Seville, one of the principal teachers of the early Middle Ages, had admitted this interpretation into his book on the Ecclesiastical Offices,[2] which was also known in Northumbria, the native country of Willibrord.[3] The latter was the first to put this canonical theory into western practice. Boniface followed this example; he had in his last days at least two chorepiscopi, the Anglo-Saxon Lullus who succeeded him as bishop of Mainz,[4] and Eoba, whose name also manifests his English origin, whom he made bishop at Utrecht 'ad subveniendum suae senilis aetatis debilitate', and who was to be one of his companions in martyrdom.[5] It was also a principle that only a 'civitas', not a village or small town, should be made the see of a bishop, 'ne vilescat nomen episcopi'. In the missionary lands very few 'cities' existed, and the choice of places in accordance with the canons

[1] The so-called Isidorian version of the canons of Ancyra, c. 13, Neocaesarea, c. 13, and Antiochia, c. 8, ed. C. H. Turner, *Ecclesiae Occidentalis monumenta iuris antiquissima*, ii. 1, Oxford, 1907, pp. 84, 138, and ii. 2, 1913, pp. 254, 256 (col. 2). On the origin of this version of the 5th century cf. Eduard Schwartz, 'Die Kanonessammlungen der alten Reichskirche' (*Savigny-Zeitschr.* lvi, 1936, *Kan. Abt.* xxv, pp. 11 ff., 60 ff., 83 ff.).

[2] Isidore, *De ecclesiasticis officiis*, ii. 6 (Migne, *P.L.* lxxxiii. 786 f.), based on the canons of Neocaesarea (loc. cit.) and Antiochia, c. 10 (loc. cit., pp. 260, 262, 264, col. 2). Cf. Paul Séjourné, *Saint Isidore de Séville: son rôle dans l'histoire du droit canonique*, Paris, 1929, pp. 56 f.; A. C. Lawson, 'The Sources of the *De ecclesiasticis officiis* of S. Isidore of Seville' (*Rev. Bén.* l, 1938, p. 29).

[3] The unknown monk of Lindisfarne, who between 698 and 705 composed the earliest Life of St. Cuthbert, when describing the latter's qualities (iv. 1, ed. Colgrave, pp. 110, 112), first copied some lines from the Life of St. Martin by Sulpicius Severus, the next from the Letters of St. Paul, and the rest from Isidore's work, ii. 5, §§ 17–18 (col. 785 f.); cf. Colgrave, p. 331. The same work is quoted in a letter of Bishop Megingoz of Würzburg, preserved in the Vienna MS. of the correspondence of Boniface and Lullus, which also contains another extract from Isidore's book; cf. Appendix VII, below, pp. 282 f. *De ecclesiasticis officiis* was one of the sources of the *Collectio canonum Hibernensis*; cf. Séjourné, loc. cit., pp. 380 f. On existing MSS. of Isidore's work see C. H. Beeson, 'Isidor-Studien' (Traube, *Quellen*, iv. 2), 1913, pp. 49 ff.

[4] Boniface, *Epist.* 93 (p. 213) of the year 752. Lullus was presbyter at least till November 751; cf. ib., nos. 86, 87, 90 (pp. 192, 200, 205).

[5] Willibald's *Vita Bonifatii*, c. 8 (ed. Levison, p. 47). The form 'Eoban' here, in Boniface's *Epist.* 35 and 41 (pp. 60, 66), and in an addition to Bede's Martyrology (H. Quentin, *Les Martyrologes historiques du moyen âge*, Paris, 1908, pp. 51, 115) is the oblique case of the name Eoba; but it was considered a nominative as early as about 900 (Levison, loc. cit., p. 60) and is often erroneously used so to-day also.

was difficult; this fact may have contributed to the spreading of the chorepiscopal office.

The example of Willibrord and Boniface was decisive;[1] the number of chorepiscopi in the Frankish Church grew quickly, not only in missionary districts, but in many dioceses. Friction soon arose, the chorepiscopi being inclined to enlarge their rights, the bishops to restrict them. Anyone who has studied one of the most famous forgeries of all times, the Pseudo-Isidorian Decretals of the middle of the ninth century, knows that opposition to the chorepiscopi is not their principal aim, but an obvious secondary purpose. The forgers succeeded; the chorepiscopal institution gradually disappeared in the course of the next centuries. But the problem remained how to find, for an overburdened or sick bishop, assistants endowed with the right to confer spiritual gifts reserved to a bishop; so there arose the bishops 'in partibus infidelium' and other auxiliary bishops, England's suffragans, Germany's 'Weihbischöfe' of later times. We need only note here that it was Willibrord who first set the example of appointing a chorepiscopus of the Western type. Boniface was the next to follow him in this Anglo-Saxon contribution to the constitution of the Occidental Church.

But the importance of Willibrord's work belongs to the missionary field. In this he continued and established the Northumbrian tradition, which had been accidentally created by Wilfrid, and he also had successors in the north after he had left the scene. During his lifetime a man of even greater ascendancy came to the front, Wynfrid or Boniface, who combined missionary enthusiasm with organizing ability. He and his companions represented another part of England, Wessex. The continental enterprises of the English thus proceeded from groups dwelling in the borderlands of Anglo-Saxon civilization, from the two kingdoms remotest from each other and from Kent, which provided the usual route to and from the Continent. West

[1] Chorepiscopi were mentioned in a general way in 747 by Pope Zacharias, when he answered questions of canon law which the bishops and abbots of *maiordomus* Pippin had addressed to him; in his answer he referred to the canons of Antiochia and Neocaesarea (*Codex Carolinus*, 3, cc. 1 and 4, *MG. Epist.* iii. 480 f.). The same Pope in the following year answered a letter written to him by Frankish bishops (the names of whom are given) 'et ceteris amantissimis chorepiscopis' (Boniface, *Epist.* 82, p. 182). The relation to the Anglo-Saxon continental circle is evident in both cases.

Saxons and Northumbrians were the most ready of all Englishmen to receive the ecclesiastical learning, and the first to show
the fruits of their newly acquired scholarship, as is testified by
the names of Aldhelm and Bede. Northumbrians and West
Saxons similarly led the way as missionaries; after Willibrord
came Boniface, equally zealous to enlighten by his labours what
he believed to be the darkness of continental heathendom.

IV

BONIFACE: GERMAN MISSION AND REFORM OF THE FRANKISH CHURCH

LIKE the other Englishmen of extensive religious enterprise of whose origin we know something, Wynfrid came from the class of free landowners. In an early letter he calls himself 'ignobili stirpe procreatum', the offspring of an ignoble stem, adopting a kind of humility which was habitual among churchmen.[1] But his kinsmen and later collaborators, the brothers Willibald and Wynnebald, are ascribed to a noble family, and Leobgytha or Leoba, who similarly followed him to Germany and was his relative on his mother's side, also had parents of noble stock. He was born in Wessex about 675. Crediton in Devonshire is reputed to have been his birthplace; but there is no earlier authority for this than the liturgical books of Bishop John Grandisson of Exeter (1327–69),[2] and the foundation of this late statement is unknown. Nevertheless his paternal home cannot have been far away. For he was committed in his

---

[1] See the anonymous letter to Sigebert, ed. Dümmler, *MG. Epist.* iv, p. 565. 1, and (complete) ed. Paul Lehmann, 'Ein neuentdecktes Werk eines angelsächsischen Grammatikers vorkarolingischer Zeit' (*Historische Vierteljahrschrift*, xxvi, 1931, p. 754, l. 54). Dümmler ascribed this letter to the first part of the 9th century. Recently Lehmann has for the first time published the later portion of it, which is lacking in Dümmler's edition ('Mitteilungen aus Handschriften I', *SB. München*, 1929, no. 1, pp. 20–2; cf. p. 15). In the article mentioned above (loc. cit., pp. 738–56) he added an edition of the whole text, recognized rightly its conformity with Aldhelm's style, and tried to show that the latter himself was the author. But N. Fickermann, *Neues Archiv*, xlix, 1932, pp. 763 f., subsequently discovered that this text was written by Boniface as a dedicatory letter to his grammatical compilation which has long been known. Lehmann at once joined him in this attribution, notwithstanding differences on minor points, nor can there be any doubt that Boniface is the author ('Die Grammatik aus Aldhelm's Kreise', *Historische Vierteljahrschrift*, xxvii, 1932, pp. 758–71). Cf. also Fickermann, 'Der Widmungsbrief des hl. Bonifatius' (*Neues Archiv*, l, 1935, pp. 210–21).

[2] Ed. J. N. Dalton, *Ordinale Exon.*, vol. ii (H. Br. Soc., vol. xxxviii), 1909, p. 407 (the words 'ex civitate Criditonie iuxta Exoniam' are inserted in a sentence taken from the Martyrology of Usuard, Migne, *P.L.* cxxiv. 123), and vol. iii (loc. cit., vol. lxiii), 1926, pp. 247 f. (the name of the birthplace is added to an extract from Willibald's *Vita Bonifatii*; cf. my edition of the latter, p. xxix). Crediton is first mentioned in a grant of 739, ed. Napier and Stevenson, *The Crawford Collection of Early Charters*, p. 1, no. 1; cf. pp. 37 ff. On the date of Boniface's birth (672/73?) cf. F. Flaskamp, *Zeitschr. für Kirchengeschichte*, xlv, 1927, pp. 339–44.

childhood to the monastery of Exeter nearby, in a country which probably had been conquered from the Britons and colonized by Saxons only a short time before. From Exeter he went later to the monastery of Nursling near Southampton.

In these houses he was trained in the spirit of St. Benedict; he acquired a sense of steady ecclesiastical order and of firm connexion and conformity with the Roman Church, features which were revealed in all his life and work. He also absorbed a considerable amount of the new learning which was cultivated in those monasteries. This was derived from the Canterbury school of Theodore and Hadrian and from Celtic sources, and culminated in these years in the teaching and writing of Aldhelm, the abbot of Malmesbury and bishop of Sherborne, with his elaborate, affected prose style and his liking for alliteration and unusual wording, quite different from the simpler, more natural manner of the Northumbrian writers Bede and Alcuin. Wynfrid has left, besides his letters, poems and compilations on grammar and metrics. The influence of Aldhelm is obvious in his early letters, so much so that the dedicatory letter of his grammatical treatise, which had been published anonymously, was attributed to Aldhelm a few years ago, until the true authorship was demonstrated.[1] He proved an impressive preacher and an effective teacher. His interpretation of the Scriptures, which was no doubt largely allegorical in the manner of his age, attracted many disciples from other monasteries and convents; the friendship of learned nuns, which is reflected by his letters,[2] originated in these years. He also displayed practical abilities; on the advice of several abbots, King Ine of Wessex and a synod chose him as their envoy to the Archbishop of Canterbury. An ecclesiastical career in his country might have been foretold for him, and he was even elected abbot of Nursling (717). But the desire to spread the Gospel abroad overcame all his other longings and ambitions. Nor was his firm resolution deflected by the failure of a first attempt, when he went to Friesland in 716, at a time of insurrection against the Frankish domination and of the persecution of Christianity (p. 63), and was forced to return to England. In 718 he sailed a second time; it was the decisive moment of his

[1] See above, p. 70, n. 1.
[2] On the letters of Boniface and Lullus cf. Appendix VII, pp. 280 ff.

life. He never lost touch with his native country, but he did not see it again, and the remaining thirty-six years of his life were devoted to his work in Germany. They can be divided into two or rather three parts. Missionary activity occupied the first and longest period; then, from 739 onwards, followed years devoted to organizing the German and reforming the Frankish Church. At the end of his life he resumed the task of preaching the Gospel to the heathen and suffered martyrdom.

The Mission in Germany

One feature of his activity is the close connexion and co-operation with the Papacy. Before the resumption of his work in 718 he followed the precedent set by Willibrord; he went to Rome to obtain the permission and help of the Pope. Gregory II on the 15th of May 719 commissioned him to preach to the unbelieving Gentiles, and this mandate is the earliest example of such a document that has been preserved. On the same occasion the Pope changed Wynfrid's name, as Sergius had changed that of Willibrord at his consecration (p. 59), and conferred on him the name of Bonifatius, a martyr whose church was situated on the Aventine Hill, and whose festival fell on the eve of the day on which the papal mandate of commission was dated. Henceforth his official designation was Boniface, and this almost entirely displaced his original Germanic name. Only in a few letters written to and from England was the name of Wynfrid occasionally used side by side with the new one, with which the fame of his achievements is connected. This also was a symptom of the Roman influence prevailing in his work.

After his first successes he was invited to visit Rome again. Gregory II consecrated him bishop there on the last day of November 722, the festival of St. Andrew, the apostle and brother of St. Peter. To that saint Gregory I had dedicated his Roman monastery, from which his first English missionaries proceeded. The mass of the apostle in the Gregorian Sacramentary (c. 184) not only emphasizes the apostolic foundations of the Church but also celebrates Andrew as 'praedicator', preacher; the day of this fisher of men could therefore be considered appropriate to the occasion. Thus the nucleus of a new German Church was established, a church self-sufficient in the sphere of episcopal order. Boniface had first to offer a profession of faith, as was usual for bishops of the immediate metropolitan district of the Pope,[1] and after his consecration he made a sworn promise of obedience and fidelity to St. Peter and to the Pope and his successors. The promise was based on the formula contained in the *Liber Diurnus*, of an oath which such Italian bishops on the occasion of their consecration were required to deposit on the tomb of St. Peter. Only an obligation to the Roman Empire, which was out of place for a Frankish bishop, was replaced by another; Boniface promised to have no communion or connexion with bishops living in opposition to the ancient institutions of the Fathers, to oppose them with all his might, or to inform the Pope. This obligation became a heavy burden for a conscientious, scrupulous man such as Boniface, who met at the Frankish court worldly bishops living in defiance of all canon law, nor could he avoid having contact with them in the interest of his own work. But the fact of the oath was in itself of importance; the sphere of the new bishop was thereby brought into closer connexion with the Roman Church than any diocese of Frankish rule had hitherto been, except perhaps Willibrord's Frisian province. The Roman origin of the English Church began to exert an influence overseas through the ideas of ecclesiastical unity which the English missionaries disseminated.

After ten more years of hard work and success the last stage was reached; the next Pope, Gregory III, sent Boniface the pallium, probably in 732, and made him archbishop. The provincial organization of the Church had disappeared in the Frankish countries, but had taken root in England and had been transferred first to Willibrord's Frisian Church (p. 62). It was now applied to the sphere of action of Boniface, who was to be the head of a new German Church. It was a plan for the future, and several years passed before bishops were consecrated by him. He was a metropolitan without bishops subject to him and without dioceses. Did the secular power, did Charles Martel, oppose the creation of new bishoprics? Or did opposition come from the Frankish bishops in the Rhineland, who may have included the districts east of the Rhine in their spheres of interest?

[1] On the professions of Boniface cf. Tangl, *Neues Archiv*, xl, 1916, pp. 739 ff.; xli, p. 49, no. 4.

The above is merely a sketch of the relations between Boniface and Rome. The first papal mandate of 719, the episcopal consecration in 722, and the conferment of the metropolitan dignity about 732, are the notable landmarks in their progress. This sketch requires to be supplemented from a large correspondence, partly extant, partly lost. Boniface sent reports on the progress of his work and asked the Pope for information and instruction on problems of ecclesiastical practice arising in a soil new to Christianity. There were questions and answers recalling the 'interrogationes' and 'responsa' of Augustine and Gregory the Great. The essential fact was the kind of union and unity which Boniface tried to maintain: when a Pope died, he offered his subjection and service to the successor and asked to carry on the 'familiaritas' and 'amicitiae communio' with the Roman See.

In the early continental years of Boniface, Charles Martel gained the mastery over all opponents as the real ruler of the Frankish kingdom; he governed as mayor of the palace in the name of a powerless king, and in his last years without any king at all. Gregory II recommended Boniface to him after his episcopal consecration, and Charles granted the missionary his protection, without which the work of foreigners was practically impossible. Charles was the right man for this iron age, above all a warrior avid of power and endowed with force of will, who smashed the local 'tyrants', as Einhard said; nor did he spare worldly bishops and abbots who stood in his way. He conferred bishoprics and abbacies according to temporal considerations. Because the royal estates were not sufficient for his purposes, he seized more possessions of monasteries and churches than his predecessors had done, and bestowed their revenue on his followers, so as to have an army of mounted professional warriors at his disposal. This 'forced loan' or 'secularization' of church property, which contributed to the development of the feudal system, earned him a bad reputation in ecclesiastical circles from the ninth century onwards; there is even a hint in this sense in a letter of Boniface written a few years after the death of the *maiordomus*.[1] Certainly Charles was not interested

---

[1] Boniface, *Epist.* 73 (p. 153, n. **), the version which represents the definitive text sent to England, as it is recorded by William of Malmesbury, *Gesta reg. Angl.* i. 80 (ed. Stubbs, i. 81). The words are missing in the continental manuscripts derived from another copy. Cf. Tangl, *Neues Archiv*, xl. 715 ff.; below, p. 280 f.

in church reform as was his son Carloman; but he was religious after the usual manner of his age. He protected Willibrord and made gifts to him, to his church of Utrecht, and to his monastery of Echternach (p. 64); similarly he gave Boniface his protection. Frankish dominion and Christian interests harmonized with each other. Charles fought several times to repress insurrections of Frisians and Saxons, for whom Christianity was connected with Frankish lordship. In spite of tribal antagonisms and aspirations, the difference of religion was one of the strongest dividing lines. To a Christian Bavarian, who was captured by robbers and sold to Thuringia, no fate seemed to be worse than to fall into the hands of the neighbouring Saxons, 'who do not know God' and whose life he detested as an 'abyss of death'.[1] Working for Christianity, the English missionaries contributed to the consolidation of the State.

When Boniface first came to the Continent in 716 he turned to Friesland, the scene of Willibrord's labours. He went there again when the news of Radbod's death reached him in Thuringia in 719, and he assisted the old archbishop in his endeavours to restore the Frisian Church and to recover lost ground. Willibrord tried to secure his permanent co-operation by offering him consecration as bishop (p. 65). But Boniface declined; obviously he preferred a sphere of independent activity.[2] He left Frisia in 721, though he returned to that country at the end of his life to gain there the crown of martyrdom. He found his proper field of action in central Germany; it is here that he acquired the name of the 'Apostle of Germany'. Coming from Rome in 719, he went to Thuringia, where Christianity had already taken root,[3] but an element of paganism had still to be extirpated. After leaving Willibrord and after his consecration in Rome, he chose Hesse as his field of work, later to be exchanged once more for Thuringia. These were years of hardship, of privations and dangers, but also of success in his fight against heathendom, pagan survivals, and heretics (among whom some Anglo-Saxon names are found), and for the observance of canon law. Everybody knows the story how he destroyed the oak of Donar at

---

[1] Arbeo's *Vita Haimhrammi*, cc. 37–43 (ed. Krusch, *SS. rer. Merov.* iv. 512–20, and *Arbeonis Vitae SS. Haimhrammi et Corbiniani*, pp. 84–95).

[2] Cf. Tangl, 'Bonifatiusfragen' (*Abhandl. Berlin*, 1919, no. 2, pp. 7 ff.).

[3] Cf. also above, pp. 47, 64,

Geismar in Hesse and thereby manifested to the heathen the
defeat of their god and the might of Christ. Monasteries were
founded as strongholds and places of rest and refuge, Amöneburg
east of Marburg and Fritzlar in Hesse,[1] Ohrdruf near Gotha
in Thuringia. The Rule of St. Benedict, which, since the seventh
century, had been of some influence in France, won new centres
in Germany.

The correspondence of Boniface shows with what lively
interest, with what contributions of spiritual and material help,
advice, suggestions, and presents, his fellow countrymen and
women followed his activities. What was more important,
compatriots came overseas to join in his work and that of his
first companions. The English colony in Germany increased
through an influx of clerics, monks, and nuns, 'plurima multitudo', as his biographer Willibald says (c. 6, p. 34), who was
himself of English origin. Among them were men and women
of learning. Rudiments of ancient civilization, which had been
brought to England directly from the Mediterranean or from
Ireland together with Christianity and in its service, now came
back to the Continent. The new-comers were dispersed in
Hesse, Thuringia, and northern Franconia; it became gradually
possible to spread the network of preachers and teachers. There
were helpers of whom we do not know more than their names;
but I may here mention at least Wigbert, the first abbot of
Fritzlar, and Leobgytha or Leoba, a relative of Boniface (p. 70),
one of the most amiable women in this circle, who had been
educated in the convents of Minster in Thanet and of Wimborne
in Dorset.[2] Boniface made her abbess of Tauberbischofsheim

---

[1] Hesse in the later meaning. Amöneburg was situated in the Lahngau, the
inhabitants of which have to be distinguished from the Hessians in the strict sense
of this age. Cf. H. Boehmer, 'Zur Geschichte des Bonifatius' (*Zeitschr. des Vereins für
hessische Geschichte*, l, 1917, pp. 175 ff.).

[2] Our main source, besides some letters in the correspondence of Boniface, is the
Life of Leoba by Rudolf of Fulda of 836 (ed. Waitz, *MG. SS.* xv. i, pp. 118–31).
It is based on the relations of four of her disciples written down by a priest and
monk Mago. But Rudolf adorned the narrative by drawing not only on Willibald's *Vita Bonifatii* but also on sources which had no direct connexion with his
subject, such as Athanasius's *Vita Antonii*, Jerome's *Vita Hilarionis*, Paulinus's *Vita
Ambrosii*, Constantius's Life of Germanus of Auxerre, the fabulous *Actus Silvestri*,
and the Dialogues of Gregory the Great. Not all the statements in the work therefore can be taken at their face value. Cf. my paper, 'Bischof Germanus von
Auxerre' (*Neues Archiv*, xxix, 1904, pp. 153–6) and the thesis of W. Finsterwalder,
'Beiträge zu Rudolf von Fulda', an extract from which has been published in

in Franconia, to-day in the north-eastern part of Baden. The house won high prestige under her guidance; other convents took abbesses from it, and noble families of the country sent their daughters there. Another convent in Franconia under Anglo-Saxon leadership was Kitzingen on Main; its abbess Thecla, a relative of Leoba, also governed, according to medieval tradition, Ochsenfurt near by. Boniface, like Willibrord, very soon found native pupils and helpers; among them was the young Gregory from the neighbourhood of Trier, a member of the Frankish aristocracy,[1] who as abbot of Utrecht after the death of Boniface became head of the Frisian Church. The Frisian Liudger, the first bishop of Münster, was one of his disciples. Thus east of the Rhine a new church developed, inspired with missionary zeal and sense of vocation. Personalities such as Gregory and Liudger show the lasting influence of the Anglo-Saxon action and example.

The year 738 was a turning-point in the work of Boniface. Charles Martel defeated the Saxons of Westphalia; they had to give hostages and promised to pay tribute.[2] A new area of missionary work seemed to become accessible to the Anglo-Saxons. Boniface asked all English people to pray for the conversion of their kinsfolk, who themselves said: 'We are of one blood and one bone with you.' A bishop of Leicester rejoiced in the hope that this nation of his own race ('gens nostra') should believe in Christ; he knew that the thoughts of Boniface dwelt day and night upon the conversion of the pagan Saxons. Probably this prospect induced Boniface to undertake his third journey to Rome in 738. Gregory III issued an appeal to the whole people of the 'Old-Saxons' ('Altsaxones'), a letter largely consisting of biblical quotations, which were hardly likely to make any impression on pagans. But the whole plan was premature. The success of Charles Martel over the Saxons was merely temporary; it was reserved for his eminent grandson

---

Jahrbuch der Philosophischen Fakultät der Albertus-Universität zu Königsberg, 1921, p. 57 f.

[1] On Gregory cf. the conjectures of Tangl, *Neues Archiv*, xl. 766 ff.

[2] Cf. H. Wiedemann, *Die Sachsenbekehrung* (Missionswissenschaftliche Studien, ed. J. Schmidlin, New Series, v), Hiltrup, 1932, pp. 27 ff.; M. Lintzel, 'Untersuchungen zur Geschichte der alten Sachsen XIV' (*Sachsen und Anhalt*, xiii, 1937, pp. 59–65). Cf. also E. Hennecke, *Zeitschr. für Kirchengeschichte*, liv, 1935, pp. 62–9.

to master this last independent German tribe and to open their country to missionary endeavour.

Church Organization and Church Reform

Nevertheless, this Roman journey of Boniface initiated a new chapter of Anglo-Saxon work on the Continent. The notions of a 'legatio' and of Boniface being the legate of the Apostolic See came more to the front. The organization and supervision of all existing churches in Germany east of the Rhine was now contemplated, also of southern Germany, of Bavaria and Alamannia; the meeting of a synod there under the leadership of Boniface was asked for by the Pope. The archbishop by an effort extending over twenty years had gained a position which gave him authority and prestige beyond his missionary field. During his stay at Rome in 738–9 he attracted not only Anglo-Saxons but also Romans, Franks, Bavarians, and others. He induced new helpers to join him in Germany, among them his relative Wynnebald, who had remained as a monk in Rome. Probably Boniface also gained there the adherence of a second Anglo-Saxon, Lullus, who was destined to succeed him as bishop of Mainz. Then the Pope sent him Wynnebald's brother Willibald, who, after his journey to the Holy Land (p. 43), had lived as a monk in St. Benedict's monastery of Monte Cassino, which, having been destroyed by the Langobards, was now rising again.

After so many years of missionary activity a new epoch of Boniface's life began; it was shorter than the previous period, but its importance was even greater. Southern Germany was already a Christian country, at least on the surface. Christianity had survived there in the south from Roman times, and in the lands of the Alamanni there were even some bishoprics, Basle, Constance, Chur, and Augsburg. I have mentioned the work of Irishmen and their followers (p. 47). A contemporary of Boniface was a Bishop Pirmin or perhaps Priminius. His nationality has been the subject of much controversy; he has been regarded as a Frank, an Irishman, and an Anglo-Saxon. But there is now some agreement that he came from the Visigothic kingdom, from Spain or the Visigothic part of southern Gaul, and had probably been forced to emigrate by the Arab invasion.[1]

[1] Cf. Gall Jecker, 'St. Pirmins Herkunft und Mission' (in *Die Kultur der Abtei*

He gained like Boniface the protection of Charles Martel and contributed to the spiritual and economic development of the Alamannian country by his monastic foundations following the Rule of St. Benedict, above all Reichenau on an island in Lake Constance (724), which monastery became a cultural centre rivalling its neighbour St. Gall, and Murbach in Alsatia (728). Similar centres had risen in Bavaria, at Regensburg, Freising, Salzburg, and elsewhere. While ancient bishoprics had survived in southern Alamannia, such remains of an organization were lacking in Bavaria, where the Christian dukes of the house of the Agilolfings were almost independent. As early as about 735 Boniface had preached in their country, had there visited many churches, and had proceeded against the leader of a 'sect', Eremwulf, who from the Roman point of view was considered a schismatic and heretic. Probably on this occasion Boniface obtained the fellowship of a young noble Bavarian, Sturmi, who went with him to Hesse to be educated at Fritzlar by Abbot Wigbert (p. 76); he was to become the first abbot of Boniface's later foundation, the abbey of Fulda. In Bavaria there were some bishops residing in monasteries and wandering bishops after the Irish pattern. There was also a Bishop Vivilo working in Passau, whom Pope Gregory III had consecrated between 731 and 736. But no organization of the Bavarian Church existed, no dioceses with fixed frontiers in spite of a previous attempt to create them. When in 716 Duke Theodo visited Rome as the earliest Bavarian pilgrim, Pope Gregory II conceived the plan of organizing a Bavarian Church province like the English and the Frisian Churches. Three papal legates were to be sent there; but the plan was not carried out (p. 62).

Such a scheme was put into effect on the invitation of Duke Odilo by Boniface, when he returned from Rome in 739. There was no need of a metropolitan, because Boniface himself could act in that capacity in Bavaria also. He divided the country into four dioceses and selected as the sees of the new bishops places, partly of Roman tradition, with which the activity of Vivilo and of monastic or wandering bishops had been connected. Boniface as yet was an archbishop without bishops subject to his supervision; now Vivilo of Passau and the newly consecrated bishops of Regensburg, Salzburg, and Freising became the first suffragans under his leadership. The structure of the Bavarian Church as conceived by him proved stable, based as it was on the political framework of the territory of the Agilolfings. A new phase came when Charles the Great made an end of their dukedom in 788 by deposing Duke Tassilo. Ten years later, on the request of the king, Pope Leo III made Salzburg the metropolitan see of Bavaria; Bishop Arno of Salzburg, the intimate friend of another Anglo-Saxon, Alcuin, in 798 received the pallium from Rome and became the first Bavarian archbishop. The development initiated by Boniface in 739 thus came to its natural completion.

The example of Bavaria had a sequence. In the last year of Charles Martel, 741, dioceses and bishops were established in Hesse, Thuringia, and Franconia. In Bavaria the new bishops, so far as we are informed, were men connected with the Bavarian churches; in 741 at least three bishops were chosen from amongst the Anglo-Saxon collaborators of Boniface, in the same way as Willibrord had selected his 'antistites' of the Frisian Church. The fortified hill of Buraburg near Fritzlar[1] became the seat of a Hessian bishop, the Anglo-Saxon Witta. In Thuringia proper Erfurt was given the same position; the name of its bishop (Dadanus?) is uncertain.[2] The dominion of the Thuringians originally stretched southwards to the Danube near Regensburg; we have seen that the last Thuringian duke gave Willibrord possessions in northern Franconia (p. 64). Here Würzburg on the Main, which place preserved the memory of the Irish martyr Kilianus (p. 47), was made the episcopal see of Burghard (Burchard), another Anglo-Saxon pupil of Boniface.

[1] On recent (1926–31) excavations on this derelict hill cf. J. Vonderau, 'Ausgrabungen am Büraberg bei Fritzlar' (Germania, xii, 1928, pp. 34–45; Veröffentlichungen des Fuldaer Geschichtsvereins, xxvi, 1934). We find the church in later times dedicated to the Irish virgin St. Brigid (whose name is entered, e.g., in Willibrord's calendar); but the dedication is not attested before 1330, and it would be rash to refer it to the origin of the church.

[2] I cannot accept the conjectures of others and, lastly, F. Flaskamp, 'Das Bistum Erfurt' (Zeitschr. für vaterländische Geschichte und Altertumskunde [Westfalens], lxxxiii, 1925, i, pp. 1–26), that Willibald of Eichstätt had first been bishop of Erfurt. His views have been partly approved by A. Overmann, 'Probleme der ältesten Erfurter Geschichte' (Sachsen und Anhalt, vi, 1930, pp. 26–38).

Lastly Willibald, the latter's relative, whose journey to the Holy Land and residence at Monte Cassino I have previously mentioned (p. 43), was consecrated bishop. He was given his diocese on the northern side of the Danube between the districts of Würzburg and Regensburg; the monastery of Eichstätt in southern Franconia, which later grew into a small city, became the centre of this diocese. The monastery of Heidenheim north-west of it (near Gunzenhausen) was founded some years after and committed to Willibald's brother Wynnebald. It is the only double monastery of monks and nuns to be found in Germany during the eighth century,[1] and was obviously organized after the model of double monasteries existing in England, in other parts as well as in Wessex, the native country of the two brothers. After the death of Wynnebald (761) his sister Waldburg became head of the monastery, the same whose name was connected in a later age with the strange beliefs of the 'Walpurgis Night', the eve of one of her festal days (1 May): 'soror eius quae post obitum beati viri monasterium servando habebat'[2]—the sister succeeded the brother as ruler of the community; one is reminded of the 'family monasteries' of England. The convent of nuns was now the more prominent; it is one of its members, the English nun Hugeburc, to whom we are indebted for having written the substantial Lives of the two brothers, bishop and abbot.[3]

Thus the episcopal organization of the German Church east of the Rhine, so far as the Frankish dominion extended, was completed to some degree in 741. Boniface, archbishop without bishops till 739, now had eight suffragans; there were a few other bishops of the older dioceses in Alamannia who also accepted his leadership. One anomaly remained. In the Mediterranean system, as transferred to England, the archbishop was not only the president of a union of bishops but also their colleague, having himself a diocese, the metropolitan diocese or archdiocese such as Canterbury and, after 735, York. Boniface had yet no metropolis nor a diocese; he had to rely on the goodwill of his 'coepiscopi'. Pope Gregory III in 739 admonished him not to stay at one place when his work there

---

[1] Cf. Hilpisch, loc. cit., p. 50; above, pp. 22 f.
[2] *Vita Wynnebaldi*, c. 13 (*MG. SS.* xv. 1, p. 116).
[3] Cf. p. 294.

M

was done, nor to shrink from hard and varied journeys for the preaching of the Gospel;[1] these were the transitional conditions of a missionary sphere.

In October 741 his protector, Charles Martel, the mayor of the palace (without a king), died, a victor on many battlefields. Like the Merovingians of the sixth century he divided the kingdom between his two sons, Carloman and Pippin III. The younger, Pippin, became ruler of the western countries; on Carloman devolved the administration of Austrasia, the east, which included the scenes of the activity of the Anglo-Saxons. Pippin was predominantly a politician and warrior like his father. Carloman, besides warlike abilities shown in the following years, had stronger spiritual inclinations, which made him accessible to the influence of Boniface and to the ideas of Church reform. At last, in 747, he surrendered his power and went to Italy, as English kings had done before, to live there as a monk, first near Rome on Mount Soracte, later at Monte Cassino. His few years of rule enabled Boniface to make further progress towards his goal; they saw almost the culmination of his work.

Two years before, in 739, Willibrord had died in old age; the Frisian Church as a separate province came to an end. Willibrord was the first and, for more than eight centuries, the last archbishop of the Frisians at Utrecht (p. 63). For Carloman committed the see to Boniface to institute and consecrate there a new bishop, possibly the Anglo-Saxon Wera,[2] who did not

---

[1] Boniface, *Epist.* 45 (p. 73).

[2] Wera is one of the seven continental bishops of English origin who about 746 joined Boniface to send a letter of admonition to King Ethelbald of Mercia (Boniface, *Epist.* 73, p. 146). Some scholars believe him to be the bishop of Utrecht who after 741 was appointed by Boniface (ib., no. 109, p. 235) and in or before 753 was followed by Eoba (cf. above, p. 67; below, p. 90 f.); cf. Tangl, 'Das Bistum Erfurt' (*Geschichtliche Studien Albert Hauck dargebracht*, Leipzig, 1916, pp. 113 ff.). Others deny this identity; but there are good reasons for accepting it. Wera is very likely the 'sacerdos' (often meaning bishop) Vira, whom Alcuin mentions side by side with Suidbert, *De sanctis Euboric. eccl.* v. 1073 (*MG. Poetae*, i. 193; Raine, *The Historians of the Church of York*, i. 380). He is commonly identified with St. Wiro, whose cult was centred at Odilienberg (formerly St. Peter's Berg) near Roermond in Dutch Limburg (on this place cf. W. Fabricius, 'Erläuterungen zum geschichtlichen Atlas der Rheinprovinz', *Publikationen der Gesellschaft für Rheinische Geschichtskunde*, xii, vol. v. I, Bonn, 1909, p. 396 f.). When Utrecht had been destroyed by the Vikings, King Lothar II in 858 provided its cathedral church with the monastery of this (Odilien-) Berg (mentioned by Alcuin, *Carm.*, no. 31, *Poetae*, i. 249) as a place of refuge for the canons (Böhmer and Mühlbacher, *Regesta Imperii*, i, 2nd ed., 1908, no. 1283). The translation of relics of an earlier bishop of Utrecht to Odilienberg

receive the pallium. Boniface was to be the sole archbishop of all the missionary dioceses and the other Austrasian churches under his authority and influence. After the years of organizing, ideas of church reform predominated. The young churches of Germany were endeavouring to realize the ancient ideals of ecclesiastical law and custom, whereas these had lost ground in the Frankish Church during the struggle of the factions for power. Restoration of the old order became the aim, a Carolingian 'Renaissance' in the sphere of the Church. These ideas, as manifested in the work of the Anglo-Saxons, had taken possession of Carloman. He co-operated at once with Boniface with a view to co-ordinating the Frankish with the German Church and restoring ecclesiastical order and discipline in the ancient dioceses, first of course in the east within the reach of Carloman's authority. He invited Boniface to see him and to summon a synod, the first Frankish synod for more than forty years (p. 47).

They acted quickly. Charles Martel had died in October 741. On the 21st of April in the following year a synod of Austrasia met at an unknown place; its usual designation is therefore 'Concilium Germanicum'.[1] The mode of dating of its decrees is characteristic in itself: 'anno ab incarnatione Christi septingentesimo XLII' and shows the influences under which the text of the decrees was formulated: it was the first time that the year was indicated by the era of the Incarnation in an official Frankish document. More than two centuries earlier the Roman abbot Dionysius 'Exiguus' (as he is called

may be considered to be in consonance with these facts. It is evident that later nothing was known about 'Wiro'; he and a second bishop venerated with him, Plechelm, whose name (Anglo-Saxon Pleghelm, as it is spelt in a litany of Utrecht of the late 10th century; cf. M. Coens, *Anal. Boll.* lv, 1937, p. 67) also suggests an English origin, were made Irishmen in their legendary and commonplace Lives (*BHL*. ii, nos. 6867, 8973). There is no need to date the Life of St. Wiro earlier than 858; it is rather considerably later than have assumed L. Van der Essen, *Étude critique et littéraire sur les Vitae des saints mérovingiens de l'ancienne Belgique*, Louvain and Paris, 1907, pp. 105 ff., and J. F. Kenney, *The Sources for the Early History of Ireland*, i, New York, 1929, p. 509. Another possibility is that Wera and Pleghelm were among the bishops consecrated by Willibrord (p. 62) or were chorepiscopi. We are also unable to ascribe two others among the seven Anglo-Saxon bishops of 746, Werberht and Leofwine (cf. p. 109, n. 3), to particular sees. Utrecht was the only continental diocese with a cult of St. Mildred of Thanet; cf. Coens, loc. cit. liv, 1936, p. 138, and lv, p. 67.

[1] On the Bonifatian synods cf. also Carlo de Clercq, *La Législation religieuse franque de Clovis à Charlemagne*, Louvain and Paris, 1936, pp. 114 ff.

through a misunderstanding of a formula of humility) had created this era for his Paschal Tables, in order to substitute a Christian starting-point in the numbering of years for the Egyptian era named after the persecutor Diocletian. This method of dating was handed down with his tables, but apart from that was not put into practice for about two centuries. The Anglo-Saxons, like the other Germanic peoples, reckoned time by the regnal years of their kings. For example, the laws of King Wihtred of Kent were dated: 'the fiftan wintra his rices.' But if bishops of several of the little Anglo-Saxon king-doms came together at a synod and had to date its decrees by the years of each of their kings, this kind of reckoning became troublesome and moreover did not correspond with the unity of the English Church. To Anglo-Saxon clergymen the paschal writings of Dionysius were a manual of practice; so the suitability of the Dionysian era, as being applicable to all English kingdoms, became obvious about 700. Bede used it to indicate the years in his *Ecclesiastical History* (731);[1] but Willibrord also adopted it in 728 in an entry of his calendar (p. 65). The dating of the 'Concilium Germanicum' by the year of the Incarnation is therefore a sign of Anglo-Saxon influence. But a Carolingian interest was involved at the same time. Charles Martel governed during his last years (from 737) without a king; so did his sons at the outset, until in 743 they gave the royal name once more to a Merovingian, Childeric III, in order to deprive the adherents of the legitimate royal house of a pretext for opposition. The throne was still vacant in 742; accordingly, by using the year of the Incarnation, the redactors of the synod's decrees avoided the numbering of the years from the death of the last king and a consequent reminder of unpleasant facts. Thus these decrees, by their very dating, mark the alliance of Carloman and Boniface.

It is also evident in another respect. The decrees were the outcome of an ecclesiastical synod, but they were published in the name of Carloman, 'dux et princeps Francorum', as he was styled; so they were made laws of the realm. The practice was different in the case of the Merovingian synods. These also referred to the will of the king as the reason for their assembling, but their decrees became canon law by the decisions

---

[1] Cf. Appendix VI, pp. 265 ff.

of the bishops who constituted the synod and appended their signatures to the 'canones', the decrees. Now the agreements of the bishops in 742 and at the following assemblies were only proposals submitted to the ruler; he published them in his own name and gave them the character of law.[1] Carloman acted in accordance with the wishes of the reformers; but, formally, he reserved the final decision to himself. The synod of 742 and its successors differ in another respect from the Merovingian synods. Not only did bishops and priests take part in the reform meetings, but also 'optimates', secular magnates; at least the two next synods, in 743 and 744, were held at the beginning of March, obviously in connexion with the 'campus Martius', that is, the regular meeting of the army and its leaders. Both differences corresponded, as Hans von Schubert[2] has pointed out, with the legislation of Anglo-Saxon kingdoms about 700; one has only to read the introductions of the laws of King Wihtred of Kent or of Boniface's own king, Ine of Wessex, to perceive this similarity. Boniface therefore had little reason to object to this mode of procedure, the more so as he had to rely on the protection and help of Carloman.

Meetings of bishops had been an important means of Church co-operation and unification since the fourth century. Theodore of Canterbury also used synods of the English Church for this purpose; the synod of Hertford in 672 decreed, in accordance with early canon law, that such a meeting should be held every year. The 'Concilium Germanicum' similarly demanded annual synods for the restoration and amendment of Church law and life. A second Austrasian synod in fact assembled the following year at Estinnes in the Belgian Hainaut. But the idea of Church reform and of synods to promote it was now also accepted by Carloman's brother Pippin, the ruler of Neustria and Burgundy. The first western synod met in the following year 744 at Soissons; part of the decrees were based almost verbatim on those of the Austrasian synods. But the 'regnum Francorum' was a unit, though the administration may have been divided. Now both brothers supported the reform movement; so, after the separate

---

[1] Cf. Hans Barion, *Das fränkisch-deutsche Synodalrecht des Frühmittelalters* (Kanonistische Studien und Texte, ed. Koeniger, v–vi), Bonn, 1931, pp. 252 ff.

[2] Loc. cit., p. 308; Karl Voigt, *Staat und Kirche von Konstantin dem Grossen bis zum Ende der Karolingerzeit*, Stuttgart, 1936, pp. 312 ff.

Austrasian and Neustrian meetings, a synod of the whole kingdom assembled in 745 and again at least in 747. The current
began to react upon England: the Frankish decrees of 747
influenced an English reform synod of the same year which
met at Clovesho.[1]

The aim of the synods was the restoration and improvement
of Church order and Church life: 'how the law of God and the
religion of the church fallen into decay in the days of former
princes, might be re-established, and how the Christian people
might gain salvation of their souls and not perish through the
deceit of false priests', were the words defining the scope in 742.
The hierarchical order and a regular church administration had
to be restored for this purpose, provinces under an archbishop
in direct contact with Rome, dioceses with a monarchical bishop
supervised by the archbishop and controlling the whole clergy
of his district. The life of clergy and laymen had to be constituted in accordance with canon law; I may mention the
celibacy of the clerics, the marriage laws, and the fight against
surviving pagan customs. Boniface was recognized as the archbishop of the East in 742, 'qui est missus sancti Petri', the
delegate of St. Peter, as was significantly added to his name.
He was recognized as the archbishop not only of the missionary
dioceses but of all the lands governed by Carloman; 'Boniface
était par l'autorité du pape archevêque de Germanie, il devient,
par la volonté du prince franc, l'archevêque des États de
Carloman', as Lesne has described the situation.[2]

There was as yet the anomaly of an archbishop without his
own diocese and without a metropolitan seat. The synod of
745 bestowed on him the city and diocese of Cologne to supply

---

[1] The decrees of the Frankish synod of 747 are only known from the letter of
Boniface to Archbishop Cuthbert of Canterbury (no. 78, ed. Tangl, p. 163 f.; *MG.
Concilia*, ii, p. 47). They were partly based, directly or indirectly (through the lost
decrees of 745?), on the decrees of 742 and, to a smaller extent, of 743. A comparison with the canons of Clovesho, especially cc. 3, 19, 21, 25 (H. and S. iii,
pp. 363 f., 369, 371), makes it evident that the latter were influenced by the
Frankish decrees of 747, as reported in Boniface's letter, and not vice versa. Cf.
also Hauck, loc. cit. i, p. 571, n. 1; Hefele-Leclercq, *Histoire des conciles*, iii. 2, Paris,
1910, pp. 895 (n. 2), 903 (n. 4). The definitive form of Boniface's letter, as received
by the addressee (cf. pp. 280 f.), was copied together with the canons of Clovesho in
the same Anglo-Saxon MS. of the later part of the 8th century, Cotton Otho A.I,
of which fragments only have survived. Cf. Lowe, *Codices Lat. ant.* ii, nos. 188, 229;
N. R. Ker, *The British Museum Quarterly*, xiv, 1940, p. 79 f.

[2] *La hiérarchie épiscopale*, p. 40. Cf. Hauck, loc. cit. i. 522.

this need. Cologne was well situated, in the neighbourhood
of Friesland, of Hesse, and of the pagan Saxons, whose conversion was again the order of the day. Carloman continued the
expeditions of his father against them. In 744 many accepted
Christian baptism; the combination of Frankish dominion
and Christianization began to appear in sight. Cologne as
metropolis of Boniface must therefore have been considered
appropriate in 745, and the choice of it was confirmed by the
Pope.[1] But the decision met with opposition; Cologne had to
be abandoned and was given to another bishop, while Mainz
became the seat of Boniface. So this question was settled, at
least for his lifetime. For after his death diocese and metropolitan dignity were again separated; his successor in Mainz,
his compatriot Lullus, had to remain a simple bishop for many
years,[2] till Charles the Great carried out the programme of
Boniface in this and in other respects and definitely established
the ecclesiastical provinces of his kingdom. The high position
which the archbishops of Mainz later gained in the organization
and constitution of Germany[3] was largely based on the work
and, even more, on the memory of Boniface.

When Pippin joined the reformers the first step was taken
towards restoring in Gaul also the provincial organization of
ancient times. The bishops of Rheims[4] and Sens were constituted archbishops by the synod of Soissons in 744, and the
Pope was asked to grant the pallium to both and also to the

---

[1] Cf. Boniface, *Epist.* 60, 80, 88 (pp. 124, 179, 201 f.); Tangl, *Neues Archiv*, xl.
785 ff.   [2] Cf. Appendix II, pp. 234 f.
[3] Cf., e.g., Karl Wenck, 'Die Stellung des Erzstiftes Mainz im Gange der deutschen Geschichte' (*Zeitschr. des Vereins für hessische Geschichte*, xliii, 1909, pp. 278–
318); U. Stutz, *Der Erzbischof von Mainz und die deutsche Königswahl*, Weimar, 1910.
[4] The new archbishop of Rheims, Abel (*MG. Concilia*, ii. 34; Boniface, *Epist.*
57, 58, pp. 103, 106), was among the seven bishops who joined Boniface about 746
in sending King Ethelbald of Mercia a letter of admonition, and were all, according
to Boniface, 'de eadem Anglorum gente nati et nutriti' (ib., nos. 73, 74, pp. 146,
156. 2). Consequently I do not identify Abel, in opposition to this express statement, with an Irishman of the same name, who, we are told by Folcwin (*Gesta
abbatum Lobiensium*, cc. 5, 7, *MG. SS.* iv. 58), lived in the Belgian monastery of
Lobbes under Abbot-Bishop Ermino (who died in 737). Either there were two
namesakes, or Folcwin, who wrote in the late 10th century, was ill informed of
Abel's nationality. Many scholars have accepted Folcwin's report and his con-
jectural identification of the Irish monk with the archbishop; cf. Frank, 'Die
Klosterbischöfe des Frankenreiches' (loc. cit.), pp. 33 ff. Abel, who is said to have
been ejected from Rheims by Milo, was succeeded in 748 by Tilpin; cf. below,
pp. 234 f.

bishop of Rouen, that is, to three bishops of what had formerly been metropolitan sees. He did so 'pro adunatione et reformatione ecclesiarum Christi'; but he was astonished to receive in the same year another letter from Boniface asking for only one pallium, for the bishop of Rouen alone. There has been much speculation on the causes of this change. Was the opposition of Frankish bishops to supervising archbishops too strong, and was the limitation of the number to one a compromise? Or did the opinion prevail that it would be better to concentrate the archiepiscopal powers, intermediate between bishops and Pope, in one man in the West, in the same way as Boniface alone, after the death of Willibrord, was archbishop in the East? Or was the reduction of the number of pallia the result of demands for money made at the papal curia? Boniface objected to such a practice, implying that canon law had been violated and the heresy of simony committed. Pope Zacharias denied emphatically that there had been an offence of this kind.[1] Whatever had happened, this episode of the metropolitans shows that Boniface, in remodelling the Frankish Church after the Roman and English pattern, met with serious difficulties, which could only be overcome in process of time. The reconstitution of the provincial organization and of the metropolitan sees was completed only during the reign of Charles the Great.

The correspondence of Boniface reveals various other instances of trouble and antagonism, of opponents in the higher and lower ranks of the Church; occasionally he had even to suffer a reprimand from the Pope. He had to fight against heretics, among whom were strange wandering enthusiasts of robust superstitions, or against what he believed to be heresy. The most famous incident is that of the learned Irish Presbyter Virgil, on whom Odilo of Bavaria conferred the diocese of Salzburg. This he governed for many years (745–84), first in the Irish manner as abbot, then as bishop. Boniface sent a report to the Pope on the heresies of this man, who held the doctrine, if it is accurately represented, that there is below the earth another world and other men and also a sun and a moon. It was a reminiscence, somewhat confused, of ancient learning on the spherical form of the earth and on the existence of antipodes, a doctrine opposed by Boniface from the biblical

[1] Cf. Appendix III, p. 242.

point of view, a controversy well known in the history of science.[1]

But in spite of all difficulties Boniface and his compatriots must have had hours of satisfaction. They had advanced Christianity among pagan and semi-pagan peoples; their principles of Church life were accepted in the Frankish Church, though their ideas were not fully realized. But a great change had in fact been made since 738. A reform of the Church had been started to bring it into line with canon law and with the practice of the Roman See. The influence of the Pope on the Merovingian Church had been almost negligible. This relation was now altered by Anglo-Saxon influence, as two examples will show. In 746 Pippin, his bishops, abbots, and great men ('principes') sent Pope Zacharias a questionnaire on no less than twenty-seven points of canon law;[2] thus the vicar of St. Peter was recognized as the authoritative head of the Church. The synod of the next year, 747, sent to Rome an impressive formal declaration, bearing the signatures of all the bishops present: 'that we will maintain the catholic faith and unity and the subjection to the Roman Church till the end of our lives; that we will be subjects of St. Peter and his vicar; that we shall hold a synod every year; that the metropolitans will ask for their pallia from that see; and that in all things we desire to follow the precepts of St. Peter according to the canons, so that we may be counted among the sheep entrusted to him.' A similar profession by a Merovingian synod may be sought for in vain. It was the theory (though not always the practice) of Anglo-Saxon churchmen who were conscious of their Roman origins and instilled their views into the minds of their continental followers. Instruction and advice were sought from Rome not only by Boniface, the 'legatus Germanicus sedis apostolicae', as he was called and called himself, but also by Pippin, and even opponents of Boniface now appealed against him to the Pope.

---

[1] See particularly H. Krabbo, 'Bischof Virgil von Salzburg und seine kosmologischen Ideen' (*MIÖG.* xxiv, 1903, pp. 1–28); H. Vander Linden, 'Virgile de Salzbourg et les théories cosmographiques au VIIIᵉ siècle' (*Bulletins de l'Académie royale de Belgique, Classe des lettres*, 1914, pp. 163–87). On Virgil cf. also Krusch, *SS. rer. Merov.* vi. 517 ff. (=*Arbeonis Vitae*, pp. 130 ff.).

[2] *Codex Carolinus*, 3 (*MG. Epist.* iii. 480–7). A similar question on marriage law had been submitted as early as 742; cf. *MG. Concilia*, ii. 21. 3.

But there was an important limitation. The reform was set in motion by Carloman; the decrees of the first reform synods were promulgated by him and Pippin. While the reform was inspired by the ideas of Boniface and his circle, the Carolingians did not surrender the reins of Church government. In spite of the approach to the Papacy and of the recognition of its authoritative ecclesiastical position, the reformed Church remained a territorial church, in which the secular ruler exerted the chief influence. He could be the promoter and, as has been said of a later period, 'the instigator of reform and at the same time the master of the church in his dominions'.[1] Hence the necessity of compromise; here also were the roots of the struggles of later ages, which nobody could foresee in the eighth century.

The first impetus of the reform subsided in 747. Its progress thereafter was brought about by the zeal of the bishops and of their clergy in the dioceses and by the educational work of monasteries and convents, rather than by the decrees of synods. Boniface was more than seventy years old. He made provision for the security of his monastery of Fulda in Hesse, which he had founded in 744 and where he wished to have his last place of rest; I have mentioned the privilege of exemption which he procured for it from Pope Zacharias in 751 (pp. 26 f.). He obtained a promise from Pippin that his Anglo-Saxon pupil and chorepiscopus Lullus should succeed him as bishop of Mainz. Missionary enthusiasm had stimulated him to bring the Gospel to his heathen kindred overseas. Now in his old age he resumed those plans of his manhood. With his chorepiscopus Eoba, who was now bishop of Utrecht, and many other helpers, he returned in 753 to Friesland, where in 716 he had started his continental work, to preach to the heathen north-east of the Zuider Zee. Thousands were christened. Winter suspended his endeavours, but they were continued in the following year. He was about to administer confirmation to many new Christians, when they were attacked by furious pagans near Dokkum (in the modern Dutch province of Friesland). He forbade resistance and was killed on the 5th of June 754[2] with fifty-three companions,

[1] Z. N. Brooke, *The English Church and the Papacy from the Conquest to the Reign of John*, Cambridge, 1931, p. 132.

[2] The sources, strangely enough, disagree about the year of Boniface's martyrdom. The tradition of Mainz, as represented *inter alia* (cf. p. 240, n. 2) by his biographer Willibald, ascribes it to A.D. 755. But the tradition of Fulda, in accor-

among them Eoba and other Anglo-Saxons. His body, according to his wishes, was transferred to Fulda. His end corresponded with his continental beginnings; the fame of the 'Apostle of Germany', as he was and is called, was crowned by the glory of martyrdom. But important as his apostolic work was for Germany, his organizing and reforming activity was of greater consequence.

He was not a man of new ideas but of firm belief, of enterprise and action. He was convinced of the truth of his faith as the basis of salvation and impelled by the desire to communicate this light to others who were still in darkness. He was conscious of what he left in England; the 'peregrinatio' was also to him a self-chosen exile, and he calls himself occasionally 'exul Germanicus'. The difficulties of the beginnings, the struggle with opponents in later years, irruptions of pagan Saxons into his missionary field, where they destroyed in 752 more than thirty churches, conduced to keep these feelings alive: 'Everywhere is struggle, everywhere grief' ('Undique labor, undique meror'), so he once wrote to an English abbess. When he started on his last journey, he thought of the uncertain conditions of his pupils living in a foreign country and recommended them to Pippin: 'They are almost all pilgrims, foreigners' ('Sunt enim pene omnes peregrini'). During all his life he kept the closest connexion with his native country, as his correspondence amply shows. He remained in touch with former pupils and friends, with bishops, abbots, and priests; his exchange of letters with learned abbesses and nuns is particularly remarkable for the warm expressions of friendship and affection. After he had received the pallium we find him corresponding with the English bearers of the same distinction, the archbishops of Canterbury and York. When the reform of the Frankish Church had been

dance with Northumbrian Annals (*Continuatio Bedae*), attributes his end to the previous year 754, and this earlier date has been sufficiently established by M. Tangl, 'Das Todesjahr des Bonifatius' (*Zeitschr. des Vereins für hessische Geschichte*, xxxvii, 1903, pp. 223-50); cf. his note, *Neues Archiv*, xl. 788 ff. and Flaskamp, *Histor. Jahrbuch*, xlvii, 1927, pp. 473-88. Recently L. Levillain, 'L'Avènement de la dynastie carolingienne et les origines de l'État pontifical' (*BECh*. xciv, 1933, pp. 256 ff.), has examined anew the chronology of Pippin's Italian expeditions and tried to prove that the king's first campaign against the Langobards did not take place in 754, but in 755, and that the end of Boniface also belongs to the later year. But, in my opinion, not all his arguments on this second question are conclusive, and others prevail in favour of 754.

started, he asked not only for advice but also thought it his duty to give it. Some decrees of the English synod of Clovesho in 747 show the influence of the letter in which he reported to Archbishop Cuthbert of Canterbury the decrees of the Frankish synod of the same year and remonstrated against evil practices in English life (p. 86). Along the same lines is the letter which he and seven continental bishops of English origin sent to King Ethelbald of Mercia to admonish him and reprove him for his dissolute life and his encroachments on possessions and privileges of monasteries.

His connexions began more and more to cover the whole of England, from his native Wessex to the Isle of Thanet, from Canterbury to York, Wearmouth, and Whithorn. As the English Church paved the way for the national unity of England so the continental missionary effort became a matter of interest to all her people. 'Angli' as well as Saxons are mentioned in the letters, but there, as in other sources, we find almost no difference between these names. Boniface, who came from Wessex, called his home country 'transmarina Saxonia', but he also described himself as of the race of the Angles and asked all Angles to pray for the conversion of the continental Saxons, men of the same blood and bone (p. 77). A bishop of Leicester named these Saxons 'our people' ('gens nostra', ib.), while Boniface called the Northumbrian (that is, Anglian) Willibrord 'of Saxon race' ('generis Saxonum'). Thus the difference between Angles and Saxons was disappearing. As the feeling of national identity prevailed in Bede's works, so the continental mission was regarded as a national undertaking of the whole English people and undoubtedly contributed to this feeling of belonging together and being homogeneous. The combined title of 'Anglo-Saxon' originated and coalesced on the Continent.[1]

[1] The name of the Anglo-Saxons was intended to designate the 'Anglian Saxons' in contrast to the Saxons of the Continent; it coalesced gradually into a single word. I add the earliest examples known to me, only a part of them being mentioned by others (cf. Freeman, *Norman Conquest*, i.³, pp. 540 ff.; W. H. Stevenson, *Asser's Life of King Alfred*, pp. 148 ff.; J. Hoops, *Reallexikon der Germanischen Altertumskunde*, i. 90; Liebermann, *Gesetze*, ii. 2, p. 283): Report on the Legatine synods of 786 (*MG. Epist.* iv. 20), headlines: 'Synodus, que facta est in Anglorum Sax[o]nia.'—Paulus Diaconus, *Hist. Langob.* iv. 22 (*MG. SS. rer. Langob.*, p. 124): 'Vestimenta . . . qualia Angli Saxones habere solent'; v. 37 (p. 157): 'ex Saxonum Anglorum genere'; vi. 15 (p. 169): 'Cedoal rex Anglorum Saxonum.'—*Vita Alcuini*, c. 18 (*MG. SS.* xv. 1,

The synod of Clovesho in 747 (c. 17) had ordered the celebration of the days of Gregory the Great and his delegate Augustine. After the martyrdom of Boniface a general English synod added the anniversary of the new patron and of his companions to these festivals, to be celebrated with solemnity every year.[1] It was also entered in the archetype of Bede's Martyrology.[2]

p. 193): 'Aigulfus praeterea presbiter, Engelsaxo et ipse.'—Prudentius of Troyes, *Annales Bertiniani*, 844: 'Brittaniam insulam, ea quam maxime parte, quam Angli Saxones incolunt'; 855: 'rege Anglorum Saxonum'; 860: 'ad Anglos Saxones navigant' (ed. Waitz, *SS. rer. Germ.*, 1883, pp. 31, 45, 53).—Hrabanus Maurus, *De inventione litterarum* (below, p. 291): 'Bonifacius . . . ab Angulsaxis veniens.'—*Vita Bertuini Maloniensis*, c. 1 (*SS. rer. Merov.* vii. 177): 'Bertuinus ex provintia Anglisaxonis oriundus fuit.'

[1] Boniface, *Epist.* 111 (p. 240).
[2] Henri Quentin, *Les Martyrologes historiques*, p. 51; cf. p. 115.

V

FROM PIPPIN TO CHARLES THE GREAT

Some consequences: Currents and Countercurrents between England and the Continent

THE lively attachment of Boniface to his native people and country was combined, as we have seen, with the firm belief in the unity of a universal church, a unity maintained by a hierarchical system under the authority of St. Peter and the Pope as his successor. He did not shrink from denouncing abuses existing in Rome. But, except for such rare cases, the law and custom of the Roman Church were guides to him from his first Roman journey to the letters of his last years addressed to Pope Stephen II. Again and again he sought to obtain papal decisions on difficulties of canon law or to be informed on the rites of the Roman Church: 'sciscitando, qualiter teneat vel doceat haec sancta apostolica Romana aecclesia.'[1] He asked an English abbess to make him a copy of the Epistles of his master, the apostle St. Peter, written in gold, not only to impress honour and reverence for the Sacred Scriptures upon the eyes of the carnally minded in his audience, but also to have ever present before himself the words of that apostle who had pointed the way for him.[2] This spirit was alive, to some extent, in the English Church, and it was one of his momentous achievements to instil a similar spirit into the German and the Gallic churchmen. Certainly the result was not an unlimited influence of the Pope on the Frankish Church, for the king remained its ruler; but the connexion with Rome became much stronger and more effective than before, though it also included problems of conflict which later times had to face.

Nor must we forget that the new approach to the Papacy was intensified by the needs of the other side. The Eastern Empire struggling against Slavs and Moslems was unable to protect those parts of Italy which it still held against the renewed offensive of the Langobards. Spheres of imperial administration exercised over Rome and its surroundings gradually passed into

[1] Boniface, *Epist.* 26 (p. 44).
[2] Ib., no. 35 (p. 60).

the hands of the bishop of Rome, while the Iconoclastic controversy contributed to estrange West from East. The danger
of losing his semi-independence and of becoming a Langobard
bishop induced the Pope, a few months before the martyrdom
of Boniface, to cross the Alps and ask for Pippin's help. The
Frankish intervention in Italy and the establishment of the
Pontifical State followed (cf. p. 59). It is difficult to say how
far the continental work of the Anglo-Saxons and their affection
for Rome contributed to prepare the way for this development;
certainly a part falls to their share. The king practically kept
the Church government in his hands. Charles the Great
occasionally identified his decisions with the will of God,[1] and
his attitude during the contest on the cult of the images is a
famous example of his independence of the Pope. Nevertheless,
the reform spirit created by the Anglo-Saxons was alive in the
Frankish Church, and the ecclesiastical policy of these Carolingians on the whole may be regarded as the continuation and
heritage of the work of Boniface. There were reform synods in
the years 755–7, at Ver, Verberie, and Compiègne, others in
Bavaria, and a large part of the extensive legislation of Charles
the Great was devoted to the reform of the Church, while, after
the times of Willibrord and Boniface, another Anglo-Saxon,
Alcuin, was in the forefront of the king's helpers.

We have seen that the attempt to restore the provincial and
metropolitan organization of the Frankish Church had stopped
half-way in the age of Boniface, but that Charles the Great in
process of time made it complete (pp. 87 f.). About 781 Lullus
of Mainz received the pallium; the bishop of Trier seems to
have received it earlier,[2] the bishop of Cologne later. Willibrord's Frisian church had ceased to be a separate ecclesiastical
province (p. 82). After the martyrdom of Boniface and Eoba
it was committed to the former's Frankish disciple, Abbot
Gregory of Utrecht, who remained a presbyter (cf. p. 77); one

---

[1] Letter of Charles, discovered in a Munich palimpsest and edited by E. Mund-
ing, *Königsbrief Karls d. Gr. an Papst Hadrian* (Texte und Arbeiten herausgeg. durch
die Erzabtei Beuron, I. Abteilung, Heft. 6), Beuron, 1920, p. 4: 'Cor enim regis in
manu Dei consistere credimus nutuque illius huc illucque verti. Ideoque non
nostro arbitrio, sed Dei cre[dimus esse] pastorale illi culmen concessum' (the
bishopric of Pavia to Abbot Waldo of Reichenau). On the letter cf. also my
review, *Neues Archiv*, xliii, 1922, pp. 464 ff.; W. Erben, ib. xlvi, 1926, pp. 11 ff.

[2] Cf. below, p. 235, n. 5.

of his English collaborators, Aluberht, in 767 was consecrated at York bishop of the 'Oldsaxons' and co-operated with the abbot as his chorepiscopus. After the death of Gregory (775?) the situation was normalized. He was succeeded by his nephew Alberic, who after a few years received at Cologne the episcopal consecration; the bishopric of Utrecht became a diocese of the province of Cologne. When Saxony was won over by King Charles to Frankish dominion and to the Christian Church, the new Saxon dioceses were divided between the provinces of Cologne and Mainz, and the archbishop of Mainz also incorporated in his own diocese the shortlived bishoprics of Buraburg and Erfurt founded by Boniface (p. 80). We have also seen that in 798 Salzburg was made the metropolitan see of the Bavarian churches (ib.), when, by the destruction of the power of the Avars, a vast missionary field had been opened to the Bavarian bishops. Almost all the provinces of Gaul were also re-established. When the old emperor in 811 disposed of his treasure, sixteen metropolitan seats, besides those of Italy, were named to be provided for. Thus the system of provincial church organization, transferred to England by Gregory the Great, was restored after the vicissitudes of a transitional period, in all the lands of Frankish rule. The possession of the pallium as the condition of administering the archiepiscopal functions, and the right of the Pope to confer it, were also recognized. Whenever afterwards there was occasion to found a new province of the Church, we see the secular power negotiating with the Pope, with whom rests the grant of the pallium. One may note, for instance, the northern province of Hamburg in 831, the eastern of Magdeburg in 968, the province of Gnesen in Poland in 1000, all connected with a field of missionary work, not to speak of later times, when, after the reforms of the eleventh century, the growing centralization of the Church had immensely strengthened the influence of Rome. Nor is there any need to dwell again on the payments demanded for the pallium, one of the abuses complained of in the later Middle Ages, which contributed to the Reformation movement; we have found an early hint of such charges in the letters of Boniface (p. 88).

Frankish synods, renewed by Boniface since 742, were now a relatively regular feature of Church life. The authority of the bishop in his diocese and the discipline of the clergy were strengthened by the policy adopted at the reform synods. Wandering bishops and other bishops without dioceses but attached to monasteries, who upset the diocesan order, ceased in time to exist. On the other hand, we have seen that the institution of the chorepiscopi, who were introduced as auxiliary bishops of the diocesan by Willibrord and Boniface, spread in all directions, till friction arose between bishops and chorepiscopi and the Pseudo-Isidorian forgers began to attack the institution (p. 68).

The idea of conformity with Roman ritual and discipline existed in the English Church from the outset, as is shown by the struggle against the Celtic observances. Church song 'more Romanorum' spread from Kent to the north in the seventh century. The synod of Clovesho in 747 ordered uniformity of ritual in accordance with the appropriate Roman books (cc. 13, 15, 16, 18). In a letter of the same year Boniface borrowed (without mentioning the source) some words from the so-called Gelasian Sacramentary,[1] which had a Roman basis with Gallican elements added. The same words are also found in another form of this sacramentary, which came into use in Gaul about this time and to-day is named the Frankish Gelasianum or the Gelasianum of the eighth century; there exist fragments of both forms and connected texts written by Anglo-Saxon hands,[2] and it was conjectured that the later form of this liturgical book originated in Wessex and was brought to the Continent by Boniface himself.[3] This opinion has been contested, and most scholars refer the sacramentary rather to an order of Pippin to adopt the Roman liturgy, an order presumed to have been made on the occasion of his alliance with Pope Stephen in 754.[4]

[1] Cf. below, Appendix VII, pp. 283 f.

[2] H. M. Bannister, *J.T.S.* ix, 1908, pp. 398–411; xii, 1911, pp. 451–4; A. Baumstark, *Jahrbuch für Liturgiewissenschaft*, vii, 1927, pp. 130–6 (British Museum, Add. MS. 37518, fol. 116, of the 8th century). P. Siffrin, ib. x, 1930, pp. 1–39 (Berlin, MS. Lat. fol. 877, of the same century).

[3] A. Baumstark, *Die älteste erreichbare Gestalt des Liber Sacramentorum anni circuli der römischen Kirche* (Liturgiegeschichtliche Quellen, xi–xii), Münster i. W., 1927, pp. 134* ff.; *Missale Romanum*, Eindhoven and Nijmegen (1929), pp. 86 ff., 183 ff.

[4] Cf. C. Mohlberg, 'Note liturgiche' (*Rendiconti della Pontificia Accademia Romana di archeologia*, vii, 1931, pp. 19–33); Th. Klauser, 'Die liturgischen Austauschbeziehungen zwischen der römischen und der fränkisch-deutschen Kirche vom 8. bis zum 11. Jahrhundert' (*Historisches Jahrbuch*, liii, 1933, pp. 173 f.). Both authors mention other literature.

Bishop Chrodegang of Metz, who escorted the Pope from Italy to Pippin's court and, after Boniface's martyrdom, was made archbishop in the latter's place, was one of the promoters of the romanization of the liturgy; the fame of the Roman song established at Metz was great. A Northumbrian priest, Autbert, took his nephew Sigulf, a friend of Alcuin, with him to Rome 'ad ecclesiasticum ordinem discendum'; then the young cleric was sent to Metz 'causa cantus'.[1] Even Englishmen might now occasionally take a lesson from the reformed Frankish Church. Charles the Great showed the same inclination as his father to the unification of the ritual in conformity with the Roman liturgy. He asked Pope Hadrian for the pure text of the sacramentary ascribed to Gregory the Great, and about 785 received the *Sacramentarium Gregorianum*; the authentic copy was deposited at the palace for transcription. The real character of the text does not concern us here. Alcuin had to correct it and to compose a supplement from other sources for the requirements of the Frankish Church; his edition of the Gregorianum is the principal foundation of the Roman mass-book up to the present day. Only the general trend is relevant in this connexion: the Anglo-Saxon missionaries had inspired in the Frankish churchmen and rulers the ideal of unity and uniformity with the Roman Church. This ideal persisted. But now, when the direct communication between Rome and the Carolingians had become a reality, the indirect intercourse through England and through her missionary sons lost its momentum.

There are other features of continental church life in which the English influence is even more evident. The early Church had a public penitential system for grave sins; there was a public order of penitents, who were admitted to penance only once and were subject to certain obligations for the rest of their lives. There has recently been much discussion concerning the origin of the confession of lesser sins and how and when 'private' penance consequently arose alongside of 'public' penance. This 'private' penance was associated with the imposition by the priest of an appropriate act of penitence and with his absolution, and could be repeated by an absolved penitent as often as was necessary. The early beginnings of private penance, which gradually replaced the public system, need not be discussed

---

[1] *Vita Alcuini*, c. 8 (*MG. SS.* xv. 1, p. 189).

here; there is agreement to-day that the predominance of private penance originated in the Celtic churches and was carried by Irish monks to England and by Columbanus and his successors to the Continent. This system found expression in the production of Penitential Books, handbooks for the guidance of the priest; they gave him a list of sins and of corresponding forms of penance, of 'medicamenta paenitentiae' in different sorts and gradations, comparable with medical drugs for the diseases of the body, and with the catalogues of wrongs and compensations or 'compositions' of the secular laws of the Celtic and Germanic peoples. While the ancient system permitted penance only once in a lifetime, the practice of yearly recurring confession of sins was extended from the monks to the laymen outside the monasteries; in England from the days of Archbishop Theodore people came before Christmas to confess their sins to their 'confessores'.[1] Theodore gave many answers and decisions on questions of penance and of other canon law. He had in mind an Irish penitential as well as Greek and Roman practice, as one would expect from the course of his life. His 'judgements' ('iudicia') were soon written down in smaller and larger collections. The most influential were two books composed by an anonymous writer who called himself 'discipulus Umbrensium', disciple of the Humber people; other books of the same kind followed. The English missionaries took such manuals as these with them as aids in their pastoral work. Side by side with the Irish penitentials the English books gained ground on the Continent, where similar collections were composed more or less after the insular models.[2] Theodore's 'iudicia' are first mentioned not by an English author but by Paul the Deacon, the historian of the Langobards,[3] and almost all the manuscript tradition of the penitentials connected with Theodore's name belongs to the Continent, so much so that the last editor wrongly ascribed the 'discipulus Umbrensium' to the

---

[1] Dialogue of Archbishop Egbert, c. 16 (H. and S. iii. 413).

[2] Cf., e.g., M. L. W. Laistner, 'Was Bede the author of a Penitential?' (*Harvard Theological Review*, xxxi, 1938, pp. 263–74).

[3] *Hist. Langob.* v. 30 (*MG. SS. rer. Langob.*, p. 154). From Paulus the words were inserted in 1142 by Petrus Guillermus into the Life of Pope Vitalian in the version of the *Liber Pontificalis* finished after 1130 (ed. Duchesne, ii, pp. xxvf.; ed. Mommsen, p. 188, note to l. 9 on MSS. H[1.2]); but they are absent from the original text of this version, as discovered in a Tortosa MS. and published by Jos. M. March, *Liber Pontificalis prout exstat in codice manuscripto Dertusensi*, Barcelona, 1925, p. 114.

circle of Willibrord.[1] In fact he wrote in England;[2] but his books were soon employed overseas to help the priests to educate the people, to combat their vices, and to improve their moral level, according to the Christian standards of the times. It is not for me to dwell on the merits and deficiencies of these penitential writings, on commutation and money redemption of penance, on vicarious penance and other abuses, on the objections to which the unauthorized and often conflicting multiplicity of penitentials gave rise in the Frankish Church of the ninth century, on the modifications of books and practice.[3] Here it is sufficient to note the share of eighth-century England in this development and her continental influence.

One aspect of this influence was the revival of food restrictions and prohibitions, in which Irish and Greek influences were combined.[4] The canon law of the Continent with its ancient foundations of Church administration was dominated by decrees of synods and decretals of Popes. In Ireland, with a less strict organization of the Church, moral and legal rules taken directly from the Bible and particularly from the Old Testament occupied a relatively larger place in canon law; the title of an Irish 'Liber ex lege Moysi' based on the Pentateuch, and the many biblical quotations in the influential Irish collection of canon law called the *Hibernensis*, give an idea of this biblical tendency of the Irish.[5] Thus food restrictions in accordance

---

[1] P. W. Finsterwalder, *Die Canones Theodori Cantuariensis und ihre Überlieferungs-formen*, pp. 155 ff. His text is amended from the MSS. in the translation by J. T. McNeill and H. M. Gamer, *Medieval Handbooks of Penance*, pp. 179–217 (cf. pp. 58–60).

[2] Cf. my review, *Savigny-Zeitschr.* l, 1930, *Kan. Abt.* xix. 705 f.; P. Lehmann, *Histor. Jahrbuch*, li, 1931, pp. 544 f.; G. Le Bras, *Revue historique de droit français et étranger*, 4th series, x, 1931, pp. 95–115.

[3] Cf., e.g., Boehmer, 'Das germanische Christentum' (loc. cit., pp. 267 ff.); P. Fournier and G. Le Bras, *Histoire des collections canoniques en Occident*, i, Paris, 1931, pp. 56 ff., 84 ff., 98 ff., 108 ff.; Hodgkin, loc. cit. ii. 432 f.

[4] Cf. Karl Böckenhoff, 'Die römische Kirche und die Speisesatzungen der Buss-bücher' (*Theologische Quartalschrift*, lxxxviii, 1906, pp. 186–220), and his book, *Speisesatzungen mosaischer Art in mittelalterlichen Kirchenrechtsquellen des Morgen- und Abendlandes*, Münster, 1907; P. Fournier, 'De quelques infiltrations byzantines dans le droit canonique de l'époque carolingienne' (*Mélanges offerts à M. Gustave Schlum-berger*, i, Paris, 1924, pp. 67–71); Jecker, 'Die Heimat des hl. Pirmin' (loc. cit.), pp. 109 (n. 18), 115 ff.

[5] Cf. P. Fournier, 'Le Liber ex lege Moysi et les tendances bibliques du droit canonique irlandais' (*Revue Celtique*, xxx, 1909, pp. 221–34); Fournier and Le Bras, loc. cit. i. 62 ff.

with the Mosaic law and the Apostolic Decree (Acts xv. 29) were revived in Irish Christianity. There was the distinction between clean and unclean food; this was partly founded on rational considerations, but other bans, such as the avoidance of horse-flesh, are to be derived rather from biblical precepts. These orders and customs were also expressed in the penitentials. The Irish example came into contact in England with similar Greek practice, which was brought over by Theodore from his native country, Asia Minor. His penitential judgements ordered abstinence from the drinking of blood and from eating what is strangled and meat that is unclean or torn by beasts, and gave some reasonable advice for distinguishing clean and unclean food and drink; the ecclesiastical penance prescribed in relevant cases shows the biblical connexion. Such prescripts, as they are found even in the laws of King Alfred, were transferred to the Continent by the Irish and English. Boniface objected to the eating of the flesh of horses, hares, beavers, crows, and storks, and asked for the advice of the Popes, who insisted on the prohibition of such food;[1] the see of St. Peter was occupied during this period by several Popes of eastern origin. The English Legatine synods of 786 (c. 19) also opposed the eating of horse-flesh as a pagan custom and referred to the example of the Christians of the East. These Irish and Greek customs, transferred to England and thence to the Continent, were repeated there in the penitentials; some centuries were to pass before these habits and the ideas connected with them disappeared again.

The institution of ecclesiastical 'confraternities' was also brought overseas from England.[2] The belief in the efficacy of prayer for one another was their foundation. Diptychs were deposited on the altar containing the names of departed members or benefactors to be commemorated during the mass. Such diptychs were the origin of larger lists, of books devoted to

---

[1] Letters of the Popes Gregory III (a Syrian) and Zacharias (a Greek), in Boniface, *Epist.* 28 and 87 (pp. 50, 196).

[2] Cf. H. Hahn, 'Die Namen der Bonifazischen Briefe im liber vitae ecclesiae Dunelmensis' (*Neues Archiv*, xii, 1887, pp. 112 ff.); A. Ebner, *Die klösterlichen Gebets-Verbrüderungen bis zum Ausgange des karolingischen Zeitalters*, Regensburg, 1890; A. Molinier, *Les Obituaires français au moyen âge*, Paris, 1890, pp. 24 f., 29 f.; J. Duhr, 'La confrérie dans la vie de l'Eglise (*Revue d'histoire ecclésiastique*, xxxv, 1939, pp. 450 ff.).

whole communities, the 'Libri vitae' or Confraternity Books, which could be enlarged and continued through centuries by the inclusion of additional names. Single persons asked to be inscribed in the book of a monastery; entire monastic congregations formally agreed to pray for each other's members in life and death, forming a guildship, 'communio', 'familiaritas', 'fraternitas', 'confraternitas', &c. This kind of religious alliance was early established in England. Bede, for example, when he had finished his Lives of St. Cuthbert, asked that the monks of Lindisfarne should grant him their intercession as a reward, including his name in the 'album' of the congregation.[1] Such confraternities were taken by the missionaries to the Continent; they were one of the links connecting them with their native country. The correspondence of Boniface, Lullus, and Alcuin contains a number of examples, embracing not only bishops and abbots with their 'familiae', but also Anglo-Saxon kings who wished to obtain 'subsidies' of prayers. The parties concerned exchanged lists of their living and departed members; the names of associates had to be communicated when they died. The Vienna MS. of the letters of Boniface and Lullus includes even a formula for sending such a 'rotulus mortuorum' (no. 150);[2] a letter of Boniface asking to be admitted to the confraternity of Monte Cassino (no. 106) precedes it in the manuscript, and a letter of Lullus follows notifying the archbishop of York of the names of deceased brethren and friends (no. 125). These examples give a notion of the extent of this 'unitas fraternae dilectionis et societatis spiritalis', to quote one of the letters. Such associations now took root in the Frankish kingdom. During a synod at Attigny in 762 twenty-seven bishops and seventeen abbots joined in such an agreement, among them Chrodegang of Metz, the successor of Boniface as archbishop, Lullus of Mainz, and Willibald of Eichstätt.[3] The earliest existing Confraternity

---

[1] *Two Lives of St. Cuthbert*, ed. B. Colgrave, p. 146 (cf. p. 342). Cf. Plummer, *Baedae Op. hist.* i, pp. xxvii f.

[2] Also in Zeumer, *MG. Formulae*, p. 571, no. 34.

[3] *MG. Concilia*, ii. 72 f. Alcuin in 794 was formally admitted by the synod of Frankfurt 'in suo consortio sive in orationibus' (ib., p. 171, c. 56). On the 'societas' between Ferrières and York cf. Lupus of Ferrières, *Epist.* 61 (*MG. Epist.* vi. 61). A. Wilmart, 'Le règlement ecclésiastique de Berne' (*Rev. Bén.* li, 1939, pp. 37-52), has published from a French MS. of about 830 (though the text is perhaps of the 8th century) the curious rules of a confraternity of clerics founded in honour of St. Peter. He refers the statute to a group of clerics or monks who had come from

Books belong to the end of the eighth and to the first part of the ninth century.

We have already seen that the Rule of St. Benedict had spread in England with the progress and victory of the Roman party in the seventh century. At the same time its influence increased in the Frankish monasteries, side by side or combined with other Rules such as those of Columbanus or Caesarius. Its position was strengthened by the English missionaries who came from Benedictine houses; their foundations, Fulda and others, accepted it from the outset. Benedict's famous monastery of Monte Cassino, restored about 720 after its destruction by the Langobards, was considered by these 'pilgrims' and their adherents as a model house, 'the source and origin of all religion'[1] (that is, monasticism). Willibald, the future bishop of Eichstätt, when he returned from Palestine (p. 43), stayed there for ten years (729–39), holding several monastic offices. There has been some speculation how far Anglo-Saxon experience of the Benedictine Rule thus may have contributed to its restoration in its place of origin: *ignorabimus*. Willibald's brother Wynnebald, the abbot of Heidenheim, wished to end his life in the same monastery, though infirmity prevented him from going there.[2] Sturmi, the first abbot of Fulda (p. 79), and Liudger, the future bishop of Münster and founder of the monastery of Werden, acquired at Monte Cassino the practice of the Rule. This respect for the monastery of St. Benedict was a symptom of the high regard paid to his Rule. It became one of the aims of the Frankish Church reform to impose it on all monasteries

the British Isles (p. 39). But several names in the included litany (p. 52, § 6) rather point to a French 'societas' ('Dionisi cum sociis. Mauriti cum sociis. . . . Simphoriane. . . . Exuperi. Candide. Victor. . . . Germane. Remigi. Vedaste. Amande. . . . Genovefa . . .'), and nothing but the invocation of the widely venerated Irish saint 'Brigida' shows any connexion with the British Isles (on her cult cf. L. Gougaud, 'Le Culte de sainte Brigide de Kildare dans l'Europe continentale', *Archiv für Elsässische Kirchengeschichte*, xi, 1936, pp. 35–56).

[1] Paschasius Radbertus, *Vita Adalhardi*, c. 12 (*MG. SS.* ii. 525): 'venit Casinum, quo totius fons religionis et origo putabatur.'

[2] In the 12th century an old copy of the Rule existing at Heidenheim was referred there to Monte Cassino. Cf. Adelbert, *Relatio de restitutione monasterii Heidenheimensis* (Jac. Gretser, *Opera*, x, Ratisbonae, 1737, p. 811; Mabillon, *Acta*, iii. 2, p. 190): 'Sed et regula S. Benedicti a Cassino monte deportata et alii libri ecclesiasticae aedificationi necessarii, quos pius confessor (Wynnebald) in asino suo ad Heidenheimensem cellam advexerat, licet propter vetustatem inutiles, tamen propter reverentiam praedicti patris usque adhuc apud nos habentur.' This tradition may be added to the textual history of the Benedictine Rule.

and convents and to eliminate other Rules. The Concilium Germanicum of 742 ordered that monks and nuns, 'ancillae Dei', were to live according to the Rule of St. Benedict; the synod of Estinnes in the following year declared that abbots and monks had accepted this Rule to restore 'normam regularis vitae'. Many similar decrees followed. There was only one monastic Rule thenceforth, which was often simply called 'regula', 'sancta regula', or 'monastica regula' without the name of its author, and we hear of monasteries which abandoned another Rule for that of Benedict.[1] Its victorious career, promoted by the Anglo-Saxons, caused Charles the Great in 787 to ask the abbot of Monte Cassino for an authentic copy of the Rule,[2] just as he requested Pope Hadrian to send him the text of the Gregorian Sacramentary (p. 98); it was an expression of the same aim at unity and uniformity in the monastic field.

The monopoly given to the Rule of St. Benedict had further effects which reacted upon England. At cathedrals and other churches where a number of clergymen officiated there was a tendency to arrange a common life for them according to the apostolic example and the precedent of St. Augustine of Hippo, who lived together with his clergy a 'quasi-monastic' life in a 'monasterium'. Augustine of Canterbury instituted the same for his clergy at Christ Church, while the monastery of SS. Peter and Paul was erected for monks. Willibrord also seems to have had a clerical and a monastic community at Utrecht. So long as Frankish monasteries followed manifold rules, the clerical congregations of 'canonici', a name which was used in Gaul as early as the sixth century, did not appear too different from other 'monasteries'. But when the Rule of St. Benedict gained predominance or even exclusive control, the difference between the monks and the clergy without monastic vows who performed pastoral duties became more evident, and an attempt was made to bring the clergy of cathedrals and other larger churches (the 'collegiate' churches of later times) likewise into uniformity, and to impose upon them a 'quasi-monastic' life with common dormitory and refectory. The life of the clerics according to

---

[1] Cf. my remarks on the convents of St. Radegundis at Poitiers and of Remiremont, *Westdeutsche Zeitschr. für Geschichte und Kunst*, xxvii, 1908, pp. 495 f., 504 f.

[2] Cf. the letter of Abbot Theodemar to Charles, *MG. Epist.* iv. 510, and L. Traube's famous *Textgeschichte der Regula S. Benedicti* (Abhandl. München, xxi, 1898; 2nd ed. by H. Plenkers, ib. xxv. 2, 1910).

the canons of the Church was now opposed to the life of the
monks according to the Benedictine Rule. The restoration of
the common life of the clergy was a consequence of the reforms
initiated by the Anglo-Saxons, rather than their direct aim.
Boniface occasionally mentions 'canonici clerici' side by side
with bishops, priests, and deacons, and with abbots, abbesses,
monks, and nuns, obviously meaning clerics in minor orders
who probably were subject to a common life.[1] But his synods
considered the restoration of the canonical order generally;
they did not yet raise the special question of the common life
of the clergy. It was only after his death that its restoration
became an object of synodical legislation and of practice. Bishop
Chrodegang of Metz (742–66), the successor of Boniface in his
archiepiscopal dignity, composed for his cathedral clergy the
earliest 'regula canonicorum', in which the imitation of the
Rule of Benedict is obvious. The same ideas were also applied
to those 'ancillae Dei' or 'sanctimoniales' who were not inclined
to accept the Benedictine Rule and the complete vows of a nun;
consequently there arose 'canonicae', canonesses, side by side
with the 'canonici', the male canons. The name of canonesses,
which had had some meaning in the early Church, was perhaps
transmitted to the Continent from England, for its first appearance in this period is in the Penitential ascribed to Archbishop
Egbert of York (732–66), which not only mentions the 'ancilla
Dei' and 'virgo sanctimonialis' but also the 'canonica'.[2] The
development came to an issue at the synod of Aachen in 816;
this published Rules for canons and canonesses, the history of
which we need not pursue.[3] England did not actively participate
in this evolution, and there would be no need to mention it at
all if it had not reacted on the English Church. Anglo-Saxons
had revived the spirit of reform overseas; now the roles began
to be exchanged. First the Legatine synods of 786 (c. 4) issued

---

[1] Boniface, *Epist.* 46 (p. 74, l. 20). The comma between 'canonicis clericis' in
the modern editions requires to be deleted; cf., e.g., *MG. Concilia*, i, p. 77, l. 12.

[2] Penitential of Egbert, preface and c. 5. 8 (F. W. H. Wasserschleben, *Die Buss-
ordnungen der abendländischen Kirche*, Halle, 1851, pp. 232, 236 f.; H. and S. iii. 417,
422). Cf. *Westdeutsche Zeitschr.*, loc. cit., p. 497.

[3] Cf. the edition of the *Institutio canonicorum* and *sanctimonialium* of Aachen by
A. Werminghoff, *MG. Concilia*, ii. 307–464 (with an additional letter of Emperor
Louis to Agobard of Lyons; cf. M. Conrat, *Neues Archiv*, xxxvii, 1912, pp. 771 f., and
Levison, ib. xxxviii, 1913, pp. 508 f.) and Werminghoff's article, *Neues Archiv*, xxvii,
1902, pp. 605–75.

a decree concerning the life of canons, who were to be distinguished from monks as well as from seculars.[1] The term
'canonici', employed on this occasion after the continental
pattern, remained an exception in Anglo-Saxon England for
centuries. But we have now an example of the restoration in
England of the common life of the clergy. Kent was the natural
entrance-gate for continental goods and ideas; so, several years
later, we find the theory put into practice there. The community
of Christ Church at Canterbury at the end of the eighth century
had either preserved or recovered at least a part of their common
life; there existed a 'common table' ('mensa') of the 'familia
Christi'. In the early years of the next century Archbishop
Wulfred (805–32) restored their 'monasterium', bestowed new
property on the 'common congregation', and prescribed the
use of a common refectory and dormitory (813).[2] Now it was
England's turn to follow the continental example, though in
this case the effect was only ephemeral.

The Legatine synods of 786 also marked an advance in
another respect. The payment of a tenth of the annual produce
of the soil to the Church was based on the Old Testament
and for centuries was recommended or demanded as a moral
obligation. It was insisted on, for example, in Irish sources,
and by Caesarius of Arles; tithes were also mentioned in the
Penitential Books containing the 'judgements' of Theodore,
and by Boniface. Their payment may have been customary
to some extent.[3] On the Continent King Pippin made it by
public law a general duty, perhaps to compensate the Church
for the losses incurred through the transfer of ecclesiastical
property to royal vassals.[4] Charles the Great renewed the same
law, and Alcuin had grave scruples lest the strict enforcement

---

[1] Almost forty years before, in 747, the synod of Clovesho (c. 29, H. and S. iii.
374) forbade not only monks and nuns but also clerics to reside with laymen in the
houses of seculars, instead of living in 'monasteries'.

[2] M. Deanesly, 'The Familia at Christchurch, Canterbury' (*Essays in Medieval
History presented to Thomas Frederick Tout*, Manchester, 1925, pp. 1–13); J. A. Robin-
son, 'The Early Community at Christ Church' (*J.T.S.* xxvii, 1926, pp. 225–40).
Cf. Hodgkin, loc. cit. ii, pp. 418, 428 f.

[3] Cf. also *Vita Wilfridi*, c. 64 (ed. Levison, p. 260. 6; ed. Colgrave, p. 140,
c. 65).

[4] Boniface, *Epist.* 118 (p. 254). Cf. U. Stutz, 'Das karolingische Zehntgebot'
(*Savigny-Zeitschr.* xxix, 1908, *German. Abteil.* pp. 180–224); E. Perels, 'Die Ursprünge
des karolingischen Zehntrechtes' (*Archiv f. Urk.* iii, 1911, pp. 233–50).

of the payment might impair the cause of Christianity in the lands of the newly converted Saxons and Avars. It may be a reflection of this continental situation that the Legatine synods (c. 17) were the first to make demand for this payment in an English official document, whatever may have been its legal significance. It was the first public command to pay tithes, but, we may assume, without general effect; for it was not until the tenth century that royal laws threatened penalties for a refusal of payment.[1]

Kent was also the doorway through which the office of archdeacon was introduced about 800 from the Continent.[2] The institution of the 'archidiaconus', the first of the deacons, whose function it was to assist the bishop in his administrative duties, was very common overseas, but was yet unknown in England, until it is found at Canterbury in the early ninth century. Wulfred, later archbishop, whom I have mentioned before, is the first English archdeacon on record; we find him with this title in the years 803–5, the years immediately before he was enthroned on the seat of Augustine. A few successors occur in 830 and about 858. The single archidiaconate began to be divided in France in the course of this century, and a part of the diocese was assigned to each archdeacon. Canterbury also followed this example; three or four archdeacons are found at the same time among the witnesses in charters of the years 863–70. A single archdeacon occurs in 889 in the other diocese of Kent, at Rochester.[3] There is no further trace of this office in England until the eleventh century; it was only the Norman Conquest that made it there a permanent institution. Thus the introduction of this continental official of the Church about 800 had no lasting effect. But the facts adduced show that the current of the early eighth century was reversed at its end. It is significant that the two papal legates of 786 were accompanied by an envoy of Charles the Great, Abbot Wigbod.

[1] On tithes in early England I may mention Liebermann, *Gesetze*, ii. 2, pp. 748–50; E. W. Watson, *The Cambridge Medieval History*, vi. 534 f.; Stenton, *Anglo-Saxon England*, pp. 154 ff.
[2] W. H. Frere, *Visitation Articles and Injunctions*, i (loc. cit.), pp. 41–7; M. Deanesly, 'The Archdeacons of Canterbury under Archbishop Ceolnoth' (*E.H.R.* xlii, 1927, pp. 1–11). Cf. Stenton, *Anglo-Saxon England*, p. 434.
[3] Birch, ii, no. 562; Earle, *A Hand-book of the Land-charters*, p. 153.

Charles the Great

At the end of the eighth century the Frankish kingdom was at its zenith under the rule of King Charles, to whom posterity has rightly granted the title of the Great. He was a war-lord, whose conquests extended the frontiers of his realm from Hungary to the north of Spain, from Holstein to southern Italy. But he was also a great administrator and civilizer, whose manifold legislation in quantity and, what is more, in cultural substance surpassed all that had preceded it from the decay of the Roman world to his own age. He worked for an organized and unified Church, but governed it himself, though recognizing in theory the spiritual authority of the Pope. He was conscious of the value of knowledge and education, particularly of the worth of an educated clergy and, striving for the promotion of his aims with personal interest, he also impressed nations outside his rule by his personality and achievements.

The first purpose of the English missionaries had been the conversion of their continental kinsfolk. We have seen that the Christianization of the pagan Saxons became the ambition of Boniface during his later years (p. 77); this object was now attained. As is common knowledge, Charles put an end to the numerous frontier wars with this, the last independent German people of the Continent. In a struggle which lasted (with intervals) for more than thirty years, he overcame their resistance and incorporated them in his empire as members with equal rights. Their surrender was one of the foundations of medieval and modern Germany, much as the subduing of Aquitania by Pippin was one of the bases of future France. The submission of the Saxons was not only political; the acceptance of Christianity became after some years a condition of surrender, enforced by severe law. The preaching of missionaries was the spiritual complement; missionary districts entrusted to bishops and monasteries gradually became normal dioceses.

Anglo-Saxons took part in this last chapter of German Christianization, which included the clearing up of the remains of Frisian heathenism. Utrecht, Willibrord's see, was one of the centres of these endeavours. After the death of Boniface the diocese was committed, as has been said (pp. 95 f.), to his Frankish pupil Gregory, who was never consecrated bishop but remained presbyter and abbot up to his death (775?); his helper in episcopal functions was an Anglo-Saxon chorepiscopus Aluberht, consecrated at York in 767 'ad Ealdsexos',[1] as has also been mentioned. In his monastic school at Utrecht Gregory's disciples, who came from almost all the German tribes, included also Anglo-Saxons.[2] His Frisian pupil Liudger became at the beginning of the ninth century the first bishop of the diocese of Münster, which embraced Saxon and Frisian territories. From England also came Presbyter Liafwine or, as he was called on the Continent, Lebuin, to join Gregory, who sent him to the eastern Netherlands. He worked there, in the borderland of Franks and Saxons, near the river Yssel, where, in the dangerous neighbourhood of pagans, the church of Deventer became the centre of his activities and his last place of rest.[3] His earliest Life, probably written about the middle of the ninth century, has only recently been published;[4] the most impressive part of this short text is the lively account of Lebuin's appearance and preaching at Marklo, the annual meeting-place of the deputies

[1] Northumbrian Annals in Symeon of Durham's *Hist. regum*, § 46 (ed. Arnold, ii. 43); Liudger, *Vita Gregorii*, c. 10 (*MG. SS.* xv. 1, p. 75); Altfrid, *Vita Liudgeri*, i. 10 (ib. ii. 407; ed. Diekamp, p. 15).

[2] Liudger, loc. cit., c. 8 (p. 73): 'Sed et pueros duos cum consensu magistri (Boniface) in discipulatum suum, Marchelmum videlicet et Marcwinum germanos de gente Anglorum, secum inde adduxit' (Gregory from Rome); ib., c. 11 (p. 75): 'quidam (discipuli) autem et de religiosa gente Anglorum.' On (another?) Marchelm, who is said to have been a disciple of Willibrord, cf. *Vita Liudgeri*, i. 13, 18, 24 (cc. 13, 16, 21, in *SS.* ii).

[3] *Vita Liudgeri*, i. 13–15. Altfrid expressly calls Liafwine 'presbiter' and refers his coming from England to the time after the death of Boniface. If he had been consecrated bishop, it is highly improbable that his episcopal dignity would have been forgotten as early as the second quarter of the 9th century, even at Deventer. I am therefore not prepared to identify him, as has been done by Tangl, with Leofwine, one of Boniface's seven 'coepiscopi', who about 746 sent the admonishing letter to King Ethelbald of Mercia, *Epist.* 73 (p. 147, l. 1, the name being transmitted in the *Vita Ecgwini*; cf. below, Appendix VII, pp. 280 f.); A. Hofmeister in his edition of the *Vita Lebuini antiqua*, p. 791, and M. Lintzel (see n. 4), p. 77, n. 10, have similarly denied the identity.

[4] See the edition by Hofmeister, *MG. SS.* xxx. 2 (1926–34), pp. 789–95. To the MSS. has to be added Berlin Theol. Lat. fol. 706, written by the Carthusian Hermann Greven of Cologne, who died in 1477; cf. B. de Gaiffier, *Anal. Boll.* liv, 1936, p. 348. Besides the literature recorded by Hofmeister, cf. M. Lintzel, 'Untersuchungen zur Geschichte der alten Sachsen VIII' (*Sachsen und Anhalt*, vii, 1931, pp. 76–108; cf. Hofmeister, *Neues Archiv*, xlix, 1932, pp. 653–6); K. D. Schmidt, '"Nuntius Dei" in der Germanenmission' (*Zeitschr. für Kirchengeschichte*, lv, 1936, pp. 437–44); Gerhard Eis, 'Drei deutsche Gedichte des 8. Jahrhunderts aus Legenden erschlossen' (loc. cit.), pp. 43–57. There are many doubtful assumptions in these latest studies.

of all Saxon districts and classes, the earliest medieval assembly of a representative character that is known.

We are better informed about the life of another Anglo-Saxon, the Northumbrian Willehad, a friend of Alcuin.[1] About 770 he was formally sent, in accordance with his wishes, to Friesland by the Northumbrian king and a synod of his home country,[2] and first worked amidst Frisians in the region of Boniface's martyrdom, in the adjoining eastern Frisian country, and, to the south, in the modern Dutch province of Drenthe. In 780 he was directed by King Charles to apply his missionary zeal to the Saxons between the lower parts of the Weser and the Elbe. His work was interrupted in 782 by the insurrection of the Saxons and their duke Widukind. In consequence of persecution he had to leave the country and made a pilgrimage to Rome. Then for about two years he found with his disciples a refuge in the monastery of Echternach, governed by another Anglo-Saxon and a relative of its founder Willibrord, Abbot Beornred. When Widukind made his subjection in 785 and accepted Christianity, Willehad resumed his work among the Saxons with obvious success. For in 787, by order of the king, he was consecrated the first bishop of Bremen and the first bishop of any see in Saxon lands the origin of which can be exactly dated. In 789 he consecrated the cathedral at Bremen, but died a week later, to be buried in the new church and to be venerated there as a saint of miraculous power.

We need not follow the details and vicissitudes of the missionary effort. Alcuin objected, as I said above (pp. 106 f.), to the imposition of tithes upon the new Christians, which, in his opinion, might hinder sincere Christian belief from taking root. But Christianity did strike root, and Saxony became a Christian country in spite of all surviving paganisms. German and Latin literature of the next centuries bear witness to the participation and co-operation of Saxons in the Christian civilization of the West. When Willehad died a century had passed since his Northumbrian compatriot Willibrord with his companions was sent overseas to convert the heathen kinsfolk of the English. Now this task had been achieved, though it was the strong, harsh hand of Charles the Great that accomplished its last

[1] Alcuin, *Epist.* 6 (p. 31).
[2] *Vita Willehadi*, c. 1 (*MG. SS.* ii. 380; *Acta SS. Novembris*, iii. 843).

stages. Anglo-Saxons had set about the task and in large part had carried it out.

The intercourse between England and the Continent had considerably increased in the meantime. In spite of all wars, internal conditions on both sides of the Straits were more settled and in better order than a century before. England also had about this time an eminent king, Offa of Mercia (757–96), whom I have had occasion to mention several times already, 'active, many-sided, ambitious',[1] and whose kingdom or over-lordship in the end comprised all England south of the Humber. Let us recall his relations with the Apostolic See: the sending of papal legates for the reform of the Church in 786, and Offa's promise to pay 365 mancuses to the Roman Church every year, which gift may be regarded as one of the origins of Peter's Pence (p. 31); the ephemeral establishment of a special Mercian Church province with Lichfield as metropolis (p. 19); the foundation and acquisition of monasteries by the king and the papal privilege in regard to these houses granted to him and his family (p. 30). We have also seen that this 'King of the English' ('rex Anglorum') issued a better coinage and probably first adopted the new Frankish monetary system of 240 pennies corresponding to a pound (p. 11). Offa was, like the Frankish king, a patron of building; he asked Charles to send him 'black stones' of a special length, while the latter suggested that English cloaks should be manufactured such as were imported into his realm in old days from overseas. English pilgrims, like all pilgrims, enjoyed exemption from customs in the countries of Charles; but he insisted, as we have heard (p. 38), that English merchants, posing as pilgrims, should not abuse this privilege but pay their dues, though merchants should be protected by both kings against injustice and oppression. This letter of Charles has been called with some exaggeration the record of the first commercial treaty ever negotiated by an English king. Abbot Gervold of St. Wandrille in Normandy was administrator of customs at several ports, particularly at Quentavic, and, we may suppose, met there many Anglo-Saxons; this fact may have qualified him to be sent by Charles on a number of missions to Offa.

The importance of the traffic between the two countries

[1] Hodgkin, loc. cit. ii. 386. Cf. also Stenton, *Anglo-Saxon England*, pp. 204 ff.

became evident when a quarrel arose between the two rulers. Charles, the eldest son of the Frankish king, sought the hand of a daughter of Offa; but the English king, to emphasize the equality of rank, made it a condition that Bertha, a daughter of Charles the Great, should be given to his own son Egfrid, whom he had made co-regent of the Mercians. The Frankish king, who did not give away any of his daughters during his lifetime, refused, perhaps offended in his pride. Tension arose (790), and the commercial traffic was stopped first by Charles, then on the other side also (p. 10). We have reason to be grateful for the failure of this marriage scheme; for Bertha had a love-affair with Angilbert, one of her father's favourites, a poet, the 'Homer' of the palace circle and abbot of St. Riquier in Picardy, and became by him mother of Nithard, a soldier as well as one of the few lay-writers of the early Middle Ages, to whom we are indebted for the history of the struggle between the sons of Louis the Pious. As to Charles and Offa, harmony and the former alliance were restored after a while. There exist letters of Offa's last years in which Charles calls him his brother and friend, and speaks of 'antiquum pactum' and 'foedus'; after the defeat of the Avars he sent him as presents silken cloaks, an Avar sword, and a sword-belt.

There was also some co-operation in ecclesiastical politics. The strange rumour arose that Offa had suggested to Charles the deposition of Pope Hadrian, and the Frankish king at Offa's request informed the Pope that the report was unfounded. When Charles entered the Iconoclastic conflict, he sent the controversial acts of the Nicene council of 787, which were favourable to the cult of the images, to England in 792. Alcuin, who was residing in his native country at this time, composed a letter against these decrees, and brought it to Charles in the name of the English bishops and kings;[1] England seconded his action. Alcuin and other English theologians took part in the synod of Frankfurt in 794, where the Frankish point of view on this controversy was maintained. Charles also showed his interest in the English Church in the fashion of his age by bestowing alms on English monks and anchorites to obtain the benefit of their prayers. After the death of Hadrian he sent

---

[1] Northumbrian Annals in Symeon of Durham's *Hist. regum*, § 55 (ed. Arnold, ii. 53 f.; *MG. SS.* xiii. 155).

vestments to the English cathedrals with the request that prayers should be offered for the soul of the Pope.

English refugees sought the shelter of the Frankish kingdom. Charles asked the archbishop of Canterbury and another bishop to intercede for them with Offa; he sent others to Rome to be judged by the Pope and the archbishop of Canterbury, who was there at this time. Even a daughter of Offa himself took refuge with Charles, Eadburg, the wife of King Beorhtric of Wessex (786–802); after the death of her husband, being hated for her cruelty, she fled to the Continent. The emperor made her abbess of a large convent; but, expelled for her profligate life, she died in misery at Pavia. She had a predecessor of more importance at the emperor's court: Egbert, who succeeded her husband Beorhtric in Wessex (802–39), had been driven by him and Offa into exile and remained for three (thirteen?) years in the Frankish countries before he was able to return to England and obtain his throne.[1] We can only conjecture that he may have had an opportunity there of learning methods of government from the great emperor, as William of Malmesbury afterwards surmised; everybody knows that at a later date Egbert for some time won the ascendancy over all the Anglo-Saxons, and is with Offa one of 'two all-important unknown quantities in the formation of a united England'.[2] All these facts, trifling as many of them are, show how close were the relations between England and the Continent in the political as well as the ecclesiastical sphere at the end of the eighth century.

Nor were these relations confined to the southern part of England. The power of Charles was felt even by the Irish. Envoys sent by him to Ireland ('Scotia') are occasionally mentioned by Alcuin.[3] Einhard, the biographer of the emperor, tells of the submissiveness shown by the Irish kings in their letters to Charles. Northumbria, the native country of Willibrord and Alcuin, was of course nearer to the sphere of Frankish interests. We hear of presents sent by Pippin to King Eadbert[4] (737–58), who after reigning for more than twenty years resigned the throne and the world like Pippin's brother Carloman (he

[1] *Saxon Chronicle*, 836 (ed. Earle–Plummer, i. 62 f.). Cf. ib. ii. 75; Stenton, *Anglo-Saxon England*, p. 218, n. 4.
[2] Hodgkin, loc. cit. ii. 415. Cf. Stenton, loc. cit., pp. 230 ff.
[3] *Epist.* 101 (p. 147).
[4] Symeon, *Hist. Dunelm. eccl.* ii. 3 (ed. Arnold, i. 48).

died in 768). Alchred, one of the next Northumbrian kings (765–74), the same with whose consent Willehad came to Germany (p. 110), dispatched envoys to Charles and asked Bishop Lullus of Mainz to help him in the preservation of peace and friendship (773). The murder of King Ethelred in 796 shocked the Frankish ruler so deeply that he withheld gifts which had been destined for the northern cathedrals.[1] Eardwulf, who succeeded Ethelred after the expulsion of a pretender, even brought about a diplomatic intervention by Charles. Eardwulf had stood his ground in the blood-stained soil of Northumbria against hostile factions for ten years; he was then expelled and went to the Continent in 808, first to Charles, whom he found in his palace at Nijmegen on the Rhine, thence to Rome to see Pope Leo also. After some misunderstanding, both united to support him. Two abbots of northern France as envoys of the emperor, and a deacon of English origin as legate of the Pope, reconducted him to his kingdom in 809.[2] But Eardwulf disappears at once from history. He may have died or resigned, and his son now became king for many years. There is a notice in the so-called Annals of Lindisfarne (in 797), that Eardwulf's wife was a daughter of King Charles: 'Iste duxit uxorem filiam regis Karoli.'[3] The notice is unique; no other source confirms this statement of the Annals, which are a Durham compilation of the early twelfth century.[4] This tradition if true would explain the emperor's interest in the re-establishment of Eardwulf. But Einhard, who had enjoyed intimate familiarity with Charles, has expressly stated that the emperor did not permit his daughters to leave him for marriage during his lifetime.[5] Perhaps we have here a confusion with the famous marriage of King Ethel*wulf* of Wessex with Judith, the daughter of Charles the Bald, in 856.[6] In any case it is better not to rely on this unique late account.

---

[1] Alcuin, *Epist.* 101 (p. 147).

[2] Cf. K. Hampe, 'Die Wiedereinsetzung des Königs Eardulf von Northumbrien durch Karl den Großen und Papst Leo III' (*Deutsche Zeitschr. für Geschichtswissenschaft*, xi, 1894, pp. 352–9); Tillmann, loc. cit., pp. 7–10.

[3] Ed. Pertz, *MG. SS.* xix. 506.

[4] They are not early Lindisfarne Annals, as I hope to show elsewhere.

[5] *Vita Karoli Magni*, c. 19 (6th ed. by Waitz and Holder-Egger in *SS. rer. Germ.*, 1911, p. 25). Cf. above, p. 112.

[6] Cf., e.g., Symeon's *Hist. regum*, § 90 (ed. Arnold, ii. 103): '(Ethelwulf) ad patriam suam remeavit, afferens secum Juditham, *Karoli Francorum regis filiam*,'

The influence of Carolingian political practice can probably be traced in the adoption of a new feature in the inaugural rites of English kings, the anointing. We have heard that Carloman and Pippin during their troublesome early years had given their government a more legitimate foundation by once more instituting in 743 a Merovingian sham king, Childeric III, in whose name they ruled (p. 84). Some years after Carloman's resignation Pippin felt strong enough to get rid of the incongruous separation between the actual power and the empty name of a king, who, in spite of his lack of authority, yet by his royal blood signified something to traditional dynastic feeling and could be used as a pretext by all opponents of the régime. The closer relations now existing between the Carolingians and the Papacy helped to provide a substitute for the want of royal descent; the consent of the people was supplemented and sanctified by the authority of the Church. After consultation and agreement of the assembled magnates, Bishop Burchard of Würzburg, the Anglo-Saxon disciple of Boniface, and Abbot Fulrad of St. Denis, the archchaplain (that is, head of the court clergy), in 750 were sent to Rome to ask Pope Zacharias, as we are told in the semi-official so-called Annals of the Frankish kingdom, whether the existence of Frankish kings without any royal power was right or not. The Pope answered that the holder of the real power, rather than one who had no power, should also have the name of king, and by apostolic authority ordered Pippin to be made king to avoid disturbances. In view of the part played by the Pope, the event was to become a famous precedent in later times. The Pope was in fact recognized as the highest spiritual authority, whose decision was used to salve the conscience of the Carolingian party for the removal of the legitimate royal house.[1] When the expected papal answer had arrived, Pippin was elected king at Soissons by an assembly of the Franks and enthroned with his wife, while King Childeric and his son were tonsured and thus deprived of their long hair, the sign of the Merovingian 'reges criniti', and placed in monasteries. This happened in the last two months of 751 or in January 752, perhaps at

---

[1] We do not know whether the personal influence of Boniface had a part in this action. Cf., e.g., G. W. Sante, 'Bonifatius und die Begründung des Mainzer Erzbistums' (*Histor. Jahrbuch*, lvii, 1937, pp. 175 f.).

Christmas.[1] But the election of Pippin was also sanctified by unction performed by bishops and particularly by Boniface. His name is given in the semi-official Annals which I have mentioned above, and there is no sufficient reason to doubt the fact. The performance of the anointing by the papal delegate with the assistance of other bishops accorded with the participation of the Pope in the preliminaries of this *coup d'état*.

This papal co-operation had been prepared, at least in part, by the continental activity of the Anglo-Saxons, who had strengthened the connexion between the Roman See and the Carolingian house, and had asserted the authority of the Pope in the Frankish Church. Can Anglo-Saxon influence be recognized in the action itself? The accession to the throne of the Merovingians was a secular act, devoid of any ecclesiastical ingredient; Pippin was the first Frankish king to be anointed. The unction was repeated by Pope Stephen II in 754 at St. Denis, when he had come to Gaul to ask for Pippin's assistance against the Langobards; the sons of the king, Charles and Carloman, were also consecrated kings on this occasion. The purpose of securing the succession to the new dynasty is evident, the more so as the Pope constrained Pippin's subjects by the 'law of excommunication' never to elect a king from the loins of another. Charles the Great took similar advantage of his visit to Rome in 781; his sons Pippin and Louis were then anointed kings by Pope Hadrian. Thenceforward the anointing of kings took its place side by side with other inaugural rites: 'from this time onwards it was essential to the medieval king that he should not only receive the insignia of office but should also be anointed at the hands of the clergy'.[2] Nor is there any doubt as to the prototype and significance of this act. It referred to the record in the Old Testament that Samuel and other priests consecrated Jewish kings with oil, a magical practice, which was compared in Christian times with the use of oil in conferring sacraments, baptism, confirmation, and extreme unction. In the eighth century ceremonial anointing was introduced, first in Gaul, in the ordination of the priest, then also

---

[1] Cf. Krusch, *SS. rer. Merov.* vii. 508 ff.

[2] Percy Ernst Schramm, *Geschichte des Englischen Königtums im Lichte der Krönung*, Weimar, 1937, p. 8; translated by L. G. Wickham Legg, *A History of the English Coronation*, Oxford, 1937, p. 8.

in the consecration of the bishop.[1] The anointing of a king
therefore became one of the sacraments, before their number
was reduced to seven; one has only to refer to Peter Damian
in the eleventh or the so-called Anonymous of York in the early
twelfth centuries, to find examples of this development. The
king, by virtue of the unction, became 'the Lord's Anointed'.[2]
The participation of bishops was based on the biblical precedents. The coronation was added to the unction after the
imperial coronation of Charles the Great in 800; 'ordines
coronationis' were composed from the ninth century onwards.
Now the peculiar purpose of the act of 751–2, which was the
starting-point of this momentous process, was obvious: as Saul
was refused by God, and David became the 'christus Domini'
by Samuel's unction 'and the spirit of the Lord came upon
David from that day forward', so Childeric was rejected and
Pippin made the sacred king by the anointing, which was to
counteract and to conceal the deficiency of blood-right.

Did the Frankish bishops and particularly Boniface in introducing the new practice directly rely on the pattern of the Old
Testament, which they knew of course, or did they also imitate
and resume an earlier Western practice, which had similarly
been based on the Bible? Visigothic kings were in fact anointed
in the seventh century.[3] British anointed kings were mentioned
in the sixth century by Gildas (c. 21); but it is doubtful whether
his words permit the assumption of a real 'physical' anointing
or are only a biblical reminiscence.[4] Scottish kings of Dalriada
were 'ordained', as is evident from a story of St. Columba told
by Adamnan. 'Ordinationis regum liber' is there shown in a
vision, which suggests the existence of such a book in reality.
Columba employed 'ordinationis verba'; he ordained Aidan
'in regem' and 'in regnum': 'imponensque manum super caput
eius, ordinans benedixit.' Adamnan also calls a high-king of

---

[1] Cf. Gerald Ellard, *Ordination Anointings in the Western Church before 1000 A.D.*
(Monographs of the Mediaeval Academy of America, No. VIII), Cambridge
(Mass.), 1933, pp. 14 ff.

[2] Cf. Fritz Kern, *Gottesgnadentum und Widerstandsrecht im früheren Mittelalter* (Mittel-
alterliche Studien, i. 2), Leipzig, 1914, p. 78 (224) f.; translated by S. B. Chrimes,
Kingship and Law in the Middle Ages (Studies in Mediaeval History, edited by
G. Barraclough, iv), Oxford, 1939, pp. 36 f.; Schramm, loc. cit., pp. 6 f.

[3] Cf., e.g., my edition of Julian of Toledo's *Historia Wambae*, c. 4 (*SS. rer. Merov.*
v. 503 f.).

[4] Cf. Ellard, loc. cit., pp. 9 ff.

Ireland 'Deo auctore ordinatum'.[1] There thus appear to have been ecclesiastical ceremonies (though possibly not anointing) connected with the 'ordination' of those Celtic kings.[2] Were such customs adopted by Anglo-Saxons and transferred to the Franks? But there is no trace of an ecclesiastical element in the royal initiation of the Anglo-Saxons before the late eighth century. In former days the Pontifical attributed to Archbishop Egbert of York (732–66) was thought to some extent to prove English precedence in this respect; but to-day all agree that this text is much later and derives from Frankish practice.[3] Boniface came from the borderland of British and English life; he may therefore have known of a religious element in the initiation of British kings. But this is a mere possibility, nor can we assert that it was the Anglo-Saxons and not others who introduced the idea and the act of anointing into the Frankish proceedings of 751. Too many unknown quantities are involved.

But there is every probability that the ceremony, when established among the Franks, was transferred to England. A few years after the sons of Charles the Great had been anointed in Rome by Pope Hadrian (781), the two legates of the Pope and an envoy of Charles came to England in 786. In the twelfth of the 'capitula' offered by the legates and accepted by the two 'Legatine' synods it was declared that 'in ordinatione regum' nobody should permit the counsels of bad men to prevail.[4] Admonitions follow on the election of a king and against con-

---

[1] Adamnan's *Vita Columbae*, iii. 5 and i. 36 (2nd ed. by J. T. Fowler, pp. 167 f., 111). The Life of St. Columba ascribed to Cummeneus is not a source of Adamnan but an extract from his work, as Gertrud Brüning has shown, *Adamnans Vita Columbae und ihre Ableitungen*, Dissertation of Bonn, 1916 (reprinted from *Zeitschr. für Celtische Philologie*, xi), pp. 260 ff. J. F. Kenney, 'The Earliest Life of St. Columcille' (*Catholic Historical Review*, New Series, v, 1926, pp. 636–44) has not refuted her arguments (cf. also Kenney's *Sources for the Early History of Ireland*, i. 428 f.). Therefore c. 5 of this text (Brüning, pp. 294 f.) has not the value of an independent source but derives from Adamnan, iii. 5.

[2] The Irish collection of canon law, xxv. 1 (ed. H. Wasserschleben, 2nd ed., Leipzig, 1885, p. 76), has a chapter 'De ordinatione regis', describing the anointing of Saul, as related in 1 Reg. (Samuel) x. 1.

[3] Cf. Schramm, 'Die Krönung bei den Westfranken und Angelsachsen von 878 bis um 1000' (*Savigny-Zeitschr.* liv, 1934, *Kan. Abt.* xxiii, pp. 152 ff., 209 ff.).

[4] *MG. Epist.* iv. 23 f. The term 'ordinatio' may be influenced by Rom. xiii. 1 and 2, quoted a few lines later; possibly it refers here to the election, not to a consecration. Nor am I disposed to lay stress on Bede, *H.E.* iv. 11 (p. 225), speaking of King Sebbi of the East Saxons: 'Unde multis visum et saepe dictum est, quia talis animi virum episcopum magis quam regem *ordinari* deceret.'

spiracies and attempts to slay him; he is twice called the
Anointed of the Lord, 'christus Domini', though there is no
clear indication of a consecration rite. But in the following
year 787 King Offa of Mercia actually had his son Egfrid
consecrated king.[1] In the *Saxon Chronicle* the word 'gehalgod'
is used on this occasion, which had previously been applied to
the consecration of bishops only. One of his next successors,
Ceolwulf I (821–3), himself mentions his 'consecratio' performed
by the archbishop of Canterbury.[2] In the meantime, at the
latest in 796, consecration of kings was introduced into Northumbria: King Eardwulf was in that year consecrated in the
cathedral of York.[3] We need not follow the history of the
English coronation ceremonies, as it has been recently told by
Percy Ernst Schramm;[4] only the beginnings concern us here.
There are three possibilities: either Franks and Anglo-Saxons
resumed the prototype of the Old Testament independently of
each other, or one imitated the example of the other. The first
possibility is improbable in these times of lively intercourse
between the two countries. The few known facts favour the
opinion that Pippin and Boniface inaugurated the practice in
751, which was repeated by the Pope in 754 and 781, and that
the Mercians followed the example in 787 to secure during
Offa's lifetime an undisputed succession. In Northumbria in
796 one king had been murdered, his successor expelled after
less than a month; Eardwulf came to the throne from exile.
Thus his consecration, which to some extent strengthened his
position spiritually, fits in well with the circumstances of his
accession. Offa was, as we have heard, inclined to set himself
on an equality with Charles; probably it was he who transferred
the Frankish example to England and first introduced a Christian element into the initiation of English kings. It developed
and has stood its ground till the present day. The unction gave
the ruler a kind of sacramental character and contributed to
the later doctrine of the divine right of kings.

There is another expression of ideas connected with the royal
anointing, which has also been referred to English example and

---

[1] *Saxon Chronicle*, 785 (that is, 787), ed. Plummer, i. 52–5; cf. ii. 57.
[2] Birch, i, no. 370.
[3] Symeon, *Hist. regum*, § 58 (ed. Arnold, ii. 57 f.); *Saxon Chronicle*, DEF, 795 (ed.
Plummer, i. 57; ed. Thorpe, i. 103).
[4] Cf. above, p. 116, n. 2; p. 118, n. 3.

precedent, the formula 'gratia Dei', by the grace of God, added
to the royal style. The formula was originated by the apostle
St. Paul; it was a symbol of humility, particularly used by
bishops and other members of the clergy to declare that they
did not owe their position to personal merit but only to God's
condoning grace. The addition of these and similar words to
the title of rulers gradually gave the formula another aspect
and meaning: the king is indebted for his dignity not to men
but only to God; there is no other superior power. The formula
became an expression of sovereignty, to employ a term fixed
in the sixteenth century. The Merovingian kings did not use
such a formula nor did Pippin in most of his charters. But it
is found in a few documents of his last years only copies of
which exist; these few instances may be therefore considered
not absolutely established. But 'gratia Dei' certainly became
a regular addition to the royal title after the accession of Pippin's
sons Charles and Carloman (768): the new dynasty had to find
in the grace of God an additional substitute for legitimacy and
a counterpoise to the lack of lawful descent.

Now the opinion has been held that herein the Carolingians
were also following English precedent.[1] In earlier English charters such formulas were in fact added not only to the style of
bishops but also of kings. But there is a variety of these formulas,
if such a formula was added at all (which often it was not),
and the use of the precise form 'gratia Dei' is comparatively so
scarce in the eighth century[2] that English influence in this
matter upon the Frankish chancery may be regarded as doubtful
and has been considered improbable by scholars.[3] Nor are there
sufficient grounds for adopting the converse explanation of the
facts and deriving the English practice from Frankish influence
in the age of Charles and Offa.[4] English ecclesiastics used
'gratia Dei' in many cases from Archbishop Theodore onwards.
No royal chancery existed at this time in England and clergy-

---

[1] Cf., e.g., H. Brunner, *Deutsche Rechtsgeschichte*, 2nd ed., ii (by Cl. Freiherrn von
Schwerin), München, 1928, pp. 17 f.

[2] Birch, i, nos. 218, 223, 234, 241, 244, &c.

[3] Karl Schmitz, *Ursprung und Geschichte der Devotionsformeln bis zu ihrer Aufnahme in
die fränkische Königsurkunde* (Kirchenrechtl. Abhandl. lxxxi), 1913, pp. 169 ff.

[4] Ib., pp. 173 ff. This opinion of Schmitz has been accepted by Marc Bloch, *Les
Rois thaumaturges* (Publications de la Faculté des lettres de l'Université de Strasbourg,
xix), 1924, pp. 466 f.

men or monks drew up the charters of kings as occasion arose; they may also have introduced the formula of St. Paul in some English royal charters. Englishmen used it also in their continental connexions. It is found, for instance, in the oath delivered in 722 by Boniface on the occasion of his episcopal consecration. Thirty years later, in a letter, he employed first the papal formula of humility 'servus servorum Dei', thereby anticipating the word 'Dei', but then added to his title of 'episcopus' the formula 'gratia Christi'. An English priest Wigbert inscribed two letters 'Lullae gratia Dei episcopo'.[1] Thus the possibility of Anglo-Saxon influence in this matter upon the Frankish chancery remains; but it is no more than a possibility. For the same formula in these centuries was not only used by Frankish bishops, but the pattern of papal documents has also to be considered, a number of which show the ancient formula inserted in the signatures of the Popes.[2] Thus it may have found its way into royal charters independently and through different channels on both sides of the sea; at least no dependence on one side or the other can be proved. We do not know the particular circumstances which induced the Frankish chancery to add the two words to the royal style, occasionally at the end of Pippin's reign and regularly after his death. It is better therefore to refrain from definite conclusions.

Another question arises, similarly relating to the history of political ideas. Had Englishmen a share in preparing the restoration of the Empire in the West? They did not co-operate of course in the momentous event of Christmas Day 800 in St. Peter's, when Pope Leo placed the imperial crown on the head of Charles and the latter was hailed Emperor of the Romans, nor need we consider the political conditions of the Byzantine Empire or the special occurrences at Rome preceding the coronation, or the reasons for Charles's aversion to it according to Einhard's much-discussed account. After all, Charles accepted the imperial dignity conferred upon him. Now it has long been observed that though Charles was not called and could not be called emperor before the end of 800, nevertheless his kingdom had already been named 'imperium' by an Englishman of his intimate circle, by Alcuin, just in the years immediately

[1] Boniface, *Epist.* 16, 93, 137, 138 (pp. 28, 212, 275, 277).
[2] Schmitz, loc. cit., pp. 142 ff.

preceding the event. The word 'imperium' was sometimes applied to kingdoms in the sixth and later centuries when their rulers were not 'imperatores'.[1] We must not forget the various meanings of the expression: command, control, government, supreme power, &c., besides empire and imperial government in the strict later sense. The early English had no special word to distinguish 'regnum' and 'imperium', which were both translated by 'rice'; 'Caserdom' for 'imperium' is quite exceptional. Alcuin occasionally called the kingdom of Charles before 797 not only 'regnum' but also 'Francorum imperium'.[2] In 799 he declared that the 'regalis dignitas' of Charles was superior by power and wisdom to the Roman See and to the dignity of the second Rome.[3] Moreover he used 'imperium' with some stress in five letters of the years 798–800, three of which are addressed to Charles himself.[4] In these he spoke of the 'Christianum imperium', the government of which God had committed to the king; he contrasted it with the 'Romanum imperium' of former days and set it side by side with the Holy Church and its needs. He employed the same expression 'Christianum imperium' after the coronation as well as before it.[5] It was, as has been observed,[6] a theological conception taken from liturgical usage. Among the prayers for Good Friday in the sacramentaries is one for the 'imperium Romanum'. In some texts of the eighth century the name of the Franks was added:

[1] W. Sickel, 'Die Kaiserwahl Karls des Grossen' (*MIÖG.* xx, 1899, p. 2, n. 3).
[2] Alcuin, *Vita Willibrordi*, i. 23 (*SS. rer. Merov.* vii. 133); cf. ii, c. 23, v. 8 (*MG. Poetae*, i. 215; *Acta SS. Nov.* iii. 455). [3] *Epist.* 174 (p. 288).
[4] Ib. nos. 148, 177, 185, 200, 202 (pp. 241, 292, 310, 331, 336). Cf. also no. 136 (p. 205): 'cuncto christianitatis imperio', 'sacratissimi gubernacula imperii'; no. 170 (p. 279. 2): 'decus imperii.'
[5] Ib. nos. 234, 245, 249 (pp. 379, 397, 402).
[6] Cf. G. B. Ladner, 'The "portraits" of Emperors in Southern Italian *Exultet* Rolls and the Liturgical Commemoration of the Emperor' (*Speculum*, xvii, 1942, p. 197 f.), who quotes the relevant studies of Hans Hirsch, 'Der mittelalterliche Kaisergedanke in den liturgischen Gebeten' (*MÖIG.* xliv, 1930, pp. 1 ff.); G. Tellenbach, *Römischer und christlicher Reichsgedanke in der Liturgie des frühen Mittelalters* (Sitzungsberichte der Heidelberger Akademie der Wissenschaften, Philos.-histor. Klasse, xxv, 1934–5, No. 1); C. Erdmann, 'Der Heidenkrieg in der Liturgie und die Kaiserkrönung Ottos I' (*MÖIG.* xlvi, 1932, pp. 129 ff.); cf. also K. Heldmann, *Das Kaisertum Karls des Grossen* (Quellen und Studien zur Verfassungsgeschichte des Deutschen Reiches, founded by K. Zeumer, vi. 2), Weimar, 1928, pp. 18 ff., 31 ff., 54 ff. I have not seen Heinz Löwe, *Die Karolingische Reichsgründung und der Südosten* (Forschungen zur Kirchen- und Geistesgeschichte, xiii), Stuttgart, 1937, pp. 143 ff., nor Ludwig Biehl, *Das liturgische Gebet für Kaiser und Reich* (Görres-Gesellschaft, Sektion für Rechts- und Staatswissenschaft, lxxv), Paderborn, 1937.

'sive (atque) Francorum', while in others 'Christianum' was
substituted for 'Romanum'. 'It is therefore obvious', so it has
been remarked,[1] 'that the liturgical association of the ancient
Empire with the Empire to come preceded the actual renovation
of the Western Christian Empire by Charlemagne.' In any
case Alcuin, in identifying Charles's realm with the Christian
Empire of the liturgy, set it on a higher level, and he made this
meaning even plainer when, in a letter to the king in 796–7,
he called it an 'imperial realm', declaring it his aim, 'ut plurimos
ad profectum sanctae Dei ecclesiae et ad decorem *imperialis regni
vestri erudiam*'.[2] Alcuin may therefore be said to have made
the notion of 'empire' more familiar to the king, to have contributed to his readiness and disposition to accept the papal
action of 800 in spite of his aversion to the manner of its execu-
tion, and to have played a part in the spiritual prelude of the
medieval Empire of the West.

When Alcuin wrote those letters the territories ruled by
Charles had almost reached their widest expansion. The last
insurrections of the Saxons were approaching their end, the
Spanish marches south of the Pyrenees were in the making, the
defeat of the Avars had opened a large new field of activity to
German settlers and Christian missionaries. The last quasi-
independent dukedom had been abolished; Charles was not
only king of the Franks but also of the Langobards, two of his
sons being under-kings. This situation may have made the
conception of 'imperium' even more obvious to Englishmen
such as Alcuin, as E. Stengel has recently commented.[3] Bede
had often used the word 'imperium', for the Roman Empire of
course, but also for the Anglo-Saxon kingdoms, employing the
terms 'regnum' and 'imperium' indifferently;[4] but he showed
some preference for the word 'imperium' when speaking of those
kings who had acquired an overlordship, a hegemony over other
kingdoms besides their own, as did the seven kings (*H.E.* ii. 5)
who, with Egbert of Wessex, are called 'bretwaldas' in the *Saxon
Chronicle* (827); he ascribed 'imperialis auctoritas' to Pippin II
in Friesland (*H.E.* v. 10). He was not alone in this usage.

[1] Ladner, loc. cit., p. 198.
[2] Alcuin, *Epist.* 121 (p. 177). Cf. below, p. 125, n. 1.
[3] 'Kaisertitel und Suveränitätsidee' (*Deutsches Archiv für Geschichte des Mittelalters*,
iii, 1939, pp. 1–56). Cf. also E. Pfeil, loc. cit., pp. 98 ff.
[4] Cf. P. F. Jones, *A Concordance to the Historia Ecclesiastica of Bede*, p. 252.

Aldhelm spoke of King Aldfrid of Northumbria 'aquilonalis imperii sceptra gubernanti', and of Ine of Wessex 'qui nunc imperium Saxonum iure gubernat',[1] and Boniface applied Aldhelm's words on Aldfrid to Ethelbald of Mercia 'inclita Anglorum imperii sceptra gubernanti'.[2] Adamnan of Iona went even farther, when he said of King Oswald of Northumbria, 'totius Britanniae imperator a Deo ordinatus est'.[3] Empire in this sense was the government and rule of a king who was also overlord over other kings or territories. Let us look at a few examples of the style in charters of such kings of Mercia, as collected by F. M. Stenton in his essay on 'the supremacy of the Mercian kings'.[4] Ethelbald is called 'rex non solum Marcersium, sed et omnium provinciarum quae generale nomine Sutangli dicuntur'[5] or 'rex non solum Mercensium, sed etiam in circuitu populorum';[6] his successor Offa, 'rex Merciorum simulque aliarum circumquaque (in circuitu) nationum'.[7] His successor Cœnwulf, who did not maintain the hegemony, nevertheless was styled in an early charter 'rector et imperator Merciorum regni, anno secundo imperii nostri'.[8] Now let us quote for comparison the title given to Charles in the so-called 'Libri Carolini', the famous treatise against image-worship, written not only at the order but also under the supervision of the king, as W. von den Steinen has recently shown: 'Caroli nutu Dei regis Francorum, Gallias, Germaniam Italiamque sive harum finitimas provintias Domino opitulante regentis.'[9] The parallelism is obvious, and the simpler style of Charles's charters from 775 to 800, 'rex Francorum et Langobardorum ac patricius Romanorum', points in the same direction. Anglo-Saxons applied the notion of 'imperium' to those of their kings (though not to them alone) who had

---

[1] Aldhelm, *De metris et enigmatibus* (ed. Ehwald, p. 61); *Carm. eccles.* iii. 37 (ib., p. 16).

[2] Boniface, *Epist.* 73 (p. 146).

[3] *Vita Columbae*, i. 1 (2nd ed. by Fowler, p. 92).

[4] *E.H.R.* xxxiii, 1918, pp. 433–52.

[5] Birch, i, no. 154; cf. no. 157.   [6] Ib., no. 181.

[7] Ib., no. 234; cf. no. 236.

[8] Ib., no. 289. Cf. Stenton, loc. cit., pp. 450 (n. 73), 452.

[9] Ed. H. Bastgen, *MG. Concilia*, ii, *Supplementum*, 1924, p. 1. On Charles's personal part cf. W. von den Steinen, 'Karl der Grosse und die Libri Carolini' (*Neues Archiv*, xlix, 1932, pp. 207–80). On his claim to summon a 'universal' synod cf. Bastgen, 'Das Capitulare Karls d. Gr. über die Bilder' (ib. xxxvi, 1911, pp. 665 f.). On Charles's styles cf., e.g., E. Caspar, 'Das Papsttum unter fränkischer Herrschaft' (*Zeitschr. für Kirchengeschichte*, liv, 1935, pp. 260 f.).

authority also outside their own territory.[1] Charles came within the same category, as the ruler of the largest realm of the West that had existed since the days of the ancient Roman Empire, the more so because liturgical texts of the eighth century insinuated the continuity of the 'imperium Romanum' and of his 'imperium'. I follow Stengel in thus explaining Alcuin's share in preparing the revival of the imperial idea.

We should not overrate the importance of this share. Without the action of Pope Leo or some other restoration of the imperial dignity in the West, nobody would probably have paid much attention to the words of Alcuin. It would have appeared to most a mere matter of terminology, like the use of another Anglo-Latin expression. The office of the German 'graf' ('gravio') was almost always translated in the Frankish countries by 'comes', particularly in official documents, a late Roman title of rank, which had become the designation of a Frankish functionary. But there are some exceptions; in sources of the eighth and the next centuries the 'graf' or count is sometimes called by another Latin word, 'praefectus'.[2] All passages illustrating the use of the latter term that were written in Germany during the eighth century, and some during the ninth century, came from the pen of Anglo-Saxons[3] or are found in documents or places connected with their activity;[4] only a certain number belonging to the latter century when the usage had obviously

---

[1] Cf. Alcuin, *Epist.* 129 (p. 191), addressed to 'Nobilissime genti et populo laudabili et *regno imperiali* (cf. above, p. 123) Cantuariorum', of whom he says: 'Vos vero principium salutis Anglorum, . . . et a vobis *imperii* potestas prima processit et fidei catholicae origo exorta est.' Ethelbert of Kent had been, according to Bede, *H.E.* ii. 5 (p. 89), the third of the seven overlords: 'qui tertius quidem in regibus gentis Anglorum cunctis australibus eorum provinciis . . . *imperavit*'; cf. i. 25 (p. 45): 'qui ad confinium usque Humbrae fluminis . . . fines *imperii* tetenderat.'

[2] Cf., e.g., G. Waitz, *Deutsche Verfassungsgeschichte*, ii. 2 (3rd ed.), Berlin, 1882, p. 26; iii (2nd ed.), 1883, p. 383.

[3] Boniface, *Epist.* 95 (p. 216); Willibald, *Vita Bonifatii*, cc. 8, 9 (ed. Levison, pp. 53, 57); *Vita Wynnebaldi*, c. 12 (*MG. SS.* xv. 1, p. 115).

[4] *Concilium Germanicum*, c. 2 (*MG. Concilia*, ii. 3): 'unusquisque praefectus' (afterwards 'gravione'), and of Estinnes, c. 1 (ib., pp. 6 f.): 'comites et praefecti'.—Addition to a Fulda charter of 806, ed. E. Fr. J. Dronke, *Codex diplomaticus Fuldensis*, Cassel, 1850, p. 120, no. 228; cf. Tangl, *MIÖG*. xx, 1899, p. 204.—Charters forged at Fulda in the early 9th century, in the name of Boniface (ed. E. Stengel, *Urkundenbuch des Klosters Fulda*, i. 1, no. 6, p. 10) and King Pippin (ib., no. 20, p. 43; *MG. Dipl. Karol.* i, no. 32, p. 45); cf. Stengel, 'Fuldensia I' (*Archiv f. Urk.* v, 1913, pp. 56, 148, 151).—Rudolf of Fulda, *Annales Fuldenses*, 852 and 863 (ed. F. Kurze in *SS. rer. Germ.*, 1891, pp. 42 f., 57); cf. the continuation of Altaich, 898 (ib., p. 132).

spread, come from other hands.[1] There has been some discussion about the meaning of this term; it has also been connected with the name of the later 'burggraf', 'praefectus urbi' or simply 'praefectus'.[2] But it is very doubtful whether there is a connexion between the earlier and the later use. They may have been independently based on a Roman term which was found in many sources and combinations. It also formed part of the vocabulary of the Vulgate and was employed by the Anglo-Saxons to translate the vernacular 'gerefa' and 'ealdorman'. This usage is evident from many charters,[3] from Eddi Stephanus and Bede,[4] and from letters of Abbess Eangyth and of Boniface, referring to English institutions.[5] When Anglo-Saxons came to the Continent they used the Latin translation familiar to them to designate an office of which they probably oftener heard the German name than the Latin 'comes'. It is significant that the combination of 'comes' and 'praefectus' was also occasionally employed by Anglo-Saxons in England and overseas.[6] This word is thus another sign of English influence in Germany during the eighth century.[7]

On the other hand, the Germanic word which was to give a common name to the German language, people, and state, 'theodisc', the modern 'Deutsch', does not first occur in Germany but in England, and is there applied to the English, not to the continental German language; it is the language of the 'theod',

[1] I may mention Walahfrid Strabo, *De exordiis vel incrementis rerum ecclesiasticarum*, c. 32 (*MG. Capitularia*, ii. 515): 'comites vel praefecti'; Collectio Sangallensis no. 10 (*MG. Formulae*, p. 403); Rimbert, *Vita Anskarii*, c. 16 (ed. Waitz in *SS. rer. Germ.*, 1884, p. 37); Adalbert's continuation of Regino's *Chronicon*, 949 (ed. Kurze, ib., 1890, p. 164).

[2] A. Meister, 'Burggrafenamt oder Burggrafentitel?' (*Histor. Jahrbuch*, xxvii, 1906, pp. 253 ff.); O. Oppermann, 'Untersuchungen zur Geschichte von Stadt und Stift Utrecht' (*Westdeutsche Zeitschr.* xxvii, 1908, pp. 190 f.); K. A. Eckhardt, 'Präfekt und Burggraf' (*Savigny-Zeitschr.* xlvi, 1926, *German. Abteil.*, pp. 166 ff.).

[3] Cf., e.g., H. M. Chadwick, *Studies on Anglo-Saxon Institutions*, Cambridge, 1905, pp. 251, 259, 282 ff., 344, 370 ff.; Stenton, *E.H.R.* xxxiii, 1918, p. 443, n. 48.

[4] *Vita Wilfridi*, cc. 17, 18, 36 (afterwards 'comes'), 38 (pp. 211, 213, 229, 231); Bede, *H.E.* ii. 16, iii. 14, iv. 1, v. 24 (ed. Plummer, pp. 117, 155, 203, 356), and *Epist. ad Egbertum*, c. 13 (ib., p. 416).

[5] Boniface, *Epist.* 14, 73 ('prefecti et comites tui'), 78 ('aliquis prefectorum vel comitum'), ed. Tangl, pp. 23, 152, 169.

[6] Cf. above, p. 125, n. 4; p. 126, nn. 1, 5; Birch, i, no. 194: 'Ecgbaldi comitis atque praefecti.'

[7] I gave this explanation of the term in *Westdeutsche Zeitschr.* xxvii, 1908, p. 498, n. 20. Cf. also Lesne, *La hiérarchie épiscopale*, p. 39, n. 4.

the (German) people, contrasted with the Latin language of
the Church. When the papal legates and their companions in
786 came to the southern part of England with the decrees of
the northern synod, whose meeting had already taken place, a
synod of the Mercians and of the other kingdoms under Offa's
overlordship assembled. Offa himself with his great men, the
archbishop of Canterbury, and Alcuin and Pyttel as envoys of
the king of Northumbria and of the archbishop of York, took
part in the meeting. The decrees of the north were confirmed at this synod of the south. The several chapters were
read in a clear voice in Latin and in the vernacular, 'tam Latine
quam theodiscae', so that all could understand them, that is,
not only the clergy but also the laymen.[1] The word 'theodisc'
did not develop as a proper name in England[2] but became the
common designation for the continental German idioms and
peoples. The earliest known continental example is two years
later than the English occurrence, which certainly must be
referred to an importation from overseas.[3]

The report on the Legatine synods was composed for Pope
Hadrian by one of the legates, Bishop George of Ostia, who had
many connexions with the Frankish court.[4] In 753-4 he accompanied Pope Stephen II on his journey to France,[5] and in the
following years he was several times employed by Stephen and
his successor Paul I as envoy to Pippin.[6] Thus in 757 he

[1] *MG. Epist.* iv. 28. Cf. Alfred Dove, 'Das älteste Zeugniss für den Namen
Deutsch' (*SB. München*, 1895, pp. 223–35, repeated in Dove, *Ausgewählte Schriftchen
vornehmlich historischen Inhalts*, Leipzig, 1898, pp. 324–33); Fritz Vigener, *Bezeich-
nungen für Volk und Land der Deutschen vom 10. bis zum 13. Jahrhundert*, Heidelberg,
1901, pp. 29 ff.; C. Erdmann, 'Der Name Deutsch' (in *Karl der Große oder Charlemagne? Acht Antworten deutscher Geschichtsforscher*, Berlin, 1935, pp. 94–105); Willy
Krogmann, *Deutsch* (Deutsche Wortforschung, i), Berlin, 1936; L. Weisgerber,
'Vergil Aen. VII 741 und die Frühgeschichte des Namens Deutsch' (*Rheinisches
Museum*, lxxxvi, 1937, pp. 97–126), &c.

[2] The notion of language is found in *King Alfred's Old English Version of Boethius*
(c. 19), ed. W. J. Sedgefield, Oxford, 1899, pp. 46, 165: 'on manig theodisc' (in
many languages). I omit other meanings of the word. Cf. Krogmann, loc. cit.,
pp. 7 ff.

[3] As recent additions to the much discussed history of the word I may quote the
'gens Teudisca' mentioned by the famous Godescalc (G. Morin, 'Gottschalk re-
trouvé', *Rev. Bén.* xliii, 1931, p. 309); 'Teutonica Francia' in the second *Passio Kiliani* of
the late 9th century (*SS. rer. Merov.* v, p. 720, n. 8; p. 722, n. 3); the 'regnum Teuton-
icorum' in the *Annales Iuvavenses maximi*, 920 (ed. Bresslau, *MG. SS.* xxx, 2, p. 742).

[4] On George cf. Duchesne, *Liber Pontificalis*, i. 457 (n. 25), 482 (n. 30), 515 (n. 19);
Fastes épiscopaux, iii. 128 f.   [5] Duchesne, *Lib. Pontif.* i. 446.

[6] *Codex Carolinus* 8, 9, 11, 16–18 (*MG. Epist.* iii. 497, 500, 507, 514, 517 f.).

participated in the synod of Compiègne; his consent to several of the decrees is specially recorded.[1] He obviously became a favourite of the king, for in the sixties of that century Paul granted the latter, at his request, permission to keep the bishop of Ostia with him.[2] When the short-lived successor of Paul, Constantine II (767–8), withdrew this permission,[3] George nevertheless remained in France and was provided with the bishopric of Amiens. He was sent together with twelve Frankish bishops to take part in the Roman synod of 769, and while its acts call him bishop of Ostia, the list of the bishops in the 'Liber Pontificalis' (preserved in a French MS. of the ninth century, B[4] of Duchesne) styles him bishop of Amiens:[4] his twofold position is evident. Charles in 773 and about 782 used his services as an envoy to Pope Hadrian.[5] Alcuin, writing in 790 from England to Abbot Adalhard of Corbie (which is situated in the proximity of Amiens), requested him to remember him to 'his father' George.[6] The relation of the bishop of Ostia to the diocese of Amiens is also shown by his taking part in the consecration of the churches of the monastery of Saint-Riquier in the nineties.[7] His name occurs for the last time on the 23rd of October 798, when, as bishop of Ostia, he was among the members of a Roman synod;[8] in the following year another bishop occupied the see of Amiens. Thus the activities of George belonged to the Frankish kingdom as well as to Italy, and we may assume without hesitation that it was among the Franks that he had acquired the use of the term 'theodisc'. We need not refer it to Charles's envoy, Abbot Wigbod, who in 786 accompanied the two papal legates to England, nor to Alcuin, who joined them there and had previously been on the Continent.[9] George may have been regarded as specially suited for

---

[1] *MG. Capitularia*, i, pp. 38 f. George is said to have been also at a synod of Estinnes (ib. ii. 433; Migne, *P.L.* cxxvi. 142 = *MG. Concilia*, ii. 5); but the letters of Hincmar stating his participation are unreliable.

[2] *Cod. Carol.* 21, 37 (pp. 524, 549).   [3] Ib., no. 99 (p. 653).

[4] Duchesne, *Lib. Pontif.* i. 473; *MG. Concilia*, ii. 75, 80.

[5] Duchesne, *Lib. Pontif.* i. 494; *Cod. Carol.* 73 (p. 604).

[6] Alcuin, *Epist.* 9 (p. 35. 23).

[7] Angilbert, *MG. SS.* xv. 1, p. 174; also in Hariulf, *Chronique de l'abbaye de Saint-Riquier*, ed. F. Lot, 1894, p. 58.

[8] *MG. Concilia*, ii. 202.

[9] Cf. Dove, *Schriftchen*, pp. 329 ff. To Abbot Wigbod we are probably indebted for the preservation of the report. It is found in a Wolfenbüttel MS. of the 10th century (cf. above, p. 16, n. 3) amidst a collection of canon law, which also contains

a legation to England in view of the situation of his Amiens diocese.

In any case, as the report is a document significant of English and continental relations in the late eighth century, so this first example of the relevant use of 'theodisc', not yet a real proper name, requires to be considered. We do not know where the new meaning of the word originated. Some have thought of the circle of Charles, who united all German nations or tribes; but the word had obviously taken root before 786, and others therefore have preferred Boniface, to whom in his missionary work the German tribes must also have appeared as a unity, and who, with the Popes, often used the Roman conception of 'Germany'[1] and also included, like Aldhelm, the Anglo-Saxons among the German peoples.[2]

The word 'theodisc' arose from the point of view of the Latin tongue. The language called by the new name was the speech of the Germans as differing from Latin, the language of Church and learning, and from the Romance idioms derived from it, the 'sermo vulgaris'. Learned ecclesiastics familiar with Germanic dialects and probably of Germanic origin may have been the first to sum up all these dialects under the term 'theodisc'. Anglo-Saxon monks as well as King Charles were interested not only in Latin but also in their native tongues; a glimmer

a report on the Roman synod of 769 (*MG. Concilia*, ii. 78 f.) and had probably been compiled at Trier in the monastery of St. Maximin; cf. M. Sdralek, *Wolfenbüttler Fragmente* (Kirchengeschichtliche Studien i. 2), Münster, 1891, pp. 87 ff. Fournier and Le Bras, loc. cit. i. 304 f., similarly refer the collection to the Rhenish countries but suggest a Strasburg origin. Now there existed at St. Maximin's a manuscript written between 775 and 800 by order of King Charles 'ad opus suum', which contained a compilation of 'Quaestiones in Octateuchum' composed from the Fathers by Wigbod and dedicated to Charles. A part has been published by Martene and Durand, *Veterum script. et monum. ampliss. collectio*, ix, 1733, cols. 293–366 (= Migne, *P.L.* xcvi. 1101–68). The poetical preface (*MG. Poetae*, i. 95–7; cf. p. 88) is almost entirely a plagiarism from Avitus of Vienne and Eugenius of Toledo (cf. Peiper, *Auct. ant.* vi. 2, pp. lv–lviii, and *CSEL.* xxiii, pp. ii ff.; Vollmer, *Auct. ant.* xiv, pp. xxi, xliii, 27, 67, 69); cf. also H. Omont, *Notices et extraits des mss. de la Bibliothèque nationale*, xxxviii, 1903, pp. 358–61, on a kindred text from St. Maximin's. The facts pointing in both cases to this monastery make the identification of the compiler with the abbot of 786 very probable, as Dove, *Schriftchen*, p. 329, has perceived.

[1] Cf. Tangl's edition of Boniface's letters, pp. 291 and 294, s.v. 'Bonifatius' and 'Germania'.

[2] Aldhelm, *De metris*, c. 142 (ed. Ehwald, p. 202): 'neminem nostrae stirpis prosapia genitum et Germanicae gentis cunabulis confotum'; Boniface, Dedicatory letter to Sigebert (ed. Lehmann, loc. cit., p. 754, cf. p. 740; *MG. Epist.* iv. 565): 'me pene de extremis Germaniae gentibus ignobili stirpe (cf. above, p. 70) procreatum.

of more than 'half-realized national feeling' is embodied therein.[1]
When Bede discussed the Hebrew, Roman, and Greek names
of the months, he considered it incongruous to pass over in
silence the corresponding forms in his own language. He was
translating St. John's Gospel when he died; his Death Song,
with Caedmon's Hymn, is one of the earliest existing documents
in Anglo-Saxon, while all the vernacular poems of Aldhelm
have perished.[2] Charles the Great had similar aims. He gave
German names to the months and winds, caused poems on the
exploits and wars of ancient kings, only orally preserved up to
his time, to be written down, and even began a German grammar. German studies and a written German poetry originated
on the background of Latin learning; that was the soil from
which a word such as 'theodisc' sprang into existence, whether
Anglo-Saxons were connected with it or not.[3]

[1] Cf. V. H. Galbraith, 'Nationality and Language in Medieval England'
(*T.R.H.S.*, 4th series, xxiii, 1941, p. 119).

[2] An anonymous letter, no. 146 (p. 283) among those of Boniface and Lullus, has
preserved a 'Saxonicum verbum', an Anglo-Saxon proverb of four short-lines
(Sweet, *The Oldest English Texts*, pp. 151 f.; Grein and Wülker, *Bibliothek der Angelsächsischen Poesie*, ii, 1894, p. 315). The recipient of the letter, whose name is replaced by *N.* in the Vienna MS., was almost certainly a bishop, as the epithets
'Reverentissimo atque sanctissimo' suggest (cf. Bede, *H.E.* i. 24, 28, 29; Boniface,
Epist. nos. 7, 24, 26, 28, 45, 51, 57, 58, 60, 68, 77, 80, 87; *Liber Diurnus*, no. 1. 9,
p. 2, &c.); probably he was starting for missionary work, as may be inferred from
the quotation of Matt. ix. 37 (cf. Bede, *H.E.* i. 29; Willibald, *Vita Bonifatii*, cc. 5, 6,
pp. 24, 33; Alcuin, *Vita Willibrordi*, i. 5). If the recipient was in fact a bishop, the
writer, who was in the humbler position of a monk 'sub regula alterius', must have
been familiar with him, as the whole tenor of the document shows. He mentions
the poverty of his own and his companions' lives, 'nihil habentes nisi cotidiana sti-
pendia'. Tangl has compared these conditions with the 'paupercula vita' of Boniface's priests 'prope marcam paganorum' stated in *Epist.* 93 (p. 213) and had no
doubt that the writer of no. 146 was among these collaborators of the archbishop.
The sender calls himself 'ego minimus nomine latito'. 'Minimus' is a frequent
formula of humility (like 'exiguus', 'ultimus', &c.; cf. p. 284. 4: 'De me quid dicam
minimo?') suggested by 1 Cor. xv. 9; cf. Schmitz, loc. cit., p. 189, s. v. The word
'latito' means 'I hide myself', Anglo-Saxon 'hyde' (from 'hydan'). Did the writer
intend to conceal his name playfully by a Latin rendering? Was it Hiddi (Birch,
i, no. 37=Aldhelm, ed. Ehwald, p. 509; *Liber vitae Dunelmensis*, fol. 24, ed. Sweet,
loc. cit., p. 158), and are we justified in identifying the sender with Hiedde, a monk
of Fritzlar in Hesse, whom Boniface made 'praepositus' there, probably in 737/8
(*Epist.* 40, p. 65)? But 'hydde' is preterite, not present, and corresponds with
'latitavi', not 'latito'. Thus this attempt at an explanation remains daring and
doubtful, and 'latito' possibly is a misreading of the name, though I have not found
a satisfactory emendation. Or is 'latito', as has been suggested to me, the ablative
of the unusual passive participle of 'lateo', agreeing with 'nomine' (and rhyming
with 'Domino')?

[3] Cf. the conjectures of W. Braune on the influence of the Anglo-Saxon mis-

Here we have reached another field, in which their efforts had lasting influence and laid firm foundations, the sphere of learning and scholarship. The name of Alcuin, who has already been mentioned so often, bears witness to this fact.

sionaries upon the ecclesiastical vocabulary of Germany, 'Althochdeutsch und Angelsächsisch' (*Beiträge zur Geschichte der Deutschen Sprache und Literatur*, xliii, 1918, pp. 361–445).

LEARNING AND SCHOLARSHIP

A RELIGION, the sacred books of which were available only in a foreign language—Latin, the liturgy of which had to be performed in the same tongue, was necessarily based on some knowledge of this language and its literature, dominated and limited as the range and scope of its study might be by theological views. Let us remember to what a high level Latin scholarship rose in England during a few generations, what part Archbishop Theodore[1] and Abbot Hadrian of Canterbury had in this development, and what Irishmen also contributed to it, in Ireland itself, in Northumbria, or at Malmesbury. Continental tradition directly derived from Italy and Gaul blended with Irish tradition to bring forth the Anglo-Latin learning and literature of the late seventh and of the eighth centuries, as seen in the works of men such as Aldhelm, Bede, and Alcuin, who represented the schools of Malmesbury, Wearmouth–Jarrow, and York. The schools varied in the authors they studied, as is apparent from the different styles cultivated by Aldhelm, the 'discipulus Umbrensium' (p. 99), Guthlac of Crowland's biographer Felix (p. 262), and the Northumbrians. From the beginning of the Roman mission books were imported into England, at first for the proper needs of divine service and elementary religious instruction; in the second part of the seventh century libraries with a wider scope began to be established. Benedict Biscop and Ceolfrid laid the foundations of the libraries of Wearmouth and Jarrow. Benedict on his journeys to Rome acquired books in Italy and Gaul, 'an innumerable amount of books of every kind', as Bede says on one of these occasions.[2] Bishop Acca of Hexham between 710 and 731, to quote Bede again,[3] founded 'amplissimam ibi ac nobilissimam bibliothecam'. About the

[1] Paul Lehmann, 'Wert und Echtheit einer Beda abgesprochenen Schrift' (*SB. München*, 1919, no. 4), pp. 4 f., has called attention to an example of Theodore's exposition of the Scriptures. Cf. Baeseke, loc. cit. [cf. p. 136, n. 1], pp. 10 ff.

[2] *Hist. abb.* c. 6 (p. 369). When in the second part of the 7th century Abbess Bertila of Chelles was asked by kings of 'Saxony' to dispatch some disciples overseas for the foundation of monasteries, relics and 'many volumes of books' were sent with them (*Vita Bertilae*, c. 6, *SS. rer. Merov.* vi. 106 f.).

[3] Bede, *H.E.* v. 20.

same time, between 716 and 731, Bishop Cuthwine of Dunwich
collected precious illuminated manuscripts. He imported from
Rome a volume with many pictures, representing the 'passiones
sive labores' of St. Paul.[1] It is lost; but an illuminated manuscript of Sedulius's 'Carmen Paschale' at Antwerp (Museum
Plantin-Moretus no. 126, from St. James at Liége) has preserved
the subscription of the same lover of books: 'FINIT · FINES ·
FINES · CUĐUUINI'; it was copied in the early ninth century from

[1] Cf. L. Traube, 'Paläographische Anzeigen III' (*Neues Archiv*, xxvii, 1902,
pp. 276 ff.; Traube, *Vorles*. iii. 239 ff.); P. Lehmann, 'Wert und Echtheit einer Beda
abgesprochenen Schrift' (loc. cit.), pp. 6 ff. A. St. Cook, 'Bishop Cuthwini of
Leicester (680–691), amateur of illustrated MSS.' (*Speculum*, ii, 1927, pp. 253–7) has
tried to show that Bede in his *Liber quaestionum*, c. 2 (Migne, *P.L.* xciii. 456; emended
in Lehmann, p. 12) made a mistake in calling Cuthwine 'Orientalium Anglorum
antistes', and referred the statement about him to the first bishop (of the same
name) of the *Middle* Angles at Leicester. But the existence of this bishop is very
doubtful, though he has been admitted into Stubbs's *Registrum Sacrum Anglicanum*
(2nd ed., pp. 6, 224) and into Powicke's *Handbook of British Chronology*, 1939, p. 152.
Florence of Worcester reports in his Chronicle (ed. Petrie, p. 622) that Cuthwine
in 679 was made bishop of Lichfield by Theodore of Canterbury; in the episcopal
lists added to his work Cuthwine is the first bishop of Leicester, not of Lichfield (ib.,
pp. 623 f.). He is not mentioned in the lists of Cotton MS. Vespasian B. VI of 811–14
(Sweet, *The Oldest English Texts*, p. 168), which was a Lichfield MS. (K. Sisam,
'Cynewulf and his Poetry', *P.B.A.* xviii, 1932, p. 306), and of William of Malmesbury, *Gesta pontif*. iv. 172, 176 (ed. Hamilton, pp. 307 f., 311), and probably he owes
his origin to some confusion. On the other hand, the existence of the *East* Anglian
bishop of Dunwich is confirmed by his inclusion among the 'Nomina episcoporum
Orientalium Anglorum' in the early list of the Cotton MS. mentioned above, which
has not been used by Lehmann and Cook. The archetype, from which this text and
the lists of Florence (Petrie, p. 618) and of William of Malmesbury (loc. cit. ii. 74,
p. 148) derive, was evidently arranged, after the division of the East Anglian diocese,
in two columns, the left with the names of the bishops of Elmham, the right with
those of their colleagues of Dunwich; this bi-columnar list of the archetype ended
with Ethelwulf of Elmham (after 742, died between 781 and 785) and Ecglaf of
Dunwich (bishop in 742, died before 781). Bishop Cuthwine has there his place
between Heardred I who in 716 took part in the synod of Clovesho (H. and S. iii,
300; Birch, i, no. 91), and Aldberht who governed the diocese of Dunwich when
Bede in 731 finished his *H.E.* (v. 23, p. 350). In the signatures of early charters
giving the names of bishops but not of their sees, the contemporaneous bishops of
Elmham and Dunwich are often found following each other. There is not the least
reason to doubt Bede's authority in this case; the opinion of Lehmann is right, while
Cook went astray. On the *Liber quaestionum*, cf. also Laistner, *A Hand-List of Bede
Manuscripts*, Ithaca, 1943, pp. 155 ff., and the important contribution by H. Weis-
weiler, *Das Schrifttum der Schule Anselms von Laon und Wilhelms von Champeaux in
Deutschen Bibliotheken* (Beiträge zur Geschichte der Philosophie und Theologie des
Mittelalters, xxxiii. 1–2), Münster i. W. 1936, pp. 54–69: The chapters 1–8 come
in fact from Bede, but c. 9 from Isidore of Seville, 10–12 from Gregory the Great,
and cc. 13–15 are much later and connected with the studies of the early schoolmen
of the 12th century (cf. the texts, ib., pp. 281–354, so far as Q = Pseudo-Bede is
involved).

an 'insular' exemplar which itself was derived from an Italian manuscript.[1] The library of York Minster has been rendered famous by the verses in which Alcuin celebrated this centre of studies. There must have been many more collections of books, smaller and larger, than are rather casually mentioned in the scanty records. We hear incidentally, for instance, of two anonymous pilgrims to Rome who brought back with them 'volumina numerosa' (before 705).[2]

The imported texts were often copied and thus spread to other places. The Irish monks were industrious transcribers of manuscripts. Sulpicius Severus had told how St. Martin of Tours was always praying or reading; Adamnan of Iona adapted this statement to St. Columba, but he added writing as a third occupation.[3] The Englishmen similarly became diligent copyists, as, in spite of all losses, their existing manuscripts show, books some simple, others magnificent, with or without illuminations, manifesting Italian and Celtic influences. A precious manuscript of the Gospels written by order of Bishop Wilfrid of York for his monastery of Ripon was not only recorded in his Life but was also considered worthy to have a special mention in his epitaph.[4] A Northumbrian poem composed about a century after his death shows that the estimation of calligraphy had not diminished in the meantime.[5] The effect of such zeal may be gathered from the survey of Bede's library by Professor Laistner,[6] and from J. D. A. Ogilvy's list of 'Books known to Anglo-Latin writers from Aldhelm to Alcuin'.[7] I need only deal with the continental results.

---

[1] On the Antwerp MS. cf. also C. Caesar, *Rheinisches Museum*, lvi, 1901, pp. 247–71 (the name of Cuthwine, p. 264); W. Koehler in Paul Clemen, *Belgische Kunstdenkmäler*, i, Munich, 1923, pp. 7–11.

[2] Æthilwald, *Carmina rhythmica*, ii. 107 ff. (ed. Ehwald, *Auct. ant.* xv. 531).

[3] *Vita Martini*, c. 26. 3 (*CSEL.* i. 136); *Vita Columbae*, 2nd pref. (2nd ed. by Fowler, p. 87). I have mentioned this dependence and difference, 'Die Iren und die Fränkische Kirche' (*Historische Zeitschr.* cix, 1912, p. 19); cf. also G. Brüning, *Zeitschr. für Celtische Philologie*, xi, 1916, p. 248.

[4] Eddi, *Vita Wilfridi*, c. 17 (p. 212); Bede, *H.E.* v. 19 (p. 330).

[5] *Ædilvulfi Carmen*, c. 8, v. 5 and 45; c. 20, v. 40 (ed. Dümmler, *MG. Poetae*, i. 589 f., 599; ed. Arnold, *Symeonis Opera*, i. 274 f., 288).

[6] *Bede Essays*, pp. 237–66.

[7] *The Mediaeval Academy of America, Studies and Documents*, no. 2, Cambridge (Mass.), 1936. On the books known to Aldhelm cf. also M. R. James, *Two Ancient English Scholars: St. Aldhelm and William of Malmesbury* (Glasgow University Publications, xxii), 1931, pp. 12 ff.

Anglo-Saxon Script on the Continent

The migration of Englishmen overseas carried their books in its train. Moreover, Anglo-Saxons settled on the Continent continued to write in their usual characters; their peculiar script therefore, different as it was from the continental scripts, is found alongside of these in French and German libraries.[1] Among the Italian books imported into England were uncial biblical manuscripts, which were there copied and imitated; the Bibles written in Jarrow about 700 by order of Abbot Ceolfrid are a celebrated example. Some of these volumes found their way to the Continent, such as the 'Codex Amiatinus', which in 716 Ceolfrid took with him as a gift to St. Peter. But manuscripts in uncials taken from Italy to England, or imitated there, were exceptions; they were too magnificent and valuable to be produced very often, though uncial script was even employed for early Anglo-Saxon charters. The script which was the habitual hand of the Anglo-Saxons working on the Continent had another origin.

The Irish script was derived from the Roman half-uncial hand of Gaul; it developed its peculiar patterns in the insularity of Ireland and was introduced into England through the island monasteries of Iona and Lindisfarne and wherever the Irish monks settled among the English. The Roman party won the victory over the Irish in the English Church; but the Irish influence had been so powerful during a generation before 664, that the Irish script was adopted by the Anglo-Saxons and 'was destined to remain for centuries the national hand of England'.[2] It became the usual script of books and charters, so much so that formerly it was often difficult, and is so sometimes even now, to distinguish Irish from Anglo-Saxon script; modern scholars have given to these two scripts the common name of 'insular' writing to distinguish them from the continental scripts. The national trend of English civilization manifested itself by the gradual addition of two letters for *th* and of a third for *w*; two of them, *wyn* and *thorn*, were taken from the runic alphabet, which the immigrant Anglo-Saxons had brought with them overseas; but Latin texts did not offer many opportunities of

[1] Cf., e.g., Paul Lehmann, *Lateinische Paläographie* (Einleitung in die Altertumswissenschaft, ed. A. Gercke and E. Norden, i. 10), Leipzig, 1925, pp. 55 ff.; Fr. Steffens, *Lat. Paläographie*, 2nd ed., pp. xiv ff.   [2] Lowe, *Codices Lat. ant.* ii, p. x.

using these distinguishing letters. Irishmen imported their books
and script into the Frankish countries and Italy, and so did the
English: a continental insular script, to use this 'contradictio in
adiecto', was the result. The 'libri Scottice scripti', that is, the
manuscripts in Irish hands, which for example are specially
mentioned in a ninth-century catalogue of the St. Gall library,
also comprised Anglo-Saxon books, as the presence of works of
Bede under this heading suggests.[1] Manuscripts in English
hands (mostly in minuscule script) in the eighth and ninth
centuries could be found in churches and monasteries where
Englishmen had settled, or in houses connected with them, such
as Echternach, Fulda, Mainz, Lorsch, Amorbach,[2] Würzburg,
Salzburg, Corbie, and Tours. There were what has been called
islands of insular script, which had to maintain their existence
against the overwhelming prevalence of the indigenous handwriting, the more so since in the late eighth century the so-
called Carolingian minuscule emerged; in a struggle of some
centuries this new script conquered almost all the West to become the ancestor of all future occidental kinds of writing.
In the transitional period Anglo-Saxon influence in the continental 'scriptoria' led also to some blending of forms;[3] it can

---

[1] On Anglo-Saxons and Anglo-Saxon MSS. in St. Gall cf. K. Löffler, 'Die Sankt
Galler Schreibschule in der 2. Hälfte des 8. Jahrhunderts' (*Palaeographia Latina*, ed.
Lindsay, vi, 1929, pp. 12 f., 15 f., 17); Georg Baeseke, *Der Vocabularius Sti. Galli in
der angelsächsischen Mission*, Halle, 1933, p. 31. In the neighbouring monastery of
Reichenau, according to the Chronicle of Gallus Oehem (ed. K. Brandi, *Quellen und
Forschungen zur Geschichte der Abtei Reichenau*, ii, Heidelberg, 1893, pp. 41 f.; repeated
by A. Holder, *Die Handschriften der Grossherzoglich Badischen Hof- und Landesbibliothek
in Karlsruhe*, vii. 1, 1916, pp. 66 f., cf. vii. 2, p. 216, and by Th. Längin, *Die Kultur der
Abtei Reichenau*, ii, München, 1925, pp. 699 f., cf. pp. 647, 1148, 1161), two Anglo-
Saxons became monks, between 759 and 786 Ethelfrid ('Edefridus'), between 786
and 806 a former bishop Heardric ('Hartrichus'), who perhaps had previously
joined the monastery of Maursmünster in Alsatia (*MG. Libri confraternitatum*, ed.
Piper, p. 246, col. 314. 5: 'Hartricus episcopus'; cf. *MG. Epist.* iv. 529, n. 5). The
former left several books written by himself in the Saxon tongue ('ettliche bücher
von im in Saxischer zungen geschriben'—probably a mistake by Oehem for 'Saxon
script'); the latter brought many books with him.

[2] The monastery of Amorbach was not founded in the late 10th century, as F. J.
Bendel has tried to show and E. Hennecke, *Zeitschr. für Kirchengeschichte*, liv, 1935,
pp. 77 f., has accepted, but existed at least as early as the middle of the 9th century
(P. Kehr, *MG. Die Urkunden der Deutschen Karolinger*, i. 1932–4, p. 73, no. 54) and
probably in the 8th century. Cf. also A. Brackmann, *Germania pontificia*, iii. 175. On
the library cf. P. Lehmann, *Studien und Mitteilungen zur Geschichte des Benediktiner-
Ordens*, xlviii, 1930, pp. 264–300.

[3] Cf., e.g., P. Lehmann, *Aufgaben und Anregungen der lateinischen Philologie des Mittelalters* (SB. München, 1918, no. 8), pp. 10 ff.

even be recognized later in the survival of insular abbreviations or in the misreading of certain insular letters.[1] But the
period of Anglo-Saxon immigration ended in the early ninth
century, and so the use and teaching of Anglo-Saxon script
ceased on the Continent and gave way to the Carolingian
minuscule.

Two examples may show the introduction of English usage
overseas and its withdrawal before the mighty continental
current. A manuscript in the Cathedral Library of Cologne
(no. CVI), containing writings of Alcuin and Bede, was written
there about 805 by seven scribes; one used, according to the
subtle statement of a modern scholar, 'an Irish hand trained in
an English scriptorium', another an Anglo-Saxon hand, but
five transcribers employed continental script.[2] The oldest existing cartulary of Fulda was written about 828 in an Anglo-Saxon
hand, but additions were made during the same century in
Carolingian script;[3] about the middle of this century the continental handwriting prevailed even near the tomb of St.
Boniface. The use of Anglo-Saxon script on the Continent was
an expression of Anglo-Saxon expansion and influence; the
cessation of the migration brought it to an end. In the tenth
century, in connexion with the monastic reform, the Carolingian
minuscule made its appearance in England;[4] the juxtaposition
of the two scripts, their influence upon each other, and their
rivalry occurred a second time. Once more the continental
script won the victory, though a peculiar English development
of the survivor was the result.

The English missionaries not only took their habitual script

---

[1] Cf., e.g., Traube, 'Die Ueberlieferung des Ammianus Marcellinus' (*Mélanges
Boissier*, Paris, 1903, pp. 443–8; Traube, *Vorles.* iii. 33–8).

[2] Leslie Webber Jones, *The Script of Cologne from Hildebald to Hermann* (The
Mediaeval Academy of America, Publication No. 10), Cambridge (Mass.),
1932, pp. 40–3 and pls. 31–45; W. Arndt, *Schrifttafeln*, 4th ed. by M. Tangl,
ii, 1906, pls. 39, 40, 44–7. For other examples of Anglo-Saxon hand employed
side by side with continental script see Lowe, *Codices Lat. ant.* ii, no. 196 *a, b*; iii,
no. 297 *a, b*.

[3] Cf. E. Heydenreich, *Das älteste Fuldaer Cartular im Staatsarchive zu Marburg*,
Leipzig, 1899; Steffens, loc. cit., 2nd ed., pl. 54 *a*. Cf. Stengel, 'Fuldensia II'
(*Archiv f. Urk.* vii, 1921, pp. 1 ff.). On another example from Fulda cf. Paul Lehmann, 'Quot et quorum libri fuerint in libraria Fuldensi' (*Bok- och Bibliotekshisto-
riska Studier tillägnade Isak Collijn*, Uppsala, 1925, pp. 51 ff.).

[4] Cf. A. Hessel, 'Studien zur Ausbreitung der karolingischen Minuskel' (*Archiv
f. Urk.* viii, 1923, pp. 16–20).

across the sea; the Fulda tradition of the ninth century also attributed to St. Boniface the importation of cryptographic puzzles, which enjoyed some popularity in the Middle Ages.[1] The ancient Greeks and Romans had already used particular methods for concealing the meaning of a written text to un-initiated people; for example, as Suetonius tells us, Augustus substituted the next letter of the alphabet for the letter intended, Julius Caesar the third following letter. In the Middle Ages two similar but simpler methods were often employed to disguise the name of a writer or a few other words. The five vowels only were replaced either by the next consonants (e.g. *a* by *b*, *u* by *x*) or by a series of one to five dots; both methods were also sometimes combined. One of the ablest disciples of Alcuin, Hrabanus Maurus, whose life (*c.* 784–856) was connected with Fulda and Mainz, is credited with a little treatise on the in-vention of letters; there he attributed the origin of the two cryptographic systems to the 'ancients', but he referred to the tradition that Boniface had taught these methods of writing to the predecessors of the author, and there is every probability that the tradition was well founded, and that Anglo-Saxons in fact carried these devices to Germany or at least diffused them there. The early English taste (shared by Boniface) for riddles, for hiding the answers to these or the dedicatory verses of an intricate poem in acrostics or in the middle of the poem, may be compared with these cryptographic puzzles. The Vienna MS. of the correspondence of Boniface and Lullus has also preserved some examples of a special alphabetical system; it was derived, as Tangl has shown,[2] partly from Greek letters and partly from runes, which themselves were employed for the same purpose by others.[3] This use of 'secret' script is more of antiquarian than of historical interest; but unimportant as it may be, it remains a sign of the continental Anglo-Saxon in-fluence. We do not know whether the knowledge of it was derived directly from Italy or from Ireland. In a Munich MS. (from Augsburg) the two 'varieties' employed by Boniface are combined with a third trick which reminded Lindsay of the

[1] Cf. Appendix VIII, pp. 290 ff.

[2] *Neues Archiv*, xl. 723–31.

[3] Cf., e.g., Fr. Tupper, *The Riddles of the Exeter Book*, Boston, 1910, p. lxxix. The name of Cynewulf is written in runic letters in the Exeter and Vercelli Books; cf. K. Sisam, 'Cynewulf and his Poetry' (loc. cit., pp. 315 ff.).

Ogham-script of the Irish,[1] who occasionally used this script as a kind of cryptography.[2]

Books and Libraries

The appearance of Anglo-Saxon script on the Continent indicates that the English emigrants transferred thither the studies developed in their native country. Another symptom was the continuous importation of books. Libraries were established in their new homes, books being acquired from England as well as from Gaul and Italy, and their number was multiplied and texts disseminated by transcribing exemplars. When, for instance, the Northumbrian Willehad was forced by the insurrection of the Saxons to leave his missionary field and, from 783 to 785, was living at Echternach (p. 110), he used his involuntary leisure to copy the Epistles of St. Paul 'aliaque quam plurima'.[3] Questions arose in missionary practice itself, for which a solution was sought in earlier writings. Boniface asked a Roman deacon for letters of Pope Gregory the Great; on another occasion to solve a problem of marriage law he tried in vain to obtain from Rome the questions of Augustine of Canterbury with the answers of Gregory, and he applied for the same text to Archbishop Nothelm of Canterbury. Later he was able to send Egbert of York a copy of letters of the Pope, which he had transcribed at Rome.[4] Books were sent him as presents by English friends, such as Abbess Eadburg of Thanet or Archbishop Egbert,[5] and he himself asked for others, for Passions of the martyrs, a magnificent copy of the letters of St. Peter (p. 94), a manuscript of the Prophets suited to his failing

---

[1] W. M. Lindsay, *Early Irish Minuscule Script* (St. Andrews University Publications, no. VI), Oxford, 1910, p. 46, n. *n*; cf. A. Meister, *Die Anfänge der modernen diplomatischen Geheimschrift*, pp. 7 f. The MS. in question, Munich Lat. No. 4115 (formerly Cim. IV. 3. g), a copy of the *Lex Ribuaria, Alamannorum*, and *Salica* written about 800, did not come from Fulda, as A. Holder has conjectured and Lindsay repeated. Cf. B. Krusch, *Die Lex Bajuvariorum*, Berlin, 1924, p. 316, n. 4; Karl Christ, *Die Bibliothek des Klosters Fulda im 16. Jahrhundert* (64. Beiheft zum Zentralblatt für Bibliothekswesen), Leipzig, 1933, p. 247.

[2] Cf., e.g., Traube, *Vorles.* i. 4 f.; Steffens, loc. cit., pl. 50.

[3] *Vita Willehadi*, c. 7 (*MG. SS.* ii. 382; *Acta SS. Nov.* iii. 845).

[4] Boniface, *Epist.* 54, 33, 75 (pp. 96, 57, 158). Cf. E. Posner, 'Das Register Gregors I.' (*Neues Archiv*, xliii, 1922, pp. 251 ff., 285 ff.). On books imported from England by Boniface and Lullus cf. Baeseke, loc. cit., pp. 83 ff.

[5] Boniface, *Epist.* 30, 35, 75 (pp. 54, 60, 157).

eyesight, treatises on St. Paul;[1] the letters of Lullus contain similar requests.[2] When Boniface left England, Bede was unknown to him, nor had he seen his *Ecclesiastical History* when, in 735, he inquired about the answers of Pope Gregory and about the date of the arrival of his emissaries,[3] both to be found in this work. But the fame of Bede reached him in his later years; in the forties he requested Egbert of York and Abbot Hwætbert of Wearmouth and Jarrow to provide him with some treatises of Bede, that new light shining in the province of York. Egbert complied with these wishes, and Boniface asked him later for other writings of Bede, particularly for those which were useful to a preacher.[4] Lullus expressed similar wishes about writings of Aldhelm;[5] but he also sent presents to the tomb of Bede, in return for which Abbot Cuthbert, Hwætbert's successor, sent him Bede's two books on St. Cuthbert; he would have provided more, had not the cold winter hampered the hand of the scribe. Meanwhile Lullus acquired the *Ecclesiastical History*, which contains at the end a short autobiography of Bede with a list of his writings; Lullus quoted this list, when he wanted to have other works of Bede, and at least one more of these writings reached Mainz.[6]

The English emigrants not only relied on their native country for the enrichment of their libraries, but naturally also took advantage of continental opportunities. Boniface had been living overseas for almost twenty-five years, when we find him acquainted with books no trace of which can be found up to his time in England, with the Sermons of Caesarius of Arles[7]

---

[1] Boniface, *Epist.* 15, 35, 34, 63 (pp. 27, 60, 59, 131).

[2] Ib., nos. 124, 142; cf. no. 145 (pp. 261, 282 f.).

[3] Ib., no. 33 (pp. 57 f.).   [4] Ib., nos. 75, 76, 91 (pp. 158 f., 207).

[5] Ib., no. 71 (p. 144).

[6] Ib., no. 116 and (quoting from Bede, *H.E.* v. 24), nos. 125, 126 (pp. 251, 263. 9–12, 264. 9–11). In the same way about the middle of the 9th century Bede's list was copied in the monastery of Murbach to record his works in the catalogue of the library, those which were found there as well as those which the monastery was yet unable to acquire; cf. H. Bloch, *Strassburger Festschrift zur XLVI. Versammlung Deutscher Philologen und Schulmänner*, Strasburg, 1901, pp. 267 f., cf. 281.

[7] According to Laistner, 'Was Bede the author of a Penitential?' (loc. cit., pp. 272 f.), Caesarius's Sermons were not included in the English libraries in the 7th, 8th, and perhaps even in the 9th centuries (but cf. below, p. 299, n. 4). Boniface in 742 (*Epist.* 50, p. 85) quoted *Sermo* no. 54. 5 (ed. Morin, p. 229. 2–7) and about the same time or later (*Epist.* 104, p. 228; cf. below, p. 284) *Sermo* no. 29. 1 (p. 120), both under the name of St. Augustine, to whom many Sermons of Caesarius were ascribed.

and the *Historia Tripartita* compiled on the instructions of Cassiodorus.[1] Friends in England began to ask for books not available at home; Bishop Cyneheard of Winchester requested Lullus, if he should find ancient books unknown to him, particularly books of secular science such as medicine, to let him have a share of these.[2] But, on the whole, during the eighth century the libraries of England were one of the main sources from which the continental Englishmen and their associates drew their copies.[3] When the Frisian Liudger, after studying with Alcuin at York, returned to Utrecht about 773, he took with him 'copiam librorum'.[4] Alcuin, when at Tours, missed the exquisite books which had been at his disposal at York, and asked King Charles for permission to send thither some 'pueri' to bring back such flowers of Britain.[5]

Italian texts found their way to Germany and France not only directly but often by way of England. The calendar of Willibrord, which I have occasionally mentioned, was early bound up with the Echternach copy of the so-called 'Martyrologium Hieronymianum', a copy written in Anglo-Saxon script by Willibrord's Presbyter Laurentius. The Martyrology itself was the foundation of all later similar Western calendar lists of martyrs and other saints; it is a compilation which developed gradually and about 600 produced in eastern Gaul the archetype on which all existing manuscripts are based. The controversial question does not concern us, whether this archetype was written in St. Columbanus's monastery of Luxeuil after his death (615) or a few years earlier in Auxerre, nor do the manuscripts which were derived from this archetype in Gaul interest us here. But another copy went to Northumbria during the seventh century;

---

[1] Bede, *In Marcum*, ii, c. vi. 29 (Migne, *P.L.* xcii. 190 f.) relied on Rufinus, *Hist. eccl.* xi. 27, 28 (ed. Mommsen, pp. 1033f.), not on Cassiodorus's *Historia Tripartita*, vi. 15, ix. 27, 28, as Laistner has stated (*Bede Essays*, pp. 245, 264); cf. Bede's *Chronica maiora*, §§ 436, 490 (*Auct. ant.* xiii. 297, 304) and *Martyrology* (Quentin, loc. cit., p. 108, where the Chronicle of Marcellinus Comes 453, *Auct. ant.* xi. 84 f., is to be substituted for Dionysius Exiguus; cf. Quentin, p. 693). Nor have I been able to find that Bede made any other use of the *Hist. Trip.* (*Bede Essays*, p. 133). Boniface employed this work about 745 in *Epist.* 63; cf. below, p. 283.

[2] Boniface, *Epist.* 114 (pp. 246 f.).

[3] Cf. also E. Lesne, *Histoire de la propriété ecclésiastique en France*, iv (Mémoires et travaux publiés par des professeurs des Facultés catholiques de Lille, xlvi), Lille, 1938, pp. 56 ff.; Baeseke, loc. cit., passim.

[4] Altfrid, *Vita Liudgeri*, i. 12 (*MG. SS.* ii. 408; ed. Diekamp, p. 17).

[5] Alcuin *Epist.* 121; cf. no. 309 (pp. 177. 4, 474. 24).

the Echternach transcript of Laurentius and an extract written in Wales in the eleventh century[1] descend from it, and Bede also used a similar copy.[2] The Northumbrian origin of this text is shown by entries on Northumbrian saints; but what is of importance in this connexion is the fact that there are additions on saints of Campania and some other places of southern Italy in the Epternacensis (including Willibrord's calendar) as well as in the kindred Welsh epitome.[3] Links with south Italy are also manifest in other manuscripts of northern England and of continental Anglo-Saxons.[4] Three copies of the Gospels of the Northumbrian type contain a list of lessons for feasts at Naples: the Lindisfarne Gospels of about 700 (Cotton MS. Nero D. IV), a Royal MS. of the British Museum (i. B. VII) of the eighth century, and the so-called Burchard Gospels of Würzburg. The 'Codex Amiatinus' written about 700 in Wearmouth or Jarrow is commonly connected with a biblical text of Cassiodorus, whose monastery was situated in the southernmost part of Italy. Lastly, the Echternach Gospels (Paris 9389) have at the end a note obviously copied from an ancestral manuscript, to the effect that it was corrected in 558 from a book in the library of Abbot Eugippius, the biographer of St. Severinus, living near Naples. The 'Codex Bonifatianus' no. 1 of Fulda, a Gospel Harmony, was written in uncials by order of Bishop Victor of Capua and read by him in 546 and 547. Later it was taken to the north and glossed by an Irishman; then it was owned by Boniface to become one of the treasures of Fulda.[5] Another example of more complicated wanderings is the

---

[1] H. Delehaye, 'Martyrologium Hieronymianum Cambrense' (*Anal. Boll.* xxxii, 1913, pp. 369–407); H. J. Lawlor, *The Psalter and Martyrology of Ricemarch*, i (H. Br. Soc. xlvii), 1914, pp. 1–28, cf. pp. xxv ff.   [2] Quentin, loc. cit., p. 109.

[3] Cf. L. Duchesne, *Acta SS. Novembris*, ii. 1, 1894, p. [ix], to be checked by the edition and commentary of the *Martyr. Hieron.* published by Quentin and Delehaye, ib. ii. 2, 1931; Delehaye, *Anal. Boll.* xxxii. 374 f.; H. A. Wilson, 'The Calendar of St. Willibrord' (loc. cit.), pp. xx f.; P. Siffrin, 'Zwei Blätter eines Sakramentars in irischer [rather Anglo-Saxon] Schrift des 8. Jahrh. aus Regensburg' (*Jahrbuch für Liturgiewissenschaft*, x, 1930, pp. 22 ff.), and 'Das Walderdorffer Kalenderfragment saec. VIII und die Berliner Blätter eines Sakramentars aus Regensburg' (*Ephemerides Liturgicae*, xlvii, 1933, pp. 216 ff., 221 f.). Some of the names are also found in the marble calendar of Naples of the 9th century (ed. Delehaye, *Anal. Boll.* lvii, 1939, pp. 5 ff.).

[4] E. A. Lowe, *Codices Lat. ant.* ii, pp. xiv f. (cf. p. 27, no. 213); Baeseke, loc. cit., p. 89. Of earlier authors I may mention John Chapman, *Notes on the Early History of the Vulgate Gospels*, Cambridge, 1908, pp. 1 ff.

[5] Literature in Traube, *Vorles.* i. 185 f. Cf., e.g., Carl Scherer, 'Die Codices

'Codex Laudianus' of the Acts of the Apostles in Oxford.[1] It was in all likelihood written in Sardinia in sixth-century uncials and was probably afterwards acquired for Wearmouth and Jarrow, where Bede seems to have used it. But it soon passed to Hornbach in the Palatinate, one of the monasteries founded by Pirmin (cf. pp. 78 f.). It remained there only for a short time; for probably from the eighth century onwards it belonged to the cathedral of Würzburg, the first bishop of which was Burchard, the Anglo-Saxon disciple of Boniface. These examples, taken only from biblical manuscripts, however they are to be combined and explained,[2] illustrate how Anglo-Saxons and England contributed to bring about the wanderings of books in this early age. Let us realize once more the countries and places mentioned in this connexion: Campania with Naples and Capua and southern Italy in general, Northumbria with Lindisfarne and Wearmouth–Jarrow, Echternach, Würzburg, and Fulda—the English settlements on the Continent were importing centres, England a transit country for Italian texts, though other books were taken directly from Italy to houses in Germany and Gaul that were English or were under English influence.[3]

Nor does this statement apply only to biblical and theological books; it is valid for a large part of ancient Latin literature, pagan and Christian, for the preservation of which posterity is indebted to Anglo-Saxon scholars and their continental pupils.[4]

Bonifatiani', *Festgabe zum Bonifatius-Jubiläum*, Fulda, 1905, pp. 6–12; Baeseke, loc. cit., pp. 90 f.

[1] Cf. Lowe, 'An Eighth-century List of Books in a Bodleian MS. from Würzburg' (*Speculum*, iii, 1928, pp. 12 ff.), and *Codices Lat. ant.* ii, no. 251; Laistner, 'The Latin Versions of Acts known to the Venerable Bede' (*Harvard Theological Review*, xxx, 1937, pp. 43 ff.), and his edition of *Bedae Venerabilis Expositio Actuum Apostolorum*, Cambridge (Mass.), 1939, pp. xxxix f.

[2] Abbot Hadrian of Canterbury, coming from the proximity of Naples, and Benedict Biscop and Ceolfrid of Wearmouth–Jarrow have been mentioned in this connexion. There may have been other possibilities.

[3] When Gregory, the later abbot of Utrecht, accompanied his master Boniface to Rome, he acquired there several volumes of the Scriptures and took them to Germany; see Liudger's *Vita Gregorii*, c. 8 (*MG. SS.* xv. 1, p. 73). Before his death (775?) he distributed books among his disciples, giving Liudger Augustine's *Enchiridion* (ib., c. 14, p. 78).

[4] Cf. Traube, 'Paläographische Anzeigen III' (*Neues Archiv*, xxvii, 1902, pp. 265 ff.; Traube, *Vorles.* iii. 230 ff.); P. Lehmann, 'Fulda und die antike Literatur (in *Aus Fuldas Geistesleben, Festschrift . . . der Landesbibliothek Fulda*, ed. J. Theele, Fulda, 1928, pp. 9–23), and 'Deutschland und die mittelalterliche Ueberlieferung der Antike' (in *Zeitschr. für Deutsche Geistesgeschichte*, i, Salzburg, 1935, pp. 65–74, 136–48).

Manuscripts copied from English exemplars bear witness to this fact, as has been more and more recognized since the advance of palaeographical science has made it possible to distinguish English 'symptoms' in derived copies. Let us consider again a few examples. The minor works of Tacitus have been preserved only in a ninth-century manuscript belonging to Hersfeld, the monastic foundation of Bishop Lullus (several leaves of it were rediscovered in an Italian library about fifty years ago); the *Germania* of Tacitus was known in the ninth century in Fulda also, as were the first books of his *Annales*.[1] What exists of the histories of one of the best successors of Tacitus in the fourth century, Ammianus Marcellinus, comes from the same Anglo-Saxon foundations, Hersfeld and Fulda.[2] The tradition of Suetonius's 'Caesares' seems to be derived from a lost copy which was at Fulda in the ninth century.[3] I have mentioned the old Vienna MS. of Livy, which alone has preserved half his fifth decade, and which belonged to a bishop of Duurstede near Utrecht in the eighth century (above, p. 62); we are here at least in the sphere of Willibrord, Gregory, and Liudger.[4] One of the two existing early copies of Columella's *De re rustica* (in Milan) was written by an Anglo-Saxon hand of the first part of the ninth century, probably in Fulda.[5] The tradition of the poet Lucretius to some extent also shows Anglo-Saxon symptoms; the Leiden MS. came from Mainz. Vitruvius's work on architecture found its way from Italy to the Frankish kingdom, at any rate in part, through England.

Lastly I quote a letter which Bishop Milret of Worcester sent to Lullus after the death of Boniface (754); a copy exists in the Vienna MS. of the correspondence. There is a postscript:

[1] The works of Tacitus were unknown in medieval England. The archetype from which the copies of Hersfeld and Fulda were derived was possibly an Irish exemplar. Cf. Weisgerber, loc. cit. (p. 127, n. 1), pp. 119 ff.

[2] R. P. Robinson, 'The Hersfeldensis and the Fuldensis of Ammianus Marcellinus' (*The University of Missouri Studies*, xi, 1936, pp. 118–40), tries to prove that the Fuldensis derives from the Hersfeldensis. He accepts the opinion that the text is based on insular tradition; this alone concerns us here.

[3] The different view of E. K. Rand, 'On the History of the De vita Caesarum of Suetonius in the Early Middle Ages' (*Harvard Studies in Classical Philology* xxxvii, 1926, pp. 1–48), has not convinced Lehmann, loc. cit., pp. 16 f. and 137, nor myself.

[4] Cf. P. Lehmann, 'Das älteste Bücherverzeichnis der Niederlande' (loc. cit., pp. 210 ff.).

[5] Steffens, loc. cit., pl. 54 b. Cf. Lehmann, 'Fulda und die antike Literatur', loc. cit., pp. 13, 22; Christ, loc. cit., p. 214.

'Librum pyrpyri metri ideo non misi, quia Gutbertus episcopus adhuc reddere distulit.'[1] Lullus desired to have a book (or a copy of it) which Archbishop Cuthbert of Canterbury (740–60) had borrowed from Worcester. 'Librum pyrpyri metri': either the writer of the letter or the transcriber of the unique manuscript has misspelt the title. But E. Kylie has restored it correctly:[2] 'Librum Porfyri metri', that is, the poems of the fourth-century author Optatianus Porfyrius, whose artificial, even absurd picture poems, directly or indirectly, were a favourite object of imitation and served to exercise the ingenuity of readers in the Middle Ages.[3] Bede knew his writings.[4] Boniface imitated them in the picture poem at the beginning of his 'Grammar', composed before he left England.[5] Lullus also attempted these devices, as the description of a poem in one of his letters makes evident.[6] An English copy of his model actually reached the Continent. In the library of the monastery of Lorsch near Mainz, which owned other Anglo-Saxon manuscripts, 'metrum Porfilii' existed in the early ninth century.[7] Fulda also had a transcript of these strange poems;[8] they were there imitated by Hrabanus Maurus, more than by any other writer, not to mention further authors. The part of England in transmitting these ingenious trifles of the late Empire is obvious; Alcuin and his Irish pupil Joseph also produced 'poetry' of this sort.[9]

These examples may suffice to show the role of early England as a country of transit of ancient literature. Even a Spanish work of the late seventh century, the 'Grammar' of Archbishop Julian of Toledo, compiled a few years before his death (690),

---

[1] Boniface, *Epist.* 112 (p. 245).

[2] Edward Kylie, *The English Correspondence of Saint Boniface*, London, 1911, p. 209. Cf. Ogilvy, loc. cit., p. 74; Baeseke, loc. cit., p. 85.

[3] I refer to the edition of Elsa Kluge, Leipzig, 1926, and to her article, 'Studien zu Publilius Optatianus Porfyrius' (*Münchener Museum für Philologie des Mittelalters*, iv, 1924, pp. 323–48). In the 7th century Ansebert of St.-Wandrille composed a poem of this kind (*SS. rer. Merov.* v. 541 f.), not to speak of Ennodius and Fortunatus.

[4] *De arte metrica*, ed. Keil, *Grammatici Latini*, vii. 258. Cf. also Aldhelm, *Aenigmata*, pref., and *Carmen de virginitate*, pref. (ed. Ehwald, pp. 97–9, 350–2).

[5] *MG. Poetae*, i. 16 f. Boniface gave a description of this poem in his letter to Sigebert; cf. above, p. 70, n. 1.   [6] Boniface, *Epist.* 98 (pp. 220 f.).

[7] Gustav Becker, *Catalogi bibliothecarum antiqui*, Bonn, 1885, pp. 110 (no. 422), 123 (no. 78). On the date of the Lorsch catalogues cf. Lindsay, *Palaeographia Latina*, iii, 1924, p. 10. On Anglo-Saxon MSS. at Lorsch cf., e.g., ib., pp. 30–3.

[8] Christ, loc. cit., p. 122, no. 282; cf. p. 202.

[9] Alcuin, *Carm.*, nos. 6, 7 (*MG. Poetae*, i. 224–7); Joseph, *Carm.*, nos. 3–6 (ib., pp. 152–9).

seems to have taken the same route to France and Germany. It was probably known to Aldhelm and Bede, and all the manuscripts of this work which exist to-day are derived from an 'insular' archetype.[1] How much the continental libraries were indebted to Anglo-Saxons is also manifest from the number of Anglo-Latin writings of this age which perished in England itself in the period of Viking devastations, but survived overseas. The emigrants desired to read 'modern' works of their compatriots; we have heard how eager Boniface and Lullus were to acquire writings of Bede. Cuthbert's letter on the death of Bede was also sent to the Continent and was disseminated there at an early time.[2] Similarly other literary compositions of Englishmen followed their fellow countrymen to Germany and France. The first Life of St. Cuthbert, written about 700 at Lindisfarne, exists to-day in seven manuscripts, all either written or preserved on the Continent.[3] The earliest Life of Pope Gregory the Great, composed about the same time at Whitby,[4] has been saved in a single copy at St. Gall. Bede's Martyrology survived in continental transcripts; the earliest existing Anglo-Saxon calendars were also preserved overseas.[5] The rhythmical

---

[1] C. H. Beeson, 'The ars grammatica of Julian of Toledo' (*Miscellanea Francesco Ehrle*, i = *Studi e Testi*, xxxvii, 1924, pp. 50–70). Cf. also Christ, loc. cit., p. 198; Baeseke, loc. cit., p. 109.

[2] Cf. Dobbie, loc. cit., pp. 49 ff. and Ker; above, p. 42, n. 4. See also R. Brotanek, *Anglia*, lxiv, 1940, pp. 159 ff.

[3] B. Colgrave, *Two Lives of Saint Cuthbert*, pp. 17 ff. The 'Sacramentarium Fuldense saeculi X' (Göttingen, Cod. Theol. 231), c. 41 (ed. Gr. Richter and A. Schönfelder, *Quellen und Abhandlungen zur Geschichte der Abtei und der Diözese Fulda*, ix, Fulda, 1912, p. 31), contains a mass of St. Cuthbert, the same as that found in England about the middle of the 11th century in 'the Missal of Robert of Jumièges' (ed. H. A. Wilson, H. Br. Soc. xi, 1896, pp. 166 f.; also in F. E. Warren, *The Leofric Missal*, Oxford, 1883, p. 284, cf. ib., pp. 205 f., 308). Fulda in 819 owned relics of St. Cuthbert (*MG. Poetae*, ii. 208); his Lives by Bede existed there in the 16th-century library (Christ, loc. cit., pp. 143, 257 f., 301; Colgrave, p. 39).

[4] Cf. above, p. 8, n. 4.

[5] Besides the calendar of Willibrord from Echternach (above, p. 54, n. 1), there are two 8th-century fragments of Anglo-Saxon calendars, which were early imported into Bavaria and were recently discovered there. One fragment (July–October), belonging to Count Walderdorff at Regensburg, has been published by P. Siffrin, loc. cit. (cf. p. 142, n. 3), pp. 201–24; cf. the Bavarian entries in F. L. Baumann, *MG. Necrologia*, iii. 369 (with two plates) and Krusch, *SS. rer. Merov.* iv. 454. The other fragment (3 May to 24 June) was found in the Bavarian Record Office at Munich ('Raritätenselect', No. 108) and has been edited by R. Bauerreiß, 'Ein angelsächsisches Kalendarfragment des bayrischen Hauptstaatsarchivs in München' (*Studien und Mitteilungen zur Geschichte des Benediktiner-Ordens*, li, 1933, pp. 177–82, extracts in Baumann, loc. cit., pp. 103 f., 534; there are some wrong interpretations

poems of Æthilwald would have perished but for the copy in the Vienna MS. of the correspondence of Boniface and Lullus, which comes from Mainz. The Grammar of Boniface, though written in England, is found in a Vatican MS. from Lorsch and in another Carolingian transcript at Paris.[1] Alcuin's great poem on York was published from two copies in Rheims, one of which was recently rediscovered there.[2] His pupils at York sent him new poems on the Miracles of St. Ninian of Whithorn; they were believed to be lost but were found some years ago in a Bamberg MS., which contains the copy of a 'florilegium' collected by Alcuin.[3] Probably more early English writings would have survived if the Fulda library had not been dispersed and the greater part lost. Even in the sixteenth century they had there the 'Ymnarius Edilwaldi', most likely composed by the bishop of Lindisfarne of this name (721–40) and possibly one of the sources of the so-called Book of Cerne; it appears no longer to exist.[4] These examples show the eagerness of the Anglo-Saxons on the Continent to remain in contact with the intellectual achievements of their native country and to bring their own libraries up to date.

It would be absurd to attribute to their influence the whole development of French and German libraries in the eighth and early ninth centuries. Besides importing many manuscripts, Anglo-Saxons brought with them the conviction of the usefulness of books for ecclesiastical education and a pride in the possession of beautiful volumes; they instilled new life into the rudiments of libraries saved from former days, and set a current in motion which spread everywhere in the time of Charles the Great, who

in both editions). It comes evidently from Northumbria (after 729, death of King Osric) and seems to have belonged to the monastery of either Tegernsee or Ilm-münster, as later entries show. A calendar of the 9th century from Lorsch, which afterwards was in the monastery of St. Maximin at Trier, now Berlin MS. Lat. no. 131 (Phillipps MS. no. 1869), is based on a Northumbrian calendar of the late 8th century (after 780, death of Archbishop Ælbert of York); cf. V. Rose, *Verzeichniss der Lateinischen Handschriften der Königlichen Bibliothek zu Berlin*, i. 1893, pp. 293 ff.; M. Manitius, *Neues Archiv*, xxii, 1897, pp. 763–7; P. Miesges, *Der Trierer Festkalender* (Trierisches Archiv, Ergänzungsheft xv), Dissertation of Bonn, 1915, p. 8.

[1] Above, p. 70, n. 1. The picture poem belonging to the 'Grammar' of St. Boniface has survived in a Würzburg MS. On this work, mentioned in a Würzburg list of books in an Anglo-Saxon hand of about 800, see Lowe, *Speculum*, iii, 1928, p. 9.

[2] MS. No. 426 (E. 335) of the 9th century, from St. Thierry. Cf. H. Loriquet, *Catalogue général des mss., Départements*, xxxviii, 1904, p. 568.

[3] Cf. above, p. 34, n. 4.

[4] See Appendix ix, p. 295.

encouraged the movement himself. The early-ninth-century chronicle of the monastery of Saint-Wandrille in Normandy[1] devotes attention to the growth of the monastic library and thus furnishes an example of this increasing interest in books outside the direct Anglo-Saxon sphere of action; a number of other library catalogues of the same century also testify to the effect of this zeal.[2]

Studies: Charles the Great and Alcuin

The books of the Anglo-Saxons were not regarded as unproductive capital; their libraries were intended to promote the education of clerics and monks. The study of the Scriptures was the centre of their endeavours, connected with that of the Fathers; but in acquiring this knowledge there was ample room for general, liberal, or secular learning, to use the terms employed by Bede, who, for example, mentioned Theodore's and Hadrian's teaching of metrics, astronomy, and ecclesiastical arithmetic. Alcuin's description of Ælbert's teaching at York similarly reveals studies of a wide scope. The decline of ancient scholarship and the ecclesiastical purpose set limits to this larger culture, and objections were sometimes raised against secular knowledge in general; but in practice the idea of its usefulness for the understanding of the Scriptures prevailed. Boniface, admonishing his young friend Nithard to study strenuously the Scriptures in order to acquire divine wisdom, did not forget to mention 'liberalium litterarum scientiam'.[3] Alcuin condemned the study of Virgil and his 'lies' as an end in itself, but he considered secular learning a means of obtaining spiritual knowledge and therefore promoted it;[4] all his poetry, including his own epitaph, bears witness to his interest in the poets of ancient Rome. He dedicated to King Charles a recension of the spurious correspondence of Seneca with the Apostle St. Paul;

[1] Cf. p. 15, n. 1; W. Bartz, 'Studien über die Gesta abbatum Fontanellensium' (*Histor. Jahrbuch*, lvii, 1937, pp. 584–95), and my own remarks, *Rev. Bén.* xlvi, 1934, pp. 256 f.

[2] On book 'trade' in this age cf. also Paul Kletler, *Nordwesteuropas Verkehr, Handel und Gewerbe im frühen Mittelalter* (Deutsche Kultur, Historische Reihe, ed. A. Dopsch, ii), Vienna, 1924, pp. 62 ff., who, in my opinion, overstates the commercial part.

[3] Boniface, *Epist.* 9 (pp. 5 f.).

[4] Cf. Hans Frederichs, *Die Gelehrten um Karl den Großen*, Dissertation of Berlin, 1931, pp. 30 ff.; Eva M. Sanford, 'Alcuin and the Classics' (*The Classical Journal*, xx, 1924–5, pp. 526–33).

similarly a part of the manuscript tradition of the letters exchanged between Alexander the Great and the Indian sage Dindimus is derived from Alcuin's recension.[1] And he wrote to Charles:[2] 'My master often used to say to me: "It was the wisest of men who discovered these arts concerning the nature of things, and it would be a great disgrace to allow them to perish in our day." But many are now so pusillanimous as not to care about knowing the reasons for the things the Creator has established in nature.' There was a greater tendency to communicate the existing tradition than to put independent questions; to make extracts from the available books and to combine them, as Bede and Alcuin did in their exegetical and other work; to imitate the ancient poets, even employing their very words, rather than to be original and creative. Notwithstanding these limitations of 'traditionalism', such studies gave a literary training, awoke new interests, and helped to develop mental faculties. It was a new beginning after the breakdown of ancient civilization in the West.

The English missionaries took this respect for teaching and learning with them overseas, and the very necessity of educating a native German clergy who had to officiate in Latin called for a minimum of scholarly acquirement. When Boniface, before his last Frisian journey, recommended his disciples to King Pippin, he also mentioned children who were learning to read their letters.[3] But more than elementary knowledge was the missionaries' aim. Boniface was a missionary who followed the impulse of his vocation; but he was also a scholar and had been a beloved teacher at Nursling. He compiled from earlier authors treatises on metrical and grammatical subjects and even prefixed a picture poem to one of them.[4] Nor did his missionary zeal banish these interests from his mind. From the Continent he sent a sister a poem of nearly 400 verses on virtues and vices in the form of riddles;[5] riddles were a favourite subject of

---

[1] C. W. Barlow, *Epistolae Senecae ad Paulum et Pauli ad Senecam* (Papers and Monographs of the American Academy in Rome, x), 1938, pp. 58 ff., 94 ff.; B. Kuebler, *Juli Valeri Alexandri Polemi Res gestae Alexandri Macedonis*, Leipzig, 1888, p. xxvii; cf. *MG. Poetae*, i. 300.

[2] Alcuin, *Epist.* 148 (p. 239). I use, with some variation, the translation by Andrew Fleming West, *Alcuin and the Rise of the Christian Schools*, London, 1893, p. 37.

[3] Boniface, *Epist.* 93 (p. 213).

[4] Cf. above, p. 145.

[5] *MG. Poetae*, i. 3–15; cf. pp. 1 f. On the MS. tradition cf. also Traube, 'Die

Anglo-Saxon poetry, and he had been preceded by Aldhelm in this field of composition. The early letters of Boniface show his indebtedness to Aldhelm in the use of his phraseology and of some Greek words; that he transmitted the Aldhelmian model to others can be seen from the letters of Lullus. English nuns who had been Boniface's pupils sent him letters containing borrowings from Virgil, Jerome, Pseudo–Seneca,[1] or the legendary 'Actus Silvestri'.[2] The nun Bugga asked him to compose for her a collection of scriptural sentences;[3] his relative Leobgytha, who followed him afterwards to Germany, requested him to correct the letter which she was addressing to him and added some verses, having learned the 'poetical tradition' from his disciple Abbess Eadburg.[4] During his last sojourn at Rome he gave Lullus lessons in metrics; this new pupil sent an English friend an artificially framed poem as a specimen of his art, asked Boniface to correct other verses, 'in litterarum studio devotissimo eruditori', and was directed by him to Thuringia for the continuation of his studies.[5] A Lorsch manuscript of the early ninth century has preserved the epitaph of an Anglo-Saxon Dombercht, whom Boniface 'docuit, nutrivit, amavit' and who is called 'grammaticae studio, metrorum legibus aptus'.[6] There is a certain playfulness in the products of these arts; they show that literary interests lived on side by side with the missionary tasks.

In Gaul considerable remains of ancient learning existed in the sixth century; one has only to recall the writings of Gregory of Tours or of his friend, the Italian poet Venantius Fortunatus settled at Poitiers. Then the decline became more marked. There was very little that could be called literature in the early eighth century; the short 'Liber historiae Francorum', several

---

älteste Handschrift der Aenigmata Bonifatii' (*Neues Archiv*, xxvii, 1902, pp. 211–16; *Vorles*. iii. 164–7).   [1] Cf. below, p. 283.

[2] Ib., p. 285.   [3] Boniface, *Epist*. 15, 27 (pp. 27, 48).
[4] Ib., no. 29 (p. 53).   [5] Ib., nos. 98, 103 (pp. 220 f., 225 ff.).
[6] *MG. Poetae*, i. 19 f.; K. Neff, 'Die Gedichte des Paulus Diaconus' (Traube, *Quellen*, iii. 4), 1908, pp. 178 ff. Cf. Lindsay, *Palaeographia Latina*, iii, 1924, p. 45. The identification of Dombercht with Abbot Tunberht of Glastonbury suggested by H. Hahn, *Bonifaz und Lul*, p. 165, is unacceptable. The words 'docuit, nutrivit, amavit' seem to be borrowed from a poem of Peter of Pisa (*Poetae*, i. 74, v. 6; Neff, loc. cit., p. 160) and are also used by Alcuin, *De sanctis Euboric. eccl*. v. 1450 (*Poetae*, i. 201) and in his verses for the church of St. Peter at Salzburg, *Carm*. 109, xxiv, v. 5) ib., p. 340).

Lives of saints, and a number of rhythmical poems may be mentioned. The written Latin was often extremely barbarized by the influence of the idioms of daily life, the Romance languages in the making; a glance at an original Merovingian charter of this time will give an idea of this strange hybrid language intended for Latin but influenced by the beginning of French. Copies of books were spoilt by misreadings and misspellings. The level of knowledge sometimes fell surprisingly low. There is a sermon in which the gods and the customs of the heathen are attacked in the usual way, most of the arguments being borrowed from Caesarius of Arles, the celebrated preacher of about 500; but it contains one blunder which it would be difficult to parallel earlier: the goddess Venus is represented as a man—the writer knew the bare name but little else.[1] East of the Rhine written literature did not yet exist; Latin was a foreign language as in England, not connected with but also not contaminated by a native idiom, only by ignorance. A priest in Bavaria perverted the baptismal formula, saying: 'Baptizo te in nomine patria et filia et spiritus sancti'; Boniface ordered the baptisms to be repeated but was rebuked by Pope Zacharias, because there was no heresy, only lack of learning.[2]

A clergy living in accordance with canon law but also better educated became one of the objects of Church reform, as it was inspired by the Anglo-Saxon missionaries. Charles the Great showed himself in this respect their heir and executor; the English stream flowed into the greater river that is usually called the 'Carolingian Renaissance'.[3] The stream gave the river its direction, other tributaries reinforced the movement. Charles, as I have stated above, held throughout the reins of Church government, but he desired to govern in the spirit of the reformers. The education of the clergy was one of the aims of his legislation; they should be able to understand the Latin texts they had to deal with, and to interpret them to the laymen. A minimum of knowledge was repeatedly prescribed, and was to be tested by examinations. The king showed concern for the

---

[1] See Appendix X, p. 311.
[2] Boniface, *Epist.* 68 (p. 141).
[3] Cf. what I have said in defence of this expression against modern objections, 'Eine Predigt des Lupus von Ferrières' (*Kultur- und Universalgeschichte, Walter Goetz dargebracht*, Leipzig, 1927, pp. 3 f.); Frederichs, loc. cit., pp. 29 ff.; Hans Naumann, *Wandlung und Erfüllung*, Stuttgart, 1933, pp. 73 ff., 154 ff.

exact correctness of biblical and ecclesiastical texts, which were to be emended in accordance with the classical standard, in so far as it was known. In his famous circular on the cultivation of letters he insisted that devotion and right sense should find expression in the right form, and that study of the arts was a prerequisite to the understanding of the scriptural mysteries. This circular was first sent to the monasteries, afterwards, it seems, to the metropolitans to be forwarded to their suffragans. Only the text for the abbot of Fulda has survived in two copies, one nearly contemporaneous in a manuscript in continental Anglo-Saxon minuscule from Würzburg, now a 'codex Laudianus' of Oxford.[1] Charles and his helpers did not work in vain; everyone who has studied Merovingian and Carolingian manuscripts knows the success of those endeavours and the improvement they effected.

But Charles in his desire for learning had higher aspirations. Few rulers of the Middle Ages attached so much importance to scholarship as the Frankish king, and he was anxious to attract from everywhere the best scholars with a view to the promotion or rather the revival of science and learning.[2] They came from his wide dominions and from the lands beyond; their activity was concentrated in the palace school and in the fellowship of what has been called the palace academy, with the king himself as its centre. There were Italians: the grammarian Peter of Pisa, the historian of the Langobards Paul the Deacon, and Paulinus who became patriarch of Aquileia; a Visigoth, Theodulf, the future bishop of Orléans, whose country of origin, Spain, before the Arab invasion could in her literature rival the nascent scholarship of England; there were Irishmen and, last not least, the Anglo-Saxon Alcuin. Several nations thus contributed to the Carolingian 'Renaissance' and 'Humanism'; they made the Continent once more the seat of a learning which was to spread and to increase in extent and intensity, and very soon produced native representatives, such as Angilbert, Einhard, Hrabanus Maurus, and Walahfrid Strabo, to recall a few names. The seed sown by Boniface and his disciples in

---

[1] Charles's 'Epistola de litteris colendis' (between 780 and 800), ed. Boretius, *MG. Capitularia*, i, pp. 78 f., and from the Laudianus (Misc. 126) ed. P. Lehmann, 'Fuldaer Studien, Neue Folge' (*SB. München*, 1927, no. 2), pp. 4–13.

[2] Cf., e.g., Frederichs, loc. cit.

Fulda and elsewhere had taken root, and other seeds were now added. The personality of Alcuin entitles us in this connexion to dwell afresh on the relations between England and the Continent in the eighth century. Willibrord had inaugurated the missionary work of Anglo-Saxons, Boniface continued it and began to organize and to reform the Frankish Church; the educational effort which was involved in both tasks culminated in the work of Alcuin, who, under the impulse of the great king, brought to a close this epoch of English activity overseas. The history of his life bears witness to the growth of international intercourse and to the existence of a spiritual heritage now common to England and the Frankish kingdom.

Alcuin's English and continental activities are not divided by a sharp line, as they are in the lives of Willibrord and Boniface. Born about 730, he was a relative of Willibrord and came like him of a noble Northumbrian family. The school of York Minster now occupied in England the place which Canterbury held in the times of Theodore and Hadrian, Wearmouth and Jarrow in the age of Bede. Archbishop Egbert continued Bede's tradition; his successor Ælbert was head of the school before he was raised to the archiepiscopal throne. Alcuin, who was educated there, has celebrated this seminary of learning and its library in the great poem which he devoted to York, its church and bishops; the knowledge of the Seven Arts paved the way for the study of the Scriptures. Alcuin there imbibed the truism that 'discere' is the foundation of 'docere';[1] when Ælbert became archbishop, Alcuin was made master in his place. He was not a man of original ideas but had the gift of transmitting traditional learning and has been rightly called 'the born teacher'.[2] He did not aspire to high dignities in the Church, nor did he ever take another order than that of deacon, a humble deacon, 'humilis levita', as he styled himself in many letters with the customary humility of medieval times. It is uncertain whether he was a professed monk or a clergyman who had not taken the vows; there are reasons for both opinions, perhaps better reasons for considering him a monk who did not

---

[1] Alcuin, *Epist.* 19, 31, 88, 117, 168, 243, 270 (pp. 55, 73, 132, 173, 277, 390, 429).
[2] Hauck, loc. cit. ii. 139; C. J. B. Gaskoin, *Alcuin, his Life and his Work*, London, 1904, p. 54.

live up to strict monastic principles but held a *via media*.[1]
Certainly the stability of the Benedictine monk, which was so
conspicuous in Bede's life and work, had less part in Alcuin's
career, and he confessed as late as 796 his vain attempts 'ad
portum stabilitatis venire'.[2] For all his piety and humility he was
also a nobleman of worldly abilities, of which his superiors
availed themselves. He first met Charles when his teacher
Archbishop Ælbert sent him to the king, we do not know when
and why.[3] He went again to the Continent in 780, when
Ælbert's successor Eanbald ordered him to Rome to receive
the archbishop's pallium from Pope Hadrian. It was a decisive
moment in his life; for, returning about Easter in the next year
781, he again met Charles in Parma and was invited to join
him in his educational efforts. So he came back to the Frankish
court, perhaps in 782. In 786 he was in England; he was one
of the two envoys of the king of Northumbria and of the Archbishop of York who, after the northern synod, accompanied the
papal legates to King Offa and the synod of the south. He
stayed once more in his native country during the years 790 to

---

[1] I may mention W. Pückert, *Aniane und Gellone*, Leipzig, 1899, pp. 248 ff.;
Gaskoin, loc. cit., pp. 249–52; Walter Delius, 'War Alchvin Mönch?' (*Theologische
Studien und Kritiken*, ciii, 1931, pp. 465–73). Not all the arguments which have been
adduced in both directions are to the point. Carmelo Ottaviano, 'Un opuscolo
inedito di Alcuino' (*Aevum*, ii, Milan, 1928, pp. 3–16), also in his 'Testi medioevali
inediti' (*Fontes Ambrosiani*, iii), Florence, 1933, pp. 3–18, has published from
Ambrosianus S. 17 sup. of the 10th century, fol. 57v–61v, an anonymous 'Opus-
culum interrogationum' on the acceptance of novices according to the Rule of St.
Benedict, and has ascribed it to Alcuin, whose works 'De Trinitate', 'De Trinitate ad
Fredegisum quaestiones', and 'De ratione animae' (Migne, *P.L.* ci. 11–64 and 639–
47; cf. *MG. Epist.* iv, pp. 414, 447, 473, nos. 257, 289, 309) precede it in this MS.
But I am not certain that there are sufficient reasons for attributing the fourth text
also to the same author.   [2] *Epist.* 97 (p. 141).

[3] *Vita Alcuini*, c. 9 (*MG. SS.* xv. 1, p. 190). Alcuin accompanied Ælbert to Rome,
before the latter became archbishop in 767; his mission to the king must have been
later. In 773 Charles sent 'Albuinus deliciosus ipsius regis' with Bishop George of
Ostia-Amiens (cf. above, p. 128) and Abbot Wulfard (of St. Martin's at Tours) as
envoy to Pope Hadrian (*Vita Hadriani*, c. 26, ed. Duchesne, *Lib. Pontif.* i. 494).
There is much controversy whether this Albuin is Alcuin, who called himself
Albinus, or not. Most scholars deny the identity, or at least consider it unlikely in
this early year, e.g. E. Dümmler, 'Zur Lebensgeschichte Alchvins' (*Neues Archiv*,
xviii, 1892, pp. 57 f.) and Moore, loc. cit., p. 74, n. 1, while others accept the identification, such as Duchesne, loc. cit., p. 515, n. 19, and, lastly, Marcella Papetti,
'Intorno ai viaggi di Alcuino in Italia' (*Sophia*, iii, Toledo and Naples, 1935,
pp. 216–18), emphasizing that we do not know of any other namesake to whom the
designation of 'deliciosus ipsius regis' could apply (the other arguments are of no
importance).

793; but then the Continent became his permanent home, from
793 to his death in 804.[1] Charles in 796 bestowed on him the
abbey of St. Martin of Tours, after he had already made him
abbot of the monasteries of St. Lupus at Troyes and of Ferrières,
which also was to become a centre of learning in the next century.
But most of the time he had to accompany the royal court, and
only the sickness of his last three years allowed him a stable
residence at St. Martin's. So, measured by time, his continental
activity was less than that of Willibrord, who worked there
almost half a century, or than the thirty-six years of uninter-
rupted stay of Boniface; but these fewer years overseas were
none the less effective, different as Alcuin's aims and obligations
were.

His learning, limited by the conditions of his age, was
traditional;[2] I have pointed out his lack of originality. But by
transmitting the spiritual heritage which he had received at
York he helped both to create new ground and to build on the
foundations laid by Boniface, whom many like-minded men
now followed. Alcuin could impress his tendencies of learning
and teaching on the monasteries committed to him, as at St.
Martin's, where, according to his own words, he fought a daily
struggle 'cum Turonica rusticitate'.[3] But, what was of greater
moment, he became one of the principal or rather the principal
collaborator of the king in his educational efforts centred in the
'palace school'. Not only young people, members of the royal
family as well as others like Einhard, were educated there; the
palace offered a wide opportunity for a kind of 'adult education',
of which Alcuin's letters and some works of his and of other
members of this circle give a vivid picture. There was a lively
system of question and reply, the king himself often leading the
discussion, interrogating on subjects of grammar, of scriptural
interpretation and theology, of chronology and astronomy, and
so on.

The personal part taken by Charles in such discussions,

---

[1] The day of his death, 19 May (*Vita Alcuini*, c. 26, p. 196), is also marked in a
9th-century manuscript from Freising, Munich Lat. no. 6399 (G. Becker, *Catalogi
bibliothecarum antiqui*, p. 41, no. 19; Baumann, *MG. Necrologia*, iii. 79): 'Migravit
Albinus levita Christi' (not identified by the editors).

[2] On his lack of a real knowledge of Greek cf. M. L. W. Laistner, *Thought and
Letters in Western Europe A.D. 500 to 900*, London, 1931, p. 192.

[3] *Epist.* 172 (p. 285).

playful and serious, was made even more evident by the discovery of Wolfram von den Steinen that the Vatican MS. of the 'Libri Carolini', the famous manifesto of the Frankish Church against image worship, was the very copy discussed at the palace in the presence of the king;[1] many Tironian notes, that is, remarks in shorthand, represent his opinions and decisions, which caused erasures and alterations to be made in this volume, a large portion of which is unfortunately lost. Alcuin had no part in composing this haughty official pronouncement against the Greek and even the papal policies on the image question; the Frankish Church, not without misinterpretations of the views it condemned, refused alike iconoclasm and superstitious worship of the images, and kept a middle course. Alcuin was in England at this time; but in 792 he wrote a manifesto of the English Church, which agreed with the Frankish point of view, and two years later he represented with other Englishmen his native country at the synod of Frankfurt, which was one of the culminations of this struggle (cf. p. 112). He contributed more to a second theological question, which was also treated at this synod, the controversy over the Spanish doctrine of Adoptionism and the conflict with its protagonists, Bishop Felix of Urgel (in the Spanish Marches) and Archbishop Elipand of Toledo. Alcuin's dossier on this question comprises letters and some treatises, and was enlarged a few years ago by a letter discovered in Spain, written by him to one of the champions of the 'orthodox' tenets, Beatus of Liébana.[2] In these dogmatic discussions he was only one of the debaters; Paulinus of Aquileia was perhaps intellectually his superior. At any rate, Alcuin's disputation with Felix at Aachen in 800, in the presence of the king, secured the external submission of Felix.

But another fact was of greater relevance: the revival of theological and 'philosophical' literature in the Frankish countries, which was to some extent involved in these dogmatic contests, though at first foreigners such as Alcuin and Paulinus were the principal writers. It is impossible here to enter into the merits and defects of Alcuin's share in this revival, to discuss his three systematic books on the Holy Trinity, largely derived

---

[1] Cf. above, p. 124, n. 9. Cf. also Tangl, *Neues Archiv*, xxxvi, 1911, pp. 752–4; D. De Bruyne, 'La Composition des Libri Carolini' (*Rev. Bén.* xliv, 1932, pp. 227–34).   [2] See Appendix XI, pp. 314 ff.

from Augustine, or his biblical commentaries[1] and his moral writings on Virtues and Vices or on the Soul; some of his letters also have the character of informative treatises. He had no constructive mind;[2] he extracted and compiled rather from former writers, as Bede had done. But this study of earlier authors opened the way for comparison of texts, the discovery of contradictions and gaps, for the reawakening of dialectical exercises in the field of theology so as to 'blend religious faith with rational speculations'.[3] The result was that already in the ninth century we find thinkers of greater independence, and these had wider scope since the love of books had taken root and ampler material for comparison was available.[4]

Alcuin's biblical studies were also influential in another respect. As I have said above, it was one of the aims of Charles the Great to secure that, in contrast with the period of Merovingian barbarization, only correct Latin texts should now be used by the clergy. Alcuin was one of his helpers in providing an emended text of the Bible. Much scholarly research has been recently devoted to his part in this work. Textual criticism by theologians and philologists, studies in palaeography and the history of art have been applied to determining the kind of text (or texts) to be ascribed to his emendation, a matter on which he touches only slightly in his letters; scholars have sought to discover the manuscripts which were written at the palace or at Tours under his directions, biblical and other books, sumptuous and simpler volumes. It is difficult to establish how far his personal suggestions and instructions contributed to the revival of a real art of writing and illuminating beautiful manuscripts and to the development of the different styles to be found at Tours in this age.[5] Whether particular books are to be attributed

[1] Cf. P. Lehmann, *Fuldaer Studien* (SB. München, 1925, no. 3), p. 52, on unpublished works. On Alcuin's Commentary on St. John's Gospel cf. A. E. Schönbach, *Ueber einige Evangelienkommentare des Mittelalters* (SB. Wien, cxlvi, 1903, no. 4), pp. 43–67.

[2] Cf., e.g., Boehmer, 'Das germanische Christentum' (loc. cit., pp. 211 f.), on Alcuin's *Epist.* 307 (pp. 466 ff.).

[3] E. Gilson, *Reason and Revelation in the Middle Ages*, New York, 1939, p. 15.

[4] Cf., e.g., the remarks of Beryl Smalley, *The Study of the Bible in the Middle Ages*, Oxford, 1941, pp. 24 f.

[5] There are the fundamental works of E. K. Rand, *A Survey of the MSS. of Tours*, Cambridge (Mass.), 1929, and W. Köhler, *Die Karolingischen Miniaturen*, i. 1, Berlin, 1930, pp. 33 ff. Cf. both authors and D. De Bruyne, *Göttingische gelehrte Anzeigen*, 1931, pp. 321–59. I may also mention the cautious remarks of

to his influence or not is matter of controversy; some of them may have been written only after his death. But all agree that the 'Alcuinian' revision of the Bible, probably a Northumbrian text emended by the reception of variant readings from other sources, had great importance in the following centuries.[1]

King Charles likewise endeavoured to provide the Frankish clergy with correct and uniform liturgical books and in this effort Alcuin co-operated. He made a recension of the 'Lectionary', the text of the Epistles of the Mass (a part of the so-called 'Comes').[2] Like Paul the Deacon, he compiled a collection of homilies. His sacramentary for private devotion, a mosaic composed from different sources, influenced even the development of the official liturgy of the Church. But more important was his recension of the Gregorian Sacramentary which I have previously mentioned (p. 98). The 'Sacramentarium Gregorianum' was sent by Pope Hadrian to Charles, who wished to give uniformity to the Frankish liturgy in conformity with the Roman Church. Alcuin corrected this text, which was to be the official liturgy of the countries ruled by Charles; but it was incomplete, and because there was need of a supplement for the Frankish Church, Alcuin added a second part. He compiled this appendix from the so-called Gelasian Sacramentary, in which Roman and Gallican elements were combined (p. 97), and from other sources, in which Spanish influences may be observed. The corrected Gregorian text and Alcuin's supplement were originally separated by an anonymous preface to the appendix, in which we are informed of the relation of the two parts; Alcuin's authorship was discovered in modern times and is now generally recognized. The two parts were later merged and even became a liturgy book of the Roman Church and of almost all the churches under its leadership; on the whole they are the main foundation of the modern 'Missale Romanum',

A. Hessel, 'Zur Entstehung der karolingischen Minuskel' (*Archiv f. Urk.* viii, 1923, pp. 210 f.).

[1] I need only mention Henri Quentin, 'Mémoire sur l'établissement du texte de la Vulgate I' (*Collectanea Biblica*, vi), Rome and Paris, 1922, pp. 207 f., 267 ff.; E. K. Rand, 'A Preliminary Study of Alcuin's Bible' (*Harvard Theological Review*, xxiv, 1931, pp. 323–96); L. W. Jones, 'The Text of the Bible and the Script and Art of Tours' (ib. xxviii, 1935, pp. 135–79), who refer to earlier literature. Cf. also H. H. Glunz, *History of the Vulgate in England*, Cambridge, 1933, pp. 24 ff.

[2] A. Wilmart, 'Le Lectionnaire d'Alcuin' (*Ephemerides Liturgicae*, li, 1937, *Analecta histor.-ascet.*, pp. 136–97).

certainly a momentous contribution of this Englishman of the eighth century to the spiritual heritage of the Catholic Church.[1] Evidently his textual criticism and the choice of supplementary texts corresponded with the needs of his age. A competent scholar has said that in the liturgical field Alcuin's work was of the first class and no contemporary could claim the same rank.[2]

Some special additions to the ecclesiastical practice of the Continent are probably also attributable to his influence. A small but significant outcome of the contest about Adoptionism has been recently ascribed by Dom B. Capelle to Alcuin with good reason.[3] The singing of the symbol in the canon of the mass was unknown to the Roman Church; it originated in the sixth century in the East and was adopted by the Spanish Church in 589 at the conversion of the Visigoths from Arianism to Catholicism. From Spain the custom was adopted by Irishmen, as the Stowe Missal shows, and then by the Church of Northumbria, the native country of Alcuin. Now it was as a pronouncement against Adoptionism that the singing of the Creed (in the words of Paulinus of Aquileia) was introduced into the canon of the mass in Frankish Churches, to emphasize its importance to the community of the believers, and there is great probability that this act was inspired by Alcuin. The custom spread during the next century in the Frankish kingdoms and to the Roman Church; it became and is to-day the common practice of the catholic world.

If Capelle's assumption is correct, the importation of this practice from Ireland to Northumbria, and from this country

[1] Cf. (after S. Bäumer), e.g., Edmund Bishop, *Liturgica Historica*, Oxford, 1918, pp. 39–61 ('The earliest Roman Mass Book'); H. Lietzmann, *Das Sacramentarium Gregorianum nach dem Aachener Urexemplar*' (Liturgiegeschichtliche Quellen, iii), Münster i. W., 1921, pp. xviii ff., and 'Handschriftliches zu Alkvins Ausgabe und Sacramentarium' (*Jahrbuch für Liturgiewissenschaft*, v, 1925, pp. 68–79). Cf. below, p. 315.

[2] F. Cabrol, 'Les Écrits liturgiques d'Alcuin' (*Revue d'hist. ecclés.* xix, 1923, p. 521); cf. his earlier article on Alcuin, *Dictionnaire d'archéol. chrét. et de liturgie*, i. 1, col. 1072 ff. On the 'Liber de psalmorum usu', wrongly ascribed to Alcuin except for a small part, cf. A. Wilmart, 'Le Manuel de prières de saint Jean Gualbert' (*Rev. Bén.* xlviii, 1936, pp. 262 ff.). On Alcuin's share in establishing the baptismal order after the defeat of the Avars (796) cf. von Schubert, loc. cit., pp. 646 ff.

[3] 'Alcuin et l'histoire du symbole de la messe' (*Recherches de théologie ancienne et médiévale*, vi, 1934, pp. 249–60); cf. Capelle's earlier paper, 'L'Origine antiadoptianiste de notre texte du symbole de la messe' (ib. i, 1929, pp. 7–20). On doubtful assumptions of his, which demand further research, cf. Th. Klauser, *Jahrbuch für Liturgiewissenschaft*, xiv, 1938, p. 454.

to the Continent may be compared with another fact also related
to Alcuin's personal history. The festival of All Saints on the
first day of November was unknown in the Frankish kingdoms
before his age. It is found in Northumbria after the middle
of the eighth century, probably introduced from Ireland, and
it began to take root in the lands of King Charles at the end of
the same century. Once more in all probability it was Alcuin
who was the connecting link in this transmission.[1]

Alcuin in his own style continued the Northumbrian tradition
embodied in the works of Bede; he wrote a plain, lucid Latin,
avoiding the excessive ornaments of Aldhelm's difficult prose.
His Latin was not that of the ancient classical age, of course.
Modern critical editions of some of his works, based on early
copies, have brought out more orthographical and grammatical
deviations than would have been expected; he did not always
conform with the rules prescribed in his own compilations on
grammar and orthography.[2] But he was obviously considered
a writer of distinction and experience and was asked to compose
or revise Lives of saints. He had in this respect a position
similar to that held in Gaul by the two Italians Venantius
Fortunatus in the sixth, and Jonas of Susa in the seventh century,
or by the Fleming Goscelin in England in the eleventh century.
The very number of the existing manuscripts and of the excerpts
from these writings shows his influence in this field of literature.
As an historical source the most important of the Lives written
by Alcuin is the biography of his relative St. Willibrord, though
he composed it too late to give much more than a collection of
miracle stories.[3] But his literary aims are perhaps better revealed

---

[1] The festival of All Saints is first found in the Metrical Martyrology of York of
the 8th century (after 745), v. 68 f. (Quentin, *Les Martyrologes historiques*, p. 125;
A. Wilmart, 'Un témoin Anglo-Saxon du calendrier métrique d'York', *Rev. Bén.*
xlvi, 1934, p. 68), in Ireland about 800 in the 'Martyrology of Oengus' (ed. Stokes,
H. Br. Soc. xxix, 1905, p. 232). On the Continent Alcuin in 800 recommended the
celebration of the day to his friend Archbishop Arno of Salzburg (*Epist.* 193, p. 321).
He may have done this before; for the Bavarian synod of Riesbach which assembled
two years earlier, authorized the celebration of the festival (*MG. Concilia*, ii. 197).
Thus the conjectures of A. Wilmart, loc. cit., pp. 50–6, on the introduction of the
festival from Ireland into Northumbria and by Alcuin overseas seem reasonably
justified. Cf. also Quentin, loc. cit., pp. 636–41.

[2] Cf. Traube, *Vorles.* ii. 102 f. According to E. Dümmler, 'Alchvinstudien' (*SB.
Berlin*, 1891, pp. 499 f.), the orthography of most of Alcuin's early manuscripts has to
be referred to his scribes, who reproduced his dictation, not to the author himself.
But cf. *SS. rer. Merov.* iii. 405, iv. 385, vii. 96.   [3] Cf. above, p. 53, n. 1.

by his rewriting of two earlier Lives: the Life of St. Vedast
(to-day St. Vaast) of Arras which had first been written by that
Jonas of Susa who was the biographer of St. Columbanus,[1] and
the Life of St. Richarius, the saint of St. Riquier in Picardy,
whose first Life composed in rhymed but barbarous Latin has
only recently been discovered.[2] The comparison of Alcuin's
revised versions with the earlier ones discloses the revival of
higher literary ambitions, the desire for a correcter language
and a better story, though some verbosity and much commonplace are included. The purpose of edification was also made
more evident: besides other additions due to this tendency,
Alcuin appended homilies to the Lives of Willibrord (i, c. 32)
and Vedast which found special favour with medieval writers
as models of preaching;[3] the last chapter of the Life of Richarius
(c. 18) has a similar feature.

His literary work was not confined to prose. He was not a
poet in the higher sense; but he was skilful in the art of versifica-
tion as it was practised in his native country. Aldhelm, Bede,
and Boniface were his English predecessors; but the art was also
exercised in his own age in the northern country from which he
came. Pupils of York sent him overseas the versified Miracles
of Ninian, the saint of Whithorn in Galloway;[4] the poem which
Ædilvulf composed in the early ninth century on a monastery
in the proximity of Lindisfarne[5] testifies to the continuity of the
tradition. On the same lines was Alcuin's longest poem, on
York, its saints and bishops, among them his master, Archbishop
Ælbert, whose teaching and library he praised in this work. A
great part of it was based on Bede's *Ecclesiastical History*; Alcuin
recognized thereby the ancient tradition that the same subject
could be treated either in prose or in verse with little difference
and without much difficulty.[6] Sedulius' double Paschal work

---

[1] B. Krusch has edited Jonas's and Alcuin's versions, *SS. rer. Merov.* iii. 399–427
(cf. iv. 770, vii. 819 f.), Jonas's text also in *Ionae Vitae sanctorum Columbani*, &c.,
pp. 295–320. But he excluded Alcuin's Homily on St. Vedast (*BHL.* ii, no. 8509),
Acta SS. Febr. i. 800, and Migne, *P.L.* ci. 678–81; cf. Alcuin, *Epist.* 296 (p. 455. 36).

[2] Krusch has published the first *Vita Richarii* in *SS. rer. Merov.* vii. 438–53,
Alcuin's revision ib. iv. 381–401 (cf. ib., pp. 778 f.).

[3] Cf. ib. vi. 147 (n. 16), vii. 97, and my paper, 'Eine Predigt des Lupus von
Ferrières', loc. cit., pp. 6 (n. 1), 7 (nn. 2, 3).

[4] Cf. above, p. 34, n. 4, and p. 147.   [5] Cf. below, pp. 300 f.

[6] Cf. E. R. Curtius, 'Dichtung und Rhetorik im Mittelalter' (*Deutsche Viertel-
jahrsschrift für Literaturwissenschaft und Geistesgeschichte*, xvi, 1938, pp. 439 ff.).

was in this respect the most famous example of ancient Christian poetry; Bede imitated it in his twofold treatment of the Life of St. Cuthbert. Alcuin continued this practice by adding to his prose Life of St. Willibrord a second, metrical book for scholars only, in which the same stories were told in hexameters with the addition of some elegiac couplets; he thus created a medieval continental tradition for such double treatment of a literary subject. There are many other smaller, metrical and perhaps some rhythmical[1] poems from his pen, which to some extent justify the name of Flaccus, that is, Horace, which he was given in the scholarly circle round King Charles. Many occasional productions are among them, poetical letters sent to friends, metrical inscriptions (*tituli*) for the walls and altars of churches and monastic buildings,[2] prefaces and end verses of books, some riddles, and proverbial sentences of moral wisdom.[3] I may mention his prefaces to the Bible in distichs,[4] and the epitaph which he composed for himself:

'Alchuine nomen erat sophiam mihi semper amanti'[5]

the words of which were soon after used for the epitaph of Angilbert. He was not the only poet of this circle; there are poems by Paul the Deacon, Paulinus of Aquileia, Theodulf of

---

[1] ed. Strecker, *MG. Poetae*, iv. 2, pp. 903–10.

[2] The so-called 'Sylloge Cantabrigiensis', a collection of papal inscriptions which has first been published by myself (*Neues Archiv*, xxxv, 1910, pp. 350–66; cf. ib. xxxviii, 1913, pp. 645 ff., 652 ff.), seems to have been among Alcuin's models. For the latest text of this Sylloge, the epitaph of Pope John VII (who died in 707), no other copy of which seems to exist, obviously was used by Alcuin. Cf. v. 9 of this epitaph (I also refer to the edition by Fedor Schneider and W. Holtzmann, 'Die Epitaphien der Päpste . . . des Mittelalters', *Texte zur Kulturgeschichte des Mittelalters*, vi, Rome, 1933, pp. 22 f., no. 27):

'Non parcens opibus, pretiosum quicquid habebat
    in tua distribuit munera, sancta parens',

with Alcuin's inscription for the tomb of St. Amandus (*Carm.* 88, xiv, v. 3, *Poetae*, i. 308; cf. Angilbert, ib. p. 364):

'*Non parcens opibus*; miseris nam *quidquid habebat*
    sparserat et Christi compsit sacra templa sacerdos.'

On Alcuin's 'occasional poetry' cf., e.g., F. J. E. Raby, *A History of Secular Latin Poetry in the Middle Ages*, i, Oxford, 1934, pp. 183 ff.

[3] On the 'Praecepta vivendi' (*Poetae*, i. 275–81) cf. lastly M. Boas, *Alcuin und Cato*, Leiden, 1937. On Alcuin's hymns cf. G. M. Dreves, *Analecta hymnica medii aevi*, l, Leipzig, 1907, pp. 152 ff.

[4] *Poetae*, i. 287–92; H. Quentin, *Biblia sacra iuxta Latinam Vulgatam versionem*, i, Rome, 1926, pp. 44–51 (cf. p. xl).

[5] On Alcuin's notion of 'wisdom' cf. M. Roger, *L'Enseignement des lettres classiques d'Ausone à Alcuin*, Paris, 1905, pp. 441 ff.

Orléans, Angilbert, the so-called 'Hibernicus exul', Alcuin's Irish pupil Joseph, and others; but his poems by their number, extent, and influence, if not by their merit, occupy the first place, though 'real inspiration is rare'.[1] Certainly he contributed to the revival of the ancient poetical tradition, based not only on Christian but also on pagan poetry, at least so far as it offered the new poets useful formal instruction.

The ancient form of dialogue which he used in some of his works, even in his short commentary on the Book of Genesis, reminds us of his activity as a teacher. His personal influence at York, as master of the palace school, and in his Frankish monasteries was probably of greater moment than his literary work. His books on Rhetoric and Dialectic, compiled as they were from earlier works, without any originality, have met in the past, as has been said, with 'the almost unanimous contempt of the historians of philosophy'.[2] They were written as dialogues between the King and Alcuin; I may also quote one of the introductory distichs of the *Rhetoric*:[3]

> Scripserat haec inter curas rex Karulus aulae
> Albinusque simul: hic dedit, ille probat.

Poor and unoriginal as these and other writings of Alcuin appear to the modern scholar, they were the beginning of medieval philosophy, which had to start, like a schoolboy, by mastering parts of earlier teaching, and we must not forget that in this age 'philosophy consisted in little more than the dialectical exercises of the old schools of the rhetors'.[4] How discussions among the palace people helped to open their eyes to problems and to develop a primitive dialectic may also be seen from a letter of the next generation, written by Fridugis, an English pupil of Alcuin, who became his successor as abbot of St. Martin's. He gave his opinion on the question under discussion whether

---

[1] Laistner, *Thought and Letters*, p. 281.
[2] Gaskoin, loc. cit., pp. 195 f. On Alcuin's sources cf. P. Lehmann, 'Cassiodor-studien VIII' (*Philologus*, lxxiv, 1917, pp. 361–83); W. S. Howell, *The Rhetoric of Alcuin and Charlemagne* (Princeton Studies in English, xxiii), Princeton, 1941, pp. 22 ff., 159 ff. Cf. also R. McKeon, 'Rhetoric in the Middle Ages' (*Speculum*, xvii, 1942, pp. 13 f.); J. W. H. Atkins, *English Literary Criticism: the Medieval Phase*, Cambridge, 1943, pp. 51 ff.
[3] *MG. Poetae*, i. 300; C. Halm, *Rhetores Latini minores*, Leipzig, 1863, p. 525; Howell, p. 66.
[4] A. J. Macdonald, *Authority and Reason in the early Middle Ages*, Oxford, 1933, p. 7.

Nothing and Darkness are real things, the question of the existence of 'Nihil' having also been touched upon by Alcuin.[1]

Such writings show the endeavours of the great king to enlarge his own learning, to obtain an educated clergy, and to spread knowledge amongst laymen, to create perhaps, as Alcuin has said,[2] a new Athens in Francia. Charles's consort Liutgard and his children were among Alcuin's pupils. A small work, the Disputation of 'Albinus' with Charles's son Pippin, gives an idea of a special method of teaching: exercises in the learning of Latin words by playful paraphrasing, by employing 'kenningar', to use a Norse term.[3] As a result of such zeal on the part of Charles and his helpers, we find among the next generation of writers a few laymen, such as Einhard, the biographer of the emperor, and Nithard, Angilbert's son, the historian of the struggle of Charles's grandsons. This development was short-lived, as was also the beginning of a more extended school attendance in 'scholae legentium puerorum'. But in spite of all setbacks there was no general decline of learning among clerics and monks such as occurred in the Merovingian age; if it decreased in some churches and monasteries, it survived in others to kindle a new flame.

It has been said with some reason that Alcuin rapidly became and remained for long the spiritual ruler of Europe.[4] His correspondence in its range is suggestive of the part which this Englishman played in furthering the new intellectual movement. Almost all the existing letters of Boniface are addressed to his fellow countrymen and to the Popes and a few other Romans. Alcuin also exchanged letters with his compatriots in Northumbria and in other parts of England; he wrote to kings of Northumbria and Mercia, to archbishops of Canterbury and York, to English bishops, abbots and abbesses, monks and nuns, to great laymen, always inclined in his old age to give religious

[1] *Disputatio Pippini cum Albino*, c. 100 (ed. W. Wilmanns, *Zeitschr. für Deutsches Altertum*, xiv, 1869, p. 544); Fridugis, *MG. Epist.* iv. 552–5; cf. the letter of Charles to Dungal, ib., p. 552. On Fridugis as 'philosopher' cf. J. A. Endres, *Forschungen zur Geschichte der frühmittelalterlichen Philosophie* (Beiträge zur Geschichte der Philosophie des Mittelalters, xvii. 2–3), Münster, 1915, pp. 4–15; Macdonald, loc. cit., pp. 29–35, 50 f., 58 f.   [2] *Epist.* 170 (p. 279).
[3] It has been used in this connexion by W. P. Ker, *The Dark Ages*, London, 1923, p. 87; Helga Reuschel, 'Kenningar bei Alkuin' (*Beiträge zur Geschichte der Deutschen Sprache und Literatur*, lxii, 1938, pp. 143–55).
[4] Traube, *Karolingische Dichtungen*, p. 25.

and moral admonitions and warnings. But the number of his continental correspondents is much larger. The master of York, on his journeys to and from Rome, had made many friends in the countries of Charles, even before he settled there.[1] Afterwards his position in the palace school, near the king, whom he sometimes accompanied on his journeys, brought him into contact with a wide circle of churchmen and of the secular aristocracy in Gaul, Germany, and Italy; he had a long list of correspondents, headed by the king, Queen Liutgard, their sons and daughters, and Charles's sister Gisla. Young men who appeared qualified were sent to the palace school or later to St. Martin's, and after having been trained went to help in the educational work at other places such as Salzburg, where Bishop (from 798 Archbishop) Arno was a particular friend of Alcuin. Among his disciples and friends there were some who occupied high places in the Frankish Church, archbishops of Trier and Mainz, bishops of Autun and Worms, and the first bishop of Münster, the Frisian Liudger who had been educated at Utrecht but was also twice sent to the school of York when Alcuin was teaching there; also abbots of Fulda and Lorsch. The three next abbots of his monastery of Ferrières were also among his disciples. The last of them became archbishop of Sens; the first was the Anglo-Saxon Sigulf, who had been his pupil at York and, like others, followed him overseas.[2] Some Anglo-Saxons gained important positions in the service of the great king. We may recall Willehad, a friend of Alcuin, who continued the missionary line of Northumbrian activity, became the first bishop of Bremen, and died in 789 (p. 110). Another English friend, Beornred, a relative of Willibrord, was made abbot of the latter's monastery of Echternach (775) and also bishop (785) and lastly archbishop of Sens (he died in 797). Alcuin's pupil Fridugis, whose philosophical interests have already been mentioned (p. 163), succeeded his master as abbot of St. Martin's at Tours; the monastery of SS. Audomar and Bertin (St. Omer)

---

[1] Cf. Alcuin's *Carm.* no. 4 (*Poetae*, i. 220 ff.).

[2] About the middle of the 9th century Lupus of Ferrières wrote to Archbishop Wigmund of York offering to renew the confraternity initiated by the predecessors of the abbot, *Epist.* 61 (*MG. Epist.* vi. 61 f.). At the same time he asked Abbot Altsig of York to send him some books for transcribing, ib., no. 62 (p. 62), 'the last glimpse of the existence of the famous schools of learning in the North' (H. and S. iii. 636).

was also bestowed on him, situated not far from the English
Channel and near the most important continental route of
English travellers. Under Louis the Pious he became the head
of the imperial chancery, from 819 to 832, two years before his
death in 834.[1] He closed the series of Anglo-Saxon immigrations
in the Carolingian age.

But the seed sown by Alcuin had grown up and was produc-
ing fruit. The leadership in the intellectual revival had passed
from the Anglo-Saxons to the great king and emperor; side by
side with Echternach, Fulda, and Hersfeld other monasteries
which had no English founders now followed the same line.
We have heard that Italians, Spaniards, and Irishmen also
contributed to the work of Charles, and that natives of the
Frankish countries had been educated to take a full part in
this renascence. Foreign contribution, like that of the Irishmen
John (Eriugena) and Sedulius, became the exception; on the
contrary, the Continent was now able, in the person of Grimbald,
to help King Alfred in his endeavours to restore learning in
England when its decay had been aggravated by the invasions
of the Vikings, not to speak of later times.

How much the intellectual conditions overseas had been
changed may easily be recognized, if the decline of scholarship
in Gaul and the few literary achievements of the seventh and
early eighth centuries are compared with the manifold richness
and advancing refinement of Carolingian writings. The ancient
Christian and also pagan tradition served as standard and
model; it was in fact an intentional 'receptio' of an earlier
heritage. It will suffice to mention, for example, the works of
Paschasius Radbertus and Ratramnus, of the unfortunate Godescalc, of whom we hope to know more in a near future,[2] of
Agobard of Lyons, the letters of Lupus of Ferrières, or the first
secular biography of the Middle Ages, Einhard's Life of Charles
the Great, to give an impression of the new growth, which
persisted in spite of all temporary and local setbacks. It is not easy
to distinguish the English from the native and the other foreign
elements in this Frankish rebirth of learning and scholarly work.

---

[1] On Fridugis cf. W. Pückert, *Aniane und Gellone*, pp. 259 ff.; *SS. rer. Merov.* v.
736 f.; Bresslau, *Handbuch der Urkundenlehre*, 2nd ed. i. 375, 386. On the manuscripts
written at Tours during his abbacy cf. the literature quoted above, p. 157, n. 5.
[2] Cf. Morin's article quoted above, p. 127, n. 3.

But the facts, of which I have tried to sketch at least some outline, leave no room for doubt that the English part in laying the foundations of this 'Renaissance' and creating the right atmosphere for it was really large.

Occasional remarks and the existing manuscripts written by English hands indicate that the number of English monks and nuns working on the Continent in this age was much greater than the names handed down to posterity seem to show. But for the existence of the earliest monastic chronicle of the West, that of St. Wandrille in Normandy, there would be no mention of an Anglo-Saxon monk Baga, who led in this monastery an exemplary life until his death after 710.[1] We do not know who brought to the same house Bede's *Ecclesiastical History*; the chronicle which I have quoted, and some Lives composed there about 800 show the influence of this famous work. But they also had in the same monastery Bede's books *De natura rerum* and *De temporibus* and Cuthbert's letter on his death.[2] Who gave a Gospel book written about 770 in southern England to the convent of Aldeneyck in Belgian Limburg?[3] There was another small monastery in the same diocese of Liége, Malonne near Namur on the Sambre, of whose connexion with England we should know nothing had we not the legendary Life of the founder, Bertuin, written in the ninth century.[4] We are told that he came of noble English stock, 'ex provintia Anglisaxonis', and was educated in a monastery Otbellum, which seems not to be mentioned elsewhere (Outwell near Wisbech, on the frontiers of Cambridgeshire and Norfolk?), and it is added in the true English manner: 'et ipsum monasterium eiusdem sancti viri Bertuini erat hereditas atque possessio.' He is said to have been a bishop but to have left his diocese after a vision; his foundation of Malonne is ascribed to the time of King Pippin. Two early abbots of St. Bavo's at Ghent, probably of the eighth century,

---

[1] Cf. above, p. 56, n. 2.

[2] Cf. my paper, 'Zu den Gesta abbatum Fontanellensium' (*Rev. Bén.* xlvi, 1934, p. 257, n. 1).

[3] On the Gospel book preserved at Maeseyck cf. E. H. Zimmermann, *Vorkarolingische Miniaturen*, Berlin, 1916, pp. 142 f., 303 f., and pls. 318–20. The *Vita Harlindis et Renulae* does not give any reliable explanation; cf. L. Van der Essen, loc. cit., pp. 109 ff.; *SS. rer. Merov.* vii. 130, n. 4.

[4] *Vita Bertuini*, ed. Levison, *SS. rer. Merov.* vii. 175–82. The invocation 'sancte Berahtwine' is found in a Tegernsee litany of the middle of the 11th century; cf. M. Coens, *Anal. Boll.* liii, 1935, pp. 138 f., and liv, 1936, p. 34.

have English names, Wilfrid and Egilfrid; but we know nothing about them beyond this.[1] Another mere shadow is Philip, 'genere Anglus', who, according to his legend, after staying at Rome for some time, settled under King Pippin as a hermit near the river Pfrimm in the Palatinate at a place which to the present day is called Zell after his cell.[2] These are a few examples of English continental relations which we are unable to refer to the exploits of great men such as Willibrord or Boniface. How many more of this kind may have existed?

There are also persons mentioned in the correspondence of Boniface and Lullus who remain for us more or less unsubstantial. The names of others who similarly went to the Continent do not occur in these letters, such as Sola who became a hermit in the diocese of Willibald, where the village of Solnhofen west of Eichstätt has preserved the memory of his cell; he died in 794, having committed it to the monastery of Fulda.[3] The monasteries of Hersfeld in Hesse and of Bleidenstadt in Nassau (near Wiesbaden) were founded by Lullus of Mainz; were compatriots of his among the earliest monks settled there? The probability of this is suggested by manuscripts of Hersfeld (p. 144) and by the name of its first abbot, Baldhart, who died in 798 and seems to have been of Anglo-Saxon extraction.[4] In the case of Bleidenstadt we have nothing on which to found even such conjectures.[5]

We learn from the letters of St. Boniface that his ecclesiastical policy met with various kinds of opposition. Did the fact that he and others we have spoken of were aliens also provoke hostility? People often dislike foreigners, and such aversion occasionally found expression in an attack on their nationality even in the early Middle Ages. When Bishop Eligius near

---

[1] Ph. Grierson, 'The Early Abbots of St. Bavo's of Ghent' (*Rev. Bén.* xlix, 1937, pp. 40 f., 42 f., 61); 'The relations between England and Flanders before the Norman Conquest' (loc. cit., p. 83).

[2] *Vita Philippi presbyteri Cellensis,* ed. A. Hofmeister, *MG. SS.* xxx. 2, pp. 796–805. The entry of his name in Vatican MS. Palat. Lat. 834 was also published by Quentin, *Les Martyrologes historiques,* p. 19.

[3] Ermenric of Ellwangen's *Vita Soli,* ed. O. Holder-Egger, *MG. SS.* xv. 1, pp. 151–63. The donation of a village to Sola by Abbot Wynnebald is recorded by Adelbert of Heidenheim (see above, p. 103, n. 2), ed. Gretser, pp. 808 f., Mabillon, iii. 2, p. 184, n. *a.*

[4] Cf. Boniface, *Epist.* 147, 148 (pp. 284 ff.); Tangl, ib., p. 284, n. 2.

[5] On the beginnings of Bleidenstadt cf. Meginhard of Fulda's *Sermo de S. Ferrucio,* ed. Holder-Egger, loc. cit., pp. 148–50.

Noyon preached against heathen customs he was reviled as a Roman. Corbinianus, the Bavarian saint, who seems to have been of Romanic descent, was abused by a Bavarian duchess as a bishop of British origin. Bishop Liudger of Münster attributes some opposition encountered by Boniface to his being a foreigner.[1] Another story of a more harmless kind also shows that the large number of Anglo-Saxon immigrants was viewed with some disfavour, and it is significant that raillery, as in the case of Corbinianus, took the form of a mis-statement of their race. When Alcuin was old and sick, so we are informed by his biographer,[2] another Anglo-Saxon, Aigulf, came to visit him at Tours, and heard four brethren of St. Martin's, who thought he would not understand them, saying: 'This Briton or Irishman has come to see the other Briton who lies within. O God, deliver this monastery from these Britons, who all come to this man like bees returning from every direction to their queen.' We need not follow the rest of the story. It seems to be just an expression of dislike for these Englishmen as aliens. But if such feeling existed in some places, it was without practical consequence; these foreigners were supported by the protection and favour of the royal house and particularly of the great king and emperor, ruler over many nationalities, and no doubt the influence of the great personalities among these Anglo-Saxons was weighty.

Nor did this impulse cease when the emigration of English missionaries and scholars came to an end in the early ninth century. It was propagated through their books and disciples. Their literary influence is frequently evident. The example of Bede's works mentioned above could be multiplied[3] and be extended to Alcuin's writings. Bede's Martyrology gave direction and character to all subsequent literature of this kind, which was abundant in the ninth century. His two books on chronology, notable for their lucidity, and the Chronicles of the World, which constitute their last chapters but were also copied

---

[1] *Vita Gregorii abb. Traiect.* c. 4 (*MG. SS.* xv. 1, p. 71): 'non esse eum dignum episcopatu, quia peregrinus erat.'

[2] *Vita Alcuini*, c. 18 (ib., p. 193).

[3] Bede's influence through the centuries is evident from the number of existing manuscripts; cf. the impressive lists published by M. L. W. Laistner and H. H. King, *A Hand-List of Bede Manuscripts*, Ithaca, 1943, and Laistner's instructive introduction.

as separate works, were favourite text-books of medieval com-
putists and chroniclers.[1] The Paschal Table based on that of
Dionysius, which Bede prefixed to his larger work on chronology,
became the foundation of a new kind of annals destined to a
great future; they originated in western Germany in the eighth
century as an addition to the framework of Christian years in-
herent in these tables. I have already mentioned (pp. 83 f.) that
the Christian era of Dionysius, the era of the Incarnation, was
adopted by the Anglo-Saxons first at home, then also on the
Continent; in process of time it was accepted by nearly the
whole Christian world. Bede's and Alcuin's compilations of
biblical commentaries were copied and excerpts were made
from them again and again. I might speak of Bede's chapters
on visions of the other world in the fifth book of his *Ecclesiastical
History* and of a similar story told by Boniface, which give them
a place among the forerunners of Dante,[2] and of the influence
of Anglo-Latin riddles and other poetry on the Latin continental
poems. The early Christian vernacular poetry of Germany also
followed in some measure the precedent of Anglo-Saxon poems
in the native tongue; it was soon to react upon England, as the
famous case of the Old Saxon and the Old English 'Genesis'
has made manifest.[3]

Continental art entered England in the seventh century and
mingled there with 'northern' models.[4] The penetration from
Gaul and Italy is evident in ecclesiastical architecture, in the
monumental crosses, and in the illumination of books; the
activities of Wilfrid and of Benedict Biscop include famous

---

[1] Bede's chronology of the ages of the world met with early opposition not only
in England (*Bede Essays*, p. 115; cf. pp. 120 ff.) but also in Rome, if the conjecture
of L. Traube is well founded, that the author of the anonymous 'Laterculus impera-
torum Romanorum Malalianus' (*Auct. ant.* xiii. 424 ff.), when attacking Irishmen
and their pupils ('Scotti', 'Scottorum scolaces') was in fact confronting Bede and his
chronological system. Cf. Traube, 'Chronicon Palatinum' (*Byzantinische Zeitschr.*
iv, 1895, pp. 489–92; Traube, *Vorles.* iii. 201–4). But such opposition was ineffective.

[2] *Bede Essays*, p. 144; Laistner and King, loc. cit., pp. 103, 106 ff.; below, p. 281.

[3] The Latin Preface and verses (the latter also in *MG. Poetae*, ii. 668 f.) on the
poet of the *Heliand* (*Heliand*, ed. Sievers, Halle, 1878, pp. 3–6) offer a later example
of English influence. Some features of Cædmon's story (Bede, *H.E.* iv. 24), as is
almost generally recognized, have there been transferred to the German poet of the
9th century. Cf. Baeseke, loc. cit., pp. 120 ff.

[4] On art I may refer to the works of G. Baldwin Brown (1903 ff.), E. H. Zimmer-
mann (1916), A. W. Clapham (1930), T. D. Kendrick (1938), and to the essay of
R. Krautheimer, 'The Carolingian Revival of Early Christian Architecture' (*The
Art Bulletin*, xxiv, March, 1942).

examples of such importation.[1] Mediterranean art, after the age of Roman dominion, was once more advancing to the north. King Naiton of the Picts about 710 employed architects from Jarrow to build him a stone church 'iuxta morem Romanorum'; Benedict, a generation before, had brought masons from Gaul for the same purpose. Benedict also introduced glassmakers from the same country, who taught Englishmen their art.[2] The knowledge thus acquired died out or was insufficient; the abbot of Wearmouth and Jarrow in 764 asked Lullus of Mainz to send him a man able to make vessels of glass well, 'qui vitrea vasa bene possit facere'. But about the same time English art began to react upon the Continent. Illuminated manuscripts which the English emigrants took with them contributed to the Carolingian styles of book illumination. On the other hand, the magnificent new books of the Continent soon began to influence the insular illuminators; an American scholar has recently sought to trace this influence in some pages of the famous Book of Kells finished shortly after 800 in northern Ireland.[3] Carolingian architecture early left its mark in England. A reciprocal give and take went on; this was possible, because the continental missionaries to England in the seventh century and the English emigrants to the Continent in the eighth had created a common ground which both parties could cultivate: 'we see', a historian of art has said,[4] 'that the British Isles represent the North European aspect of the medieval artistic spirit and that a constant influence on the southern element and a constant mingling with southern ingredients produced the richness of medieval

---

[1] I may also mention the pilgrims to Rome, who returning brought with them 'toraciclas' showing 'imagines Christi matris'; see Æthilwald's *Carm. rhythm.* ii, vv. 171 ff. (Aldhelm, ed. Ehwald, pp. 532 f.). On 'thoracic(u)la' (not 'thoracida') cf. my remarks, 'Konstantinische Schenkung und Silvester-Legende' (*Miscellanea Francesco Ehrle*, ii = *Studi e Testi*, xxxviii, Rome, 1924, pp. 195 f.).

[2] Wilfrid fitted the windows of York cathedral with glass (*Vita Wilfridi*, c. 16, p. 211. 2; cf. Colgrave's edition, p. 163). The churches of Bugge (Aldhelm, *Carm. eccl.* iii. 67, p. 17) and in Ædilvulf's monastery (*Carm.* c. 20. 25, *MG. Poetae*, i. 599; *Symeonis Op.* ed. Arnold, i. 288) also had glass windows. Cf. also G. Baldwin Brown, *The Arts in Early England*, iv. 480 ff.

[3] A. M. Friend, 'The Canon Tables of the Book of Kells' (*Medieval Studies in Memory of A. Kingsley Porter*, ii, Cambridge, Mass., 1939, pp. 611–66). But cf. also the different views of Françoise Henry, *Irish Art in the Early Christian Period*, London, 1940, pp. 134 (n. 2), 144 (n. 2).

[4] Adolph Goldschmidt, 'English Influence on Medieval Art' (*Medieval Studies in Memory of A. Kingsley Porter*, ii. 728).

art.' They had a common soil, fertilized by the pagan and Christian heritage of ancient times, on which to develop the rich crop of medieval Western civilization in its special forms.

It is the historian's principal task, to use the words of a philosopher,[1] 'humanas actiones non ridere, non lugere neque detestari, sed intelligere'. There are some who have censured and condemned the achievements of Boniface and his followers, and regard them as a misfortune for Germany and even Europe. Heirs of the 'rabies theologorum' of the sixteenth century, in the spirit of the Magdeburg Centuries (whose merits I do not deny), they substantiate such a judgement on the ground of the connexion of the Anglo-Saxons with the Roman Church and the Papacy, while the Irishmen are praised as predecessors of Protestantism. Protestant theologians such as Loofs, Hauck, and von Schubert have sufficiently disposed of this fallacious reasoning of historical dilettanti, who transpose the opinions and controversies of later times into the past and disregard its different conditions and beliefs.[2] We find in modern times another ground of condemnation, which is more comprehensive and fundamental; it demands that a culture should be absolutely native, without any importation of a 'universal' religion having its origin in another soil and race. Charles the Great, enforcing Christianity upon the Saxons, was for some time particularly obnoxious to such critics. We do not know what development would have taken place had there been no Anglo-Saxon emigrants and no great emperor. The historian is no prophet, and to divine what would have happened in the past if certain events had not occurred is even more difficult than to prophesy. The historian may find it suggestive to ruminate upon the possibilities, latent but unfulfilled, at some decisive moment of history; but he should not forget that such speculations are based on a 'conditio irrealis'. I doubt whether there was or is any culture of a higher level some part of which did not proceed from the acceptance and adaptation of the legacy of other

[1] Spinoza, *Tractatus politicus*, i. 4.
[2] I have in mind the naïve, uncritical books of Otto Wissig, *Wynfrid-Bonifatius: Ein Charakterbild nach seinen Briefen gezeichnet*, Gütersloh, 1929, and *Iroschotten und Bonifatius in Deutschland*, ib., 1932, not to mention earlier works of the same tendency. Cf. the reviews by Stach, *Historische Vierteljahrschrift*, xxvii, 1932, pp. 414–16, and myself, *Deutsche Literaturzeitung*, 1932, col. 850 f.

civilizations. 'A truly rich nation becomes rich by accepting much from others and developing it.'[1] One may dislike and disapprove of numerous features and tendencies of medieval life; but one cannot but recognize that, notwithstanding all the prejudices and other deficiencies of that age, many of the noblest products of Western civilization have grown up on medieval foundations, from a common heritage which is even now a living reality among the individual nations in spite of their differences and their present struggles. The devotion and the enterprise of English emigrants in the eighth century had a large share in creating this common soil and atmosphere. When the legions of Emperor Claudius had conquered a part of Britain, a Roman poet wrote words which might have been repeated with a deeper meaning about 800:

'Coniunctum est quod adhuc orbis et orbis erat.'[2]

[1] Jacob Burckhardt: 'Ein wahrhaft reiches Volk wird dadurch reich, daß es von anderen vieles übernimmt und weiterbildet'; quoted by Andreas Heusler, 'Germanentum' (*Kultur und Sprache*, viii), Heidelberg, 1934, p. 88.

[2] 'Now joined is what before were separated worlds.' *Anthologia Latina*, ed. A. Riese, 2nd ed. i, 1, p. 326, no. 426 ('Laus Caesaris'). Cf. Edward A. Freeman, 'Alter Orbis' (*Historical Essays, Fourth Series*, London, 1892, pp. 219–48); Arnold J. Toynbee, *A Study of History*, 2nd ed. i, Oxford, 1935, pp. 17–22, 29 f.

APPENDIX
STUDIES AND SOME TEXTS

I

THE CHARTERS OF KING ETHELBERT I OF KENT AND THE DESCENT OF THE ANGLO-SAXON CHARTERS

THERE exist three charters purporting to be granted in 605 by Ethelbert of Kent, the first Christian English king, to the abbey of SS. Peter and Paul in Canterbury, later known as St. Augustine's. They are considered commonly and rightly to be forgeries; the question is whether they contain genuine elements, whether these can be recognized and furnish evidence regarding the origin and descent of the earliest Anglo-Saxon charters in general. Thomas of Elmham, the historian of the abbey at the beginning of the fifteenth century (*Historia monasterii S. Augustini Cantuariensis*, ed. Ch. Hardwick, Rolls Series, 1858), not only copied the text of these 'earliest' documents of his house, but also added facsimiles of the charters of Ethelbert and of the 'Bulla plumbea' of Archbishop Augustine of Canterbury. The latter (Birch, no. 7) and one of Ethelbert's charters (no. 6) are written in an imitation of uncial script; the other two (nos. 4 and 5) exhibit a different kind of writing. Margaret Deanesly[1] recently stated that these 'are clearly copies of a Merovingian cursive script', that 'a very old papyrus' much emended was the foundation of the existing texts, and that one of them 'incorporates certain elements from an original grant' made by Ethelbert to St. Augustine's. In a charter of Rochester Cathedral which is also ascribed to Ethelbert and to the previous year 604 (Birch, no. 3), she discovered 'old Frankish formulas' and conjectured that Bishop Liudhard, the companion of Queen Bertha, Ethelbert's Frankish wife, was the connecting link, having introduced Frankish chancery customs into England. From the list of witnesses who attested the charters for St. Augustine's, she also concluded that the king of Kent in arranging his court followed the example of Bertha's Merovingian relatives. This would be another consequence of early connexions between Kent and the Franks which are obvious, and one may also recall

---

[1] M. Deanesly, 'Early English and Gallic Minsters' (*T.R.H.S.*, 4th series, xxiii, 1941, pp. 25–69); 'Canterbury and Paris in the reign of Æthelberht' (*History*, xxvi, no. 102, 1941, pp. 97–104); 'The Court of King Æthelberht of Kent' (*The Cambridge Historical Journal*, vii, no. 2, 1942, pp. 101–14).

the golden triens with the name of 'Leudardus episcopus' found at Canterbury as furnishing proof of such influence exercised by Bertha's bishop. But as to Ethelbert's charters things are less simple, and Miss Deanesly herself destroyed one of the foundations of her opinions by publishing a reproduction of Elmham's facsimile of Birch, no. 5 (in her third article after p. 114): as everybody familiar with early medieval script can see and Neil Ker has already pointed out (ib., p. 107, n. 11; cf. p. 101, n. 3), it is not an imitation of Merovingian cursive but of an Anglo-Saxon minuscule hand perhaps of about 800. Nevertheless these charters do actually show connexions between England and the Continent, but connexions of quite a different nature.

A critical edition of the charters of St. Augustine's does not yet exist. Elmham's published work, which comprises many of them, is the latest of a number of medieval cartularies of the abbey.[1] The author of a future definitive edition of the charters will have to establish the characters of the different cartularies as entities, and the relations between these collections and the few existent and the many lost originals or pseudo-originals, before the value of the individual texts transmitted to us can be assessed;[2] he will have to pay attention to details referring to these original documents which are found in the cartularies[3] and in the histories of the monastery by Thomas Sprott, William Thorne, and Thomas of Elmham. Birch, whose *Cartularium Saxonicum* includes the charters up to 975, did not make use of all the available material, and sometimes neglected the very earliest copies. Therefore any effort in this field of research, at a time when manuscripts are not accessible, cannot but be provisional. However, in spite of these limitations, the printed texts are sufficient to justify an attempt in this direction, though subject to revision.

The list of witnesses in Birch, no. 5, is the centre of Miss Deanesly's conjectures regarding Ethelbert's court and its relations to a Merovingian model. There may be prima-facie doubts whether this document will bear such conclusions. The introductory formula of 'notification' or 'promulgation': 'Notum sit omnibus tam praesentibus quam posteris, quod . . . ', is continental in fact, but it belongs to

---

[1] Cf. G. J. Turner (and H. E. Salter), *The Register of St. Augustine's Abbey Canterbury commonly called the Black Book*, i (The British Academy, Records of the Social and Economic History of England and Wales, ii), London, 1915, pp. xiv ff.; Holtzmann, *Papsturkunden*, at the pages indicated, i, p. 648, and ii, p. 486.

[2] According to Holtzmann, i, p. 69, Cotton MS. Julius D. II (*c.* 1250) was a source of Elmham.

[3] Cotton MS. Claudius D. X (*c.* 1290) was based on the originals, according to Holtzmann, i, p. 82. Elmham already saw differences between originals and cartularies (viii. 51, p. 237).

a later age. Charters of the Merovingians also contain formulas of notification but in different terms; diplomas of Frankish kings do not exhibit this particular kind of formula before the times of Pippin and Charles the Great, and it is an arbitrary assumption that a transcriber 'modernized' the transmitted words. It will later become clear how such a continental formula, unusual in early England, found its way into this document. The dating by the year of the Incarnation also points to an age later than Ethelbert's. The form of the signatures of the witnesses compels the same conclusion:

+ Ego Agustinus gratia Dei archiepiscopus libenter subscripsi.
+ Ego Eadbaldus regis filius favi.
+ Ego Hamigisilus dux laudavi.
+ Ego Hocca comes consensi.
+ Ego Augemundus referendarius approbavi.
+ Ego Graphio comes benedixi.
+ Ego Tangisilus regis optimas confirmavi.
+ Ego Pinca consensi.
+ Ego Geddi corroboravi.

The genuine early Anglo-Saxon charters, originals and copies, are simpler and even monotonous in this respect. Persons who were able to write gave their signatures in the form +*Ego N.* (the name) *subscripsi* or *consensi et subscripsi* or in a similar formula without any differentiation of the words; those who could not write 'signed' by a cross, while the scribe of the charter added to each cross the formula *Signum manus N.* This is not the place to discuss how far the first kind of signatures and the crosses of the 'signa' were in fact made by the witnesses 'manu propria'; certainly very often there was no real difference between the two ways of signing, and all signatures were written alike by the scribe, to give a list of the witnesses; therefore all these formulas were dropped occasionally for a simple list of names (and titles). Here it is only the uniformity of the formulas in the early genuine charters that is essential. The tenth century brought about a change. From *c.* 930 onwards the fashion started of diversifying the verbs of the episcopal signatures, while names of minor clerics and of laymen were added usually with the same verb or, more often, without any verb. The earlier custom did not disappear entirely; e.g. a charter of King Edgar of 958 (Birch, iii, no. 1040) has 18 times, another one of 967 (no. 1198) 15 times, the same formula *consensi et subscripsi*. But the liking for variation prevailed, in so far as members of the royal house and bishops were concerned. I will only quote a charter of 956 (no. 926): *consensi, roboravi, impressi, consignavi, adquievi, subscripsi, conclusi*, or another of 1061 (Kemble, iv, no. 811), where two abbots join the bishops: *laudavi, corroboravi, affirmavi, consolidavi, confirmavi, laudavi*; in the eleventh century such a verb was also added, though exceptionally, to names of laymen (e.g. ib., nos. 727, 817). The difference between the earlier and the later fashions was already emphasized by Kemble (i, pp. xcv f.), who justly considered variations of the later kind 'one of the strongest evidences of forgery when found in charters professing an earlier date'; he mentioned expressly Ethelbert's charter Birch, no. 5, which obviously cannot be earlier than the tenth or eleventh centuries, either itself or indirectly through a document of that age used in fabricating the royal grant. It is possible of course that a copyist changed the original words in accordance with the fashion of his times (cf. Kemble, ii, pp. ix f. on the difference between the original and the later texts of Birch, i, no. 312); but several of the names also cause difficulties (below, p. 220).

And is there any reason for presupposing an underlying papyrus fragment? Letters and charters of the Popes (and probably others) which were sent to England in Ethelbert's time and after were certainly written on papyrus (cf. below, p. 255); it is possible and even probable that papyrus was also imported for the correspondence of the Roman missionaries. But it is another question whether it was also used for Anglo-Saxon legal affairs. It is a mere possibility, and no trace of it remains. The survival of the Laws of Ethelbert, which were written down 'iuxta exempla Romanorum' (Bede, *H.E.* ii. 5, p. 90), is no evidence; Roman law-books were copied in this age not only on papyrus but also on parchment, which could easily be produced in England as elsewhere. The Florentinus of Justinian's Digests, the Verona MS. of his Codex, the Turin and Vatican fragments of the Codex Theodosianus may be mentioned; some years after Ethelbert, even in Italy, King Rothari used 'membrane' for the first Langobardic codification (643) and also knew charters written on parchment (*Edict.* c. 243). Although in the Mediterranean countries papyrus prevailed longer for charters and letters, imperial rescripts existed already in 470 written 'in chartis (papyrus) sive membranis' (*Cod. Iustin.* i. 23. 6); in Ethelbert's time Columbanus wrote a letter on parchment (*Epist.* 4, *MG. Epist.* iii, p. 169. 26). It may be that papyrus was never used for Anglo-Saxon charters. Nor do we know whether the 'exotic' use of charters was introduced so early in England as 'a new and a better form of testimony'[1] side by side with the oral declarations of will familiar to the Germanic peoples. No original Anglo-Saxon charter has survived earlier than of 679, no copy of a charter which can be considered reasonably genuine, earlier than of 670, and it is not certain that the lack of documents during the previous seventy years is connected with the

---

[1] Cf. above, p. 4, n. 1.

A a

use of papyrus. In the chancery of the Merovingians a transition from this material to parchment took place between 660 and 670;[1] but in Gaul, where the Romanic population persisted in spite of all invasions and immigrations and continued to employ written legal documents without any interruption, the conditions were quite different from those prevailing in England, notwithstanding the Roman survivals in Britain which have been the subject of modern discussion. There is therefore no sound basis for conjectures founded on the assumption of the preservation of a fragmentary papyrus text in what is evidently a late forgery.

The charters of King Ethelbert should not be singled out for consideration. There are other documents of St. Augustine's which are also obvious forgeries or at least raise well-founded suspicions, and these require to be examined together with Ethelbert's grants. We are even informed of occasions when some of them were employed as weapons in the conflicts of the abbey during the 'golden age of forgers',[2] the late eleventh and the twelfth centuries. After the Norman Conquest the monastery had to acquiesce in encroachments of royal vassals on its lands; it defended its 'liberty' against the diocesan, the archbishop of Canterbury; it resisted inroads on its possessions and demands for payments made by the archbishop and by the archdeacon and the chapter of Christ Church, the cathedral. The monks claimed for their cemetery the right of *generalis sepultura* and strove against its limitation. They objected to an abbot nominated by Archbishop Lanfranc (1087) and maintained the principle of the free election of the abbot by the monks. Abbots refused the profession of canonical obedience demanded by the archbishops in connexion with the benediction of a new abbot; there was also the special question whether the benediction should be performed only within the abbey, or whether the abbot was obliged to receive it at another place also. The aim was 'exemption' of the monastery from the jurisdiction of the diocesan and from any ecclesiastical authority but that of the Pope, and maintenance of its own ecclesiastical jurisdiction in parishes belonging to the abbey.

Genuine and forged documents were the usual weapons in such

---

[1] Cf., e.g., H. Bresslau, *Handbuch der Urkundenlehre*, ii[2], Berlin, 1931, pp. 488 f. The erroneous statement that a Frankish royal diploma was written on papyrus as late as 692 should not have been repeated by R. S. Lopez, 'Mohammed and Charlemagne: a revision' (*Speculum*, xviii, 1943, pp. 15, 28). Therefore the change cannot be referred to an embargo on the export of papyrus enforced by the Caliph 'Abd al-Malik about this time. I should rather attribute it to the influence of the reconquista-politics of Emperor Constans in the sixties of that century (cf. above, p. 13).

[2] A. de Boüard, *Manuel de diplomatique française et pontificale*, i, Paris, 1929, p. 16, n. 2; cf. Bresslau, loc. cit. i[2], Leipzig, 1912, p. 12.

contests in England as on the Continent, and we know that charters were used for these purposes at St. Augustine's at least from the early twelfth century onwards. When at the end of 1107 Archbishop Anselm, himself being ill, intended to have the benediction of Abbot Hugh of St. Augustine's carried out in his cathedral, Christ Church, by the bishop of Exeter, the monks resisted and claimed to possess privileges by which their abbot should not be consecrated elsewhere than in his own monastery; these privileges were declared null and void by King Henry I and his great men at a meeting in London early in 1108.[1] In the year 1124 the Augustinians relied upon a privilege of Pope Calixtus II granted in 1120, which referred to privileges of his predecessors Boniface (IV), Adeodatus, Agatho, and John (XII); the beginning of the privilege is mostly based on the existing charter of Boniface.[2] The contents were considered by Archbishop William to encroach on the rights and dignity of Christ Church; he asked to have presented the *privilegium bullatum* itself; the monks refused. Under Archbishop Theobald (1139–61) in the time of Abbot Hugh II (1126–51) the monks again pleaded 'ancient privileges' against the other side, claiming to be a Roman house. After the election of the next abbot, Silvester, in 1151, the question of the place of his benediction was once more raised; papal privileges were produced by the monks, but their authenticity was challenged by the archiepiscopal party.[3] When the conflict regarding the benediction and profession of the abbot reached its climax in the later part of the century, Pope Alexander III decided in favour of the monastery in 1178: 'inspectis antiquis privilegiis ecclesiae vestrae et praecipue privilegio beati

---

[1] Eadmer, *Historia novorum in Anglia*, ed. M. Rule, pp. 188 f.: 'Nam ecclesiam suam privilegia habere commentati sunt, per quae abbatem suum nonnisi in sede sua ordinari debere manifesta allegatione se probaturos asseruerunt.' But the discussions in London proceeded, 'omissis privilegiis suis, quae nulla vel non rata a rege et principibus comprobata sunt et damnata'. The claim of the monks may have referred to the Bulla Plumbea of Augustine and to the privileges of the Popes Boniface IV and John XII; cf. below, pp. 181 f.

[2] The complete text of Calixtus's privilege was published by Holtzmann, *Papsturkunden*, i, p. 231, no. 10; cf. Jaffé, i. 6878. D. Knowles, 'The Growth of Exemption' (*The Downside Review*, l, 1932, p. 406, n. 2), considered the forged privilege of Boniface IV dependent on that of Calixtus; but analysis of the sources shows the reverse relation; cf. below, pp. 190 f.

[3] *Ioannis Sarisberiensis Historia Pontificalis*, c. 42 (ed. R. L. Poole, Oxford, 1927, p. 89; ed. W. Arndt, *MG. SS.* xx. 544): 'Sed de loco benedictionis contentio suborta est ex causa quorundam privilegiorum statuentium ut abbas eiusdem loci in proprio monasterio benedictionem recipiat nec alio trahatur. Ipsa tamen privilegia suspecta habebantur, tum quia concepta non erant in ea scribendi forma quam sequitur ecclesia Romana, tum quia ex collatione scripture et bulle (cf. below, p. 207, n. 4) videbantur non esse pontificum quorum nomina preferebant.' Cf. Poole, loc. cit., pp. xlviii ff.; Knowles, 'The Growth of Exemption' (loc. cit., p. 409, n. 3).

Augustini Cantuariensis archiepiscopi, quod vestro monasterio indulsit' (Elmham, pp. 420 ff.; Jaffé, ii. 13039/40). But Archbishop Richard declared the documents to be forged,[1] and in 1181 the Pope commissioned the bishop of Durham and the abbot of St. Albans to examine the privileges of St. Augustine's and to send sealed copies with two or three originals to Rome, while the monks carried there the 'original' privileges of Boniface and Agatho (Holtzmann, i, p. 477, no. 205; cf. Elmham, pp. 441 f.=Jaffé, ii. 14380). According to the report of Gervase of Canterbury (ed. Stubbs, i. 296) who represents the views of the archbishop and Christ Church, the monks produced in England also two documents:

'Protulerunt itaque tandem aliquando monachi abbatis scedulas duas, quas sua originalia constanter esse dicebant. Quarum prima vetustissima erat rasa et subscripta, acsi esset emendata, et absque sigillo. Hanc dicebant regis Ethelberti esse privilegium. Alia vero scedula multo erat recentior, de qua bulla plumbea cum iconia episcopi nova valde dependebat. Hanc cartulam sancti Augustini dicebant esse privilegium. In his autem privilegiis intuentium iudicio haec maxime notanda fuerunt. In prima laudabilis quidem fuit vetustas, sed rasa fuit et inscripta nec ullius sigilli munimine roborata. In alia vero reprehensione dignum fuit, quod nova extitit eius littera et bulla. . . . Fuit etiam notatum, immo notorium et notabile, quod bulla ipsius plumbea fuit, cum non soleant Cisalpini praesules vel primates scriptis suis autenticis bullas plumbeas apponere. Modus etiam Latini et forma loquendi a Romano stilo dissona videbantur. Haec duo solummodo privilegia in medium prolata sunt, cum alia nonnulla se habuisse monachi iactitarent.'

There is no need to dwell on the rudimentary criticism of this age.[2] Alexander's successor Lucius III failed to recognize the true value or rather worthlessness of charters the spuriousness of which is obvious to-day to every historian versed in medieval diplomatics. King Henry II effected a compromise in 1182 to end these controversies, which in fact persisted; but their later history does not concern us, nor have I mentioned many details which are told in the *Acta Lanfranci* (ed. Plummer, *Two Saxon Chronicles*, i. 290 f.), by Gervase, Thorne, Elmham, and in charters and letters.[3] Gervase's

---

[1] Cf. also Holtzmann, loc. cit. ii. 388 ff., nos. 190, 191.

[2] Cf., e.g., Bresslau, loc. cit. i. 15 ff.; M. Spaethen, 'Giraldus Cambrensis und Thomas von Evesham über die von ihnen an der Kurie geführten Prozesse' (*Neues Archiv*, xxxi, 1906, pp. 638 ff.); R. L. Poole, *Lectures on the History of the Papal Chancery*, Cambridge, 1915, pp. 143 ff.

[3] Cf. J. B. Sheppard, *Literae Cantuarienses*, i (Rolls Series), 1887, pp. lv ff.; Georg Schreiber, *Kurie und Kloster im 12. Jahrhundert*, i (Kirchenrechtl. Abhandl. lxv–lxvi), 1910, pp. 134 ff.; R. C. Fowler, *V.C.H., Kent*, ii, 1926, pp. 128 f.; D. Knowles, 'The Growth of Exemption' (*Downside Review*, l, 1932, pp. 401–15), 'Parish Organization' (ib. li, 1933, pp. 515–17), and *The Monastic Order in England*, pp. 115 f., 588; Jean-François Lemarignier, *Étude sur les privilèges d'exemption et de juridiction ecclésias-*

statement that Ethelbert's charter 'erat rasa et subscripta, acsi esset emendata', suggests that the monks had employed an older parchment and had erased the script but not completely, so that traces of the original writing could be seen under the new ('*sub*scripta').[1]

This sketch of the background against which the contested documents must be examined does not touch all subjects of controversy nor all charters involved.[2] But the following may reasonably be included:

1. King Ethelbert grants lands for the foundation of a monastery (of SS. Peter and Paul) near the eastern wall of Canterbury in 605, *Omnem hominem qui*, Birch, i, no. 4. The list of witnesses is missing in some of the manuscripts and may have been added afterwards from the next document; it existed when the 'inspeximus' and confirmation of charters were granted to the monastery by Edward II in 1326 (*Calendar of Charter Rolls*, iii, 1908, p. 492; cf. the 'inspeximus' of 1362, ib. v, 1916, p. 174). Elmham depicted the 'originals' of nos. 1–4 (above, p. 174); Leland also saw one of Ethelbert's charters (*Collectanea*, ed. Th. Hearne, 2nd ed., vol. iv [tomus iii], London, 1774, p. 8).

2. Ethelbert makes the same grant in 605, giving a more detailed description of the boundaries, *Notum sit omnibus*, Birch, no. 5. Cf. above, pp. 175 f.

3. Ethelbert grants to the monastery 'villam nomine Sturigao (Sturry), alio nomine dictam Cistelet' (Chislet), *Largiente summi regis*, Birch, no. 6. The date: 605, 9 January ('Actum sane quadragesimo quinto anno regni nostri . . .'), which is in contradiction with the beginning of the charter ('iam per decem quinquennia sceptrigera potestate potitus'), is missing in some of the manuscripts, which also shorten the list of witnesses, omitting the name of Aldhun. This charter was no doubt the privilege produced in 1181.

4. The privilege of Bishop Augustine, called 'Bulla plumbea' on account of its seal, which was described by Elmham (ii. 29, p. 124; cf. p. 119, n. 3) and Leland (loc. cit.), *Patet omnibus quod*, Birch, no. 7.

5. Privilege of Pope Boniface IV of 611, 27 February, *Omnipotentis Dei institutione*, Birch, no. 11; cf. Jaffé, i, no. 1997.

6. Grant of lands at Northbourne by King Eadbald in 618, *Ego Aedbaldus rex*, Birch, no. 13. Leland (loc. cit.) saw the original.

---

tique des abbayes normandes jusqu'en 1140 (Archives de la France monastique, xliv), Paris, 1937, pp. 111 f., 154, 176 f. Holtzmann's *Papsturkunden* have recently added new material.

[1] It is hardly possible to apply these words to a papyrus, as Miss Deanesly has done.

[2] I abstain from examining the grant of William I suspected by H. W. C. Davis, *Regesta regum Anglo-Normannorum*, i, p. 10, no. 35 (= p. 119, no. viii).

7. Privilege of Pope Adeodatus (672–6), *Evangelicis atque apostolicis*, Birch, no. 31; cf. Jaffé, i, no. 2104.

8. Privilege of Pope Agatho of 679, *Quoniam semper sunt*, Birch, no. 38; cf. Jaffé, ii, no. 2105*a* (p. 741).

9. Privilege of Pope John XII (955–63) addressed to King Edred (946–55), *Studio divini cultus*, Birch, iii, no. 915; cf. Jaffé, i, no. 3678.

10. Second privilege of Pope John XII, addressed to King Edred and Archbishop Odo of Canterbury (942–58), *Inter praeclaras sacrae*, Birch, iii, no. 916; cf. Jaffé, i, no. 3679.

11. Grant of the island of Thanet by King Edward the Confessor (1042–66), *Conditor caeli terraeque*, Kemble, iv, no. 900.

Notwithstanding the diversity in the main subjects of some of these charters, there is more connexion and interdependence between them and even more unity than may appear at the first glance. Even the short grant no. 1 acquires a peculiar aspect by the addition: 'et res quam supra memoravi in potestate abbatis sit qui ibi fuerit ordinatus', a theme which is developed positively and negatively in other documents. The 'liberty' of the monastery from the control of other powers, royal and ecclesiastical, and from their demands and encroachments is stressed, the 'perpetua libertas' (2, 4, 5, 11); there should be no subjection (3, 4, 10) or subjugation (4), no *servitium* (5), *consuetudo* (5),[1] *ius consuetudinarium* (4), no tribute (4); a freedom is conferred on the monastery's churches and parishes (4, 10) and *iudicia* (4) as well as on its other possessions. The free election of the abbot is emphasized (4, 5, 7, 8, 9); his ordination must be performed by the diocesan in St. Augustine's: 'in eodem monasterio . . . ordinet' (4), 'in eodem loco consecretur' (5, 9); nor should there be any other interference of the archbishop without the invitation of the abbot and the brethren. The monastery is the first in England (5, 9, 10), and it should be the resting-place of the departed kings and archbishops, as we are repeatedly informed (3, 4, 5, 6, 9, 10, 11), 'ex auctoritate apostolica' (3, 4, 10), 'ex praecepto . . . Gregorii' (9): the burial rights claimed by the abbey[2] and their limitation were, according to Gervase (ed. Stubbs, i. 81), the origin of all the quarrels. The connexion with the Apostolic See is not only shown by the number

---

[1] On the meaning of *consuetudo* cf., e.g., Lemarignier, loc. cit., pp. 46, 72 ff.

[2] In Ethelbert's third grant the claim that all archbishops should be buried at St. Augustine's, that is, outside the city of Canterbury, is referred to the Scriptures: 'Scriptura dicente, non esse civitatem mortuorum sed vivorum.' Mark xii. 27 (Matt. xxii. 32; Luke xx. 38) quoted by Birch, speaks of God: 'Non est Deus mortuorum sed vivorum', but has no relation to burial-grounds. There is a similar sentence in Alcuin's *Vita Vedasti*, c. 9 (ed. Krusch, SS. rer. Merov. iii. 424) in connexion with the interment of the saint: 'quod nullus intra muros civitatis sepeliri debuisset, quia omnis civitas locus debet esse vivorum, non mortuorum.' Is there a common source?

of papal privileges (5, 7, 8, 9, 10) but also by the express order that there shall be free access to it in case of need (5).

Bede's *Ecclesiastical History* (i. 33, ii. 3–6, iv. 5) was drawn upon in several of these charters (3, 4, 5, 6, 7, 11);[1] the origin of the monastery is told in what I may call the *hortatu*-formula; forgers are often more talkative than the authors of genuine charters:[2]

Bede, *H.E.* i. 33: Fecit autem et monasterium non longe ab ipsa civitate ad orientem, in quo eius *hortatu* Aedilberct ecclesiam beatorum apostolorum Petri et Pauli a fundamentis construxit ac diversis donis ditavit.

3: monitu et *hortatu* beatissimi papae Gregorii et sancti patris nostri Augustini ipsi beatissimo apostolorum principi Petro et doctori gentium Paulo ecclesiam *a fundamentis construxi* illamque terris variisque possessionum *donariis* decorare studui.

4: rex Aethilberhtus . . . nostra *instantia* (cf. 6) . . . monasterium . . . condidit et regalibus opibus amplisque possessionibus *ditavit*, dilatavit, magnificavit.

5: ut *ecclesia beatorum apostolorum Petri et Pauli ad orientem civitat*is Doroberniae sita, quam . . . sanctissimorum patrum tuorum Gregorii (cf. 3) atque Augustini *hortatu* ammonitus . . . *a fundamentis construxi*sti et . . . *diversis donis dita*sti.

6: ecclesias Dei, quas viriliter *instantia* (cf. 4) patris Augustini fundavit et terris multisque honoribus *ditavit*. . . .

9: quod Athelbertus rex . . . *hortatu* eiusdem patris et apostoli vestri Augustini *a fundamentis construxit*.

11: aecclesiam, quam *hortatu* beati Augustini rex Aethelberht in honore apostolorum Petri et Pauli *a fundamento constituit diversisque donis ditavit*.

I omit other examples which show the same kind of workmanship; the dependence on Bede is manifested even by such unimportant phrases as in 3: 'Hanc igitur *ecclesia*m *ad provectum debiti culminis promovere* desiderans' (cf. *H.E.* ii. 4, p. 87. 6) or by the date of 5 which was taken from the same chapter of Bede.

There is much interdependence, as I said before, between the documents, in tendencies and wording.[3] The local aims of 3, 6, and 11 are connected with the more general demands of the other charters referring to the powers of the abbot and the rights of the

---

[1] I am not prepared to say whether in Ethelbert's third charter the list of presents is partly derived from Bede ('speculum argenteum, . . . camisiam ornatam'; cf. *H.E.* ii. 10, 11: 'camisia cum ornatura', 'speculum argenteum') or depends on an unknown inventory. The misreading *armilcaisia* for *armilausia* (*cai* for *au*), corrected already by Du Cange (s.v.), may perhaps support the second possibility.

[2] Cf. the remarks of Hans Hirsch, 'Die Urkundenfälschungen des Klosters Ebersheim' (*Festschrift Hans Nabholz*, Zürich, 1934, p. 23).

[3] Cf. e.g. 3: 'Hanc donationem meam . . . *per omnia* cum consilio . . . Augustini condidi'; 9: '*per omnia*, sicut sancti praedecessores nostri viri apostolici Deoque digni in suis privilegiis eidem contulerunt aecclesiae'; 10: '*per omnia*, sicut sancti et Deo dilecti filii sedis apostolicae . . . se habuere'.

abbey to be exercised *intus et foris* (3, 4, 5; cf. Exod. xxv. 11). The
rights claimed by the monastery in Chislet (3), Northbourne (6),
and the isle of Thanet (11) were subjects of dispute during the
twelfth century; in the compromise of 1182, when 'pax et concordia'
between Archbishop Richard and Abbot Roger were restored by
the king, the abbatial churches of Minster in Thanet, Northbourne,
and Chislet were exempted from the payments which the other
churches belonging to the monastery had to make to the archdeacon
(Elmham, p. 451). The grievances against the neighbouring cathedral monastery of Christ Church found an outspoken echo in the
command ascribed to Pope John XII (9): 'Unde *canonicis* de monasterio S. Salvatoris illi loco invidentibus praecipimus omnimodis,
ne sanctae huius devotionis cultum inquietare praesumant. Quod si
fecerint, eodem anathemate puniantur.' This outburst against the
'canons' was either written before Lanfranc (1070–89) directed his
energies 'towards making Christ Church a model monastery',[1] or is
a malicious reflection on the previous period, when the community
was, 'more than any other house, secular in outlook under the
Confessor'.[2]

These charters vary in point of diction; some exhibit, at least
in parts, rhymed prose (4, 5, 6, 7, 9, 10, 11), others do not. But the
style is no doubt influenced by the sources which the forger or
forgers employed in composing the new 'originals'. There are of
course biblical quotations and allusions; I have already mentioned
the use made of Bede (p. 183). Several sources can be recognized
on which the composition largely depended. The first charter of
King Ethelbert alone can claim to comprise genuine elements of an
early Kentish charter, though this was not earlier than the middle
part of the eighth century. A comparison with a charter of King
Sigired of 762 preserved in the *Textus Roffensis* (Birch, i, no. 193)
and with some other charters (ib., nos. 177, 199, 255) is conclusive.

Birch, no. 193	*Birch, no. 4*
In nomine domini nostri Iesu Christi. Omnem hominem, qui secundum Deum vivit et remunerari a Deo sperat et optat, oportet ut piis precibus assensum hilariter ex animo praebeat, quoniam certum est tanto facilius ea, quae quisque[3] a Deo poposcerit, consequi posse, quanto	*In nomine domini nostri Iesu Christi. Omnem hominem qui secundum Deum vivit et remunerari a Deo sperat et optat, oportet ut piis precibus consensum hilariter ex animo praebeat, quoniam certum est tanto facilius ea, quae ipse[3] a Deo poposcerit, consequi posse, quanto et ipse libentius Deo aliquid concesserit. Quo-*

---

[1] Knowles, *The Monastic Order*, p. 130; cf. pp. 122 ff.

[2] Ib., p. 697. Cf. R. R. Darlington, 'Ecclesiastical Reform in the Late Old English Period' (*E.H.R.* li, 1936, p. 403, n. 2).

[3] 'ipse' Birch, i, no. 177 and ii, no. 855.

et ipse libentius hominibus recte postulata concesserit. Quocirca ego Sigiraed rex Cantiae tibi venerabili Eardvulfo episcopo, ut diligenter postulasti, aliquam particulam terrae iuris mei, id est quasi unius ac semis iugeri, in civitate Hrofi ad augmentum monasterii tui aeternaliter possidendam concedo ac describo, cum omnibus scilicet ad eam pertinentibus rebus. . . .

circa ego Aethilberhtus *rex Canciae* cum consensu venerabilis archiepiscopi Augustini ac principum meorum[1] dabo et *concedo*[2] in honore sancti Petri *aliquam partem terrae iuris mei,* quae iacet *in* oriente *civitatis* Doroberniae, ita dumtaxat,[3] ut monasterium ibi construatur, et res quam supra memoravi in potestate abbatis sit, qui ibi fuerit ordinatus.

No. 189 (Eadbert of Kent)

Hinc igitur praecipio et precor in nomine omnipotentis Dei . . . , ut haec nostra concessio in Dei donatione aeternaliter sit confirmata, ita ut nec mihi nec alicui successorum meorum regum sive principum seu cuiuslibet conditionis dignitatibus nefario temeritatis ausu de supradicta donatione nostra aliquid fraudare vel minuere liceat.

Igitur adiuro *et praecipio in nomine* domini *Dei omnipotentis,* qui est omnium rerum iudex iustus[4], *ut* praefata terra sub scripta *donacione* sempiternaliter sit confirmata, ita ut nec mihi nec alicui successorum meorum regum aut principum sive cuiuslibet conditionis dignitatibus et ecclesiasticis gradibus de ea aliquid fraudare liceat.

No. 193

Si quis autem contra hanc donationem meam aliquando venire invido malivoloque animo temptaverit, sit in praesenti separatus a

Si quis vero de *hac donacione* nostra aliquid minuere[5] aut irritum facere[6] temptaverit, sit in praesenti separatus a sancta communione corporis et sanguinis

---

[1] Ib., no. 190 (Eadbert of Kent, 761): 'una *cum consensu* reverentissimi *archiepiscopi* Bregwini aliorumque servorum Dei *et principum meorum*'; no. 196 (Egbert of Kent, 765): '*cum consensu* scilicet *venerandi archiepiscopi* Genberhti . . . necnon et *principum meorum*'; no. 199 (Eardwulf of Kent): '*cum consensu venerabilis* episcopi nostri Eardvulfi necnon et *principum meorum*', &c.

[2] The formula *dabo et concedo* is found, e.g., in nos. 88, 213, 214, &c. On the use of the future cf. Kemble, i, pp. xxviii ff.; H. Brunner, *Zur Rechtsgeschichte der Römischen und Germanischen Urkunde,* i, Berlin, 1880, p. 165; Napier and Stevenson, *The Crawford Collection of Early Charters,* pp. 37 f.

[3] Birch, no. 199: 'terram iuris mei . . . possedendam concedo, *ita dumtaxat, ut,* quicquid de ea fieri volueritis, . . . liberam sempiternaliter *potestatem* habeatis.'

[4] Cf. Birch, ii, no. 779 (Edmund, 942–6): 'Unde *adiuro* in nomine domini Dei nostri Iesu Christi, *qui est omnium iustus iudex*' (cf. Ps. vii. 12); ib. iii, no. 1295 (Edgar, 973?): 'Ita *adiuro* in nomine domini Dei nostri Iesu Christi, *qui est omnium iudex iustus,* ut nec michi nec alicui successorum meorum regum seu cuiuslibet dignitatis aliquid fraudare vel minuere liceat.'   [5] Cf., e.g., n. 4 and above, no. 189.

[6] Cf., e.g., Birch, no. 199: 'Quisquis igitur ex quolibet vel ex *ecclesiastico gradu* vel ex saeculari dignitate . . . praefatam donationem nostram *inritam facere* temptaverit, sciat se sine dubio et in praesenti *ob meritum malitiae suae* iuste excommunicatum fieri a *corpore et sanguine Christi.*'

communione sanctae aecclesiae Christi et in futuro a societate sanctorum omnium segregatus. . . .

Christi et in die iudicii[1] ob meritum malitiae suae[2] *a* consortio *sanctorum omnium segregatus.*

No. *192, &c.*

Haec terra circumcincta est hiis terminibus: . . .

Circumcincta est haec terra his terminibus: . . .

No. *191, &c.*

Actum in civitate Dorovernis anno incarnationis Domini DCCLXII.

Acta in civitate Doroberni anno ab incarnatione Christi DCV, *indictione* VIII.

No. *177*

Actum mense Maio in civitate Lundonia indictione XIIII, anno ab incarnatione Christi DCCXLVIII.

No. *193*

✠Ego Sigiraed rex Cant. hanc donationem meam signo sanctae crucis roboravi.

✠*Ego* Aethilberhtus *rex Canciae* sana mente integroque consilio[3] *donacionem meam signo sanctae crucis propria manu roboravi* confirmavique.

No. *160*

✠Ego Aethilberhtus rex Cantiae hanc donationem a me factam propria manu signo sanctae crucis roboravi.

The comparison shows that the author of the 'foundation charter' of St. Augustine's used a grant by one of the Kentish kings of the middle of the eighth century, which probably comprised the formulas of our text, such as they are found separately in the documents of

[1] Birch, no. 316: 'sciat se separatum esse *in die iudicii a consortio sanctorum*.'

[2] See note 6 on p. 185.

[3] Cf. Birch, nos. 34 and 81 and the spurious charter no. 39: 'sana mente integroque consilio.' The formula had its origin in the last wills and testaments of Roman times and was used in Italian and Gallic testaments, but was transferred to other charters also; cf., e.g., Krusch, *Neues Archiv*, xx (1894), 540 f. and my remark, ib. xxvii (1902), 341, also my edition of the testament of Adalgisel-Grimo of Verdun of 634, *Trierer Zeitschr.* vii (1932), 75, n. 35. I add early Italian examples in Marini, *I papiri diplomatici*, Rome, 1805, pp. 110, 112 f. and *Historiae patriae monumenta*, xiii, Turin, 1873, col. 74, no. 39. Frankish charters which are not last wills are in C. Zeuss, *Traditiones possessionesque Wizenburgenses*, Spire, 1842, p. 25, no. 18, and C. Wampach, *Geschichte der Grundherrschaft Echternach*, i. 2, p. 21, no. 4 (= *Dipl. Merov.* p. 174, no. 56). The formula was also inserted into Ethelbert's third charter (Birch, p. 11, l. 18 f.), taken either from the first document or from its source.

those times which I have quoted. He may have employed a charter of King Ethelbert II (725–62), though this obvious conjecture cannot be really proved. The dating by the year of the Incarnation came into use in this age; the year 605 which he substituted may have been suggested by the beginning of Bede's second book of *H.E.*: 'His temporibus (that is, of King Ethelbert I of Kent and Ethelfrid of Northumbria), id est anno dominicae incarnationis DCV, beatus papa Gregorius . . . defunctus est.'

This foundation charter was partly copied, partly changed and enlarged, in Ethelbert's second charter. The royal style of this and · of the third grant manifests the greater distance from the source of the first document: while Ethelbert there calls himself rightly *rex Cantiae*, he appears in the two other texts as *rex Anglorum* (*Dei gratia* precedes in 2). The forger may have been influenced by Pope Gregory's letter to the king (*H.E.* i. 32) or rather by the practice of his own times; about 600 even *rex Cantuariorum* would have been more appropriate than *rex Cantiae*. The other charters have very little in common with early English documents. The names of the witnesses in 2 were repeated in 3 and supplemented by some names from Bede (cf. p. 198). The different verbs used in the list of witnesses of the grant of King Eadbald (6) correspond with 2 and also show that the author was familiar with English charters of the tenth and eleventh centuries (cf. pp. 176 f.). At the same time Eadbald's grant is connected with 3 by the phrase 'in solio paterno confirmatus' (3: 'solio paterno confirmatus').[1] The strange signature of 'Aemma, Francorum regis filia, regis Aeadbaldi copula', is obviously drawn either from the treatise on the Saints of England[2] or rather from a Genealogy of the Kentish kings, such as was also known to Florence of Worcester[3] and to William of Malmesbury.[4] The charter of Edward the Confessor (11) shows even more clearly the acquaintance of its author with the legends of the Kentish royal house, of the brothers Ethelred and Ethelbert, their sister 'Domneva' and their murderer Thunur.[5]

Papal privileges were another source of help in fabricating these charters. In fact one of the texts was thus adapted with very little change at St. Augustine's; the comparison of the privilege of Pope

---

[1] Cf. Livy xxxix. 53. 4: 'Romanos Demetrium *in paterno solio* locaturos'; Lactantius, *Institut.* i. 10. 10 (*CSEL.* xix. 35): 'cum paternum solium . . . cepisset.'

[2] Ed. Liebermann, *Die Heiligen Englands*, pp. 1 f., c. 6: 'Ymme, Eadbaldes cwén, Franca cynges dohtor', 'Eadbaldus vero habebat in uxorem filiam regis Francorum, nomine Ymmam'; cf. p. vi, n. 2.

[3] Ed. Petrie, p. 635.   [4] *Gesta regum*, i. 11 (ed. Stubbs, 1. 15).

[5] Liebermann, loc. cit., pp. 1 ff., cc. 7, 10–12; cf. pp. iv ff. Cf. also Ernst A. Philippson, *Germanisches Heidentum bei den Angelsachsen*, Leipzig, 1929, p. 137; Plummer, *Two Saxon Chronicles* II, 21 f.

Agatho (8) with the formula no. 32 of the *Liber Diurnus* (ed. Sickel, p. 23) makes this evident:

Liber Diurnus, no. 32

Birch, no. 38

Agatho episcopus, servus servorum Dei, Adriano religioso abbati[1] monasterii sanctorum apostolorum Petri ac Pauli, quod ab Athelberto primo Christiano rege Anglorum fundatum iuxta Doroverniae metropolitanam civitatem est situm,[2] eiusque congregationi pacis prosperitatem in perpetuum.

Quoniam semper sunt concedenda, quae rationabilibus congruunt desideriis, oportet ut devotio conditoris pie constructionis oraculi in privilegiis praestandis minime denegetur. Igitur quia postulasti a nobis, quatenus monasterium sancti ill. situm in locum ill. privilegiis sedis apostolicae infulis decoretur, ut sub iurisdictione sanctae nostrae, cui Deo auctore deservimus, ecclesiae constitutum nullius alterius ecclesiae iurisdictionibus summittatur; pro qua re piis desideriis faventes hac nostra auctoritate id quod exposcitur effectui mancipamus. Et ideo omnem cuiuslibet ecclesiae sacerdotem in praefato monasterio dicionem quamlibet habere hac auctoritate praeter sedem apostolicam prohibemus,

Quoniam semper sunt concedenda, quae rationabilibus desideriis congruunt, oportet ut nostrum studium[3] *p*ii petitoris devocioni *in praestandis privilegiis minime denegetur. Igitur postulasti*s *a nobis, quatenus* vestrum *monasterium* supra nominatum *privilegi*o apostolic*o decoretur, ut sub iurisdictione sanctae nostrae, cui Deo auctore deservimus, ecclesiae constitutum nullius alterius ecclesiae* dicioni in posterum *submittatur. Pro qua re piis desideriis faventes* seu et praedecessorum nostrorum beatae memoriae pontificum privilegia confirmantes, apostolica *auctoritate id quod exposcitur effectui mancipamus.* Hoc modo *omnem cuiuslibet ecclesiae sacerdotem in praefato monasterio dicionem quamlibet* aut *auctoritate*m *praeter sedem apostolicam habere prohibemus.* Et cum abbatem loci illius obisse contigerit, nullus monachis eisdem praeferatur, nisi quem sibi ex se ipsis regulariter praeelegerint patrem. Et *nisi ab abbate monasterii* quisquam *fuerit invitatus, ne missarum solemni*a *ibi praesumat*

ita ut, nisi ab abbate monasterii fuerit invitatus, nec missarum ibidem sollemnitatem quispiam

---

[1] Cf. the address of Gregory II's letter to Abbot Hwætberht of Wearmouth and Jarrow of 716 (*Vita Ceolfridi*, c. 39, ed. Plummer, p. 403): 'Gregorius episcopus, servus servorum Dei, Hwaetberhto *religioso abbati*', &c.

[2] Cf. the privilege of Innocent II of 1139 (Elmham, p. 369; Jaffé, i. 8004): 'Hugoni *abbati monasterii sanctorum apostolorum Petri et Pauli, quod iuxta Doroberniae metropolitanam civitatem situm est, eiusque* successoribus . . .'

[3] Cf. the privilege of John XIII to Old Minster, Winchester (below, p. 197): 'vestrae piae petitionis studium.'

praesumat omnimodo celebrare, ut profecto iuxta id quod subiecti apostolici privilegii consistunt, inconcusse dotandus permaneat. Constituentes per huius decreti nostri paginam atque interdicentes omnibus omnino cuiuslibet ecclesiae praesulibus vel cuiuscumque dignitati praeditis potestate sub anathematis interpositione, qui ei praesumpserit praesenti constituti a nobis praefati monasterii induIti quolibet modo existere temeratur.

agere, *sub anathematis interpositione* nobis placuerit statuere.

*Interdic*imus eciam *omnibus omnino ecclesiae praesulibus vel* qua*cumque dignitate* seu regali *praeditis potestate*, ne vel ipsi haec nostra infringere decreta audeant nec aliis contraire volentibus consenciant. Si quis haec despexerit, a Deo omnipotente anathema sit.

Data Idus Maii, imperantibus dominis piissimis augustis Constantino maiore imperatore anno xxv, post consulatum eius ix, sed et Heraclio atque Tiberio novis augustis eius fratribus anno xxi, indictione v.

The privilege of Agatho is obviously based on a genuine charter of the Pope, though the existing text reproduces its exemplar in details less correctly than do the privileges of Gregory II or III for monasteries at Beneventum (see p. 26) and of Zacharias for Fulda (pp. 26 f.). One may question the authenticity of the words 'primo Christiano' in the address, but the superscription 'religioso abbati' and a topographical addition on the situation of the privileged house are confirmed by the Beneventan charter and by the privilege of Pope Constantine (708–15) for Bermondsey and Woking (Birch, i, no. 133). The changing of the end cannot be attributed to a tendentious purpose (except perhaps for the words 'seu regali'), but rather to the defective condition of the papyrus original and to the incomplete formula of the sanction clause. On the other hand, the reference to predecessors is more suspect and may have been interpolated in view of the privileges of Boniface IV (5) and Adeodatus (7), which are evident forgeries. The insertion of the election clause may have been occasioned by the struggles for the free election of the abbot in the late eleventh century, but it need not be an interpolation; a similar insertion, more explicit and better placed, is found in the Beneventum document, and Agatho's lost privilege to Wearmouth contained a clause of the same kind (see p. 24).

The formulation of the date also proves the genuineness of the underlying charter and, moreover, certain abbreviations confirm this; early 'suspensions' are found in Cotton MS. Claudius D.X according to Birch: *Dd. piiss.* (=dominis piissimis), *Novv. Augg.* (=novis augustis), and *post* c(*onsulat*)*um*. The numerals are wrong;

a privilege granted by Pope Agatho on the 15th of May can belong only to 679 or 680. The year of Emperor Constantine IV in May 679 was XXVI (not XXV), his post-consulate XI (not IX); the year of his brothers may be right;[1] but the indiction should be VII (not V). Misreadings of this kind are found, e.g., in the papal letters to St. Boniface in spite of their survival in early copies, and also disfigure the acts of the Roman synod held in October of the same year 679, the first and genuine part of which was preserved in a Life of Archbishop Theodore of Canterbury, where the text was interpolated during the contest between Canterbury and York on the primacy question.[2] Anyone who has seen papyri damaged even in a small degree will understand the origin of such misreadings.

The privileges of the two earlier popes are open to much stronger objections. The dates of the charter of Pope Adeodatus (7) are copied from the Agatho text (except the day) with the blunders in numerals mentioned above, all numbers being reduced by three[3] so as to refer to A.D. 675, 673, 676, and again 673. The words on Abbot Hadrian: 'ab apostolica sede ordinato atque destinato' are probably derived from the acts of the synod of Hertford of 672 transmitted by Bede, H.E. iv. 5 (p. 215. 5), where Hadrian's companion, Archbishop Theodore, calls himself 'ab apostolica sede destinatus'.[4] The idea that the Pope 'conceded' to Hadrian, in compliance with his petition, his monastery with all its income and rights, is evidently connected with the design of obtaining exemption from the diocesan. The election clause seems partly to be influenced by the privilege of Agatho ('nisi quem ipsa sibi prorsus Deo servientium congregatio de proprio videlicet monasterio communi assensu regulariter praeelegerint'; cf. above, p. 188. A part of the sanction may be derived from a papal document not yet traced; cf., e.g., the words: 'ex auctoritate videlicet beati Petri apostolorum principis, cui dominus Iesus Christus Deus noster ligandi solvendique in caelo et in terra potestatem concessit' with the acts of the Roman synod of 679 (H. and S. iii. 132 f.; my edition p. 280, c. 6, with parallels in n. 4; cf. also below, p. 197, &c.).

The elements of the privilege ascribed to Pope Boniface IV and to the year 611 (5) can to a greater extent be traced to their sources.

---

[1] They became emperors in 659 between 26 April and 9 August. Therefore their imperial year in May 679 was XXI or XX.

[2] See my paper, 'Die Akten der römischen Synode von 679' (Savigny-Zeitschr. xxxiii, 1912, Kan. Abt. ii, pp. 265 f., 277). On the MS. tradition of the text cf. ib. l (1930), Kan. Abt. xix, 672 ff. Both manuscripts come from St. Augustine's.

[3] The only exception is the number of the indiction, XV. But it is written over an erasure in Elmham's text and may have been originally II according to the MS. used by Wilkins ('secunda'), as Haddan and Stubbs, iii. 124, n. a, have already pointed out; cf. Birch i, p. 53, n. 4.   [4] Cf. below, p. 191, n. 3.

The historical background and the date are borrowed from Bede's *H.E.*:

Bede, H.E.	Boniface IV
i. 33 (p. 70). Fecit autem et monasterium non longe ab ipsa civitate ad orientem, in quo eius hortatu Aedilberct ecclesiam beatorum apostolorum Petri et Pauli a fundamentis construxit ac diversis donis ditavit, in qua et ipsius Augustini et omnium episcoporum Doruvernensium, simul et regum Cantiae poni corpora possent.	Laudabilis atque Deo placita petitio tua haec est, ut *ecclesia beatorum apostolorum Petri et Pauli ad orientem civitat*is Doroberniae sita, quam . . . patrum tuorum Gregorii atque Augustini *hortatu*[1] ammonitus, in sepulturam[2] tui et successorum tuorum *regum et* praefatae urbis praesulum *a fundamentis construxi*sti et . . . *diversis donis dita*sti, *in qua et* monachorum religiosorum congregationem sub abbate Iohanne *ab hac apostolica sede directo*[3] collocasti, ubi et ipse vir praefatus vere *Deo dilectus et in gloria resurrecturus pater Augustinus requiescit*, . . . perpetua libertate donaretur. . . .
ii. 3 (p. 86). Defunctus est autem Deo dilectus pater Augustinus . . . Hic requiescit domnus Augustinus...	
ii. 1 (pp. 75. 2, 79. 7). ab apostolica sede directus est . . . cum ceteris sanctae ecclesiae pastoribus resurrecturus in gloria.	
ii. 4 (p. 88). His temporibus venit Mellitus Lundoniae episcopus Romam, de necessariis ecclesiae Anglorum cum apostolico papa Bonifatio tractaturus. Et cum idem papa reverentissimus cogeret synodum episcoporum Italiae, de vita monachorum et quiete ordinaturus, et ipse Mellitus inter eos adsedit anno VIII. imperii Focatis principis, indictione XIII, tertio die Kalendarum Martiarum, ut quaeque erant regulariter decreta . . . secum Anglorum ecclesiis mandanda atque observanda deferret. . . . Hic est Bonifatius, quartus a beato Gregorio. . . .	Haec itaque nostrae institutionis *decreta* in *synod*o *episcoporum Italiae*, cui etiam *inter*fuit tuae dilectionis legatus *Mellitus*, . . . roborari fecimus tibique et *ecclesi*ae tuae . . . custodienda *atque* perpetualiter *observanda*, tibi et genti tuae per manum ipsius direximus. . . . Data *die III. Kal. Mart.*, imperante piissimo augusto[4] *Foca anno VIII. imperii*[5] eiusdem *principis, indictione* XIIII.[6]

[1] Cf. above, p. 183.   [2] Ib., p. 182.

[3] Cf. our documents 3: 'virum secum ab apostolica sede directum', and 9: 'Petrum monachum ab hac apostolica sede directum.' Cf. also below, p. 242, n. 1.

[4] The author would find this formula in papal letters inserted by Bede, *H.E.* i. 23, 24, &c.: 'Data die . . . , imperante . . . piissimo augusto . . .'. The words 'in initio nascentis Christianae religionis' (Birch, i, p. 17, l. 33) are also possibly reminiscent of Bede, i. 27 (§ 1), iv. 27 (pp. 48, 270): '*initio nascentis* ecclesiae.' Cf. the first privilege of John XII (9): 'ab initio vestrae nascentis ecclesiae'; Birch, i, no. 312.

[5] The editions (and MSS.?) have 'imperatoris', perhaps by a wrong interpretation of the suspension 'imper'.

[6] The MS. of Bede which was used for the charter had probably this variant number.

The author had obviously studied Bede's work and had his words in mind. He had also read letters of Gregory I relating to monasteries; reminiscences of the *Registrum* of the Pope intermingle with the words of Bede:

Registrum, ix. 216 (*MG. Epist.* ii. 203)

Igitur gloriosae memoriae Childebertus Francorum rex, catholicae religionis amore succensus, intra muros Arelatensis civitatis monasterium virorum . . . constituens quaedam ibidem pro habitantium sustentatione concessit. . . . Unde . . . a praedecessore nostro Vigilio . . . ad praedecessorem vestrum Aurelium scripta transmissa sunt, ubi omnia, quae amplectendae voluntatis studium deposcebat, apostolicae auctoritatis libenter adnisu firmata sunt, quia difficultatem pati non potuit huiusmodi res petita. . . .

Boniface

Quapropter, rex inclite ac fili karissime,[1] *omnia, quae* tuae *amplectendae voluntatis studium* per coepiscopum nostrum Mellitum *poscebat, apostolica auctoritate libent*issime concedimus, *quia* nec aequum videtur *difficultates pati huiusmodi rem petita*m. Laudabilis atque Deo placita petitio tua haec est, ut ecclesia . . . , quam, *catholicae religionis amore succensus,* . . . construxisti et ob honorem divini cultus *habitantium sustentatione*m diversis donis ditasti. . . .

These are phrases without substance, though they help us to see the forgeries in the making.[2] The privilege of Boniface is based to a much greater extent on another document ascribed to Pope Gregory, though this is itself spurious. Monastic houses have some place in the letters of this Pope, who founded monasteries, became a monk himself, and also transmitted to posterity the legendary stories about St. Benedict. There are letters, not yet of exemption, but of protection granted to particular monasteries;[3] there was no general monastic privilege in his *Registrum*. Later times tried to supply such a document. Parts of the letters viii. 17, vii. 12, and v. 49 (*MG. Epist.* ii, p. 19, i, pp. 455, 348) and of a canon of the synod of Carthage of 535 (Mansi, *Concil.* viii. 841) were combined and a clause was added taken from the acts of the Roman synod assembled under the second Pope Gregory in 721, which were found in several collections of canon law (ed. P. Hinschius, *Decretales Pseudo-Isidorianae*, 1863, p. 753 f.). Thus a general monastic privilege was created which is absent from all early manuscripts of Gregory's Register but existed

---

[1] The same address: 'rex inclite ac fili karissime' is found in the first privilege of John XII (9).

[2] At the end of the 15th century they had two MSS. of the *Registrum Gregorii* at St. Augustine's; cf. M. R. James, *The Ancient Libraries of Canterbury and Dover*, Cambridge, 1903, p. 233, no. 395 f.

[3] Cf. F. H. Dudden, *Gregory the Great*, ii, London, 1905, pp. 185 ff.; Caspar, loc. cit. ii. 416 f., 500, n. 7; McLaughlin, loc. cit., pp. 148 ff., 177 ff.

in the eleventh century.[1] It was edited by the Benedictines of St.
Maur as Appendix VII of their edition of the letters of the Pope
(Migne, *P.L.* lxxvii. 1340–2; cf. Jaffé, i. 1366) and even haunts
some minds to-day as a decree of a legendary Roman synod of 601.[2]
There are also texts in which the end is missing and the beginning
has been displaced by that of *Registr.* v. 49 (ii. 41 of the Benedictines,
Migne, loc. cit., col. 579 f.; cf. Jaffé, i. 1362), the so-called enlarged
form of this letter.[3] Some form or other of the Pseudo-Gregorian
privilege was the main source of the charter ascribed to Boniface IV:

Pseudo-Gregory	*Boniface IV*
Sed ne ex ea quae magis emendanda est consuetudine quisquam monachis *quicquam molestiae praesumat inferre, necesse est ut haec . . . debeant custodiri, ut ex eis non possit ulterius inferendae inquietudinis occasio reperiri.* Interdicimus *igitur* in nomine domini nostri Iesu Christi et ex auctoritate beati Petri apostolorum principis, cuius vice huic Romanae ecclesiae praesidemus, prohibemus, ut *nullus* episcoporum aut saecularium *ultra* praesumat *de reditibus, rebus vel chartis* monasteri*orum vel de* cellis vel villis *quae ad ea pertinent quocumque modo, qualibet* occasione *minuere vel dolos* vel *immissiones facere.* . . . *Defuncto vero abbate* cuiusquam congregationis, *non extraneus nisi de eadem congregatione, quem sibi propria*	Huius igitur beatissimi apostolorum principis Petri auctoritate ordinamus atque perpetua stabilitate stabilimus, ut praefatum monasterium . . . ab omni servitio sit liberum, ab omni mundiali[4] strepitu inconcussum nec *ecclesiasticis*[5] *conditionibus seu angariis vel quibuslibet obsequiis saecularibus ullo modo subiaceat, nullis canonicis iuribus deserviat.* . . . Unde *interdicimus in nomine domini nostri Iesu Christi, ex auctoritate* ipsius *beatissimi apostolorum principis Petri, cuius vice huic Romanae praesidemus ecclesiae, ut* a praesenti *nullus* praesulum, nullus *saecularium* praesumat in dominium huius ecclesiae aliquo *modo* sese ingerere *vel quamlibet imperandi potestatem* sibi usurpare vel alicuius *inquietudinis*[6] *molestia*s *inferre*

[1] Cf. n. 3. L. M. Hartmann, *MG. Epist.* ii, p. xxv, mentions the Chartres MS. 50 (71) of the 12th century.

[2] Cf. W. Wisbaum, *Die wichtigsten Richtungen und Ziele der Thätigkeit des Papstes Gregors des Grossen*, Dissertation of Bonn, 1884, pp. 37 ff.; Caspar, loc. cit. ii, p. 416, n. 4; McLaughlin, p. 181, n. 2. They do not mention the dependence on the synod of Carthage. In the Codex Flaviniacensis of the Benedictines signatures were added from *Registr.* v, 57 a (*MG. Epist.* i. 365 ff.); cf. Migne, loc. cit., col. 1342, n. *c.*

[3] This text was added in the 11th century to the famous Codex Aemilianus (from San Millan de la Cogolla) of the Escorial (to-day d. I. 1) according to P. Ewald, *Neues Archiv*, vi, 1881, p. 238; cf. *MG. Epist.* i, p. 348, l. 42. G. Antolín, *Catálogo de los códices latinos de la Real Biblioteca del Escorial*, i, Madrid, 1910, p. 364, does not distinguish the two forms of v. 49 (ii. 41).

[4] This is a reminiscence of a formula very common in Anglo-Saxon charters of the 10th century: 'Sit praedicta terra *libera ab omni mundiali* obstaculo (censu, iugo, servitio)'; cf. Birch, ii, nos. 642, 660, 670, 714, 734, 741, 748, 749, 753, 756–9, 764, 767, 781, 789, 808, 821, 824, 828, 833; iii, nos. 888, 891, 927, 1025, &c.

[5] From the later part of Pseudo-Gregory.

[6] From the beginning of the same.

voluntate concors fratrum societas *elegerit, et qui electus fuerit, sine dolo vel venalitate aliqua ordinetur. Quodsi aptam inter se personam invenire nequeant, sollerter sibi de aliis monasteriis similiter eligant ordinandum*[4]... Nec (episcopus) audeat ibi *cathedram collocare*[5] vel quamlibet *potestatem habere*[6] imperandi *nec aliquam ordinationem, quamvis levissimam, fac*iendi, *nisi* ab abbate loci fuerit rogatus, quatenus *monachi* semper maneant *in abbatum suorum potestate.*[5] ... *Hanc* ergo *scriptorum nostrorum paginam omni in futuro tempore ab* omnibus *episcopis firmam statuimus illibatamque servari, ut et* suae *ecclesiae iuvante Domino tantummodo* sint *iure* conten*ti et monasteria*[10] *ecclesiasticis conditionibus* seu *angariis* vel quibuslibet obsequiis saecularibus nullo modo *subiace*ant,[5] *nullis canoni*cis *iuribus de-serv*iant, sed *remotis vexationibus ac cunctis gravaminibus divinum opus cum summa animi devotione perficiant.*[10]...

vel *aliquam* omnino consuetudinem, *quamvis levissimam,* sibi attribuere vel etiam, *nisi rogatu abbat*is aut fratrum, in ea *missas facere.* Sed communis filius[1] noster abbas Iohannes libere teneat, possideat, cum consilio fra-trum[2] omnem utilitatem loci intus vel foris[3] bene ordinet atque disponat, et sic *remota vexati*one et *cunct*o *grava-mine, divinum* servitium *perag*ant *cum* tota *animi devotione.*[7] Post cuius obitum *non extraneus* assumatur, sed *de eadem congregatione* et *quem sibi propria voluntate concors fratrum societas elegerit, et qui electus fuerit, sine dolo vel venalitate aliqua ordinetur* atque in eodem loco consecretur.[8] *Si* autem, quod non optamus,[9] *aptam inter se personam invenire nequ*iverint, *sollerter sibi de aliis monasteriis similiter eligant ordinandum.* ...

The privilege of Pope Adeodatus (above, pp. 182, 190) not only has another phrase in common with that of Boniface (5: 'praefatum monasterium apostolicis praerogativis praemunitum'; 7: 'praefatum monasterium apostolicis praerogativis nunc et in perpetuum prae-munire'), but it also shows the influence, though to a small extent, of the same Pseudo-Gregorian document:

'praecipientes *ex auctoritate* videlicet apostolicae sedis .... omnes omnino tam ecclesiae praesules quamque sublimium *saecularium* dignitates .... sese a praefati monasterii inquietudinibus atque *gravaminibus* suspendere nec per *quam*libet *occasion*em tibi tuaeque congregationi .... quoquo modo dispendia vel *inquietudin*um *molestia*s irrogare'.

[1] Gregory's *Registr.* viii. 17 (*Epist.* ii, p. 19): 'communis filius Claudius abbas', x. 21 (p. 257): 'communi filio nostro Anatolio diacono', &c.; cf. ib., p. 546, s.v. *filius.*
[2] *Regula S. Benedicti,* c. 65: 'per decanos *ordinet*ur ... *omnis utilitas* monasterii, prout abbas *dispo*suerit...; quemcumque elegerit abbas *cum consilio fratrum* timentium Deum, *ordinet* ipse sibi praepositum.' The same words recur in Ethelbert's third charter: 'Sed abbas ipse ... *intus* et *foris cum consilio fratrum* secundum timorem Dei (= Regula Benedicti, c. 64) *libere* eam regat et *ordinet*'. The words of 3: '*sciat se aequissimo iudici Deo* et beatis apostolis Petro et Paulo *rationem* esse *redditurum*' also are a reminiscence of St. Benedict (*Regula,* c. 3).
[3] Cf. above, p. 184.
[5] From the synod of Carthage.
[7] See note 5 on p. 193.
[9] Cf., e.g., below, p. 196 (*Liber Diurnus,* no. 86).
[4] From *Registr.* viii. 17.
[6] From *Registr.* vii. 12.
[8] Cf. above, p. 182.
[10] From *Registr.* v. 49.

I may also mention, what is a trifle by itself, that the word *praesules* was substituted in both charters for the *episcopi* of the source (Ps.-Greg. 'nullus episcoporum', 5 'nullus praesulum', 7 'ecclesiae praesules'). The word is very common; but we are perhaps justified in seeing in this detail also the work of the same man, who had in his mind, probably unconsciously, the end of the privilege copied in Agatho's charter (p. 189): 'interdicentes *omn*ibus *omnino* cuiuslibet *ecclesiae praesul*ibus vel cuiuscumque *dignitat*i praediti potestate'.

The forger or forgers also employed a papal privilege of John XII (955–64) or XIII (965–72) for concocting the charter of John XII (9) addressed to King Edred (946–55) and the other charter of this Pope (10) inscribed to the same king and to Archbishop Odo of Canterbury (942–58). Both are evident fabrications. I would not stress the fact that Edred died some weeks before the young and worldly Octavian added the papal dignity to the inherited secular lordship of Rome; the death of the king may have been unknown there in the early months of the pontificate. But the very date of the first document: 'Datum x. Kal. Mai., imperante domino piissimo augusto[1] Ottone anno II. regni eius (A.D. 938 of the regnal years, 963 of the imperial years of Otto I), indictione XI' (938, 953, 968), is impossible in a papal privilege of this age and inconsistent with the names of pope as well as king. There are words which are suspect stressing the position of St. Augustine's as the earliest English monastery (as in 5, 10) and its burial rights 'ex praecepto . . . Gregorii' (p. 182); there is the outburst against the canons of Christ Church (p. 184). But the author undoubtedly had before him a papal privilege. The clauses on the election of the abbot and on a bishop being precluded from celebrating the mass in the monastery unless invited by the abbot are to be referred to a privilege on the lines of Agatho's. It was a papal charter of the tenth century which combined (probably indirectly) formulas of the *Liber Diurnus* nos. 87, 32, and 86:

Liber Diurnus, no. 87 (*p.* 114)	*John XII*
Credite speculationis impellimur cure, etiam ardore Christiane religionis et studio divini cultus permovemur pro venerabilium locorum percogitare stabilitate atque Deo servientium securitate, ut, hoc proveniente pio labore, et anime Christo dicate, quae se illi diebus vitae eorum serviture decreverunt, perseverent inper-	*Studio divini cultus permovemur pro venerabilium locorum semper percogitare stabilitate,* quatinus, *proveniente pio labore, animae Christo dicatae, quae se illic diebus vitae eorum servi*re *decreverint,* sub regulari institutione *perseverent imperturbatae necnon illa maneant fine*[2]

[1] Cf. above, p. 191, n. 4.
[2] The editions have 'fide'.

turbate necnon et illa maneant fine tenus, quae a Christianis in Dei laude constructa sunt. . . .

tenus inconvulsa, *quae* ob religionis cultum *in Dei laude constructa sunt.* . . .

Agatho (above, p. 188)

Et cum abbatem loci illius obisse contigerit, nullus monachis eisdem praeferatur, nisi quem sibi ex se ipsis regulariter praeelegerint patrem. Et *nisi*[1] *ab abbate monasterii quisquam fuerit invitatus, ne missarum solemni*a *ibi praesumat* agere. . . .

Cum vero *abbatem* ipsum *obisse contigerit*, non aliunde quam ex eadem congregatione, *quem ips*i communi consilio *elegerint*, constituatur, in loco eodem consecretur[2] et ovili dominico *praeficiatur*. Nullus ibi praesulum[3] aliquam sibi auctoritatem usurpet, sed *nec ibi, nisi ab abbate invitatus,* illorum *missam* celebrare (= Liber Diurnus) *praesumat.* . . .

Liber Diurnus, no. 86 (p. 113)

Si quis autem, quod non optamus, nefario ausu presumpserit haec quae a nobis . . . statuta sunt refragare aut in quoquam transgredi, sciat se anathematis vinculo innodatum et cum . . . Iuda traditore domini nostri Iesu Christi aeterni incendii supplicio concremandum deputatus.

Si quis vero hoc sanctae religionis propositum contaminare vel delere conaverit, *sciat se* auctoritate apostolica *anathematis vinculo innodatum et cum Iuda traditore Domini aeterni incendii supplicio concremandum.*

There are other papal privileges of the tenth century which also comprise the preamble 'Creditae speculationis' and a sanction of this kind.[4] But the very address at the beginning of John's charter and the salutation at its end can also be referred to a genuine papal document of this age sent to England. A privilege of John XIII connected with the English monastic revival of his times makes this evident. When King Edgar and Bishop Ethelwold of Winchester had introduced monks into the Old Minster there in the place of secular canons (964), the Pope ordered that in future the bishop of Winchester should be a monk chosen from this house, if a suitable person could be found therein.[5] The papal charter was based,

[1] *Liber Diurnus*, no. 32; above, p. 188.   [2] Cf. above, p. 182.   [3] Ib., p. 195.

[4] Cf., e.g., Leo VII for Subiaco, 938 (Jaffé, i. 3608; Kehr, *Italia pontificia*, ii. 88, no. 12); Gregory V for S. Genesio (Santa Maria) de Besalù, 998 (Jaffé, i. 3885; cf. Kehr, 'Papsturkunden in Spanien I', *Abhandl. Gött., Neue Folge*, xviii. 2, 1926, p. 148), Migne, *P.L.* cxxxii, 1078, cxxxvii. 924.

[5] W. Stubbs, *Memorials of Saint Dunstan*, pp. 364 f.; Birch, iii, no. 1275; cf. Jaffé, i. 3753. On MSS. see Holtzmann, *Papsturkunden*, ii, pp. 39 f., 42. On the question of the genuineness of this privilege cf. Stubbs, loc. cit., p. 364, n. 1, who compared it rightly with the preface of the *Regularis Concordia* (*Mon. Angl.* i, p. xxviii; W. S. Logeman, *Anglia*, xiii, 1891, p. 372; Birch, iii, no. 1168, p. 424). Cf. Knowles, *The Monastic Order*, pp. 45, 621.

mutatis mutandis, on a monastic privilege similar to that which was used for fabricating the charter of John XII:

John XIII

Johannes episcopus servus servorum Dei Edgaro regi excellentissimo atque omnibus episcopis, ducibus, comitibus, abbatibus et cuncto fideli populo Anglicae gentis Christianam salutem et apostolicam benedictionem.

Quoniam semper sunt concedenda, quae rationabilibus quaeruntur *desideriis, oportet ut* vestrae *piae* petitionis studium *in privilegiis minime* offendatur *praestandis.*[1] Scimus enim, gloriose fili, imperii vestri dignitatem zelo divinae legis ita undique munitam, ut indesinenter *pro venerabilium locorum percogit*et *stabilitate, quatenus, proveniente pio labore,*[2] schola dominici multiplicetur servitii[3] et largitori omnium Deo abunde fructus referantur milleni. Quare, rex inclyte ac fili carissime. . . .

Illeque eorum vitam ita sanctitatis moribus exornet, ut, pastore ad laboris sui praemium vocato, non aliunde quam ex illa congregatione alter in locum regiminis succedat. Quodsi . . . in eadem congregatione idoneum invenire minime posse contigerit, auctoritate apostolorum principis Petri, cui dominus ac salvator noster ligandi solvendique potestatem contradidit,[4] praecipimus, ut nemo e clericorum ordine ad huius regimen ecclesiae promoveatur; sed potius ex alia qualibet congregatione, qui dignus inventus fuerit, monachus assumatur et huic ecclesiae praeficiatur.

Si quis enim interea, quod non credimus, haec apostolicae sedis

John XII

Johannes episcopus servus servorum Dei Eadredo *regi excellentissimo atque omnibus episcopis, ducibus, comitibus, abbatibus et cuncto fideli populo Anglicae gentis* carissimam salutem et apostolicam benedictionem.

Studio divini cultus permovemur *pro venerabilium locorum* semper *percogit*are *stabilitate, quatinus, proveniente pio labore,* animae Christo dicatae . . . constructa sunt (above, pp. 195 f.). *Qua*propter mando tibi, *rex inclite ac fili karissime.* . . .

Cum vero abbatem ipsum obisse *contigerit, non aliunde quam ex* eadem *congregatione* . . . constituatur, in loco eodem consecretur et ovili dominico *praeficiatur.* . . .

Si quis vero hoc sanctae religionis propositum *contaminare* vel delere

---

[1] The words in italics correspond to formula 32 of the *Liber Diurnus;* above, p. 188.
[2] From formula 87, ib., p. 195.
[3] *Regula Benedicti*, pref.: 'Constituenda est ergo a nobis *dominici scola servitii*.'
[4] Cf. above, p. 190.

privilegii decreta irrita facere et ea quae a nobis pie indulta sunt contaminare[1] praesumpserit, auctoritate eiusdem caelestis clavigeri Petri omniumque successorum eius sciat se anathematis vinculo innodatum et in illo magni iudicii die perpetualiter damnandum.

In Christo valeas, domine fili.

conaverit, *sciat se auctoritate* apostolica *anathematis vinculo innodatum et* cum Iuda traditore Domini aeterni incendii supplicio concremandum. . . .

In Christo cum omnibus tuis, *domine fili, valeas.*[2]

The address of the second letter of John XII (10) is partly founded either on the first letter or on its source. But on the whole it is much more a piece of free invention. Stress is laid on the burial claims, on the precedence of St. Augustine's as the earliest monastic foundation of England—the 'mater primaria' of all English monasteries—and on its freedom from 'secular' servitude, episcopal or royal. The archbishop of Canterbury should not consider the abbot a subject, but his equal, 'Romanum legatum et comministrum evangelii pacis', and should neither claim any power or office nor receive anything from the places and parishes of the monastery without the favour of abbot and brethren, while the abbot as the first-born and 'vice Romana' should have the first place among his colleagues, though 'affectuose magis quam imperiose'.

In tendencies and their formulation the 'Bulla plumbea' of Augustine (4) is a kind of counterpart to this privilege;[3] in other respects it approaches the third charter of Ethelbert (3) and the grant of his son Eadbald (6). The manner of giving the list of witnesses, not by separate signatures, but in the usual way of a later age by an ablative absolute[4] is significant:

3: 'Confirmata est haec donatio praesentibus testibus reverentissimo patre Augustino . . . , Mellito quoque et Iusto', etc.

4: 'praesente glorioso rege Aethilberhto cum suo filio Aedbaldo et collaudante cum ipso et omnibus optimatibus regiis atque ultro volentibus reverentissimis fratribus nostris . . . , scilicet Laurentio . . . et Mellito . . . obnixe postulantibus. . . .'

6: 'assidentibus et collaudantibus archiepiscopo . . . Laurencio et subscribente cum regina mea Aemma filiisque meis . . . , cum duobus

---

[1] The editions have 'intaminare'.

[2] Cf. the privilege of Boniface IV; below, p. 203.

[3] Even such a rare word as *excommunicatorius* is common to both texts; cf. 4 'apostolica sancti papae Gregorii interminatione excommunicatoria', 10 'excommunicatorio sancti Petri principis apostolorum gladio'.

[4] Cf., e.g., charters of William I and II in Davis, *Regesta regum Anglo-Normann.* i, p. 122, no. 16 (1082): 'praesente archiepiscopo Guillelmo et abbate Gilberto, testibus episcopis . . . , abbatibus . . . , clericis vero . . . , laicis . . . , et aliis multis'; p. 132, no. 52 (1093): 'audientibus istis et videntibus', &c.

episcopis . . . ceterisque multis comitibus et optimatibus meis confaventibus et subscribentibus. . . .'

The ablative constructions of 4 and 6 include even a sanction formula. But 6 has a peculiar position in this series, because it adds after this ablative list of witnesses a number of signatures with the anachronistic variety of verbs, as it is found in the second charter of Ethelbert (p. 176). The ablatives *collaudante, collaudantibus*, and *confaventibus* of the other lists show that they also derive from this fashion, which belongs to the tenth and eleventh centuries (2 has *favi, laudavi*, 6 *laudo*, &c.).

Further research may reveal other sources of the charters here discussed, and may also distinguish, among these documents, different periods and strata. I am not prepared to affirm that all of them were made by one man or at the same time; but so much intermingling and interdependence are apparent that most of them may be referred to one author without hesitation. They are not mentioned in connexion with the disputes of the late eleventh century. The privilege of Calixtus II shows that at least four of the papal documents existed in 1120 (p. 179). The Cotton MS. Vespasian B.XX of the early twelfth century, in which this privilege was added by another hand, contains the charter of Edward the Confessor (11, inserted by a later hand),[1] two of Ethelbert (2, 3),[2] and those of the Popes Boniface IV (5), Adeodatus (7), Agatho (8), and John XII (9, 10).[3]

[1] This charter, referring to the grant of the island of Thanet, is preceded in the MS. by the *Libellus Goscelini contra inanes usurpatores S. Mildrethae*; in this the author claimed for St. Augustine's the possession of the true relics of St. Mildred, which King Canute (d. 1035) had given to the monastery together with the property of Mildred's church, that is, Minster in Thanet (Kemble, vi, No. 1326); cf. Lemarignier, loc. cit., pp. 111 f., 176 f. On the other hand, the canons of St. Gregory's at Canterbury, founded by Archbishop Lanfranc (1070–89), asserted that the latter had transferred there the real relics of Mildred; cf., e.g., John of Tynemouth, ed. C. Horstman, *Nova Legenda Anglie*, ii, Oxford, 1901, p. 197. The charter of King Edward seems not to be connected with this controversy but only to refer to the ownership of Minster and the pertinent rights in Thanet. But the treatise of Goscelin (cf. Hardy, *Descriptive Catalogue*, i. 1, p. 381) has never been published and may give more information. A modern edition and study of Goscelin's writings, printed and unprinted, is a desideratum of more than literary history; cf. A. Wilmart, 'Ève et Goscelin' (*Rev. Bén.* l, 1938, pp. 42 f.), 'La légende de Ste Édith par le moine Goscelin' (*Anal. Boll.* lvi, 1938, p. 5) and Ph. Grierson, 'Grimbald of S. Bertin's' (*E.H.R.* lv, 1940, pp. 539 f.). The study begun by a pupil of mine some years ago (cf. *Savigny-Zeitschr.* l, 1930, *Kan. Abt.* xix. 672) was not finished. Cf. also R. W. Southern, 'The First Life of Edward the Confessor' (*E.H.R.* lviii, 1943, pp. 398 ff.).

[2] The MS. is not accessible at present, and no editor of Ethelbert's charters used this earliest of the existing copies. I rely on some notes made years ago for other purposes.

[3] Cf. Holtzmann, *Papsturkunden*, i. 98, 231 and the two printed catalogues of the Cottonian MSS. Birch used the MS. for the two privileges of John XII (9, 10), Kemble for Edward's charter (11).

About the same time Goscelin, the monk of Saint-Bertin, who came to England some years before the Norman Conquest and, 'in laudibus sanctorum Angliae nulli post Bedam secundus', was asked to write a number of Lives of English saints, composed the history of the translation of St. Augustine and of other saints of his church; their remains were translated in September 1091 into the new church of St. Augustine's where the author had settled at last. He also related the miracles that occurred during the first seven years after the translation, and finished his work some time after the fall of Jerusalem (1099)[1] and certainly before 1109; for he dedicated it to Archbishop Anselm who died in this year. The Cotton MS. mentioned as the earliest copy of several of our charters contains, in the part which precedes, an almost contemporaneous *corpus* of Goscelin's works connected with his stay at St. Augustine's. Now, in his *Translatio Augustini* (ii. 25, 26, p. 440) he mentions charters of Ethelbert and obviously alludes to the third charter, stressing also the burial claims of the abbey:

'Construxit et monasterium principale extra urbis muros a fronte orientali in honore principum apostolorum Petri et Pauli, ubi et rex et pontifex cum omnibus successoribus suis perpetualiter ("in perpetuum" 10) requiescerent. . . . Illud vero apostolicum domicilium, quo cum suo apostolo Augustino cunctaque successione, ut praenotatum est, ex decreto beati papae Gregorii ("ex praecepto eiusdem Gregorii" 9) requiem hereditaret, tanto scilicet praestantius nobilitare curavit, quanto specialius hoc sibi cum tot sanctis et excelsis divinitus praerogatum fore perpendit. Foris hoc regiis amplificavit possessionibus, intus ("intus et foris" 3, etc.; see p. 184) decoravit regiis ornatibus (cf. 3), regia libertate cum apostolica auctoritate perpetuis stabilivit sanctionibus. *Sunt chartae, sunt privilegia ipsius ac tot primorum testimonio signata.*'

Goscelin also mentions the grant of Northbourne by King Eadbald (6); there is a reminiscence of this charter, when he calls Augustine *protodoctor* (ib. ii. 9, 23, pp. 434, 439). His designation of the abbey as 'monasterium regale et apostolicum'[2] reminds us of the charter of Augustine (4 'hoc dominicum vel apostolicum monasterium') and of the second of John XII (10 'Sit [ecclesia], inquam, regia et apostolica confirmatione regalis et apostolica').

This charter of John was incorporated almost completely with other elements into one of the spurious Peterborough charters, a

---

[1] *Translatio Augustini*, i. 43, § 46 (*Acta SS. Maii*, vi. 426). Wilmart, *Ève*, p. 51 and *Édith*, p. 7, n. 1, dissented from F. Liebermann's statement that Goscelin was living in 1107, and dated his death before the end of the 11th century. But he overlooked this chapter, which was omitted by Mabillon and in Migne's reprint. If the dedication to Anselm was not written beforehand, Goscelin cannot have added it before the end of 1100, when Anselm returned from his exile.

[2] *Vita Augustini maior*, c. 23 (there is also an allusion to the burial claims) and 52 (*Acta SS. Maii*, vi. 384, 395); *Vita minor*, Migne, *P.L.* cl. 752.

clumsy privilege ascribed to Pope Agatho.[1] The author's knowledge of this Pope and of his Roman synod of 125 bishops was derived from Bede (*H.E.* v. 19, pp. 326 f.); the year 680 came from the same source (ib. iv. 17, v. 24, pp. 238 f., 355). This lengthy document existed in or shortly after 1121, when an Anglo-Saxon abbreviated adaptation of it was inserted, together with other Peterborough additions, in the so-called MS. E of the *Saxon Chronicle*. The exemplar of the *Chronicle* then copied and interpolated at Peterborough came from St. Augustine's.[2] The use made of the second charter of Pope John shows the same relationship between the two abbeys: a charter originating from St. Augustine's was employed at Peterborough for forging another document.

Certainly the charters 2, 3, and 5–10 existed about 1100; the same probably applies to 1 and 11, and it may be a mere chance that there is no certain trace of Augustine's 'Bulla plumbea' (4) before the examination of 1178–81. But we have to go back into the eleventh century for about thirty more years. Canterbury produced in this age another famous series of forged or interpolated charters connected with Christ Church and with the archbishop's struggle for primacy over his colleague of York. The true nature of these documents, which were suspect long before, has been shown in an excellent little book by Heinrich Boehmer.[3] His main subject does not concern us here,[4] nor the controversy whether and how far

[1] Birch, i, no. 48; cf. Jaffé, i. 2111. On this charter cf. F. M. Stenton, 'Medeshamstede and its colonies' (*Historical Essays in Honour of James Tait*, pp. 314 f.).

[2] Cf. Plummer, *Two of the Saxon Chronicles*, ii, pp. xlv, xlix ff., lxxvii.

[3] *Die Fälschungen Erzbischof Lanfranks von Canterbury* (Studien zur Geschichte der Theologie und der Kirche, ed. Bonwetsch and Seeberg, viii. 1), Leipzig, 1902. Cf. A. J. Macdonald, *Lanfranc*, Oxford, 1926, pp. 271–91, and 'Eadmer and the Canterbury privileges' (*J.T.S.* xxxii, 1931, pp. 39–55); M. Dueball, *Der Suprematstreit zwischen den Erzdiözesen Canterbury und York* (Historische Studien, ed. Ebering, 184), Berlin, 1929, pp. 24 ff.; E. Hora, 'Zur Ehrenrettung Lanfranks' (*Theologische Quartalschrift*, cxi, 1930, pp. 288–319); Z. N. Brooke, *The English Church and the Papacy*, pp. 120 ff. On *canones*, which Boehmer has connected with the privileges, cf. H. Frank, 'Zwei Fälschungen auf den Namen Gregors d. Gr. und Bonifatius IV.' (*Studien und Mitteilungen zur Geschichte des Benediktiner-Ordens*, lv, 1937, pp. 19–47).

[4] I will only mention that Boehmer, pp. 100–2, has rightly assumed that No. 10 of the series, that is, the pallium-privilege granted to Archbishop Dunstan by Pope John XII (ib., pp. 159–61; Birch, iii, no. 1069), is genuine except for the interpolation of one sentence. For the authentic text exists also. The Pontifical of Sherborne, which formerly was ascribed to Dunstan, was written (at Canterbury?) in the later part of the 10th century, belonged to bishops of Sherborne about 1000, and is now Paris MS. Lat. no. 943, has preserved the genuine version, as can be seen from the facsimile of fol. 7 published by Franz Steffens, *Lateinische Paläographie*, 2nd ed., Trier, 1909 (Berlin, 1929), pl. 71 a (1st ed., Fribourg, 1903, pl. 42 c). As early as 1685 Mabillon in his edition of the privilege (*Acta*, v. 658) observed that the words *Primatum* to *dinoscitur* are missing in this MS., that is, the primacy clause rejected by Boehmer. Stubbs added Mabillon's variant readings to his reprint of the charter

Archbishop Lanfranc was himself responsible for the fraud; on the whole the views of Z. N. Brooke may be right. The first document in this series[1] has nothing to do with the primacy contest; by it Boniface IV grants King Ethelbert's petition that Archbishop Laurentius should be authorized to establish at Christ Church a house of monks living according to the Rule. The foundation of a monastic chapter at the cathedral is the purpose of the charter; its text was added to the primacy series rather accidentally. The larger part of it, except the address, introduction, salutation, and date, was quoted as early as 1072 by Pope Alexander II in a letter which he then wrote to Lanfranc for the protection of this chapter of monks;[2] obviously he had received this text from the archbishop, whose (lost) letter probably also provided the Pope with the words introducing the quotation and possibly based on Bede:

Bede, H.E. ii. 4	*Alexander II*
Hic est Bonifatius, quartus a beato Gregorio Romanae urbis episcopo...	Hinc habetur epistola Bonifacii, qui *quartus a beato Gregorio* ecclesiae Romanae, cui auctore Deo praesidemus, praefuit. ...

The date of the complete letter of Boniface, as it is transmitted, cannot be genuine and is, directly or indirectly, derived from Bede; but A. J. Macdonald[3] and D. Knowles[4] have tried to show that this

(*Memorials of Saint Dunstan*, pp. 296–8) but did not see the consequences, nor did Jaffé-Loewenfeld (*Regesta*, i, no. 3687), or von Hacke (loc. cit., pp. 42, 80 f.) distinguish between the two versions of the text. The forger not only added the primacy interpolation, but changed also the 'vitae tuae tantummodo' formula (cf. von Hacke, pp. 70, 122) into 'vitae perpetuae' and omitted the enumeration of the days on which Dunstan should be entitled to wear the pallium (cf. ib., pp. 70 f.). Forgers often used genuine documents for their fabrications and, having finished their task, destroyed the authentic texts. But sometimes they did not know that copies of the original version existed elsewhere and thus escaped. As continental examples of a similar fortune, which have been the subject of discussion in modern times, I may mention the famous Austrian privileges and Nortbert's Life of Bishop Benno of Osnabrück. On the Pontifical which contains the authentic form of John's charter see also Henderson, *Liber Pontificalis Chr. Bainbridge archiepiscopi Eboracensis* (Surtees Society, vol. lxi), 1875, p. xviii; L. Delisle, *Le Cabinet des MSS. de la Bibliothèque nationale*, iii, 1881, pp. 268–70 and pl. 30. 5; *New Palaeographical Society*, First Series (1903–12), vol. i, pls. 111–12; Ellard, loc. cit., pp. 78 ff.; V. Leroquais, *Les Pontificaux manuscrits des bibliothèques publiques de France*, ii, Paris, 1937, pp. 6–10 and Planches vii–x.

[1] Boehmer, pp. 145 f.; cf. H. and S. iii. 65; Birch, i, no. 10; Jaffé, i, no. 1998.

[2] Eadmer, *Historia novorum*, ed. Rule, pp. 19–21; cf. Jaffé, i. 4761.

[3] *J.T.S.* xxxii. 48 ff. with a facsimile of Cotton MS. Claudius A. III of about 1100. The second form of the date, as transmitted in other MSS., does not concern us. Possibly the letter contained originally both dates, of *Actum* and *Missa*.

[4] 'The Early Community at Christ Church, Canterbury' (ib. xxxix, 1938, pp. 128 ff.); *The Monastic Order*, p. 620.

date was added only afterwards and was absent from the text as it was known to Lanfranc and was sent by him to Alexander, by whom it was partly reproduced as the essential portion of a genuine privilege of Boniface. But I doubt whether these parts of the document can be separated; for there is a relationship between this letter of Boniface and that for St. Augustine's which suggests a different conclusion:

Gregory I, Registr. ix. 216 (above, p. 192)	*Boniface IV to Ethelbert for St. Augustine's*	*Boniface IV to Ethelbert for Christ Church*
ubi omnia, quae amplectendae voluntatis studium deposcebat, apostolicae auctoritatis libenter adnisu firmata sunt, quia difficultatem pati non potuit huiusmodi res petita.	Quapropter, rex inclite ac fili karissime,[1] *omnia quae* tuae *amplectendae voluntatis studium* per coepiscopum nostrum Mellitum *poscebat, apostolica auctoritate libentissime* concedimus, *quia nec aequum* videtur *difficultates pati huiusmodi rem petitam.* . . .	*Quapropter,* gloriose *fili, quod* ab apostolica sede *per coepiscopum nostrum Mellitum postulastis, libenti* animo[2] *concedimus...*
	Haec itaque nostrae institutionis decreta. . . . Quae si quis successorum tuorum regum sive episcoporum, clericorum sive laicorum contempserit aut irrita facere temptaverit, ab officio cleri submotus, apostolicae auctoritatis reus et sanctorum communione iudicetur alienus, quoadusque, quod temerario ausu praesumpsit, congrua satisfactione recognoscat et tanti excessus poenitudinem gerat. . . .	*Quae nostra decreta si quis successorum* vestrorum *regum sive episcoporum, clericorum sive laicorum irrita facere temptaverit, a* principe apostolorum Petro et a cunctis successoribus suis anathematis vinculo[3] subiaceat, *quoadusque, quod temerario ausu* peregit, Deo placita *satisfactione paenit*eat et huius inquietudinis vestrae[4] emendationem promittat.
	In[1] Christo, domine fili, valeas.	*In Christo valeas, domine fili.*

---

[1] From a letter of the 10th century; see pp. 197 f.

[2] The words '*animo nos decet libenti concedere*' occur in the preamble 'Quotiens illa a nobis' of papal letters; cf., e.g., Jaffé, i, nos. 3033, 3742; Migne, *P.L.* cxxvi. 660, cxxxv. 982.   [3] Cf., e.g., above, p. 196.

[4] This is the reading in the letter of Pope Alexander and in Eadmer. Cotton MS. Claudius A. III has 'inqu. veram emend. faciat'; 'vestrae' was meaningless and was changed accordingly.

Bede, H.E. ii. 4

et ipse Mellitus inter eos adsedit anno VIII. imperii Focatis principis, indictione XIII, tertio die Kalendarum Martiarum.

Data *die III. Kal. Mart.*, imperante piissimo augusto *Foca, anno VIII. imperii*[1] *eiusdem principis, indictione* XIIII.[2]

Actum sane anno incarnationis sescentesimo quarto decimo, *imperante Foca augusto piissimo anno imperii eiusdem principis octavo, indictione XIIII*[ma3], *tertia die Kalendarum Martiarum*, Athelberti regis regni anno quinquagesimo tertio.[4]

So far as I can see, there is only one conclusion to be drawn from this comparison: the Christ Church text depends on that for St. Augustine's and is likewise spurious; therefore the Augustinian document already existed in 1072, when Alexander sent the other letter to Lanfranc.

But the privilege of Boniface to St. Augustine's had not long been in existence at that time; the leaden bull attached to it makes this evident. The monks were proud of its possession: 'Et nota quod ista est prima bulla papalis plumbea totius ecclesiae Anglicanae', remarked Thomas of Elmham (ed. Hardwick, p. 131, n. 1). But the 'forma et quantitas signi bullae plumbeae eiusdem papae Bonifacii Quarti', which precedes these words, disproves his statement. The bull had the legends: 'Bonifatii papae IIII' and the Leonine hexameter: 'Petro catholicas fidei dat Christus habenas'. Leo IX (1049–54) was the first Pope to add an ordinal number to his name on his seals; such numbers are lacking in the bulls of all earlier Popes and even in the first ones of Leo himself. Therefore a leaden seal fixed to a forged papal charter and having an ordinal after the name must have been made after the middle of the eleventh century, when the bulls of the Popes exhibited this item to an imitator as a regular feature. The other legend forces us to look some years ahead. The second part of this century from Leo IX onwards is a transitional period in papal diplomatics in general and in the development, in particular, of the papal seals, before their definitive type emerged with the pontificate of Paschalis II (1099–1118).[5] We need not

---

[1] The editions have 'imperatoris'; cf. above, p. 191, n. 5.

[2] Cf. ib., n. 6.

[3] Boehmer, p. 146, has the misprint 'XIIIma'; but cf. pp. 54 f. of his book and Macdonald's facsimile.

[4] The year of the Incarnation as well as Ethelbert's regnal year do not correspond with the imperial year of Phocas nor with the indiction.

[5] Cf., e.g., L. Schmitz-Kallenberg, *Urkundenlehre*, ii (Grundriss der Geschichtswissenschaft, ed. A. Meister, i. 2), 2nd ed., Leipzig, 1913, pp. 89 ff.; R. L. Poole,

follow the whole of this process; the only fact here relevant is that
three Popes in this age used a Leonine hexameter on their bulls and
three only at all, viz. Victor II (1055–7), Alexander II (1061–73),
and the imperial antipope of Gregory VII, Wibert of Ravenna or,
officially after his enthronization (1084), Clement III (1080–1100).
The three legends are related to some representation of St. Peter
being addressed by Christ:

> Victor, 'Tu pro me navem liquisti, suscipe clavem'.
> Alexander, 'Quod nectes nectam, quod solves ipse resolvam'.
> Clement, 'Corrige, parce, feri, Petre, pande, memento mederi'.

Wibert kept up some connexion with England and met there, if not
an ephemeral recognition, certainly neutrality;[1] but the device of
Boniface follows the pattern of the two earlier mottoes in form and
idea. We may also leave aside the short pontificate of Victor II,
though later the abbey of Peterborough inscribed his verse on its
seals.[2] The lively relations between William I and the Papacy may
have brought so many documents of Alexander II to England that
after some years their features might easily be considered a model
for the fabrication of a papal privilege,[3] and such an impression may
have been strengthened by the fact that a Leonine hexameter
appeared on obverse and reverse of the seals of the Conqueror;[4] no
other English king followed his example, frequent as legends of this
kind were later on. This assumption fits in with the *terminus ante quem*
reached from the other side, 1072; we shall not be far from the truth

---

Lectures on the History of the Papal Chancery, pp. 98 ff.; especially on bulls, Bresslau,
loc. cit. ii, pp. 608 ff. and, fundamental, Serafini, loc. cit. i, pp. lxxxiv, lxxxix. Cf.
also Heinz Hartmann, 'Über die Entwicklung der Rota' (*Archiv f. Urk.* xvi, 1939,
pp. 399 ff.).

[1] Cf. F. Liebermann, 'Lanfranc and the Antipope' (*E.H.R.* xvi, 1901, pp. 328–
32); P. Kehr, 'Zur Geschichte Wiberts von Ravenna' (*SB. Berlin*, 1921, pp. 356–60);
Tillmann, loc. cit., p. 18; Brooke, loc. cit., pp. 144 f.

[2] Cf. W. de Gray Birch, *Seals*, London, 1907, p. 128; *Catalogue of Seals in the
Department of MSS. in the British Museum*, i, 1887, p. 700, no. 3827. There exist
privileges granted by Victor to Ely (Jaffé, i. 4350) and Chertsey (Holtzmann,
Papsturkunden, i, p. 221).

[3] Alexander II conferred on Abbot Æthelsige of St. Augustine's during his stay
in Rome the privilege of wearing mitre and sandals. The text seems to be lost (cf.
Jaffé, i. 4541), except for the short account in Goscelin's *Translatio Augustini*, ii. 1,
§ 6 (*Acta SS. Maii*, vi. 433) on which the Chronicles of Thorne, c. vi. 8 (ed. Twysden,
Historiae Anglicanae Scriptores X, 1652, col. 1785) and Elmham, p. 89, depend, only
adding the year 1063. Cf. Ph. Hofmeister, *Mitra und Stab der wirklichen Prälaten ohne
bischöflichen Charakter* (Kirchenrechtl. Abhandl. civ), 1928, pp. 6 f.

[4] A. B. and A. Wyon, *The Great Seals of England*, London, 1887, pp. 5 f. and pl. II.
Bresslau, 'Internationale Beziehungen im Urkundenwesen des Mittelalters' (*Archiv
f. Urk.* vi, 1918, p. 57), has conjectured that William I took as model a (lost) seal of
Canute the Great.

in dating at least a part, if not all, of the spurious charters of St. Augustine's about 1070.

The first archbishop who was buried at Christ Church, not at St. Augustine's, was Cuthbert in 760, and others followed. We do not know when the claims of the Augustinians for their cemetery became the subject of a feud which is reflected in the later histories of the abbey and in some of our charters and did not relate to the burial of the archbishops alone: '*Primo* etenim nostrum invaserunt cimiterium, nobisque generalis sepultura subtracta est, unde tanta quam auditis praesens discordia sumpsit *initium*', was the opinion of the monks as represented by Gervase (ed. Stubbs, i. 81). We are told by a contemporary writer how the nomination of Abbot Wido in 1087 aroused the fierce resistance of the monks.[1] Are we justified in assuming that there was also opposition and strife in 1070, when after Abbot Æthelsige had gone into exile to Denmark, Scotland, a Norman monk of Mont St. Michel in Normandy, was designated for election by the king?[2] The free election of the abbot was obviously another aim of the charters. In 1070 a new archbishop, Lanfranc, was on his way, after Stigand had been deposed. Was there, as in 1087, opposition to the nomination of a Norman abbot, and did the monks seize the occasion to further their claims by fabricating documents purporting to show that these claims had been authoritatively upheld in earlier days? Abbot Scotland was blamed in the traditions of his abbey for having contributed to the decline of its autonomous 'jurisdictions' by his support of the archiepiscopal synods of his compatriot Lanfranc;[3] but on the whole he left a good reputation. That is no refutation of these conjectures. But we must be conscious of the limits set to our knowledge, and speculations such as these may go too far.

On the inferences and conjectures to which an examination of the charters gave rise an unexpected light is thrown, from another direction, by a document among the 'Cartae antiquae' (A. 62) in the Chapter Library at Canterbury. It was first published about 250 years ago by Henry Wharton (*Anglia Sacra*, ii, 1691, pp. iv–vi) and has been reprinted several times[4] and newly edited half a century

---

[1] *Actus Lanfranci*, ed. Plummer, loc. cit., pp. 290 f.

[2] Cf. Freeman, *History of the Norman Conquest*, iv. 338, 750 ff.; H. Böhmer, *Kirche und Staat in England und in der Normandie*, Leipzig, 1899, pp. 106 ff.; Knowles, *The Monastic Order*, pp. 103 ff. on the 'Norman plantation'. Scotland was 'elect' when Lanfranc came to Canterbury (*Actus Lanfranci*, loc. cit., p. 288).

[3] Thorne, *Chron.* vii. 8 (ed. Twysden, col. 1790 f.). Cf. Lemarignier, loc. cit., pp. 176 f.

[4] Petrus Coustant, *Vindiciae veterum codicum confirmatae*, Paris, 1715, pp. 680–3; (Pierre) Le Brasseur, *Histoire civile et ecclésiastique du comté d'Évreux*, Paris, 1722, Actes et preuves, pp. 4 f. (cf. the text of the author, p. 154); M. Brial, *Recueil*

ago by J. B. Sheppard,[1] but has received little attention since.[2] The controversy on the profession of canonical obedience to be made to the archbishop by the abbot reached a climax in the times of Archbishop Richard (1174–84) and Abbot Roger of St. Augustine's elected in 1176; the question of the authenticity of the monastic privileges was brought before the Pope (p. 179). Then Giles I du Perche, bishop of Évreux in Normandy (1170–9), copied for the information of Pope Alexander III a letter which his late uncle Hugh III of Amiens, archbishop of Rouen (1130–64), had written to Pope Hadrian IV (1154–9). Hugh, so he told Hadrian, had assisted at the council of Rheims held by Pope Innocent II in October 1131. Two of his companions were the abbots Raginfred of St. Ouen in Rouen (1126–41) and William II of Jumièges near by (1127–42); both were 'electi nec benedicti'; there were the same controversies at Rouen as at Canterbury, and Hugh informed the Pope of this state of affairs. Innocent asked the abbots whether they could prove their immunity from subjection to their metropolitan 'privilegiis autenticis'; the abbot of St. Ouen hesitated to answer. By chance another bishop was present, Gaufrid of Châlons (1131–42), who had just been raised to the episcopal dignity after having been abbot of the ancient monasteries of St. Thierry near Rheims (1112–19) and of St. Medard at Soissons (1119–31).[3] He put an end to the debate by his intervention:

'Ait enim, quod, dum in ecclesia Beati Medardi abbatis officio fungeretur, quendam Guernonem nomine ex monachis suis in ultimo confessionis articulo se falsarium fuisse confessum, et inter cetera, quae per diversas ecclesias figmentando conscripserat, ecclesiam Beati Audoeni et *ecclesiam Beati Augustini de Cantuaria* adulterinis privilegiis[4] sub apostolico nomine se

des historiens des Gaules et de la France, xv, Paris, 1808, pp. 961 f.; Migne, *P.L.* cc. 1411 f.

[1] *Literae Cantuarienses*, iii, 1889, pp. 365–7 (Appendix, nos. 21, 22); cf. i, 1887, pp. 341 f., no. 329.

[2] The document has been mentioned, apart from Sheppard's introduction (vol. i, pp. lix ff.) and his earlier notice in the *Fifth Report of the Royal Commission on Historical MSS.*, 1876, p. 431, by P. Hébert, 'Un archevêque de Rouen au XIIᵉ siècle, Hugues III d'Amiens' (*Revue des questions historiques*, lxiv, 1898, p. 342); by Ernst Müller, 'Die Nithard-Interpolation und die Urkunden- und Legendenfälschungen im St. Medardus-Kloster bei Soissons' (*Neues Archiv*, xxxiv, 1909, p. 692, n. 1), and by A. H. Davis, *William Thorne's Chronicle of St. Augustine's Abbey, Canterbury, rendered into English*, Oxford, 1934, p. lv.

[3] Cf. *Gallia Christiana*, ix. 186 f., 415 f., 879 f.

[4] Cf. the letter of Archbishop Richard of Canterbury to Alexander III among the letters of Peter of Blois of about 1181 (Migne, *P.L.* cc. 1456 ff.; cf. ccvii. 213) deploring the use made by abbeys and especially those of Malmesbury and St. Augustine of forged privileges of exemption against their diocesans; he speaks of 'bullis adulterinis' and asks for their examination 'ex collatione scripturae et bullarum' (cf. above, p. 179, n. 3).

munivisse lacrimabiliter poenitendo asseruit; quin et ob mercedem iniqui-
tatis quaedam se preciosa ornamenta recepisse confessus est et ad Beati
Medardi ecclesiam detulisse.'

The bishop of Châlons was willing to take oath to the truth of his
declaration. Then the Pope ordered Archbishop Hugh to perform
the benediction of the two abbots 'sub professione canonica'. The
forged privileges, obviously those of St. Ouen, were ordered to be
handed over to Hugh[1] and were burnt at his command by his
nephew, the future bishop of Évreux, whom he had made archdeacon
of Rouen, with his own hand;[2] we shall see that copies survived.
Giles received from Hugh a transcript of his letter to Hadrian and
transmitted it under Hugh's seal to Archbishop Thomas of Canterbury between 1162, the first year of the latter's pontificate, and 1164,
in which year Hugh died and Thomas went into exile; we know that
in 1163 Pope Alexander studied papal privileges sent him by the
Augustinians.[3] But Hugh's letter, as it is preserved, belongs to the
next decade, when Giles was bishop of Évreux and the dispute arose
between Abbot Roger and Archbishop Richard, reaching its height
between 1176 (election of Roger) and 1179 (death of Giles). Giles
added to Hugh's letter under his own seal a certificate addressed to
Pope Alexander to be presented to him by 'the church of Canterbury'.
The letter and the certificate which accompanied it have survived
at Canterbury in this form.

These documents were the subject of controversy in the early
eighteenth century during the quarrels roused by Mabillon's excellent fundamental work *De re diplomatica*. They were quoted from
Wharton in a book connected with the beginnings of modern
biblical criticism: *Lettres critiques où l'on voit les sentimens de Monsieur
(Richard) Simon sur plusieurs ouvrages nouveaux*, Basle, 1699, pp. 131 ff.,
to support an attack against the Benedictine monks. Then Bar-

---

[1] Hugh stated the spurious character of the charters ('ea esse falsa') when he
arranged a *compositio* with the monks of St. Ouen. This document, mentioned by
Lemarignier, pp. 213 f., has no date, but is certainly later than the synod of Rheims;
it does not belong to the year 1130 (ib., p. 213, n. 125), to which the authors of
Gallia Christiana, xi, 138, 144 have ascribed it, probably by misinterpretation of
Fr. Pommeraye, *Histoire de l'abbaye royale de S. Ouen de Rouen*, Paris, 1664, pp. 163,
261, 391, who mentioned 1130 as the first year of Hugh's pontificate, but not as the
year of the charter.

[2] There is, according to A. H. Davis, loc. cit., p. 257, n. 4, a similar statement in
Thorne's MS. at Corpus Christi College, Cambridge, in the record of 1272, that the
privileges which had been impugned as forgeries by Archbishop Richard of Canterbury, were handed over by Abbot Nicholas of St. Augustine's (1273–83) to be
burnt. 'This statement was cancelled by a later hand.' The Latin text is to be
found among the variant readings (col. 1921. 2) at the end of Twysden's edition
(after col. 2768).

[3] *Materials for the History of Thomas Becket*, ed. J. C. Robertson, v, 1881, pp. 60 f.

thélemy Germon, the notorious hypercritical opponent of Mabillon, utilized this quotation, at haphazard, in his polemics on the un-reliability of old manuscripts: *De veteribus haereticis ecclesiasticorum codicum corruptoribus*, Paris, 1713, pp. 193 f. One of the ablest disciples and champions of Mabillon, Pierre Coustant, answered and, blinded by controversial partisanship, tried to show that the documents under Giles's name were falsifications, loc. cit. (1715), pp. 673–98.[1] An anonymous writer[2] defended their authenticity in the periodical published at Trévoux, *Mémoires pour l'histoire des Sciences et des Beaux Arts*, March 1716, pp. 501–43: 'Défense d'un acte qui fait foi qu'un moine de S. Medard de Soissons, nommé Guernon, fabriqua de faux privilèges au nom du S. Siége, en faveur de plusieurs Eglises.' The Benedictine diplomatists of the next generation, Toustin and Tassin, used the occasion of their *Défense des titres et des droits de l'abbaye de Saint-Ouen de Rouen*, Rouen, 1743, pp. 260 ff.,[3] to renew this 'bellum diplomaticum' and to attack again the reliability of the texts, and when no regard was paid to this article in a new edition of the much read *Histoire de France* of the P. Gabriel Daniel (enlarged by the P. Henri Griffet), Paris, 1755, vol. ii, p. 157, they repeated their challenge in the *Nouveau Traité de Diplomatique*, iii, Paris, 1757, p. xv, n. 1 (cf. vol. vi, 1765, pp. 173 f.). There the discussion ended, except for the notes by J. A. Fabricius in his *Bibliotheca Latina mediae et infimae aetatis*, *Liber VII et VIII* (=vol. iii), Hamburg, 1735, pp. 357 f., and by Brial in the *Histoire littéraire de la France*, xiv, Paris, 1817, pp. 20 f. (cf. xii, 1763, p. 665), and this little *cause célèbre* was forgotten.[4]

There is no reason to doubt the reliability of the story notwith-standing the common interests of the bishops. All dates relating to persons and facts mentioned in the letters of Hugh and Giles fit well together. Moreover, the benediction and profession of the abbots ordered by the Pope at Rheims are confirmed by other documents. The procedure aroused the indignation of King Henry I, who objected 'benedictionibus scilicet et extortis professionum scriptis extra ducatum' of Normandy, he himself not having been consulted.

[1] A part of the argumentation rested on the fact that the address 'Domino Adriano papae dominus Hugo Rothomagensis' was missing in Wharton's edition and was only supplied by Sheppard.

[2] He was an advocate of Rouen, Clerot, according to J. Lelong, *Bibliothèque historique de la France*, new edition by Fevret de Fontette, i, Paris, 1768, p. 792, no. 12810. The authors of the *Nouveau Traité*, loc. cit., mentioned the rumour that Germon wrote this article with the assistance of M. des Thuilleries. It was reprinted by Le Brasseur, loc. cit., on 14 pages without numbering between pp. 5 and 6 of the 'Actes et preuves.'

[3] I have not seen this book.

[4] Only U. Chevalier in his *Répertoire des sources historiques du moyen âge*, Bio-Biblio-graphie, 2nd ed. i, 1905, col. 1910, has devoted some lines to Guerno.

Innocent had to write conciliatory letters to king and archbishop.[1]
Further, Abbot Silvester of St. Augustine's (1151–61) induced Pope
Eugenius III in 1152 to order his benediction to be performed by
Archbishop Theobald 'sine professione'. But Eugenius's successors
Anastasius IV and, in 1156 and 1157, Hadrian IV reversed this decision and demanded that the abbot should make a profession, if his
predecessors could be proved to have done so;[2] there exists a declaration of seven bishops concerning this temporary end of the controversy.[3] The letter of Archbishop Hugh to Hadrian has its place
in this development between 1154 and 1157. The forgeries were of
course executed many years before this; for Guerno, the forger, died
as monk of St. Medard during the abbacy of Gaufrid, that is, between
1119 and 1131, obviously in old age.

The case of one man doing such reprehensible work for several
monasteries is not unique. In the same age a monk of Reichenau
provided his own and a number of other monasteries of southern
Germany with useful documents.[4] Guerno, according to his deathbed confession, worked 'per diversas ecclesias'. Of these Archbishop
Hugh, for the purposes of his letter, named only St. Ouen and St.
Augustine's; but the remark was made long ago that a monk of
St. Medard engaged in work of this kind would hardly have failed
to provide his own house with his fabrications.[5] St. Medard is
notorious for its frauds in respect of relics, hagiography, and charters.[6]
The monks pretended to have received there in 828 the bodies of
the Roman martyrs Tiburtius, Marcellinus, and Petrus, and did not
scruple to falsify and plagiarize a work of the famous Einhard which
must have proved to them the frivolity of this claim.[7] The number

---

[1] *Recueil des historiens des Gaules et de la France*, xv, pp. 377, 378 (Jaffé, i. 7585–6).
Innocent II also urged Abbot Alan of St. Wandrille to make his profession to Hugh,
ib., p. 373 (Jaffé, i. 7523). On the Cluniac Hugh of Rouen cf. J. G. Fotheringham,
Dict. of Nat. Biogr. xxviii. 163 f.; Hébert, loc. cit., pp. 325–71; Böhmer, *Kirche und
Staat*, pp. 276 f.; see also A. Wilmart, *Rev. Bén.* xlvi, 1934, p. 307; Knowles, *The
Monastic Order*, p. 282. On the position of the monasteries in Normandy and their
relations to the dukes cf. also C. H. Haskins, *Norman Institutions*, Cambridge (Mass.),
1918, pp. 25 ff., 35 ff.

[2] Gervase of Canterbury, ed. Stubbs, i. 76, 163 f.; Elmham, pp. 400 f., 404 ff.,
411 ff. Cf. also *Chronicon monasterii de Bello*, London (Anglia Christiana Soc.), 1846,
p. 88; F. Liebermann, *Ungedruckte Anglo-Normannische Geschichtsquellen*, 1879, p. 83;
Holtzmann, *Papsturkunden*, ii, 309, no. 118.

[3] Sheppard, loc. cit. iii, p. 367, no. 23; Gervase, i. 164 f.

[4] Cf. Bresslau, *Handbuch*, i², p. 12 with reference to the studies of Brandi and
Lechner and to the review of Bloch. Cf. also Hans Hirsch, *Neues Archiv*, xxxvi
(1911), 395 ff. and *Festschrift Hans Nabholz*, Zürich, 1934, pp. 23 ff.; *MG. Urkunden
der Karolinger*, i, nos. 219, 222–4, 281, and *Urkunden der Deutschen Karolinger*, i (1934),
p. 252, no. 177; ii (1937), p. 293, no. 178.

[5] Müller, loc. cit., p. 692, n. 1.   [6] Cf. Müller's article.

[7] *Translatio Tiburtii, Marcellini et Petri*, ed. Holder-Egger, *MG. SS.* xv. 1, pp. 391–5.

of doubtful relics in their possession was increasing and included even those of Gregory the Great, which were said with better right to rest in Rome. At last a tooth of Christ appeared there and aroused the scorn of one of the celebrated writers of the early twelfth century, Abbot (1104–21) Guibert of Nogent-sous-Coucy near by (dép. Aisne, arr. Laon), north of Soissons; this pretension induced him to write his book *De pignoribus sanctorum*, a part of which is directed expressly against the assertions of the monks of St. Medard.[1]

The monastery of St. Ouen in Rouen had many relations with St. Medard, personal and literary. The legend made St. Medard, the bishop of the Vermandois who died after the middle of the sixth century, the twin brother of Gildard of Rouen who was already bishop in 511; the identity of their festivals (8 June) was probably the starting-point of the legend. Gildard was translated from Rouen to St. Medard in the ninth century;[2] on the other hand, St. Ouen was provided about 1090 (?) with relics from St. Medard.[3] Of relics sent from Soissons to Rouen I will mention only (it will be seen why) those of Bandarid, an obscure bishop of Soissons in the sixth century.[4] There was another spiritual link between this city and the abbey of Rouen. St. Ouen (*Audoin* or *Dado*) was the most celebrated bishop of Rouen of the Merovingian age (641–84), and his tomb in St. Peter's at Rouen gave his name to church and abbey. He was born in the territory of Soissons; Sancy, in the proximity of the city, his birth-place, became a possession of the Rouen monastery in the third quarter of the eighth century.[5] The veneration of this saint connected Rouen with Canterbury also; Christ Church claimed to have received relics of him in the time of Archbishop Oda (942–58); biographies of Ouen which as usual spread with the cult, were copied in England from the eleventh century onwards,[6] and other writings in his honour soon followed.[7] When after the times

---

[1] Migne, *P.L.* clvi. 607–80. Cf. also the *Narratio de dente S. Iohannis* edited by A. Poncelet, *Catalogus codicum hagiograph. Latin. bibliothecae Vaticanae*, 1910, pp. 541–8, and the version of the *Miracula Gregorii et Sebastiani* published by the Bollandists in their *Catalogus codicum hagiograph. bibliothecae Regiae Bruxell.* i. 2, 1889, pp. 238–48; the passages mentioning the tooth of Christ are absent from the other version, *Acta SS. Martii*, ii. 749–51; cf. Müller, p. 708. There is a connexion between c. 2 (p. 239) and the interpolation of Nithard's Histories, iii. 2, which led to Müller's investigations.   [2] Poncelet, *Anal. Boll.* viii, 1889, pp. 402 ff.

[3] *Acta SS. Octobr.* x. 83 ff.   [4] Cf. ib., *August.* i. 60 ff.

[5] Cf. *SS. rer. Merov.* v. 554, n. 3. On St. Ouen cf. the introduction to my edition of the earliest *Vita Audoini*, ib., pp. 536 ff. and E. Vacandard, *Vie de saint Ouen*, Paris, 1902; cf. also Lemarignier, loc. cit., pp. 21 ff.

[6] *SS. rer. Merov.* v. 545, 549 (n. 2), 550 (nn. 5, 12), vii. 847.

[7] Fragmentary *Miracula S. Audoeni* from a Christ Church MS. of the 12th century were published by A. Wilmart, 'Les Reliques de Saint Ouen à Cantorbéry' (*Anal. Boll.* li, 1933, pp. 285–92); cf. my review, *Neues Archiv*, l (1935), 681. He also

of the Vikings the monastery of St. Ouen was restored, the abbot asked for King Edgar's (959–75) help.[1] There were other material links connecting the abbey with England; according to Domesday Book, the monastery owned property at West Mersea in Essex even before the Conquest,[2] and some monks were sent from Rouen to supervise this foreign possession.

We do not know the personal history, the range of the wanderings and other doings of Guerno. His name, as it is spelt by Archbishop Hugh, suggests a continental, a French, perhaps Norman origin; against the background sketched above we may guess how a monk who died at St. Medard came to fabricate charters for St. Ouen and St. Augustine's. The principal aim of all the documents which we may reasonably ascribe to his 'skill', was to secure the protection and independence of the monasteries against the diocesans and their officials and against the inroads of laymen. There are of course many differences in the details according to the particular conditions of the several houses and to the sources employed for the falsifications.

I give a short list of the charters involved and, first, of two papal privileges granted to St. Medard, clumsy forgeries which were the subject of one of the *Bella diplomatica* of the seventeenth century, when their genuineness was contested by Jean de Launoi:

I*a*. Privilege of John III of 562 (11 March), ⟨*Summum*[3] *esse*⟩ *quos*

edited the complete text of Eadmer's work *De reliquiis sancti Audoeni . . . quae Cantuariae in aecclesia domini Salvatoris habentur* (*Revue des sciences religieuses*, xv, 1935, pp. 362–70).

[1] Stubbs, *Memorials of St. Dunstan*, pp. 363 f.

[2] Cf. Fr. Pommeraye, loc. cit., pp. 483–8; *Mon. Angl.* vi. 2. 991 f.; J. H. Round, *Calendar of Documents preserved in France*, i, 1899, pp. 29 ff., and *V.C.H., Essex*, i (1903), 341 f., 454; R. C. Fowler, ib. ii (1907), 196 f. Philip Morant, *The History and Antiquities of the County of Essex*, i, London, 1768 (Chelmsford, 1816), p. 426, n. *F*, published a charter 'found amongst the Archives of Colchester', by which King Edward granted in 1046 a part of the island of Mersege (that is, Mersea) to SS. Peter and Audoen. The charter, which is not in Kemble's *Cod. dipl.*, was considered 'most suspicious' and 'doubtful' by Round (p. 341, n. 8) and Fowler. The style of Edward as '(rex) Anglorum atque Northanhumbrorum' would be more appropriate in the 10th than in the 11th century, and the invocation and preamble correspond almost entirely with a grant of Edgar in 967 (Birch, iii, no. 1196). Unfortunately the editor omitted the signatures of 19 'archbishops, bishops, abbots, officers and great men', a list which might have helped towards a more substantiated criticism. On the description of the boundaries, which seems to be a later addition, cf. P. H. Reaney, *The Place-names of Essex* (*E.P-N.S.* xii), 1935, p. lx. *Deramys-Diche, -Flete, -Strete, -Peete*, and *-Stone* mentioned therein, have probably to be referred to a tenant of the Conqueror, Deorman or Dereman; cf. Davis, *Reg. regum Anglo-Normann.* i, nos. 84, 141, 399; Freeman, *Norman Conquest*, v. 791; Round, *Domesday Studies*, ed. Dove, ii, 1891, pp. 556, 558; M. Gibbs, *Early Charters of St. Paul, London*, 1939, p. xxii, n. 2.

[3] Here and in II*b* the preamble begins probably with the words 'Quos divinae', and 'Summum (var. Suum, Summam) esse' is the end of the address, the *salutatio*,

divinae fidei (Pardessus, *Diplomata . . . ad res Gallo-Francicas spectantia*, i, Paris, 1843, p. 122, no. 166, has an incomplete text, obviously abbreviated), cf. Jaffé, i. 1039. Even the first editor, A. du Chesne (Quercetanus), recognized the fraud, *Petri Abaelardi et Heloisae Opera*, Paris, 1616, pp. 1168 f.; cf. p. 1167. The author used, directly or indirectly, a Frankish monastic privilege; the charter of Bishop Burgundofaro of Meaux[1] granted in 637 or 638 to the monastery of Rebais which Audoin, the future bishop of Rouen, and his brothers had founded, and the preceding privilege of King Dagobert I[2] may be compared as examples:

Burgundofaro	*John III*
quia nihil de canonica auctoritate convellitur, quicquid domesticis fidei pro quiete tranquillitatis tribuitur ('conceditur' Dagobert).	quia nihil de canonica auctoritate minuitur, *quicquid pro quietis tranquillitate* et servitute Dei ad loca venerabilium sanctorum *conceditur*.

The Pope granted the privilege 'praecellentissimi regis Clotharii suadente clementia', although Chlothar I had died in the previous year 561. It was 'consensu Bandaridi episcopi Suessorum (above, p. 211) factum, insuper et septuaginta episcoporum tali anathemate solidatum'.

This document is quoted in and closely connected with

I*b*. The privilege of Gregory I of 593 (26 or 27 May), *Quando ad ea catholicorum*: Pardessus, i, pp. 163–6, no. 201; Migne, *P.L.* lxxvii. 1330–4 (Appendix IV of the Benedictine edition of Gregory's letters);[3] cf. Jaffé, i. 1239. The preamble and other sentences are borrowed from one of the three identical privileges in Gregory's Register XIII, 11–13 (*MG. Epist.* ii. 376–81). Bishop Anseric, who occurs in other sources from 614 to 637, occupies here the place of Bandarid ('suadente nobis viro apostolico Anserico Suessorum urbis pontifice'); the Roman senate promotes the papal decision ('voluntate totius senatus Romani'),[4] and not only Gregory but also thirty bishops add their signatures. The names of seventeen were taken at random

---

containing a formula of good wishes: the Pope wishes the princes the highest state of being, *summum esse*.

[1] Pardessus, *Diplomata*, ii, no. 275, p. 40; V. Leblond and M. Lecomte, *Les Privilèges de l'abbaye de Rebais-en-Brie*, Melun, 1910, p. 55 (on this edition cf. *Neues Archiv*, xxxvii, 1912, pp. 869 f.).

[2] *Dipl. Merov.*, no. 15, p. 17; Leblond and Lecomte, p. 52.

[3] The Benedictines knew a MS. of St. Victor of Paris containing this privilege, to-day Paris 14300 of the 12th century (cf. *MG. Epist.* ii, p. xxiii; Ewald, *Neues Archiv*, iii, 1878, p. 501). Escorial MS. a. I. 6 of the 14th century contains the same text (Ewald, ib. vi, 1881, p. 226; Antolín, loc. cit. i. 16). The so-called interpolated text of Pardessus is the original one, except for some misreadings.

[4] This was repeated in II*b*, *c*.

from the register of the Pope,[1] to which the signatures of the Frankish king Theodoric II (who did not become king till the end of 595!) and of his grandmother Brunichild are also to be referred; but five names (Gregory—or rather George—of Porto, Andrew of Albano, Sergius of Palestrina, Agnellus of Sutri, Tiberius of Silva Candida) owe their appearance in this place to the acts of Gregory II's Roman synod of 721, with the consequence that the signatures of two bishops of Porto are to be found there. Bede also made his contribution: the names of *Etherius Arelatensis* (a mistake of Bede's for Lyons!), *Augustinus Cantuariorum* and *Mellitus Lundoniae episcopus* are taken from his *H.E.* There remain three fictitious names (Sutellius of Bordeaux, Vitalis of Besançon, Boniface of Piacenza); Flavius of Rheims, who belongs to an earlier age (*c.* 535),[2] and Anseric of Soissons mentioned above, conclude the series. The sort of abortive notarial signatures show, like other items, the relationship of I*a* and I*b*:

'Ego Simplicius ("Petrus" I*b*) notarius sanctae Romanae sedis subscripsi et sigillavi';

Petrus was also found by the forger in Gregory's register. We need not follow his methods further. One sentence common to both charters may show his design:

'ne tantae sublimitatis locus vilescat, quem caput constituimus monasteriorum totius Galliae nulliusque ditioni patimur esse subiectum.'

Spurious privileges to St. Pierre in Rouen, the later St. Ouen, betray the same workshop and hand. The reasons for the forgery were also the same. The bitterness of the antagonism between the parties was manifested in 1073 in an armed affray between the monks of the abbey and the followers of the archbishop.[3]

II*a*. Privilege of Leo I, *Nobis residentibus in ecclesia Calcedonensi, concilio inibi habito*, edited by J. Ramackers, *Papsturkunden in Frankreich*, Neue Folge II (Abhandl. Gött., 3. Folge, no. 21), 1937, pp. 48–51, no. 1, from copies of the fourteenth century in Paris, and of the fifteenth and seventeenth in Rouen. This charter was ascribed to Leo II and to the years 682–3 (Jaffé, i. 2124), because it is addressed to a King Chlothar as the founder of St. Pierre, and bishops are also mentioned in it who lived in a very different age from that of Leo the Great. But no Frankish king of the name of Chlothar was

---

[1] Some misreadings of names can be corrected from the register.

[2] Flavius has an impossible place also in another forged charter ascribed to King Dagobert I (*Dipl. Merov.*, p. 152, no. 33) which likewise seems to come from St. Medard but may be of later origin than I*a, b*. Cf. Vacandard, loc. cit., p. 18, n. 3.

[3] Annals of Rouen in F. Liebermann, *Ungedruckte Anglo-Normannische Geschichtsquellen*, pp. 46, 129; *Acta archiep. Rothomag.*, ed. Mabillon, *Vetera Analecta*, 2nd ed. (1723), pp. 224 ff., &c. Cf. Lemarignier, loc. cit., p. 155, n. 81.

contemporaneous with Leo II; therefore in the late Rouen copies the name of Pope Vigilius (537–55) was substituted for that of Leo, the more so because Vigilius actually took refuge in Chalcedon in 551–2 (cf. the *initium* printed above), and the editor of the document accepted this date, but wrongly.[1] The injudicious forger had in mind Leo I; for in the next charter of this series (II*b*) Gregory I refers to the privilege of Pope Leo (there was no Pope Leo before Gregory's time except Leo the Great), and Eugenius II (II*d*) mentions the privileges of his predecessors in the order of Leo, Gregory, and Martin; the forger obviously meant the first Pope Leo and the famous council of Chalcedon of 451. The fact that Leo was not at the council would present no difficulty to a forger of this type.

Considerable parts of this privilege, beginning with the formula of humility ('meritorum . . . qualitate infimus'), are copied more or less verbatim from the St. Medard charter of Pope John III (I*a*). The consent of Bandarid and the anathemas of seventy bishops also have their analogies: '*hoc* ipsum *privilegium consensu* et voluntate Flavii Rothomagensis archiepiscopi (he lived about 540)[2] . . . *firmatum et sexaginta episcoporum* sub *anathemate* in contradicentes *solidatum.*' There are signatures of forty-nine bishops,[3] two chorepiscopi, an archdeacon of Rome, and 'Sinelicius sanctae Romanae ecclesiae sedis vicarius', who sealed the charter in the same way as the notaries of I*a*, *b*; a 'protonotarius' John also gave his signature. Many of the bishops are from Gaul, and the reason is obvious: as the names of

---

[1] Lemarignier, pp. 26 (n. 48) and 214 (n. 126) has not observed the identity of the privileges of Leo and Vigilius. He connects these forgeries with the conflict in the time of Archbishop Hugh III (above, pp. 207 f.); but he did not know of Guerno's confession. The first words of the document remind us of the date of several charters of Duke Richard II of Normandy of 1025 (?), quoted by Lemarignier, pp. 252 f.: '*considentibus nobis* Fiscanni palatio.'

[2] The author of the second *Vita Audoini* (about 800) rightly connected the 24th year of Chlothar I (= A.D. 534–5) with the episcopate of Flavius, but wrongly identified this year with A.D. 500 (*SS. rer. Merov.* v. 565, n. 1): our forger had predecessors in such mistakes. But he attributed, like this biographer of St. Ouen, the origin of St. Pierre to King Chlothar I (511–61), whereas in the *Vita Chrothildis*, c. 13 (ib. ii. 347), the *re*-establishment of this monastery is ascribed to Chlothar's mother Chrothildis and its original foundation to the time of St. Dionysius (of Paris) who is said to have consecrated this monastery. This story probably developed after St. Nicasius had been introduced between 1079 and 1110 into the episcopal list of Rouen, from which his name was absent before; his legend had made him a companion of St. Dionysius. The earliest extant MS. of the *Vita Chrothildis* belongs to the 12th century. Thus the late 11th century as the date of the forged charters of St. Ouen receives some confirmation from this side. Cf. E. P. Sauvage, *Anal. Boll.* viii, 1889, pp. 422 ff.; Duchesne, *Fastes*, ii², pp. 202 ff.

[3] A few more seem to have been omitted in the edition; for Ramackers, p. 48, mentions two bishops of Autun as well as of Orléans, although only one of each of these sees is to be found in his text.

most of the bishops in I*b* were copied at haphazard from the *Registrum* of Gregory I, so the author of II*a* used a Martyrology for the same purpose, probably the widely circulated work of Usuard of St. Germain-des-Prés, where I have found twenty-two of the names.[1] Many additions were made in the different copies of this Martyrology, and some signatures of our privilege may have their origin in such supplements to Usuard. Five bishops owe their inclusion in the list to the Dialogues of Gregory I (Fortunatus of Todi, Julian of the Sabina, Anastasius of Nepi, Marcellinus of Ancona, Boniface of Ferento). Among the remaining names Bandarid of Soissons again finds a place. No wonder that the list of bishops is inconsistent and embraces men of different dates, even of different centuries.

II*b*. Privilege of Gregory I, (*Summum esse*)[2] *quos divinae fidei*, edited by J. von Pflugk-Harttung, *Acta pontificum Romanorum inedita*, iii, Stuttgart, 1886, p. 1, no. 1; cf. Jaffé, i, no. 1927 and ii, p. 698 (on MSS. see Ramackers, loc. cit., pp. 9, 12). The beginning is copied from the St. Medard privilege of John III (I*a*), but a larger part is based on that of Gregory (I*b*), which also furnished the signatures of the Pope, ten bishops, King Theodoric, Queen Brunichild, and notary Peter. But for the names of the bishops Venantius of Luni and Melantius of Rouen the 'author' returned to the register of the Pope. While his source I*b* attributed to St. Medard the dignity of 'caput monasteriorum totius Galliae' (p. 214), St. Ouen was assured the lesser position of 'caput monasteriorum ('ecclesiarum' II*c*) totius Neustriae'.

II*c*. Privilege of Pope Martin I of 649, *Apostolicae dignitatis status*, edited by J. von Pflugk-Harttung, loc. cit., ii, 1884, p. 18, no. 44; cf. Jaffé, i. 2077 (on MSS. Ramackers, pp. 9, 12). The text is derived to a large extent from Gregory's privilege to St. Medard (I*b*); that of John III (I*a*) and II*b* are also utilized. A Roman notary, Fortunatus, seals the charter; four of nine episcopal signatures belong to Gaul, three of them to famous saints of this age, Eligius of Noyon, Faro of Meaux (cf., e.g., Bede, *H.E.* iv. 1), and Audoen of Rouen; the other six are fictitious. The date is added in a *Traditum* formula (as it is, combined with the name of the notary, in II*d*): 'Traditum pridie Kalendas Septembris, indictione septima.'

II*d*. Privilege of Pope Eugenius II (824–7), *Quotiens illa a nobis*, edited by J. Ramackers, loc. cit., pp. 52–5, no. 2; cf. Jaffé, i. 2562. A part of this charter also is copied from the St. Medard privilege of Gregory (I*b*); a few sentences are taken from that to St. Ouen (II*b*). But the preamble is derived from another, genuine document

[1] A number of misreadings can be corrected from this source, and nearly all the variant readings of the earlier MSS. are confirmed thereby.

[2] Cf. above, p. 212, n. 3.

of St. Medard, the privilege of Pope John VIII of 876 (Migne, *P.L.* cxxvi. 660–2; cf. Jaffé, i. 3033); the words relating to the Roman visit of the Emperor Charles the Bald are transferred to Abbot Hildvin of St. Denis, St. Medard, St. Germain, and (obviously) St. Ouen.[1] The *Traditum* formula (cf. II*c*): 'Traditum *per manum* Iohannis notarii sancti Petri octavo Ydus Aprilis, indictione quintadecima' (rather V=827, not XV), may be a misinterpretation of the abbreviation for *Datum per manum* in an original papal privilege of this age; this abbreviation has also given trouble to others.[2] The list of possessions of the abbey confirmed by the Pope is in a large measure identical with that in a charter of the Emperor Charles of 876 (Bouquet, *Recueil*, viii. 650), as Ramackers, p. 52, has observed.[3]

This survey shows the close connexion which exists between the charters of St. Medard and St. Ouen, and the dependence of the latter on the former. This fact is the best confirmation of Archbishop Hugh's assertion that a monk of St. Medard, Guerno, before dying (after 1118), confessed to the forgery of papal privileges for St. Ouen —and for St. Augustine's. Are we justified in ascribing to his work the papal privileges and other charters of the latter which are here under consideration, or at least a number of them? Hugh mentioned only the two churches and 'adulterina privilegia' of Popes fabricated for them; speaking to Innocent II and writing to Hadrian IV he had no reason for referring to other charters. But his words are open to a wider interpretation: '*inter cetera*, quae per diversas ecclesias figmentando conscripserat.' There are naturally differences between the French and the English charters, since the particular circumstances and the 'sources' drawn upon were different. Guerno had to study, no doubt during his stay in England, Anglo-Saxon documents with their special features, and there may have been a considerable interval, perhaps of many years, between the forging of the English (*c.* 1070) and of the French texts. One of the St. Ouen privileges (II*b*) contains a strange word which astonished the editor

---

[1] On the privilege of John VIII cf. Müller, loc. cit., p. 694. On Hildvin cf., e.g., M. Buchner, *Das Vizepapsttum des Abtes von St. Denis*, Paderborn, 1928 (cf. my review, *Savigny-Zeitschr.* xlix, 1929, *Kan. Abt.* xviii. 578 ff.). Buchner, p. 183, defended the authenticity of the charter of Eugenius II, when only a fragment of it was known.

[2] Cf. below, p. 256, n. 8. The name *Rainowardi* (*Ramoluardi* Ramackers) . . . *archiepiscopi* may have been taken from a genuine source; Ragnoward became archbishop of Rouen between 825 and 828.

[3] F. Pommeraye, loc. cit., pp. 163, 238 f. mentions a privilege of Gregory V granted to St. Ouen on the 14th or 4th of May in the first year of his pontificate, that is, 996. It seems to be lost, and was perhaps also spurious. The author remarks that it was *donnée à Latran, à S. Iean de Latran*. The statement of the place of issue would be, though not impossible, a rare exception in papal privileges of this age. Cf. also *Gallia Christiana*, xi. 138.

(von Pflugk-Harttung, iii, p. 2); it occurs in a passage regarding the rights of the monks when taking part in a procession: 'In exeundo autem cantor monachorum, quamcumque sibi placuerit, primitus antiphonam incipiat, atque ad nutum abbatis et cantoris clerici *singant*, et processio uti disposita fuerit fiat.' The expression *singant* (for *cantent*) in a 'papal' privilege to an abbey of Normandy is less surprising, if it is employed by a man like Guerno, whose stay in England may have been of some duration; *singan*, a word common to the Germanic languages, is already found in Anglo-Saxon.

Other facts confirm the identity of authorship. We have seen that the forger of the Canterbury charters used, naturally enough, the *Registrum* of Gregory the Great and Bede's *History*; now it has been shown that the same sources were employed overseas (Gregory in I*b*, II*b*, Bede in I*b*).[1] Rhymed prose is sometimes conspicuous both in the English (p. 184) and in the French groups of documents. Here is an example from each:

Boniface IV (5): 'Ipsa vero saepe dicta ecclesia, | tua largiente regali munificentia, | ab hac, ut ita dicam, sede apostolica | constructa, ordinata atque edocta, | si qua sibi contigerint adversa, | indurata aliquorum pestilentum pertinacia, | ad matris ecclesiarum recurrat limina, | apostolica utatur audientia | ipsiusque in perpetuum consoletur et regatur vigilantia.'

John III (I*a*): 'Totius orbis principibus | machinam mundi sub Christo principe regentibus, | praesentibus scilicet et futuris, Iohannes meritorum qualitate infimus, | sed Christi gratia sanctae Romanae sedi praelatus. | . . . Ob hoc, divina inspirante gratia | et praecellentissimi regis Clotharii suadente clementia | . . .'

There are also smaller coincidences which I need not stress. I will mention only

Boniface IV (5): 'Laudabilis atque Deo placita petitio tua haec est, ut . . .'; Adeodatus (7): 'Quam ob causam annuentes tuae petitioni. . . .'
Leo (II*a*): 'venit ad nos petitio tua devotione plena. . . . Petitio tua, inquam, fuit, ut. . . . Unde annuentes tuae regiae petitioni. . . .'

But, what is more important, in spite of all differences in detail and wording, we may recognize not only similar tendencies but also the same technique of fabrication.

Guerno confessed that he had executed his forgeries 'per diversas ecclesias'. Further research may discover more of his 'work'.[2] Pos-

---

[1] A MS. of the *Registrum* at St. Ouen was one of the main sources for establishing its text in the Benedictine edition of Gregory's Works (vol. ii. 482 f. = Migne, *P.L.* lxxvii. 439), now Rouen no. 518 (O. 17) of the 12th century (cf. H. Omont, *Catalogue générale des mss.*, *Départements* [8°], i, 1886, p. 114).

[2] But I doubt whether the spurious privileges of the Popes John IV and Martin I to the monastery of Rebais near Meaux (Pardessus, ii, pp. 74, 85, nos. 302, 311; Leblond and Lecomte, loc. cit., pp. 57, 60; Jaffé, i. 2048, 2075) can be attributed

sibly, perhaps with some probability, his hand may be recognized in three spurious charters in favour of Peterborough Abbey, which existed in 1121 or a little later (cf. p. 201) and show the same type of composition and style:

(*a*) Charter of King Wulfhere of Mercia, 664 (Birch, i, no. 22A).[1] The list of witnesses is similar to those of Ethelbert's second charter for St. Augustine's and to that of Eadbald (cf. pp. 176, 187); Bede was used for the signatures of ecclesiastics. The author also employed a genealogy of the Mercian kings similar to that which Florence of Worcester inserted into his Chronicle (cf. p. 187). He quoted Matt. xvii. 24–5 with the same intention with which the passage is cited in the 'Bulla plumbea' of Augustine, and he called the latter by the hybrid name of *protodoctor*, which is also applied to him in the grant of Eadbald (cf. p. 200), no doubt after the example of St. Alban, the *protomartyr Angliae*. The intention may be recognized from a few words: 'Haec, nobis beato Petro principante, principalis in sua regione et specialius Romana sit ecclesia.'

(*b*) Privilege of Pope Agatho, 680 (Birch, no. 48; cf. above, pp. 200f.). The second letter of Pope John XII to St. Augustine's is incorporated almost verbatim; Bede's *H.E.* and a Mercian genealogy are other sources. Ethelbert 'regaliter condidit' the monastery of SS. Peter and Paul according to the 'Bulla plumbea'; so the Mercian kings 'regaliter condidere' Medeshamstede and would make its church 'Romanam et apostolicam'. The forger treated the problem of the relation of St. Augustine's to Peterborough in the same way as he has treated that of St. Medard to St. Ouen. St. Medard should be the head of the monasteries of Gaul, St. Ouen of the monasteries of Neustria, that is, of northern Gaul and particularly Normandy (cf. p. 216). St. Augustine's was the first monastery of Britain and should have precedence of all her abbeys; consequently Peterborough, as it was 'primitiva abbatia' and 'mater primaria' in its region, should have the precedence of the monasteries north of the Thames. The archbishop of Canterbury is called the vicar of the Pope; that may perhaps presuppose knowledge of the forged charters produced in 1072 on the primacy of Canterbury over York.[2]

(*c*) Charter of King Edgar, 972 (Birch, iii, no. 1280; repeated by Pseudo-Ingulf, ib., no. 1258).[3] The signatures were borrowed from

---

to the forger of the St. Ouen charters, which Lemarignier, loc. cit., p. 215, n. 131, has compared to them.

[1] Birch, no. 22, is a copy much enlarged by interpolations (pp. 34. 7–26; 35. 6–35; 35. 40—36. 3; 36. 4—38. 29).

[2] Cf. Boehmer, *Die Fälschungen Lanfranks*, pp. 154, 158 f.; Tillmann, loc. cit., p. 30.

[3] Birch's text no. 1258 (also in his edition of *The Chronicle of Croyland Abbey by Ingulph*, Wisbech, 1883, pp. 78–80) is incomplete; the list of witnesses is to be

a charter of the same king of 971 (ib., no. 1270). Some words recall
the privilege of Boniface IV to St. Augustine's. But there seem to
be several strata of Peterborough forgeries[1] which require special
examination.

The fabrication of the Canterbury charters by a continental monk
like Guerno explains certain special features in Ethelbert's second
charter, from which this discussion started. We now see why the
continental type of notification (p. 175), 'Notum sit omnibus tam
praesentibus quam posteris, quod . . .' is adopted,[2] and the difficulties connected with the names and titles of the witnesses are similarly
accounted for. Most of the names, except those of Augustine and
Eadbald, were probably borrowed from an earlier charter; but
Guerno, who may at first have had little experience in reading
insular script, made mistakes. The spelling of *Hocca* is confirmed by
Eddius's Life of Wilfrid, c. 18 (p. 213. 33), while the name is written
without *h* elsewhere. *Tangisilus* and *Geddi* may be misreadings for
Eangislus and *Aeddi*: insular initial letters have given rise to other
misinterpretations.[3] *Hamigisilus* and *Augemundus*[4] may have been
Haemgislus and *Agemundus*, and the emendation of *Pinca* is even nearer
at hand. Miss Deanesly found in it the misunderstood abbreviated
title of *pincerna* and bethought her of the office of butler after the
pattern of the Frankish court. It may be doubted whether there
would have been any need to go abroad for this office: the household
dignity of the *byrele* was common to the banquet halls of most
Germanic peoples;[5] and is there any example of an abbreviation of
pincerna in this early age which could be misread? Is not the simpler
assumption obvious that a continental transcriber misunderstood the
Anglo-Saxon rune ƿ, that is *w*, taking it for *p* (a frequent stumbling-

---

supplied from the edition of Pseudo-Ingulf by W. Fulman, *Rerum Anglicarum scriptorum veterum tom.* i, Oxford, 1684, pp. 46 f.

[1] Cf. Stenton, *Medeshamstede and its Colonies* (loc. cit.).—In view of Guerno's
relations to St. Medard I may mention that among the relics at Peterborough there
were some 'de sancto Medardo'; see Hugo Candidus, ed. J. Sparke, *Historiae Anglicanae scriptores varii*, London, 1723, p. 35.

[2] The word *posteris* for the usual *futuris* is also found, e.g., in a grant of William I
to St. Wandrille (Davis, *Reg. regum Anglo-Normann.* i. 28, no. 110; *Mon. Angl.* vi. 2.
1108; F. Lot, *Études critiques sur l'abbaye de Saint-Wandrille*, 1913, p. 82, no. 36):
'Notum sit omnibus tam posteris quam presentibus, quod. . . .'

[3] On the corruption of Anglo-Saxon letters by transcribers cf., e.g., W. H. Stevenson, 'An Old-English Charter of William the Conqueror' (*E.H.R.* xi, 1896,
p. 739, n.).

[4] *Augemundus* is read in the facsimile of Elmham published by Miss Deanesly, for
the *Angemundus* of the editions.

[5] Cf., e.g., L. M. Larson, 'The King's Household in England before the Norman
Conquest' (*Bulletin of the University of Wisconsin*, no. 100), Madison, 1904, pp. 124 ff.;
Liebermann, *Gesetze*, ii. 2, p. 590; Birch, i, nos. 160, 232, 328.

block to copyists), and that we may see underlying *Pinca* the name of *Wineca* or *Winca*, which has survived in several place-names?[1]

The office of *Augemundus referendarius* also finds its explanation in the same direction. The heads of the Merovingian chancery bore this Roman title; but there is no trace of even a rudimentary English chancery before the ninth century;[2] it would be rash to assume on the unstable ground of this document that King Ethelbert had at his court such an official after the Frankish model. If Guerno forged this charter, it is easy to see how he came to introduce this dignity into his fabrications. Audoin-Dado, 'St. Ouen', the future bishop of Rouen (641–84), was born near Soissons and was buried in his episcopal city in the church of St. Peter, which was afterwards called by his name (see p. 211). Soissons and St. Ouen of Rouen were the very places in France with which Guerno's falsifications were connected; no doubt he knew something of the life of St. Ouen. Now the bishop had been referendary under King Dagobert I and, as he became a saint of widespread fame, perhaps no holder of this office was better known during the Middle Ages. There were no referendaries in Gaul after the close of the Merovingian period; but the title lived on in literature. I need only quote the widely read *Gesta Dagoberti*, which were composed in the earlier part of the ninth century at St. Denis, c. 38 (*SS. rer. Merov.* ii. 416): 'Dadonis referendarii, qui alio vocabulo Audoenus dictus est posteaque episcopus Rotomorum extitit.' It is therefore not surprising that a forger who had relations with Rouen as well as with the native country of the saint, should place this title in one of his productions side by side with other titles which he probably found in Anglo-Saxon charters, *dux, comes, regis optimas*. The name of referendary and its significance were known in the close neighbourhood of Soissons in the age of Guerno. Waldric was chancellor of King Henry I of England from 1103 to 1106, when he was made bishop of Laon[3] to find there an untimely end in 1112 at the hands of the citizens, who had formed a 'commune'. Abbot Guibert of Nogent (cf. p. 211), whose monastery was situated west of Laon, north of Soissons, told the history of Waldric in his famous autobiography and, when mentioning his

---

[1] E. Ekwall, *The Concise Oxford Dictionary of English Place-Names*, 1936, pp. 498 f. has found the name of Win(e)ca in Wincle, Winkburn, Winkfield, Winkleigh, Winkton. A charter of 929 (Birch, ii, no. 665) mentions *on þincan* (Kemble read *pincan*) *hammes díc* (near Aust, Gloucestershire).

[2] Cf. Bresslau, *Internationale Beziehungen im Urkundenwesen* (loc. cit., pp. 50 f.); R. Drögereit, 'Gab es eine angelsächsische Königskanzlei?' (*Archiv f. Urk.* xiii, 1935, pp. 335–436).

[3] Cf. H. W. C. Davis, 'Waldric the Chancellor of Henry I' (*E.H.R.* xxvi, 1911, pp. 84–9); W. Farrer, 'An Outline Itinerary of King Henry the First' (ib. xxxiv, 1919, pp. 320 ff.).

episcopal election, did not call him by his official title of *cancellarius*, but said: 'Galdricum eligunt quendam regis Anglorum *referendarium*.'[1] We need not dilate on this parallel, which speaks for itself.

There remains a last signature which looks like a line from a glossary: 'Ego Graphio comes benedixi.' *Graphio* is the Old German equivalent of *comes*, and the use of the word as a proper name was at the best an exception.[2] In the age of Guerno the term had spread to England; it is found in spurious charters of Abingdon (Birch, i, nos. 366, 413)[3] and in the law-books of the *Quadripartitus* (arg. 24) and the *Leges Henrici* (7. 2) of the early twelfth century (Liebermann, *Gesetze*, i, pp. 534, 553). But was it the intention of the forger simply to give to this continental synonym of 'count' the meaning of a proper name, or had he a hidden motive for choosing the word? There is a surprising analogy in the documents from St. Ouen; one of the many bishops whose signatures are read under the privilege of Pope Leo (II*a*) has a curious resemblance to Count Graphio: 'Graphius Calcalaunensium episcopus subscripsi.' Obviously the name of 'Elaphius Catalaunensium episcopus' underlies the signature; this bishop of Châlons died in 580 as ambassador of Queen Brunichild to Visigothic Spain and gained a local cult as a saint,[4] which may be supposed to have been known to a monk living in the same province of the church. Have the names of bishop and city been corrupted by the mistake of a copyist (there are no variant readings in Ramackers, p. 51), or were they deliberately altered by the forger himself? A slip of the pen which alters *El-* into *Gr-* and *-t-* into *-lc-* does not appear very likely, even less so, if we consider the parallel form *Graphio*. Both names are reminiscent of the Greek γράφειν. We must not suppose that the author had a knowledge of this language; but the root of the word and its meaning were familiar to medieval scholars. I refer to Isidore's *Etymologies*, vi. 9. 2: 'Graphium autem Graece, Latine scriptorium dicitur, nam γραφή ('grafia' or 'gravia' other MSS.) scriptura est'; also to the *graphium* or *graphius* or even *graphio*, the writing implement of the stylus, and to other derivatives of the same stem.[5] Again, one may quote

---

[1] Guibert de Nogent, *De vita sua*, iii. 4 (ed. G. Bourgin, *Collection de textes pour servir à l'étude et à l'enseignement de l'histoire*, xl), Paris, 1907, p. 137.

[2] A Merovingian charter of St. Bénigne at Dijon (Pardessus, *Diplomata*, ii, p. 366, no. 554, of 609?) has the signature: 'Signum Graffiono'; but the reliability of the copy may be considered doubtful.

[3] On these charters cf. Stenton, *The Early History of the Abbey of Abingdon*, Reading, 1913, pp. 23, 30.

[4] Gregory of Tours, *Hist.* v. 40 (ed. Krusch, *SS. rer. Merov.* i. 1, 2nd ed., 1937, p. 247). Cf. H. Moretus, *Anal. Boll.* xxxiv–xxxv, 1915–16, pp. 270–6.

[5] Cf., besides Du Cange, W. Wattenbach, *Das Schriftwesen im Mittelalter*, 3rd ed., Leipzig, 1896, pp. 220 f., 261.

a much read poet like Ovid, in his *Amores*, i. 11. 23: 'Quid digitos opus est graphio lassare tenendo?' or the story of St. Medard's translation from Soissons to Dijon, the author of which sets out by saying: 'quamvis exilem, nostrae tamen narrationis flectamus graffionem' (*Acta SS. Junii*, ii. 96). The minds of forgers sometimes work in queer ways; did Guerno intend to perpetuate secretly and playfully the testimony of his knowing 'pen' in the disguise of Count Graphio and Bishop Graphius? The other witnesses use the words *libenter subscripsi, favi, laudavi, consensi, approbavi, confirmavi, corroboravi*; Graphio adds the more solemn *benedixi*. The term is not unique in this connexion, but it is found only exceptionally among many hundreds of signatures, and is always employed by bishops of the tenth and eleventh centuries.[1] That a count should give his blessing to a grant may appear anomalous and rather favours the idea that a covert joke was intended by the author. But perhaps too much stress has been laid on the word and all these considerations may be rash, though the coexistence of Graphio and Graphius in two spurious charters which we are justified in ascribing to the same man is in any case remarkable. Be that as it may, the court officials of King Ethelbert dissolve into thin air. No doubt his charters to St. Augustine's manifest the existence of relations between England and France, but of a different character and age.

There is another charter, by its date the earliest of the first Christian English king, his grant to Rochester Cathedral of 604 (Birch, i, no. 3); it is the first document of the so-called *Textus Roffensis*. It is less open to objection than the charters of St. Augustine's; but there is a difficulty here also. The text is addressed directly to St. Andrew, the patron-saint of Rochester Cathedral: 'Ideoque *tibi*, sancte Andrea, *tuae*que ecclesiae ... trado aliquantulum telluris mei.' This manner of addressing the grantee is also found in other early Rochester charters (ib., nos. 193–6, 227, 228, 242, 257, 260; ii, no. 439) and elsewhere (ib. i, nos. 148, 173, 187, 199), and is not in itself open to criticism (cf. below, p. 225).[2] But an address to the king's son Eadbald: 'Ego Aethelberhtus rex filio meo Eadbaldo'[3] is inserted at the beginning, between the date

---

[1] I have found *benedixi* in Birch, ii, no. 769; iii, nos. 917, 1050, 1190; Kemble, iii, nos. 636, 638, 692 ('benedicendo corroboravi'), 714 ('cum benedictione corroboravi' and 'benedixi'); vi, no. 1291. The signature of Archbishop Theodore in the spurious privilege of Pope Agatho to Peterborough (Birch, i, no. 48; cf. above, p. 219) ends: 'cuius inviolatores dampno et excomunico, defensores vero gratifico et *benedico*.'

[2] Cf. V. H. Galbraith, 'Monastic Foundation Charters of the Eleventh and Twelfth Centuries' (*Cambridge Historical Journal*, iv, 1934, p. 209).

[3] The strange formula of salutation with an admonition which follows these words in all editions, 'admonitionem catholicae fidei optabilem', would be unusual

and the preamble; this 'inscription' and the direct address to St. Andrew do not go well together. Moreover, the date of the document is: 'Mense Aprilio, sub die[1] IIII. Kal. Maias, indictione VII', that is, A.D. 604, in which year Augustine according to Bede (*H.E.* ii. 3) consecrated Justus first bishop of Rochester; his new dignity is already mentioned in the charter: 'ubi praeesse videtur Iustus episcopus.' It was granted during the lifetime of Augustine, who died in this or one of the following years (before 610)[2] on the 26th of May, having consecrated before his death his successor Laurentius (ib. ii. 4). The name of the latter occurs in the text: 'Hoc cum consilio Laurencii episcopi et omnium principum meorum signo sanctae crucis confirmavi'; but should we not expect the name of Augustine side by side with that of his junior partner? One may object that possibly Augustine was not present on the occasion of the grant and that, because his signature was not added, he was not to be mentioned. It may also be a mere chance that no other Rochester charter for more than a century has survived, and that the next one belongs to the year 734 (Birch, i, no. 152).[3]

In any case this charter of Ethelbert is no secure starting-point for establishing the origins of Anglo-Saxon diplomatics. Miss Deanesly has observed that it comprises certain formulas which are also found in the Frankish formulary of Marculf. He dedicated it to a Bishop Landeric whose identity is a subject of controversy.[4] She identifies him, in agreement with L. Levillain, with Bishop Landeric of Paris (about 654), and draws the conclusion that Ethelbert's scribe relied on Frankish formulas 'used later by Marculf and stored among the archives of the bishop of Paris: the very probable channel of

in this age and was evidently printed in this way under the influence of Bede (*H.E.* ii. 5, 6), who relates that Eadbald did not accept Christianity with his father but after the latter's death caused a pagan reaction, although it was ephemeral and was ended by his conversion. The words 'admonit. cath. fid. optab.' do not belong to the address but are the beginning of the preamble, and the text should read: 'Ego Aethelberhtus rex filio meo Eadbaldo. Ad monitionem catholicae fidei optabilem nobis est aptum semper inquirere, qualiter per loca sanctorum . . . aliquid . . . debeamus offerre.'

[1] The formula 'sub die' is very common in inscriptions and charters of this age; cf., e.g., E. Diehl, *Inscriptiones Latinae Christianae veteres*, iii, 1931, pp. 307 ff.

[2] Cf. W. Bright, loc. cit., p. 105; Plummer, *Baedae Op. hist.* ii. 81.

[3] The sanction of Ethelbert's charter is similar to that of a grant of 'Ethelbert of Wessex and Kent' of 781, which date is corrected from 761 (Birch, i, no. 242; Earle, *A Hand-book to the Land-charters*, p. 332). A charter of 781 (perhaps of Egbert II of Kent) seems there to have been mixed up with another one of Ethelbert of Wessex (860–6) of 861, who is sometimes styled, like Ethelwulf (839–58) and Ethelred (866–71), 'rex Occidentalium Saxonum necnon et (seu, seu etiam) Cantu(u)ariorum' (Birch, ii, nos. 442, 444, 449, 467, 486, 502, 506, 507, 516, 518, 538, 853, 855).

[4] I have mentioned recent literature on the subject in my note 'Zu Marculfs Formularbuch' (*Neues Archiv*, l, 1935, pp. 616 ff.).

connexion being Bertha, daughter of the king of Paris, her chaplain-bishop Lothar [rather Liudhard or Leudard] and, or, her notary'.[1] But we must not forget that the Frankish charter is an offspring of the late Roman charter, like the charters of Roman and Langobardic Italy (Spain can be left aside here), in the same way as the 'Merovingian' script originated in late Roman cursive writing; there are differences of development but there also is common ground. A particular connexion of the Frankish derivative with the Anglo-Saxon charter can only be assumed if the pertinent formulas are specific features of the Merovingian offshoot. That is not the case; the same formulas are found also in Italy. Here are a few examples:

The formula 'Regnante in perpetuum domino nostro Iesu Christo salvatore', a favourite invocation of the early Anglo-Saxon documents (cf., e.g., the synod of Hertford in 672, Bede, *H.E.* iv. 5; Birch, i, nos. 162, 174, 189, 195, 201, 207, 224, 230, &c.), also introduces the decrees of the Roman synod of 595 (*MG. Epist.* i. 362): 'Regnante in perpetuum domino nostro Iesu Christo.'[2]

'ecclesiae, . . . ubi *praeesse videtur* Iustus episcopus'; cf. a charter of Ravenna of 572 (Marini, *I papiri diplomatici*, Rome, 1805, p. 137): 'sancte ecclesiae catholicae Ravennati, in qua venerabilis Petrus archiepiscopus praeesse videtur.'

Sanctions with *Si quis* (cf. pp. 196, 197 f.) are very common in papal privileges and synodal decrees.

The formula 'pro animae remedio' occurs in charters of Ravenna and Dalmatia (Marini, loc. cit., pp. 121, 139, 144, 147) and in a Roman inscription (E. Diehl, *Inscriptiones Latinae*, Bonn, 1912, pl. 37*e*): 'pro remedium (remedio) animae meae (nostrae).'

We have already seen that Ethelbert addresses St. Andrew directly. Miss Deanesly has compared this form of speech with Marculf, ii. 17 (ed. Zeumer, *MG. Formulae*, pp. 86 ff.), that is, the formula of a Roman testament which has parallels in Gaul and Italy. The number of genuine Western sixth-century charters is small; but a Ravenna papyrus again helps (Marini, p. 113; cf. p. 115=K. Brandi, *Urkunden und Akten*, 3rd ed., Berlin, 1932, p. 18): '*Te* itaque, sanctam ecclesiam catolicam Ravennatem, in cuius servitio crevi, heredem mihi ex axe (= asse) esse iubeo ac volo.' I may also quote a Roman grant preserved on stone (Diehl, loc. cit., pl. 38*b*; Brandi, p. 23): 'renuntiamus et emittimus ecclesia(m) beate Barbarae virginis *tibi*, domino Iesu Christo.' It follows that the alleged formulas do not prove the descent of Anglo-Saxon charters from a Frankish model, even if Ethelbert's Rochester grant should be genuine.

---

[1] Deanesly, *Transactions* (cf. above, p. 174), p. 53, cf. 66–9; *History*, pp. 102 ff.; *Cambridge Hist. Journ.*, pp. 102 (n. 5), 110.

[2] Poole, *Studies*, pp. 174 f., has also overlooked this Italian example.

The introduction of writing and of written records into legal business, which had previously been based solely on oral declarations and appropriate symbols, had far-reaching consequences. To discover who imported the new, securer kind of testimony we must proceed from those early English charters which can be reasonably assumed to be originals or reliable copies. There is no doubt that the Anglo-Saxon charter, like those of Gaul and Italy, is an offspring of the late Roman charter, developing from the outset its special features, as they have been described by Kemble, Earle, Hubert Hall, H. Brunner, and others.[1] The arrangement is almost the same as in Frankish and Italian charters; the ideas, e.g., of the preambles are more or less identical, but only the ideas, while they receive on the whole a new formulation; the structure in general is imitated, without being copied. Even the script makes this evident; the scribes do not imitate continental charter-hands. There are some early examples of majuscule (uncial) writing, that is, of book-hand; later 'insular' minuscule script prevailed and shows that charters obtained a greater place in Anglo-Saxon life, after the Irish predominance in the English Church between 635 and 664 had also given preponderance to the Irish script.

As to the formulas, there is a single text among early Anglo-Saxon charters in which the influence of Gallic documents can be traced. It is 'the oldest West Saxon charter of which a good text has survived'[2] (in the Shaftesbury cartulary, Harley MS. 61, of the fourteenth century), and it records the grant of land on the river Fontmell in Dorset by Coinred to an Abbot Bectune (Kemble, i, no. 104; Birch, i, no. 107). Birch dated the charter about 704; but the signature of Bishop Leutherius of Wessex (Winchester) points to the years 670–6 which comprise his pontificate (cf. Plummer, *Baedae Op. hist.* ii. 144, 147); the witnesses occur in the same sequence, with two additional signatures, under a grant of 675, by which Bishop Leutherius conferred the monastery of Malmesbury on Aldhelm (Birch, i, no. 37; *Auct. ant.* xv. 507). The other charter was preserved by an 'inspeximus' (to use a later term) of Bishop Cyneheard of Winchester in 759 (Kemble, loc. cit.; Birch, i, no. 186), when controversies between the monastery of Tisbury and the (unknown) house of Abbot Bectune were settled (cf. Brunner, loc. cit., pp. 176 f.). On this occasion the words 'beatae memoriae' may have been in-

---

[1] I will cite only H. Brunner, *Zur Rechtsgeschichte der Römischen und Germanischen Urkunde*, i. 149 ff.; Oswald Redlich, *Urkundenlehre*, iii (part of v. Below and F. Meinecke, *Handbuch der Mittelalterlichen und Neueren Geschichte*), München, 1911, pp. 43 ff.; cf. also Bresslau, 'Internationale Beziehungen im Urkundenwesen des Mittelalters' (loc. cit., pp. 44 ff.); Galbraith, loc. cit., pp. 205 ff.

[2] Stenton, *Anglo-Saxon England*, p. 65.

serted in the earlier document before the name of Bishop Leutherius
in contradiction to his signature, if they are a later addition; for
Eddi and probably Aldhelm applied these words also to living
persons (cf. *SS. rer. Merov.* vi, pp. 217. 7, 252. 1, 259. 28; *Auct. ant.* xv,
493. 3). This grant of 670–6 on the whole does not differ from other
Anglo-Saxon charters; the preamble is found, with some variants,
in several documents (exactly with the same wording in Birch, i,
no. 308); there is the ancient form of handing over by the symbol
of *caespites* which were laid on a Gospel Book (cf. Brunner, pp. 188 f.).
But one formula is unusual in early English charters, the words
added at the end of the sanction:

'. . . ita ut ab hac die tenendi, habendi, possidendi in omnibus liberam et
firmam habeat potestatem. Si quis vero episcoporum seu regum contra
hanc definitionis cartulam propria temeritate vel potius sacrilega debaca-
cione venire temptaverit, inprimis iram Dei incurrat, a liminibus sanctae
ecclesiae sit ('et' MS.) separatus, *et hoc quod repetit vindicare non valeat.*'

The sanction itself presents nothing remarkable, but the final clause
ranges it by the side of numerous Frankish charters. I will quote
only Marculf, ii. 6 (ed. Zeumer, p. 79):

'. . . *habendi, tenendi* vel quicquid . . . elegerint faciendi *liberam in omnibus
habeant potestatem. Si quis vero* . . . calliditate commotus aut cupiditate pre-
ventus *contra hanc* epistolam donationis nostrae . . . *venire* aut eam infrangire
conatus fuerit, *inprimi*tus *iram* trine maiestatis *incurrat* . . . *et quod repetit
vindicare non valeat.* . . .'

A grant by Abbess Irmina to Willibrord's monastery of Echternach
in 699 may serve as a second example (*Dipl. Merov.*, p. 175; C.
Wampach, *Geschichte der Grundherrschaft Echternach*, i. 2, p. 26, no. 6):

'ut . . . faciendi, *habendi, tenendi,* commutandi *liberam et firmissimam in omnibus,*
Christo propitio, *habeat*is *potestatem*. . . . Nam *si quis contra hanc cart*am
donationis . . . *tempta*re conaverit, . . . *inprimi*tus *iram Dei* omnipotentis *incurrat* . . . *et hoc quod repetit* nullatenus *valeat evendicare.*'

There are many similar examples from the Frankish kingdom, some
of which correspond even more closely with the words of the Wessex
charter (as the Formulae Salicae Lindenbrogianae, no. 1, Zeumer,
p. 267: '*a liminibus sanctae* Dei *eclesiae* excommunus et sequestratus
appareat').

  Coinred's charter is exceptional also in another respect. The names
of the scribes were not mentioned in Anglo-Saxon charters, while
Frankish and Italian 'private' charters regularly include their signatures, as does this document: 'Ego Wimbertus presbyter qui hanc cartulam rogante supra effato[1] abbate *scripsi* et subscripsi.' Wynbercht,

---

[1] Cf. the charter of Leutherius mentioned above: 'quibus ita caelesti oraculo
effatus est.'

who was afterwards abbot of Nursling near Southampton (cf. my edition of the *Vitae S. Bonifatii*, p. 9), likewise recorded his part in the writing or composition of two charters of King Ine of Wessex (Birch, i, nos. 100, 103: 'hanc cartam *scripsi* et subscripsi', 'hanc donacionem *dictans* subscripsi'). These few deviations of early Wessex charters from Anglo-Saxon custom and this approach to continental usage need not raise suspicion,[1] as they are due to particular circumstances. Bishop Leutherius, who was the first to give his signature to the grant of Coinred, was a nephew of Agilberct, who, after having been bishop of the West Saxons, returned to his native country, Gaul, and died as bishop of Paris; invited to resume his English see, he sent Leutherius, who was consecrated bishop by Theodore of Canterbury (Bede, *H.E.* iii. 7, iv. 12, pp. 141, 227). These personal relations explain sufficiently the slight and ephemeral appearance of Frankish custom in a few Wessex charters and especially in Coinred's grant, the wording of which may have been dictated more or less by Leutherius.

But these are very rare exceptions and had no lasting effect. The early Anglo-Saxon charters on the whole show no connexion with Merovingian charters, either with the particular form of the royal diplomas or with 'private' charters. They contain a punitive clause, the royal charters of the Franks do not; but this clause threatens the transgressor with 'spiritual' sanctions only, while the Frankish private charters also demand a payment for the infringement of their provisions, nor is their usual formula *stipulatione subnexa* found in early England. The limitation of the 'sanctio' to spiritual threats and promises points to the ecclesiastical origin of the English charter;[2] nor can there be any doubt that Italian and especially Roman documents were the models. The sanctions of early English charters *Si quis . . . , Quisquis . . . , Quicumque . . . , Quod si . . .* , &c., have their parallels in papal and other Roman documents and in the formulas of the *Liber Diurnus*. The negative penal clauses[3] are often accompanied by a positive invocation of a blessing on whoever may promote the intentions of the grantor, ending sometimes in early Kentish charters with a quotation from Matthew xxv. 34;

---

[1] Cf. J. Aronius, *Diplomatische Studien über die älteren angelsächsischen Urkunden*, Dissertation of Königsberg, 1883, pp. 13 ff.; Stenton, *The Early History of the Abbey of Abingdon*, pp. 11 f., 16.

[2] Cf. Joachim Studtmann, 'Die Pönformel der mittelalterlichen Urkunden' (*Archiv f. Urk.* xii, 1932, pp. 262 ff., 271 ff.).

[3] The legendary end of the Ostrogothic King Theodoric the Great was inserted in the sanctions of some royal charters of the 10th century, the *olla Vulcani* being borrowed from the Dialogues of Pope Gregory, IV. 31 (ed. Moricca, p. 275; *MG. SS. rer. Langob.*, p. 540); cf. Birch, ii, no. 818, iii, nos. 1142, 1265. A. Giry, *Manuel de diplomatique*, p. 564, n. 5, mentions a later French example.

it is introduced with words after the pattern of sermons of this age:

Birch, nos. 36, 42: 'audiatque in die novissimo tremendi examinis ab ipso iudice omnium Christo domino aeternae benedictionis vocem: Venite, benedicti patris mei, percipite regnum, quod vobis paratum est ab origine mundi.'

Ib., nos. 160, 194: 'auribus percipiant ('audiant' for 'aur. perc.' 194) vocem clementissimi iudicis ('arbitri' ib.) inquientis ad pios: Venite, benedicti. . . .'

Ib., no. 189: 'et beatissimam vocem audire mereatur cum sanctis: Venite, benedicti. . . .'

Ib., no. 199: 'et illam beatam vocem audire meruerint: Venite, benedicti . . . .'[1]

It was thus that Caesarius of Arles ended many of his homilies.[2] But this kind of preaching was adopted in Rome also; a papal allocution in the *Liber Diurnus*, no. 85 (pp. 109 f.), contains a close parallel: 'ut *in die* adventus domini et salvatoris nostri Iesu Christi a dextris consistens *illam* desiderabilem de evangelio *mereamur vocem audire* dicentem: *Venite, benedicti . . .*'; cf. also the letters of Pope Stephen II in the Codex Carolinus 8, 9, 11 (*MG. Epist.* iii, pp. 497. 23, 500. 19, 507. 20), of Hadrian I, no. 57 (ib., p. 583. 13), and of Leo III (ib. v, p. 63. 5). A similar sentence taken from the end of a sermon or a letter was obviously the foundation of the Kentish formula.

Frankish and Italian 'private' charters were provided with the signature of notary or scribe; no such formula is to be found in papal documents of this early age with a few exceptions of a special kind,[3] and its omission is also a characteristic feature of the Anglo-Saxon charters, as I have stated above.

Many English charters begin with an 'invocation', and two types occur very often. The *Regnante*-form, which is at the head of Ethelbert's Rochester grant, is seen in the acts of the Roman synod of 595 (p. 225). Another type is also found very often in early English charters (with some variants of course): *In nomine domini Dei (et) salvatoris nostri Iesu Christi*;[4] we find it at the beginning of the grant which Gregory, the future Pope, made to his Roman monastery in 587 (*MG. Epist.* ii. 437), of Roman synodal decrees of the years 600 (ib., p. 275), 721 (Hinschius, *Decretales Pseudo-Isid.*, p. 753), 732

---

[1] A charter of this kind was used in Ethelbert's third grant to St. Augustine's (Birch, no. 6): '*ut in die* Domini dulcem illam piissimi Redemptoris nostri *vocem mereatur audire* dicentis: Euge, serve bone . . .' (Matt. xxv. 23).

[2] *Caesarii Arelatensis Sermones*, ed. G. Morin, Maredsous, 1937, pp. 74. 6, 87. 31, 116. 9, 504. 3, 551. 1, 590. 32, 638. 4, 683. 20, 719. 26, 768. 17, 810. 26, 918. 26, &c.

[3] Cf. Schmitz-Kallenberg, loc. cit., pp. 75 f.

[4] Cf. W. H. Stevenson, 'Trinoda necessitas' (*E.H.R.* xxix, 1914, pp. 702 f.).

(O. Günther, *Neues Archiv*, xvi, 1891, p. 244), and 745 (Boniface, *Epist.* 59, ed. Tangl, pp. 108, 113, 116), and of two formulas of the *Liber Diurnus* (nos. 74, 83, pp. 74, 90). The grant of Gregory of 587 and a decree of Gregory II (Diehl, *Inscriptiones Latinae*, 1912, pl. 38*d*; cf. Kehr, *Italia pontificia*, i. 136, no. 8) have a preamble which in part recurs verbatim in a few English charters of the late seventh century (Birch, i, nos. 34, 72, 81).[1]

There were two kinds of signatures, as I have already said (p. 176), the *subscripsi*-type and the *signum*-type, the first used originally by persons skilled with the pen, the other by those who were unable to write because of illiteracy or illness. The reason for using a *signum* was not stated as a rule; but there are some Kentish charters of the late seventh century where an explanation is added, either in the so-called 'corroboratio', the formula indicating the signs (signatures, &c.) employed to give the document the character of a valid testimony, or in the signature of the grantor itself:

Birch, i, nos. 34, 73, 86, 90, 97–9: 'pro ignorantia litterarum signum sanctae crucis (in hac cartula) expressi(mus)' [no. 69 is spurious but depends on a text similar to no. 86, and the two seem to be somehow combined in no. 296, cf. below, p. 249, n. 3]. This formula continues in nos. 73, 90, 97, 98: 'et testes (97, 98 add 'idoneos') ut subscriberent rogavi(mus).'

In many cases no reason is given for the absence of a real *subscriptio*; but the above formula (without the *ignorantia*-clause) is frequently employed to announce the *signum* of the grantor, e.g.

Ib., no. 45 (the earliest existing original): 'manu propria signum sanctae crucis expraessi et festes ut subscriberent rogavi'; no. 175: ' signum sanctae crucis impressi.'

Ravenna papyri of the fifth and sixth centuries prove once more the Italian origin of these formulas:

Marini, loc. cit., p. 112: '*litteras ignorans* subter *manu propria signum* feci'; p. 114 (= Brandi, loc. cit., p. 17): 'faciente nequissima egritudine podagrae quia suscribere non potui, *signum* tamen beatae *crucis* ut potui coram testibus inpressi'; p. 124: '[si] . . . ipse in eadem *manu propria signum inpraess*erit *testes*que *ut suscriberent* conrogav*erit . . .* in qua *pro ignorantia litterarum* subter *signum* feci'; p. 131: 'cuique quia *ignoro litteras signum* feci, ad quod Castorium v. c. carum meum *ut* pro me *suscriberet* conrogavi'; p. 133: 'cui *propriae manus* tam ego quam Felithanc vir subli(mis) iugalis meus *propter ignorantiam litterarum signa inpraessimus*'; p. 139: 'in qua subter . . . *mano propria p*[*rop*]*ter ignorantia litterarum signum sanctae crucis* feci'; p. 145: 'in qua subter *propria*

---

[1] Cf. Stevenson, *E.H.R.* xxix, 1914, p. 702; Stenton, ib. xxxiii, 1918, p. 435, n. 11. The first two words of the original, Birch, i, no. 160: 'Provabilibus desideriis' correspond with the beginning of some papal charters (*MG. Epist.* i. 170, ii. 196; Jaffé, ii, p. 805) and of *Liber Diurnus*, no. 6 (p. 5), and also indicate a slight Roman reminiscence.

manu pro ignorantia litterarum signum venerabilem *sanctae crucis* feci'; p. 182:
'manibus nostris suscribtiones vel *signa inpraessimus*, simul *et testes* pariter *ut
suscriberent conrogavimus*'; p. 183: 'ipso praesente ... et subter *manu* [sua
prop]ria pro ignorantia literarum signum faciente et [*testes*] *ut suscriberent conrogavit*',
&c. Cf. also *Liber Diurnus*, no. 74 (p. 78. 8): 'in qua et ego manu propria
subscripsi *et testes ut subscriberent rogavi*.'

The ignorance formula[1] was employed in Italy for centuries; Kemble
(i, pp. xcviii f.) has referred to a 'Notitia iudicati' of 874 from the
monastery of Casauria near Chieti (Mabillon, *De re diplomatica*, 1681,
p. 544; Muratori, *Rerum Italic. scriptores*, ii. 2, col. 946):
'Signum Heribaldi comitis sacri palatii, qui ibi fui et *propter ignorantiam
litterarum signum sanctae crucis* feci.'

The 'corroboratio' is often introduced by some words indicating
the purpose of the signs of validity. A few Kentish charters are once
more reminiscent of an Italian model. I arrange them according
to the development which in my opinion the formula underwent:

Birch, i, no. 99: '*Ad cuius cumulum firmitatis* manu propria signum sanctae
crucis expressi'; no. 191: 'per crucem dominicae passionis adiuro, *cuius*
signum *ad cumulum firmitatis* in hac paginela descripsi.'

Ib., no. 86 with the spurious nos. 69 and 296: '*Ad cuius cumulum* etiam
affirmationis ('confirmationis' 296) ...'; no. 69: '*Ad cumulum* autem confirmationis. ...'

Ib., nos. 73, 90: 'manente hac cartula perpetualiter nihilominus donationis
meae in sua *firmitate* ('m. h. c. nostrae don. in sua nichilominus firmitate' 90).
Ad cuius (etiam) confirmationem. ...'

Ib., nos. 97, 98: 'Quam donationem meam volo *firm*am esse in perpetuum.
... *Ad cuius* confirmationem. ...'

The spurious privilege of Pope Adeodatus to St. Augustine's (above,
p. 182) also borrowed the formula from a similar charter (Birch, p. 52, l. 28):
'*Cuius ad cumulum firmitatis* praevidimus. ...'

The formula *ad cumulum firmitatis* ('to give the highest degree of
security') certainly is not common; the new *Thesaurus linguae Latinae*
(s.v. *cumulus, firmitas*) does not indicate any example of this combination. But it is found in a Ravenna papyrus of 551, an agreement
between the clergy of the Gothic church of Sant' Anastasia and
the Defensor Petrus, famous for the number of Gothic names and
signatures that it presents (Marini, p. 181; E. Spangenberg, *Juris
Romani tabulae negotiorum sollemnium*, Lipsiae, 1822, p. 267; H. F.
Massmann, *Die gothischen Urkunden von Neapel und Arezzo*, Vienna,
1838, p. 14, l. 52):

'et *ad cumulum* tuae *firmitatis* dominii suprascripta [c]a[utio] centum viginti

---

[1] Cf. also the Visigothic formula, no. 7 (*MG. Formulae*, p. 578). Many Greek
papyri from Egypt may also be compared. In these a person very often writes in
place of another, μὴ εἰδότος γράμματα, ἀγραμμάτου ὄντος, διὰ τὸ μὴ εἰδέναι αὐτὸν
γράμματα, &c.

solidorum a nobis tibi emissa pro tui dominii ut dixi[mus] firmitatem penes te placuit resider[i].'

These are small coincidences; but they confirm the descent of the Anglo-Saxon charters from the Roman part of Italy, in accordance with the opinion of scholars such as Brunner (loc. cit., pp. 70, 187), W. H. Stevenson (*E.H.R.* xxix, 1914, pp. 695, 702), R. L. Poole (*Studies*, pp. 50, 175), Redlich (loc. cit., pp. 43 f., 46), Brandi (*Ausgewählte Aufsätze*, Oldenburg, 1938, pp. 136, 154), and Brandileone.[1] This written kind of testimony was in use a few years after the arrival in England of Theodore and Hadrian (669); we do not know whether it had taken root there before.[2] It was a heritage of Roman times and was transferred overseas as an ecclesiastical implement and developed there its particular features: the use of the vernacular not only to define boundaries but also for the inditing of entire charters finds a parallel in the Anglo-Saxon law-books. Frankish influence also operated to some extent. The style of 'rex Anglorum', applied in charters first to Offa of Mercia,[3] probably came into use by analogy with the 'rex Francorum', Charles the Great.

The beginnings of a royal chancery in Wessex, perhaps in the ninth century (p. 221), followed Frankish example. But England also contributed to continental diplomatics. The 'chirographum' or 'cyrographum'[4] in the technical sense, the charter written in duplicate for contracting parties, a 'charter-party', first appears in England about the middle of the ninth century; it was transferred in the next century to the Continent and helped there to bridge the gulf created by the breakdown of the charter of Roman origin until the development of new forms of written evidence, such as the sealed charter or the notarial instrument.[5] About the end of the first millennium England initiated a new kind of royal charter, the 'writ', which also had its influence abroad.[6] This simpler form of royal

---

[1] Fr. Brandileone, 'Preliminary Notes upon the Anglo-Saxon Documents of the Eighth and Ninth Centuries' (*Celebration Legal Essays in honor of John H. Wigmore*, pp. 384–93 = *Illinois Law Review*, xiii, Chicago, February–March, 1919, pp. 592–601). Cf. also Galbraith, loc. cit., pp. 209 f.

[2] Now cf. Stenton, *Anglo-Saxon England*, pp. 141, 303.

[3] See Stenton, 'The Supremacy of the Mercian Kings' (*E.H.R.* xxxiii, 1918, pp. 433–52).

[4] The word does not point, in my opinion, to Graeco-Byzantine influence (Hazeltine in Whitelock's *Anglo-Saxon Wills*, p. xxiv, n. 2) but derives rather from the vocabulary of the Latin Bible, where it is found several times in the Book of Tobit and in Col. ii. 14; it is consequently often found in ecclesiastical literature (cf. *Thesaurus linguae Latinae*, iii. 1009 f.) and belongs, e.g., to the Latinity of the Liber Pontificalis and of Aldhelm.

[5] Cf., e.g., Bresslau, *Handbuch*, i². 667 ff., 745 f.; Redlich, loc. cit., pp. 46, 97 ff.

[6] Cf. Bresslau, *Internationale Beziehungen im Urkundenwesen* (loc. cit., pp. 48 ff.);

testimony may have been a reaction provoked by increased use of Aldhelm's inflated, pompous style in English documents of the tenth century, which also had some repercussion overseas.

But these are questions beyond the scope of these pages, which are intended to suggest anew the Roman and ecclesiastical origin of the Anglo-Saxon charter. The history of ancient and early medieval diplomatics to some extent is the history of the acceptance of documentary evidence as a legal means, which passed from the 'Hellenistic' countries to the West and from the Mediterranean world to the North. In this 'chain of Receptions'[1] the Anglo-Saxon charter is connected with late Roman or Byzantine Italy.

II

LULLUS'S PROFESSION OF FAITH

A BISHOP who was to receive the distinction of the *pallium* was required to send a written profession of his faith to the Pope. There is early mention of the custom in two formulas of the *Liber Diurnus*:

No. 45 (ed. Sickel, p. 35): 'Fidem autem, quam in tuis epistolis breviter adscripsisti, licet planius explanare debueras, Redemptori tamen nostro gratias agimus, quod eam in ipsa etiam brevitate rectam esse cognovimus', and

No. 46 (p. 37): 'Fidem autem fraternitatis tuae, quamvis in epistola quam direxisti subtiliter debuisses exponere, verumtamen letamur in Domino, quia eam rectam esse ex sollemnis symboli confessione didicimus.'

There exist a number of papal pallium charters from the end of the eighth century onwards, which are based on formula 45 and include the sentence about the profession of faith, and other texts confirm the existence of the practice.[2] Pope Zacharias, when in 744 he sent the pallium to the bishops of Rouen, Rheims, and Sens, informed them,

'quomodo fidem suam exponere debeant hi, qui pallium uti licentia conceduntur'.[3]

M. Treiter, 'Die Urkundendatierung in angelsächsischer Zeit' (*Archiv f. Urk.* vii, 1921, p. 64).
[1] H. Steinacker, *Die antiken Grundlagen der frühmittelalterlichen Privaturkunde* (Grundriss der Geschichtswissenschaft, ed. A. Meister, Ergänzungsband i), Leipzig, 1927, pp. 19, 23, &c.
[2] Cf. von Hacke, loc. cit., pp. 132 ff.; Th. Gottlob, *Der kirchliche Amtseid der Bischöfe* (Kanonistische Studien und Texte, ed. A. M. Koeniger, ix), Bonn, 1936, pp. 14, 29 f.
[3] Boniface, *Epist.* 57 (p. 104). Boniface himself had presented such a profession, when he was consecrated bishop by the Pope in 722, like the bishops of the papal metropolitan district (cf. *Liber Diurnus*, no. 73, pp. 69 ff.). Cf. Willibald, *Vita Bonifatii*, c. 6 (p. 28); above, pp. 72 f.

Only one profession of this kind of the eighth century has survived, that of Lullus, the Anglo-Saxon successor of Boniface as bishop of Mainz. His succession had been secured, in accordance with the latter's wishes but contrary to canon law, during the lifetime of Boniface. This circumstance, it has been conjectured, may have induced Pope Hadrian I to order an examination of the consecration of Lullus when Charles the Great continued the re-establishment of the provincial organization of the Frankish Church (above, pp. 95 f.), and the petition was made shortly before 780 that Lullus should receive the pallium. The mandate of Hadrian, which was sent to Archbishop Tilpin of Rheims to arrange this examination, was interpolated in Rheims in the ninth century; the forger, probably Archbishop Hincmar (845–82), a prelate notorious for his ambition, inserted between the beginning and the end of the document a long intermediate passage connected with his aspirations. This enlarged text, preserved by Flodoard, the historian of Rheims in the tenth century,[1] has been the subject of much controversy; but É. Lesne has shown that the first and the last part of the 'privilege' represent the genuine text of Hadrian's letter to Tilpin.[2] Only the last part concerns us here:

'Iniungimus etiam fraternitati tuae, ut, quia de ordinatione episcopi nomine Lul sanctae Mogontinae ecclesiae ad nos quaedam pervenerunt,[3] assumptis tecum Viomago et Possessore episcopis et missis gloriosi ac spiritalis filii nostri Karoli Francorum regis, diligenter omnia de illius ordinatione inquiras et fidem ac doctrinam illius atque conversationem et mores ac vitam investiges, ut, si aptus fuerit et dignus ad episcopalem cathedram gubernandam, *expositam et conscriptam et manu sua propria subscriptam catholicam et orthodoxam fidem* per missos suos cum litteris ac testimonio tuo seu aliorum episcoporum, quos tecum esse mandavimus, ad nos dirigat, ut pallium illi secundum consuetudinem transmittamus[4] et ordinationem illius firmam iudicemus et in eadem sancta ecclesia Mogontina archiepiscopum constitutum esse faciamus.'

The three bishops appointed by the Pope were bishops of metro-politan sees. Tilpin, who was bishop of Rheims from 748 to his

---

[1] *Historia Remensis ecclesiae*, ii. 13 (from *Vita Rigoberti*, c. 14, *SS. rer. Merov.* vii. 71; cf. p. 856), 16, 17 (*MG. SS.* xiii. 461–4), repeated by É. Lesne, 'La lettre interpolée d'Hadrien I à Tilpin et l'église de Reims au IXᵉ siècle' (*Le Moyen Age*, xxvi, 1913, pp. 349–51). Cf. Jaffé, i. 2411.

[2] Lesne, loc. cit., pp. 325–51 and 389–413. Cf. E. Perels, *Neues Archiv*, xliv, 1922, p. 53 (n. 2); xlviii, 1930, p. 157.

[3] Cf. *Liber Diurnus*, no. 46 (p. 37): 'pervenit ad nos, quod . . .'; Gregory I, *Registr.* vii. 17 (*MG. Epist.* i. 460): 'dum ad nos quaedam de Maximo pervenissent', &c.

[4] *Liber Diurnus*, no. 46 (p. 36): 'Palleum preterea iuxta antiquam consuetudinem fraternitati tuae transmisimus.'

death in 794,[1] had already received the pallium, as the beginning of Hadrian's letter shows. The same probably applies to Possessor, who has been questionably regarded as bishop of the Tarentaise;[2] he went to Italy as 'missus' of Charles in 775 and 781, and while he is called *episcopus* on the earlier occasion, he was archbishop in 781.[3] The third bishop was Weomad of Trier, who is first mentioned in 762 and died in 791.[4] The title of *archiepiscopus* is given to him in a charter of Charles between 781 and 791, probably of 782–3, though only fourteenth-century copies exist and *archi-* may be, but need not be, a later addition.[5] It is therefore probable that the three bishops asked to examine the case of Lullus in or shortly before 780 were already themselves invested with the rights of metropolitans.

The profession of Lullus has not been transmitted among his letters; the Vienna MS. does not contain any piece of his correspondence which can be attributed with certainty to a year later than 773 (nos. 119–21). The document survived only in a late medieval cartulary of Fritzlar in Hesse, where Boniface had founded a monastery; the book is now in the Archives of the State at Marburg (Lahn). The exemplar from which the text was copied in the fifteenth century may have been preserved in Lullus's monastic foundation and last place of rest, Hersfeld, which is mentioned in the headline, and the profession is followed in the manuscript by the 'Epithaphium sanctissimi Lulli, *patroni nostri*', which also points to Hersfeld. There were early connexions between Fritzlar and Hersfeld. The first abbot of Fritzlar, the Anglo-Saxon Wigbert, died during the lifetime of Boniface, perhaps about 738 (*Epist.* 40, p. 65), and was buried in his monastery. In 774, in the time of the Saxon wars, his relics were taken for safety to Buraburg nearby, and after

---

[1] Cf. L. Duchesne, *Fastes épiscopaux de l'ancienne Gaule*, iii, 1915, p. 86; Levison, 'Das Formularbuch von Saint-Denis' (*Neues Archiv*, xli, 1917–19, pp. 301 f.). On Tilpin's death see also *Historiae Francorum Steinveldenses* (*MG. SS.* xiii. 728).

[2] Cf. Duchesne, loc. cit. i², p. 244, n. 7; S. Abel and B. Simson, *Jahrbücher des Fränkischen Reiches unter Karl dem Großen*, i², 1888, p. 240, n. 4.

[3] *Codex Carolinus*, 51, 52, 56, 57, 67 (*MG. Epist.* iii, pp. 572, 574, 580, 582, 594 f.).

[4] Duchesne, loc. cit. iii. 40.

[5] *MG. Dipl. Karol.* i, no. 148, p. 201, ll. 34 and 45 (cf. p. 566). Alcuin called his friend Ricbod, Weomad's successor, in a letter (*Epist.* 191, p. 318) *patriarcha*; the word applies to an archbishop rather than to a bishop. The case of Amalar, to whom the see of Trier was entrusted about 811 for some time, and who was not made a metropolitan at once (*MG. Epist.* v. 243 f.), does not justify the usual conclusion that the metropolitan rights of the see had not been restored some years earlier, though limited for a time by the archiepiscopal position bestowed on Angilramn of Metz in or soon after 784 (*SS. rer. Merov.* vi. 265, n. 4). Cf. Lesne, *La Hiérarchie épiscopale*, p. 67, n. 6; Hauck, loc. cit. ii³, pp. 56 (n. 3), 214; Duchesne, loc. cit. iii. 41. The case of Amalar was obviously exceptional; his correspondence with the Emperor shows that Trier was considered by Charles a regular metropolitan see.

some years were translated to Hersfeld by order of Witta, the bishop of Buraburg, when Lullus had conveyed to him the consent (command?) of King Charles.[1] Wigbert thus became the special saint of Hersfeld, side by side with and even more than the original patron-saints Simon and Thaddaeus and than Lullus the founder.[2] It was natural therefore that interest should be taken in the latter at Fritzlar also, the more so because Lampert of Hersfeld in his Life of Lullus written about 1070, besides other misrepresentations, attributed the translation of Wigbert from Buraburg to Hersfeld to Lullus himself.[3] Accordingly the presence of texts referring to Lullus in a Fritzlar book is not surprising.

The document was published from this manuscript by C. B. N. Falckenheiner, *Geschichte Hessischer Städte und Stifter*, Cassel, 1841, vol. ii, pp. 165–7 (= F.), and reprinted by J. Fr. Böhmer and C. Will, *Regesta archiepiscoporum Maguntinensium*, vol. i, Innsbruck, 1877, pp. 40–1, no. 49.[4] But it is not included in any of the editions of the letters of Lullus, nor edited among the 'epistolae variorum' of the age of Charles the Great in the *Monumenta Germaniae historica (Epist. iv)*, nor in the *Mainzer Urkundenbuch* by M. Stimming (vol. i, 1932). But this profession of a continental Anglo-Saxon is our only eighth-century example of the whole series of such documents, a large number of which must have existed, and a new edition may be thought to be justified, the more so since the printed text is spoilt by bad misreadings either of the copyist or rather of the first editor.[5]

The manuscript is of course not accessible for the present; but the text can be restored with some certainty from its sources, which have not hitherto been established. Fr. W. Rettberg stated that it was

[1] Lupus, *Vita Wigberti*, cc. 13–25 (ed. Holder-Egger, *MG. SS.* xv. 1, pp. 41 ff.).

[2] Cf. the charters in H. Weirich, *Urkundenbuch der Reichsabtei Hersfeld*, i. 1, Marburg, 1936.

[3] *Vita Lulli*, c. 17, ed. Holder-Egger, *Lamperti monachi Hersfeldensis Opera* (in the collection *SS. rer. Germ.*), Hanover, 1894, pp. 330 f.; *Institutio Herveldensis ecclesiae*, ib., pp. 346 f.; cf. pp. xxvi f.

[4] I have not seen the reprint in Falckenheiner, *Geschichte Fritzlars*, Eschwege, 1925, pp. 501 ff., quoted by F. Flaskamp, *Histor. Jahrbuch*, xlvii, 1927, p. 486, n. 92. Paul Hinschius, *Das Kirchenrecht der Katholiken und Protestanten*, i, Berlin, 1869, p. 603, n. 5, has reprinted only the first and the last sentences.

[5] The epitaph of Lullus was also edited by Falckenheiner, loc. cit., p. 167, and reprinted by others, as by Dümmler, *MG. Poetae*, ii, p. 649. After the manuscript had been rediscovered at Marburg, Dümmler published a new edition in the *Forschungen zur Deutschen Geschichte*, xxv, 1885, pp. 177 f., repeated by Holder-Egger, *Lamperti Opera*, p. 355, and by Tangl, *Neues Archiv*, xli, p. 27. For the text of Falckenheiner was proved to contain serious blunders; e.g. the *Venneticos—patres*, to whom Britain is said to have sent Lullus, and who puzzled his biographers (see, e.g., H. Hahn, *Bonifaz und Lul*, 1883, p. 332), were nothing but a misreading for *Romanos—patres*.

based on the whole ('ziemlich') upon the symbol *Quicumque* (the so-called Athanasian Creed), and that Lullus also paid attention to the doctrine of Adoptionism.[1] This attention would be surprising as early as 780: the relevant words did not refer in fact to the doctrinal controversies of the late eighth century, but were borrowed from another profession of faith which had been composed nearly four centuries before. The profession of Lullus comprises parts which were copied more or less verbatim from earlier declarations of the Creed. The borrowed words are here printed in italics, and the different main sources are marked by numerals in the margin:

I. The Nicene Creed, as translated by Rufinus, *Historia ecclesiastica*, x. 6 (ed. Mommsen, pp. 965 f.; C. H. Turner, *Ecclesiae Occidentalis Monumenta Juris Antiquissima*, i, p. 175; cf. Aug. Hahn, *Bibliothek der Symbole und Glaubensregeln der alten Kirche*, 3rd ed., Breslau, 1897, p. 162, § 143).

II. The profession of faith by Gregorius Thaumaturgus of Neocaesarea, also as translated by Rufinus, loc. cit. vii. 28 (ed. Mommsen, pp. 955 f.; Hahn, p. 253, § 185). But Lullus took much larger parts from

III. The *Libellus fidei* of Pelagius of 417, which was ascribed in the Middle Ages to Jerome (as in Augiensis no. xviii, fol. 16 v [see p. 238] and in the *Libri Carolini*, iii. 1, ed. Bastgen, pp. 106–8) or, by an irony of fate, even to Augustine (Migne, *P.L.* xxxix. 2181–3, xlv. 1716–18, xlviii. 488–91; Hahn, pp. 288–92). The formula against the doctrine of the adoption 'nec adoptivus', which I have mentioned above, is also borrowed from Pelagius, who by the words 'aut adoptivum' opposed the teaching of Bonosus and his followers, 'qui', to quote Isidore of Seville (*Etymol.* viii. 5. 52), 'Christum filium Dei adoptivum, non proprium adserunt'. Lullus used, to a smaller extent:

IV. The symbol of the synod of Toledo of 675 (Hahn, pp. 242–8, § 182; K. Künstle, *Antipriscilliana*, Freiburg, 1905, pp. 74–83), to which J. Madoz recently devoted his book, *Le Symbole du XIe concile de Tolède* (Spicilegium Sacrum Lovaniense, xix), Louvain, 1938;[2] the text is to be found there pp. 16–26. Opposition to the Bonosians is also here indicated (§ 9: 'non adoptione'; cf. ib., pp. 47 f.).

Thus the profession of Lullus is longer and more complicated than the profession which Hincmar of Rheims presented to his consecrators in 845, probably to be sent to the Pope,[3] and than the declarations

---

[1] *Kirchengeschichte Deutschlands*, i, Göttingen, 1846, p. 576. Hahn, loc. cit., p. 277, followed Rettberg.

[2] Cf. the supplement by Madoz, 'Eugène de Tolède, une nouvelle source du symbole de Tolède de 675' (*Revue d'histoire ecclésiastique*, xxxv, 1939, pp. 530–3).

[3] Migne, *P.L.* cxxv. 1199 f. (from Marlot, *Metropolis Remensis historia*, i, 1666, p. 388). Cf. H. Schrörs, *Hinkmar Erzbischof von Reims*, Freiburg i. Br., 1884, p. 56,

of faith which English bishops of the province of Canterbury inserted
into the professions of obedience offered to the archbishops from 796
onwards, as published by Haddan and Stubbs and in the *Cartularium
Saxonicum* of Birch. But the study of these documents, of their different types and their connexions, goes beyond the scope of these pages.[1]
In compiling his profession Lullus perhaps used a collection of symbols comparable with that of the Augiensis no. xviii of Karlsruhe
of the early ninth century, which has been studied by K. Künstle.[2]

Fidem meam catholicam, quam in ecclesia Christi[3] didici,
exponere cupiens, qualiter a me creditur vel docetur, iuxta
praeceptum[4] apostolici pontificis Adriani papae et missorum eius
Viemadi, Tilpini, Possessoris pontificum et missorum domini nostri
5   Carli regis gloriosissimi,[5] ego Lullus servus servorum Dei[6] et
ecclesiae Magontinensis absque meritorum adiumento[7] antistes
iuxta capacitatem sensus[8] mei nunc edissero. *Credo in unum Deum* I
Patrem omnipotentem, omnium visibilium et invisibilium factorem, | qui ex IV
nullo ducit originem et *ipse est origo divinitatis, ex quo* omnia; | ipse est II
10 *pater verbi viventis, sapientiae subsistentis et virtutis suae et figurae, perfectus*

1 *The headline preceding reads* Fides sancti Lulli archiepiscopi, fundatoris magne
aecclesie Hersfeld   4 nostri] rever. *F*   6 Magoncicensis *F*   meritorum]
mortalium *F*   8 omnivisibilem et invisibilem *F*   10 subsistentis] substantie *F*.

n. 20 (cf. pp. 518 and 561, no. 1); Gottlob, loc. cit., p. 31. The text is identical with
a formula of a MS. from Fleury in Zeumer, *MG. Formulae*, pp. 555 f.

[1] Cf. Gottlob, loc. cit., pp. 138 ff.

[2] *Eine Bibliothek der Symbole und Theologischer Traktate* . . . (Forschungen zur christlichen Litteratur- und Dogmengeschichte, ed. Ehrhard and Kirsch, i. 4), Mainz,
1900, pp. 7 ff., 26 ff.

[3] That is, in the Christian Church, not Christ Church at Canterbury; cf. below,
p. 240. 11: 'Hanc fidem in catholica didicimus ecclesia' (the words are derived
from Pelagius). Lullus came no doubt from Wessex, like Boniface; for he was educated at Malmesbury (*Epist.* 135, p. 274), and Bishop Cyneheard of Winchester
(754–759/78) was a relative of his (ib., no. 114, p. 246).

[4] Cf. Lullus, ib., no. 98 (p. 220): 'iuxta praeceptum Domini' (= Exod. xl. 23,
&c.).   [5] Cf. the mandate of Pope Hadrian; above, p. 234.

[6] Lullus uses this form of humility, which Gregory the Great had introduced into
the papal letters, in his letters 125 and 126 (pp. 262 f.). On its history cf. Schmitz,
loc. cit., pp. 38 ff., 85 (n. 1), 86, 94, 102 (n. 1), 109 ff., 113 ff., 118 (n. 1), 120 ff.,
144 f., 147 (n. 3), 150 (n. 1). Cf. also Levison, *Savigny-Zeitschr.* xxxvii, 1916, *Kan.
Abt.* vi. 384 ff. on a sermon of St. Augustine (ed. G. Morin, *Miscellanea Agostiniana*,
i, Rome, 1930, pp. 563 ff.); L. Levillain, *Le Moyen Age*, xl, 1930, pp. 5 ff.

[7] Cf. Lullus, *Epist.* 98 (p. 219): '*absque* praecedente *meritorum* amminiculo';
no. 71 (p. 144): 'sine praerogativa *meritorum*', after the pattern of Aldhelm, *Epist.* 4
(ed. Ehwald, p. 481): 'sine *meritorum* praerogativa' (= Boniface, *Epist.* 106, p. 231),
and *De virginitate*, c. 15 (p. 244): 'sine ceterarum *adiumento* virtutum' (cf. pp. 202. 13,
244. 9); King Ethelbald of Mercia 757 (Birch, i, no. 181): 'sine *meritorum* suffragio.'

[8] Cf., e.g., Hilarius, *De Trinitate*, xi. 17 (Migne, *P.L.* x. 411): 'secundum *capacitatem sensus* nostri.'

perfecti genitor, pater filii unigeniti. | Credo *et in dominum nostrum Iesum* III
Christum, verum Deum, per quem creata sunt omnia, | *Filium Dei, de Patre* I
natum, unigenitum, hoc est de substantia Patris, Deum verum ex Deo vero,
lumen de lumine, natum, non factum, eiusdem cum Patre substantiae, | qui II
5 est *solus ex solo Deo, filius verus veri* patris, *invisibilis ex invisibili, incorru-*
ptibilis ex incorruptibili, inmortalis ex inmortali, sempiternus ex sempiterno, |
ante omnia saecula natus ex Patre,[1] *non factus* nec *adoptivus sed genitus* III
atque ita per omnia aequalis Deo Patri. Credo in Spiritum sanctum, Deum
verum, ex Patre procedentem et Filio,[2] non factum nec genitum sed pro-
10 cedentem, *aequalem per omnia Patri et Filio,* | *per quem* Pater *et Filius* II
Deus solus *super omnia et in omnibus cognoscitur.* Sic itaque sancta
Trinitas Pater et Filius et Spiritus sanctus *perfecta maiestate, sempiter-*
nitate regnoque | *inseparabilis. Haec Trinitas unus Deus est,* ex quo IV
omnia, per quem omnia, in quo omnia.[3] Ita *Pater* et *Filius* et *Spiritus*
15 *sanctus* et *in singulis* quisque horum *Deus* et simul omnes *unicus Deus,*
id est *in* una *substantia deitatis* manentes, et simul omnes *una sub-*
stantia. | *Ipsum autem Dei Filium, qui absque initio aeternitatem cum* III
Patre et Spiritu sancto possidet, confiteor *in fine saeculorum perfectam*
naturam hominum suscepisse absque patre, *et Verbum carnem esse factum,*
20 *assumendo hominem, non permutando deitatem. Spiritum sanctum* confiteor
non *fuisse pro semine, sed potentia ac virtute creatoris operatum* in Filio. *Sic*
autem confiteor in Christo unam Filii esse personam, ut dicamus duas perfectas
atque integras substantias esse deitatis et humanitatis. Passus est et Filius
vere omnia, quae Scriptura testatur, non secundum deitatem suam, in qua
25 *inpassibilis est ut Pater* et Spiritus sanctus. *Mortuus est ergo Dei Filius*
*iuxta id quod mori poterat; resurrexit tertia die, ascendit in cel*os, sedet ad

---

6 ex corruptibili *MS*   7 natus] novus *F*   8 atque in premium equalis
F   12 perfecta] persecula *F*   17 autem] unicum *F*   19 carnem] tamen
F   20 Spiritum] Ipsum *F*   21 creatoris] recreacionis *F*   22 personam,
in dies dierum perfectum imaginospicium substantie esse *F*; *perhaps* integrasque
is to be written for atque integras.   26 poterat] potenter *F*   celes *MS*

---

[1] The Nicene-Constantinopolitan Creed has this formula (Hahn, p. 166, § 145;
A. E. Burn, *Facsimiles of the Creeds*, H. Br. Soc., vol. xxxvi, 1909, p. 17): 'natum ex
Patre ante omnia saecula', followed by later texts.
[2] On the *Filioque* cf., e.g., the so-called Athanasian Creed § 22 (23) (Hahn, p. 176,
§ 150; Burn, loc. cit., p. 23; C. H. Turner, *J.T.S.* xi, 1910, p. 408): 'Spiritus sanctus
a Patre et Filio, non factus nec creatus nec genitus, sed procedens', &c. The doctrine
of the Procession of the Holy Ghost from the Son as well as from the Father began to
be accepted by the Frankish Church in the time of the first Carolingian kings and
so of Lullus, from the synod of Gentilly in 767 onwards.
[3] This sentence is derived from Augustine's *Confessiones*, i. 2, who rendered thus
Rom. xi. 36. The words were used, in accordance with the 'Confession' of the Emperor
Justinian of 551 against the Three Chapters and with the anathematisms of the
synod of Constantinople of 553, c. 1 (Mansi, *Concil.* ix. 539, 375), in the profession
of the synod of Milan in 680 (Migne, *P.L.* lxxxvii, 1265; Hahn, p. 248, § 183):
'Patrem ex quo omnia, Filium per quem omnia, Spiritum sanctum in quo omnia',
and likewise by St. Columbanus, *Epist.* 3 (*MG. Epist.* iii. 165), and in the papal
allocution of the *Liber Diurnus*, no. 85 (p. 106). Cf. also Leo III, Migne, *P.L.* cii.
1031 (cf. *MG. Epist.* v. 67, n. 1): 'a quo omnia, per quem omnia, in quo omnia.'

dexteram Dei Patris, manente ea natura carnis, in qua natus et passus est III
et resurrexit; non enim exinanita est humanitatis substantia, sed glorificata
et in aeternum cum deitate mansura. Credo Dominum *venturum ad iudicium*
vivorum et mortuorum, ut et iustos remuneret et puniat peccatores, resurrectionem
5 *carnis ita cred*ens, *ut dicam nos in eadem, in qua nunc sumus, veritate mem-*
brorum esse reparandos, qualesque semel post resurrectionem fuerimus effecti,
in perpetuo mansuros. Anim*ari quoque credimus* occulto Dei iudicio
infantes in utero materno, non *partem esse* deitatis.[1] *Liberum sic*
*confite*or *arbitrium, ut dicam nos semper Dei indigere auxilio, hominem et*
10 *peccare et non peccare posse, ut semper nos liberi confiteamur esse arbitrii.*

　　*Hanc fide*m *in catholica didicimus ecclesia; in qua si in*caute *vel minus*
*perite aliquid dic*tum *sit, a* doctioribus *cupimus emendari.*

　　Hanc fidem meam ego Lullus Moguntinensis civitatis antistes
exposui anno duodeno regni domini nostri Carli regis gloriosissimi,
15 pontificatus mei anno xxv.[2] Similiter huic sanctae Dei ecclesiae,
cui Deo annuente praesidet sanctitas Adriani papae, sacramento
iuxta praeceptum[3] sanctitatis eius per quattuor ewangelia Christi
fidelitatem promisi, cuius sanctitatem incolumem Christus Dominus
custodiat.[4] Amen.

---

2 enim] cum *F*　　　5 membrorum] morituros *F*　　　7 perpetue *F*

---

[1] Pelagius wrote: '*Animas* a Deo dari *credimus*, quas ab ipso factas dicimus, ana-
thematizantes eos, qui animas quasi *partem* divinae dicunt *esse* substantiae.' Lullus
stated the doctrine of 'Creationism' more clearly, using an addition to the book *De*
ecclesiasticis dogmatibus (sometimes attributed to Gennadius), c. 14 (ed. C. H. Turner,
J.T.S. vii, 1906, p. 92; Migne, *P.L.* lviii. 984, lxxxiii. 1231): '*Dei* vero *iudicio animari*
('coagulari' other MSS.) in vulva . . . ac formato iam corpore animam creari et
infundi, ut vivat *in utero* homo . . .'; similarly c. 17 (18).

[2] The 12th year of Charles the Great began on the 9th of October 779 and ended
on the 8th of the same month 780. It corresponded to the 25th year of Lullus's
episcopate, if his inauguration was dated in 755. Willibald, who had his information from Lullus, assigned the death of Boniface (5 June) to the year 755 (*Vita*
Bonifatii, c. 8, p. 55), while according to the Fulda tradition Boniface died in 754.
Cf. above, p. 90, n. 2.　Lullus is called *episcopus* in a royal charter of 780 (8 March),
archiepiscopus the first time in 782 (4 July); see *Dipl. Karol.* i, nos. 129 and 142.

[3] Cf. above, p. 238, n. 4.

[4] One of the usual formulas of salutation in the papal letters of this age is: 'Deus
te *incolumem custodiat*', imitated, e.g., by Archbishop Berhtwald of Canterbury
(Boniface, *Epist.* 7, p. 2): '*Incolumem* reverentiam tuam aevo prolixiore Iesus *Christus*
dominus noster *custodiat*.'

III

THE PROTEST OF THE BISHOPS OF BRITAIN AGAINST PAPAL DEMANDS IN CONNEXION WITH THE PALLIUM

HENRY WHARTON, *Anglia Sacra* (1691), i. 461, first published from a Cotton MS. a letter in which the bishops and priests of 'the whole of Britain' made complaints to a Pope Leo of grievances connected with the conferment of the pallium. The 'immense trouble' of the archbishops travelling in person to Rome to receive this token of their dignity, and the 'Simoniac heresy' of payments asked in respect of it, are contrasted with the different practice of former times; Bede and Alcuin are quoted in proof of this difference. Wharton and his successors: Wilkins (*Concilia*, i, 1737, p. 166), Migne (*P.L.* cii. 1033 f.), Haddan and Stubbs (*Councils*, iii. 559) printed the letter with this heading: 'Omnes episcopi et sacerdotes totius Britanniae insulae venerabili papae Leoni salutem in Christo'; it was—and is—referred to Leo III and to the year 805, though Haddan and Stubbs (ib., p. 561, n. *a*) felt some hesitation about this dating:

'As this letter appears to have been written on the occasion of a vacancy of the see of Canterbury, and as the only such vacancy during the pontificate of Leo III was that caused by the death of Ethelheard, it may be regarded as probably to be dated in A.D. 805, and possibly to have been drawn up in the council in which Wulfred was elected. . . . It may be questioned whether the Pope Leo in question were Leo III or one of the later popes bearing that name. On the one hand, there is scanty evidence of the prevalence of the custom of going to Rome for the pall before this date; and the Archbishops of York certainly did not do so; moreover, the reference to Alcuin as a great authority, within so short a time after his death, may seem to point to a later date. It is, on the other hand, almost impossible to point out the coincidence of a vacancy at Canterbury with the pontificate of any of the later popes of the name of Leo; and the letters which appear in close proximity with this in the Cotton MS. can be referred only to Leo III.'

This opinion was almost generally accepted[1] but cannot be maintained: the letter belongs to a later age.

---

[1] I will mention only W. Hunt, *The English Church from its Foundation to the Norman Conquest*, 1899, p. 248; Plummer, *Baedae Op. hist.* ii. 51, and *Two of the Saxon Chronicles*, ii. 67; Hodgkin, loc. cit. ii[2], p. 451; R. R. Darlington, 'Ecclesiastical Reform in the Late Old English Period' (*E.H.R.* li, 1936, p. 418, n. 2); W. E. Lunt, *Financial Relations of the Papacy with England to 1327*, Cambridge (Mass.), 1939, p. 179. Only H. Boehmer, *Die Fälschungen Erzbischof Lanfranks*, p. 94, n. 1, referred the document to Leo IX, and J. Haller, *Das Papsttum*, ii. 2, Stuttgart, 1939, p. 454, also questioned its early date. K. Hampe, *Deutsche Zeitschr. für Geschichtswissenschaft*, xi, 1894, p. 357, n. 3, had doubts about its authenticity.

Objections to payments demanded for the pallium were raised as early as the time of Gregory the Great; at the Roman synod of 595 he forbade all payments for ordinations as well as for the grant of the pallium (*Registr.* v. 57*a*, *MG. Epist.* i. 364 f.; cf. v. 62, ib., p. 377). But there remained the subterfuge of voluntary presents permitted after the grant. Pope Leo II (682–3) ordered that the archbishop of Ravenna after his consecration should not pay a 'custom' *pro usu pallei* (*Liber Pontificalis*, ed. Mommsen, p. 201). When the metropolitan organization of the Frankish Church began to be restored and pallia were requested for the bishops of Rouen, Rheims, and Sens in 744 (above, p. 88), demands of money were evidently made by members of the Roman curia. Boniface complained of them to Pope Zacharias. His letter is lost; but the answer of the Pope, who denied too emphatically the truth of the accusation, shows that in 744 the same catchwords were used as in the letter of the bishops of Britain: the objection to Simoniac heresy and to the selling of spiritual gifts. After seven years Zacharias again stated that he acted in accordance with the Lord's command (Matth. x. 8): 'Freely you have received, freely give' (Boniface, *Epist.* 58, 87, pp. 107, 195 f.). The same arguments could of course be advanced in 805.

But the situation is different in another respect. Extracts from Bede's *Ecclesiastical History* (i. 23, 27; ii. 4, 7, 8, 3, 9, 17, 18) and particularly from letters of the Popes Boniface V and Honorius (ib. ii. 8, 18) are quoted to prove that in former days the archbishops were consecrated by colleagues, the pallia were sent to them, and they were not required to receive them personally at Rome: 'quod non tam ingens labor incumbebat anterioribus nostris, scilicet pallii gratia *Romam usque fatigari*, quemadmodum postea mos inolevit,'— the wording is also here influenced by Bede (ii. 18): 'ne sit necesse ad *Roma*nam *usque* civitatem per tam prolixa terrarum et maris spatia pro ordinando archiepiscopo semper *fatigari*.' The archbishops of Canterbury travelled to Rome to receive the pallium in the tenth century, at least from 927, those of York a century later, from 1026. There may have been some earlier unrecorded cases;[1] but certainly

---

[1] Archbishop Berhtwald of Canterbury was consecrated in 693 (29 June) by Bishop Godin of Lyons according to Bede (*H.E.* v. 8, p. 295; cf. c. 11, p. 302), but by Pope Sergius according to the *Liber Pontificalis* (ed. Mommsen, p. 216: 'Hic ordinavit Bertoaldum Britanniae archiepiscopum'). He is described as 'sent from the apostolic see' in the *Vita Wilfridi*, cc. 52, 57 (pp. 246. 36, 247. 29, 253. 20: 'ab (hac) apostolica sede emisso,' 'ab huius apostolicae sedis monarchia directo'; cf. Pope John VI, ib., c. 54, p. 250. 13: 'quem auctoritate principis apostolorum archiepiscopum ibidem confirmavimus'). H. Boehmer, *Die Fälschungen Erzbischof Lanfranks*, pp. 89 ff., has suggested, probably rightly, that Berhtwald went to Rome after his consecration to receive the pallium.

here was no such established custom in 805. During the eighth century he Popes sent the pallium to the archbishops of Canterbury and York, so far as the sources give explicit information:[1]

Canterbury

733. *Continuatio Bedae* (Plummer, p. 361) = Symeon, *Hist. regum*, c. 32 (ed. Arnold, ii. 30): 'Tatwini archiepiscopus, accepto ab apostolica auctoritate pallio[2]. . . .'

736. Symeon, c. 34 (pp. 31 f.): 'Nothelmus, pallio a Romano pontifice suscepto . . .'; *Saxon Chronicle* 736 (Plummer p. 44 f.): 'Her Nothhelm aercebiscep onfeng pallium from Romana biscep.'

766. *Sax. Chr.* 764 (p. 50): 'Her Iaenbryht aercebiscop onfeng pallium.'

806. Ib. 804 (pp. 58 f.): 'Her Wulfred aercebiscop pallium onfeng.'

834. Ib. 831 (p. 62): 'Her Ceolnoth aercebiscop onfeng pallium.'

York

735. *Cont. Bedae* (p. 361) = Symeon, c. 34 (p. 31): 'Ecgberctus episcopus, accepto ab apostolica sede pallio, primus post Paulinum in archiepiscopatum confirmatus est'; *Sax. Chr.* DEF (p. 45): 'Her onfeng Ecgbriht biscop pallium *aet* Rome' (*aet,* is a mistake for *from*); Alcuin, *De sanctis Euboric. eccl.* v. 1279 (*MG. Poetae*, i. 197): 'Hic ab apostolico humeris fert pallia *missa*.'

773. Symeon, c. 47 (p. 45): 'Eodem tempore Alberht Eboracae antistes ecclesiae pallii ministerium ab Adriano papa sibi directum accepit.'

780. Ib., c. 50 (p. 47): 'Eodem etiam anno Eanbald episcopus pallium ab apostolica sede sibi directum accepit; qui eo suscepto in episcopatum solemniter est confirmatus'; *Sax. Chr.* DE 780 (p. 53): 'Aelfwold cining (of Northumbria) sende man aefter pallium to Rome,' F (p. 52): 'Alwold cing sende to Rome aefter pallium to Eanboldes arcebiscop behove.' It was Alcuin who was sent to Rome by Eanbald, 'ut sibi pallium impetraret ab apostolico', and returning in the spring of 781 met Charles the Great at Parma (*Vita Alcuini*, c. 9, *MG. SS.* xv. 1, p. 190).

797. Symeon, c. 58 (p. 58): 'Eanbaldus ille posterior, accepto ab apostolica sede pallio, in archiepiscopatum genti Northanhymbrorum solemniter confirmatus est VI. Idus Septembris'; *Sax. Chr.* DEF 797 (p. 57):

---

[1] The first part of the list of Popes who sent pallia to Canterbury compiled about 1100 (ed. A. Whelock, *Historiae ecclesiasticae libri V a Venerabili Beda scripti*, Cambridge, 1644, p. 568; R. Flower and H. Smith, *The Parker Chronicle and Laws*, Early English Text Society, Original Series, No. 208, 1941, fol. 54 *b*), is unreliable. Radulf de Diceto (*Abbreviationes Chronicorum, Opera*, ed. Stubbs, i. 16 f.), Gervase of Canterbury (*Actus pontificum, Works*, ed. Stubbs, ii. 330 ff.), and an anonymous History of the Popes and the Archbishops of Canterbury (in Canterbury, *Cartae antiquae* A. 42 of the late 13th century; see my extracts, *Neues Archiv*, xxxviii, 1913, p. 655, n. 2; pp. 658 f., 662) are founded on this list.

[2] Cf. Bede's *Chronica maiora*, c. 532 (*Auct. ant.* xiii. 309) and his letter to Egbert, c. 9 (Plummer, p. 413): '*accepto a sede apostolica pallio*, metropolitanos esse debere' ('metropolitanus esse deberet').

'Eanbald onfeng pallium on VI. Idus Sept.' Alcuin asked Pope Leo III to grant this pallium, *Epist.* 125 (p. 184): 'Sed et pro his missis—qui de patria mea venerunt et civitate mea, more canonico atque apostolico beati Gregorii praedicatoris nostri praecepto sacri pallei depraecari dignitatem—humiliter vestrae pietatis excellentiam obsecro, ut benigne ecclesiasticae necessitatis accipias postulationes,' &c.; cf. his poem 43 to Pope Leo v. 39 (*MG. Poetae*, i, p. 255).

The practice revealed by the correspondence of Boniface conforms with the English examples of the eighth century. In these circumstances, in spite of all gaps in our knowledge, the letter of the bishops cannot have been written about 805, but only in a later period, when the custom had taken root and had been accepted by the archbishops, personally 'pallii gratia Romam usque fatigari'. The wording of the letter confirms this conclusion. The times of Alcuin are contrasted with those of the letter-writer in such a way as to indicate a considerable interval between the two ages; for, after a quotation from Alcuin, the text goes on:

'*Tunc temporis* impleverunt sancti et apostolici viri illud laudabile praeceptum Salvatoris nostri, dicentis: "Gratis accepistis, gratis date." *Tunc* sine viribus elanguit Simoniaca haeresis, quia non pecunia emebatur donum Dei (cf. Acts. viii. 20), sed gratis, sicut ipse iusserat, donabatur.'

Words such as these cannot have been written a year after Alcuin's death.

His letter to King Offa, which is quoted immediately before these words, is not to be found in the editions of his letters, but was published by Paul Lehmann in his *Holländische Reisefrüchte* (SB. München, 1920, No. 13), 1921, pp. 29–34, from the MS. 70. H. 7 of the early tenth century in the Royal Library of the Hague, fols. 58–9, where it is preceded by Cuthbert's letter on the death of Bede[1] and Bede's letter to Egbert of York.[2] When Alcuin wrote this letter there were two metropolitans in the kingdom of Offa, after Lichfield had been made a metropolitan see at the cost of Canterbury in 788. The king had asked Alcuin how to proceed when one of the two archbishops died and a new one had to be consecrated. The death of Archbishop Jaenberht of Canterbury in 792 (12 August) and the succession of Ethelhard, who was consecrated in the next year (21 July

---

[1] Published from this MS. by N. R. Ker, *Medium Aevum*, viii, 1939, pp. 40–4. Cuthbert's report is here introduced by a letter sent by an unknown person to an Albinus, only the last lines of which have been preserved. Ker identified the recipient, Albinus, with Alcuin; R. Brotanek, *Anglia*, lxiv, 1940, pp. 161 ff., regarded Abbot Albinus of Canterbury, Bede's contemporary, as more probable.

[2] Plummer, *Baedae Op. hist.* i, pp. cxli f., did not know of this MS., having found two others only.

793), probably occasioned Offa's application to Alcuin's authority, as Lehmann has conjectured, and the letter may have been written between these two events, at a time when Alcuin was residing in England. He answered by pointing out that the Pope, when he set up two metropolitan sees in seventh-century England, intended to make it possible for an archbishop elect after the death of his predecessor to be consecrated by the surviving metropolitan, that is, in 793, for an archbishop of Canterbury to be consecrated by the new metropolitan of Lichfield. It seems not to have been observed that this answer of Alcuin's was, together with Bede, the source on which the bishops of Britain drew in framing their protest. I therefore repeat this short text from Lehmann's edition, side by side with the part of the bishops' letter derived from it.

INCIPIT EPISTOLA ALCHUINI

Domino pio et praeclaro Offano regi humilis levita Alchuinus salutem.

5   Beatae memoriae Gregorius papa predicator noster[1] idcirco statuit duas in Britannia metropolitanas esse civitates easdemque pallii dignitate honorari voluit,[2] ut non opus esset, defuncto
10   metropolitano episcopo, Romam ire propter ordinationem metropolitani episcopi, qui in locum eligeretur defuncti.[3] Quod perspicue invenire potes in libro secundo Ecclesiasticae Hystoriae,
15   quem beatus presbiter Beda scripsit, capitulo XVIII. et XVII. ibique invenies, quod ad ordinationem beati Honorii pontificis Doruvernensis ecclesiae sanctus Paulinus Lindocoloniam occurrit ibique eum
20   ordinavit archiepiscopum, quod idem beatissimus Honorius papa in sua epistola confirmavit.[3] Quae epistola eidem praefato capitulo adiuncta est, et ideo non mihi opus est ea latius scribere, quae
25   apud te scripta scimus. Sed regum dissensiones aecclesiasticum turbaverunt

Letter of the bishops.

Item Albinus vel Alquinus maximus librarius[4] scripsit ad Offam regem Anglorum, dicens, quod *archiepiscopus semper ab archiepiscopo* debeat

2 Olfanno *MS.*

---

[1] Alcuin also speaks of 'beati Gregorii (papae) praedicatoris nostri' in *Epist.* 124, 125, 128 (pp. 182, 184, 189); cf. Pope Honorius in Bede, *H.E.* ii. 17 (p. 119. 19).
[2] Bede, ib. i. 29.   [3] Ib. ii. 18.
[4] Anglo-Saxon *bōcere*, 'scholar', 'writer'.

ordinem, ut non potuerit [fieri] quod
fieri debuit, licet sancti canones firmis-
sime decrevissent, numquam ob regum
dissensiones aecclesiastica statuta violari
5 debuisse. Idcirco tua excellentia fir-
missime sciat iustius esse, ut archy-
episcopus semper ab archyepiscopo
ordinetur. Et quia in regno tibi a Deo
dato duos habes metropolitanos, necesse
10 est, ut aecclesiasticum iubeas servare
decretum, id est, ut in loco defuncti a
supravivente ordinetur archyepiscopo.
Pallium tamen quivis eorum primo in
propria ecclesia a sibi subiacentibus,
15 cum a domno apostolico directum ei
fuerit, accipere debet, sicut mihi viri
Romanorum peritissimi tradiderunt.

*ordin*ari, et *pallium ei debet*
mitti *a domno apostolico. Sed*
regum dissensiones hanc *turba-*
*verunt ordin*ationem, ita *ut non*
potuerit fieri quod fieri debuit,
quamvis *sancti canones firmis-*
sime decrevissent, nunquam ob
regum dissensiones ecclesiastica
statuta violari debuisse.

1 fieri *is missing in MS.*   4 violare *MS.*
by B. Schmeidler, Neues Archiv, xlvi, 1926, *p.* 185.

13 quivis] quis *MS., corrected*

Alcuin's letter confirms the view that it was papal practice in his
age to send the pallia to England ('cum a domno apostolico directum
ei fuerit'), and that the letter of the bishops belongs to a later period.
But I doubt whether the name of Pope Leo is to be read in the
manuscript at all, at least in the *original* text of that manuscript
which alone has transmitted the document to our times, Cotton MS.
Vespasian A. XIV, fol. 178 (176). It is not accessible in the present
conditions; therefore the following argument must be tested *visu*,
when the book is once more available. First, the two printed catalogues of the manuscripts of the Cottonian Library, of 1696 and 1802,
do not categorically declare the text to be a letter written to a Pope
Leo, but 'ad papam, scilicet Leonem'. It is hardly possible to explain
this formula, except on the assumption that the name of the addressee
does not or did not originally exist in the manuscript. It may be a
gloss of a later reader, who identified the Pope in the light of a letter
of Leo III which he had seen 'in close proximity' on fol. 174 (172),
a letter of Leo to King Cœnwulf of Mercia (Jaffé i. 2494; H. and S. iii.
523; Birch, i. 398, no. 288; *MG. Epist.* iv. 187, no. 127). Moreover, W.
Holtzmann, who saw the manuscript in recent years, printed among
some notes on it the headline of the bishops' letter, differing from
the published texts in *one* word: he read 'uenerabili pape tt salutem
in Christo', substituting a double *t* for the name *Leoni* of the editions
(*Papsturkunden* i, p. 96). Therefore the name of the Pope can be
assumed to be in fact missing in the manuscript, and to be nothing
but the conjecture, either of Wharton or some earlier reader. I

cannot explain the meaning of *tt* with certainty; it may be a mis-reading for *ill(i)*, as it was substituted for a name in some other texts of the same manuscript (the letters *ll* crossed by a line), or for *tl.*, that is, *t(a)l(i)*, or it may perhaps be a capital letter *N*, the diagonal line crossing the two shafts, as it was often used as an abbreviation of *nomen* or *nomine* in the Middle Ages. The copy may have been taken from a first draft which did not contain the name, or the scribe thought to give it more of the character of a formula for later use: either assumption would also explain the fragmentary character of the text, which lacks an appropriate conclusion. In any case, there is no need to ascribe the document to an age with the customs of which it does not accord, that is to an earlier century than the tenth.

The manuscript was written in the early eleventh century for Wulfstan II, archbishop of York (1003–23), who had been bishop of London (996–1003) and also occupied for some years (1003–16) the see of Worcester.[1] It contains not only letters of Alcuin and other texts of the eighth and early ninth centuries[2] but also the pastoral letter and 'canons' of Archbishop Oda of Canterbury (942–58),[3] several letters of the later part of the tenth and the beginning of the eleventh centuries edited by Stubbs,[4] and verses written in honour of Wulfstan, when he was archbishop of York.[5] The letter of the bishops of Britain is the penultimate document of the manuscript; it is followed only by a letter addressed to Wulfstan when he was bishop of London and this brings the manuscript to an end.

It is even probable that the text is to be ascribed to the time of Archbishop Wulfstan himself. When King Canute was returning from his famous pilgrimage to Rome in the spring of 1027 (after the 26th of March), he sent home a letter, the seventh paragraph of which is relevant here (Liebermann, *Gesetze*, i. 276; cf. iii. 189 ff.):

'Conquestus sum iterum coram domino papa et mihi valde displicere causabar, quod mei archiepiscopi in tantum angariabantur immensitate pecuniarum, quae ab eis expetebatur, dum pro pallio accipiendo secundum morem apostolicam sedem expeterent; decretumque est, ne id deinceps fiat.'

Wulfstan died before 1027; his successor Ælfric is the first archbishop of York known to have gone to Rome to receive the pallium person-

---

[1] Cf. D. Whitelock, 'A Note on the Career of Wulfstan the Homilist' (*E.H.R.* lii, 1937, pp. 460–5; on the MS. cf. pp. 463 f.); 'Archbishop Wulfstan, Homilist and Statesman' (*T.R.H.S.*, 4th Series, xxiv, 1942, pp. 25–45; on the MS. pp. 30 f., 32, and 43, n. 5).

[2] Cf. *MG. Epist.* iv. 9; H. and S. iii. 121, 394 (= Birch, i. 262, no. 184), 579; below, p. 297.   [3] Wilkins, *Concilia*, i. 212.

[4] *Memorials of St. Dunstan*, 1874, pp. 369 f., 380 f., 383–9, 404 f. (= Birch, iii. 57, no. 897); cf. pp. liv f.

[5] Stubbs, p. liv, n. 4; Birch, iii. 57, no. 896; *MG. Epist.* iv. 9, n. 1.

ally from Pope John XIX; this he did in 1026.[1] But Canute made complaint of the 'immensity' of the papal demands for payments in respect of the pallium not only in 1027 but also on an earlier occasion ('Conquestus sum *iterum* coram domino papa . . .'), we may assume, in connexion with another exaction of the same kind. Wulfstan himself became archbishop before Canute won the crown of England, but two archbishops of Canterbury received the pallium from Pope Benedict VIII (1012–24), Lyfing (1013–20), and Æthelnoth (1020–38).[2] Lyfing went to Rome, if not earlier, perhaps in 1017;[3] Æthelnoth received the pallium there in 1022.[4] The second occasion seems to be too late, since the manuscript containing the letter was written for Wulfstan, who died in 1023; the occasion of Lyfing's journey may be more appropriate. But the document may also have been drafted after Wulfstan had been transferred to York in 1003, or on the accession of another archbishop of Canterbury in the late tenth century, when papal demands might have roused similar opposition, and it need not be connected with Canute's endeavours to reduce them, though one may be inclined to suppose a connexion with known events rather than with unknown possibilities. In any case, we may be sure that we are not far from the truth in dating the letter about the year 1000. The form of the designation: 'episcopi et sacerdotes *totius Britanniae* insulae,' corresponds with this age. Canute is called in several charters '*totius Britanniae* monarchus', 'telluris *Britanniae totius* . . . rex ac rector', '*Brittanniae totius* Anglorum monarchus'.[5] But there were also precedents for this from the time of King Æthelstan (925–39) onwards.[6]

[1] *Sax. Chr.* D (p. 156); Raine, *Historians of the Church of York*, ii. 342 f.

[2] List in the Parker MS. (see above, p. 243, n. 1): 'Benedictus Aelfstano (id est Living) atque Aegelnotho.'

[3] Liebermann, iii. 186; cf. Canute's constitution of 1020, § 2 (ib. i. 273).

[4] *Sax. Chr.* DEF (pp. 154 ff.; cf. Plummer, ib. ii. 204).

[5] Kemble, *Codex dipl.* iv, nos. 728, 730, 736, 743 f. Cf. Freeman, *History of the Norman Conquest*, i³ (1877), pp. 558, 595 f.; Liebermann, *Gesetze*, iii. 190 c.

[6] Cf., e.g., Hubert Hall, *Studies in English Official Historical Documents*, Cambridge, 1908, pp. 343 f.; R. Drögereit, 'Gab es eine angelsächsische Königskanzlei?' (*Archiv f. Urk.* xiii, 1935, p. 395). There were a few early precedents: the report of the synod of Hatfield in 679 spoke of 'Theodoro gratia Dei archiepiscopo *Brittaniae insulae* et civitatis Doruvernis' and 'ceteris episcopis *Brittaniae insulae*' (Bede, *H.E.* iv. 17); Bishop Waldheri of London called Theodore's successor in 705 'Berctvaldo *totius Brettaniae* gubernacula regenti' (H. and S. iii, p. 274; Birch, i, no. 115); cf. *Vita Wilfridi*, c. 46 (p. 240, l. 9): 'cum sancto archiepiscopo Berhtwaldo et *totius poene Brittanniae* episcopis,' c. 52 (p. 246, l. 36): 'iudicia sancti archiepiscopi Berhtwaldi Cantuariorum aecclesiae et *totius Brittanniae*,' c. 60 (p. 254, l. 16; cf. p. 256, l. 6): 'Berhtvaldus Cantuariorum aecclesiae et poene *totius Brittanniae* archiepiscopus.' Cf. Bede, *H.E.* i. 27, § 7 (p. 53. 22).

IV

WINCHCOMBE ABBEY AND ITS EARLIEST CHARTERS

At Winchcombe in Gloucestershire, according to the annals of its monastery, King Offa of Mercia founded a convent of nuns in 787, his second successor, King Cœnwulf (796–821), a monastery of monks in 798;[1] the dedication of the church is ascribed to the year 811.[2] The monastery ten years later became the last resting-place of Cœnwulf and also of his son Cynhelm, to whom Pope Leo III in 798 confirmed the monastery of Glastonbury (above, p. 32).[3] Cynhelm was buried at Winchcombe perhaps in or shortly after 812; for, as E. S. Hartland[4] and J. A. Robinson[5] have conjectured, we may take it as probable that he was the Cynehelm or Cynhelm princeps[6] or dux[7] who signed a number of charters from 803 to 811 (1 August), but whose name does not occur later. Legends developed around his tomb. When Bishop Oswald of Worcester (961–92) restored monastic life at Winchcombe in the next century, Cynhelm had gained the fame of a martyr; calendars from about 975 onwards show the name 'Cynelmi martiris' or 'sancti Kynelmi martiris' on the 17th of July.[8] At the end of the tenth century a sacramentary, written probably at Winchcombe, was sent as a present to the monastery of Saint-Benoît-sur-Loire (Fleury), to-day MS. 127 (105) of Orléans; there Cœnelmus, Kœnelmus, or Kenelmus, as the name

---

[1] *Mon. Angl.* ii. 300; Annals of about 1130 in Cotton MS. Vitellius C. VIII, see Liebermann, *Ungedruckte Anglo-Normann. Geschichtsquellen*, p. 19. On Winchcombe cf. David Royce, *Landboc sive Registrum monasterii beatae Mariae Virginis et sancti Cenhelmi de Winchelcumba*, 2 vols., Exeter, 1892–1903; Rose Graham, *V.C.H., Gloucestershire*, ii, 1907, pp. 66 ff.; also the sketch by F. W. Potto Hicks, *The Story of Winchcomb Abbey*, Elkstone Rectory, 1945. There is a fragmentary original of a grant of land at Aldington (Worcestershire) made by Cœnwulf to Wulfled, with the reservation of a rent for '(ecclesia) quae sita est aet Wincelcumbe' (Birch, i, no. 364). [2] See below, p. 253.

[3] There is also the signature 'Cenelm filii regis' under a grant made by Cœnwulf to Christ Church, Canterbury, in 799 on the 17th of July, that is, the day of St. Kenelm (Birch, i, no. 296). The text is unreliable and seems to be a conflation of two charters, one connected with that ascribed to King Cædwalla and to the year 687 (ib., no. 69), the other a charter of King Wihtred (ib., no. 86). Cf. above, p. 230.

[4] 'The Legend of St. Kenelm' (*Transactions of the Bristol and Gloucestershire Archaeological Society*, xxxix, 1916, p. 16).

[5] *Somerset Historical Essays*, London, 1921, p. 38, n. 3.

[6] Birch, i, nos. 308, 335.

[7] Ib., nos. 313, 316, 321, 322, 326, 328, 339.

[8] Fr. Wormald, *English Kalendars before A.D. 1100*, vol. i (H. Br. Soc., vol. lxxii), 1934, pp. 22, 64, and later calendars. Cf. also Liebermann, *Die Heiligen Englands*, pp. 17, 19: 'Đonne resteð sancte Kenelm *cynebearn* on Wincelescumbe'; cf. p. 18: 'Sanctusque Kynelmus *martir* in loco qui dicitur Winclescumbe.'

is variously spelt, has his proper prayers and mass and occupies a prominent place among the martyrs, next to the protomartyr St. Stephen.[1] In the eleventh century the fanciful story of his martyrdom and of its revelation was told. The original text of the legend has not yet been published,[2] only an abbreviated version by John of Tynemouth;[3] Florence of Worcester[4] and William of Malmesbury[5] seem to have known this *Passio Kenelmi*. Kenelm, we are told, succeeded his father Kenulf in 819 as king, when he was a child of seven years, but was murdered after a few months, at the instigation of his ambitious sister Quendritha, by his tutor Ascebert (Æscberht) in a wood—I omit the miraculous story of his revelation at Rome and of his invention.[6] The year 819 is derived from the *Saxon Chronicle*, where the death of Cœnwulf and the succession of Ceolwulf are ascribed to this year. The author of the legend, of course, did not know that all events in this part of the *Chronicle* are recorded two years too early and that entries under 819 in fact belong to the year 821. There is no need to distinguish an elder Cynhelm who died during the lifetime of his father Cœnwulf, and a younger brother of the same name who was born in 814, was killed after the death of Cœnwulf and was succeeded by Ceolwulf.[7] This second 'Kenelm' no doubt is no more than a shadow of the real bearer of the name, whose history was forgotten but whose tomb in the family monastery of Winchcombe gave rise to legends to supply the lack of knowledge when some cult was offered to his relics. The real son of King Cœnwulf may in fact have been killed on an unknown occasion, e.g. in one of the wars with Welshmen; there were other saints who by the misinterpretation of a sepulchral inscription were considered to have been martyrs:[8] *ignoramus*. Certainly the words of the *Saxon*

---

[1] Cf. L. Delisle, 'Mémoire sur d'anciens sacramentaires' (*Mémoires de l'Institut national de France, Académie des Inscriptions et Belles-Lettres*, xxxii, 1, 1886, pp. 211–18). Cf. also Royce, loc. cit. ii, pp. 1 ff.; V. Leroquais, *Les Sacramentaires et les missels manuscrits des bibliothèques publiques de France*, i, Paris, 1924, pp. 89 ff., no. 35; below, p. 258.   [2] See Hardy, *Descriptive Catalogue*, i. 2, p. 508.

[3] Last edition by Carl Horstman, *Nova Legenda Anglie*, ii, Oxford, 1901, pp. 110–13.

[4] *Chronicon* 819 and Genealogies (ed. Petrie, *Mon. Hist. Brit.* i, pp. 547, 630, 638).

[5] *Gesta regum Angl.* i. 95, ii. 211 (ed. Stubbs, i, pp. 94 f., 262 f.); *Gesta pontif.* iv. 156 (ed. Hamilton, pp. 294 f.). Cf. also Henry of Huntingdon, *Hist. Angl.*, book ix of the 4th ed. (ed. Arnold, p. xxvi); Roger of Wendower, *Chron.* 821 (ed. Coxe, i, pp. 273 f.) = Matthew Paris, *Chronica maiora*, 821 (ed. Luard, i, pp. 372 f.).

[6] The martyrdom was revealed (in 819!) according to Huntingdon, 'Silvestro iuniori papae' (999–1003), according to Tynemouth to Pope Leo Junior (795–816). The MSS. of the *Passio* not being accessible, it is impossible at present to establish the original version.   [7] So Robinson, loc. cit.

[8] Cf. my paper, *Das Werden der Ursula-Legende*, Cologne, 1928 (= Bonner Jahrbücher, cxxxii), pp. 35 f.

Chronicle in 819 (that is, 821) justify in this case the 'argumentum e silentio' that Ceolwulf followed Cœnwulf immediately, that there was no nominal reign of Cynhelm between them.

But his sister Quendritha had a real existence. This name of 'Quœnthryth' (or Cwœnthryth) seems to have been occasionally mixed up by copyists with that of Cynethryth. The latter also occurs in the history of Mercia, being the name of King Offa's consort (p. 30). The privilege by which Pope Leo III confirmed to Cynhelm the monastery of Glastonbury in 798 was corroborated by King Cœnwulf, his two archbishops, nine bishops, thirteen abbots, and six 'principes'; Abbess Kynedrith also added her signature with her relatives ('cognatae' in William of Malmesbury's retranslation) Æthelburh and Ælfled.[1] These signatures probably refer to Offa's widow and daughters; a grant of the king to Chertsey Abbey in 787 (Birch, i, no. 251) mentions among his children Abbess Ethelburga and 'Ælfleda virgo' (thus in the signatures of the charter; the text of the copy has the name 'Æthelflede').[2] I doubt also whether Quœnthryth is to be identified, as Robinson has suggested, with Abbess Cynedrytha of Cookham (Berkshire), who at the synod of Clovesho in 798 gave Archbishop Ethelhard of Canterbury lands in Kent in exchange for his claims to her monastery, and also received from him the monastery of Pectanege;[3] she was obviously connected with King Offa and may have been his queen, whereas nothing points to a relationship with Cœnwulf.[4] Certainly the latter's daughter gave her signature in 811 to a grant of the king as 'Quœnðryð filia regis' (Birch, i, no. 339), and it was also his daughter on whom Archbishop Wulfred of Canterbury (805–32) made some demands, when she had become abbess of Suthmynstre (Minster) in Kent. He recovered from her and her 'familia' of Suthmynstre at a synod of Clovesho in 824 lands at Œsewalum (to-day Easole Street) in the same region (ib., no. 378).[5] Her father had occupied other posses-

---

[1] Thus I correct the names Etheburh and Celfled in William's retranslation of an Anglo-Saxon translation of Leo's privilege (Birch, i, no. 285).

[2] We have three or four letters of Alcuin to Ethelburga, whom he also addressed with her (ecclesiastical?) surname of Eugenia (*Epist.* 36, 102, 103, 300, pp. 78, 148 ff., 458); she was abbess of Fladbury near Worcester (Birch, i, no. 238). Her sister Ælfled married in 792 King Ethelred of Northumbria, who was murdered in 796; then she may have entered a convent in conformity with Alcuin's advice (pp. 149, 15, 150. 7).

[3] H. and S. iii. 512; Birch, i, no. 291. Pectanege may be Patney on Avon (Wiltshire); cf. ib. iii, no. 1118; J. E. B. Gover, A. Mawer, and F. M. Stenton, *The Place-names of Wiltshire* (E.P-N.S. xvi), 1939, p. 314.

[4] Thus also Hartland, loc. cit., pp. 42 f.

[5] The lands had been given to Wulfred by *comes* Aldberht and his sister Abbess Selethryth of Lyminge (Birch, i, no. 317), who are known from grants of King Offa of Mercia and Cuthred of Kent of 785, 786, and 805 (ib. i, nos. 247, 248; iii,

sions and rights at Suthmynstre and Reculver, which were also claimed by the archbishop; for several years there were quarrels,[1] which were settled only after the death of Cœnwulf and of his brother and successor Ceolwulf, at the next synod of Cloveshó in 825. On this occasion Abbess 'Cwœnthryth' is expressly called daughter and heiress of Cœnwulf. Wulfred made it a condition of the reconciliation that the names of some lands given to him should be erased 'de antiquis privilegiis quae sunt aet Wincelcumbe';[2] the monastery of Winchcombe was evidently used for preserving the family records, the 'archives' of the former royal house. The Winchcombe foundation of Cœnwulf and his charters were also mentioned at the end of the century, when Duke Ethelwulf 'investigavit hereditarios libros Cenwulfi regis et in privilegiis illius scriptum inveniebat, quod nullus heres post eum licentiam haberet hereditatem Cenvulfi quae pertinet ad Wincelcumbe alicui hominum longius donandam vel conscribendam quam dies unius hominis'. Now 'Cynethryth', Cœnwulf's daughter Quœnthryth, rather than Offa's widow, had granted land at Upton-on-Severn (Worcestershire)[3] belonging to this 'hereditas' to the father of a certain Wullaf for three generations, and Ælflæd had later extended the grant to Wullaf himself for three more generations. This Ælflæd was evidently a member of the former royal house, probably the daughter of King Ceolwulf (821–3), Cœnwulf's brother, and a cousin of Quœnthryth; she married Wigmund, the son of King Wiglaf (827–40) of Mercia (*Genealogies* in Florence of Worcester, Petrie, pp. 630, 638), and may have inherited some of the possessions and rights of Cœnwulf's family. In 897 Quœnthryth's and Ælflæd's grants were annulled; Wullaf was obliged to return 'pristinos libellos a Cyneðryða et Ælflæda conscriptos'. The land was granted to him again, but for his lifetime only, to be given after his death to the church of Worcester for the 'renovation' of the peace between the 'families' of Worcester and Winchcombe to settle 'discords' of these communities, and to confirm the peace which Bishop Werfrid of Worcester (873–915) and Duke Æthelwulf had established between them in the presence of King Alfred and Æthelred, the ealdorman of the Mercians, his son-in-law (Birch, ii, no. 575). These

no. 1336). Œsewalum has been identified by J. K. Wallenberg, *Kentish Place-names*, Uppsala, 1931, p. 147; *The Place-names of Kent*, Uppsala, 1934, pp. 534 f.

[1] Cf. also a letter of Pope Leo III of 808 (H. and S. iii. 563; *MG. Epist.* v. 90).

[2] H. and S. iii. 596 ff.; Birch, i, no. 384, cf. 385. I have no doubt that this place is identical with the monastery in Gloucestershire, while Birch, p. 531, n. 1, suggested Great and Little Winchcomb near Godmersham in Kent, mentioned in the boundaries of a grant of 823–5 (ib., no. 378, p. 518; cf. no. 372). Cf. Wallenberg, loc. cit. (1931), pp. 149 f.

[3] Cf. Birch, iii, no. 1088; A. Mawer and F. M. Stenton, *The Place-names of Worcestershire* (E.P.-N.S. iv), 1927, p. 174.

few facts known of the early history of Winchcombe illustrate the life of a proprietary monastery of a royal house. In 942 a witenagemot met 'in loco celeberrimo qui Wincelcumb nuncupatur' (ib., no. 771); but there is no mention of the monastery.

The community seems to have been in decay in the tenth century. Monastic life was restored, as I have already said, by Bishop Oswald of Worcester (961–92), one of the promoters of the monastic reform movement of this age, who introduced monks there and made Germanus, who had stayed with him at Fleury in France, abbot of the new monastery. It was probably Germanus who gave Fleury the sacramentary in which St. Kenelm had so prominent a place among the martyrs (above, p. 249); the origin of his cult was perhaps connected with the establishment of the monastery of Bishop Oswald. The records of this house are very scanty for two centuries, because during the war of King Stephen and Henry II, in 1151 (28 September), the monastery was burnt 'cum scriniis, vestementis, libris et cartis ac edificiis omnibus' (Royce, loc. cit. i, p. 83); when a cartulary of the abbey was made in the thirteenth century, there were only three documents earlier than charters of Pope Alexander III of 1175. They have been preserved in and printed from two manuscripts: (1) the twelfth-century manuscript of the *Annales de Winchcumba* continued up to 1205, now Cotton MS. Tiberius E. IV in the British Museum,[1] from which Birch edited the three documents; and (2) the cartulary begun in the thirteenth and continued into the fourteenth century, owned by Lord Sherborne and published by David Royce (above, p. 249, n. 1).

One of the above documents is the so-called foundation charter of Winchcombe in the name of King Cœnwulf (H. and S. iii, p. 572; Birch, i, no. 338; Royce, i. 18). It is ascribed to the 9th of November 811, but mentions 'precepts' of Pope Paschalis (817–24) as well as the presence of King Cuthred of Kent (his signature is also added) who died in 807; thus it is an evident forgery, as Haddan and Stubbs (p. 574, n. *a*) have pointed out. But they also saw that a genuine charter, probably of a synod, was used for its fabrication, as is proved by the list of bishops and *duces* witnessing the document. The date and some details of the wording may also be considered. The 9th of November in 811 was a Sunday, a day on which synods sometimes assembled and dated decrees in this age, at Chelsea in 816 (27 July) and at Clovesho in 824 (30 October). We may also compare the date: 'anno vero incarnationis eiusdem salvatoris mundi domini nostri Iesu Christi DCCCXI, indictione autem IIII, imperii vero nostri

---

[1] There are other Winchcombe annals (1050–1231) in Cotton MS. Faustina B. I, extracts from which have been published by Pertz, *MG. SS.* xvi. 481 f.

a Deo dati anno xv⟨i⟩' with that of a witenagemot of the same year 811, 1 August (H. and S., p. 570; Birch, i, no. 335, cf. 341): '*anno autem incarnationis eiusdem domini salvatoris mundi Iesu Christi* DCCCXI, *indictione* vero IIII, porro quoque *imperii*[1] piissimi regis Merciorum Coenvulfi anno xv.' The latter document, an original, has also, like the Winchcombe charter, the formula 'pro expiatione piaculorum eius (meorum)'[2] and mentions side by side with other great men *procuratores* ('sive principum seu ducum vel procuratorum'; Winchcombe charter: 'principes, comites, procuratores').[3] The foundation is said to have been made 'famoso in loco (cf. e.g. H. and S. iii. 465, 579, 617, 619; Birch, i, nos. 256, 358, 421, 423: 'in loco famoso', &c.), quem solicoli antiquo nomine Wincelcumbam appellare suescunt'. Place-names were often referred to the 'ruricolae' or 'solicolae', 'solicoli' of the region in documents from the ninth to the middle of the eleventh centuries (in vernacular 'eorð-buende'); but I have found wording similar to the above only twice, in two charters of about 800, one of King Offa of 785 (Birch, i, no. 245): 'quandam partem terrae . . . ubi *solicoli* clamare *suescunt* aet Aeldenham', the other of Bishop Deneberht of Worcester (800?–22): 'in alio quoque loco . . . ubi *solicoli suescunt appellare* aet Collesburnan' (ib., no. 304). Cœnwulf is called 'Kenulfus Dei *arridente* gratia rex Merciorum'; the same formula, in place of the simple 'Dei gratia' or other expressions of this idea, is also employed in three charters of the king of 816–17 (ib., nos. 357, 359, 360): 'cuius melliflua gratia *adridenti*', 'eius *arridenti* gratia'.[4] The sanction is also partly derived from a genuine document. The forger seems to have used a synodal charter of 811 and another document giving the name of King Cuthred of Kent. His main intention may have been to assert for the abbey rights of asylum and property; the prohibition to grant 'agros meae hereditatis' for more than a single lifetime is probably derived from the original document of 811, as Haddan and Stubbs (p. 575, n. *b*) have assumed (cf. above, p. 252, and the decrees of the synod of Chelsea of 816, c. 7).

---

[1] Years *imperii* for *regni* are also found in other charters of Cœnwulf; cf. Birch, i, nos. 289, 293, 303, 366, cf. no. 332. The addition 'imperii vero nostri *a Deo dati*' may be compared with Birch, i, nos. 321, 322, 326, 343, 350, 356, 357: 'regni (autem, vero) nostri (mei) *a Deo concessi*', &c.; cf. above, p. 246. 8.

[2] Cf. also Birch, i, nos. 225, 332, 426; ii, nos. 438, 466, 467. *Expiatio, piaculum, famosus* are words used by Aldhelm.

[3] Cf. ib. i, no. 45; ii, nos. 676, 677, 689–92; iii, no. 1343. The 'procuratores' were probably reeves; cf. F. Liebermann, *The National Assembly in the Anglo-Saxon Period*, Halle, 1913, p. 36; *Gesetze*, ii. 2, p. 718 (Ic).

[4] Cf. Birch, i, nos. 419, 426; ii, nos. 444, 734, 752, &c. (cf. e.g. Bede, *H.E.* v. 23: 'Qua *adridente* pace'). With the words 'omnibus *archontis* Merciorum' cf. Birch, ii, no. 430 of 840: 'coram suis archontis.'

The sources utilized by the forger of this so-called foundation charter of Winchcombe are lost; but two papal privileges mentioned in the latter have been preserved, though in a fragmentary condition, privileges of the Popes Leo III (795–816) and Paschalis I (817–24), who granted King Cœnwulf comprehensive confirmations of his monasteries and their possessions. Both are based on formulas known to us from the *Liber Diurnus* (cf. above, pp. 29 ff.). The privilege of Leo (Birch, i, no. 337; Royce, i, pp. 21 f.)[1] is derived largely, *mutatis mutandis*, from formula 86, from which several words of the defective text can be corrected.[2] There is a particular reference to Winchcombe, because not only 'omnia monasteria vel varia loca sita in ipsa insula Saxonia' acquired by Cœnwulf and the right to dispose of them freely were confirmed to him by the Pope, but particularly 'monasteria vicique ac praedia ad illud monasterium pertinentia, ubi corpus tuum sepultum fuerit', were freed 'ab omni iugo secularique servitio'. The end of the text with the date has perished.

The privilege of Pope Paschalis (Birch, i, no. 363; Royce, i, p. 23) continues the series of charters based on no. 93 of the *Liber Diurnus*, which was itself derived from a privilege granted by Leo's predecessor Hadrian I to King Offa of Mercia (pp. 29 f.). When the text was copied, only the former part and the end of the papyrus original had survived, while the middle part giving the names of monasteries and possessions confirmed to Cœnwulf by the Pope either had been destroyed or was illegible. The copyist also had difficulty in deciphering the cursive writing of the papal chancery; everyone who has had experience of modern reproductions of the surviving, more or less fragmentary, originals of papal papyrus charters will sympathize with him. He sometimes misread *s* for *r* and *u* for (open) *a*, and combined in a strange manner the deciphered fragments of the 'great date' which is characteristic of the papal privileges from the time of Hadrian onwards, endeavouring to discover words rather than sense. But his combinations, in comparison with the other existing texts, obviously show the underlying formulas; his mistakes were not those of a forger but the effect of bad preservation of

---

[1] Royce, p. 22, has *in piis* and *quod non* for the wrong readings in Birch, p. 470, ll. 13 and 23, *impiis* and *non quod*.

[2] The dependence of the two privileges on formulas of the 'Liber Diurnus' has been stated by L. Santifaller, loc. cit., pp. 251, 268 f., 301 f. Some words of Leo's different from formula 86 are confirmed by other formulas, Birch, p. 470, l. 19: 'cuius vel immeriti vicem gerimus' (cf., e.g., *Lib. Diurn.*, nos. 90, 96, 97) and l. 25: 'et a regno Dei alienum' (ib., no. 89). W. H. Stevenson, 'Trinoda Necessitas' (*E.H.R.* xxix, 1914, p. 700, n. 49) thought that the text of Leo also contained 'extraneous and probably later matter'. I should rather surmise some gaps and words misread in consequence of bad preservation of the original.

the papyrus and of insufficient knowledge of the script. The date reads:

Hanc kartam scripsit Ianuasius presbiter anno[1] Theodosii summi[2] imperatoris Constantinopoleos. Signum vero Ludouuici Romanorum piissimi augusti a Deo coronati in magni imperii iure, anno vero regni sui xi. Signum[3] etiam Lotharii novo imperatore eius filio. Anno primo[3] indictione xi[a].

The underlying words can easily be restored from similar privileges, regard being also paid to the usual abbreviations[4] such as *p(ost)c(onsulatus)*,[5] which caused some misinterpretations:

[D]a[t(um) . . .] Ka[lenda]s Ianua[r]i[a]s p[e]r [m]an[um] Theodo[r]i [n]um[encul]atoris[6] [s(an)c(t)ae] s[edis a]po[stolicae, imp(erante) d(omi)n(o) n(ostro) H]ludouuic[o] piiss(imo) [p(er)p(etuo)] august[o] a Deo coronat[o] magn[o] imper[ato]re anno [q]u[a]r[t]o [et p(ost)c(onsulatus) eius anno quarto], s[ed] et [H]lothari[o] novo imperatore eius filio anno primo, indictione xi[a].

The day was no doubt given in the Roman style; thus the month of January could be used to cover the period from the 14th of December 817 to the 13th of January of the next year; but in view of 'Hánc kartam[7] scripsit Ianuasius' the reading '[D]a[t(um)[8]. . .] Ka[lenda]s Ianua[r]i[a]s' seems very probable and a date comprising the words 'Nonas' or 'Idus' can be disregarded: the privilege may be ascribed without hesitation to the second part of December 817 or, at the latest, to the first day of January 818. The year is established by the eleventh indiction; it fell, during the pontificate of Paschalis I, between the beginning of September 817 and the end of August 818; the first imperial year of Lothar I who was crowned emperor in July 817, corresponds to this indiction. The nomenculator

---

[1] 'II' was added afterwards in the Cotton MS. according to Birch.

[2] 'summi' is missing in Birch's text.

[3] 'Signum' to 'primo' is missing in the same text.

[4] On abbreviations in early papal privileges cf. P. Kehr, *Die ältesten Papsturkunden Spaniens* (Abhandl. Berlin, 1926, no. 2), p. 12. I have not seen L. Santifaller, *Die Abkürzungen in den ältesten Papsturkunden, 788–1002*, Weimar, 1939.

[5] The letters 'p̄c̄' for 'post consulatum' or 'postconsulatus' embarrassed other copyists also. Cf., e.g., Krusch, *SS. rer. Merov.* vi. 499; Tangl, *Die Briefe des hl. Bonifatius*, p. 18, n. 1 (cf. p. 304, s.v. 'consulatus') and *Neues Archiv*, xl, 1916, pp. 701 f.; A. Menzer, 'Die Jahresmerkmale in den Datierungen der Papsturkunden . . .', *Römische Quartalschrift*, xl, 1932, pp. 41 (n. 48), 43.

[6] On other misreadings of the title of 'nomenculator' or 'numenculator', which was unknown outside Rome, cf. Bresslau, *Handbuch der Urkundenlehre*, i², p. 204, n. 4; Tangl, 'Die Fuldaer Privilegienfrage' (*MIÖG.* xx, 1899, p. 233).

[7] The later MS. published by Royce has 'cartam', as it also has twice 'largiri' for 'largire' and the spelling 'Lodovici' for 'Ludouuici'.

[8] On misinterpretations of the difficult abbreviation of 'Dat(um)' in these privileges cf. Kehr, loc. cit., p. 12.

Theodore is mentioned in other sources from May 813 to February 817; at the beginning of this year he acted as 'datarius' in a charter of Pope Stephen IV and on the 1st of February of the same year in a charter of Paschalis, who succeeded Stephen on the 25th of January. He is probably identical with the 'primicerius (notariorum)' Theodore who held this higher office in 821 and two years later was killed together with his son-in-law Leo, who was then nomenculator.[1] The privilege granted by Paschalis to King Cœnwulf preceded by more than a year his privilege for the church of Ravenna of July 819, the oldest papal privilege whose original has survived to our days.[2] The formula no. 93 of the *Liber Diurnus*, which originated on the occasion of the Offa-privilege of Pope Hadrian, was used in this Ravenna charter of Paschalis in drafting the 'arenga'; in the document for King Cœnwulf the rest of the formula could also be employed to a large extent.

Thus we have at least some fragmentary knowledge of the early history of Cœnwulf's foundation; the privilege of Paschalis gave the sanction, as it were, of ecclesiastical law to the fact that the king's daughter Quœnthryth was not only abbess of Suthminster in Kent but probably also of Winchcombe, at least disposed of property connected with this monastery (and possibly with others), and that her cousin Ælfled seems to have been the heiress of this 'hereditas' of formally ecclesiastical endowments. By the papal privilege such proprietary church rights were confirmed to Cœnwulf's house.

According to the annals of the monastery, a convent of nuns established at Winchcombe by Offa in 787 preceded the foundation of Cœnwulf; by adding a monastery of monks in 798, the latter may have made the house a 'double' monastery, of which his daughter could be abbess.[3] I have conjectured (above, p. 31) that Offa's foundation at Winchcombe was one of the monasteries erected or acquired by him, all dedicated to St. Peter, as we learn from the

[1] Cf. L. Halphen, *Études sur l'administration de Rome au moyen âge* (Bibliothèque de l'École des Hautes Études, Sciences hist. et philol. clxvi), 1907, pp. 93, 131 f.; cf. Jaffé, i, pp. 316, 318. The identity of the nomenculator with the primicerius Theodore is also assumed by Bresslau, loc. cit., p. 205, and by B. Simson, *Jahrbücher des Fränkischen Reichs unter Ludwig dem Frommen*, i, Leipzig, 1874, p. 202.

[2] Cf. Jaffé, i. 2551, and Kehr, *Italia pontificia*, v, 1911, p. 38, no. 94, on editions and facsimiles. The reproductions of the whole document in *Pontificum Romanorum Diplomata papyracea quae supersunt in tabulariis Hispaniae Italiae Germaniae phototypice expressa*, Rome, 1929, pl. I *a*, *b*, *c*, and of a part by I. Battelli, *Acta pontificum* (= *Exempla scripturarum . . . bibliothecae et tabularii Vaticani* iii), Rome, 1933, pl. I, have to be added.

[3] When Oswald reformed Winchcombe and six other monasteries of his diocese there may have been a survival of some kind of double monasteries; cf. Eadmer, *Vita Oswaldi*, c. 17 (ed. Raine, *The Historians of the Church of York*, ii. 20 f.): 'eiectis clericis feminarum consortium ecclesiis anteponentibus.'

privilege of Pope Hadrian which survived as formula 93 of the *Liber Diurnus*. Certainly in later times Winchcombe had other patron saints, St. Mary and St. Kenelm; but these may have supplanted St. Peter, as happened at Worcester. Here, after the reform of Bishop Oswald, a new, larger church of St. Mary was erected side by side with the older and smaller church of St. Peter; the Virgin later became the patroness of the cathedral and of the diocese, while St. Peter's ceased to be the principal church.[1] The sacramentary written probably at Winchcombe in the late tenth century and sent to Fleury, which I have previously mentioned in connexion with St. Kenelm (p. 249), contains a litany, in which a threefold invocation is found to St. Benedict, as was appropriate in a house of Benedictine monks, and to St. Peter, but not to St. Mary.[2] At Winchcombe there also existed a church of St. Peter, which later was regarded as a chapel of the church of St. Kenelm;[3] it was situated in the proximity of this church within the precincts and became the parish church of the place, appropriated and united to the abbey. There were the usual quarrels between the monastery, as the owner having the 'ius patronatus', and the incumbents of the church of St. Peter with their parochial duties.[4] The annals of Winchcombe dated the dedication of the abbey church 'in honore sanctae Trinitatis sanctaeque virginis Mariae et sanctae Crucis et Omnium Sanctorum' as early as the year 811.[5] But they may be supposed to draw in this respect on the forged foundation charter, and the assumption that St. Mary originally stood in the background is confirmed by the fact that her mass was celebrated at Winchcombe Abbey 'secretly and with subdued voice', that is, a low mass, almost to the end of the twelfth century; not until 1194 did abbot and chapter introduce its

---

[1] Cf. J. A. Robinson, *St. Oswald and the Church of Worcester* (The British Academy, Supplemental Papers, v), 1919, pp. 3 ff. and 22 ff. on charters which seem to contradict Robinson's assumption, but were, in his opinion, either altered in later times or forged altogether. Cf. below, p. 263, on Malmesbury.

[2] Delisle, loc. cit., pp. 367 f.: 'S. Petre, ter. . . . S. Benedicte, ter.' N. R. Ker, *Medieval Libraries of Great Britain*, London, 1941, p. 111, has rejected the sacramentary from the list of Winchcombe books. Robinson, *The Times of St. Dunstan*, Oxford, 1923, p. 97, n. 2, thought that it was probably sent from Ramsey, where Germanus, the first abbot of the reformed monastery of Winchcombe, later became abbot. But the prominence given in the book to St. Kenelm applies to no other house but Winchcombe, neither to Fleury to which the importance given to St. Peter and St. Benedict might be referred, nor to Ramsey where St. Mary and St. Benedict were the patron saints.

[3] Pope Alexander III confirmed in 1175 'abbati monasterii beate Marie et sancti Kenelmi Wynchecumbie' among its possessions 'ecclesiam beati Kenelmi cum capella sancti Petri' (Royce, i, pp. 25 f.; cf. Jaffé, ii. 14148).

[4] Cf. Royce, ii, pp. 12, 32, 94, 139 ff.; cf. i, pp. xcvii f.

[5] Birch, i, p. 469.

'solemn' celebration.[1] Good reasons seem therefore to exist for
including Winchcombe among the religious houses founded by Offa
and dedicated to St. Peter.

V

THE PATRON SAINTS OF ENGLISH CHURCHES IN THE SEVENTH AND EIGHTH CENTURIES

A COMPLETE list of English church dedications to the beginning of
the ninth century cannot of course be compiled. But, in spite of the
limits and uncertainty of our knowledge and of the many gaps and
deficiencies, a list of the known facts may prove suggestive. I shall
not accumulate *all* available proofs; if there is reliable evidence (such
as Bede's *H.E.*), I shall abstain from adducing all other authorities,
all charters, &c. I include some less certain dedications. Only the
first three churches have survived from Roman times.

ALBANUS: Verulamium (St. Albans), p. 34.

MARTINUS:
    Canterbury, Bede, *H.E.* i. 26.
    Whithorn (Wigtown), p. 34.
    Canterbury, 'porticus' in SS. Peter and Paul's (St. Augustine's),
      Bede, *H.E.* ii. 5 (p. 90).
    Dover, church, monastery (cf. Birch, i, no. 91), ascribed to King
      Wihtred of Kent (690–725), Liebermann, *Die Heiligen Englands*,
      p. 7 (c. 27), the Genealogies of the Chronicle of Florence of
      Worcester (Petrie, *Mon. hist. Brit.* i. 635), and later sources.
    'Oratorium' near Lyminge (Kent), Birch, i, no. 160.
    Martineseye (Somerset), 'ecclesia' near the river Axe (near Blea-
      don?), ib., no. 128, identified by J. A. Robinson, *Somerset Histo-*
      rical Essays, p. 34.

SALVATOR: Canterbury Cathedral, Bede, *H.E.* i. 33 and charters.
      Later 'ecclesia Christi', Christ Church, Birch, i, nos. 214, 291
      (side by side with 'ecclesia Salvatoris'), &c.

PETRUS ET PAULUS:
    Canterbury, monastery (later St. Augustine's), Bede, *H.E.* i. 33.
      ii. 3, 5, 6, and charters. Called after St. Peter alone as early as

---

[1] Royce, i, p. 93: 'ut missa de beata Maria, quam retroactis temporibus secreto
et suppressa voce celebrare consueverant, ad honorem ipsius ac pro salute omnium
ecclesie Winchecumbe beneficia inpendentium singulis diebus in eorum monasterio
solempniter celebraretur perpetuo.'

Bede, *H.E.* ii. 7 (pp. 93, 95), iv. 1 (p. 204), v. 8; Bede's *Hist. abb.* c. 3 (p. 367), &c.

Winchester, cathedral, Bede, *H.E.* iii. 7 (p. 140) and charters.

Glastonbury (Somerset), monastery: church of (Salvator and) SS. Peter and Paul, erected by King Ine of Wessex, William of Malmesbury, *Gesta regum*, i. 35 (ed. Stubbs, i. 36), *De antiquit. Glaston. eccl.* (Migne, *P.L.* clxxix. 1704); cf. Birch, i, no. 168.

Malmesbury (Wiltshire), Birch, i. no. 105 = Aldhelm, ed. Ehwald, p. 513 (Sergius I, Jaffé, i. 2140). Cf. Aldhelm, *Carm. eccl.* i (p. 11; cf. Ehwald, p. 5) and his verses on altars of the Twelve Apostles, which perhaps refer to the same church, ib. iv (pp. 19–31; cf. p. 8).

Medeshamstede, the later Peterborough, monastery founded in the 7th century (Bede, *H.E.* iv. 6): there seems to be no early attestation of the patron saints. The *Saxon Chronicle* E 656 (p. 30) gives the names of SS. Peter, Paul, and Andrew; forged charters (Birch, i, nos. 22, 48, &c.) and other sources usually mention only St. Peter in accordance with the later name of the place.

Isle of Thanet, monastery near Minster founded by Abbess Eadburg, Birch, i, no. 177; 'monasterium sancti Petri', ib., no. 189.

On the combined monasteries of Wearmouth (St. Peter) and Jarrow (St. Paul) see below, p. 261.

PETRUS:

York, cathedral (627), Bede, *H.E.* ii. 14, 20.

Lichfield, second church, ib. iv. 3 (p. 212).

Lindisfarne (consecrated by Theodore of Canterbury), ib. iii. 17, 25, v. 1 (pp. 160, 181, 282); Bede, *Vita Cuthberti*, c. 40 (ed. Colgrave, p. 288).

Worcester, cathedral, Birch, i, nos. 75, 164, 171, 183, 216, 217, 220, 239, &c.; A. J. Robertson, *Anglo-Saxon Charters*, Cambridge, 1939, p. 2, no. 1.

Bamburgh, Bede, *H.E.* iii. 6 (p. 138).

Bath, monastery, Birch, i, no. 327 (A.D. 758) = W. Hunt, *Two Chartularies of the Priory of St. Peter at Bath*, 1893, i, p. 23, no. 19.

Bermondsey (London), monastery, Birch, i, no. 133.

Beverley (Yorkshire), 'porticus' in the monastery, Bede, *H.E.* v. 6 (p. 292).

Bredon (Worcestershire), monastery, Birch, i, no. 234, 236; ii, no. 847.

Bruton (Somerset), church of St. Peter built according to tradition by Aldhelm, William of Malmesbury, *Gesta pontif.* v. 222 (ed. Hamilton, p. 374).

Chertsey (Surrey), monastery (Bede, *H.E.* iv. 6), Birch, i, nos. 33,

34, 56, 251, 394 (some of these charters are forged or doubt-ful).

Gloucester, monastery: early sources mentioning the dedication to St. Peter do not seem to exist. Cf. W. H. Hart, *Historia et cartularium monasterii S. Petri Gloucestriae*, i, 1863, pp. 3 ff.; Birch, i, no. 60.

Henfield (Sussex)? Birch, i, no. 206.

St. Osyth (Essex), 'on sancte Petres mynstre', Liebermann, *Die Heiligen Englands*, p. 13 (c. 22). Later sources mention SS. Peter and Paul.

Ripon, monastery, *Vita Wilfridi*, cc. 17, 45, 48, 65, 67 (pp. 211, 239, 243, 261, 263); Bede, *H.E.* v. 19 (pp. 322, 330).

Selsey (Sussex), monastery (*Vita Wilfridi*, c.41, p. 234; Bede, *H.E.* iv. 13, p. 232), Birch, i, no. 262.—At Chichester, to which the see of Selsey was transferred in the late 11th century, 'antiquitus et sancti Petri monasterium et congregatio fuerat sanctimonia-lium', according to William of Malmesbury, *Gesta pontif.* ii. 96 (ed. Hamilton, p. 205).

Wearmouth, monastery, *Vita Ceolfridi*, cc. 9, 18, 25, 30 (ed. Plum-mer, pp. 391, 394, 396, 399); Bede, *Hist. abb.* cc. 1, 4–7, 9, 14, 19, 20, 22 (ib. pp. 364, 367–70, 373, 378, 383, 385 f.). Bede, when mentioning this monastery together with the combined house of St. Paul of Jarrow, calls them the monastery of SS. Peter and Paul, ib., c. 15 (p. 379); *H.E.* v. 21, 24 (pp. 332, 357).

Westminster, Birch, i, no. 245. I omit certain forged charters and later sources. Cf. above, p. 31, n. 5.

Whitby, monastery, Bede, *H.E.* iii. 24, iv. 26 (pp. 179, 267); *Vita I. Gregorii papae*, c. 19 (ed. Gasquet, p. 23).

Woking (Surrey), monastery, Birch, i, no. 133.

Naiton, the king of the Picts, promised that he would have the stone church built in his country consecrated in the name of St. Peter (about 710), Bede, *H.E.* v. 21 (p. 333).

On the monasteries of King Offa of Mercia dedicated to St. Peter, see above, p. 30.

The monastery near Lindisfarne celebrated in the poem of Ædilvulf (see pp. 300 f.) had a church of St. Peter; cf. c. 4, v. 11; c. 6, v. 35; c. 21, v. 2 (*MG. Poetae*, i, pp. 585, 587, 600; *Symeon*, ed. Arnold, i, pp. 269, 271, 289). The heading of c. 21 calls it 'apostolorum oratorium'.

PAULUS:

London, cathedral, Bede, *H.E.* ii. 3, iv. 11 (pp. 85, 227); cf. Birch, i, no. 265; M. Gibbs, *Early Charters of the Cathedral Church of St. Paul, London* (Camden Third Series, lviii), 1939, pp. 7 f.

Rochester, 'porticus' in the cathedral of St. Andrew, Bede, *H.E.*
v. 23 (p. 348).

Jarrow, monastery, *Vita Ceolfridi*, cc. 11, 12, 17, 18, 23, 29 (ed.
Plummer, pp. 391 f., 394, 396, 398); Bede, *Hist. abb.* cc. 7, 9,
13, 15, 18 (ib., pp. 370, 373, 376 f., 379 f., 382 f.); dedication
inscription of 685 (ib. ii, p. 361; H. Quentin, *Les Martyrologes
historiques*, 1908, p. 128; H. E. Savage, *Archaeologia Aeliana*,
xxii, 1900, p. 34; E. Diehl, *Inscript. Latinae Christ. veteres*, i,
no. 1820A); Boniface, *Epist.* 116 (pp. 250 f.). Cf. Wearmouth,
St. Peter, above, p. 261.

Church in the diocese of Selsey (Sussex), Birch, iii, no. 1334
(= i, no. 237).

York, altar in the cathedral of St. Peter, Alcuin, *De sanctis Euboric.
eccl.* v. 1492 (*MG. Poetae*, i. 202); Symeon, *Hist. regum* c. 58
(ed. Arnold, ii. 58).

ANDREAS:

Rochester, cathedral, Bede, *H.E.* ii. 3, iii. 14, v. 23 (pp. 85, 154,
348 f.); Birch, i, nos. 152, 159, 175, &c. A charter of 774
mentioning 'terram sancti Andreae' (near Higham-Upshire,
north of Rochester), ib., no. 213, no doubt refers to property
of the cathedral.

Ferring (Sussex): ib., no. 261.

Hexham, monastery, *Vita Wilfridi*, cc. 22, 56 (pp. 216, 251); Bede,
H.E. v. 20 (p. 331). Wilfrid felt a special veneration for SS.
Peter and Andrew, *Vita Wilfridi*, c. 67 (p. 262); cf. c. 5 (p. 198).

Oundle (Northamptonshire), monastery, ib., c. 64 (p. 259).

Church near Pagham (Sussex), Birch, i, no. 50 (Earle, *Hand-Book*,
p. 282; *Auct. ant.* xv, 511), spurious (*c.* a. 975). Cf. Stevenson,
E.H.R., xxix (1914), 691 ff., on this charter.

Wells, monastery, Birch, i, no. 200.

'Oratorium' and cell of Wilgils near the mouth of the Humber,
Alcuin, *Vita Willibrordi*, i. 1 (*SS. rer. Merov.* vii. 116).

BARTHOLOMAEUS: Crowland (Lincolnshire), monastery. The forged
charters of the monastery (Birch, i, no. 135, &c.) mention SS.
Mary and Bartholomew as the patron saints. Felix in his Life of
St. Guthlac refers to the 'oratorium' of the saint and to a new
church (c. 32, ed. Mabillon, *Acta* iii. 1, p. 279) without noting
the dedications; but he gives Bartholomew so important a part
that the inference of his patronage is obvious (cc. 14, 15, 17,
19, 32, ib., pp. 268 ff.).

MATTHIAS: church to which Aldhelm dedicated some verses, *Carm.
eccl.* iv (p. 32).

MICHAEL:

Clive (Gloucestershire), monastery, Birch, i, no. 246.

'Clymeterium' (= oratorium) near Hexham, Bede, *H.E.* v. 2 (p. 283).

Malmesbury, third church in the monastery, William of Malmesbury, *Gesta pontif.* v. 216, 231 (ed. Hamilton, pp. 361, 385).

Stanmer (Sussex), monastery, Birch, i, no. 197.

IOHANNES BAPTISTA:

Canterbury, church built by Archbishop Cuthbert (740–60), William of Malmesbury, *Gesta pontif.* i. 7 (ed. Hamilton, p. 15); Birch, i, no. 345.

Frome (Somerset), monastery, ib., no. 105 = Aldhelm, ed. Ehwald, p. 513 (Sergius I, Jaffé, i. 2140).

MARIA:

Canterbury, church in the monastery of SS. Peter and Paul, Bede, *H.E.* ii. 6, v. 20 (pp. 93, 331).—Church in the western part of the city, Birch, i, no. 317.

Abingdon (Berkshire), monastery: no certain evidence before the 10th century, only forged charters; cf. Birch, i, nos. 155, 352, 366; ii, no. 687, &c.

Barking (Essex), church in the monastery, Bede, *H.E.* iv. 10 (p. 224).

Bruton (Somerset), church built according to tradition by Aldhelm, William of Malmesbury, *Gesta pontif.* v. 222 (ed. Hamilton, p. 374).

Glastonbury, monastery (SS. Mary and Patrick), Birch, i, nos. 61, 109, &c.; cf. William of Malmesbury, *Gesta regum*, i. 19, 21 (ed. Stubbs, pp. 24 f.), &c.

Hexham, church in the monastery of St. Andrew, cf. *SS. rer. Merov.* vi. 251, n. 3 (on Wilfrid's interest in the Roman church of St. Maria Maggiore cf. *Vita Wilfridi*, c. 62, ib., p. 258).

Lastingham (Yorkshire), church in the monastery, Bede, *H.E.* iii. 23 (p. 176).

Lichfield, first church, ib. iv. 3 (p. 212).

Lyminge (Kent), monastery, Birch, i, nos. 97, 98, 148, 160–1, 317, 411, 419–20.

Malmesbury, second church in the monastery of SS. Peter and Paul, Aldhelm, *Carm. eccl.* ii (ed. Ehwald, p. 12; cf. p. 7); it became the principal church in the 10th century, William of Malmesbury, *Gesta pontif.* v. 253 (p. 405).

Minster in Thanet, monastery, Birch, i, nos. 96, 177.

Reculver (Kent), monastery (669; cf. *Saxon Chron.* ed. Plummer, pp. 34 f.; Bede, *H.E.* v. 8, p. 295; Birch, i, nos. 45, 91), Birch, i, no. 173.

Sheppey (Kent), monastery (cf. Birch, i, no. 91), Liebermann, *Die Heiligen Englands*, p. 5 (c. 18).

Wearmouth, church in the monastery of St. Peter, *Vita Ceolfridi*, c. 25 (ed. Plummer, p. 396); Bede, *Hist. abb.* cc. 9, 17 (ib., pp. 373, 381 f.).

Church in the monastery of Wilgils near the mouth of the Humber, Alcuin, *Vita Willibrordi*, ii, c. 34 (*MG. Poetae*, i. 220; *Acta SS. Nov.* iii. 457; cf. *SS. rer. Merov.* vii. 114, n. 4; 116, n. 2).

Church in the monastery of Bugge (in Wessex), Aldhelm, *Carm. eccl.* iii (ed. Ehwald, pp. 14 ff.; cf. p. 8). There were twelve altars (of the apostles?), besides St. Mary's altar in the apse (v. 40).

Second church in the monastery of St. Peter (near Lindisfarne) celebrated in the poem of Ædilvulf, c. 14 (*MG. Poetae*, i. 594 f.; *Symeon*, ed. Arnold, i. 281 f.).

On the church of St. Mary in Crowland cf. above, p. 262; in Winchcombe p. 258; in Worcester, ib.

St. Mary as patron saint of the monastery of Evesham is not attested for these early times except by forged or at least doubtful charters (cf. H. and S. iii. 278 ff.; Birch, i, nos. 116–18, 222, 229, &c.). The same applies to the monastery of Ancarig, mentioned in the Peterborough forgeries; cf. *Saxon Chron.* E 656 (ed. Plummer, p. 31); Birch, i, no. 22, p. 38.

MARTYRES ET S. CRUX: York, altar in the cathedral of St. Peter, Alcuin, *De sanctis Euboric. eccl.* v. 1502 (*MG. Poetae*, i. 203).

LAURENTIUS:

Bradford-on-Avon (Wiltshire), 'ecclesiola' in Aldhelm's monastery, William of Malmesbury, *Gesta pontif.* v. 198 (p. 346).

Malmesbury: a church of St. Lawrence is said to have existed in the 9th century, ib. v. 240 (p. 394).

Wearmouth 'oratorium' in the dormitory of the monastery of St. Peter, *Vita Ceolfridi*, c. 25 (ed. Plummer, p. 397); Bede, *Hist. abb.* c. 17 (ib., p. 382).

QUATTUOR CORONATI: 'martyrium' in Canterbury, Bede, *H.E.* ii. 7 (p. 94).

GREGORIUS I: Canterbury, altar in the north-'porticus' of the monastery of SS. Peter and Paul, ib. ii. 3 (p. 86).

Whitby, altar in the church of St. Peter, *Vita I. Gregorii papae*, c. 19 (ed. Gasquet, p. 23).

York, 'porticus' in the cathedral of St. Peter, Bede, *H.E.* ii. 20 (p. 125).

SS. CUTHBERTUS ET OSWALDUS: At 'Scyt(h)lescester iuxta murum' (the Roman Wall: Chesters near Chollerton in Northumberland?) a church was erected where King Elfwald of Northumbria had been murdered in 788, Symeon, *Hist. regum*, c. 54 (ed. Arnold, ii. 52).

VI

THE BEGINNING OF THE YEAR OF THE INCARNATION IN BEDE'S 'HISTORIA ECCLESIASTICA'

I HAVE ascribed (above, pp. 50 f.) the crisis in the life of Wilfrid of York, his downfall and his journey overseas, to A.D. 678 in accordance with Bede, *H.E.* iv. 12 and v. 24, and I have consequently attributed the first English missionary effort in Friesland to the following winter 678–9, the view that prevailed until recently. In doing so I have implicitly rejected the opinion of the late Dr. Reginald L. Poole, who contended that Bede, in the *H.E.*, did not reckon the year of the Incarnation from Christmas, but adapted it to the Indiction: 'Consequently throughout his History Bede made his Year of Grace begin in September. . . . It was by no mistake that he dated the synod of Hertford 24 September, Ind. I, in 673, or the synod of Hatfield, 17 September, Ind. VIII, in 680 (*H.E.* iv. 5, v. 24); though these assemblies were held in what we call 672 and 679.'[1] Events belonging to the last four months (September to December) of our year of the Incarnation mentioned by Bede occurred therefore in the preceding year according to our method of reckoning the year from 1 January, whereas the first month of that year was for Bede the previous September. Wilfrid left England in 677, not 678, and preached to the Frisians during the winter of 677–8, not of 678–9, and other dates have to be shifted accordingly. In view of the authority of so excellent and accurate a scholar as Dr. Poole, I must state the reasons why I cannot accept his conclusions, which have recently found the weighty approval of Professor Stenton.[2]

[1] Poole, 'The Beginning of the Year in the Middle Ages' (*Studies*, p. 9); 'The Chronology of Bede's Historia Ecclesiastica and the Councils of 679–680' (ib., pp. 38–55, reprinted from the *J.T.S.* xx, 1919, pp. 24–40).

[2] *Anglo-Saxon England*, pp. 76 (n. 1), 129, 684. Poole's results are also accepted in the *Handbook of British Chronology*, edited by F. M. Powicke, London, 1939, pp. 6 and 374 f., and by C. W. Jones, *Bedae Opera de Temporibus*, 1943, pp. 121 (n. 5), 383.

I purposely say: 'his conclusions'; for I agree with him in some of his premisses: he has rightly assigned the synod of Hertford to 672 for 673, as B. Krusch and A. Anscombe did before him, and the synod of Hatfield to 679 for 680. But the only conclusion I draw is that Bede in both cases was making a small mistake. It is one of his merits as an historian to have reduced to a single system of time-reckoning the manifold ways of dating which he found in his sources. These included consular and imperial years, regnal years of a number of English kingdoms, years of Rome and indictions, years of the World from the Creation or from Abraham, and in some annals years of the Incarnation, &c. He synchronized events by applying the era of the Incarnation to the whole field of the *H.E.*, and thus gave his work chronological unity.[1] Abbot Dionysius had devised this era two centuries before in his Paschal Tables, in order to substitute a Christian numbering of the years for the era named after the persecutor Diocletian. Bede retained of course the invention of Dionysius in the complete paschal cycle from 532 to 1063 which he prefixed to his work *De temporum ratione* in 725, and he laid thereby the foundations, or at least promoted the growth, of a new kind of annals based on the Easter tables with their Christian series of years.[2] Bede had also treated theoretically this system of numbering, in connexion with the Paschal Tables, in his two books on chronology written in 703 and 725; but he had employed, like others, this era, outside the tables, only in a few exceptional cases. In his *Ecclesiastical History* of 731, in order to indicate the years uniformly, he chose from the beginning of his work Dionysius's era of the Incarnation, as applicable to all parts of England, and thus gave an influential lead in spreading the use of this era in England[3] and on the Continent.

All agree that Bede was, within the limits of his age, an intelligent and most scrupulous writer and a model of clearness and accuracy. But his information was often insufficient, and it would also be rash to assume that in computing the years of the Incarnation Bede, though 'the greatest master of chronology in the Middle Ages, did not make mistakes' (Poole, *Studies*, p. 38)—'Indignor quandoque bonus dormitat Homerus'. There are evident contradictions in his dates, even for events which happened during his lifetime.[4] 'We may presume that his Indictions are correct, and his years of the

---

[1] I use here freely what I have written in *Bede Essays*, pp. 147 ff.

[2] Cf., e.g., R. L. Poole, *Chronicles and Annals*, Oxford, 1926.

[3] Cf. Treiter, loc. cit., pp. 68 ff., 92 ff.

[4] Cf., e.g., Plummer, *Baedae Op. hist.* ii. 329 on the year of the death of Abbot Hadrian (*H.E.* v. 20, pp. 330 f.), or the 31 regnal years attributed to Ethelred of Mercia on his abdication in 704, though his accession is ascribed to 675 (ib. v. 24, pp. 354 f.).

Incarnation are nearly always computed by himself' (Poole, ib.).
He certainly employed for this purpose the Easter Tables of Dionysius
and his continuators; the first and second of their eight columns
indicated the *anni domini nostri Iesu Christi* and the *indictiones*. In this
way he added, e.g. at the end of a letter of Pope Honorius, to the
dates after the words *indictione VII* the explanation: *id est anno
dominicae incarnationis DCXXXIIII* (*H.E.* ii. 18).[1] The letter was also
dated by imperial years and by the 11th of June; in this case hardly
any possibility of a mistake could exist. Paschal Tables were designed
to supply the elements for establishing the date of Easter; the years
of Incarnation and the indictions were suitable for distinguishing
the individual coming years in the continuous sequel of the paschal
cycle; there was no need to mark the difference between their beginnings, which had no relation to the date of Easter. It could
therefore easily happen even to a careful user of these tables to
overlook this difference on one occasion or another. That is what,
in my opinion, Bede did when he gave the dates of the synods
mentioned above, which assembled on 24 and 17 September. He
simply forgot that the indictions did not change, with the years of
Incarnation, on Christmas day, but almost four months earlier; in
identifying the indictions I and VIII with A.D. 673 and 680, he took
the years from the Paschal Tables without paying regard to months
and days in these particular cases, but not because it was his rule
to identify the beginning of the indictions with that of the years of
Incarnation.

But there is one argument which Dr. Poole considered decisive
(*Studies*, p. 9). When Bede related the unfortunate events of 678,
the dissension between King Egfrid and Bishop Wilfrid and the
latter's expulsion, he inserted between the indication of the year and
the account of these happenings some words on the appearance of
a comet in August (*H.E.* iv. 12, p. 228); similarly in the short
'recapitulatio' at the end of his work (v. 24, p. 355) he also mentioned
the comet first. The reason is evident: comets were to Bede, as to
his whole age and many other ages, signs of coming misfortunes and
disasters (cf. his *De natura rerum*, c. 24, ed. Giles, vi. 111; *H.E.* v. 23,
p. 349). This comet was not observed in fact in 678 but, as Poole
has pointed out from Chinese sources (*Studies*, pp. 42 f.), two years
earlier, from August to October 676.[2] Now one of the oldest and
best manuscripts of the *H.E.*, the so-called Moore MS. (M of Plummer's edition, to-day Cambridge University Library MS. Kk. V. 16)
originally had in the 'recapitulatio' not the year 678 but DCLXXVII,

---

[1] Cf. Napier and Stevenson, *The Crawford Collection of Early Charters*, p. 45;
Menzer, loc. cit., p. 89; *Bede Essays*, p. 148, n. 3.

[2] The *Annales Cambriae* note it under the right year.

to which one more digit seems to have been added later (Plummer, i. 355, n. 2); the year 677 is also given in a ninth- to tenth-century manuscript from St. Maximin's at Trier, now Phillipps MS. 1873 (Latin MS. no. 133) of Berlin, which was used by Pierre François Chifflet in his edition of Bede (*Bedae presbyteri et Fredegarii concordia*, Paris, 1681, p. 313 and in iv. 12 of *H.E.*, p. 210). Poole preferred this reading 677 to avoid the conclusion that Bede 'made a bad chronological mistake, which is unlikely'; the year 677, if it is reckoned from September 676 to August 677, 'included almost the whole of the time during which the comet was visible'. But this argument is untenable. Chifflet's manuscript is not only of the same type as M, as Th. D. Hardy has seen (*Descriptive Catalogue*, i. 1, p. 436; cf. Plummer, i, p. cxxxi), but probably derived from it; it is almost certain that it is a copy of M and has no independent value at all.[1] Further, it is impossible to base the text of Bede on M and its companions alone; M 'is not so uniformly correct as to be above criticism'. There are other manuscripts 'of equal weight' (ib., p. xc), and they agree in the reading 678 of the recapitulation. Moreover, in the text of Bede's narrative iv. 12 there is, according to Plummer, no variant reading of the year of the Incarnation in any of the important manuscripts, and the conclusion is to be drawn that 677 in the summary is nothing but a slip of the pen of the transcriber of M, the more so since the preceding line begins with the year 676. The manuscript tradition therefore shows that the original reading of Bede was 678, and this date cannot be identified with the autumn of 676. Thus Poole's assumption loses its decisive argument. Bede in ascribing the comet to the year 678 made a mistake in any case.

He borrowed his account of the phenomenon, as Poole has rightly stated (pp. 42 f.), from the Life of Pope Donus (676–8) in the *Liber Pontificalis* (ed. Mommsen, p. 192); there the comet is called a star ('stella') and is said to have appeared after the election of the Pope ('dum esset electus') in August and to have been visible for three months. Bede added the term 'cometa' and changed its description accordingly a little.[2] He found, of course, no years of the Incarnation in his source and had to establish the year of the comet himself. The next date which could be easily identified was 18 June in the

---

[1] Extracts from Isidore and the decrees of the Roman synod of 721 are added in M by a later hand, in the Berlin MS. by its copyist himself, as we have to assume, directly or indirectly from M. Cf. Plummer, i, pp. lxxxix f.; V. Rose, *Verzeichniss der Lateinischen Handschriften der Königlichen Bibliothek zu Berlin*, i, 1893, pp. 296 f.; K. Hampe, *Neues Archiv*, xxii, 1897, p. 667.

[2] The words '*flammae* quasi *columnam* praeferens' may perhaps be influenced by Dracontius, *De laudibus Dei*, ii. 796 (ed. Vollmer, *MG. Auct. ant.* xiv. 91): 'nubes flammaeque columna.' On Bede's (doubtful) knowledge of this work cf. Ogilvy, loc. cit., p. 36.

8th indiction (= A.D. 680) in the Life of Donus's successor Agatho (Mommsen, p. 193. 18); he could also read in the *Lib. Pontif.* that a vacancy of 2 months and 15 days occurred between the pontificates of Donus and Agatho, and that Donus died on 10 April after he had been Pope for 1 year 5 months and 10 days. If Bede worked on these data and overlooked or neglected details which were less patent, it would not be difficult for him to ascribe the death of Donus, two years late and miscalculating the days, to April 680 and consequently the comet which appeared in August after Donus's election, to the year 678, and to insert the story of its appearance in his account of the English events of this year. Anyhow, his date of the comet is wrong, whether he reckoned the year from September or Christmas, and does not prove that he treated the year of the Incarnation as beginning in September.

On the other hand, there are some facts which make it certain that he used Christmas as the starting-point of the year, before 731 as well as in the *H.E.*, in conformity with the custom of his monastery. According to the anonymous author of the *Vita Ceolfridi*, c. 17 (Plummer, p. 394), Ceolfrid was constituted abbot 'tertio anno regis Aldfridi, indictione prima' (= A.D. 688) on 12 May; 'eodem anno' Abbot Sigfrid died on 22 August; then Abbot Benedict also departed this life 'anni sequentis exordiis,[1] id est II. Id. Ian.': obviously there was no change in the year in September but either at Christmas or on the first of January. Abbot Ceolfrid arrived at Langres and died there, as we are informed by the same author cc. 35, 36 (pp. 401 f.), on the 25th of September, 'incipiente indictione XV,' that is, in 716 (this year is confirmed by the weekdays mentioned cc. 31, 32, p. 400). According to Bede (*Hist. abb.* c. 23, p. 386) this day of Ceolfrid's death, 25 September, was 'feria sexta'; it was in fact a Friday in 716. Bede adds expressly 'anno ab incarnatione Domini septingentesimo sexto decimo'. The conclusion is evident again: there was no change in the number of the year of the Incarnation on 1 or 24 September when Bede wrote his *Historia abbatum*; at this time he changed its number on a day after 25 September, that is, at Christmas or on 1 January.

Did he go back to September and adapt the year of the Incarnation to the indiction, when he made this year the foundation of dating in his *Ecclesiastical History*? The Easter Tables of Dionysius and of his continuators were of course the basis of his synchronization. The Roman abbot himself had drawn up his tables only for the period of five lunar cycles of 19 years, that is, for 95 years (A.D. 532–

---

[1] The date cannot be referred to the actual regnal years of Aldfrid, though there was probably some interval between the death of his predecessor Egfrid (685, 20 May) and his accession. Cf. also Poole, *Studies*, pp. 46 f.; below, p. 273.

626);[1] an abbot Felix[2] continued the tables for five more cycles (627–721) which expired just in Bede's time in 721. Victorius, with his different system, had given in the fifth century the example of a complete table of $28 \times 19 = 532$ years, combining the solar and the lunar cycles. Thus the corresponding table of 532 years, from A.D. 532 to 1063, was calculated according to Dionysius's rules in Bede's age,[3] and he furthered its wide diffusion by prefixing it to his larger work on chronology. These tables could also easily be applied to the preceding period of 532 years for the purpose of synchronization. Copies of the tables and other evidence show that a combination of the Easter tables with a list of the Roman emperors existed in the early eighth century in England and especially in the Northumbrian homeland of Bede, as some annals of English happenings transmitted with this list make manifest; Paul Lehmann has given the explanation of this whole complex.[4] But Bede had to synchronize here not only the years of the Roman emperors, as he had done in his larger *Chronicle of the World*, where he marked the last year of each by years reckoned from the Creation. In the *H.E.* English events above all had to be dated, and in particular the dates of the reigns of English kings had to be established. The model for synchronization of regnal years was the Chronicle of Eusebius, as it had been translated, adapted, and continued by Jerome.[5] There is a difference between the real regnal and imperial years and their

---

[1] A new edition of Dionysius was published by the late Bruno Krusch, *Studien zur christlich-mittelalterlichen Chronologie* (Abhandl. Berlin 1937, no. 8), 1938. It is a pity that the distinguished editor, to whom I owe very much, produced these studies only in his old age, when he had lost his eyesight and had no qualified assistant to help him. The text is spoiled by some misprints and other mishaps. His MS. 3, from which he printed several annals transcribed by Mommsen (p. 61), is Phillipps MS. no. 1830, now Berlin Lat. 129. It was not written in Great Britain, as Krusch assumed, but at Laon in 874 and was later taken to the monastery of St. Vincent of Metz. The annals are the *Annales Laudunenses et S. Vincentii Mettenses* edited by Holder-Egger, *MG. SS.* xv. 2, pp. 1293–5; the last two lunar cycles are reproduced by M. Tangl in W. Arndt's *Schrifttafeln zur Erlernung der Lateinischen Palaeographie*, 4th ed., ii, Berlin, 1906, pl. 49 A; cf. ib., p. 31. Cf. also Rose, loc. cit, i. 287 ff.

[2] The authorship of Felix has been denied by C. W. Jones, 'The "lost" Sirmond MS. of Bede's "Computus" ' (*E.H.R.* lii, 1937, p. 207, n. 4); cf. his note, 'Two Easter Tables' (*Speculum*, xiii, 1938, pp. 204 f.), and his book *Bedae Opera de temporibus*, p. 73 f.

[3] Probably Bede was not the first after Victorius as has been supposed to calculate the entire table. Cf. *Bede Essays*, p. 119, n. 2.

[4] Paul Lehmann, *Fuldaer Studien* (SB. München, 1925, no. 3), pp. 34–46, and *Neue Folge* (ib. 1927, no. 2), pp. 50–2, with an improved collation of MS. 641 (B. IV. 18) of the Biblioteca Casanatense in Rome, R in Mommsen's edition of *Adnotationes antiquiores ad cyclos Dionysianos* (*Auct. ant.* ix. 751–6). Cf. also H. Bresslau, *Die ältere Salzburger Annalistik* (Abhandl. Berlin 1923, no. 2), pp. 13 f.

[5] Cf., e.g., E. Caspar, *Die älteste römische Bischofsliste* (Schriften der Königsberger Gelehrten Gesellschaft, ii, Geisteswissenschaftl. Klasse, no. 4), 1926, pp. 15 (229) ff.

adaptation by Eusebius–Jerome and their followers. In official documents these years on the whole, we may suppose, were reckoned from the actual beginning of the reign, in England, e.g., in the acts of the synod of Hatfield (*H.E.* iv. 17), in the laws of King Wihtred of Kent, in charters, or in royal and episcopal lists and their derivatives, if they indicate not only 'round numbers' of years[1] but also months or months and days. But Bede's regnal years, like those of Jerome, seem to be different and adapted to the 'common' year. He could note in the narrative of the *H.E.*, as he did in the larger *Chronicle*, if his information was sufficient, not only the years but also the months and days of the duration of a reign; but to effect the synchronism and parallelism of regnal years and years of the Incarnation, he had to simplify the tradition and to neglect the minor units or to regard them as a complete year. He considered the whole year of the Incarnation, in which a king died, as his last year and reckoned the next year of the Incarnation as the first year of his successor. Only when a king died early in the year, he may occasionally have neglected a few weeks and ascribed the whole year to the next king; his *Chronica maiora* include such adaptations after Jerome's pattern.[2] The assumption that Bede in the *H.E.* similarly adapted the regnal years to the years of the Incarnation is suggested by the very wording of dates such as

> ii. 14 (p. 113): 'anno regni sui (of Edwin) XI, qui est annus dominicae incarnationis DCXXVII';
>
> iii. 26 (p. 189): 'anno dominicae incarnationis DCLXIIII, qui fuit annus Osviu regis XXII';
>
> iv. 12 (p. 228): 'Anno dominicae incarnationis DCLXXVIII, qui est annus imperii regis Ecgfridi VIII, apparuit mense Augusto stella . . .';
>
> v. 23; see below, p. 274.

This practice may, with all probability, be attributed to Bede in his account of the Northumbrian kings, who were best known to him; several difficulties disappear if this assumption is accepted.[3]

---

[1] As in the Northumbrian list of Bede's Moore MS. (Petrie, *Mon. hist. Brit.* i. 290; Sweet, *The Oldest English Texts*, p. 148).

[2] Cf. what Bede says, in connexion with the indictions, in 725, *De temporum ratione*, c. 48 (ed. Jones, p. 268): 'Dum enim verbi gratia quilibet imperator medio anni tempore vita vel regno decederet, poterat evenire, ut eundem annum unus historicus eiusdem regis adscriberet temporibus, eo quod eius partem regnaret, alter vero historicus eundem successori illius potius attitulandum putaret, eo quod et hic partem aeque eius haberet in regno', &c.

[3] From the same point of view there is no contradiction between *H.E.* iii. 4 and v. 22, 24. In the first chapter A.D. 715 is mentioned as the last year in which the monks of Iona clung to their Irish observances; in the other two chapters (= *Chron. mai.*, c. 586, p. 319) 716 is the year in which Egbert converted them to the acceptance of the Roman customs.

King Ethelfrid of Northumbria defeated the Scottish king Ædan in his 11th year = 603, and reigned for 24 years = 593–616 (i. 34, v. 24). King Edwin, who slew him, was christened in 627, 12 April, in his 11th year (ii. 14, v. 24; *Chron. mai.* c. 541, ed. Mommsen, p. 311); so his first year was 617. He reigned 17 years = 617–33, and fell in battle 633, 12 October (ii. 20, v. 24; his name under 13 October in Willibrord's calendar). The 'infaustus annus' of his successors, Osric in Deira and Eanfrid in Bernicia, who forsook Christianity and were also slain (the former in the following summer, the latter after a whole year) was ascribed to King Oswald, who succeeded them, by all 'regum tempora computantibus' (iii. 1, 9), that is, 634 was reckoned as Oswald's first year. This year being added, he reigned 9 years = 634–42 (iii. 9) and was killed in 642, 5 August (ib. and v. 24; the day also in Willibrord's and later calendars).

Oswiu succeeded for 28 years (iii. 14) = 643–70.[1] During the earlier part of his reign Oswine was king of Deira but was killed on 20 August in Oswiu's 9th year = 651 (iii. 14, v. 24; Oswine's name is entered on 19 August in Willibrord's calendar). Penda of Mercia was defeated in 655, 15 November, in Oswiu's 13th year (iii. 24); cf. below, p. 275. The synod of Whitby met in his 22nd year = 664; this year of the Incarnation is confirmed by the eclipse of the sun in May mentioned in this connexion (iii. 26, 27, v. 24). Oswiu fell ill in 670 and died on 15 February (iv. 5); in his summary (v. 24) Bede ascribes the king's death to the same year 670. He also identifies the year of Oswiu's last illness with the second year after the arrival of Archbishop Theodore in Britain (iv. 5). Theodore reached Canterbury 669, 27 May (iv. 1, 2). 15 February therefore, in the second actual year after his coming, was in 671, not in 670 (Plummer, ii. 211); but Bede, consistently with his method of synchronization, no doubt reckoned A.D. 669 as the first year, 670 as the second year from Theodore's arrival (Poole, *Studies*, p. 41). According to the acts of the synod of Hatfield, which assembled on the 17th of September 679 (above, pp. 265 f.), Oswiu's successor Egfrid was then in the tenth (actual) year of his reign (*H.E.* iv. 17); thus he must have succeeded Oswiu in 670. Another fact points in the same direction. Egfrid fell in battle in 685, 20 May, according to Bede in the fifteenth year of his reign (ib., c. 26). Irish Annals confirm the date, adding that it was a Saturday, which corresponds with 685; but they also state that Egfrid died after having completed his 15th year (Plummer,

---

[1] The Northumbrian (and Kentish) Annals transmitted with Paschal Tables (cf. above, p. 270) ascribe the beginning of Oswiu's reign to 643; see the entries in MSS. from St. Germain-des-Prés (*MG. SS.* iv, p. 2), in Berlin Lat. 128 from Verona–Metz (Phillipps 1831, *Auct. ant.* ix. 753), and in the *Annales Iuvavenses maiores* (*SS.* i. 87): 'Osviu regnare incipit.'

ii. 261), 'which may mean a short time after the completion of his fifteenth year' (Poole, p. 45). Thus Oswiu's 28 years in Bede are obviously a round number, representing 27 complete years and a portion of the unfinished 28th year. The *Historia Brittonum* of the so-called Nennius, c. 64 (ed. Mommsen, *Auct. ant.* xiii. 208; ed. Lot, *Biblioth. de l'École des hautes études*, cclxiii, 1934, p. 204) attributes to Oswiu a reign of 28 years and six months, numbers which, reckoned from the fall of Oswald (642, 5 August), lead to February 671; but XXVIII may be a mistake for XXVII or be influenced by Bede. In all probability Oswiu died in 670, 15 February, and Bede considered this year of the Incarnation the last year of his reign.[1]

In any case, Bede regarded 671 as Egfrid's first year:

673 (really 672), 24 September = 3 Egfrid (iv. 5; v. 24).

674, Indict. II = 4 Egfrid (Bede, *Hist. abb.* c. 4, p. 368, from *Vita Ceolfridi*, c. 7, p. 390).

678, August = 8 Egfrid (iv. 12; v. 24); on the comet (really of 676) cf. above, pp. 267 ff.

679 = 9 Egfrid (iv. 21; v. 24); 'anno post hunc sequente', November 17 = 680 (iv. 23; v. 24).

680 (really 679), 17 September = 10 Egfrid (iv. 17; v. 24).

685, 20 May (his death) = 15 Egfrid (iv. 26; v. 24); cf. above, p. 272.[2]

Aldfrid succeeded Egfrid. Bede equated his first year to 686:

[1] The Northumbrian Annals transmitted in Easter Tables (cf. p. 270) are ambiguous, but on the whole weigh against 671. For the Munich MS. of the *Annales Fuldenses antiquissimi* (*MG. SS.* iii. 116*) and the *Annales Corbeienses* (Jaffé, *Biblioth. rer. German.* i. 32) ascribe Egfrid's accession to 670: 'Ecgfrid regnare coepit', and decide against the Kassel MS. of the old Fulda Annals, where the same entry is inscribed under 671. Such displacements by one year or even more are very common in annals. Irish annals do not permit of any certain conclusion about the year.

[2] The name of King Egfrid is entered on 20 May in the calendar of St. Willibrord, in the Munich fragment of the same age (ed. R. Bauerreiss, *Studien und Mitteilungen zur Geschichte des Benediktiner-Ordens*, li, 1933, p. 178: '[Ec]fridi regis', and above these words in the preceding line 'in aquilone'; cf. *Saxon Chronicle* E 685: 'be norðan sae'), and in the Lorsch calendar of the early 9th century (M. Manitius, *Neues Archiv*, xxii, 1897, p. 764). Egfrid's actual reign comprised 15 years 3 months, if my calculations are right. The *Historia Brittonum*, c. 65 (loc. cit.), ascribes to him 'novem annis'; these have been sometimes referred to a version or source written in 679 during the lifetime of the king. But his death is also related there, and the number is rather a misreading of VIIII for original XIIII, as Lot (loc. cit., p. 205, n. 4) has suggested; this number, however, would not be accurate either. The inscription in Jarrow church commemorating its dedication on 23 April in the 15th year of King Egfrid and in the 4th of Abbot Ceolfrid (cf. p. 262) is to be referred to 684, if the actual regnal year of Egfrid is meant; but 23 April was a Sunday in 685, a fact which weighs in favour of the latter year (Plummer, *Baedae Op. hist.* ii. 361) and of another kind of reckoning, like that of Bede.

688 = 3 Aldfrid (v. 7, 24); the same (12 May), indict. I, according to *Vita Ceolfridi*, c. 17 (p. 394).

He reigned 19, less than 20 years (v. 1, 18); he died in 705 according to Bede (v. 18, 24), who seems to have identified his—unfinished—20th year with this year of the Incarnation. But the northern additions in the MSS. DE of the *Saxon Chronicle* (under 705, following Bede) mark 14 December as the day of his death, that is, in 704, if he did not complete his 20th regnal year, and sources as different as the *Annales Cambriae* and the Kassel MS. of the old Fulda Annals (loc. cit.) agree on 704, the one assigning Aldfrid's death, the other the accession of his son Osred to this year, which is probably right (cf. Plummer, ii. 305 f.).[1]

After the death of Aldfrid the succession was contested; Eadwulf usurped the power for two months (*Vita Wilfridi*, c. 59, p. 254). He was then expelled, and Aldfrid's young son Osred succeeded for 11 years; he was killed in 716 (*H.E.* v. 18, 22, 24). Bede identifies his fourth year with 709 (v. 19, 24), consequently, in my opinion, his first year with 706.

Cœnred followed him in 716 (v. 22, 23), for two years according to the list of Northumbrian kings in Bede's Moore MS. (loc. cit.), the *Saxon Chronicle* (A.D. 716), and later sources (= 717–18). Then Osric succeeded for 11 years (= 719–29) and died in 729, 9 May (v. 23, 24; the day also in the Munich calendar fragment, ed. Bauerreiss, p. 178: 'Depositio Osrici regis', wrongly identified, p. 179). Bede (v. 23) identifies his seventh year (23 April) with A.D. 725 (v. 23) in words which correspond with my view of his method of synchronization: 'Anno dominicae incarnationis DCCXXV, qui erat annus septimus Osrici regis Nordanhymbrorum. . . .'

There are similar examples from Kent and Mercia. Earconbert of Kent, who died in 664, 14 or 15 July (iv. 1; v. 24),[2] was succeeded by his son Egbert for 9 years (iv. 1, 26) = 665–73. When the latter died in 673, 4 July (iv. 5; v. 24; the day in Annals from St. Germain-

---

[1] I have formerly defended 705 myself, *SS. rer. Merov.* vi. 254, n. 3. Irish annals are inconclusive here also.

[2] Bede, *H.E.* iv. 1 refers the death of Earconbert to the same day as that of Archbishop Deusdedit of Canterbury, that is, 14 July, in 664. But the king died the following day according to Kentish Annals (cf. above, p. 272, n. 1) transmitted in MS. Paris Nouv. acq. Lat. 1615 (Libri 90) from Fleury, ed. L. Delisle, *Catalogue des manuscrits des fonds Libri et Barrois*, Paris, 1888, p. 70: '664. Erconbrech filius Eodbaldi depositus Idus Iulii, feria II'; 15 July was a Monday in 664. These Kentish Annals also mark the deaths of the kings Ethelbert I (*Ann. Iuvav. mai.* and *S. Germani, MG. SS.* i. 87, iv. 2), Eadbald (*Ann. Iuvav. mai.*), Egbert (see above), Hlotheri (ib.), and Edric (*Ann. S. Germ.* and *Floriac.*) of Kent, and though there are a few mistakes in years and days, attention should be paid to these annals in a second edition of the *Handbook of British Chronology*, pp. 7 f. Plummer has used a part of them.

des-Prés, *MG. SS.* iv, p. 2, and Fleury, Delisle, loc. cit., p. 71), his brother Hlotheri followed for 11 years and 7 months (iv. 5) or, as Bede says elsewhere (iv. 26), for 12 years. This second statement obviously includes an unfinished year and may be explained by the equation A.D. 674–85 = 1–12 Hlotheri. Bede identified his 7th year, 17 September (synod of Hatfield), with A.D. 680 (iv. 17; v. 24); the right year would have been 679 (above, p. 266).

Ceolred of Mercia died in 716; his successor Ethelbald was in his 15th year in 731 (v. 24, p. 356) about the 10th of June, when Archbishop Tatwine of Canterbury was consecrated (v. 23, p. 350): Bede may have taken 717 for the first year of his reign.

I abstain from accumulating more facts of this kind. They suggest that Bede gave exact dates when they were available to him; but at the same time he tried to bring regnal years into line with the years of the Incarnation and effected their parallelism by adapting the former to the latter. Now I return to the question whether his year of the Incarnation corresponded, except perhaps for the few last days (25–31 December), with the Roman 'civil' year, as he reckoned the year in his *Historia abbatum* (p. 269), or whether he began it four months earlier in accordance with the indiction, as Dr. Poole has assumed. There are in the *H.E.* several cases which weigh against this second possibility.

Paulinus of York was consecrated on 21 July—a Sunday[1]—in 625 (ii. 9, p. 98; cf. v. 24). His episcopate comprised 19 years 2 months 21 days (iii. 14) and must therefore have ended in October 644. In fact Bede ascribes his death to the second year of Oswiu (= 644, cf. above, p. 272) and to A.D. 644, 10 October (iii. 14; v. 24), but not to 645, the number required by Poole's theory: there is no shifting of the year on 1 or 24 September.[2]

King Oswiu in his 13th year defeated the formidable Penda of Mercia on 15 November (iii. 24, p. 179), that is, in 655, if Bede considered 643 as Oswiu's first year. He attributes to Penda a reign of 22 years from Edwin's death in 633, 12 October (ii. 20: 'ex eo tempore') and puts Penda's fall in 655 (v. 24). This date conforms

---

[1] Cf. Thomas Michels, *Beiträge zur Geschichte des Bischofsweihetages im christlichen Altertum und im Mittelalter* (Liturgiegeschichtliche Forschungen, x), Münster i. W., 1927, pp. 64 f.

[2] To bring his theory into line with the tradition, Poole, *Studies*, p. 45, had to change Paulinus's xviiii years into xviii. The xxi days should in his opinion be xx (ib.). But the day beginning a period and the day ending it are very often reckoned both as full days in the Middle Ages (cf. H. Boehmer, 'Zur Geschichte des Bonifatius', loc. cit., pp. 203 ff.; on the other hand, Flaskamp, *Histor. Jahrbuch*, xlvii, 1927, pp. 473 ff.); the interval from 21 July (consecration) to 10 October (death) comprises exactly 2 months and 21 days (21–31 July and 1–10 October, besides August and September).

with the statement that the Middle Angles were converted 'biennio ante mortem Pendan regis' (iij. 21, p. 170) in 653 (v. 24). A change of the year in September is not excluded in these cases, but very improbable, as other facts show. Archbishop Honorius of Canterbury died in this same year 653 on 30 September; a vacancy of 1 year 6 months followed before the next archbishop, Deusdedit, could be consecrated on 26 March, obviously in 655 (iii. 20).[1] He died in 664, 14 July (iv. 1; cf. iii. 28; iv. 2, pp. 195, 205; cf. above, p. 274, n. 2, on the year). Bede attributes to him a pontificate of 9 years 4 months 2 days (iii. 20), about a fortnight too long, if the days of consecration and death are correctly transmitted; possibly Bede or his authorities made a miscalculation in establishing the interval between these days. But the difference would be beyond any probability, if Bede's indication of 653, 30 September, meant 652 of our usage and Deusdedit's consecration had to be dated as 654, 26 March (a Wednesday, without any festal character). The duration of his episcopate would be more than ten years, and the miscalculation of the days would be aggravated by a greater miscalculation of the years.

Bede ascribes the synod of Hertford, which assembled on 24 September in the first indiction, to A.D. 673, that is to say a year late, equating the indiction with the year of the Incarnation which corresponded with the greater part of the indiction and was found side by side with it in the Paschal Tables (above, p. 267). Consequently he attributes the death of King Egbert of Kent, who died in fact in July 673 (pp. 274 f.), to the year of the synod: 'Facta est autem haec synodus anno ab incarnatione Domini DCLXX tertio, *quo anno* rex Cantuariorum Ecgberct mense Iulio *obierat*' (iv. 5; cf. v. 24). The last word (not 'obiit') makes it evident that Bede ascribes the month of July and the 24th of the following September to the same year of the Incarnation. There is no change in the number of the year betwen the two dates.

Another date is perhaps even more decisive. King Cædwalla of Wessex died in Rome in 689, 20 April, as Bede states (v. 7) in accordance with the indiction, the imperial postconsulate, and the papal year indicated by the inscription on his tomb monument. Archbishop Theodore of Canterbury died on the 19th of September of the next year ('Anno autem post hunc . . . proximo'), which Bede identifies with 690 (v. 8, 24). Theodore arrived at Canterbury, as I have previously mentioned, in 669, 27 May (iv. 2), and administered his church for 21 years 3 months 26 (rather 24) days (ib.; in v. 8

---

[1] 26 March was Maundy Thursday in 655. It was one of the few exceptional cases of English episcopal consecrations not performed on a Sunday. Cf. Michels, loc. cit., p. 65, n. 73.

Bede attributes to him 22 years = 669–90, including again an unfinished year); these numbers also lead to September 690 according
to our method of reckoning. Moreover, Canterbury Annals transmitted through St. Germain-des-Prés (*SS*. iv. 2) and Fleury (Delisle,
loc. cit., p. 71) add the weekday also: '690 ("691" Flor.). Theodorus
episcopus depositus ("deponitur" S. Germ.) XIII. Kal. Octobr., *feria II*':
the 19th of September was in fact a Monday in 690. Thus Bede's year of
the Incarnation cannot have begun with the indiction on 1 September,
nor, as we have seen before, on the 24th day of this month, the two
beginnings of the indiction which alone have to be considered here.

Nor can there be any doubt that he did not regard the 1st of
January as the starting-point, but Christmas.[1] For in his work
De temporum ratione, c. 47 (ed. Jones, p. 267), he mentions an
inscription which was copied by monks of his community sent
to Rome: 'Denique anno ab eius incarnatione iuxta Dionysium
septingentesimo primo, indictione quarta decima, fratres nostri, qui
tunc fuere Romae, hoc modo se in natale Domini in cereis sanctae
Mariae scriptum vidisse et inde descripsisse referebant', &c. The
14th indiction began in September 700; therefore Christmas 701
as mentioned by Bede, would have been the Christmas of A.D. 700,
if the number of the year had changed on the 1st of January. Bede's
year of the Incarnation obviously changed its numeral on Christmas
itself in conformity with the beginning of the ecclesiastical year of
the Roman sacramentaries and with the original meaning of 'in-
carnatio'; in this respect only Annunciation or Lady Day could
compete with Christmas. Bede himself wrote occasionally 'anni
nativitatis Domini' for 'anni ab incarnatione Domini' (*De temporibus*,
c. 14, ib., p. 301). He also knew that the Romans began the solar
or civil year 'a bruma', the winter solstice, for which he maintained
the date of the Julian calendar, 25 December (ib., cc. 9, 7, pp. 298,
297; *De temp. rat.* cc. 36, 30, pp. 250, 235 f.); it was at the same
time the day of the Nativity and the beginning of the old English
year, midwinter (ib., c. 15, pp. 211 f.).

Thus the conclusion seems reasonably established that Bede's year
of the Incarnation began on Christmas Day, not with the indiction
on the 1st or 24th of September. The few cases which contradict
this assumption have to be regarded as possible mistakes, though
slight. At the end of the eighth century Alcuin, who came from
Bede's native country, was accustomed to begin the year after the
'Latin' use 'cum nato Christo et crescente luce', and opposed the
'Egyptian boys' at the court of Charles the Great who wanted to
shift its beginning to September (*Epist.* 145, *MG. Epist.* iv, pp. 231 f.).

---

[1] Thus also Treiter, loc. cit., pp. 76, 97.

The change to the autumn, probably to September 24, the 'harvest equinox', belongs in England to a later age; it is found in the second part of the ninth century in the *Saxon Chronicle*.[1] It cannot be ascribed to Bede, nor is it a reproach to this master of chronology to have committed some mistakes in referring the manifold kinds of dating of his authorities to a single era applicable everywhere. It was an idea full of great consequences for the future, although the application of his principle brought about some small inconsistencies and errors.

We have to accept Bede's chronology in general, and to weigh his different data when there are difficulties and contradictions. But with all respect to his ability and competence, it is incumbent on us to pay particular attention to any early sources which do not depend on him. Under this aspect I cannot agree with Dr. Poole on the date of the death of Wilfrid I of York (cf. Poole, *E.H.R.* xxxiv, 1919, pp. 22–4; *Studies*, pp. 80 f.). Bede ascribed it undoubtedly to the year 709 (*H.E.* v. 19, compared with cc. 20 and 24); but other data contradict his assertion and justify us in deviating from his authority, great as it is for an event which occurred during his lifetime and little more than twenty years before he finished his *Ecclesiastical History*. Eddi Stephanus, Wilfrid's biographer, who had known his hero for many years and whose work was also used by Bede, states that Wilfrid died on a Thursday, and mentions that an abbot (probably Tatbercht of Ripon, to whom, together with Bishop Acca of Hexham, the biography is inscribed) celebrated 'quintam feriam in qua obiit' like a Sunday in every week (*Vita Wilfridi*, c. 64, *SS. rer. Merov.* vi. 260; ed. Colgrave, p. 140, c. 65). The exact day is neither mentioned by Eddi nor by Bede; but the oldest English calendars agree on 24 April. The 'Metrical Martyrology', which was sometimes wrongly referred to Bede but was composed in the second part of the eighth century in northern England, perhaps at York, clearly says that Wilfrid departed for Heaven on this day.[2] A calendar of the early ninth century from the monastery of Lorsch, which also contains other obits from Northumbria, ascribes the 'Depositio domni Wilfridi et Egberti (d. 729, 24 April; cf. Bede, *H.E.* v. 22, p. 347) et Melliti' (d. 624, 24 April; cf. ib. ii. 7, p. 95) to the same day.[3] The 'Old English Martyrology' of the ninth

---

[1] Cf. M. L. R. Beaven, 'The Beginning of the Year in the Alfredian Chronicle, 866–87' (*E.H.R.* xxxiii, 1918, pp. 328–42); A. H. Smith, *The Parker Chronicle* (832–900), London, 1935, pp. 10 ff.

[2] H. Quentin, *Les Martyrologes historiques du moyen âge*, p. 124; A. Wilmart, 'Un témoin anglo-saxon du calendrier métrique d'York (*Rev. Bén.* xlvi, 1934, p. 66).

[3] Cf. M. Manitius, *Neues Archiv*, xxii, 1897, p. 764, from Berlin MS. Lat. no. 131 (Phillipps no. 1869). On the MS. (later in St. Maximin's of Trier) cf. also V. Rose, loc. cit. i, pp. 293 ff.; P. Miesges, *Der Trierer Festkalender*, Dissertation of Bonn (= Trierisches Archiv, Ergänzungsheft xv), 1915, p. 8.

century[1] and a northern calendar in the Bodleian Library, Digby MS. 63, of the later part of the same century,[2] similarly commemorate Wilfrid on 24 April; no sources of the eighth, ninth, and early tenth centuries give another day. Only about the year 970 calendars begin to inscribe his name, side by side with 24 April, under 12 October, or under this day alone,[3] which was a Saturday in 709 and may represent the day of a translation, either by Oswald of York (972–92)[4] or perhaps by Oda of Canterbury[5] (942–58); for the earliest calendars which place Wilfrid's name under this date belong to southern England. Now the 24th of April was a Thursday in 710 but a Wednesday in 709; the assumption that Wilfrid died in the later part of Wednesday is an evasion from the transmitted data, not to mention other conjectures even more improbable.[6] The date in the earliest calendars and the weekday mentioned by Eddi coincide in 710; the difference from the date derived from Bede is only one year. The balance of probability therefore appears, in my opinion, to be in favour of 710.[7]

---

[1] Ed. G. Herzfeld, Early English Text Society, cxvi, 1900, p. 60. On a Wessex fragment of the 9th century see 'The New Palaeographical Society', Second Series (1913–30), vol. i, pl. 102.

[2] F. Wormald, *English Kalendars before A.D. 1100*, vol. i (H. Br. Soc. lxxii), 1934, p. 5.

[3] The earliest examples known to me are ib., pp. 25, 53, 67. There are many more commemorations of this day in the same book and in the editor's later volume, *English Benedictine Kalendars after A.D. 1100*, vol. i (ib. lxxvii), 1939. Cf. *SS. rer. Merov.* vi, p. 179, n. 1.

[4] Wormald (1939), p. 164.   [5] Cf. *SS. rer. Merov.* vi, p. 189, n. 4.

[6] Another day also found some favour as the day of Wilfrid's death, 3 October, which was a Thursday in 709. This date was initiated by a mistake of Raine, as Colgrave, loc. cit., p. 186, has already stated. MS. B. IV. 24 of the Durham Cathedral Library of the late 11th century contains at fols. 12v–39 a martyrology; there (fol. 21) an entry under 24 April was partly written by a contemporary hand on an erasure: 'Eodem die sanctorum episcoporum Melliti et Wilfridi in Brittannia.' Then a hand of the 12th century made at fol. 34 in the margin an addition at the end of iiii. Idus Octobris: 'In Brittannia sancti Wilfridi episcopi.' Stevenson, *Liber Vitae ecclesiae Dunelmensis* (Surtees Society, vol. xiii), 1841, p. 146, and Colgrave, loc. cit., referred this marginal note to the following day, iii. Id. Oct. It belongs rather to the end of the previous day, to which Thomas Rud has attributed it, *Codicum MSS. ecclesiae cathedralis Dunelmensis catalogus*, Durham, 1825, p. 217, and is nothing but one of the many entries of Wilfrid's name under 12 October. Raine in W. H. Dixon, *Fasti Eboracenses*, i, London, 1863, p. 81, quoted the *Liber Vitae* edition but omitted by negligence 'Idus' and thus created the most convenient date for Wilfrid's day, repeated by W. Bright, *Chapters of Early English Church History*, 3rd ed., 1897, p. 479, n. 1, and by Plummer, *Baedae Op. hist.* ii, p. 328. The 3rd of October therefore must be absolutely dropped. Nor can a conclusion be drawn from the recitation of the Psalter at Wilfrid's deathbed; cf. Poole, *Studies*, pp. 47 f.

[7] Cf. what I have said *SS. rer. Merov.* vi. 178. But I would now ascribe Wilfrid's stay at Meaux, his return to England, and the death of King Aldfrid to 704, not to 705 (cf. above, p. 274); the result remains the same.

VII

ON THE CORRESPONDENCE OF BONIFACE AND LULLUS

The last and best edition of the correspondence of Boniface and Lullus was the work of Michael Tangl: *Die Briefe des heiligen Bonifatius und Lullus*, Berlin, 1916 (vol. I of the *Epistolae selectae* of the *MG.*).[1] It surpassed the earlier modern editions by Jaffé (1866) and Dümmler (1892) in several respects and may be considered as almost final, though Tangl himself made a few corrections and additions in his articles which accompanied or rather followed the edition: 'Studien zur Neuausgabe der Bonifatius-Briefe' (*Neues Archiv*, xl, 1916, pp. 639–790; xli, 1917–19, pp. 23–101).[2] The manuscripts were anew collated and described, not only the three early manuscripts of Munich (1), Karlsruhe (2), and Vienna (3), but also the later texts found in a 'family' of the codices of the Pseudo-Isidorian Decretals (4),[3] in Otloh's Life of St. Boniface (5), and in late copies of a lost Roman manuscript of S. Maria sopra Minerva (6), in which letters of Pope Nicholas I were added. The relations between the manuscripts were more exactly stated by Tangl than ever before; the principal manuscripts were referred to underlying earlier collections of the letters or, in the case of the Vienna manuscript, to gleanings of first drafts and original letters which were found by the scribe at Mainz about the middle of the ninth century. An expert in diplomatics as Tangl was, he paid regard to the style, the 'dictatus', of the texts and established the chronology of undated letters and the authorship of anonymous documents with greater probability than his predecessors, though one may occasionally question his opinions in details.

Many of the original letters sent to England must have existed there for a while; but only a few have left any traces. The continental tradition of nos. 73 and 78, letters of Boniface addressed to King Ethelbald of Mercia and Archbishop Cuthbert of Canterbury, derives from incomplete drafts or copies, while the English tradition originated from the finished originals. This form of no. 73, though somewhat abbreviated, is known from William of Malmesbury (*Gesta regum*, i. 80, 81, ed. Stubbs, i, pp. 80–2); the complete address and

---

[1] Tangl's numbers of the letters are identical with those of Dümmler's edition, *MG. Epist.* iii. 215–431.

[2] Cf. also Tangl, *Bonifatiusfragen* (Abhandl. Berlin, 1919, no. 2); E. Perels, 'Hinkmar von Reims und die Bonifatiusbriefe' (*Neues Archiv*, xlviii, 1930, pp. 156–60).

[3] Tangl, *Neues Archiv*, xl. 790 added a copy of this class, Rheims no. 672 of the 13th century, not used for his edition.

the final salutation were preserved by the author of the first *Vita Ecgwini*.[1] William of Malmesbury also mentioned no. 78 (ib. i. 82, p. 82; *Gesta pontif.* i. 6, ed. Hamilton, p. 11); Spelman printed the whole text, as it had reached England, from Cotton MS. Otho A. I of the second part of the eighth century. The greater portion of this volume was destroyed when the Cottonian library was burnt in 1731; but eight damaged leaves survived, including two (fols. 5, 6) of letter no. 78, which have not been employed by Tangl.[2] Letter no. 10, in which Boniface told the vision of a monk of Wenlock, gave him a place among the forerunners of Dante.[3] An altered version of this text in Italian manuscripts of the *Vitae Patrum* of about 1100 and of the fifteenth century[4] was mentioned by Tangl in an addition (p. 320 and p. xxxi, n. 2). In the meantime an Anglo-Saxon version was published by K. Sisam (*The Modern Language Review*, xviii, 1923, pp. 253–72) from Cotton MS. Otho C. I of the eleventh century. The text is obviously independent of the continental tradition.

One piece has to be added to the correspondence of Boniface. A letter by which an anonymous writer dedicated a grammatical compilation to a certain Sigeberht has recently been shown to be the work of Boniface intended as a dedication of his grammatical treatise; cf. above, p. 70, n. 1. It refers to the picture poem which 'Vynfreth' prefixed to this compilation, mentioning his pupil Dudd as his helper (*MG. Poetae*, i. 16 f.).[5] A future editor will have to

[1] *BHL.* i, no. 2432. Tangl knew only the extracts printed by Macray from Cotton MS. Nero E. 1, but not the almost complete edition of this legendary Life published by Giles, *Vita quorundam Anglo-Saxonum*, London (Caxton Society), 1854, pp. 349–96 (the quotations from the letter, p. 360). I would refer the differences of the English tradition not to changes made by Archbishop Egbert of York, as Tangl conjectured, but to the definitive text of the letter, as it reached England, and a future editor should also distinguish the shortened text of Malmesbury and the variant readings of the *Vita Ecgwini*; Tangl's 'apparatus' is there incomplete and perhaps misleading, though he made a correction himself among the additions, p. 321.   [2] Cf. *Neues Archiv*, xl, 714 f.; above, p. 86, n. 1.

[3] Some motifs of this letter and of the similar one, no. 115, derive from the Dialogues of Gregory the Great and from the Vision of St. Paul (ed. Th. Silverstein, *Studies and Documents*, edited by K. and S. Lake, iv, London, 1935), which both greatly influenced this kind of literature. Similar passages of Bede quoted by Tangl also derive from Gregory. There is a text of the *Visio Pauli* (3rd version) not used by the editor, in two MSS. of Caesarius of Heisterbach, ed. A. Hilka, *Die Wundergeschichten des Caes. von Heisterb.* (Publikationen der Gesellschaft für Rheinische Geschichtskunde, xliii), vol. iii, Bonn, 1937, pp. 150–3 (cf. p. 443).

[4] See my note, *Neues Archiv*, xxxii, 1907, pp. 380–5. Cf. Tangl, ib. xl. 723.

[5] Not only does Dudd occur as abbot in a letter of Boniface of 735 (no. 34, p. 58) and in a Glastonbury charter of 744 (Birch, i, no. 168) mentioned by H. Hahn, *Bonifaz und Lul*, pp. 164 ff., and by Tangl, but 'signum manus Duddi abbatis' was also added to a charter of King Ethelhard of Wessex granted in 739 for the foundation of a monastery at Crediton (Napier and Stevenson, *The Crawford Collection of Early Charters*, p. 3, no. 1; Birch, iii, no. 1331).

include this letter in the correspondence of Boniface; it is the earliest letter of his that exists.

On the letter of Lullus containing his profession of faith see above, pp. 233 ff.

The copyist of the Vienna manuscript not only admitted letters from and to Aldhelm and rhythmical poems of Æthilwald, which Tangl did not repeat in view of Ehwald's edition of Aldhelm's works (*Auct. ant.* xv, 1913–19), but he also inserted the letter of Isidore of Seville to Maso (Migne, *P.L.* lxxxiii. 899–902); all the modern editors of the correspondence of Boniface and Lullus omitted this letter as alien from their subject. But they included, at least in a note, the fragment of a 'treatise', which follows this letter of the Spanish scholar in the Vienna manuscript (Tangl, p. 288). A future editor might drop this text also without hesitation. It is nothing but a fragment of Isidore's work *De ecclesiasticis officiis*, ii. 5, §§ 14–15 (Migne, loc. cit., col. 784 f.) taken from his chapter on the episcopal dignity, which was used in Lindisfarne about 700 to describe the qualities of St. Cuthbert (cf. above, p. 67, n. 3) and was also copied at the synod of Aachen in 816 to describe the qualifications of a 'sacerdos' (*Institutio canonicorum*, c. 9, *MG. Concilia*, ii. 322 ff.).

The same work of Isidore has left another trace in our correspondence (no. 134, pp. 272 f.). For a letter of Bishop Megingoz of Würzburg, who succeeded the Anglo-Saxon Burchard during the last years of Boniface and died before 769,[1] can also be elucidated from this source. Megingoz asked Bishop Lullus for his opinion on a question of marriage law and compared the conflicting views of Isidore and Jerome, Augustine and Pope Leo I. The latter quotations have been identified, and the citation from Jerome was referred to his Commentary on St. Matthew (Book III on c. xix. 9, Migne, *P.L.* xxvi. 135). But the reference to Isidore has not been explained, the threefold association of whose name with that of Jerome might have given a clue: 'Essidorus ac Hieronimus', 'apud Essidorum vero vel Iheronimum', 'et Hisidori vel Hieronimi ac Leonis decretum'. The source of Megingoz was Isidore, *De ecclesiasticis officiis*, ii. 20, § 11 (col. 813), who copied and quoted Jerome's Commentary. Megingoz did not directly use the latter's work but borrowed Jerome's name and opinion from Isidore, whose book exists also to-day at Würzburg

---

[1] Cf. my edition of the *Vitae S. Bonifatii*, pp. ix f. Lately Marcel Beck has tried to show that Burchard died in 791 or shortly before, and that Megingoz and his successor Berowelp were not diocesan bishops but 'missionary' bishops acting side by side with Burchard (Beck and H. Büttner, *Studien und Vorarbeiten zur Germania pontificia*, iii, Berlin, 1937, pp. 168–73). But this opinion is untenable; cf. P. Schöffel, 'Zum Todesjahr Burchards' (*Zeitschr. für bayerische Kirchengeschichte*, xii, 1937, pp. 148–52).

in an 'insular' manuscript (Mp. Theol. Q. 18) of the eighth to ninth century formerly belonging to the cathedral of that city.[1]

There are some other quotations or allusions in this correspondence which have not yet been traced but can be identified (I do not refer to several biblical allusions); some of them enlarge the list of 'Books known to Anglo-Latin writers from Aldhelm to Alcuin', which J. D. A. Ogilvy has composed (cf. p. 134):—

No. 14, p. 24. 16: 'ut dicitur: Quid dulcius est, quam habeas illum, cum quo omnia possis loqui ut tecum'; no. 78, p. 161. 32: 'amicum, cum quo possit loqui quasi cum semet ipso'; Alcuin, *Epist.* 78 (*MG. Epist.* iv. 119. 22, with indication of the source). From Pseudo-Seneca, *De moribus*, 20 (*Senecae Opera*, ed. Haase, iii. 463), who draws on Cicero, *Laelius*, c. 6. 22, as Ed. Woelfflin has pointed out, *Publilii Syri Sententiae*, Lipsiae, 1869, p. 138. Cf. Ogilvy, p. 80.

Ib., p. 25. 24: 'Aaron, id est mons fortitudinis.' From Jerome, *Liber interpretationis nominum Hebraicorum* (ed. Lagarde, *Onomastica sacra*, 1870, p. 12), often repeated. Cf. Ogilvy, p. 53.

Ib., p. 26. 5: 'ut tua rescripta trans pontum dirigere digneris.' Cf. Aldhelm, *Carm. de virginit.* 2190 (p. 443): 'cum pia *trans pontum* pulsaret carta magistrum.'

No. 34, p. 58. 23: 'sapientis cuiusdam sententiae, qui dixit: Serva antiquum amicum.' From Ecclus. ix. 14: 'Ne derelinquas amicum antiquum'?

No. 63, p. 131. 27: 'Habes, pater mi, sicut Antonius de Didimo fertur dixisse, oculos, quibus potest Deus videri et angeli eius. . . .' From Cassiodorus's *Historia Tripartita*, viii. 8 (Migne, *P.L.* lxix. 1115).

No. 64, pp. 135. 32–136. 5, on 'utilis simulatio', largely derives from Augustine, *De mendacio*, c. 8, and more from his work *Ad Consentium de mendacio*, cc. 13. 27 f. and 10. 24 (*CSEL.* xli. 422, 507 f., 500 f.). Cf. Ogilvy, p. 18.

No. 78, p. 162. 8: 'a quo solo ('sola' first hand of MS. 2) sancta desideria, recta consilia et iusta sunt opera.' Jaffé referred these words to the Roman Processional; but there the word 'solo' is missing, as it is in Alcuin's appendix to the Gregorian Sacramentary, c. 85 (ed. H. A. Wilson, *The Gregorian Sacramentary under Charles the Great,* H. Br. Soc. xlix, 1915, p. 200: *Missa pro pace*) and in later texts such as the 'Sacramentarium Fuldense saeculi X.' (ed. Richter and Schönfelder, loc. cit., p. 224, § 1961: 'Missa pro pace'), and the Wulfstan Collectar (ed. E. S. Dewick and W. H. Frere, 'The Leofric Collectar', H. Br. Soc. lvi, 1921, p. 555). The exact words of Boniface,

---

[1] Beeson, 'Isidor-Studien', loc. cit., p. 51. Perhaps 'official(e)' in a Würzburg catalogue of about 800 (E. A. Lowe, *Speculum*, iii, 1928, pp. 6 and 8, no. 18) has been rightly identified with this work. There are other early insular MSS. of Isidore's work at Basel (from Fulda) and Leningrad (from Corbie), Beeson, pp. 50, 52.

including 'solo' or 'sola', are found in the Gelasian Sacramentary, in its earlier form, iii. 7 (ed. Wilson, Oxford, 1894, p. 228) and in the Frankish form of the eighth century; cf. K. Mohlberg, 'Das fränkische Sacramentarium Gelasianum in alamannischer Überlieferung' (*Liturgiegeschichtliche Quellen*, i–ii), Münster, 1918, p. 167, c. 196, § 1082; P. de Puniet, 'Le Sacramentaire romain de Gellone' (*Ephemerides Liturgicae*, xlix, 1935, pp. 326 f., c. 205. 2 = § 780).

No. 81, p. 181. 19: 'quia in septenario numero perfecti sepe designantur.' Cf. Augustine, *De civitate Dei*, xi. 31 (cf. xvii. 4. 4); *Quaestiones in Heptateuchum*, ii. 107 (*CSEL*. xxviii. 2, p. 163); Isidore, *Liber numerorum*, c. 8. 35 (Migne, *P.L.* lxxxiii. 186), &c.

No. 83, p. 187. 7: 'ut, dum subesse didicerit, postmodum moderate praeesse sciat.' Cf. Gregory, *Dialog.* i. 1 (ed. Moricca, p. 19): '*ut praeesse* non audeat, qui *subesse* non *dedicerit*.'

No. 104, p. 228. 21: 'Et, sicut sanctus Augustinus dixit, licet unus sit in oriente et alius in occidente, conglutinata caritate numquam ab invicem separantur.' From Caesarius of Arles, *Sermo*, 29. 1 (ed. G. Morin, *Sancti Caesarii episcopi Arelatensis Opera*, i. 1, Maredsous, 1937, p. 120 = *Augustini sermonum append.* 107, Migne, *P.L.* xxxix, 1957), who has the reading 'conglutinante'.[1]

No. 149, pp. 287 f. The two or rather three prayers which follow the fragment of Isidore (above, p. 282) in the Vienna MS. are so-called 'apologiae', confessions of the priest preparing himself for celebrating the mass (cf. F. Cabrol, *Dictionnaire d'archéol. chrét. et de liturgie*, i. 2, col. 2591 ff.). The first of these texts of private devotion is found elsewhere also, in the *Libellus precum* of Fleury (Orléans MS. 184 of the tenth century; Migne, *P.L.* ci. 1408), the Leofric Missal (ed. F. E. Warren, Oxford, 1883, p. 8), the *Missa Latina* of Flacius (Wolfenbüttel, Helmstedt MS. 115), and in MSS. of St. Gatianus of Tours and of Salzburg (E. Martene, *De antiquis ecclesiae ritibus*, i, Bassano, 1788, pp. 179, 193, 207). There is also a retouched version (recognizable by the insertion of 'redemptor mundi' after the beginning 'Domine Iesu Christe', ib., pp. 207, 209, 212; M. Gerbert, *Monumenta veteris liturgiae Alemannicae*, i, 1777, pp. 350 f.). I have not found another text of the second and third prayers; formulas in the 'Sacramentarium Fuldense' (loc. cit., p. 255, § 2205), the 'Missa Latina' of Flacius, and a Stavelot MS. from Verdun (Martene, loc. cit. i. 183, 212) partly correspond with the second prayer. The beginning of this latter: 'Suscipe, clementissime pater, hostiam placationis et laudis, quas tibi offero . . . .', derives from an early formula; cf. the Gelasian Sacramentary (ed. Wilson, pp. 197, 304,

---

[1] Boniface wrote possibly 'conglutinati'. Cf. Dag Norberg, *In Registrum Gregorii Magni studia critica*, thesis of Uppsala, 1937, p. 75.

355; Mohlberg, loc. cit., p. 178, § 1161), the *Missale Gothicum*, c. 278 (ed. Bannister, *H. Br. Soc.*, vol. lii, 1917, p. 82, and vol. liv, 1919, p. 65), Alcuin's *Liber sacramentorum*, c. 17 (Migne, *P.L.* ci. 461), the fragment of an Irish sacramentary of the ninth century from Reichenau (ed. H. M. Bannister, *J.T.S.* v, 1904, p. 56, l. 14), a sacramentary of St. Gall (Gerbert, loc. cit. i. 282, n. 1), the 'Sacramentarium Fuldense' (loc. cit., p. 260, § 2245), the 'Sacramentarium Rossianum' (ed. J. Brinktrine, *Römische Quartalschrift, Supplementheft*, xxv, 1930, pp. 168, 174, cc. 301. 2, 322. 2), and the Leofric Missal, p. 190, &c.

Two formulas of salutation which occur in several of the letters can be referred to their origin. The *Actus Silvestri*, that pseudo-historical Roman composition of late fifth century,[1] had an immense influence during the whole Middle Ages; it was read in England also, where it was known to Aldhelm, to the Lindisfarne biographer of St. Cuthbert, and to Bede. Two parts of this story are connected by a (fabricated) correspondence between the Empress Helena and her son Constantine the Great (Mombritius, *Sanctuarium*, new edition, Paris, 1910, ii. 515). The subject of these letters does not concern us here, only their closing formulas (I omit variant readings):

'Vale, domine, augustorum pater, semper auguste, fili carissime, et prosperis ad vota successibus polle.'

'Vale, domina mater, semper augusta, et cum filiis meis prosperis ad vota successibus polle.'

These letters were used as models; they were admitted as such into the formula book of Flavigny (*MG. Formulae*, ed. Zeumer, pp. 473 f.), and the words 'prosperis–successibus' became a favourite phrase of Aldhelm's (ed. Ehwald, pp. 293. 22, 298. 6, 302. 11, 303. 1). Their influence is similarly perceptible in the Boniface correspondence:

No. 14, p. 26: '*Vale . . . et prosperis successibus polle . . .*'

No. 13, p. 21: '*Vale* iugiter *prosperis successibus . . .*'

No. 34, p. 59: '*Vale*re dilectionem beatitudinis tuae *et prosperis successibus* proficere in Christo optamus.'

No. 37, p. 62: '*Vale*re te iugiter *prosperis successibus* in Christo opto.'

No. 38, p. 63: '*Vale*re beatitudinem vestram *et* sanctis *successibus* proficere in Christo diligenter optamus.'

No. 70, p. 143: 'Bene *vale*re te desidero *et* sanctis *successibus* proficere in Christo optamus.'

No. 39, p. 64: 'Longe vos in fide catholica *et* felicis *successibus* florere faciat omnipotentis Dei gloria.'

---

[1] See my paper, 'Konstantinische Schenkung und Silvester-Legende' (*Miscellanea Francesco Ehrle*, ii = *Studi e Testi*, xxxviii, Rome, 1924, pp. 159–247), and the supplementary note, 'Kirchenrechtliches in den Actus Silvestri' (*Savigny-Zeitschr.* xlvi, 1926, *Kan. Abt.* xv. 501–11).

Perhaps Aldhelm originated the fashion of this formula, though no
letter of his with this kind of salutation has survived.[1]

Undoubtedly he influenced another formula used in the superscription of letters. He concluded the 'inscriptio' of his letter to King
Geruntius with the words (Ehwald, p. 481. 2) 'optabilem in Domino
salutem', that of the dedication of his prose work on Virginity
(p. 229. 6) with 'optabilem perpetuae prosperitatis salutem' (cf.
Aldhelm's charter of 705, ib., p. 515. 16; Birch, i, no. 114: 'cum
optabili famosissimi regis Ini consensu').[2] The Boniface correspondence shows that he found followers in this form of salutation:

Nos. 36, 71, 72 (pp. 61. 4, 144. 7, 145. 9): '*optabilem in Domino salutem.*'
No. 130 (p. 268. 2): '*optabilem* supplex *in Domino* sempiternae beatitudinis
    salutem.'
Nos. 48, 96, 131, 137 (pp. 77. 2, 217. 3, 269. 17, 275. 29): '*optabilem in*
    Christo *salutem.*'
No. 98 (p. 219. 4): '*in* angulari lapide, Christo videlicet, *optabilem salutem.*'
Nos. 32–5, 59, 63, 78, 86, 94, 106, 108, 109 (pp. 55. 19, 56. 26, 58. 20,
    60. 7, 110. 5, 129. 2, 161. 29, 192. 1, 214. 13, 231. 28, 233. 26, 235. 1):
    '*optabilem in* Christo (aeternae, intimae, inmarcescibilis) caritatis *salutem.*'
No. 142 (p. 281. 21): '*in* Christo *optabilem* sempiternae sospitatis *salutem*'
    (cf. Aldhelm, p. 61. 6: '*immarcescibilem sempiternae sospitatis* salutem';
    Tangl, pp. 3. 8, 78. 13, cf. p. 192, n. 1).
No. 120 (p. 256. 7): '*obtabilem* sospitatem.'

The copyists of the Boniface and Lullus correspondence found
some difficulties in transcribing and understanding their exemplars,
as Tangl's collected materials show (*Neues Archiv*, xl. 652–62). Here
are a few more emendations (most readers may themselves have
restored the misprinted words p. 47. 5 'si tibi'; 139. 5 'tribulatio'):

No. 41, p. 66. 14: 'in certo.' The emendation by H. Boehmer,
'Zur Geschichte des Bonifatius' (loc. cit., p. 207, n. 2) 'incepto'
(or rather 'in coepto') is probably right.

No. 57, p. 103. 6: 'Et eorum (apostolorum) sequi pedem . . . tuam
sanctissimam fraternitatem in partibus illis esse credimus destinatam.'
I combine 'sequipedem'. Cf., e.g., *Liber Diurnus*, 83 (ed. Sickel,
p. 92. 14): 'ut vere eorum discipulus et sequipeda', 84 (p. 102. 14):
'eorum in omnibus esse sequipedam'; the Lives of the Popes Zacharias, c. 14, and Stephen II, c. 36 (*Liber Pontificalis*, ed. Duchesne, i,
p. 430. 11, 450. 12): 'sequipes factus est suis missis', 'sequipes etiam
eius . . . factus'; *Vita Sollemnis*, c. 1 (*SS. rer. Merov.* vii, p. 312. 3):
'eorum sequipedes', &c. (cf. *Bonner Jahrbücher*, ciii, 1898, p. 78, n. 3;

---

[1] Cf. also the privilege of King Ethelbald of Mercia of 749 (Birch, i, no. 178;
H. and S. iii, p. 386): 'quatenus sublimitas regni eius *prosperis successibus polleat.*'
Alcuin, *Epist.* 178 (p. 294. 12) similarly employed the phrase 'prosperis successibus
pollere'.
                                                  [2] Cf. also above, p. 223, n. 3.

Aldhelm, ed. Ehwald, p. 703). 'Sequipeda' of the first declension is more usual. Cf. also Larson, loc. cit., pp. 123 f.

No. 78, p. 166. 5: 'doctori' is the reading of 1 and Spelman (Cotton MS. Otho A. I), accepted by Tangl (cf. *Neues Archiv*, xl, 656); 'doti' after an empty space 3; 'sacerdoti' 2, 6, rightly. For 'sacerdoti' is the reading of the source, which is largely transcribed in this letter, Julianus Pomerius's work *De vita contemplativa*. In the archetype 'sacer' was obviously supplied between the lines or in the margin and was overlooked by some copyists; 'doctori' is a correction of 'doti', suggested by the preceding sentence.

Ib., l. 24: 'non quod humanus sensus invenerit' Tangl with 2; but 1, 3 and Spelman have 'humani sensus', rightly. For Pomerius has ' non quod praesumptio humani sensus invenerit'. The word 'praesumptio' was evidently missing in the archetype, perhaps overlooked by Boniface himself when he made extracts from Pomerius; but it was omitted against his intention, as the genitive 'humani sensus' shows, and has to be inserted.

Ib., p. 168, l. 1: 'quod' Tangl with 3; 'qui' 2, 6; 'quae' 1; 'qᴆ.' Cotton Otho A. I according to Spelman. Pomerius has the reading 'quando', which is required by the connexion. An abbreviation of this word, perhaps 'qñ' or 'qñd', might have given rise to the variants, the more so because the word 'non' follows (missing in 3), possibly written 'ñ'. On the abbreviations of 'quando' cf. L. Traube, *Nomina Sacra*, 1907, p. 263; W. M. Lindsay, *Notae Latinae*, 1915, pp. 219 ff.

No. 83, p. 187. 2: 'a congregatione quilibet eligatur, ab episcopo tamen consecretur et non a fundatore monasterii.' Tangl thought that 'substituatur' or a similar word is missing after 'monasterii'. Probably the words 'et non a fundatore monasterii' were supplied in the margin of the archetype (the 'Collectio pontificia') and inserted at the wrong place in MS. 2, which alone has preserved this letter of Pope Zacharias. If they are placed after 'eligatur', all difficulties disappear; the transcriber was misled by the ending '-tur' common to 'eligatur' and 'consecretur'.

No. 84, p. 188. 22: 'distincte incursa et vigilantius in quo angelicas et beati domini mei et singillatim protulimus aures.' This sentence in the difficult letter of the Roman archdeacon Theophylactus is restored by two slight emendations. I write 'incussa' for 'incursa' ('the things distinctly intimated'); 'incutere' has the same meaning as 'inculcare' in no. 105 (p. 229. 16: 'haec vel maxime auditui nostro inculcare curavit'). The misreading of *r* for *s* occurred also in other letters (cf. Tangl, *Neues Archiv*, xl, 654, 658 f.). Further I correct 'quo angelicas' by joining the two words and changing the last letter: 'quoangelicae' (= coangelici). The word 'coangelicus' was one of the official epithets applied to the Popes in the eighth and ninth centuries (cf. Du Cange, s.v. 'angelus'); cf., e.g., the Life of Stephen II in the *Liber Pontificalis*, cc. 25, 36, 50 (ed. Duchesne, i, pp. 447.12, 450. 15, 455. 13): 'ipsius quoangelici ('quoangelicae' MSS. B) papae', 'beatissimus et coangelicus papa', 'coangelici ('coangelicae' and—B[3.6]—'quoangelicae' B) papae'; the Roman synod of 769 (*MG. Concilia*, ii. 80. 2): 'ter beatissimo et coangelico Stephano summo pontifice'; report on the Roman 'colloquy' of 810 (ib., p. 240. 22): 'domnum Leonem sanctissimum et coangelicum papam urbis Romae'; letter of the same Theophylactus (Tangl, no. 85, p. 190. 14): 'sancto coangelico patre vestro domno apostolico.' The spelling of *quo-* for *co-* and of *-ae* for *-i* is confirmed by the B-MSS. of the *Liber Pontificalis* quoted above. The misreading of the ending *-as* for *-ae* might be referred to the form of *e* in the early script of the Roman curia. We find the same substitution some lines later, p. 189. 8: 'non tantum *occiduas*, sed usque quaque floreant nationes.' But here the transmitted form may be original; for there are other examples of the ending *-as* used in late 'vulgar' Latin and also in Rome with the function of the nominative of the plural of the *a*-declension.[1]

No. 122, a letter of Bishop Eardulf of Rochester, mentions a messenger sent by him to Lullus (p. 259. 27): 'fratrem nostrum fidelissimum presbyterum nomine Laearoredum.' This was evidently misread by the scribe of the unique copy, the Vienna MS. (3); the real name was obviously 'Heardredum' (cf., e.g., Birch, *Index Saxonicus*, pp. 89 f.): the copyist mistook the letter *h* for *la* and the round, uncial form of *d* (ð) for *o*.[2]

In another letter to Lullus, no. 72 (p. 145), which is also transmitted by the Vienna MS., the name of the sender is misread: 'Ingalice indignus presbyter.' I cannot give an evident correction as in no. 122, but I venture to propose an attempt at emendation. One might think of names such as Ingeld (cf. nos. 55, 101, pp. 97. 29, 224. 29) or Inguuald; but another correction is simpler and more appropriate to most of the transmitted letters: 'In' could easily be misread for 'hi', and the name may have been Higelac (= Hygelac). The misreading of *ic* for an (open) *a* in the ending '-*lac*' would have a parallel in Willibald's *Vita Bonifatii*, c. 6 (ed. Levison, p. 31. 13), where in the second class of the manuscripts the name of 'Gaesmere' (Geismar) was changed into 'Gicesmere' (as vice versa p. 26. 19 'Dettic' into 'Detta' in 2a. b); cf. ib., p. xxxiv. The substitution of the last letter *e* for *c* would have been a minor consequence of this misreading.

On no. 146 cf. above, p. 130, n. 2.

[1] Cf. Norberg, loc. cit., pp. 56 ff., 74.

[2] In Alcuin's *Epist.* 71 (p. 114) 'Nordberet' is similarly to be substituted for 'Noroberet'.

For my edition of the *Vitae sancti Bonifatii* (in *SS. rer. Germ.*), Hanover, 1905, I have used or examined and classified all manuscripts of his medieval Lives which were known to me. A few escaped my knowledge or only came to light subsequently. I take this opportunity of briefly indicating them for the benefit of a future editor. I omit small extracts without any independent value.

To the group 2*a*, *b* of the Life of Boniface by the Anglo-Saxon Willibald (pp. xix f.) should be added *Stuttgart* MS. Theol. et philos. fol. 95, written in the early ninth century in the monastery of Reichenau by the librarian Reginbert, who died in 846; it is the 10th volume in his list of books (ib., p. xxiii, n. 1). Willibald's work is read on fols. 17–28 v; but after fol. 17 several (six?) leaves are lost, and only pp. 1–4. 13 and pp. 22. 19–58. 41 of my edition have survived. Cf. K. Preisendanz, *Die Handschriften der Großherzogl. Badischen Hof- und Landesbibliothek in Karlsruhe*, vii, 2, 1918, p. 143.

To the second class also belongs *Berlin* MS. Theol. Lat. Fol. 730, written in the later part of the fifteenth century somewhere in the country near the lower Rhine, fols. 49 v–59 (cf. *Mitteilungen aus der Königlichen Bibliothek*, ii, Berlin, 1914, pp. 14 ff.; *SS. rer. Merov.* vii. 540 f., 559). The manuscript which I examined in 1915 (cf. my paper, 'Wilhelm Procurator von Egmond und seine Miracula Adalberti', *Neues Archiv*, xl, 1916, pp. 795 ff.) is related to the common ancestor of the MSS. 2*c* and 2*e*. Formerly Phillipps MS. no. 568.

The copy of Willibald in *Klosterneuburg* MS. no. 707 of the twelfth century, fol. 134 (cf. H. J. Zeibig, *Notizenblatt, Beilage zum Archiv für Kunde österreichischer Geschichtsquellen*, ii, 1852, p. 104), is probably connected with the manuscripts of the Austrian Legendary (4*c* in my edition, p. xxv; cf. *SS. rer. Merov.* vii. 534 f.).

A transcript of a lost manuscript from Corvey made in 1648 exists in *Brussels* MS. no. 2216–22, fols. 5–22. Cf. J. Van den Gheyn, *Catalogue des mss. de la Bibliothèque royale de Belgique*, v, 1905, p. 108, no. 3153; P. Lehmann, *Corveyer Studien* (Abhandl. München, xxx. 5), 1919, p. 56, no. 45.

Fragments of Willibald's work have been found in the Bavarian Record Office ('Reichsarchiv') at *Munich*, MS. no. 3*c* from Freising, fol. 8 1/2 (it ends on p. 41. 2 of my edition; cf. Th. Bitterauf, *Die Traditionen des Hochstifts Freising*, i, Munich, 1905, p. xxiii), and in the library of the Count of Mirbach in his castle of *Harff* (twelfth century; cf. L. Korth, *Annalen des Historischen Vereins für den Niederrhein*, lv, 1892, p. ix).

To the six manuscripts of the *Vita tertia Bonifatii* employed in my edition the *Brussels* MS. no. 858–61 of 1490, the first volume of the Legendary of Korssendonck, fols. 221–3, should be added. Cf. Van den Gheyn, loc. cit. v. 92, no. 3139, I.

The three manuscripts of the *Vita quinta* also require an addition: *Cambridge*, Fitzwilliam Museum, MS. no. 101 (Phillipps, no. 4182), from the monastery of Weingarten in Suabia (G 3 fol.), of the twelfth century, fols. 115–20. Cf. M. R. James, *A Descriptive Catalogue of the McClean Collection of MSS. in the Fitzwilliam Museum*, Cambridge, 1912, p. 228; Karl Löffler, *Die Handschriften des Klosters Weingarten* (Zentralblatt für Bibliothekswesen, Beiheft xli), Leipzig, 1912, p. 100.

Some copies supplement the manuscripts used in my edition of Otloh's *Vita Bonifatii*. One of the earliest was formerly in the library (now sold) of the Princes of Hohenzollern at *Sigmaringen*, no. 9, of about 1200, from the monastery of Weissenau near Ravensburg in Suabia, fols. 75–95 v; cf. *SS. rer. Merov.* vii. 681 f. According to a number of variant readings transmitted to me in 1918 by my former pupil Dr. Georg Zilliken, the text represents the third class of the manuscripts in my edition (p. lxxiv) and thus contains also the addition pp. 216. 20–217. 10. Later transcripts are to be found at *Strasburg*, University Library no. 205 (Latin 201) of the fifteenth century, from Buxheim, fols. 135–94 (*Catalogue général des mss. des bibliothèques publiques de France, Départements*, xlvii, 1923, p. 117), and at *Utrecht* in the Archiepiscopal Museum, a manuscript of 1508, from the Carthusian monastery near Utrecht, fols. 84–142, with the addition mentioned above (*Catalogus codicum mss. bibliothecae universitatis Rheno-Traiectinae*, ii, 1909, p. 266). K. O. Müller, *Neues Archiv*, xli, 1917–19, pp. 691–704, has published a detailed description of two leaves in the Archives of the 'Erbschenken von Limpurg' deposited in the Württembergian Archives ('Staatsfilialarchiv') at *Ludwigsburg*; they are fragments of a manuscript of the second class written about 1080, the earliest manuscript of Otloh's work, a part of which has survived.

A second copy of the *Hameln Legend* of St. Boniface (p. lxxx) in *Brussels* MS. no. 858–61 of 1490 (cf. above, p. 289), fols. 270 v–71, has been notified by Van den Gheyn, loc. cit., p. 93. Of a second transcript of the *Compilation of Fulda* (pp. lxxx ff.) in *Berlin* MS. Lat. Oct. 367 of 1532, fols. 7–15 v, Professor Dr. Karl Christ kindly informed me ten years ago; chapter 30 is missing in this copy, which was taken from a Fulda MS.

VIII

ST. BONIFACE AND CRYPTOGRAPHY[1]

MELCHIOR GOLDAST in the second part of his *Alamannicarum rerum scriptores*, first published at Frankfurt in 1606 (pp. 91–3; in the reprint of 1661, pp. 66–8, in the third edition by H. C. Senckenberg,

---

[1] Cf. W. Wattenbach, *Anleitung zur lateinischen Paläographie*, 4th ed., Leipzig, 1886, p. 12; Aloys Meister, *Die Anfänge der modernen diplomatischen Geheimschrift*,

of 1730, pp. 68–70), edited under the name of Hrabanus Maurus a
short treatise 'De inventione linguarum'; the text has been reprinted
among the works of this famous pupil of Alcuin's, who became abbot
of Fulda and, lastly, archbishop of Mainz (*Hrabani Mauri Opera*, ed.
G. Colvenerius, vi, Cologne, 1626, pp. 333–4; Migne, *P.L.* cxii.
1579–84). The authorship of Hrabanus has been doubted (Traube,
Vorles. i. 26), and we do not know on the authority of what manuscript
the first editor ascribed to him this little work. But I see no decisive
argument against this origin, and in any case the treatise appears
to be connected with the Fulda circle of the ninth century. The end
of the headline, 'linguarum', is probably a misreading for the word
'litterarum'; for the author does not concern himself with the invention of languages, but surveys certain alphabets,[1] in particular the
Hebrew, Greek, and Latin, that of the so-called Philosopher Aethicus
(cf. above, p. 42, n. 1), the runes of the 'Marcomanni quos nos
Nordmannos vocamus',[2] and adds also some abbreviations ('notae
Caesaris')[3] and monograms. A few lines refer to cryptic writing
and to St. Boniface's share in its diffusion. I reproduce this passage
but correct Goldast's text from the variant readings of a Vienna
MS. (no. 1761) of the eleventh century communicated by H. F.
Massmann, and of a Heidelberg MS. of the twelfth century (from
Salem) published by K. Bartsch (*Germania*, xvi, Vienna, 1871,
pp. 257 f.; xvii, 1872, pp. 407 f.):

$$A \quad E \quad I \quad O \quad V$$
$$: \quad \vdots \quad \cdot \quad :: \quad ::$$

·NC·P·T V:RS::·S B::N·F:C·· :RCH·:P·SC::P· GL::R·::S·Q:··:
M:RT·R·S·[4]

Genus vero huius descriptionis, tam quod supra cum punctis V et vocalibus
quam subtus cum aliis vocalibus quam solitum est informatum continetur,
fertur quod sanctus Bonifacius archiepiscopus ac martyr, ab[5] Angulsaxis

---

Paderborn, 1902, pp. 4 ff., and *Die Geheimschrift im Dienste der päpstlichen Kurie*
(Quellen und Forschungen aus dem Gebiete der Geschichte, xi), ib. 1906, pp. 12 ff.
Cf. also W. Süss, 'Ueber antike Geheimschreibemethoden und ihr Nachleben'
(*Philologus*, lxxviii, 1923, pp. 142–75); F. Stix, 'Geheimschriftenkunde als historische
Hilfswissenschaft' (*MÖIG.*, *Ergänzungs-Band*, xiv, 1939, pp. 453–9). Cf. above,
p. 138.

[1] Cf. M. Manitius, *Geschichte der lateinischen Literatur des Mittelalters*, i. 299.

[2] On the designation of the Vikings as Marcomanni cf. *SS. rer. Merov.* vii. 18, n. 3.

[3] Cf. Paul Lehmann, *Sammlungen und Erörterungen lateinischer Abkürzungen in Altertum und Mittelalter* (Abhandl. München, Neue Folge, no. iii), 1929, pp. 11 f., who
mentions Munich MS. Lat. 23577 of the 10th century.

[4] 'Incipit versus Bonifacii archiepiscopi gloriosique martiris.' In medieval practice the system of dots has sometimes different starting-points, either one dot
standing for *a*, two dots for *e*, three for *i*, &c., or one for *i*, two for *o*, three for *u*, four
for *a*, five for *e*.   [5] 'de' for 'ab' the Vienna MS. (Massmann).

veniens, hoc antecessoribus nostris demonstrarit.[1] Quod tamen non ab illo inprimis coeptum est, sed ab antiquis[2] istius modi usus crevisse comperimus.

A E I O V
B · F · K · P · X ·

kbrxs xp̄p fprtks tkrp knstbr sbffkrp brchktfnfns scfptrp rfgnk xt dfcxs bxrk.[3]

These two methods of 'secret' writing, single or combined, were used in the Middle Ages on both sides of the Channel. I cite a few English examples:

(1) 36th riddle of the Exeter Book; see R. W. Chambers, M. Förster, R. Flower, *The Exeter Book of Old English Poetry*, London, 1933, fol. 109*b* and p. 63; G. P. Krapp and E. Van Kirk Dobbie, *The Exeter Book*, New York, 1936, pp. 198, 341; Fr. Tupper, *The Riddles of the Exeter Book*, pp. 28 (no. 37), 154 ff.: 'monn· h·p·m· [for 'hpmp' = homo] þiif·m·x·l·kfþ [for 'mxlkfr' = mulier] f·hors· qxxs [for 'hors· fqxxs' = equus].

(2) Cotton MS. Titus D. XXVII of the early eleventh century, *Palaeographical Society* (1873–83), vol. iii, pl. 60; W. de G. Birch, *Liber vitae: Register and Martyrology of New Minster and Hyde Abbey, Winchester*, Hampshire Record Society, 1892, p. 275: 'Frbtfr hxmkllimus ft mpnbchxs aflsknxs mf scrkpskt. Skt kllk lpngb sblxs. Bm..n.' [= Frater humillimus et monachus Aelsinus me scripsit. Sit illi longa salus. Amen].

Aflfþknp mpnbchp aeqxf dfcbnp cpmpptxm kstxm ppsskdfp vel mf ppsskdft. Bmfn.' [= Aelfwino (vel -us) monacho (vel -us) aeque decano (vel -us) compotum istum possideo vel me possidet. Amen]. Ælfwine afterwards became abbot of Hyde Abbey (1035–57), Birch, pp. xxxi f. and 33, on his family pp. 273 f. There were under him 'Aelfsige sacerdos' and 'Aelfsige levita', pp. 33 f.

(3) Cotton MS. Vitellius E. XVIII of the early eleventh century, H. Wanley, *Librorum vett. septentrionalium . . . catalogus*, Oxford, 1705, p. 223; Birch, loc. cit., p. 275; M. Förster, *Archiv für das Studium der neueren Sprachen*, cxv, 1905, p. 392, and *Englische Studien*, xxxvi, 1906,

[1] 'demonstraret' Goldast and the Vienna MS.

[2] The system of substituting dots for the vowels was known as early as the 4th century B.C. See Aeneas Tacticus, c. 31, §§ 30–1 (Loeb Classical Library, 1923, p. 170); cf. Süss, loc. cit., pp. 163 f.

[3] 'Karus Christo fortis tiro instar saffiro architenens sceptro regni ut decus auri.' I have corrected the last word; Goldast has 'bxpf. feliciter. a.' (the last letter signifying 'Amen'?), the Heidelberg MS. (Bartsch) 'xt pfcxs axrk' (='ut pecus auri'. Bartsch has printed 'axrb', obviously by a mistake; for he adds the solution 'auri'). The Vienna MS. ends with 'brchktenens [*sic*] scrkptpr' (= architenens scriptor). The words 'arc(h)itenens' and 'tiro' are expressions used by Aldhelm (ed. Ehwald, pp. 563, 720), whose diction influenced Boniface (cf. above, p. 71); the latter employed 'architenens' in his poems, *MG. Poetae*, i, pp. 4 (v. 33), 16 (v. 34).

pp. 325 f.: (key to the method with this example) 'kn npmknf dk̄ sxmmk. Bmfn. Pftfr (for 'Pbtfr') npstfr, etc.' [= In nomine dī (= dei) summi. Amen. Pater noster, etc.].

I add some continental specimens:

(4) Both methods are employed passim in E. Steinmeyer and E. Sievers, *Die Althochdeutschen Glossen*, i–v, Berlin, 1879–1922; cf., e.g., ii. 27, 28, 30, 34, 37, 38, 54–64, 75, 105–7, 501–21, 747–58, 767–9, &c.

(5) Alcuin, *Propositiones ad acuendos iuvenes*, c. 26 (Migne, *P.L.* ci. 1152): 'Propositio de cursu cbnks bc fvgb lfp :rks' [= canis ac fuga leporis]. Under the name of Bede (ib. xc. 669) without secret script. Alcuin's authorship is questioned by C. W. Jones, *Bedae Pseudepigrapha*, Ithaca, 1939, pp. 51 f.

(6) Letter of L. (from Fleury, after 974) to Archbishop Dunstan (Stubbs, *Memorials of Saint Dunstan*, pp. 376 f.): 'ut commentum Flori, quod habet domnus abbas ::scbr:ˑ:s [= Oscarus, abbot of Abingdon, 963–84, who had been sent, when a monk, to Fleury], et alios libellos, qui habentur þknt::nke [=Wintonie] quique condam sui fuerunt (that is, were owned by L.), - - - illi reddere faciatis'; at the end 'P:rkod::s' [= Periodos]. Monks of Abingdon, who replaced in 964 the canons in Winchester cathedral, may have taken books with them.

(7) Note on the repair of the 'Codex aureus' of St. Emmeramm in Regensburg (Munich, Latin MS. no. 14000) under Abbot Ramwold (975–1001), G. Swarzenski, *Die Regensburger Buchmalerei des X. und XI. Jahrhunderts*, Leipzig, 1901, p. 30: 'D::mnⁱ ·bb·tⁱs r·mu::ldⁱ iuss:::ne hˑ:nc lⁱbr:ˑ:m ·r:p:: :t ·d·lp:rt:ˑ:s r:n::v·v:r:ˑ:nt. Sⁱs m:m::r :::r'' [= Domni abbatis Ramuoldi iussione hunc librum Aripo et Adalpertus renovaverunt. Sis memor eor(um)].

(8) Note by the scribe of British Museum, Addit. MS. no. 21917 of the eleventh century, from Luxeuil, *SS. rer. Merov.* vii. 608: 'Hbfc Stfphbnxs scrkpskt þ prfcfptb brchkmb̄tk mbgkstrk' [= Haec Stephanus scripsit p(er) precepta Archimb(er)ti magistri].

(9) Letter 26 of Fulbert of Chartres (Migne, *P.L.* cxli. 212) in MS. B. II. 11 of Durham Cathedral Library, written between 1081 and 1096, fol. 111 v, has the address: 'Frī thfpdfrkcp·fxlbfrtxs·sbcfrdps' [= Fr(atr)i Theoderico Fulbertus sacerdos].

These examples, which could easily be multiplied, coming from different countries and belonging to several centuries, show how much this rather futile trifling with a 'secret' script was in favour in the West during the Middle Ages. It should be rash to refer all continental examples to the teaching of St. Boniface, though none seems to be known earlier than his age; these simple methods may have been practised to some extent before and in the eighth century in Italy or Gaul. Nevertheless, there appears to be a substance of truth in the Fulda tradition, which a discovery by Bernhard Bischoff of Munich has recently in some measure confirmed. The important Lives of two other Anglo-Saxons and relatives of Boniface, Bishop Willibald of Eichstätt and his brother, Abbot Wynnebald of Heidenheim (cf. pp. 43, 81), were composed in the third part of the eighth century by an Anglo-Saxon nun of Heidenheim, whose name was unknown. The best manuscript of these biographies is the Monacensis Lat. no. 1086 of about 800, which also contains a good copy of the earliest Life of Boniface himself;[1] but all editors, including O. Holder-Egger,[2] failed to notice four strange lines written by the scribe of the manuscript between the Lives of Wynnebald and Willibald. They were discovered a few years ago and explained by Bischoff:[3]

> Seēdgquār·quīn·npr̄i·sprīxquār·ntēr·
> cpr̄i·nquār·mtēr·nsecūn·hquīn·gseēd
> bquīnrc·qārr·dinando·hseēdc·scr̄ter·
> bseēd·bprīm·

The idea underlying this cipher is the same as in the two cryptographic systems referred to Boniface. Here also the vowels were superseded, though not by the next consonants or by various numbers of dots, but by the abbreviated names of the first five ordinal numbers (e.g. *pri* for *a*, *quin* for *u*), and the groups of letters which appeared meaningless revealed the name of the authoress, Hugeburc: 'Ego una Saxonica nomine Hugeburc ordinando hec scribebam.'[4] This example is hitherto unique, but it corresponds so much with the methods ascribed to the teaching of Boniface that it may be regarded without hesitation as a confirmation of that tradition.

[1] See my edition of the *Vitae S. Bonifatii*, pp. xvii f.   [2] Cf. above, p. 43, n. 4.
[3] 'Wer ist die Nonne von Heidenheim?' (*Studien und Mitteilungen zur Geschichte des Benediktiner-Ordens*, xlix, 1931, pp. 387–8).
[4] Bischoff has rightly compared *Vita Willibaldi*, pref. (*MG. SS.* xv. 86): '. . . *ego* indigna *Saxonica* de gente istic venientium novissima . . .', and *Vita Wynnebaldi*, pref. (ib., p. 106): 'Originem vite exordiumque virtutum beati Wynnebaldi . . . *ordinare* (cf. Luke 1. 1) edissereque me libet.'—The 'subscriptio' of the Codex Bonifatianus 2 of Fulda (script of 'Luxeuil' of about 750), fol. 143 v, may also be compared (C. Scherer, *Die Codices Bonifatiani* . . . , Fulda, 1905, p. 16): '. . . *ego* Ragyndrudis *ordinavi* librum istum . . .', and I may add the conjecture that this Ragyndrudis was 'Raegenthryth filia Athuolfi', who made presents of gold and silver to Lullus's churches (*Epist.* 110, Tangl, p. 238). The name of Aodulf inscribed in uncials on fol. 2 v of the volume (Scherer, pp. 16, 28 f.), reminds us of Athuolf, Raegenthryth's father, according to Lullus's spelling.

IX

ALCHFRID THE ANCHORITE AND THE BOOK OF CERNE

THE date of one of the most famous books of private devotion in the early Middle Ages, the so-called Book of Cerne in the Cambridge University Library (MS. Ll. I. 10), is controversial. There are some rhythmical verses forming the acrostic 'Aedeluald episcopus', and a collection of extracts from the Psalms is introduced by the words: 'Hoc argumentum forsorii (for 'versarii') Oeðelwald episcopus decerpsit.'[1] This bishop therefore was regarded as having been the owner of the manuscript, and the editor, Dom A. B. Kuypers, called the volume 'The Prayer Book of Ædeluald the Bishop' (Cambridge, 1902), and conjectured that the manuscript might have been written for the bishop of Lichfield of this name (818–30); his episcopate appeared to correspond with the age of the script. But Kuypers also considered the possibility that the two passages did not originate in the time of the copyist but were repeated from one of the sources of the book and had reference to an earlier bishop, Æthilwald of Lindisfarne (721–40), the same who, according to the tradition of the tenth century, procured the binding of the Lindisfarne Gospels. This second opinion was held and stressed by Edmund Bishop;[2] he identified the supposed source with the 'Ymnarius Edilwaldi', which existed in the sixteenth century in the library of Fulda[3] but seems to have perished like most of its books.[4] Bishop also stated that there is nothing to argue a later origin for the prayers of the Book of Cerne than the seventh or early eighth century: 'the prayers in this collection may be safely taken by the historian as representing the type of devotional feeling prevalent in England in the youth of men like Willibrord, Boniface, or Willibald, and also in many cases preserving to us . . . the very words, the very forms, in which the apostles of the Germanic lands, whether of English or of Irish race, communed with their Maker and their Redeemer.' Kenneth Sisam objected that the spelling of the name of Æthelwald with an *e*, not *i*, is decisive in favour of the opinion 'that this "Aedelvald" was the bishop of Lichfield, and not the bishop of Lindisfarne, who would certainly have signed himself

---

[1] Ed. Kuypers, pp. 41 and 174.

[2] *Liturgica Historica*, Oxford, 1918, pp. 192–7; cf. also Bishop's 'Liturgical Note' in Kuyper's edition, pp. 234–83.

[3] Karl Christ, loc. cit., p. 265 (vii. 4. 12; cf. p. 285) and 299 (no. 146; cf. p. 307).

[4] Cf. P. Lehmann, 'Iohannes Sichardus' (Traube, *Quellen*, iv. 1), 1911, pp. 108 ff.

"Aedil-" '.[1] While there are a few cases of the spelling with *e* about the middle of the eighth century in the south of England,[2] the spelling with *i* appears to admit no exception in the north up to the early ninth century, as the *Liber Vitae* of Durham shows. Ædelvald of the acrostic and Oeđelwald was the bishop of Lichfield, if the manuscript has preserved the original form of the name. He may have been the earlier bishop of Lindisfarne, if the compiler or transcriber of the Book of Cerne, wherever he worked, in both cases has substituted *e* for *i*. That could easily be done in the prose rubric of 'Oeđelwald episcopus'. In the acrostic also a slight change by the copyist may be regarded as possible. The fourth line of the poem, which contains the *e* of the name, runs: 'Ei beata praemia, ubi sancti plaudent coram Christo in aethris'; the word 'Ei' comprises both the letters in question. Are we justified in conjecturing that in the exemplar not the first but the second letter, *i*, had been taken for the purpose of the acrostic? Some rhythmical 'abecedarii' offer parallels, using, 'extolle', 'exultantes', 'excelsa', and 'exul' to exhibit the letter *x*, not *e* (*MG. Poetae*, i, p. 82, iv. 2, pp. 514, 628, 909). Thus a transcriber may have shifted the emphasis from the *i* to the more regular use of the first letter of 'Ei'. But these are mere possibilities, which cannot really be proved. The texts as they are transmitted point to the age of the bishop of Lichfield.[3]

On the other hand, the Book of Cerne comprises elements, which came in fact from the north and belong to the eighth century.

Three prayers are ascribed to an anchorite Alchfrid, no. 47: 'Oratio ad Dominum ab Alchfriđo anch(orita) conposita' ('conpositum' MS.), no. 48: 'Item alia eiusdem', no. 58: 'Oratio Alchfriđo

---

[1] K. Sisam, 'Cynewulf and his Poetry' (loc. cit.), pp. 321 and 331, n. 31; cf. pp. 305 f., 325, n. 5. On the Book of Cerne see also W. Meyer, 'Poetische Nachlese aus dem sogenannten Book of Cerne' (Nachrichten Gött. 1917, pp. 597–625); J. F. Kenney, *The Sources for the Early History of Ireland*, i, pp. 720–2; E. Heinrich Zimmermann, *Vorkarolingische Miniaturen*, Berlin, 1916, Text, pp. 135 f., 294–6, pls. 293–6.

[2] There are two relevant charters of kings of Kent which are regarded as originals. One has the year of the Incarnation 741 and the contradictory indiction III (for VIIII), Birch, i, no. 160 (*Facsimiles of Ancient Charters in the British Museum*, i, pl. 8); the other belongs at the latest to the third quarter of the same century, Birch no. 199 (*Facsimiles of Anglo-Saxon MSS.* of the Ordnance Survey, iii, pl. 3). Both are considered 'trustworthy guides' by Lowe, *Codices Lat. ant.* ii, p. xiv; on the second cf. also M. P. Parsons, 'Some Scribal Memoranda for Anglo-Saxon Charters of the 8th and 9th Centuries' (*MÖIG.*, Ergänzungs-Band xiv, 1939, p. 14, n. 13). They contain the signatures 'Signum manus Aeđelhuni' and 'Aethelnothi' or 'Aethelnothes' (side by side with 'Aethilberhtus').

[3] I may mention a continental case offering some analogy. The name of St. Ouen, the bishop of Rouen (641–84), is spelt in almost all early texts 'Audoinus', but in one MS. of about 700 'Audoenus', which form prevailed from the 9th century onwards (*SS. rer. Merov.* v. 536, n. 2), and a rhythmical poem written during his lifetime by Ansebert, has an acrostic with the spelling 'Audoaenus' (ib., p. 542).

ad sanctam Mariam.'[1] Kuypers dismissed these texts without further discussion, because he knew of no other mention of a hermit of this name; he merely observed that the familiarity of the author with Roman sacramentaries seemed to imply that he was a priest.[2] But another text by the same man in fact exists and makes it possible, to some extent, to establish his time and country. Two Cotton manuscripts of English origin, Vespasian A. XIV of the early eleventh century[3] and Tiberius A. XV of the same century, contain, with other letters and documents, certain collections of the letters of Alcuin, a number of which derive from the same exemplar; among them is a letter of Alchfrid.[4] The manuscripts (Vespasian fols. 131–4?, Tiberius fols. 48v–50v) are at present not accessible. The Tiberius volume was badly damaged in the Cottonian Library fire in 1731; but Thomas Gale (who died in 1702) had made a copy of it, now MS. O. 10. 16 of Trinity College, Cambridge. In these circumstances the following text is based on this transcript (pp. 52–5), which on the whole appears reliable, though I have removed some orthographical peculiarities of the seventeenth century, nor do I mention a few mistakes corrected by Gale himself. H. M. Adams, M.A., librarian of Trinity College, has kindly provided me with photostats of this copy. Further, I am indebted to Dr. H. Idris Bell, the then Keeper of the Manuscripts in the British Museum, for communicating to me the rubric and the end of the Tiberius text.

INCIPIT EPISTOLA ALCHFRIÐI[5] ANACHORITAE AD HIGLACUM LECTOREM ET PRESBITERUM

Igitur, o *filioli*,[6] *quietem silentiumque diligite et scientiae operam date atque exercete vosmet ipsos, ut frequenti conlatione mentem vestram puram exhibeatis Deo 'nec[7] orationes vestrae impediantur' apud Deum.* Et videte, fratres, ordinem humanae vitae miserae super terram, a terra in ignem, de igne in iudicium, de iudicio aut in gehennam aut in gloriam. De terra enim creatus es, terram calcas,[8] *in terram ibis*,[9] a terra resurges, in igne probaberis[10] et iudicium intrabis

---

[1] Kuypers, pp. 143–5 and 155 f. The third prayer is also found in two MSS. of the 11th century in the British Museum, Cotton Titus D. XXVII and Arundel 155.

[2] Ib., p. 232; cf. Bishop, ib. 265 (nos. 60–2); cf. also ib., pp. xiv ff., xix f., xxix.

[3] Cf. above, p. 246.

[4] Cf. Th. Sickel, 'Alcuinstudien I' (*SB. Wien*, lxxix, 1875, p. 507, n. 3); E. Dümmler, 'Zur Lebensgeschichte Alchvins' (*Neues Archiv*, xviii, 1892, p. 61, n. 2), and *MG. Epist.* iv. 9 f.

[5] Gale has 'Alcheridi' (which seems to be the reading of the Vespasian MS.) and 'Niglacum'.

[6] The first sentence is copied from Rufinus, *Historia monachorum*, c. 1 (Migne, *P.L.* xxi. 404).

[7] 1 Pet. iii. 7.   [8] Deut. xxviii. 23: 'terra quam calcas.'

[9] Gen. iii. 19 according to the so-called Itala ('in pulverem reverteris' Vulgate); cf. Sabatier, *Bibliorum versiones antiquae*, i. 20.

[10] Ecclus. ii. 5: 'in igne probatur aurum'; 1 Cor. iii. 13.

aeternum et horribile, post haec aut supplicium aut regnum possidebis.
Cum Susanna ergo clamandum est:[1] *Angustiae mihi sunt undique*, et cum Paulo
eiulandum est et dicendum:[2] *Infelix homo ego; quis me liberabit de corpore mortis
huius nisi gratia domini nostri Iesu Christi? Quid*[3] *ergo faciemus*: vel ignota amemus
et quaeramus, ne forte in perpetuum ignoremus et perdamus? Sine causa[4]
enim natus est, qui illa perpetua in perpetuum et illa aeterna in aeternum
ignorabit et nesciens ea peribit. O te miserum hominem: quod vides, debes
odisse, et quod amare te convenit, ignorare. Laqueus tibi tua vita, inretiris
velis nolis, in te habes quo compediris, in te non habes quo solvaris. Cave
temet, frater, in te ne confidas, quia a te laquearis nec a te solo solveris.
A te enim venderis, a Christo redimeris. Oculos habes caecus, ligaris
libensque morti duceris. O intolerabilis caecitas, o dolor incomparabilis;
o infelicissima miseria, quae favet adversariis, quae libenter se tradit per-
secutoribus, sibi nusquam parcentibus, quibusque se alligantibus et morti
tradentibus gaudens consentit. Quis umquam laetus ad mortem pergit,
quis ad iugulandum libens ducitur? Vae tibi, humana miseria: utinam
decollareris tunc et non in aeternum cruciareris! Quid te caecius, o misera
humanitas, quae sic erras videns? Licet vides usque ad caelum, non ultra;
citra caelum sapis, ultra non sapis, licet nec citra bene sapis.[5] O dura et
infringibilis ignorantia, quis tibi narrabit inenarrabilia; infelix humanitas,
quis tibi subveniet? Audi, quid sapiens dixit: *Cui pauca non sufficiunt, plura
non proficiunt.*[6] Audisti, credo, Dominum in euangelio dicentem: *Discedite a
me maledicti in ignem aeternum.*[7] Miser homo, esto misericors:[8] forte vel sic
a filio perditionis[9] subtrahere te poteris. Ne parcas cibo, ne fragili parcas
vestimento, ne tibi tua praeferas; plus temet ama quam tua, plus animam
tuam quam res tuas, plus temet amare debes quam aliena. Quid enim
tuum est praeter animam tuam? Noli ergo unicam[10] tuam perdere pro
nihilo; ne parcas caducis, ne aeterna perdas. Alienus tibi totus mundus

---

[1] Dan. xiii. 22.

[2] Rom. vii. 24, 25. The verses are combined in the same way by Priscillianus,
Tractatus, i (ed. G. Schepss, *CSEL*. xviii. 14), by Augustine, *Confessiones*, vii. 21, viii.
5 (ed. Knöll, ib. xxxiii. 167, 180), and in the 'Oratio S. Gregorii papae' in a prayer
book of Troyes (MS. no. 1742, of *c*. 800) edited by A. Wilmart, *Precum libelli quattuor
aevi Karolini*, i, Rome, 1940, p. 13, l. 4. 'Nisi' is missing in the Vulgate text (corresponding with the Greek): 'Gratia Dei per Iesum Christum dominum nostrum'; cf.
Wordsworth and White, *Novum Testamentum Latine*, ii. 1, p. 98.

[3] Luke iii. 10.

[4] That is, 'frustra', 'in vanum'; cf. *Thesaurus linguae Latinae*, iii. 674.

[5] 'sis' MS.

[6] From Sulpicius Severus, *Dialog*. i. 18. 1 (ed. Halm, *CSEL*. i. 170), but Severus
reads 'proderunt' for 'proficiunt' of our letter, which may be the mistake of a copyist
caused by the preceding 'sufficiunt'. The sentence from Severus (proverbial?) was
repeated by the synod of Orange in 529 (*MG. Concilia*, i. 52), by Gregory of Tours,
Vita patrum c. 2. 5 (*SS. rer. Merov*. i. 2, p. 672), by St. Columbanus, *Epist*. no. 7 (*MG.
Epist*. iii. 180), and in the 2nd preface of the *Vita Filiberti* (*SS. rer. Merov*. v. 584).
Cf. also Elipandus, *MG. Epist*. iv. 307. 7.

[7] Matt. xxv. 41.

[8] Cf. Ecclus. iv. 10; Luke vi. 36.

[9] Cf. John xvii. 12.

[10] Ps. xxi. 21: 'Erue a framea, Deus, *animam* meam et de manu canis *unicam* meam';
ib. xxxiv. 17: 'restitue *animam* meam a malignitate eorum, a leonibus *unicam* meam.'

est, qui nudus natus nudus sepelieris. O inremeabilis[1] dementia, quae alienum caducum tanto amore diligit, ut aeternum proprium in aeternum perdat. Cogita itaque mortem, quae finem dat mundi voluptatibus, et vide, quo amoena divitum abiit laetitia. Luxus, iocus, saltus, libido, luxuria certe evanuerunt vel conticuerunt, et cadaver nudum vermibus et putredine desolvendum limus suscepit, et miserrima anima poenis aeternis reddita periit, sicut scriptum est: *Subito defecerunt et perierunt propter iniquitatem suam velut a somno.*[2] Quid hac conditione lacrimabilius, quid hac miseria infelicius, quam ut quis usque ad corruptionem et perpetuum interitum[3] huius vitae vana sectatur?

Idcirco deprecor, obsecro et fraterna pietate praecipio: vide, lege et intellige, quomodo debes pugnare contra diabolum.[4] Ille pugnat primum gula, tu, frater, abstinentia; ille superbia, tu semper humilitate; ille luxuria, tu castitate; ille avaritia, tu vero elemosyna; ille tenacitate, tu largitate; ille mendacio, tu veritate; ille ira, tu mansuetudine et patientia; ille discordia, tu concordia pacis; ille tristitia, tu alacritate mentis et laetitia pugna contra eum; ille invidia, tu amore fraternae dilectionis expugna; ille vana gloria huius saeculi furit, tu toto corde quaere *futuram gloriam.*[5] Ille neglegentiam excitat, ut securus sis; tu Dei amore [sis] semper instinctus, quia *beatus homo, qui semper pavidus est.*[6] Ille pigritia corporis [et] torpore; tu labore et vigiliis exsupera eum. Ille pugnat astutia corporis; tu *simplicitate cordis*[7] interius animam tuam exorna. Ille impatientia, tu patientia. Ille immundas cogitationes immittit in cor tuum; tu vero sanctas et puras *et gladium spiritus quod est verbum Dei*[8] oppone. Et frequenter ora: oratio assidua *ignita diaboli*

---

[1] Perhaps 'inreme[di]abilis'. But cf. Vergil, *Aen.* v. 591: 'inremeabilis error.'

[2] The Vulgate has here (Ps. lxxii. 19, 20) 'Velut somnium'. But the 'Psalterium Romanum' used in early England reads 'velut a somno'; Cotton MS. Vespasian A. I of the 8th century (Sweet, *The Oldest English Texts*, p. 289) and Royal MS. 2. B. V of the 10th century (Fritz Roeder, *Der altenglische Regius-Psalter*, Studien zur Englischen Philologie xviii, Halle, 1904, pp. 133 f.) have this reading (the Vespasian Psalter originally read 'velut a somnio'), 'Eadwine's Canterbury Psalter' (ed. F. Harsley, *Early English Text Society*, xcii, 1889, p. 126) has 'velut somnio'. I am indebted to K. Sisam for this information. The ancient version of the Codex Sangermanensis (Sabatier, loc. cit. ii. 147) and the Mozarabic Psalter (ed. J. P. Gilson, H. Br. Soc. xxx, 1905, p. 52) have 'velut a somnio' (or 'a somnium').

[3] Cf. Boethius, *Consolatio philosophiae*, iii. 11. 14 (ed. Weinberger, *CSEL*. lxvii. 70): 'Estne igitur, inquit, quod . . . venire *ad interitum corruptionemque* desideret?'

[4] In describing the fight with the Devil, the author follows the model of Caesarius of Arles, *Sermo* no. 207 (ed. G. Morin, p. 785): 'Audiamus ergo consilium beati apostoli et *contra diaboli* insidias armis nos spiritalibus muniamus: 'Sumite', inquid, 'scutum fidei . . . *et gladium spiritus quod est verbum Dei*.' . . . Consurgit *ille* cum *infidelitate,* tu surge cum *fide*; *ille* pugnat cum *superbia,* tu cum *humilitate; ille* exhibet *luxuriam, tu* retine *castitatem*; adprehendit ille nequitiam, tu iustitiam tene; *ille* ingerit *iracundiam, tu* sectare *patientiam; ille immittit avaritiam,* tu exerce misericordiam; *ille gulam, tu abstinentiam*; ille malitiam, tu bonitatem. Similiter et in ceteris rebus semper contraria adversus nequitias diaboli studeamus arma proferre, et aut nunquam nos aut difficile poterunt illius machinamenta decipere. Ut ergo haec possimus Deo auxiliante conplere, . . . ieiuniorum, *vigili*arum *vel orati*onum arma nobis debemus iugiter providere.'

[5] Rom. viii. 18.   [6] Prov. xxviii. 14.   [7] Acts ii. 46, &c.   [8] Eph. vi. 17.

iacula[1] exsuperat. Ille pugnat infidelitate; tu vero fide resiste fortiter. Et crede *in*[2] *unum Deum Patrem omnipotentem.* Ille docet desperationem; tu vero spem tuam pone[3] in misericordiam Dei *et*[2] *in* redemptorem *nostrum Iesum Christum, qui* pro nobis *incarnatus est et passus et sepultus* et patiendo diabolum vicit et nobis victoriam dedit. Qui etiam per resurrectionem suam aeternam spem et scientiam futurae resurrectionis animarum et corporum in die iudicii donavit et nobis per ascensionem suam caelestis regni ianuam aperuit[4] et [nos] concives angelorum effecit. Et *quis contra nos* est, *si* ipse *pro nobis* est,[5] *qui est ad dexteram Dei, qui etiam interpellat pro nobis.*[6] Ipsi soli[7] Deo vivo[8] et vero virtus et honor[9] et potestas et imperium et omnis gloria in saecula saeculorum. Amen.

The preceding letter, or rather sermon, hardly needs any commentary. The vivid style may be mentioned: the liking of the author for short sentences, for a succession of similar notions, for parallelisms of contrasted ideas, by which his admonitions are emphasized. There can be no doubt of his identity with the anchorite Alchfrid of the Book of Cerne. The prayer 'ad sanctam Mariam' accords in its words on Christ with the end of the letter: 'Qui . . . inferni claustra destruxit *et caelestis regni ianuas aperuit.* . . . *Ipsi*[10] honor et gloria . . . Amen.' One may also compare a commonplace of the letter: 'Ille immundas cogitationes immittit in cor tuum', with the first 'Oratio ad Dominum': 'Et custodi *cogitationes* meas a malis *immiss*ionibus *inmund*orum spirituum.'

The letter is directed, according to the headline, 'ad Higlacum lectorem et presbiterum'. This man is known from the poem on a Northumbrian monastery, its abbots and brethren, which Presbyter Ædilvulf dedicated to Bishop Egbert of Lindisfarne (803–21).[11] He

[1] Ib. *v.* 16, as in Jerome, *Commentarius in Isaiam* vii. 21, xvi. 59, and *in Ezechielem* xi. 39 (Migne, *P.L.* xxiv. 270, 604, xxv. 381); the Vulgate has 'tela nequissimi ignea'. Cf. Wordsworth and White, loc. cit. ii. 451.

[2] Alchfrid quotes from the so-called Niceno-Constantinopolitan Creed, not from the original Nicene text, in which 'et sepultus' is missing.

[3] Cf. Ps. lxxii. 28, lxxvii. 7.

[4] Ib. lxxvii. 23: 'ianuas caeli aperuit.' The *Te Deum*, as B. Colgrave reminds me, contains similar words: 'Tu . . . *aperui*sti credentibus *regna cael*orum.'

[5] Rom. viii. 31.

[6] Ib. *v.* 34.

[7] Jude *v.* 25: '*Soli Deo* . . . *gloria* et magnificentia, *imperium et potestas* . . . *in* omnia *saecula saeculorum. Amen.*'

[8] 1 Thess. i. 9: 'servire *Deo vivo et vero.*'

[9] Rev. vii. 12: '. . . *honor et virtus* et fortitudo Deo nostro in saecula saeculorum. Amen.'

[10] By the word 'Ipsi' introducing the doxology, the author imitates Rufinus, loc. cit., epil. (col. 462): '*Ipsi gloria et honor* in saecula saeculorum. Amen' (cf. 2 Pet. iii. 18: '*Ipsi gloria et nunc et in diem aeternitatis. Amen*').

[11] The poem has been edited by Th. Arnold, *Symeonis Opera*, i, pp. 265–94 (cf. pp. xxxii–xxxix), and E. Dümmler, *MG. Poetae*, i, pp. 582–604. Cf. L. Traube, 'Karolingische Dichtungen' (*Schriften zur Germanischen Philologie*, ed. M. Roediger, i), Berlin, 1888, pp. 7–43. On the poet's acquaintance with the metrical Miracles

probably composed it in the beginning of Egbert's episcopate, when the author, as Traube has conjectured, had perhaps followed Egbert as abbot of the unknown monastery.[1] His account of Merchdeof's vision (c. 11) shows that, in spite of all conventionalities and defects of form, he had the soul of a true poet.[2] Now, the 16th chapter has the headline: 'De Hyglaco presbitero atque lectore.' The correspondence with the heading of the letter is evident, and the few details recorded by Ædilvulf on Hyglac make it possible to establish approximately his period as well as that of Alchfrid.

The monastery was founded about 710 (between 705 and 716). Six abbots are celebrated by the poet:

> Eanmund, the founder, had the cell 'diu' (c. 12. 1);
> Eorpvin;
> Aldvin, his brother;
> Sigbald, 'longo tempore' (c. 14. 40);
> Sigvin, his brother;
> Vulfsig, 'paucis annis' (c. 18. 35).

If Traube's view is right, Vulfsig was succeeded by Egbert (until 803) and by Ædilvulf himself, and it is quite possible, as Arnold has seen (p. xxxviii), that Sigbald was the 'Sibald abbas' who died in 771 according to the Northumbrian Annals preserved in Symeon's *Historia regum*, c. 47 (ed. Arnold, ii. 44). Hyglac is mentioned in connexion with the fifth abbot, Sigvin, and can be assigned to the second part of the eighth century, perhaps to the years about 780. He was a teacher of the poet (c. 22. 52), who entered the monastery as 'puer' and lived with Vulfsig for six years, before the latter became abbot (c. 18. 9–13). He calls Hyglac not only 'presbyter' but also 'lector', that is, reader, lecturer, teacher;[3] his ability as precentor

---

of St. Ninian cf. K. Strecker, *Neues Archiv*, xliii, 1922, pp. 20 ff. and the notes in his edition, *MG. Poetae*, iv. 2, pp. 943 ff.

[1] Arnold suggested Crayke (north of York) as the site of the monastery; but this identity is very uncertain. Nor am I sure that the house was situated near the sea (Traube, p. 9); for the words 'aequoris et dorso praedicti' (c. 6. 24) rather refer to the flat top of the hill previously mentioned (cf. the similar conditions in *Carm*. 28. 273 f. of Paulinus of Nola, ed. Hartel, *CSEL*. xxx. 303: 'ut nitido purgata patesceret area *dorso*'). The words 'laetatur clerus in urbe' (cc. 15. 33, 20. 13) are borrowed from Aldhelm (ed. Ehwald, pp. 15, v. 27), as Traube, p. 18 f., has observed; they are obviously applied to the monks and their monastery and cannot be related to York (Arnold, pp. xxxv ff.). Kenney, loc. cit., p. 234, raises the question whether the monastery might have been 'one of the English establishments in Ireland'; but this suggestion is highly improbable and contradicted by c. 22. 57: 'faciem dudum de Hibernia notam', which shows that the country of the monastery is not Ireland.

[2] Traube, p. 8.

[3] Cf. the additions of the Benedictines to the *Glossarium* of Du Cange s. v. (ed. Favre, v. 52); Traube, pp. 40 ff.; Dümmler, *Neues Archiv*, xviii. 61. I will mention only the Northumbrian Annals, A.D. 771 (quoted above): 'Sibald abbas obiit, et

is praised (c. 15. 27 ff.), so much so that Traube (pp. 15, 40 ff.) attributed here to 'lector' this very meaning.[1] Hyglac became blind but he could distinguish with spiritual eyes good and evil spirits. Ædilvulf saw him, after his death, in a dream on a Sunday night, sitting in white garments in heavenly surroundings; relating the vision, he calls him 'quondam meus ille magister Hyglac' and 'doctor lectorque beatus Hyglac' (c. 22).

So Ædilvulf, in conjunction with the rubric of the letter, shows that the materials of the Book of Cerne, at least in part, are a little later than Bishop assumed. The letter and the prayers of Alchfrid cannot be much earlier than the middle of the eighth century and may be contemporaneous with Bishop Æthilwald of Lindisfarne. They certainly belong to the north of England (southern Scotland included) and probably to the proximity of Lindisfarne, whence the founder of the monastery had obtained a priest as instructor of the monastic life (c. 5); the poet also saw in his dream the teacher of his early years (spent, it seems, in Ireland), Eadfrid, venerating the tomb of St. Cuthbert (c. 22. 61), who was buried in Lindisfarne. T. D. Kendrick,[2] like Kuypers and Sisam, has identified 'Aedelvald' with the bishop of Lichfield and called the Book of Cerne 'the first indubitably Mercian manuscript'. But he found there 'the northern mosaic style', the 'schematic northern tradition of drawing', and other things 'more in the style of the Rothbury [Northumberland] Christ than in that of the contemporary south English manner'. The new facts here adduced may offer a simple explanation of these characteristics.

X

VENUS, A MAN. FROM AN UNPUBLISHED SERMON

MANY years ago I copied from two manuscripts in the British Museum a sermon partly directed against the observance of pagan customs. Some portions were obviously derived from sermons of Bishop Caesarius of Arles; but the language was barbarized, and the low level of knowledge was also evident from the fact that, in

---

Egric . . . (a word is missing) *et lector* . . . migravit ad consortium electorum', and A.D. 794 (p. 56): 'His diebus Colcu *presbyter et lector* ex hac luce migravit ad Dominum.' Alcuin's Letter no. 7, inscribed 'Benedicto magistro et pio patri Colcu', has in one of the two MSS. the rubric: 'Epistola Albini magistri ad Col[c]um *lectorem* in Scotia' (*MG. Epist.* iv, p. 31, n. *a*).

[1] We may compare the connexion of the office of the Precentor or Chanter with teaching in later times. Cf. A. Hamilton Thompson, *Song-Schools in the Middle Ages* (Church-Music Society, Occasional Papers, no. 14), London, 1942.

[2] *Anglo-Saxon Art to A.D. 900*, London, 1938, pp. 165-7.

the earlier of the two manuscripts, the goddess Venus was regarded as a man. The beginning of the text (as I now know, nearly half the sermon) is missing because the first leaves of both the manuscripts are lost. I therefore kept back the text, though I mentioned it occasionally[1] as an example of the decline of classical studies in the later Merovingian age. My hope of some day finding a complete copy was realized at last, when the new catalogue of the Zürich MSS. by Dom Cunibert Mohlberg of Rome revealed a manuscript closely akin to the second of the London texts; Dom Mohlberg kindly provided me with photostats of the new copy.

These are the three manuscripts which are known to me:

(C) British Museum, Cotton MS. Nero A. II, fols. 14–45 (formerly 12–43), is a fragment of a small manuscript of the end of the eighth century. It was written in 'Pre-Caroline minuscule' probably in France, though it has not hitherto been possible to locate the script and W. M. Lindsay (*Notae Latinae*, Cambridge, 1915, p. 461) preferred northern Italy (Verona). The contents suggest that it was written at a place connected with an Irish circle. Cf. the description by E. M. Thompson, *Catalogue of Ancient MSS. in the British Museum*, ii, 1884, p. 54, with pl. 32 (fols. 27v–28).

The manuscript begins (fols. 14–25) with the later part of our sermon: 'Isaias propheta dicit: Vae vobis, qui iungitis agrum ad agrum' (= T, fol. 14). Fol. 14 evidently has been the first page for some time, without the protection of a binding; about 12 leaves may be missing at the beginning. The manuscript contains, besides some theological extracts (*De avaritia, De usura*, &c.), two texts which have already been published:

Fols. 34v–36 '*Incipit chronica de tempore mundi*. Ab exordio mundi usquae ad diluvium ... Constituit terminus gentium secundum numerum angelorum Dei' (Deut. xxxii. 8). This text was edited, a little polished, by Thomas Hearne, *Thomae Sprotti Chronica*, Oxford, 1719, pp. 167–8, from a copy by Thomas Smith; a reproduction of fols. 35v and 36 was published by Bond and Thompson, *The Palaeographical Society*, Second Series, vol. ii, part ii (1885), pl. 35. It is not a 'chronicle' but a computation of the years elapsed from the Creation to the time of the author. It is based on the Chronicle of Eusebius, as translated by Jerome (ed. Helm, pp. 14–17), up to the Passion of Christ, which is ascribed to the 16th year of the Emperor Tiberius; then the 532 years of the Easter cycle of Victurius (28–559)

---

[1] In my review of R. Stachnik, *Die Bildung des Weltklerus im Frankenreiche* (Paderborn, 1926), in *Deutsche Literaturzeitung*, 1928, no. 22, col. 1070. The allusion by Paul Kirn, *Propyläen-Weltgeschichte*, iii, Berlin, 1932, p. 121, derives from this review , as the author has kindly informed me.

are added. 'Ipsus expletus, hoc anno impleti sunt centum septuaginta et VIIII (= 738). Sunt in summa ab exordio mundi usque ad praesente tempore anni quinque milia nognenti XXVIII (rather 5939 according to the several numbers given by the author). Et remanent de sexto miliario anni LXXII; subtractus XL, remanent XXXII.' This subtraction, consequent on a lapse of forty years since the computation for the year 738 was made, involves a corresponding addition to the date of the text, and leads to A.D. 778. The exemplar of our copy was obviously written in this year and based on a computation originally made for the year 738 (cf. e.g. SS. rer. Merov. ii. 34, 176).

Fols. 37–42 *Ratio de cursus qui fuerunt ex auctores*, 'an account of the origins of six *cursus* or orders for the celebration of the canonical hours' (Kenney, *The Sources for the Early History of Ireland*, i, p. 687, no. 548). This difficult and doubtful treatise by an Irish monk living on the Continent has been printed several times, after others by Haddan and Stubbs, i. 138–40 (from the 17th-century copy Cotton Cleopatra E. I) and by J. Wickham Legg, *Miscellanea Ceriani*, Milan, 1910, pp. 149–67. Lowe, *Codices Lat. ant.* ii, p. 20, no. 186 (cf. p. 49), has published a fascimile of the upper parts of fols. 40v and 41. Kenney and Lowe mention literature bearing on this text; cf. also *Neues Archiv*, xxix (1904), 150; *SS. rer. Merov.* vii. 234; L. Gougaud, *Christianity in Celtic Lands*, London, 1932, pp. 317 f.; John Ryan, *Irish Monasticism*, Dublin, 1931, pp. 335 and 344.

The correspondence of some of the smaller texts in C not recorded here with texts in TA suggests that the sermon copied on the first pages was likewise transcribed from a *florilegium*, such as we have in TA. For these two manuscripts are copies of the same collection of texts on theological and moral subjects, which awaits a closer examination of its sources. The beginning of A is lost like that of C; but, except for this gap, the contents of T (up to fol. 167) and A are, according to the printed catalogues, identical. They include extracts from Cyprianus, Augustine, Caesarius of Arles, Gregory the Great (Homilies, Dialogues, Pastoral Care), &c.

(T) MS. no. 94 of the Central Library of Zürich, formerly C. 64 (286) of the Town Library, a volume of 211 leaves, was written in the so-called Raetian script in the early ninth century and came perhaps from the monastery of St. Gall. The collection has here the rubric: 'In nomine domini nostri Iesu Christi in hoc corpore continentur te(s)timonia plurima de sanctorum opusculis deflorata pio studio coniuncta.' On the contents see C. Mohlberg, *Katalog der Handschriften der Zentralbibliothek Zürich*, i, Zürich, 1932–6, pp. 35–8; cf. also Germain Morin, *Sancti Caesarii episcopi Arelatensis opera omnia*, i, Maredsous, 1937, pp. cxi f. (H⁷⁰) and pp. 42, 50, 196 (*Sermo* Nos. 8, 10, 46). Our sermon is found on fols. 8–19.

(A) British Museum, Arundel MS. no. 213, now consisting of 102 leaves, was written in the ninth century[1] by a continental 'insular' hand; one quaternion and the first folio of the next are lost before fol. 1 (the number of the gathering *II* is on the lower margin of fol. 7v). On the contents cf. *Catalogue of MSS. in the British Museum, New Series*, i. 1 (1834), pp. 58 f. with pl. 2 (3 lines of fol. 39v); *Catalogue of Ancient MSS. in the British Museum*, ii, pp. 56 f. and pl. 27 (fol. 90v); cf. also Morin, loc. cit. p. c (H[25]) and pp. 42 and 196 (*Sermo* Nos. 8, 46). Several entries of 1324–8 show that the volume belonged in this period to the Irish monastery of St. James ('Schottenkloster zu St. Jacob') at Würzburg founded about 1140 (cf. A. Brackmann, *Germania pontificia*, iii, 1935, p. 193); cf.

fol. 4: 'Anno Domini MCCCXXVIII° III° Idus Decembris comisit mihi Dominus istam ecleciam ad quartam partem anni';

fol. 30: 'Anno Domini milessimo CCCXXVIII° III° Idus Decembris commisit mihi Dominus abbas Condimmus ecleciam sancti Iacobi extra muros Herbipolenses usque ad terminum XIII septimanarum';

fol. 99v: 'Notum facio quod ego frater David anno Domini MCCCXXIIII° III° Idus Iuni a primo veni ad Herbipolim in habitus seculari';

fol. 101: 'Detur Scot(is) Herbipol(ensibus).'

No abbot of the name of Condimmus occurs in the printed lists of the abbots of St. James's (Ussermann, *Episcopatus Wirceburgensis*, St. Blasien, 1794, p. 281; M. Wieland, *Archiv des historischen Vereines von Unterfranken und Aschaffenburg*, xvi. 2–3, 1863, p. 121, and in J. B. Stamminger, *Franconia Sacra*, i, Würzburg, 1889, p. 53); but these derive on the whole from the catalogue of John Trithemius (*Opera*, ed. Busaeus, Mainz, 1604, p. 11) which may need rectification. A note on fol. 102v: 'Anno Domini milessimo CCCXXVIII° in die Affre martiris (August 7). Anno Domini milessimo CCCXXVIII° in die sancti Ciriaci' (cf. e.g. *SS. rer. Merov.* vii. 204), may be compared with a Würzburg charter of 1381 mentioning a procession to be performed 'sicut illa que fit in die beati Cyroiaci' (*Monumenta Boica*, xlv, 1899, p. 383). Our sermon, which was placed sixth in the complete manuscript and now, being a fragment, occupies fols. 1–4, begins 'sancti predicatores, ut Paulus dicit' (= T, fol. 14v; C, fol. 15).

C and TA represent two versions of the original sermon. A glance at the sources shows that both have to be considered in order to establish the archetype. On the whole C is nearer to it; but there are not only minor blunders to be corrected from TA: whole sentences have also been dropped in C. On the other hand TA comprises some interpolations, and the part of most interest, which will be

[1] So also E. A. Lowe in M. L. W. Laistner, 'Was Bede the Author of a Penitential?' (loc. cit., p. 274). Morin, loc. cit., p. c, ascribed the volume to the 7th–8th century.

found printed below, is omitted there. The complete text need not be published. It is a compilation from different sources, as the very headline of T suggests (the earlier part is missing in CA, as I have stated above) : 'Excarpsum de diversis auctoribus', that is, an excerpt, an extract from several authors.[1] It was obviously destined to serve as a model and help in the education of a semi-christianized people; it has its small place in the series of writings which starts with Augustine's book *De catechizandis rudibus*. The sermons of Bishop Caesarius of Arles (502–42), an industrious preacher, exerted a special influence on this kind of literature; his homiletic writings can now be easily studied, thanks to the life-work of Dom Germain Morin.[2] This influence on later preachers and writers has been examined more than once in recent years; the studies of Fedor Schneider on *Kalendae Ianuariae* and *Martiae* during the Middle Ages[3] illustrate it very clearly. It can be traced in the book of Bishop Martin of Bracara (d. 580) *De correctione rusticorum*,[4] in the sermons of Bishop Eligius of Noyon (641–60),[5] in the *Scarapsus* of Pirmin,[6] and in other writings of this kind, to which our compilation is now to be added. I give a short survey of the contents of this work.[7]

The author begins with a thanksgiving to God:

'Gratias agimus, Domine, *semper in omni tempore* (Ps. xxxiii. 2), id est in prospera et in adversa, sicut Iob fecit, largitorem et visitatorem, pugnatorem et defensorem et infinita sua beneficia, quae nobis largire dignatus est *secundum magnam misericordiam* (ib. l. 3) suam, dum dicit: Magna est, memor est, quod nos creavit et pascit. Magna est, quod nos redemit et promisit vitam aeternam, quia *misericordia eius preveniet* (ib. lviii. 11) nos, id est in fide ad credendum, et *misericordia subsequitur* (ib. xxii. 6), hoc est in perseverantia, et *misericordia coronat* (ib. cii. 4), hoc est in remuneratione futura. Ergo *oportet inquirere vel intelleg[er]e* (Caesarius, Serm. 16. 1, p. 74), quomodo dicit: *In principio fecit Deus caelum et terram*' (Gen. i. 1).

He then tells and explains the six days' work of the Creation and the story of the Fall, emphasizing the six sins of Adam, which gave power over humanity to the Devil ('qui deorsum fluens interpretatur';

---

[1] On *excarpsum* and kindred words cf. Gall Jecker, 'Die Heimat des hl. Pirmin' (loc. cit.), pp. 82 ff.

[2] His edition of Caesarius' *Sermones* comprises the 1st volume of the latter's *Opera*; cf. above, p. 284.

[3] *Archiv für Religionswissenschaft*, xx (1920–1), pp. 82–134, 360–410.

[4] C. P. Caspari, *Martin von Bracara's Schrift De correctione rusticorum*, Christiania, 1883.

[5] Only *Vita Eligii*, ii. 16 (15) concerns us here, partly edited by Krusch, *SS. rer. Merov.* iv, pp. 705–8, cf. 652 f. and 751–61. The whole text is in Migne, *P.L.* lxxxvii. 524–50 and xl. 1167–90.

[6] Ed. Jecker, loc. cit., pp. 34–73. On two more MSS. see P. Lehmann (above, p. 79, n.).

[7] Jecker, pp. 161 f., gave a survey from T.

cf. Isidore, *Orig.* viii. 11. 18), till the coming and passion of Christ put him in fetters. Christ's resurrection, the descent of the Holy Ghost, and the preaching of the Apostles are outlined. After this introductory part dealing with the story of the Fall and the Redemption, the sins to be avoided are discussed, many biblical sentences being quoted (some at least not directly but borrowed from earlier authors). The long quotation from St. Matthew's Gospel xxv, 34–46 forms the transition to a second part, in which the means to a Christian mode of life are described: the giving of alms and tithes, the sanctification of Sunday; eucharist, unction, and prayer as helps against diseases; the avoidance of pagan customs and beliefs, the need of patience; all these are enjoined. Finally the features of a good Christian are described with some repetitions; readiness for forgiveness and love of enemies, which were already touched on in the first part, are treated in greater detail at the end.

Possibly other manuscripts of this 'missionary sermon' exist; to facilitate the identification, I add the last lines of the text, having already given the beginning. They furnish at the same time an example of the difference of the two versions and show the character of the compilation; all the words printed in italics, that is, this whole portion except for the first words and the last quotation, are transcribed verbatim from Gregory the Great's Homilies on the Gospels (*Hom. in euang.* 27. 8, 7; Migne, *P.L.* lxxvi. 1208 f.).[1]

'Et pro inimicis orare oportit, ut *Veritas*[2] *dicit*: '*Cum statis ad orandum, remittite, si quid habetis*' (Mark xi. 25) *in cordibus vestris. Et pro inimicis oramus; fundit os pro adversariis precem, sed utinam cor teneat amore!*

TA

5   *Nam sepe et orationem inimicis nostris inpendimus, sed hanc ex preceptione potius quam ex caritate. Nam vitam inimicorum petimus; ne exaudiamur timemus.*

Pro inimicum nihil petit, *qui pro eum ex caritate non orat. Sed*[3] *quod* peius est, *alius* rogat *mortem inimici* sui; *eum, quem gladium non potest persequi,*
10   *persequitur oracione; et vivit adhuc qui maledicitur, et tamen his qui maledicit iam de morte illius reus tenetur. Iubit autem Deus, ut diligatur inimicus, et tamen rogatur Deus, ut occidat inimicum. Quisquis itaque sic orat, in ipsis suis*

---

[1] oportet *TA and C*[2]   ut] et *T*   dicit] ait *C*   2 demittite *A*; dimittite *T*   habeatis *A*   corde (vestr. *om.*) *TA*   3 oremus *TA*   fundit hos pro *C*; fundimus pro *TA*   adversarios *TA*[1]   preces *CA*   cor teneat] *T*; contineat *C*[1], contineat *C*[2], cor teneamus (in *later add.*) *A*   amorem *C and T*[2]   5 Nam... timemus *om. C*   8 inimico *TA*   eo *TA*   erat *A*   9 morte *T*   eumque gl. *CT*   gladio *TA and C*[2]   10 orationem *TA*   qui] quem *CA*   tamen] tunc *T* que *C*   11 Iubet *A and C*[2]   et *om. TA*   12 Qui sic itaque *TA*

---

[1] I distinguish between the original readings of the MSS. and the corrections of later hands by adding the numbers [1] and [2] to the letters C, T, and A.

[2] From c. 8.

[3] From c. 7.

precibus contra Conditorem pugnat. Unde sub Iudae speciae dicitur: 'Fiat oracio eius in peccato' (Ps. cviii. 7). *Et apostolus* (1 Cor. vi. 10): *Neque maledici regnum Dei possedebunt.'*

1 conditore *T*   dixerunt *C*   2 apostolus] dicit *add. TA*
maledicentes ... possidebunt *TA*.

The *excarpsum* exhibits a few quotations from Jerome, Augustine, and Gregory; but they give no idea of the large amount of transcription without any indication of the sources, nor have I been able to detect them all. Obviously a commentary on the Book of Genesis was used in the early part; Augustine's Treatises on St. John's Gospel are occasionally employed (*Tract. in euang. Ioh.* xi. 6, Migne, *P.L.* xxxv. 1478, on the two nativities of a Christian); other portions are taken from Gregory's Homilies mentioned above (*Hom. in euang.* 22. 6, 26. 3, 35. 7, 31. 5, 2. 8, 27. 7–9). But no author supplied the material for so many pages as did Caesarius of Arles. His sermons were a mine of quotations, exploited also for similar purposes by other writers, such as Martin of Bracara, Eligius of Noyon, and Pirmin, as I have already mentioned. The compiler made more or less use of the Sermons nos. 13, 16, 43, 44, 54, 154, 192, 207, 219, 221, 223, 233, perhaps also nos. 15, 41, and 180 (according to Morin's numbering). The text possibly needs a closer examination, should a general review be undertaken of the whole *florilegium* of TA and of similar compilations.

Only one portion of the sermon merits separate publication, the part referring to pagan customs. The beginning and the end are copied from Caesarius; but C has preserved between these extracts some lines which cannot be referred to the same source—at least not to the sermons which are known—and at the same time show relations to other writings of a similar character. The following text is found in C fols. 17v–21, in T fols. 15v–16v, in A fols. 1v–2. Most of the words printed in italics are taken from Caesarius, as indicated in the notes.

> ... *Videte,*[1] *fratres, quia qui infirmitate*m habet *ad ecclesiam currat corporis sanitatem recepere, et peccatorum indulgentiam merebitur obtenere. Cum ergo duplicia bona poss*umus *in ecclesiam invenire, quare per precantatoris et per fontes et per arbores, diabolica filactiria, per caragus et aruspicis et divinus et*
> 5 *sortilicus du*plicia *sibi mala miseri homines conantur inferre?*
>   *Verba*[2] *turpia et luxoriosa* de *ore vestro nolite proferre, ne forte detrahendo,*

1 habent ... currant *C*   corpore (?) *A*¹   2 recipere *TA and C*²
obtinere *T and C²A².*   3 ecclesia *TA*   precantatores *TA and C*²   4 filacteria
*TA and C*²   caragius *A*¹, garritus *A*²; garigŏs *C*; caraios *T*   auruspicis *C*; aruspices
(aruspicis *A*¹) et divinos et sortilegos (sortolegos *T, corr.*) *TA*   5 dublicia *C,
corr.*; multiplicia *Caes.*

----

[1] From Caesarius' *Sermo* no. 13, c. 3 (p. 65), which is also the source of the preceding lines.   [2] Ib. c. 4.

male loquendo, in sanctis festivitatibus chorus ducendo, cantica luxoriosa et turpia
proferendo, de linguas suas, unde debuerant Deo laudare, inde sibi vulnera videantur
infligere. Isti enim infelicis et miseri, qui ballationis et saltacionis ante ipsas
baselicas sanctorum exercere nec metuunt nec erubescunt, etsi Christiani ad
5 *ecclesiam venerint, pagani de ecclesia revertuntur, quia ista consuetudo ballandi*
de paganorum observacione remansit. Et iam videte, qualis est ille Christianus,
*qui ad ecclesiam venerat orare, neclecta*m *orationem, sagrileg*a cantica *non*
erubescit ex ore proferre. Considerate tamen, fratres karissimi, si iustum est, ut
*ex ore Christiano, ubi corpus Christi ingreditur, luxorios*a cantic*a quasi venenum*
10 *diaboli proferatur. Et*[1] *si adhuc aliquos cognoscit*ur illa sordidissima turpitudinem
de vecula[2] *vel cervolo [exercere] et, quando luna obscuratur,* vel contra tempe-
statem *clangoribus,* bucinis aut vocibus *defend*ere repotant,[3] *ita durissime*

1 male] et male *TA*   choros *T and A*[2]   docendo *A*   turpem sermonem
proferendo *C*   2 de *A*[1], per *A*[2]; de linguis suis *C*; de lingua sua *Caes.*   deum
TA, by corr. C   deinde *TA*   videantur vulnera *C*   3 Iste *C, corr.*   infelices *TA*
miseri sunt qui *C*   ballationes (bellat. *A*) et saltaciones (et salt. *om. TA) TA and C*[2]
4 basilicas *T and C*[2]; bassilicas *A*   sanctorum cum saltationes exercere *TA*
5 venerunt *A*; veniunt *T*   aeclesiae *A, corr.*   revertentur *T*; revertentes
A   7 venit *TA*   neglecta oratione sacrilegia *TA*; sacrilegia paganorum *for*
sacr. cant. *Caes.*   8 proferri *A*   tamen *om. T*   ut *om. TA*   9 christiani *C*
venena diaboli (diabuli *A*) proferantur *TA*   10 Et si to *p.* 312, *l.* 5 habent. Unde
om. TA   aliquo̊s *C*   agnoscitis *Caes.*   illam sordidissimam *C*[2]   11 cervulo *C*[2]
exercere *om. C*   12 reputant *C*[2]

---

[1] Ib. c. 5.

[2] Caesarius, *Serm.* 13. 5 and 193. 2 (ed. Morin, pp. 66, 743) has the reading *de
annicula vel cervulo, cervulum sive anniculam.* He speaks of and against people who,
especially on the 1st of January, assumed the disguise of a stag or an old woman
(*annicula* for *anicula*); the reading of earlier editions *hinnicula* (hind) is not original,
though it has been accepted by some modern scholars (cf. Schneider, loc. cit.,
pp. 92 ff.). But there must have been early MSS. in which *vecula* was substituted
for *an(n)icula*; that is not *vetula* for *vitula*, 'calf' (ib., pp. 94, 96 ff.; C. P. Caspari,
Kirchenhistorische Anecdota, i, Christiania, 1883, p. 175), but *vec(u)la* for *vet(u)la,* 'an
old woman', nor is *vecula* a misreading but another early form of *vetula* (cf. Fr. Diez,
Etymologisches Wörterbuch der Romanischen Sprachen, 5th ed., Bonn, 1887, p. 338;
W. Meyer-Lübke, *Romanisches etymologisches Wörterbuch,* 3rd ed., Heidelberg, 1935,
p. 775). Cf. e.g. the decrees of the synod of Auxerre between 561 and 605 (cf.
Duchesne, *Fastes,* ii[2], pp. 440, 446), c. 1 (*MG. Concilia,* i. 179): 'Non licet Kalendis
Ianuarii *vecola* (thus according to the MSS.) *aut cervolo* facere'; *Vita Eligii,* ii. 16 (ed.
Krusch, p. 705): 'nullus in Kalendas Ianuarii nefanda et ridiculosa, *vetulas aut
cervulos* vel iotticos faciat'; Pirmin, c. 22 (ed. Jecker, p. 55): 'In *cervulos et veculas*
in Kalandas vel aliud tempus nolite anbulare'; Continental penitentials, see
Schneider, p. 104 f. On the meaning cf., e.g., Caesarius, *Serm.* 192. 2 (p. 739), on
whom Isidore, *De eccl. off.* i. 41. 2 (Migne, *P.L.* lxxxiii. 775) has drawn.

[3] Caesarius, *Serm.* 13. 5 (p. 66): '*Et, si quando luna obscuratur,* adhuc aliquos
clamare cognoscitis, et ipsos admonete, denuntiantes eis, quod grave sibi peccatum
faciunt, quando lunam, quae Deo iubente certis temporibus obscuratur, *clamoribus*
suis ac maleficiis sacrilego ausu se *defen*sare posse confidunt' (used in *Vita Eligii,* ii.
16, p. 707: 'Nullus, si *quando luna obscuratur,* voci*ferare praesumat', &c.); 52. 3
(p. 221): 'Et illud quale est, quando stulti homines quasi lunae laboranti putant se
debere succurrere, qui . . . quasi aliquem contra caelum carminum credunt esse
conflictum, quem *bucina*e sonitu vel ridiculo concussis tintinabulis *putant* se superare
posse tinnitu.' Cf. Jecker, p. 149.

*increpa*te, *ut* se *penetea*nt *rem sagrilegam conmisisse*, vel ipsus, qui se tempe-starius esse dicunt,[1] similiter facite.

Sunt aliqui rustici homines,[2] qui credunt, quasi aliquas mulieres quod vulgum dicitur strias esse debeant et ad infantes vel pecora nocere 5 possint[3] vel dusiolus[4] vel aquaticas vel geniscus[5] esse debeat. Et Kalendas Ianuarias, quod maledictus Ianus docuit,[6] hoc custodiunt vel inpuras,[7] quod mensas conponunt[8] aut agurius adtendunt, avicellas

1 ut sepe metuant *C*; ut eos paeniteat *Caes.*   ipsos *C²*   4 ad *eras. C*
5 aquatiquus *Lebeuf* (*cf. p.* 313).   7 augurius *C²*   aviculas *Lebeuf*

---

[1] Pirmin, c. 22 (p. 55): 'Tempestarios nolite credere'; c. 28 (p. 68): 'Omnia filactiria diabolica, . . . auguriosus, tempistarius et cuncta alia mala . . . nolite ea credire.' On weather-makers cf. Jecker, pp. 139 ff.

[2] Caesarius, *Serm.* 192. 1 (p. 738): 'inperiti *homines* et *rustici*', and 3 (p. 740): '*Aliqui* etiam *rustici* . . .'

[3] On *stri(g)ae*, 'witches', cf., e.g., Joseph Hansen, *Zauberwahn, Inquisition und Hexen-prozess im Mittelalter* (Historische Bibliothek, xii), Munich, 1900, pp. 14 ff., 48 f., 58 ff. G. Morin, 'Textes inédits relatifs au symbole et à la vie chrétienne' (*Rev. Bén.* xxii, 1905, pp. 514–19) has published from Verdun MS. no. 64 of the 12th century, coming from Saint-Airy, fols. 98 v–100 v, a sermon which partly derives from our text or a common source; cf. p. 518: 'Multi *homines* dicunt, quia a*striae* sunt, et dicunt, quia *infantes* et boves et caballos manducant, et alia mala inde dicunt; *quod* hominem (for 'omnino') *non est credendum, quia sapientes hos refutant.* Vos, fratres, non *cred*itis istos *stult*os et insipientes, quia astria numquam fuit nec erit; sed diabolus, qui per *mille artes* quaerit hominem decipere, ipse dicit ista verba *per illos homines*, qui non sunt benedicti' (cf. below, p. 312).

[4] Cf. *Vita I. Richarii*, c. 2 (ed. Krusch, *SS. rer. Merov.* vii. 445): 'Vir beatus Richarius fuit eorum obvius, ubi gentiles Pontearii (Ponthieu in Picardy) inride-bant ei: malefacere adfirmabant stulti, quod essent *dusie*; maones (dusi hemaones 1, dusie manes 2) vocitabant, qui Deum non credebant; eis reputabant, quod segetes tollebant.' Krusch, ib., n. 5, compares Augustine, *De civit. Dei*, xv. 23. 1 (from whom Isidore, *Orig.* viii. 11. 103 derives): 'Silvanos et Panes, quos vulgo incubos vocant, inprobos saepe extitisse mulieribus et earum adpetisse ac peregisse concu-bitum, et quosdam daemones, quos *Dusios* Galli nuncupant, adsidue hanc inmun-ditiam et tentare et efficere.' On *ma(v)ones* cf. below, p. 311, n. 2.

[5] *Vita Eligii*, ii. 16 (p. 706): 'Nullus nomina daemonum aut Neptunum aut Orcum aut Dianam aut Minervam aut *Geniscum* vel cetera huiuscemodi ineptia credere aut invocare praesumat.' *Geniscus* is obviously connected with *genius*.

[6] Caesarius, *Serm.* 192. 1 (p. 738): 'Dies Kalendarum istarum, fratres dilec-tissimi, quas Ianuarias vocant, a quodam Iano homine perdito ac sacrilego nomen accepit', &c. (Isidore, *De eccl. off.* i. 41. 1, Migne, *P.L.* lxxxiii. 774 f., derives from Caesarius); the synod of Tours of 567, c. 23 (*MG. Concilia*, i. 133): 'cognovimus nonnullus inveniri sequipedas erroris antiqui, qui Kalendas Ianuarii colunt, cum Ianus homo gentilis fuerit, rex quidem, sed esse deus non potuit', &c. On this example of euhemerism cf. Schneider, pp. 366–70.

[7] *Vita Eligii*, ii. 16 (p. 705): 'Nullus Christianus *inpuras* credat . . .'; Pirmin, c. 22 (p. 55): 'Nolite hoc credere neque in *inpurias*, que dicunt homines super tectus mittere, ut aliqua futura possint eis denunciare, quod eis bona aut mala adveniat. Nolite eis credere, quia soli Deo est futura prescire.' Cf. Jecker, pp. 141 ff. who, following Caspari, derives this word from Greek ἔμπυρος, ἐμπύριος.

[8] Caesarius, *Serm.* 192. 3 (p. 740): 'Sunt enim qui in Kalendis Ianuariis ita *auguria* observant. . . . *Aliqui* etiam *rustici mens*ulas suas in ista nocte quae praeteriit, plenas multis rebus, quae ad manducandum sunt necessariae, *conpon*entes, tota nocte

cantantes vel sternutacionis rediculosas[1] et signus observant et mavonis,[2]
quasi messis et vindemia portari possint, quod hoc omnino non est
credendum, quia hoc sapientes refutant et omnino menime credunt,
quia hoc de paganorum consuetudine remansit.[3] Et sic credimus, quod
5 cultores idolorum hoc docuerunt; hoc menime convenit Christianum
credere. Et Deana scimus quia mulier fuit, in quem diabulus habitabit
et divinacionis multas faciebat. Sed post sua morte in Epheso pro dea
colebant eam, et Dimitrius faber cum alius multus sua templa de auro
et argento fabricabant, quem Paulus apostolus distruxit,[4] ut ipse dixit:
10 *Quasi*[5] *contra bestias in Epheso pugnavi.* Et alia mulier fuit Iunae-Menerva
meretrix, quia non solum sufficiebat cum aliis fornicare, sed etiam cum
patre suo Iove et fratres suos Martem et Venerem fornicata est.[6]

1 sternutaciones ridicul. et signos obs. et mauones C^2 3 refudant (?)C^1
3 *and* 5 minime *by corr.* C   6 dea nascimus C^1; deanam scimus C^2
quam diab. habitavit et divinaciones C^2 8 Demetrius faber cum aliis
multis C^2 9 quem *corr.* que C   10 iune.menerua C

sic conpositas esse volunt, credentes quod hoc illis Kalendae Ianuariae praestare
possint, ut per totum annum convivia illorum in tali abundantia perseverent'; *Vita
Eligii*, ii. 16 (p. 705): 'neque *mensas* super noctem *conponat*'; *Epist. Bonifatii*, no. 50
(ed. Tangl, p. 84): 'et *mensas* illa die vel nocte dapibus onerare'; Roman synod of
743, c. 9 (*MG. Concilia*, ii. 15): 'Si quis Kalendas Ianuarias et bromas colere praesumpserit aut *mensas* cum dapibus in domibus praeparare, . . . anathema sit.' Cf.
Schneider, pp. 115 ff., 128 ff.

    [1] From Caesarius, *Serm.* 54. 1 (p. 226): 'Similiter et *auguria* observare nolite, nec
in itinere positi aliquas *aviculas cantantes adtend*ite nec ex illarum cantatu diabolicas
divinationes adnuntiare praesumite. . . . Illas vero non solum sacrilegas sed etiam
ridiculosas sternutationes considerare et *observa*re nolite' (*Vita Eligii*, ii. 16, p. 705,
derives from Caesarius); Martin of Bracara, loc. cit., c. 16 (p. 34): 'alia diaboli
signa per *avicellas* et *sternut*us et per alia multa *adtend*itis'; Pirmin, c. 22 (p. 54):
'*sternut*us et *aguria* per *aviculas* vel alia ingenia mala et diabolica nolite facire nec
credire.'

    [2] Pirmin, c. 22 (p. 55): 'Tempestarios nolite credere nec aliquid pro hoc eis dare,
qui dicunt quod *maones* (*C*; manus *A*) fructa tollere possent.' On *ma(v)ones* cf. also
above, p. 310, n. 4.

    [3] Cf. Caesarius, *Serm.* 13. 4 (p. 65), repeated above, p. 309. 5: '*quia ista consuetudo
ballandi de paganorum* observatione *remansit*'; 192. 3 (p. 740): 'Qui enim aliquid
de paganorum consuetudine in istis diebus observare voluerint . . .'; Pirmin, c. 28 (p. 68):
'Ballationis et saltationis . . . facire non presumatis, *quia hoc de paganorum consuetudine
remansit.*' Cf. E. Seckel, 'Studien zu Benedictus Levita VII' (*Neues Archiv*, xxxv,
1910, pp. 153, 158); Jecker, p. 151, n. 112.

    [4] The compiler changed some details of Acts xix. 24–40. Cf. *v.* 24: 'Demetrius
enim quidam nomine argentarius, faciens aedes argenteas Dianae (there is no
mention of 'de auro'), praestabat artificibus non modicum quaestum', and *v.* 27:
'et magnae Dianae templum in nihilum reputabitur, sed et *destrui incipiet maiestas
eius.*'   [5] 1 Cor. xv. 32.

    [6] The compiler seems to have misunderstood and combined Martin of Bracara,
De correctione rusticorum, c. 7 (ed. Caspari, pp. 7 ff.; A. Mai, *Classicorum auctorum tomus
III*, 1831, p. 381 f.): 'ut alius Iovem se esse diceret, qui fuerat magus et in tantis
adulteriis incestus, ut sororem suam haberet uxorem, quae dicta est *Iuno, Minervam*
vero et *Venerem* filias suas corruperit', and afterwards: '*Alius* etiam daemon *Venerem*
se esse confinxit, quae *fuit mulier meretrix. Non solum cum* innumerabilibus adulteris,

Et alia heresis est, quod stulti homines credunt, quod spiritus, cum
de uno homine exit, in alium possit intrare, quod hoc omnino numquam
potest fieri, nisi daemonis hoc faciunt et per ipsus homines locuntur. Et
scimus, quia aliud nihil est nisi quod oculis videmus, nisi ipsi demones,
5   qui in isto aere volitant et mille artis nocendi[1] habent. Unde Paulus
apostolus dicit:[2] *Non est nobis conluctatio adversus carnem et sanguinem, sed
adversus principes tenebrarum.* Et alibi dicit:[3] *Ipse Satanas transfigurat se
etiam in angelo lucis. Ideo*[4] *quantum potestis circumvencionis diaboli fugite.
Scitote ante omnia, fratres, quia nec vos ipsos nec eos qui ad vos pertenent nec*
10   *animalia vestra nec reliqua substancia vel in parvis rebus diabulus potest ledere,
nisi quantum a Deo potestatem acceperit.* . . . .

3 daemones h. f. et per ipsos C^2 5 artes C^2 *In* Paulus apostolus dixit
resume TA 7 principes T *and* $C^2 A^2$ dixit A 8 angelum C *and* A^2 (Ideo
om.) Quanto TA circumvenciones C^2; circumventiones T *and* A^2 diabuli
A 9 ipsos *om.* C pertinent TA *and* C^2 10 anima TA pravis C
diabolus T; *om.* C 11 quanto (quando A^2) TA acciperit A

The text printed above does not call for much comment. The
extracts from its sources are barbarized to some extent by the
compiler in the usual manner of Merovingian Latin; there is the
substitution of *e* for *i*, *u* for *o*, of the accusative for the ablative and
vice versa, of the masculine gender for the neuter (acc. pl. *a(u)gurius,
signus*), and so on. How much the endings of the cases had lost their
meanings is shown by the appearance of Venus as a man, which was
the starting-point of the present appendix; 'barbarism' has taken
the place of the 'rusticity' which has been attributed with doubtful
justice to Caesarius of Arles.[5] The 'author' copied names of ancient
deities after the usual style of attacks on paganism; but he knew no
more of them than what he had read and misunderstood in his
exemplar. The text is a further example of the influence of Caesarius
on the literature directed against pagan customs, as Fedor Schneider,
for instance, has traced it through several centuries; the insertions
from other sources are in harmony with similar changes or additions

sed etiam cum patre suo Iove et cum *fratre suo Marte* meretricata est.' Similarly Caesarius
knew better, *Serm.* 193. 4 (p. 744): 'Venus autem meretrix fuit inpudicissima.'

[1] Caesarius, *Serm.* 207. 1 (p. 785): 'Quis enim contra tot milia *daemonum* die
noctuque ita stare potuit armatus, ut numquam fuerit diaboli calliditate percussus?
. . . de quo scriptum est (Virgil, *Aen.* vii. 337 f.): "cui nomina mille et *mille nocendi
artes*".' Cf. also Isidore, *Orig.* viii. 11. 16 f.: 'Hi (daemones) corporum aeriorum
natura vigent. . . . Lapsi vero in aeriam qualitatem conversi sunt, nec *aeris* illius
puriora spatia, sed ista caliginosa tenere permissi sunt.'

[2] Eph. vi. 12.   [3] 2 Cor. xi. 14.

[4] From Caesarius, *Serm.* 54, cc. 3, 4 (p. 228), copied with some omissions as far as
the middle of c. 5 (p. 229. 14 'duobus dominis servire'). Extracts follow from *Serm.*
16 and 233, again 16, then 219 and 223, ending with excerpts from Gregory's
Homily on the Gospels no. 27 (cf. above, p. 307).

[5] A. Malnory, *Saint Césaire, évêque d'Arles*, Paris, 1894, pp. 167 ff. But cf. also
C. F. Arnold, *Caesarius von Arelate*, Leipzig, 1894, pp. 120 ff.

made by Martin of Bracara, Eligius, and Pirmin. A part was omitted
in the archetype of TA (pp. 309. 10 to 312. 5), perhaps because its
transcriber appreciated its usefulness less than the original compiler;
that it belonged to the common ancestor of C and TA is shown by
the overlapping extracts from Caesarius. The text also furnishes a
new example of the euhemeristic method employed for centuries to
explain the existence and worship of pagan deities, who were regarded as human beings, deified for one reason or another after
their deaths.[1] But it is a particularly crude illustration of this belief,
and the whole compilation shows the need of the 'Carolingian
Renaissance' of letters.

The text has not hitherto been edited; but a part of it was indirectly known. The Latin MS. no. 5600 (Regius C. 4609.2) of the
Bibliothèque nationale of Paris, formerly no. 135 in the library of
the monastery of St. Martial of Limoges, was written in the tenth
century, rather than in the eleventh to which it is sometimes ascribed.
The first part of it contains Lives of Saints (fols. 2v–86v), the later
part a florilegium including homilies.[2] Among these is (fols. 94–103)
Martin of Bracara's work *De correctione rusticorum*, the identity of
which seems not to have been previously recognized (fol. 94 has
the heading in capital and uncial letters: 'In nomine Domini | nostri
Iesu Christi | incipit liber omelia|arum ex singulari|tate patrum
conpo|situm. Epistola', to which 'episcopi' was added by a minu-
scule hand); the text begins c. 3 (p. 2): 'Cum fecisset Deus in principio
caelum et terram'. The Abbé Jean Lebeuf, when he published his
'Lettre au sujet de deux anciennes figures gauloises, avec des
recherches sur le *Cervolus* et *Vetula*, défendus par les Pères de l'Eglise
et par quelques Conciles de France' (in his *Recueil de divers écrits pour
servir d'éclaircissemens à l'histoire de France*, i, Paris, 1738, pp. 280–308)
inserted (pp. 303–5) some extracts from this manuscript. Most of
them belong to Martin's work (cc. 3, 16, 11), and photostats of the
beginning (fol. 94) and end (fols. 100v–103 = cc. 15–19, ed. Caspari,
pp. 25–44), with which my former colleague the Rev. Professor
Dr. Camillus Wampach kindly provided me some years ago, confirmed this attribution (the text is similar to Caspari's Sangallenses).

[1] Cf. Fr. von Bezold, *Das Fortleben der antiken Götter im mittelalterlichen Humanismus*,
Bonn, 1922, pp. 3 ff.; J. D. Cooke, 'Euhemerism: a mediaeval interpretation of
classical paganism' (*Speculum*, ii, 1927, pp. 396–410); P. Alphandéry, 'L'Évhémé-
risme et les débuts de l'histoire des religions au moyen âge' (*Revue de l'histoire des
religions*, cix, 1934, pp. 5–27).

[2] Cf. (Melot), *Catalogus codicum MSS. Bibliothecae Regiae*, iv, Paris, 1744, pp. 138 f.;
the Bollandists, *Catalogus codicum hagiograph. Latin. Paris*. ii, 1890, p. 514; *SS. rer.
Merov*. vii. 643. H. J. Lawlor, 'The MSS. of the Vita S. Columbani' (*Transactions of
the Royal Irish Academy*, vol. xxxii, Section C, Part I), 1903, pl. iv (cf. p. 8) has
reproduced two pages of the first part (fols. 17v and 18).

But the words of c. 11 (pp. 14 f.): 'Qualis est homo Christianus, qui pro Domino muras (!) et tineas veneratur...' are preceded in Lebeuf's excerpts by two pieces of our text: 'Et si Christiani ad ecclesiam venerint' to 'de paganorum observatione remansit' (p. 309. 4–6) and 'Et si aliquis adhuc cognoscitur' to 'portare possint' (pp. 309.10–311.2). Only an examination of the manuscript could justify an opinion on the question whether these texts were interpolated into Martin's work from C or from an earlier exemplar or a brother-manuscript of C, or whether an interpolated copy of Martin was used by the compiler of C or a predecessor. In any case Limoges as the home of this manuscript confirms the view that C originated in France, not in northern Italy (cf. pp. 303 and 310, n. 3). P. Carpentier, *Glossarium novum ad scriptores medii aevi*, Paris, 1766, i. 265, ii. 183, 605, 1205 (s.v. *aquaticus, dusiolus, geniscus, mavones*) repeated a few extracts from Lebeuf, which were inserted into the later editions of Du Cange's *Glossarium*; Krusch, *SS. rer. Merov.* iv, p. 706, n. 3, reprinted one sentence.

XI

A LETTER OF ALCUIN TO BEATUS OF LIÉBANA

WE are indebted to Ernst Dümmler for the best and completest edition of the letters of Alcuin that exists to-day: *MG. Epistolarum tomus* iv, Berlin, 1895, pp. 1–493, with some additions ib. pp. 614–16 and vol. v, 1899, pp. 643–5. If, in a probably remote future, someone should try to prepare a new edition based on the manuscripts, he will not have to collate many codices unknown to Dümmler. A second copy of the large, important collection made in Corbie and represented hitherto by the Harleian MS. no. 208 (Dümmler, pp. 5 f., 555, 568 f.), was discovered in the Bibliothèque nationale of Paris, MS. Nouv. acqu. Lat. 1096 of the early ninth century, formerly at St. Léger in Soissons.[1] A future editor will have to pay regard to this manuscript, the more so as many letters were previously known from the Harleianus alone. A Salzburg manuscript of the middle of the ninth century, now in the University Library of Graz, no. 790 (41/10), fol. 64–72v, contains the letters nos. 113, 161, and 140, the second of which has also been published from a single transcript.[2] Paul Lehmann has added Vaticanus Reg. Lat. 598, likewise of the ninth century, fol. 25v, to the manuscripts

[1] H. Omont, *BECh.* lxxviii, 1917, p. 229; J. Ramackers, *Neues Archiv*, l, 1935, pp. 425–8.

[2] Levison, ib. xxviii, 1903, pp. 289 f.; *SS. rer. Merov.* vi. 152 f., vii. 592, where I have identified fols. 32–42 with Bede, *De temporum ratione*, cc. 69–71 (*Auct. ant.* xiii. 323–7).

of the letter to Dodo no. 65,[1] and H. Loriquet Rheims no. 438 (from St. Thierry) of the tenth century, fols. 2, 39v, and 68, to the manuscripts of Alcuin's letters to Wido no. 305, to Arno no. 243, and to the 'pueri' of St. Martin's no. 131.[2]

The number of new letters which have been found since Dümmler's edition is small. The anonymous preface of the supplement to the *Sacramentarium Gregorianum* must be included in future, as Alcuin's authorship is now recognized.[3] I have already mentioned and reprinted his letter to King Offa of Mercia, which Paul Lehmann had published from a Haag MS. of the tenth century; it was a source of the letter of the English bishops who protested against abuses connected with the conferment of the pallium.[4]

Another letter which was discovered in Spain some years ago may be said to be practically unknown. It was found in the manuscript of the Archivo Histórico Nacional of Madrid B–1007, written in 'Visigothic' script of the tenth century and mentioned as incomplete by D. De Bruyne;[5] but the whole text exists on fols. 101–102v and has been published by Agustín Millares Carlo,[6] who is known to students of medieval manuscripts by his *Paleografía Española* (Barcelona, 1929; 2nd ed., 1932). The editor, who added a facsimile of fols. 101 and 101v, purposely confined himself to the palaeographic aspects.[7] In the meantime Dom B. Capelle has given the document its place among the writings relative to the Adoptionist controversy, in which Alcuin took so large a part.[8] I here reproduce this addition to the 'Opus epistolarum Alcuini', the Spanish edition being little accessible; but I give a corrected text. I have tried to remove mistakes made by the scribe and the peculiarities of Spanish orthography. I have also substituted *ae* for *e*, without notice of the alteration, wherever Alcuin may be supposed to have followed the habitual practice.

---

[1] Lehmann, *Mitteilungen aus Handschriften I* (SB. München, 1929, no. 1), pp. 24 f. The early 9th-century Würzburg MS. of no. 144, which Lehmann has mentioned in his *Fuldaer Studien, Neue Folge* (ib., 1927, no. 2), p. 49, has been recorded by Dümmler himself in an addition, *Epist.* iv, p. 616.

[2] *Catalogue général des mss., Départements*, xxxviii, 1904, pp. 591 ff. Cf. also Sirmond's copies of nos. 307, 245, 132, and append. no. 3 in Paris, Nouv. acqu. Lat. 469, recorded by A. Werminghoff, *Neues Archiv*, xxvi, 1901, p. 21.

[3] Cf. above, pp. 98 and 158. Dümmler published the preface under the name of Abbot Grimald of St. Gall, loc. cit. v. 579 f.   [4] Cf. above, pp. 244 ff.

[5] 'Manuscrits Wisigothiques' (*Rev. Bén.* xxxvi, 1924, p. 14).

[6] *Contribución al Corpus de códices visigóticos* (Publicaciones de la Facultad de filosofía y letras, Universidad de Madrid, i), Madrid, 1931, pp. 213–22.

[7] The scribe of the MS., according to the facsimiles, made a distinction between assibilated and unassibilated *ti*; the copy therefore is not earlier than the 10th century. Cf. E. A. Loew [Lowe], *Studia Palaeographica* (SB. München, 1910, no. 12), pp. 52 ff.   [8] Cf. above, p. 159.

The letter is addressed to Beatus, the presbyter and abbot in the country of Liébana in Asturia, in the south-west of the modern province of Santander, whose Commentary on the Apocalypse[1] has been the subject of modern research less for its own sake than for its sources and illuminated manuscripts and their place in the history of art.[2] It is unnecessary to relate here the history of the Adoptionist controversy.[3] It is connected with archaic dogmatic formulas concerned with Christ's human nature, which were in use in the Spanish Church and were defended by Bishop Felix of Urgel, whose see became a part of the Spanish Marches of Charles the Great, and by Elipandus, the metropolitan of Toledo under Moslem rule. The orthodoxy of the doctrine of Adoptionism was attacked in 785 by Beatus and his pupil, Bishop Hetherius of Osma,[4] before Pope Hadrian and the Frankish Church entered the combat. Alcuin's letter belongs to a later phase of the controversy.[5] The doctrine was condemned by the synods of Regensburg in 792 and of Frankfurt in 794; Alcuin and other representatives of the English Church took part in the latter assembly side by side with members of the Frankish and Italian Churches and with papal legates.[6] About 793 Alcuin had sent a letter to Felix, endeavouring with kind words to convince him of the error of his opinions and to persuade him to accept the formulas approved by the great majority of the Western Churches.[7] Felix answered this exhortation by a letter or 'libellus' of considerable length in defence of his standpoint; it is lost, but known from the quotations of his opponents.[8] Alcuin learned from

---

[1] Edited by Henrique Florez, *Sancti Beati presbyteri Hispani Liebanensis in Apocalypsin commentaria*, Madrid, 1770, and by Henry A. Sanders, *Beati in Apocalipsin libri duodecim* (Papers and Monographs of the American Academy in Rome, vii), Rome, 1930.

[2] I refer to W. Neuss, *Die Apokalypse des hl. Johannes in der altspanischen und altchristlichen Bibel-Illustration*, 2 vols. (Spanische Forschungen der Görresgesellschaft, 2nd series, vols. ii, iii), Münster, 1931, and to other studies mentioned in his paper, 'Elementos Mozárabes en la miniatura Catalana' (*Homenatge a Antoni Rubió i Lluch*, I, Barcelona, 1936, pp. 507–23). Cf. also Zacarías García Villada, *Historia eclesiástica de España*, iii, Madrid, 1936, pp. 386 f., 443–62.

[3] I need mention only Hauck, loc. cit. ii, pp. 302 ff.; von Schubert, loc. cit., pp. 376 ff.; Hefele and Leclercq, *Histoire des conciles*, iii. 2, Paris, 1910, pp. 1001 ff., 1096 ff.; Villada, loc. cit., pp. 58–70; E. Amann in *Histoire de l'Église*, ed. A. Fliche and V. Martin, vi, Paris, 1937, pp. 129–52. I have not seen E. H. Limbach, *Alcuinus als bestrijder van het Adoptianismus*, Groningen, 1901. On Paulinus of Aquileia's *Contra Felicem libri tres* cf. now A. Wilmart, 'L'Ordre des parties dans le traité de Paulin d'Aquilée contre Félix d'Urgel' (*J.T.S.* xxxix, 1938, pp. 22–37).

[4] Hetherius and Beatus, *Ad Elipandum epistola* (Migne, *P.L.* xcvi, 893–1030).

[5] Capelle, loc. cit., pp. 251 ff.

[6] *MG. Concilia*, ii, pp. 159. 40, 171. 22. Cf. above, pp. 112, 156.

[7] Alcuin, *Epist.* 23 (pp. 60–5).

[8] Cf., e.g., *Concilia*, ii. 204 (n. 3), 221. 24 (= *Epist.* iv. 329. 33).

this answer that Beatus had been the first to attack Adoptionism. It now happened that a Spanish clergyman ('vir venerabilis'), by name Vincent, made a pilgrimage to St. Martin's at Tours,[1] and Alcuin availed himself of this opportunity to send Beatus the letter in question, stating that he had wished to recommend himself to him 'ex multo tempore'. The letter therefore is not earlier than 796, in which year Alcuin was provided to the abbey of St. Martin. In the text (p. 321. 11) he refers to an earlier writing of his against the Adoptionists, obviously, as Dom Capelle has pointed out, his first pamphlet against them,[2] which he sent through Abbot Benedict of Aniane to the monks of 'Gothia',[3] that is, Septimania, the part of southern France which had been under Visigothic rule up to the Arab invasion. Evidently he had not yet composed his larger work of seven books against Felix,[4] still less his later four books against Elipandus.[5] Nor does he allude to the submission of Felix at the debate of Aachen in 800.[6] The letter may have been written in 797 or 798.

Alcuin's books against Felix and his letters referring to the controversy may be compared with the letter; the objections that he raises against the bishop of Urgel and the arguments he advances in the letter here reproduced receive much illumination from these other writings, which enlarge upon the controversial matter, while it is only touched upon in an epistle merely intended to recommend the writer to his Spanish ally. The verses with which the document ends have their analogy in similar poetical compositions appended to other letters of friendship written by Alcuin.

---

[1] About the middle of the 9th century Paulus Albarus of Cordova in a letter to John of Seville also opposed Adoptionism and quoted some lines by a certain Vincentius side by side with Beatus and other enemies of this doctrine (*Epist.* no. 1, ed. Florez, *España Sagrada*, xi, 1753, p. 88; Migne, *P.L.* cxxi. 417 f.); the quotation (cf. Wolf Wilhelm Graf von Baudissin, *Eulogius und Alvar*, Leipzig, 1872, pp. 209 f.) was the subject of discussion in the correspondence that ensued (*Epist.* nos. 3. 7, 4. 29, Florez, pp. 99, 124; Migne, cols. 426, 444 f.). Vincentius, whom Albarus calls 'noster' and 'eruditissimus', is probably not identical with the visitor to Tours and friend of Beatus; the word 'nunc' in the sentence: 'Unde et noster nunc doctor Vincentius implorando taliter dicit', points rather to a man living at the time of Albarus' letter, as Florez has observed (loc. cit., pp. 5 f.), though M. Manitius, loc. cit. i. 425, has regarded him as a contemporary of Beatus and Elipandus. It would also be rash to refer some religious verses by a certain Vincentius (published from a Toletanus of the 10th century by Traube, *MG. Poetae*, iii, 147, no. 1; cf. p. 779), to one or another of these namesakes.

[2] *Adversus haeresin Felicis*, Migne, *P.L.* ci. 87–120. Cf. Capelle, loc. cit. vi. 252 f.

[3] *Epist.* 205 (pp. 340 f.).

[4] Migne, loc. cit., cols. 127–230.

[5] Ib., cols. 243–300.

[6] *MG. Concilia*, ii. 220 ff.

Beatissimo beati Dei famulo Beato patri perpetuae beatitudinis pacem
et lucem humilis levita Alcuinus optat.

Audiens venerabilem vestrae religionis in Christi caritate famam,
cupiens ex multo tempore me ipsum gremio vestrae sanctae dilectionis
5 inserere et vestrae sanctitatis orationibus conmendare,[1] quod statim
supplici mentis affectu facere non tardavi, dum oportunitas temporis
et portitoris nostrarum vobis litterarum advenit. Gaudens de adventu
viri venerabilis Vincentii, qui orationis gratia limina beati Martini
patris nostri et protectoris vestri[2] visitavit, qui multiplici vestrae boni-
10 tatis studium laude nobis enarravit et, quasi te ipso praesente, tui
nostris visceribus infixit caritatem, ita ut pene nihil de absentia faciei
vestrae cor meum ingemuit, dum spiritalis praesentiae iucunditatem
tecum ex verbis illius posse habere speravi, vel magis per eum, qui
mutuae caritatis dulcedinem paternis infundere cordibus solet, qui
15 nobis datus est pignus perpetuae salutis, in quo te amare me fateor et
a te amari exopto, ut in nobis sit unus spiritus et una fides et eadem
in sancta caritate concordia, sicut decet filiis lacte ecclesiasticae con-
solationis enutritis.

Legimus in cuiusdam Felicis Urgillitanae sedis[3] episcopi litteris
20 reprehensionis vestrae verba, qui vos adfirmavit primos omnium adoptionis nomini in Christo contradicere.[4] Quae reprehensio vestri nominis
valde, ut fateor, mihi placuit, dum te catholicae fidei defensorem audivi
et apostolicae doctrinae praedicatorem agnovi, quae omnes novitates
sub anathematis terrore constituit,[5] ita ut angelis quoque anathema

---

1 *The rubric precedes* Incipit ẹpistola sancti Alcoini Thoronensis diaconi.

2 et lucem *added above the line.* Alcinius obtat *MS.*   6 tardabi *MS.*
9 nostri] uši (=vestri) *MS.*   10 te] de *MS.*   tuis *MS.*
16 exobto *MS.*   17 eclesiastice consolatione *MS.*   19 in *omitted in MS.*
ẹpiscopi *MS.*   20 primo omnium adobtionis nomine *MS.*
24 constituit] conspicui *MS.*

---

[1] Alcuin, *Epist.* 168 (p. 276): '*Audiens* laudabilem in Christo unanimitatis vestrae
conversationem, multa animus meus laetitia gavisus est multoque anhelabat desi-
derio . . . *me ipsum* humili devotione vestris sacrosanctis *commendare orationibus*.' Cf.
ib. 5, 23, 31 (pp. 30. 19, 60. 26, 72. 20).

[2] Cf. *Epist.* 74 (p. 116. 2 = *SS. rer. Merov.* iii. 414. 5), 296 (p. 455. 6): 'sancti
Vedasti patris vestri et intercessoris (protectoris 296) nostri'; 159 (p. 258. 17):
'beati Martini protectoris nostri'; 186 (p. 312. 36): 'circa limina beati Martini
patris nostri et protectoris vestri'; 230 (p. 375. 22): 'ad sanctum Martinum pro-
tectorem nostrum et intercessorem vestrum'; 252 (p. 408. 7): 'ad limina beati
Martini patris nostri protectorisque vestri.'

[3] Seo de Urgel in Catalonia.

[4] Alcuin, *Adversus Felicem*, i. 8 (col. 133): 'Quod vero quendam Beatum abbatem
et discipulum eius Hitherium episcopum dicitis huic vestrae sectae primum contraire, laudamus eos in eo, quod veritatem defendere conati sunt.' Beatus ('anti-
frasius Beatus' or 'Inbeatus') was therefore a main object of attacks and abuses by
Elipandus and his circle; cf. *MG. Concilia*, ii. 111. 28, 118–21; *Epist.* iv. 301–3, 305,
307, 308.

[5] *Adv. Felicem* vi. 1 (col. 199): 'quia *omnes novitates* vocum cunctis catholicae fidei
filiis *sub anathematis terrore* interdixit.'

indixit, si aliter venirent praedicare, quam praedicatum est ab apostolis Christi.[1] Ideo obsecro, sanctissime frater, ut in populo Christiano, cui vos cum sacerdotibus Christi doctores divina statuit gratia, nihil novi, nihil apostolicis traditionibus contrarium aboriri permittatis, sed
5 intra terminos patrum[2] firma statione se ipsos retenere iubeatis.

Gradatim vero praefatus Felix semper ad peiora descendit.[3] Primo, adoptivum Iesum Christum dominum nostrum Dei Patris filium asserens;[4] secundo, baptismo eum indiguisse, sicut nos peccatores;[5] tertio, nuncupativum Deum eum cum ceteris sanctis esse adfirmabat.[6]
10 In qua assertione nullatenus effugere poterit duas personas in Christo, unam proprii filii, alteram adoptivi, et unam veri Dei, alteram nuncupativi, quia adoptio et proprietas in uno filio Dei ad unum patrem nullatenus poterit esse, nec idem potest esse verus Deus et nuncupativus, sicut tua sanctitas optime agnoscere poterit. Dicit quod homo ad-
15 sumptus a Filio Dei adoptivus sit propter adsumptionem, non intellegens absurditatem sui sensus vel sectatorum suorum. Nam si Christus propter adsumptionem adoptivus est filius, ergo adoptivus est filius illius personae, qui hominem adsumpsit, id est Filii Dei, et est nepus Patris.[7] Persona igitur Filii in utero Virginis humanam adsumpsit substantiam,
20 non Patris. Alio quoque argumento nititur, asserens, non posse adsumptum hominem proprie esse filium Dei, quia de substantia

---

3 doctoris *MS.*   4 tradictionibus *MS.*   7 adobt. *MS.*, *also in l.* 11
8 babtismo *MS.*   9 nuncupatibum *MS.*   esse *added above the line*
11 nuncupatibi. Quia adobtio *MS.*   13 nuncupatibus *MS.*   14 obtime *MS.*
15 adoptibus *MS.*, *also in l.* 17   16 si *added above the line*   19 substantia *MS.*   20 innitur *MS.*   21 adsumtum *MS.*

---

[1] Ib. i. 2 (col. 129): 'dum egregius doctor gentium *omnes novitates* vocum et inventas noviter sectas omnino firmiter prohibeat a quoquam catholico recipi (1 Tim. vi. 20), in tantum *ut* etiam *angelis* et omni homini *anathema indixi*sse non dubitaret, *si aliter praedicas*set, *quam ab* illo *praedicatum esset*' (Gal. 1. 8); *Epist.* 166 (p. 272. 40).   [2] Cf. Prov. xxii. 28.

[3] *Epist.* 148 (p. 241): 'Nuper mihi venit libellus a Felice infelice directus. Cuius propter curiositatem cum paucas paginolas legendo percucurri, inveni *peiores* hereses vel magis blasphemias, quam ante in eius scriptis legerem'; *Adv. Felicem* i. 1 (col. 128).

[4] *Adv. haeresin Felicis*, c. 2 (col. 88): 'asserens, Christum Iesum Deo Patri verum non esse filium nec proprium, sed adoptivum'; *Adv. Felicem*, i. 1 (col. 128 f.); *Adv. Elipandum*, i. 16 (col. 252), &c.

[5] *Adv. Felicem*, ii. 16 (col. 157): 'quem insuper lavacro indiguisse baptismatis'; *Epist.* 166 (p. 270): 'Refert quoque eum baptismo indiguisse . . . sicut et nos'; ib. 205 (p. 341. 18), &c.

[6] Ib. 148 (p. 241): 'Adserens Christum Iesum nec filium Dei esse verum nec etiam verum Deum esse, sed nuncupativum'; ib. 166 (p. 269); *Adv. Felicem*, i. 1, iv. 2 (cols. 129, 173), &c.

[7] *Epist.* 166 (p. 269): 'Dicit itaque propter adsumptionem Christum esse adoptivum. . . . Et si necesse est propter adsumptionem adoptivum esse Christum, cui personae est sanctae Trinitatis adoptivus? Utique Filii, quia Filii persona adsumpsit hominem in utero virginali, . . . et si adoptivus est, itaque Filio est adoptivus, qui hominem adsumpsit. Et est nepos Patris'; *Adv. Felicem*, iii. 8 (col. 167 f.); *Adv. Elipandum*, i. 22 (col. 258).

Patris non sit natus. Si igitur propter substantiae diversitatem non est proprie filius Dei, qui ex Virgine natus est, sed adoptive, ergo nec proprie filius Virginis est, qui ex Deo Patre natus est, sed adoptive, quia eiusdem substantiae non est divinitas et humanitas. Similiter
5 verus Deus et nuncupativus unus esse non poterit, quia totius Christi una est persona, unus Dei filius, unus et verus Deus, in duabus naturis. In sancta itaque Trinitate, in Patre et Filio et Spiritu sancto, una est aeternaliter substantia, tres personae. In Filio vero Dei, qui ex Virgine natus est, duae sunt naturae et una persona, sicut in simbolo catholicae
10 pacis¹ cantare solemus² et confiteri *unum unigenitum* coaeternum et *consubstantialem Patri* Dei Filium, *per quem omnia facta sunt, qui propter nos et propter nostram salutem descendit de caelo et incarnatus est de Spiritu sancto et Maria Virgine, homo natus, crucifixus, sepultus, resurgens tertia die.*³ Non enim alium indicans unigenitum, sed eundem qui natus est ex Patre
15 aeternaliter et ex Virgine temporaliter;⁴ unum semper consequenter unigenitum dicit. Unigeniti vero nomen adoptionis nomini non convenit.

Stultissimum est altissima Dei misteria humanis ratiunculis investigare velle⁵ et nostrae infirmitatis dicioni subicere, et quod nobis

2 adobtibae *MS*. 3 abtiuae *corr.* adobtiuae *MS*. 5 nuncupatibus *MS*. totus *MS*. 8 personas *MS*. 16 adobtionis nomine *MS*. 19 dicione *MS*.

---

¹ Alcuin often uses the notion of the 'catholic peace' connected with the unity of the Church. Cf., e.g., *Epist.* 23 (p. 60. 27): 'in Christi caritate et catholicae pacis unitate', 139 (p. 220. 21): 'catholicae pacis puritate', 166 (p. 272. 38): 'in unitate catholicae pacis'; letters sent in the name of the Frankish bishops and of the king in 794 from the synod of Frankfurt (*MG. Concilia*, ii. 143. 2, 164. 34): 'toto catholicae pacis clero', 'catholicae pacis auxiliatores'; *Adv. Elipandum*, i. 5 (col. 245): 'ad catholicae pacis concordiam.' Cf. Augustine, *Sermo* 71. 21 (Migne, *P.L.* xxxviii. 456): 'Schismaticus est hodie: quid si cras amplectatur *catholicam pacem?*'

² *Epist.* 23 (p. 61. 28): 'ecclesiam, de qua in symbulo catholico decantare solemus'; *Adv. Felicem*, I. 9, 16, 17 (cols. 134, 141, 143): 'omnis catholica ecclesia cantat . . . huiusmodi verba in symbolo', 'ut in symbolo cantatur', 'ut in symbolo cantitamus'; *Adv. Elipandum*, iii. 6, iv. 4 (cols. 274, 288): 'Nonne omnis sancta Dei ecclesia in symbolo catholico decantare solet', 'catholico universalis ecclesiae symbolo, in quo verissime decantatur . . .'. Cf. Capelle, loc. cit. vi. 253 ff.; above, p. 159.

³ Alcuin quotes here and *Adversus Felicem*, i. 9 (col. 134 f., corrected from MSS. by Capelle pp. 255 f.) the so-called Niceno-Constantinopolitan Creed, but, as Dom Capelle (loc. cit.) has observed, with two variant readings, which both are also found in the Irish Stowe Missal (ed. Warner, H. Br. Soc. xxxii, 1915, p. 8): 'de caelo' for 'de caelis' (ἐκ τῶν οὐρανῶν), and 'homo natus' for 'humanatus' (ἐνανθρωπήσαντα).

⁴ *Epist.* 166 (p. 273. 26): 'ut idem ipse, qui ex Deo Patre aeternaliter natus est, ex matre virgine temporaliter natus esset.'

⁵ *Adv. Felicem*, iii. 2 (col. 163 f.): 'Nullatenus ergo te, o Felix, humana ratione *investigare* nativitatem Verbi Dei . . . posse putes; non enim humana possibilitate omnipotentiam divinitatis metiri debes. Ipse . . . nec *infirmis humanae* coniecturae *ratiunculis* . . . comprehendi poterit'; ib. iii. 6 (col. 166): 'humana humilitas se ipsam coerceat intra terminum moduli sui Salvatorisque nostri mirabilem nativitatem *humanis ratiunculis* (= Augustine, *De civitate Dei*, xx. 1. 1) desinat aestimare';

inpossibile est, inpossibile Deo esse extimare, cui *omnia possibilia sunt*,[1]
qui *omnia quae vult facit in caelo et in terra*.[2] Quo modo non intellegunt
se ipsos, qui asserunt propter diversitatem humanae naturae Christum
non posse esse filium Dei Patris. Numquid non homo ex anima et
5   carne constat, caro vero sola ex paterna generatione procreatur, anima
vero, ut catholica credit doctrina,[3] Dei potentia tantummodo creata
carne inmittitur, et tamen proprius est filius totus homo anima et carne
patris sui? Et quod in omni homine fieri potest, quomodo in solo
Christo fieri non potest, ut sit totus Dei proprius Patris filius et totus
10   proprius matris Virginis filius?[4]

    Plura inde scripsimus, multis sanctorum patrum testimoniis catholi-
cam confirmantes fidem.[5] Quae litterae si forsan vestras veniant in
manus, obsecro ut benigna caritate, non severitatis pumice, si quid
perperam repperiatis in illis, corrigere studeatis.[6] Suaviter enim humili-
15   tas nostra columbinum caritatis vestrae oculum in correctione recipit.
Melius est ab amico corrigi quam reprehendi ab inimico.[7] Ubi divina
lumine veritatis cor meum inlustrat [gratia], ibi cum suis famulis in
laudem nominis sui dona sua participare segnes non ero. Ubi vero
minus intellego scripturae sanctae seriem,[8] ibi a bene scientibus doceri
20   gaudeo. Nec serpentinos invidorum dentes pertimesco, dum humilitas
discendi defendat me ab errore pertinaciae, magis optans esse veritatis

---

1 inpossibilem deo *MS.*   3 asseruit *MS.*   17 gratia *omitted in MS.*;
cf. p. 322, *l.* 3   19 scribture *MS.*   21 obtans *MS.*

---

letter of Charles from Frankfurt (*MG. Concilia*, ii. 161): 'nec *ratiotinando humano*
ingenio divina vos *mysteria investigare* arbitremini . . .'.
  [1] Matt. xix. 26.   [2] Ps. cxxxiv. 6.
  [3] Cf. e.g. above, p. 240, n. 1; Alcuin, *Epist.* 309, c. 13 (p. 474. 30): 'In hoc enim
omnes consentiunt catholici scriptores, quod anima a Deo sit condita.'
  [4] *Adversus haeresin Felicis*, c. 36 (col. 101): 'Interrogo te, profani assertor erroris:
anima rationalis, quae in te est et totum corpus tuum vivificat, vegetat et movet et,
ut sancti patres volunt, corporis origine non seminatur, sed *ex nihilo creata* aliunde
corpori *immittitur*, an non sit patri tuo adoptiva filia et caro tantummodo propria
filia? An tu *totus anima et* corpore unus et *proprius patri* tuo sis *filius*? Quid si *homo* ex
ea substantia, quae non ex se generatur, corpori coniuncta proprium et verum
poterit habere filium, cur Deum impotentem putas, quod *proprium non* possit et
verum de Spiritu sancto ex Maria virgine natum habere *filium*? Numquid tu leges
imponis ei, *qui omnia quae*cumque *vult facit in caelo et in terra*?' Cf. *Adv. Felicem*, iii. 7,
v. 3 (cols. 166 f., 190); *Adv. Elipandum*, i. 10 (col. 248); *Epist.* 204 (p. 338. 34–9).
  [5] Alcuin refers here to his first work against the Adoptionists, *Adversus haeresin
Felicis* (loc. cit., cols. 87–120). He mentioned it in similar words in his letter 205
(p. 340) to the abbots and monks of 'Gothia', when he was writing his larger work
of seven books against Felix: 'Quod *multis testimoniis* evangelicis vel apostolicis vel
etiam *sanctorum patrum* tradicionibus conprobari potest, sicut in libello ex parte
factum est, quem direximus per abbatem Benedictum (of Aniane) vobis solacium
et *confirmacionem fidei catholicae*'; cf. ib. 160 (p. 259. 15). Cf. Capelle, loc. cit.,
pp. 251 ff.
  [6] Cf. Alcuin, *Epist.* 80 (p. 123): '*si quid in* eis *perperam* dixerim, tu fraterno stilo
*corrigere studea*s.'
  [7] Ib. 149 (p. 245): 'Melius est amicum emendare quam reprehendere.'
  [8] Alcuin, *Epist.* 15 (p. 41. 34): 'sanctorum librorum series.'

discipulus quam falsitatis magister. In omnibus huiusmodi quaestionibus sanctorum sequi patrum vestigia desidero, nihil addens vel minuens[1] illorum sacratissimis litteris, quantum me divina adiuvaverit gratia,[2] sine qua nihil possumus,[3] in qua omnia vestra poterit caritas, quae ad
5 aedificationem catholicae pacis[4] pertinent. In qua pace obsecro ut me socium habeas et concivem, non peregrinum vel hospitem, dicente apostolo:[5] *Fratres, non estis hospites, sed cives sanctorum et domestici fidei.* De qua domo cecinit et psalmographus:[6] *Unam petii a Domino, hanc requiram, ut inhabitem in domo Domini omnibus diebus vitae meae.*

10
     Incolomem Christi faciat te gratia semper,[7]
     Praeveniat donis, augeat et meritis.[8]
     Partibus occiduis mundi lux luceat alma
     Per te catholicae, sancte pater, fidei,
   5 Ne corda excedat stultorum umbratilis error,
15
     Qui nova nunc gaudent [fingere][9] verba sibi
     Nec sunt contenti sanctorum dogmate patrum,[10]
     Nec placet illorum mentibus alma fides,
     Sed sibi cisternas fodiunt sine luminis unda,
  10 In quibus haud ulla est vivida fontis aqua.[11]
20
     Quos tua castiget, clarus, sapientia, doctor,
     Nec valeant populo plusve nocere Dei.
     Hoc opus est vobis merces[12] et causa perennis,
     Hoc te sanctorum consociat numero,

3 adiubauerit *MS.*   5 haedific. *MS.*   6 abeas *MS.*   10 Incolomen *MS.*   14 excedant *MS.*   15 fingere *omitted in MS.*   16 contempti *MS.*   dogmata *MS.*

---

[1] Cf. Deut. xii. 32.

[2] Alcuin, *Epist.* 200 (p. 332): 'quantum me divina adiuvaverit gratia.'

[3] Ib. 80 (p. 123): 'sine quo (God) nihil possumus.'

[4] Cf. above, p. 320, n. 1.   [5] Eph. ii. 19.   [6] Ps. xxvi. 4.

[7] Alcuin, *Epist.* 234 (p. 380): '*Incolumem Christus faciat te* vivere *semper*'; *Carm.* 29. i. 1 (p. 248): '*Incolumem Christus*, carissime, *te* mihi, praesul, conservet mitis *semper* ubique, precor'; ib. 68. 23 (p. 287): 'Ut conservet eum *Christi* pia *gratia semper.*' Cf. below, p. 323, n. 2.

[8] *Epist.* 99 (p. 144): '*Te* mihi conservet *Christi* dextra omnipotentis *incolumem, meritis augeat* aethereis'; *Carm.* 35. 14 (p. 251): '*Augeat et meritis* gratia summa Dei'; ib. 89, xiii. 4 (p. 310): 'Praeclaris Clemens *augeat et meritis*.'

[9] I have supplied 'fingere' in view of *Epist.* 23 (p. 61. 17): 'non nova fingentes nomina'; *Concilia* ii, 156. 8: 'nolite nova et incognita nomina fingere' (Frankfurt, 794); *Adv. Felicem*, i. 4 (col. 131): 'contraria toti orbi fingunt nomina', 'nova quaedam nomina . . . fingit . . .'.

[10] *Adv. Elipandum*, iv. 13 (col. 296): 'Audi me, obsecro, patienter, scholastica Hispaniae congregatio, tibi loquentem, quae novi semper aliquid audire vel praedicare desideras, *non contenta* apostolicis traditionibus nec universalis ecclesiae catholica fide.'

[11] Cf. Jer. ii. 13; Alcuin, *Epist.* 295 (p. 452. 30).

[12] Alcuin, ib. 89 (p. 133): '*Hoc est . . . opus* vestrum, haec est *merces* vestra, haec laus et gloria *vobis* sempiterna'; cf. 186 (p. 313. 13).

15 Corque tuum Christi magno repleatur amore,
   Sit tibi, sancte, potens semper[1] in ore Dei,
   Atque memor nostri valeas sine fine beatus,[2]
   Cum sanctis teneas regna beata Dei.

5   Sis memor Alcuini[3] per verba, Beate, [precandi].
   20 Per colles, montes currat haec cartula celsos,[4]
      Ut ferat egregio [pia] patri verba salutis.[5]   Amen.

5 precandi *omitted in MS., in l.* 7 pia   7 ferat ex regio *MS. After* Amen
follows Explicit epistola sancti viri Alcvini diaconi.

---

[1] *Carm.* 76, iii. 3 (p. 298): 'Pax *tibi*, vita, salus *semper sit, sancte* sacerdos   *atque
memor nostri* iam *sine fine vale.*'
[2] Bede, *De die iudicii* (Migne, *P.L.* xciv. 638; *Symeonis Opera* ed. Arnold, ii. 27):
'*Incolumem* mihi *te Christ*us, carissime frater,   protegat et *faciat semper* (cf. above,
v. 1) *sine fine beatu*m'; Alcuin, *Vita Willibrordi*, ii, c. 24. 10 (*MG. Poetae*, i. 216; *Acta SS.
Nov.* iii. 455): 'Conlaudans Christum, semper *sine fine beatus*'; *Carm.* 28. 14 (p. 247):
'Celsithroni videas faciem *sine fine beat*am.'
[3] *Epist.* 243 (p. 392) = *Carm.* 84. 2 (p. 301): '*Sis memor Albini per* tempora longa
magistri'; *Carm.* 33. ii. 6 (p. 250): '*Sis memor Alchuini* . . .', &c.
[4] *Epist.* 171 (p. 283) = *Carm.* 74. 25 (p. 296): '*Cartula, percurr*ens *colles* camposque
liquentes'; *Carm.* 46. 1 (p. 259): '*Cartula percurr*ens Friducino *fer* mea salve'; ib. 28.
18 (p. 247): '*Carta* tua *currat* . . . *per* terram, pelagus, regiones, regna, per urbes.'
[5] Ib. 35. 5, 62. 17 and 126 (pp. 251, 275, 279): 'Semper in ore tuo resonent *pia*
(bona 62. 17) *verba salutis*'; ib. 26. 35 (p. 246): '*pia verba* legenti.' Cf. also Angilbert's verse 'super cartam' (ib., p. 75; K. Neff, 'Die Gedichte des Paulus Diaconus',
loc. cit., p. 164): '*Fer*, mea *carta*, meo *patri* praecincta *salut*em.'

The preceding pages were already in proof, when I learnt from a note
by M. Alano in *Revue d'histoire ecclésiastique*, XXXVIII (Louvain, 1942),
p. 258, that I. F. Rivera has also published an edition of and a commentary on Alcuin's letter in a new Spanish periodical, *Revista española de
Teología*, I, 1941, pp. 418–33; 'A propósito de una carta de Alcuino
recientemente encontrada'.

INDEX[1]

---

[1] Place-names which are mentioned in connexion with 'church-dedications' only, are to be found under this heading. I have used the abbreviations: abb. = abbot, abp. = archbishop, bp. = bishop, da. = daughter, k. and K. = king, s. = son, w. = wife.

X x

Charters which are examined in this volume

LIBRARY NEW YORK

PRINTED IN
GREAT BRITAIN
AT THE
UNIVERSITY PRESS
OXFORD
BY
JOHN JOHNSON
PRINTER
TO THE
UNIVERSITY